NetWare Training Guide:
Managing NetWare Systems

3rd Edition

Debra Niedermiller-Chaffins
and
Dorothy Cady

NEW RIDERS
PUBLISHING

New Riders Publishing, Indianapolis, Indiana

Netware Training Guide: Managing NetWare Systems, Third Edition

By Debra Niedermiller-Chaffins and Dorothy Cady

Published by:
New Riders Publishing
201 West 103rd Street
Indianapolis, IN 46290 USA

Printed in the United States of America 3 4 5 6 7 8 9 0

Library of Congress Cataloging-in-Publication Data

```
     Cady, Dorothy L., 1953-
     NetWare Training Guide : Managing NetWare Systems/Dorothy Cady — 3rd ed.
             p.      cm.
     Second ed. by Debra Niedermiller-Chaffins. 1994
     Includes index
     ISBN 1-56205-366-3 : $70.00
     1.   NetWare (Computer file)
     2.   Operating systems (Computers)
     3.   Local area networks (Computer networks)
     I.   Niedermiller-Chaffins, Debra R., 1963-  NetWare training guide
     II.  Title.
     QA76.76.063C335              1994
     005.7'1369—dc20                                 94-2113
                                                          CIP
```

Warning and Disclaimer

Publisher	Lloyd J. Short
Associate Publisher	Tim Huddleston
Product Development Manager	Rob Tidrow
Marketing Manager	Ray Robinson
Director of Special Projects	Cheri Robinson
Managing Editor	Matthew Morrill

About the Authors

Debra R. Niedermiller-Chaffins is Education Director for Computer Data, Inc., in Madison Heights, Michigan. Ms. Niedermiller-Chaffins started the education department at Computer Data in 1988 to help organizations develop automony and self-sufficiency in training future Certified NetWare Engineer (CNE) operations. She is a Certified NetWare Instructor (CNI) and a CNE, specializing in training future CNEs. In addition to teaching, Ms. Niedermiller-Chaffins also supports a small client base, which provides her with a background of real-world networking scenarios. She is the author of *Inside Novell NetWare*, Special Edition, and *Inside NetWare Lite*, also published by New Riders Publishing.

Dorothy L. Cady is a senior technical writer for Novell, Inc., in Provo, Utah. Mrs. Cady started with Novell in 1990 as the team leader for the Software Testing Department's Document Testing Team, helping to assure the quality of the documentation that ships with Novell's NetWare 2,3,4, NetWare Lite, and Personal NetWare products. She is a Certified NetWare Instructor (CNI), Certified NetWare Engineer (CNE), and Certified NetWare Administrator (CNA). In addition to her duties as a technical writer, Mrs. Cady also is a member of the adjunct faculty at Utah Valley State College and a freelance writer. Mrs. Cady has over 20 years of experience in the computer industry, including both the private and public service sectors. In addition, Mrs. Cady is the author of *Inside Personal NetWare*, also from New Riders Publishing.

Acknowledgments

I want to dedicate this book to the many people who helped and supported me through this project. Thanks to my parents for always believing in me and my endeavors. A special thanks to my husband, Brian, without whom this book would not be possible. I also want to thank Computer Data partners and my boss, Jim Weyand, for his support in my education projects. Finally, to the fantastic group of people at New Riders, a special thanks for their guidance. I appreciate all your help. —*Debra Niedermiller-Chaffins*

I too would like to say thank you to my family, Raymond, Shana, and Ray, for their continued support during the development of this book. I also want to extend my special thanks to Drew Heywood for taking a chance on me and for continuing to support my writing endeavors. I would also like to extend one other special thanks to my manager at Novell, Vince Sondej, for his belief in me. —*Dorothy Cady*

Trademark Acknowledgments

All terms mentioned in this book that are known to be trademarks or service marks have been appropriately capitalized. New Riders Publishing cannot attest to the accuracy of this information. Use of a term in this book should not be regarded as affecting the validity of any trademark or service mark. NetWare is a registered trademark of Novell, Inc.

Product Director
Drew Heywood

Lead Editor
Sarah Kearns

Editors
Rob Lawson
Suzanne Snyder

Acquisitions Editor
Alicia Krakovitz

Technical Editor
Kim Green

Acquisitions Coordinator
Stacey Beheler

Editorial Assistant
Karen Opal

Publisher's Assistant
Melissa Lynch

Cover Designer
Dan Armstrong

Book Designer
Roger S. Morgan

Production Imprint Manager
Juli Cook

Production Imprint Team Leader
Katy Bodenmiller

Graphics Image Specialists
Clint Lahnen
Tim Montgomery
Dennis Sheehan
Susan VandeWalle

Production Analysts
Dennis Clay Hager
Mary Beth Wakefield

Production Team
Troy A. Barnes, Carol Bowers
Mona Brown, Elaine Brush
Cheryl Cameron, Elaine Crabtree
Steph Davis, Rob Falco
Kimberly K. Hannel, Angela P. Judy
Jamie Milazzo, Shelly Palma
Chad Poore, Casey Price
Ryan Rader, Marc Shecter
Tonya R. Simpson, Kim Scott
Susan Shepard, SA Springer
Marcella Thompson,

Indexer
Greg Eldred

Contents at a Glance

Table of Contents

XV

INTRODUCTION

The need for well-trained, competent individuals in today's computer industry is greater than ever. Novell, Inc., has seen the need to educate users who support NetWare products, and has created the following certifications to meet the industry's needs:

- ◆ *Certified NetWare Administrators* (CNAs) are tested to ensure basic competence with managing a specific NetWare operating system.

- ◆ *Certified NetWare Engineers* (CNEs) are tested for their knowledge of a wide variety of NetWare server products, as well as for their understanding of LAN hardware, software, and communication technologies. This certification is in high demand by systems engineers, consultants, and administrators of NetWare products.

- ◆ *Enterprise Certified NetWare Engineers* (ECNEs) are additionally certified for their competence with a variety of NetWare products, which might include network management and diagnostic tools, UNIX or Macintosh support products, or communication and gateway products.

Candidates for these certifications must pass one or more tests. A variety of preparation methods are available, including classroom instruction from *Novell Authorized Education Centers* (NAECs), *Novell Education Academic Partners* (NEAPs), and self-study kits available from Novell. The test objectives for each test are public, and candidates can choose to study by using their own materials.

Novell, Inc., also provides assessment disks with sample test questions to help users prepare for taking the necessary tests. These disks can be acquired through most NAECs, as well as through the NetWire forum on CompuServe.

Most candidates use a variety of these training methods, and many feel the need for additional training help. The *NetWare Training Guide* series from New Riders Publishing is intended to provide supplemental study information to help you pass the tests required to achieve Novell certification.

Who Should Read this Book?

NetWare Training Guide is written for individuals who need to learn more about Novell NetWare because of a job responsibility, and for those who need to know more about system administration and the operating system. This book is also written for individuals who may not yet have a job using NetWare, but who want to pass the Novell NetWare Certified Engineer tests as a step toward obtaining a job in the field. The following chapters guide you through the NetWare 3.1*x* and 2.2 products in an effort to acquaint you with the variety of securities and functionalities that NetWare offers.

What Is Covered in this Book?

Managing NetWare Systems is the first volume of NRP's *NetWare Training Guides*. It addresses the following NetWare certification requirements:

- NetWare 3.1*x* System Manager
- NetWare 3.1*x* Advanced System Manager
- NetWare 2.2 System Manager
- NetWare 2.2 Advanced System Manager

What Topics Are Not Included?

Managing NetWare Systems covers the test material with regard to the NetWare 3.1*x* and 2.2 Operating Systems, and DOS/microcomputer concepts.

CNE candidates also will be interested in the companion volume, *NetWare Training Guide: Networking Technologies*, which covers these core courses for the CNE curriculum:

◆ NetWare service and support

◆ Networking technologies

This volume does not include coverage of NetWare 4.*x*. If you are seeking certification as a NetWare 4 Administrator, you will be interested in two other titles in NRP's *NetWare Training Guide* series:

◆ *NetWare 4 Update* enables those who are currently certified on NetWare 2.*x* and 3.*x* to efficiently upgrade their certifications for NetWare 4.*x*.

◆ *NetWare 4 Administration* is a complete course in NetWare 4 administration for the new NetWare Administrator. This book will meet the needs of those who are seeking a CNA certification for NetWare 4, or who are pursuing a CNE on a NetWare 4 track.

The Details of this Book

You can flip quickly through this book to get a feel for its organization. The book is organized into five parts that lay the foundation on which you can build an understanding of the current NetWare operating systems. Each chapter is introduced, then the topics are covered in depth.

Throughout each section of each chapter, you also find the test objectives for either the NetWare 3.1*x* operating system, the NetWare 2.2 operating system, or the DOS/Microcomputer concepts tests. These objectives are intended to introduce the areas of this book that contain specific information related to these test objectives. You should use these areas as a guide for studying for your NetWare certification programs. However, studying just these sections alone is not sufficient to let you pass the tests, as you must understand a great deal of other related information that is provided throughout the text. At the end of each topic are multiple-choice Section Review questions followed by the answers to these questions. The questions are intended to give you some experience at answering the types of questions you can expect to find on the certification tests, as well as to help you see which areas you need to spend more time learning the related information.

At the end of each chapter are case studies that help you apply each of the concepts presented in the chapters. As mentioned, the specific answers to the section review multiple-choice questions are given, but the case studies can have multiple answers. Therefore, no specific case study answers are provided.

The following section provides an overview of each chapter in this book.

Part One describes networks, network workstations, and DOS:

- ◆ Chapter 1 discusses networks and network workstations.

- ◆ Chapter 2 describes DOS and shows you how it is used both on microcomputers and in networking.

Part Two describes the features common to current NetWare versions:

- ◆ Chapter 3 teaches you about directory structures, drive mappings, and moving about the network.

- ◆ Chapter 4 discusses security concepts. In this chapter, you learn about the different user types and how to create and manage users and groups. This chapter discusses rights and attributes for files and directories.

- ◆ Chapter 5 teaches you about NetWare menu utilities and several command-line utilities that enable you to create and manage users and files on the network.

◆ Chapter 6 comprehensively covers the topic of printing. In this chapter, you learn to navigate the menu utilities that apply to printing and learn about the printing command-line utilities.

◆ Chapter 7 deals with customizing the environment for the user. In this chapter, you learn about loading applications on the network, creating login scripts and menus, and creating the proper files for the workstation so that a user can log in to the network.

Part Three describes the features specific to NetWare 3.1x:

◆ Chapter 8 teaches you about the features of 3.1x that make this operating system so unique and well-liked. This chapter discusses the features that the System Administrator has at his disposal for security and functionality.

◆ Chapter 9 covers the advanced topics that deal with 3.1x, such as memory management, SBACKUP, and NetWare Naming Service.

Part Four describes the features specific to NetWare 2.2:

◆ Chapter 10 deals with basic 2.2 administration skills. In this chapter, you learn the ways in which 2.2 differs from 3.1x.

◆ Chapter 11 covers advanced 2.2 topics, such as memory management and accounting.

Part Five contains three appendixes:

◆ In Appendix A, you find an overview of Novell's NetWare certification programs and process.

◆ In Appendix B, you find comparison charts that you can use to study for the tests. These charts quickly point out many similarities and differences between the NetWare 2.2 and NetWare 3.1x.

◆ In Appendix C, you find Novell's list of test objectives for the following tests: NetWare 2.2 System Manager, NetWare 2.2 Advanced System Manager, NetWare 3.1x Administration, and NetWare 3.1x Advanced Administration.

PART 1

Network Workstations

Exploring Networks and Network Workstation Hardware

Without microcomputers, you probably would have no reason to read this book. Computers would still be expensive, and LANs would be installed only by engineers and only on large computer networks. Without inexpensive computing power on many users' desktops, NetWare would never have achieved its current popularity.

Microcomputers are more than just desktop computers, however. Microcomputers are also the heirs to the corporate mainframes. In the guise of network file servers, microcomputers have lowered the cost of sharing large databases and powerful applications. The same microcomputer revolution that put spreadsheets on your desktop made the network server possible.

Of the many types of microprocessor-based computers, two are most often used as workstations on NetWare LANs. The overwhelming favorite is based on the IBM PC architecture (classified as PC compatibles), but Macintosh computers are present in significant numbers. (NetWare also can be installed on a wide variety of UNIX workstations and minicomputers, but such installations are fewer in number.)

In this chapter, you learn about the basic characteristics and functions of a computer, and about the elements that make up the most common types of network workstations. Several of these elements are common to most PCs. The items covered in this chapter include the following:

◆ Different types of microprocessors

◆ Expansion buses

◆ Disk drives and floppy drives

◆ Ports

◆ Displays

Understanding the Characteristics of Digital Computers

Microcomputers are digital computers; they function by manipulating numbers. If you look deep into the heart of a digital computer, you see that this piece of equipment consists of millions of switches elaborately wired together. Memory, processing, and everything else revolves around on/off switches.

The basic unit of information in the computer, therefore, depends on whether a switch is turned on or off. Each switch manages a bit of data. A *bit* is the most basic unit of computer data, and can have only two values—one or zero—that correspond to the on or off condition of a switch. Number systems restricted to two values are called *binary*, and the term "bit" originates from the expression "binary digit."

If computers represented only the values one and zero, they would have limited appeal. When bits are combined, however, they can represent just about anything. Consider Morse code. The code uses only two symbols—dot and dash; when these symbols are strung together, however, they can represent letters. Letters can be combined to form words and sentences, all derived from two symbols.

Digital computers combine bits to represent more complex types of data. The most common group of bits is the *byte*, which consists of eight bits. The 8-bit pattern 01000001 is commonly used to represent the letter A in a standard code named ASCII.

The same pattern can represent the decimal number 65. Take a minute to see how.

The base-ten numbering system, also called the *decimal system*, is based on powers of the number 10. You probably are comfortable with the following approach to determining the value of the number 8,451:

8 represents 8×10^3 ($8 \times 10 \times 10 \times 10$ or 8×1000)

4 represents 4×10^2 ($4 \times 10 \times 10$ or 4×100)

5 represents 5×10^1 (5×10)

1 represents 1×10^0 (1×1)

If you keep this simple mathematical principle handy, you easily can understand two other systems used to represent values inside the computer. The value 10 is not particularly useful when working with bits. Ten is represented by the bit pattern 1010, just one of many bit patterns. A system that produces numbers such as 10, 100, 1,000, and so on is more convenient.

Describe the binary number system and explain how the microcomputer uses it to process data.

Computers work most naturally by using binary representation, which uses powers of two. The following shows how 1101 is evaluated in binary:

1 represents 1×2^3 ($1 \times 2 \times 2 \times 2$ or 1×8)

1 represents 1×2^2 ($1 \times 2 \times 2$ or 1×4)

0 represents 0×2^1 (0×2)

1 represents 1×2^0 (1×1)

If you add these values, you see that 1101 in binary is equivalent to the decimal value 13. Binary numbers are usually represented in groups of eight bits. The powers of two for a byte are as follows:

$$2^0 = 1$$

$$2^1 = 2$$

$$2^2 = 4$$

$$2^3 = 8$$

$$2^4 = 16$$

$$2^5 = 32$$

$$2^6 = 64$$

$$2^7 = 128$$

$$2^8 = 255$$

If these values are added together, you can clearly see that a byte can represent the equivalents of decimal numbers 0 through 255.

When working with computers, you may be surprised at some of the apparently random numbers that appear with reference to memory and other computer capacities. The numbers appear awkward in their decimal form, but look quite natural in binary. A *kilobyte* (KB) is 1,024 bytes decimal; this seemingly arbitrary value is easy to explain because the binary equivalent is an even 10000000000, which is 2^{10}. 1,000 bytes (binary 1111101000) would be an unusual amount of memory for a computer to have, but you can see now that 1,024 bytes is quite natural.

Long series of ones and zeros are difficult for humans to scan—you probably had trouble counting the digits in the previous paragraph—and decimal conversions of some values are awkward. This is why you frequently encounter numbers expressed in hexadecimal, hex for short. Hex uses base 16, which fits nicely alongside binary because 16 is 2^4. Table 1.1 shows the first 16-hex digits alongside their equivalent binary and decimal values.

Table 1.1
Hexadecimal Digits with Their Binary and Decimal Equivalents

Hexadecimal	Binary	Decimal
0	0000	0
1	0001	1
2	0010	2
3	0011	3
4	0100	4
5	0101	5
6	0110	6
7	0111	7
8	1000	8
9	1001	9
A	1010	10
B	1011	11
C	1100	12
D	1101	13
E	1110	14
F	1111	15

Notice that the letters A through F represent hex digits above nine. Also notice that a single hex digit is an exact fit for four bits. That makes it easy to represent long bit patterns as hexadecimal numbers. Consider the binary number 0010110101011011 in comparison to its hex equivalent:

0010	1101	0101	1011
2	D	5	B

Modern PCs generally have memory of a *megabyte* (MB) or more. Because it takes 20 bits to represent a megabyte, memory addresses are usually written in hex. Table 1.2 presents some common values. You may have wondered why DOS memory is 640 KB. In table 1.2, you see that it falls on a convenient numbering boundary.

Table 1.2
Conversions for Common Values

Value	Decimal	Binary	Hex
1 KB	1024	0100 0000 0000	400h
640 KB	655360	1010 0000 0000 0000 0000	A0000h
1 MB	1048576	0001 0000 0000 0000 0000 0000	100000h

Given the lengths of the binary numbers, you are probably glad that hex numbers exist. Notice that hex numbers are generally tagged with an "h" so they cannot be confused with decimal numbers. (Hex numbers are occasionally expressed by using the conventions of the C programming language. A hex number is prefaced with 0x, for example 0x2D5B.)

 Almost any *Bulletin Board System* (BBS) has several calculator programs that can convert hex, decimal, and binary numbers. You will find one of these to be a handy tool.

Understanding Microcomputer Functions

The computer performs many functions. Which function it performs at any given time depends on the instructions it has been given.

Describe the basic functions of a computer.

The computer performs five functions that are basic to its operation. These functions include:

♦ Bootup

♦ Input

♦ Processing

♦ Storage

♦ Output

Bootup, as discussed previously, involves testing the important parts of the PC, running startup files, and loading other necessary files, such as device drivers.

Input involves taking data from an external source and putting it into the computer. External sources may include floppy disks, the keyboard, the mouse, and so on.

Process involves manipulating the data that has been input, for the sake of producing some kind of result (output).

Storage is the process of taking any data—raw (*unprocessed*) input, processed data, and software—and saving it to a storage device, such as a hard disk, for later retrieval.

Section Review Questions

1. Which statement about the number 1011 is incorrect?

    a. It cannot be a hexadecimal number.

    b. If it is binary, it represents an eleven.

    c. If it is decimal, it represents one thousand and eleven.

    d. If it is binary, the hexadecimal equivalent of this number is B.

2. What designation is used to specify a hexadecimal number?

    a. hx

    b. x

    c. 0x

    d. Xx

3. Which of the following is NOT a microcomputer function?

    a. Bootup

    b. Processing

    c. Storage

    d. Memory

4. Adding two numbers together is a/an _____ function.

    a. Input

    b. Processing

    c. Storage

    d. Memory

5. Computers function most naturally using _____ repre-sentation.

    a. Binary

    b. Hexadecimal

    c. Base10

    d. ASCII

Answers

1. a
2. c
3. d
4. b
5. a

Exploring Microcomputer Hardware

In this section, you learn about the hardware components found on the main computer board. This circuit board also is called the *motherboard*, and boards that plug into it are called *daughterboards*.

 List and describe the major hardware components of a microcomputer.

Any computer contains at least the following components:

◆ Central processor

◆ Memory

◆ Long-term storage

◆ Input and output devices

Figure 1.1 shows the logical relationship of these components.

Figure 1.1

Logical relationship of major computer components.

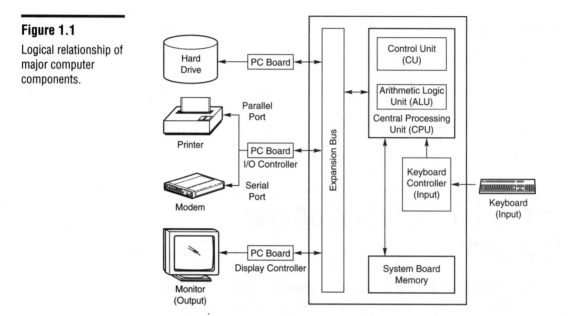

In a microcomputer, the *central processing unit* (CPU) usually is housed in a single chip, the microprocessor. This device represents the most significant cost savings of microcomputers when compared to their larger computing cousins. A modern microprocessor represents the processing power of hundreds of pounds and tens of square feet of 1970s- or even 1980s-vintage mainframe computers. The CPU is responsible for all the actual processing or data manipulation that takes place in the computer.

Memory is a high-speed "scratchpad" where the CPU stores data and programs for quick reference. Memory is electronic, usually in the form of computer chips. The two types of memory are RAM and ROM. *Random access memory* (RAM) is memory that must be under power to retain data. When data must be retained after the computer is powered off, it is stored in *read-only memory* (ROM), which cannot be easily modified, but retains data indefinitely.

Storage is slow memory that can store large amounts of data permanently and economically. Most microcomputers use floppy and hard disks for data storage.

The most common input device for a microcomputer is the keyboard, and the most common output device is a monitor. The input and output functions, however, are not always separate. Computers on LANs do much of their input and output (I/O) through network interface cards, which perform both input and output functions. Each of these systems is discussed in detail later in the chapter.

Microprocessors

The *microprocessor* is the component of your personal computer that makes it a computer. It is also known as the central processing unit, or CPU. The CPU determines and controls the computer's processing capabilities, such as what types of software programs it can process.

The microprocessor is a set of integrated circuits and transistors housed in a silicon chip. You usually can spot this chip easily on the main computer board. It is larger than most other chips and is usually square with the manufacturer's name and processor type imprinted on the face.

 Internally, the microprocessor has two major components: the control unit and the arithmetic/logic unit. These components are illustrated within the microprocessor block of figure 1.1.

The *control unit* (CU) directs the operation of the CPU. Instructions to the computer are stored in the form of programs. The control unit keeps track of and interprets the instructions given by a program, and is responsible for directing different elements of the computer to carry out specific tasks. The CU controls most I/O, memory, and storage functions.

continues

The CU interfaces with the *arithmetic/logic unit* (ALU), which is responsible for the actual computing operations. Two types of computations are performed at this level:

- Arithmetic operations include addition, subtraction, multiplication, and division.

- Logical operations involve actions dependent on comparing two data values. One such logical operation is the test and branch, which is similar in function to the IF statements in MS-DOS batch files or in NetWare login scripts.

This chapter examines two series of microprocessors. One series, developed by Intel, is the foundation of the large family of compatibles derived from the IBM personal computers. Another series, developed by Motorola, is the processor used in Apple's popular line of Macintosh computers.

Several models of microprocessors are available in each family. When comparing the various models, focus on the following characteristics:

- **Internal data bus size.** Microprocessors store data in temporary storage locations called *registers*. Data is moved among registers, the CU, the ALU, and other microprocessor components by means of a bus built into the microprocessor circuitry. The size of this bus is a measure of how much data the microprocessor can transfer in a single operation. This value can range from 8 to 32 bits—more is better.

- **Data bus size.** This is a measure of how much data can be moved between the microprocessor and outside devices in a single operation. The bus is a system of connectors and wiring that distributes data throughout the computer. The larger the data bus, the better the performance of the microprocessor. This value ranges from 8_32 bits. This measure is frequently referred to as the external data bus size to contrast it with the internal data bus size.

- **Memory address size.** The larger the memory address, the larger the amount of memory the microprocessor can manage.

- **Clock speed.** An electronic clock ensures that the many elements of the computer are properly coordinated. Higher performance computer components can operate at higher clock speeds.

- **Special features.** Many microprocessors have special features that set them apart from other, similar models.

Clock speed is a measure of how fast the CPU is operating. The measurement is taken in millions of clock cycles per second, also known as *megahertz* (MHz). It is common in the evolution of a microprocessor model to see the clock speed at which it can operate increase.

A *bus* is like a highway for moving data. The wider a highway is, the more lanes it has, and the more traffic it can move efficiently. Similarly, a wide bus with more data lines can move more bits at the same time and can move data more efficiently.

Intel Microprocessors and IBM PC Compatibles

Because the Intel 8088 microprocessor was chosen by IBM for the original IBM PC, the Intel microprocessor architecture has become the dominant force in personal computers. Most IBM-compatible PCs also use the Intel chip. In recent years, several manufacturers have introduced compatible microprocessors; however, the basic designs and features of these compatible chips are similar to those of the Intel products. In addition, Intel has developed many modified versions of its basic processors for specialized uses, such as low-power portables.

To date, five classes of Intel microprocessors have been used in IBM-compatible PCs. All have model numbers beginning with 80, and most end in 86, so the series is frequently referred to as the

21

80×86 series. (A sixth model, the Pentium, is in very limited distribution at this writing. Its features are geared toward powerful workstations and network servers.)

 List five types of microprocessor chips made by the Intel Corporation.

An IBM-compatible motherboard is illustrated in figure 1.2. This motherboard was designed for an 80386 microprocessor. It has become difficult to draw a typical motherboard, given the many new technologies that have simplified circuit board design. The original IBM AT had dozens of chips. The RAM banks shown in figure 1.2 have been superseded by memory modules on plug-in circuit boards. The functions of many chips have been integrated into chipsets that make it possible to construct an entire computer with only about four chips.

The following sections give you an overview of the basic Intel microprocessors.

Figure 1.2

Motherboard for an IBM-compatible microcomputer.

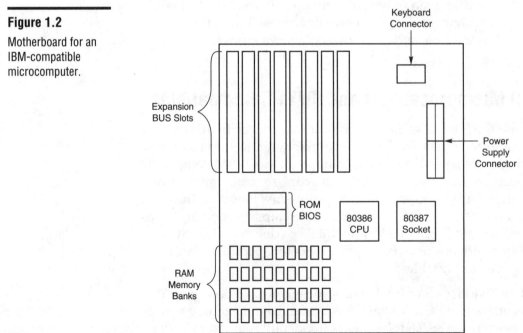

8086

The 8086 came on the market in 1978. Before its introduction, PCs were built around an 8-bit architecture. This meant that data could only be processed eight bits at a time. The 8086 introduced 16-bit processing, and had 16-bit internal and external data buses. This made the 8086 the most powerful microprocessor of its era.

The 8086 has the following features:

◆ 16-bit internal data bus

◆ 16-bit external data bus

◆ 20-bit addresses capable of addressing 1 MB

When first introduced, the 8086 was adopted by few computer designers because of the high cost of 16-bit devices. The first high-volume product to use the 8086 was the highly successful Compaq line of IBM-compatibles.

8088

The high cost of 16-bit components led IBM to choose the 8088 as the microprocessor for its popular IBM PC. The 8088 was a down-graded 8086. Internally, the chips were identical. The 8088, how-ever, had an 8-bit external data bus and could use inexpensive 8-bit components.

The 8088 has the following features:

◆ 16-bit internal data bus

◆ 8-bit external data bus

◆ 20-bit memory address capable of addressing 1 MB

◆ Clock speeds from 4.77 to 10 MHz

Note The 8086 and 8088 microprocessors set the stan-dard for IBM and DOS compatibility. The 8086 and 8088 are identical chips as far as software is con-cerned; in fact, they often are referred to collec-tively by the 8086 model number. The same DOS

continues

23

runs on both processors, as well as the same applications. All later Intel processors have the capability to function as an 8086 microprocessor does, and
the DOS operating system continues to be designed
around the features and limitations of the 8086.

80286

When first introduced, the IBM PC dazzled computer users with
its impressive features. In a day when most computers utilized a
mere 64 KB of memory, the PC's capability of addressing a full
megabyte was amazing. Few users could even afford to buy that
much memory. In addition, 4.77 MHz was a respectable clock
speed. It did not take long, however, for a new generation of
applications to test the limits of the IBM PC and the 8088/8086
microprocessors.

 Distinguish between real and protected modes of
the 80286, 80386, and 80486 microprocessors.

The 80286 was introduced in 1984 to address the demand for
better and faster processing. The 80286 retained a mode called *real
mode* that made the 80286 function like a "real" 8086 microprocessor; higher performance in this mode was achieved with a 16-bit
data bus and a faster 6 MHz clock. Real mode, however, has all
the disadvantages of the 8086/8088, particularly the 1 MB
memory limit.

Among the 80286's new features was *protected mode*. In this mode,
the 80286 can address 16 MB of memory, and can even use disk
storage to achieve virtual memory sizes up to 1 GB (one gigabyte,
or one billion bytes).

A form of multitasking made multitasking operating systems
possible. Microsoft's Xenix is an implementation of UNIX developed for the 80286 microprocessor. The first version of IBM's
multitasking OS/2 operating system also was developed for the
80286. Multitasking enables multiple applications to execute

simultaneously without interfering with each other; a malfunction of one application does not cause all applications to fail. You can easily see that large memory size and multitasking are important features for a network operating system, and NetWare relies on protected mode to turn an Intel PC into a high-performance server.

The 80286's features are as follows:

◆ 16-bit internal data bus

◆ 16-bit external data bus

◆ 24-bit memory address enabling the CPU to address 16 MB of memory directly

◆ Clock speeds from 6 to 20 MHz

◆ Virtual memory

◆ Multitasking capabilities when using a multitasking operating system

◆ Two modes of operation: real and protected

Note

New generations of software quickly outgrew the 80286. NetWare 2.*x* can probably be regarded as the most successful multitasking operating system to run on an 80286 microprocessor. Although early versions of IBM's OS/2 operating systems were designed for the 80286, they achieved little popularity among users.

When Intel designed the 80286, it was believed that after a computer was switched into protected mode, there would be no need to leave that mode. In fact, Intel's chip designers neglected to provide an instruction for switching from protected to real mode. Although a work-around was discovered, performance was slow because the procedure required a processor reset. The lack of an instruction to switch to real mode was perhaps the most serious design flaw in the 80286.

continues

Many of the limitations of the 80286 are reflected in the features of NetWare 2.*x*—in particular, the 16 MB memory limitation. A more advanced processor than the 80286 was essential to enable NetWare to reach its current potential.

80386

The 80386 can be considered the foundation for all later Intel processors. The 80386 has 32-bit registers and a 32-bit data bus, and was the first Intel processor to reach 32-bit status. The 80386 can address 4 GB of real memory and 32 TB (32 *terabytes*, or a million million bytes) of virtual memory. The 80386 is the first Intel processor whose design limits were not seriously pressed within a short time of release. The 80386 architecture leaves considerable room for growth.

 Describe the difference between the 80386DX and the 80386SX microprocessors.

Most of the PC add-on expansion boards have 8- or 16-bit designs and do not take full advantage of the 80386's capabilities. Because manufacturing costs of full 32-bit computers were high, Intel introduced the 80386SX as a low-cost alternative to the full 32-bit 80386, which is designated as the 80386DX.

The 80386SX has a 32-bit internal bus and a 16-bit external data bus. It is identical to the 80386DX internally, but is capable of external data transfers of 16 bits only.

The 80386 processors share real mode with the 8086 and the 80286, as well as the protected mode of the 80286. In addition, the 80386 has a mode called the *virtual real* or *virtual 8086 mode*. This mode enables the single processor to divide its resources and emulate multiple 8086 processors. Thus, the single processor can run multiple DOS applications at once. This mode has been used to implement multitasking in some versions of programs such as Microsoft Windows.

The features of the 80386 include the following:

- ◆ The 80386 can address up to 4 GB of real memory and 32 TB of virtual memory.

- ◆ The 80386 works in three modes: real, protected, and virtual real.

- ◆ The 80386 is equipped with instructions for switching from protected to real mode without the need for a reset.

- ◆ Clock speeds for the 80386SX are 16 MHz and 20 MHz. The 80386DX has clock speeds of 16, 20, 25, and 33 MHz. (Some manufacturers of compatible microprocessors have pushed these speeds upward in their versions.)

80486

The 80486 is a combination of the functionality of the 80386 chip, in addition to a math coprocessor, and a high-speed memory controller. The math coprocessor is built into the microprocessor chip and is used for intense mathematical calculations, such as those used in *computer-aided design* (CAD) and spreadsheets.

Note

Math coprocessors improve the capability of the computer to perform complex calculations. They make it possible, for example, to multiply large decimal numbers directly without converting them first into binary equivalents. Math coprocessors are popular for users who perform complex financial and engineering calculations using tools such as spreadsheets and CAD.

Prior to the 80486, math coprocessors were always packaged in separate chips. These chips were designated the 80287 and the 80387 as companions for the 80286 and 80386 chips. The 80486 is the first Intel microprocessor to include a math coprocessor in the same chip as the CPU.

continues

Because many users do not require a math coprocessor, Intel released a modified version of the 80486, called the 80486SX, in which the math coprocessor is disabled. The standard 80486 was relabeled as the 80486DX. Notice that SX and DX mean different things in the 386 and 486 processors. Much confusion has arisen out of this inconsistent labeling.

Unlike the 80286 and 80386 microprocessors, the 80486 does not add any new modes. In fact, the 80486 is an upwardly compatible version of the 80386. Most features are the same, but the 80486 reaches higher performance levels through better design and some new performance-enhancing features.

The 80486 incorporates a high-speed memory controller called a *cache controller*—a technology that employs high-speed memory in the CPU chip. The cache controller speeds access to memory by storing recently read bytes and by anticipating bytes that will be needed in the near future. Access to this in-chip memory is considerably faster than access to system memory.

Each successive Intel chip is compatible with add-in boards made for use with the older chip version. If, for example, you are using an 80386DX with an ISA bus (bus types are discussed later in this chapter), you can use 8-bit, 16-bit, or 32-bit boards made by almost any manufacturer.

The 80486 is available in standard clock speeds of 25 and 33 MHz. Intel has developed a clock-doubling capability that allows versions of the 80486 to function at 50 and 66 MHz internally, although they interface with the outside components at the non-doubled speed.

Pentium

The Intel processor that follows the 80486 is named the *Pentium*. The Pentium retains the 32-bit address bus width of the 80486, but dramatically expands the data bus width to 64 bits, meaning that the Pentium can move data twice as rapidly as the 80486. The Pentium incorporates two 8-bit caches (the 80486 has one) that significantly alleviate the bottleneck between the CPU and system memory. These are just some of the many performance enhancements that have been added to the Pentium.

A revolutionary difference between the Pentium and its predecessors is that the Pentium incorporates two data pipelines that enable the processor to execute two instructions at one time. Currently, Pentiums operate at 60 and 66 MHz, but faster versions are promised. The Pentium incorporates a math coprocessor.

The Pentium is equipped with twin data pipelines that can be used to support *multithreading*, the practice of running two tasks simultaneously in the CPU. Multithreading differs from multitasking, which can be performed on any CPU. In a multitasking system, each program is allowed momentary access to the CPU. The operating system (or application) switches the CPU's attention between the programs to be serviced so that each program is executed a little at a time. The microprocessor's speed gives the illusion that all programs are being executed simultaneously, but the reality is that only one program is actually being processed at any given moment. A multithreading CPU, on the other hand, is nearly like having two microprocessors at the same time.

Operating systems must be explicitly programmed to utilize the twin data pipelines of the Pentium. At present, few operating systems are capable of taking advantage of the multithreading capability of the Pentium. Windows NT is a noteworthy exception.

Summary of Features for Intel Microprocessors

Table 1.3 summarizes the features of the Intel processors discussed in this chapter.

 Identify the general differences between the 80386 and the 80486 Intel microprocessor chips.

Table 1.3
Features of Intel Microprocessors

	8086	8088	80286	80386DX	80386SX	80486DX	80486SX	Pentium
Register size	16 bit	16 bit	16 bit	32 bit	32 bit	32 bit	32 bit	64 bit
Data bus size	16 bit	8 bit	16 bit	32 bit	16 bit	32 bit	32 bit	64 bit
Address size	20 bit	20 bit	24 bit	32 bit	32 bit	32 bit	32 bit	32 bit
Max. memory	1 MB	1 MB	16 MB	4 GB	4 GB	4 GB	4 GB	4 GB
Virtual memory	None	None	1 GB	32 TB	32 TB	32 TB	32 TB	32 TB
Speed	4.77–10 MHz	4.77–10 MHz	6–20 MHz	16–33 MHz	16–20 MHz	25–33 MHz	20–25 MHz	60–66 MHz
Math coprocessor	Extra	Extra	Extra	Extra	Extra	Built-in	Extra	Built-in
Real mode	Yes	Yes	Yes	Yes	Yes	Yes	Yes	Yes
Protected mode	No	No	Yes	Yes	Yes	Yes	Yes	Yes
Virtual real mode	No	No	No	Yes	Yes	Yes	Yes	Yes

Motorola and Apple Macintosh

Apple Macintoshes are the second most popular personal computers on NetWare LANs, and you should know something about the Motorola M68000 family of microprocessor used in Macs.

MC68000

The MC68000 was introduced in 1979. It soon became popular with computers designed for engineering, graphics, and multimedia.

The Macintosh brought the 68000 series to a prominent position in the microcomputer industry.

 Describe the 68000 Motorola microprocessor chip family.

The MC68000 has a 32-bit internal data bus, but is equipped with a 16-bit external data bus.

Basic features of the MC68000 include the following:

◆ 32-bit internal data bus

◆ 16-bit external data bus

◆ 24-bit internal address bus

◆ 16 MB addressable memory

◆ 8–16 MHz clock speed

Most of the first versions of the Macintosh (as well as the first NetWare server) use the MC68000 chip. The Mac Portable, however, uses the MC68HC000, which is a low-power version of the MC68000.

MC68020

The MC68020 was introduced in 1984 and was anticipated to have many features that Intel later introduced in the 80386 and 80486 chips. The 68020 is a true 32-bit processor internally and externally. It is also equipped with a 256-byte instruction cache that enables it to hold instructions in processor memory pending execution.

The Macintosh II and the Mac LC use the MC68020, which has the following features:

◆ 32-bit internal and external data buses

◆ 4 GB of addressable memory

◆ Optional math coprocessor

◆ 12 MHz and 16 MHz clock speeds, with a potential for 33 MHz speeds

MC68030

At this writing, the MC68030 is the most popular processor in the Macintosh product line. The primary enhancement of the 68030 is a *paged memory-management unit* (PMMU), which enables Macs with 68030s to take advantage of the virtual memory features of System 7. Virtual memory swaps data between RAM and hard disk storage, making the computer appear to be equipped with much more than its physical (chip-based) memory.

The 68030 has two independent 32-bit address buses and two 32-bit data buses. The function of these buses is parallel to speed data transfers. This parallelism allows the CPU to perform multiple tasks simultaneously.

To the 68020's instruction cache was added a 256-byte data cache that holds recently used data in memory in case it is needed again.

The Macintosh SE/30 and the Macintosh IIx series use the MC68030, which has dual 32-bit buses that enable the processor to perform two things at the same time. The MC68030 boasts the following features:

◆ Dual 32-bit address buses

◆ Dual 32-bit data buses

◆ On-chip data cache and instruction caches

◆ Support for dual-processor computers

◆ Single processor can perform two simultaneous tasks

◆ Clock speeds from 16 to 40 MHz

MC68040

The MC68040 processor is found in the flagship Macintosh computer—the Quadra. It masses four times the transistors of the

68030. New features include two 4 KB caches, one each for data and instructions. The 68040 also contains a math coprocessor that handles some of the functions of a math chip.

A new feature called *pipelining* enables the CPU to decode and execute several program instructions at a time.

New features of the MC68040 are as follows:

♦ 4 KB data cache

♦ 4 KB instruction cache

♦ Math coprocessor

♦ Pipelining

Understanding the Expansion Bus

The data bus was mentioned in an earlier section in describing the features of the microprocessor. The data bus is external to the microprocessor and is found on the system board, also known as the motherboard. The data bus provides the means to transfer data among the microprocessor, memory, and add-in cards through the circuitry found on the motherboard. The data bus can resolve conflicts that occur when transferring data, and also ensure that each electrical contact carries the correct signal.

You cannot see the data bus easily. The data bus consists of printed-circuit wiring traces on the motherboard. The data bus services the memory on the motherboard. It also connects to the expansion bus.

The part of the expansion bus you can see is the series of connector slots on most microcomputer motherboards. These slots accept most add-in boards, such as network cards and floppy drive controller boards. Through these slots, data is moved between the boards and the computer circuitry.

Think of the expansion bus as the highway that moves information around in your computer, and the expansion slots as the on and off ramps. Each expansion slot contains circuits that enable devices in the slots to receive data from the expansion bus highway and send data to the bus.

Because most data enters and leaves the computer through expansion cards installed in expansion slots, the design of the expansion bus is critical to the performance of a network server. User workstations perform most of their data manipulations within the confines of their own circuitry, reaching outside only to access a server-based file or to print, for example. The file server, on the other hand, exists to share files with other computers on the network. Servers, therefore, are constantly inputting and outputting data to the network. Because the bus design determines how rapidly data I/O happens, bus design is a critical consideration where servers are concerned.

The following are the two expansion options used in Macintoshes:

◆ The *Processor Direct Slot* (PDS)

◆ The NuBus expansion bus

Bus Characteristics

Consider the following characteristics when you examine expansion buses:

◆ The number of available interrupts determines how many independent devices can perform I/O.

◆ The data bus size affects the speed of I/O operations.

◆ The address bus size determines how much memory can be located on expansion boards.

◆ The maximum clock speed that the bus can accommodate affects overall performance.

Interrupts

In a computer, virtually everything—from memory to disk storage, to keyboard I/O and interfacing with the network—is controlled by the microprocessor. One way for the microprocessor to manage all these resources is to poll each area periodically to see if it needs servicing. This requires the microprocessor to stop what it is doing, save its place, and periodically poll the devices regardless of whether the devices need attention.

The interrupt mechanism can be used by devices to notify the microprocessor that they need to be serviced. Microprocessors are equipped with *Interrupt Request* (IRQ) lines that can be assigned to subsystems. When the subsystem needs attention, it asserts its assigned interrupt, causing the microprocessor to halt its current process and service the subsystem. Because the service intervals for many systems are extremely irregular, interrupts are more efficient than polling in I/O-intensive situations.

Think of the first method in terms of driving along a street where every intersection is marked with four-way stop signs. You must stop at each sign, regardless of whether another car is at the intersection.

Interrupts replace the stop signs with intelligent stoplights that change only when a car is waiting to use the intersection. With such stoplights, your progress is not stopped unless another car trips the sensors that notify the light to change. Because you only stop when another driver demands access to the intersection, your progress is far more regular.

Because the tasks of network servers are I/O-intensive, many devices can require service. Servers, therefore, frequently require large numbers of interrupts. Careful configuration of interrupts is critical to getting the most out of a NetWare server.

Memory Address

As you learned in the discussion about microprocessors, the maximum size of the memory address determines the amount of memory a computer can use. A 24-bit address can support 16 MB of RAM, for example.

Data Bus Width

A wider data bus can move more bits of data in a single operation. Because the data bus is the highway that moves data around your computer, the more lanes it has the better. Data buses in common microcomputers range from 8–32 bits in width.

Maximum Clock Speed

You already learned about microprocessors with clock speeds of 33 MHz or more. It is important that you understand that this rating reflects the internal speed of the microprocessor. Outside the microprocessor chip, events do not happen at such high rates. When electronic circuits are pushed to high rates of speed, they begin to fail. An important goal in bus design is to increase the speed at which the bus operates.

Buses Used in PC Compatibles

Three bus designs are associated with PC compatibles:

♦ The *Industry Standard Architecture* (ISA) bus

♦ The Micro Channel bus

♦ The *Extended ISA* (EISA) bus

The connectors and cards used for each bus are illustrated in figure 1.3.

 Explain how the data bus of the IBM AT has become the ISA bus.

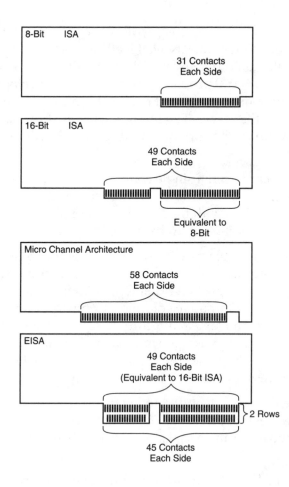

Figure 1.3

Characteristics of ISA, Micro Channel, and EISA accessory cards.

The ISA Bus

The expansion bus of the IBM AT is considered the industry standard because it combines the elements of the older IBM PC expansion bus with the newer 80286's 16-bit expansion bus. The 16-bit AT bus combination is called the *Industry Standard Architecture* (ISA) bus. (The original 8-bit PC bus was severely limited and is not a part of any currently manufactured PCs.)

The 16-bit ISA bus was defined by IBM before network file servers were common. At the time, Novell NetWare ran on a proprietary server manufactured by Novell called the 68B, which was based on the Motorola 68000 processor. Not until IBM developed the model AT did a mass-produced personal computer have the essentials for a file server. The limitations of the ISA bus, however, placed limits on the performance and services NetWare could offer.

The 8-bit ISA card used a single connector with 62 pins. When IBM designed the 16-bit connector, they simply added another 36-pin connector in line with the first. This configuration allowed the AT to accept either 8-bit or 16-bit cards in the same slot.

The ISA bus has problems with speed and compatibility. For example, the bus becomes unreliable at clock rates in excess of 10 MHz, and is seldom pushed faster than 8 MHz. This caused other vendors to create alternative solutions. Compaq Computer Corporation introduced a Flex Architecture to solve the problem of slow movement of data between the microprocessor and memory. The Flex Architecture bypasses the expansion bus so that memory and the microprocessor can communicate directly.

Most of the PCs manufactured today use variations of this type of architecture. Memory in these PCs is installed either directly on the motherboard or in special slots independent of the expansion bus.

In the original IBM PC architecture, only eight interrupts were available, numbered 0 through 7. Interrupts 2 through 7 are available to devices on the expansion bus, but several of these are usually reserved. Table 1.4 summarizes the preassigned interrupts for the original PC architecture.

Table 1.4
Interrupts for the IBM PC

IRQ	Standard Use
2	EGA display (generally available)
3	COM2 (serial port 2)

IRQ	Standard Use
4	COM1 (serial port 1)
5	Hard disk controller
6	Floppy disk controller
7	Printer

Although some interrupts (3, 4, and 7) can be reassigned if the standard resource is not being used, you can see that not many interrupts are available for use with network cards or other devices.

When the AT was introduced, IBM doubled the number of interrupts. Table 1.5 shows the available interrupts on an AT.

Table 1.5
Interrupts on an IBM AT

IRQ	Standard Use
2	Cascade to IRQ 9
3	COM2
4	COM1
5	LPT2
6	Disk controller (hard and floppy)
7	LPT1
8	Real-time clock
9	Available
10	Available
11	Available
12	Available

continues

Table 1.5, Continued
Interrupts on an IBM AT

IRQ	Standard Use
13	Coprocessor
14	Hard disk controller
15	Available

As you can see, the AT supports more interrupts, but only for expansion boards specifically designed to take advantage of them. The AT interrupt configurations have been inherited by the Micro Channel and EISA bus designs.

 In the IBM AT architecture used by most modern compatibles, interrupt 2 is a special interrupt known as the *cascade interrupt*. The interrupt circuit design uses interrupt 2 to pass interrupts on to the circuits responsible for interrupts 8 through 15. A consequence of this is that IRQ 2 and IRQ 9 are functionally the same.

 Explain why it is important to avoid interrupt, memory, and I/O address conflicts.

ISA option boards are usually configured with jumpers or switches on the boards. Because interrupts, memory addresses, and other options are set manually, it is common for installers to set two boards to the same settings. Such conflicts are common causes of system failures. More troublesome are the times when conflicts cause intermittent failures. If two devices share the same interrupt, the PC usually hangs when the devices conflict. If one device is active only occasionally, however, failures can be irregular, and the causes hard to detect.

Describe what a terminating resistor does.

Another potential source of trouble, particularly for hard disk drives, is the terminating resistor. A *terminating resistor* is an electronic component placed in a reserved socket on the last disk drive attached to the controller cable (when multiple drives are attached in a series to one controller cable). By reducing (resisting) the flow of electric current through the connecting cable, the terminating resistor successfully signals the computer that the associated drive is the last disk drive in the series. If the terminating resistor is located on the wrong disk drive, is missing, or has been damaged, an error reading the disk drives results.

Most ISA cards require you to set some options using switches or jumpers. Consult the manuals shipped with the option card to determine the correct settings.

The 16-bit ISA bus remains the most popular bus in PC compatibles. ISA expansion devices are priced competitively. In most cases, the ISA bus is well-suited for network workstations performing moderate levels of I/O. New generations of high-performance machines, however, are exceeding the limits of the ISA bus even in single-user computers.

The ISA bus is a poor choice for network servers. The 16-bit data path is narrow, 16 MB of memory is seldom enough, and ISA cards lack advanced features, such as bus mastering, that make MCA and EISA buses shine in servers.

Expansion Bus Settings

Jumpers and switches are found on many expansion boards, and often have to be set in order to avoid conflicts among add-in boards.

Explain how interrupt, memory, and I/O address settings are made on expansion boards.

Jumper settings are made by inserting a small electrical jumper over pins. Manufacturer's instructions describe whether a jumper should be present or absent for each set of pins.

Switches are frequently manufactured in packages the size of integrated circuits. Because these packages are equipped with two rows of pins that connect to the circuit board, these packages are called *Dual In-Line Pin* (DIP) switches.

Examples of jumpers and DIP switches are shown in figure 1.4.

Figure 1.4

Examples of jumpers and DIP switches.

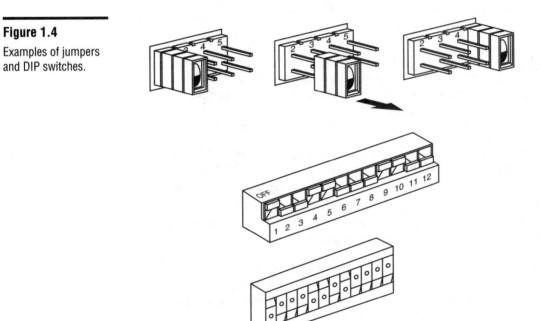

IBM Micro Channel Architecture (MCA) Bus

IBM saw the need for alternative bus architectures, and in 1987 introduced *Micro Channel Architecture* (MCA), along with the PS/2 series. The Micro Channel bus requires completely new expansion cards and remains a proprietary architecture. Many purchasers objected strongly to the need to replace their current stocks of ISA option cards with Micro Channel equivalents.

Vendors wanting to produce Micro Channel computers or expansion cards must license the technology. To date, few vendors other than IBM have produced computers incorporating the Micro Channel. A wide variety of option cards are available, although prices are generally higher than cards designed for the ISA bus. The Micro Channel architecture incorporates many advances over the ISA bus.

The primary justification IBM offered for not designing an ISA-compatible bus was that the ISA bus could not be redesigned for the speeds required by high-performance computers. The Micro Channel bus is designed to achieve a higher bus speed limit. The first Micro Channel PCs had bus speeds of 10 MHz, but the theoretical limit is much higher.

The Micro Channel bus has numerous features that improve performance, reduce susceptibility to noise, and make it easier to reduce EMI emissions.

The MCA bus has 32-bit data paths and 32-bit addressing. It can, therefore, accommodate the full capabilities of the 80386 and 80486 microprocessors.

MCA cards generally do not have any jumpers or configuration switches. They are configured instead by running a program that determines which accessory cards are installed, identifies suitable settings, and stores the settings in the computer's memory. *Non-volatile memory* is memory that retains information when the computer is turned off; it is used to store the system configuration. This procedure is called *automatic installation,* and somewhat simplifies the selection of board configuration options because the configuration program does not allow devices to conflict.

The Micro Channel architecture introduced a feature called *bus mastering* to IBM PCs. Also called *multidevice handling,* this feature allows intelligent option cards to take control of the bus independently of the main microprocessor. Network interface cards in servers are examples of cards whose performance is enhanced by bus mastering.

The MCA architecture offers the following advantages:

◆ The capability of automatically configuring added expansion boards

◆ Better transfer rates

◆ The capability of allowing expansion boards to take control of the bus for certain operations

 Not all PS/2s are equipped with the MCA bus. Table 1.6 shows the original IBM PS/2 models and their configurations.

Table 1.6
Bus Types for Original IBM PS/2s

Model Number	Bus
Model 25 & Model 30	ISA bus
Model 50 & Model 60	16-bit MCA bus
Model 70 & Model 80	32-bit MCA bus

The Micro Channel architecture had everything users wanted in a new bus, except compatibility with the old ISA bus. The prospect of replacing all their ISA option boards with Micro Channel cards made many purchasers adopt a wait-and-see attitude. Early licensing fees were substantial, and few computer manufacturers stepped forward to incorporate MCA into their designs. As a result, the MCA architecture has not been widely implemented outside of the IBM line of microcomputers.

EISA Bus

The MCA bus illuminated the inadequacies of the ISA bus, but not in a way that moved purchasers to accept the new technology overwhelmingly. The industry really wanted a new bus that could still use the old ISA cards, so a group of hardware manufacturers got together to create a new standard. This consortium consisted of AST, Compaq, Epson, Hewlett-Packard, NEC, Olivetti, Tandy, Wyse, and Zenith. The standard that they introduced in late 1988 was called *Enhanced Industry Standard Architecture* (EISA).

The connector for an EISA expansion slot has two tiers of contacts, and EISA cards have two rows of pins. The top row is identical to the pins on the 16-bit ISA card. An ISA card, when inserted into an EISA connector, makes contact only with the ISA row of contacts, and the computer accepts the card as a 16-bit device. If an EISA card is fully inserted, however, both rows of contacts come into play, and the card functions in 32-bit mode. Thus, the EISA connector design accommodates all generations of ISA cards.

EISA offers all the features of MCA, in addition to compatibility with the AT bus. For example, an EISA slot will accept an ISA board; however, only MCA boards can reside in MCA slots.

EISA was designed by a committee and has a wide variety of features. EISA uses an automatic configuration program similar to the program used to configure Micro Channel PCs. Jumpers and configuration switches are eliminated, and EISA features are stored on nonvolatile memory in the PC. The EISA bus also incorporates bus mastering.

VESA Local Bus (VL-Bus)

Changes in the network environment—along with more demanding software—are requiring higher performance levels of all computer components. More detailed graphics displays, multimedia, and graphical user interfaces such as Windows are a few of the developments that have raised performance demands. While microprocessor clock rates rose to 33 MHz and beyond, the bus designs that emerged in the 1980s were essentially limited to operating at 8 MHz speeds. Because much of a PC's performance depends on how rapidly the bus can move data among components, a variety of higher performance buses have evolved in recent years.

One approach is to bypass the bus entirely and enable the processor card to connect directly with the bus of the microprocessor, the so-called "local bus" approach. Several vendors, such as Compaq, Hewlett-Packard, and Dell, have developed proprietary standards for local buses in their PCs. This chapter focuses, however, on nonproprietary approaches.

Video displays are among the subsystems that place the highest demands on bus performance, and the *Video Electronic Standard Association* (VESA) has been a proponent of the VL-Bus primarily as a means of boosting system video performance. While video cards designed for ISA buses typically transmit video data to the screen at rates up to 600,000 pixels per second, VL-Bus video adapters frequently claim to be able to paint screens at rates up to 50–60 million pixels per second.

VL-Bus adapters have also been developed to service hard drives, which now are capable of transferring data at much higher rates than in the 1980s, when earlier buses were designed. IDE drives are capable of sustained data transfer speeds as high as 1.5 MB per second, and VL-Bus IDE controllers are claimed to move data at rates as high as 8 MB per second in short bursts.

The design for this standard incorporates a new 16-bit VL-Bus connector that is placed in-line with the ISA bus connectors on the motherboard, as shown in figure 1.5. This configuration enables a given slot location to support either ISA or VL-Bus cards. VL-Bus can support two slots when operating at 33 MHz, the most typical system configuration. Buffering enables the bus to support three slots.

VL-Bus is capable of performing 32-bit data transfers and data can be transferred at rates as high as 132 MB per second. Because VL-bus was designed primarily for video requirements, it can be difficult to adapt for other needs. Configuration of expansion cards can be difficult. At this time, VL-Bus is the most popular high-performance bus, and is incorporated into the majority of 80486 PCs being manufactured.

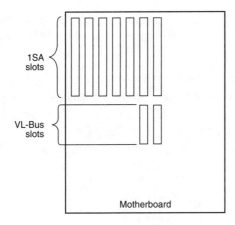

1SA slots

VL-Bus slots

Motherboard

Figure 1.5
Placement of VL-Bus slots on the motherboard.

Peripheral Component Interconnect (PCI) Bus

As mentioned, PCs are limited to a maximum of three VL-Bus slots. Cards for VL-Bus can be difficult to implement and require a high chip count that raises costs. The *Peripheral Component Interconnect* (PCI) bus has been promoted by Intel as an alternative high-performance bus. PCI was the first bus adapted to the Pentium processor and is incorporated into the majority of Pentium-based PCs. (VL-Bus cards designed for the 80486 will not currently work with the Pentium.)

When the PCI bus was designed, high performance was a concern, and the bus was designed with 32- and 64-bit data paths and 33 MHz or 66 MHz clock rates. Besides performance, an important design goal was to reduce the difficulty of configuring plug-in cards, a feature known as "plug-and-play." New operating systems, expected in 1995, will be required to take advantage of plug-and-play.

The PCI bus is not a local bus, but is commonly described as a *mezzanine* bus because it is a hardware layer away from the processor's bus. The PCI bus connects to the CPU by means of buffer chips that transfer data between the CPU bus and the PCI bus. A PCI chipset generates the data and signals that connect to PCI peripherals, such as video cards, disk controllers, and SCSI controllers. Another chipset translates PCI signals to the ISA bus, enabling PCI systems to use both PCI and ISA cards.

PCI bus has a 64-bit data path, matching the width of the Pentium data path, and operating at the same 60 and 66 MHz speeds as the Pentium processor.

As shown in figure 1.6, PCI connectors are installed parallel to the ISA connectors on the motherboard. Systems can incorporate independent ISA and PCI slots, or slots that incorporate both ISA and PCI connectors. For example, a Pentium system might be configured with four ISA slots, two PCI slots, and one PCI/ISA slot.

Figure 1.6

Placement of PCI bus slots on the motherboard.

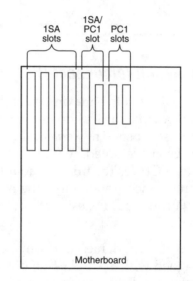

Motherboard

Characteristics of IBM PC Buses

As you have seen, each IBM PC bus has its own characteristics.

Explain the basic characteristics of the ISA bus, the MCA bus, and the EISA bus.

Table 1.7 summarizes the characteristics of the four buses just discussed.

Table 1.7
Comparison of IBM PC Buses

	8-Bit ISA	16-Bit ISA	Micro	EISA	VL-Bus	PCI Channel
Data bus width	8 bits	16 bits	32 bits	32 bits	32 bits	64 bits
Address bus	20 bits	24 bits	32 bits			
Speeds	4.77 MHz	4.77–8 MHz	10+ MHz	8 MHz	to 33 MHz	60–66 MHz
Bus mastering	No	No	Yes	Yes		
Configuration	Manual	Manual	Automatic	Automatic	Manual	Plug-and-Play

Buses Used in Apple Macintoshes

Two types of expansion slots are used in Macintosh computers.
One is the *Processor Direct Slot* (PDS), found in models such as the
Macintosh SE. Most expandable Macs, however, are equipped
with NuBus expansion slots.

Explain the basic bus characteristics of the Apple
Macintosh.

Processor Direct Slots (PDS)

Processor Direct Slots give expansion devices direct access to the
microprocessor. The PDS offers high performance with the
Motorola 68000 line of microprocessors because it gives the expansion board direct access to the microprocessor. The microprocessor, however, can handle only one slot, and the slot design is
processor-specific. This means that options designed for a 68030
PDS slot do not work with a 68040 PDS.

49

Most Macintosh computers are equipped with PDS slots, although the designs vary widely among computer models.

NuBus

NuBus originated in the laboratories at MIT. It has been standardized by an IEEE committee with members including AT&T, Texas Instruments, and IEEE. NuBus has a rich set of features, such as bus mastering.

Although Macs use interrupts and memory addresses to facilitate communication with expansion cards, you do not need to configure the cards or the computer. With the Macs, NuBus configuration is completely automatic. You do not even need to run a setup program, as is required with Micro Channel and EISA. Instead, each NuBus card stores its configuration information in a memory chip read by the Mac during the boot sequence. The configuration information is used to configure the Mac automatically for the option cards present.

Some of the most significant features of NuBus are as follows:

◆ 32-bit address and data buses

◆ Self-configuring option boards

◆ 10 MHz operation

◆ Bus mastering

Section Review Questions

6. Which statement is true?

    a. 8086 has 8-bit buses.

    b. 8088 has a 16-bit external bus.

    c. 8086 can address 1 MB of RAM.

    d. 8088 can address 2 MB of RAM.

7. Which combination is incorrect?

   a. 8088: 16-bit internal bus, 1 MB addressable RAM, 10 MHz maximum clock speed

   b. 80286: 16-bit internal bus, 16 MB addressable RAM, 20 MHz maximum clock speed

   c. 80386: 16-bit internal bus, 4 GB addressable RAM, 33 MHz maximum clock speed

   d. 80486: 32-bit internal bus, 4 GB addressable RAM, 33 MHz maximum clock speed

8. The most popular Macintosh processor is:

   a. MC68030

   b. MC68040

   c. MC68000

   d. MC68020

9. Which statement is most false?

   a. The amount of memory a computer can use is determined by the size of the memory address.

   b. The maximum clock speed reflects the speed of the internal bus.

   c. The wider the data bus, the more data can be moved in a single operation.

   d. IRQs are more efficient than polling I/Os.

10. Which is NOT a PC bus?

   a. MCA

   b. MFM

   c. ISA

   d. EISA

11. Which bus do PS/2 PCs use?

    a. MCA

    b. ISA

    c. EISA

    d. a and b

Answers

   6. c

   7. c

   8. a

   9. b

   10. b

   11. d

Exploring Microcomputer Memory

Central processors are fast. To function at their optimal capacity, they need to be capable of storing and retrieving data from an equally fast storage environment. Floppy disks and even hard drives do not qualify. To keep up with an electronic CPU, you need electronic memory. This section covers the types of electronic memory used by microcomputers. It also examines the way memory is arranged in an IBM PC.

Think of memory as a large number of boxes, each of which contains data. The capacity of a box is usually a byte (eight bits), and each box has a number that uniquely identifies it. In computer memory terms, the boxes are storage or memory locations, and the identification numbers are addresses. You encountered addresses during the discussion about microprocessors earlier in this chapter.

Types of Memory

Recall that a microcomputer can have two primary types of memory: RAM and ROM. The following sections discuss how each memory type functions.

Random Access Memory (RAM)

You learned from the previous discussion in this chapter that RAM is the microprocessor's scratchpad. The CPU can store byte values in any RAM memory location and can retrieve any given byte. RAM works like a file drawer filled with numbered folders. A byte can be written to any folder. If the CPU knows the number address for a folder, it can go directly to the folder and retrieve the data.

The term "random" is contrasted with "sequential." To access data sequentially, you must start at one end and examine every piece of data until the desired item is reached. A good example is music on an audio cassette. To reach the fifth song, you must fast forward the cassette past the first four.

If the song is recorded on a CD, however, you can tell the player to go directly to the fifth track, bypassing the first four. This is an example of random access. You can access the data in any order, without the need to examine intermediate data items.

Actually, most types of computer memory—including ROM—can be accessed randomly. The defining characteristic of RAM is that the CPU can change the data stored in RAM. As you will learn in a later section of this chapter, the contents of ROM are relatively permanent.

 Describe the main function of RAM.

RAM is used to store programs and data used by the CPU. When a program is executed, the program instructions must be read into RAM from storage such as a floppy disk. Program instructions, like everything else in computers, consist of binary numbers that represent coded orders to the CPU. After they are in RAM, the instructions can be retrieved and executed by the CPU. While executing the instructions, the CPU can use RAM to store data values for later access. Virtually every process in a computer involves some sort of manipulation of RAM memory.

 Explain the differences between dynamic memory and static memory.

Microcomputers commonly use two types of RAM: dynamic and static. Both types of RAM are *volatile,* meaning that they must be kept under power to retain their data. Most types of RAM cannot store data after the computer is turned off.

 Most types of modern microcomputers contain a type of RAM called *complementary metal oxide silicon* (CMOS) that requires very little power. CMOS is used to store machine configuration settings between sessions. CMOS is still volatile memory. If the battery runs down, the CMOS contents are lost.

Dynamic RAM (DRAM)

A *Dynamic RAM* (DRAM) memory chip consists of millions of *capacitors,* devices that can store an electric charge. You are familiar with the phenomenon of capacitance if you have ever shuffled across a carpet and been shocked when you touched a doorknob. Shuffling introduces a difference in voltage between you and the doorknob. This voltage difference remains because no conductor exists between you and the doorknob, and the electrons have nowhere to go. When you touch the doorknob, a current can flow, and the voltages are equalized. Until you touch the doorknob, you and the doorknob are forming a capacitor with the air between you acting as an insulator. The voltage charge remains intact for fairly long periods of time, and the right equipment can detect that the charge exists.

When data is stored in DRAM, a charge is introduced to one of the tiny capacitors, each of which corresponds to a bit. This charge can be detected, and the bit value stored in the capacitor can be read out of memory.

The advantage of DRAM is that it is extremely inexpensive; however, DRAM is relatively slow. Another disadvantage is that the charge is small and dissipates fairly rapidly. The computer, therefore, must frequently check each storage location and refresh its charge.

In summary, DRAM is inexpensive, but requires a refresh mechanism.

Static RAM (SRAM)

Static RAM (SRAM) functions like a large bank of switches. When a switch is set to a particular position, it remains in that position until the CPU explicitly changes it. As long as power is applied, SRAM remembers stored data, so no refresh mechanism is required.

SRAM is faster than DRAM. It is used infrequently, however, because the cost of SRAM is much higher.

Newer microcomputer designs take advantage of the higher performance of SRAM by using small banks of SRAM chips as data caches. SRAM cache memory stores data that may be needed by the CPU. Access to this data is much faster than if the data had to be read from DRAM main memory.

In summary, SRAM is faster than DRAM and does not require a refresh mechanism; however, SRAM is significantly more expensive than DRAM.

Read-Only Memory (ROM)

The data in ROM is stored permanently. Your computer can read from ROM, but cannot write new data to it. In most cases, the data is stored in the memory chip at the factory and cannot be modified after that time. Turning a computer off does not affect the contents of ROM.

ROM sounds inflexible, but it has some important purposes. Have you ever wondered how your computer is smart enough to boot DOS from your hard disk when you first turn it on? The program that gives a PC or a Mac its basic functionality is stored in ROM.

  Describe the purpose of ROM.

In the case of an IBM PC compatible, the ROM is called the *Basic Input/Output System* (BIOS). The BIOS performs simple disk operations, accepts keyboard input, displays text on the monitor, and performs other simple but essential tasks. When you turn on your PC, special circuitry activates the programs stored in the BIOS, which then tests your computer and looks for DOS on a boot disk. BIOS is a program stored in ROM. Software stored in ROM is often referred to as *firmware*.

  The ROM in your PC works with the configuration data in your PC's CMOS memory to start your system. CMOS contains data about your machine, including the type and number of disk drives. That information is used by the BIOS (or by the Mac ROMs) to find DOS and start your PC.

How Memory Is Organized

Recall that the basic unit of information in a computer is the *bit*, which corresponds to a single memory location. As you already discovered, a single bit is not very useful, so bits are generally grouped into larger units. As you have learned, the most common such unit is the *byte*, which consists of eight bits.

The chips in PCs are usually organized in terms of bits. A typical one-megabit chip is organized as one bit wide by one megabit long. To group these million bits into a million bytes, eight chips are wired in parallel, as shown in figure 1.7. Such a grouping of chips is called a *memory block*.

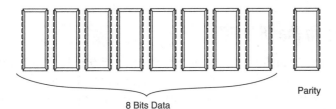

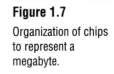

Figure 1.7

Organization of chips to represent a megabyte.

Parity

8 Bits Data

 Describe parity checking and its purpose.

In the case of the IBM PC, a ninth chip is added, which stores *parity*, an elementary error checking mechanism. The bit in the parity chip is adjusted so that the total number of bits in a byte plus parity will be odd. When the byte is read, the parity bit is checked to see if the total of bits is still odd. If not, the byte is assumed to be in error, and the PC signals a parity error. The designers of the IBM PC had the philosophy that bad data was worse than no data at all, so they designed the PC to lock up when a parity error is detected. Frequent parity errors are an indication that a memory chip is developing problems.

Macintosh computers do not implement a parity chip. Eight chips are used to construct a memory block. The Macintosh organizes memory in a long, continuous block. End users do not need to be concerned about how memory is installed or organized in their Macs.

With PCs running DOS, however, memory organization is fairly complicated. You need to have a good understanding of DOS memory when configuring DOS PCs to work with NetWare networks.

DOS PC Memory Organization

DOS memory has had a complicated evolution since the days of the original PC. The following sections examine this evolution, starting with the design limits established by the designers of the first PC.

Memory in the IBM PC

As mentioned earlier, DOS was programmed for the Intel 8086/ 8088 microprocessors, which can manage a maximum of 1 MB of memory. With DOS on the original PC, the memory was configured, as shown in figure 1.8.

Figure 1.8

DOS memory organization.

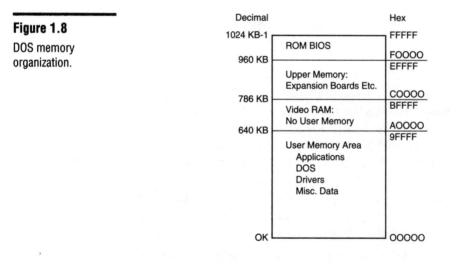

The most infamous number in DOS is 640 KB. This number represents the amount of memory that the PC's designers set aside for programs. Because the first PCs could have only 64 KB of memory on the motherboard, 640 KB seemed like a huge amount of memory in 1981.

The 640 KB memory allocation was locked in by putting video memory in the space right above. Video boards expect to find memory in a particular location, and video memory could not be easily relocated after this arrangement was established.

Above video memory is a block shared by the ROM BIOS and by various expansion boards. This 256 KB system memory block was unavailable to DOS programs in the original PC.

Expanded Memory

It did not take long for PC software to outgrow the 640 KB program memory allocation. The application that sold business on the PC was Lotus 1-2-3, a spreadsheet application used to develop extremely elaborate business models. By the time Lotus 1-2-3 was loaded into the 640 KB DOS memory, however, not much room remained for a large spreadsheet.

 Explain the difference between extended memory and expanded memory.

Three partners, Lotus, Intel, and Microsoft, developed the *Expanded Memory specification* (EMS—sometimes called the LIM specification) to work around this crippling limit.

The 8088 and 8086 processors absolutely cannot read a byte more than 1 MB, and the original PC design allocated most of that megabyte. An accessory board, however, can have memory of its own that it manages. EMS works by swapping small portions of this accessory memory into memory that DOS can see. Figure 1.9 shows how this works, based on version 4.0 of EMS, the most recent version.

EMS defines a *page frame*, which is a section of RAM mapped into the 256 KB ROM memory area. The EMS 4.0 page frame can be as large as 64 KB and is broken into 16 KB chunks. Each 16 KB chunk can be swapped in and out of EMS memory, which originally consisted of chips on an EMS expansion card.

EMS therefore makes the memory on the expansion card available, but only 64 KB at a time. This is not as useful as having all the memory available at the same time, but it is much better than being locked in to a 640 KB memory limit.

Figure 1.9

Expanded memory.

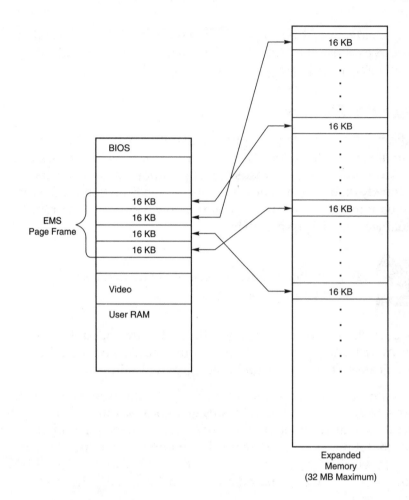

PC compatibles based on 80386 and later microprocessors can use extended memory to emulate an EMS option board (see the next section). These computers do not need any extra option boards to use applications that require EMS memory.

Extended Memory

The 80286 microprocessor in the IBM AT made it possible to access more than a megabyte of memory. 80386 and 80486 micro-processors can address up to 4 gigabytes of memory. Figure 1.10 shows how this works.

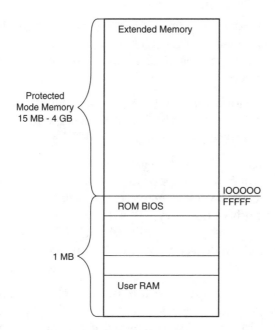

Figure 1.10
Extended memory.

With DOS alone, this memory is not all that useful because DOS remains saddled with the old 640 KB memory limit. Microsoft Windows is probably the most popular add-on software that enables DOS to use extended memory.

Operating systems such as OS/2 and UNIX can use extended memory directly by taking advantage of protected mode available in 80286 and later Intel processors. In fact, these operating systems make a PC function much like a Mac because the memory is not divided into chunks. A new version of Windows, Windows NT, also accesses memory in protected mode.

Memory Packaging

Until recently, memory chips were packaged in discrete chips. Incidentally, the typical computer chip, which consists of a black piece of plastic with two lines of pins on either side, is referred to as a *Dual In-Line Pin* chip (DIP).

61

These discrete chips are plugged into sockets on the motherboard or on memory expansion cards. They must be grouped in accordance with the wiring on the circuit board, and the proper chips must always be used.

Memory chips are identified by the width and length of their bit patterns. A typical chip might be 1×256 KB, for example, and consist of bits organized one wide and 256 KB long.

A second specification for memory chips is access time. A given chip design has a maximum speed at which it can be accessed. If this speed is exceeded, serious errors occur. The faster a PC runs, the more it demands of memory chips. Low-performance memory chips have access times in the neighborhood of 100 nanoseconds, but high-performance PCs can require 70-nanosecond or better chips.

Few PCs are now designed to require discrete chips. More popular now are *Single In-Line Memory Modules* (SIMMS). SIMMs consist of small circuit boards to which are attached a group of memory chips. The circuit board can be plugged into a special slot on the motherboard or on a memory expansion board. SIMMs are usually installed in groups of four to provide a memory block.

 Unfortunately, many types and configurations of memory are available for use in personal computers. Always consult with a knowledgeable hardware technician before you purchase memory to expand the capacity of a computer.

Section Review Questions

12. Which statement about memory is false?

    a. DRAM is commonly used as PC memory.

    b. Cache memory and CMOS are examples of SRAM.

    c. ROM is for permanently storing data.

    d. CMOS is a ROM.

13. The main difference between expanded and extended memory is:

    a. Extended is called XMS; expanded is called EMS

    b. Only expanded needs a memory driver

    c. Extended is addressable directly by the microprocessor; expanded is a special purpose 64 KB page memory

    d. Expanded uses SRAM; extended uses DRAM

14. Parity is best described as:

    a. An elementary mechanism for error checking

    b. An indicator of developing memory chip problems

    c. A memory block

    d. A Macintosh computer's means of completing a block of data

15. Which of the following is NOT a purpose of ROM?

    a. Accept keyboard input

    b. Display text on the monitor

    c. Perform disk operations

    d. Store information for access by the CPU

16. Which of the following is a main function of RAM?

    a. Accept keyboard input

    b. Display text on the monitor

    c. Perform disk operations

    d. Store information for access by the CPU

Answers

12. d

13. c

14. a

15. d

16. d

Understanding Storage Options: Floppy Disks and Hard Disks

RAM is fast, but it has two problems. First, the contents of RAM are erased when the computer is turned off, and second, RAM usually is present only in quantities of a few megabytes. Most PCs have a maximum of 4–16 MB of RAM—enough to support some elaborate processing, but not enough to store large databases or dozens of program files. Floppy disks and hard disks are alternatives to these restrictions.

 Explain the purpose of hard disks and floppy disks.

These disks enable users to store many megabytes of programs and data in relatively permanent form. Disk drives are the computer's filing cabinet; they store large quantities of data in an organized form.

Magnetic storage media store data much as music is stored on a cassette tape, by storing magnetic fields in the magnetic material that coats the disk. Computer disks, however, store data in digital form. If the magnetic material is polarized in one direction, a 1 is stored. If the material is polarized in the opposite direction, the magnetic field represents a 0.

Floppy disks are the most prevalent removable media used in microcomputers. Also called floppies, these disks are inexpensive, and each can store between 360 KB and 1.44 MB of programs and data. Floppies are slow, however, and 1.44 MB is rarely enough storage in today's world of huge programs and massive databases.

Hard drives can store many megabytes of data and are reasonably fast. They have become the primary storage devices on most microcomputers.

How Data Is Stored

Disks and hard drives are magnetic media. They use magnetic patterns recorded on a magnetic coating to represent bits of data. This is the same principle used to record sound on a cassette tape. Instead of being pulled across a playback/recording head, however, computer disks rotate.

Computer disk storage is managed by a disk operating system. In an IBM PC compatible, this is usually MS-DOS (Microsoft Disk Operating System) or PC DOS (IBM's version of DOS, which is very similar to MS-DOS). Novell has recently begun to distribute a version called DR DOS or Novell DOS, which is compatible with MS-DOS.

Before a disk is used for storage, it is divided into small units, each of which can hold a fixed amount of data. These units, called *sectors*, are indexed so that they can be located easily by DOS. Figure 1.11 shows how the disk is organized.

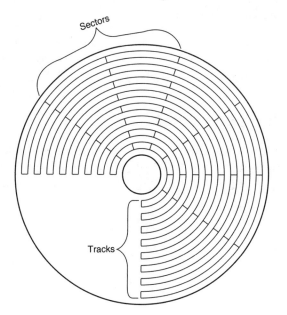

Figure 1.11

Organization of a formatted disk.

Explain why a disk is formatted.

Before a disk can be used to store computer data, it must be formatted. Chapter 2, "Using DOS on the Network," explains how to format a disk with MS-DOS. With a Mac, the process is called *initialization*, which is performed automatically whenever an uninitialized disk is inserted into the disk drive.

When formatted, the disk—floppy or hard—is divided into concentric tracks. Each track is further divided into sectors. The specific number of tracks and sectors depends on the type of disk. Typically, a sector holds 512 KB. The details of floppy disk and hard disk storage are discussed in the following sections. Figure 1.11 shows how tracks and sectors are organized on a disk, although the actual numbers of tracks and sectors can vary considerably depending on the disk type.

DOS views floppy disks in terms of *clusters*, which can range in size from 512 to 8,096 bytes depending on the disk type and DOS version. A cluster consists of one or more sectors.

Floppy Disk Drives

A floppy disk is named for the soft, flexible metallic oxide-coated mylar disk where the information is actually stored. The two most popular sizes of floppy disk are 5 1/4-inch and 3 1/2-inch.

5 1/4-Inch Floppy Disks

5 1/4-inch floppy disks are popular on PC compatibles, but are rapidly being replaced by 3 1/2-inch disks. 5 1/4-inch floppy disks are not used by Macintoshes. The features of these disks are illustrated in figure 1.12.

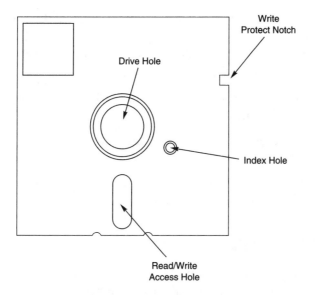

Figure 1.12

Features of a 5 1/4-inch disk.

The flexible disk material is enclosed in a stiff plastic jacket. This jacket has several cutouts:

◆ **Drive Hole.** Through this hole in the center, the drive spindle grasps and rotates the disk.

◆ **Read/Write Access Hole.** Through this hole, the read/write heads—one for each side—contact the disk. The heads slide back and forth in this slot to access different tracks. This hole does not have a cover, and makes the disk vulnerable to damage.

◆ **Index Hole.** This hole is not used in modern disk drives.

◆ **Write Protect Notch.** This notch, if covered, disables the drive's capability to write data to the disk. This is a hardware override and cannot be circumvented by software.

Identify the capacity of 5 1/4-inch and 3 1/2-inch disks.

67

5 1/4-inch disks used in PC compatibles are available in double-density and high-density versions, which hold 360 KB and 1.2 MB of data, respectively. The magnetic material on these disks is different. As a result, the following rules apply:

◆ A double-density disk drive can read or write double-density floppies.

◆ A double-density disk drive can neither read nor write high-density floppies.

◆ A high-density disk drive can read and write high-density or double-density floppies.

3 1/2-Inch Disks

3 1/2-inch disks are used by Macintoshes and by most PC compatibles currently being manufactured. Figure 1.13 shows the structure of a 3 1/2-inch disk.

Figure 1.13

Features of a 3 1/2-inch disk.

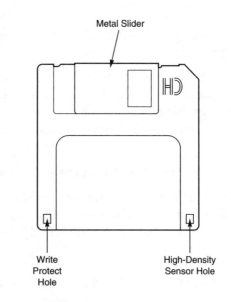

The disk has the following features:

◆ A rigid plastic case that protects the magnetic disk much better than the semirigid case of a 5 1/4-inch floppy.

◆ A write protect notch with a slider, which replaces the tape used to cover the write protect notch in a 5 1/4-inch disk. If the slider covers the hole, data can be written to the disk. If the slider is moved to uncover the hole, data cannot be written to the disk.

◆ A high-density sensor notch enables the disk drive to determine whether the disk is high-density (1.44 MB) or double-density (720 KB).

◆ A metal slider covers the read/write hole through which the read/write heads—one for each side—contact the disk surface. The metal slider provides excellent protection for the magnetic medium, and disk sleeves are not ordinarily required.

3 1/2-inch disks are available in two densities.

Double-density disks can store 720 KB of data. High-density disks can store 1.44 MB of data.

Describe the compatibilities of 5 1/4-inch disk drives and 3 1/2-inch disk drives.

The rules for disk usage on a PC compatible are as follows:

◆ Double-density disk drives can read and write double-density disks, but cannot read or write high-density disks.

◆ High-density disk drives can read and write both double-density and high-density disks. Many disk drives can sense the disk type by using the high-density sensor notch.

Macintosh computers also use double- and high-density disks. Double-density disks are formatted (or initialized in Mac terminology) to contain 800 KB. An interesting twist is that 800 KB Mac disks have different numbers of sectors on different tracks, with more sectors on outer tracks that have larger diameters. (Older Macs used single-sided disks that contained 400 KB of data.)

Macs equipped with 1.4 MB high-density disks (called Super-Drives) work differently. Each side of the disk has 80 tracks, and each track has 18 sectors regardless of position.

Table 1.8 summarizes the characteristics of the floppy disk types discussed in this section.

Table 1.8
Characteristics of Floppy Disk Types

Disk Size	Density	Tracks per Side	Sectors per Track	Total Sectors	Bytes per Sector	Sectors per Cluster	Unformatted Capacity	Formatted Capacity
5.25 IBM	Double	40	9	720	512	2	368,640	362,496
5.25 IBM	High	80	15	2,400	512	1	1,228,800	1,213,952
3.5 IBM	Double	80	9	1,440	512	2	737,280	730,112
3.5 IBM	High	80	18	2,880	512	1	1,474,560	1,457,664
3.5 Mac	Double	80	8-12	1,600	512	n/a	819,200	
3.5 Mac	High	80	18	2,880	512	n/a	1,474,560	

Note You can determine the theoretical capacity of a disk by using the following formula:

capacity = number of disk sides ×

number of tracks ×

number of sectors per track ×

sector size in bytes

The calculation performed for a 3 1/2-inch high-density disk is as follows:

capacity = 2 × 80 × 18 × 512 = 1,474,560

If, however, you examine a formatted disk with CHKDSK (see Chapter 2, "Using DOS on the Network"), you discover that its reported capacity is 1,457,664, which is somewhat less than the value you are led to expect from the preceding formula.

This is the difference between the formatted capacity and the unformatted capacity of the disk. When a disk is formatted, DOS reserves some of the disk for bookkeeping. This space is used for information about sector addresses, system files, file allocation tables (see Chapter 2 for more about FATs), and directories. In other words, not all the theoretical, unformatted capacity of the disk is available for data storage. This principle applies to hard drives as well as floppies.

Refer back to table 1.8 to see the difference between formatted and unformatted capacities for the various types of PC compatible disks.

Hard Disk Drives

The term *hard* derives from the fact that hard disk drives have multiple rigid, magnetic platters capable of storing much more data than a floppy disk. Hard drives also work significantly faster than floppy disks. Most hard drives have multiple disks that rotate on the same spindle. Each disk surface has its own read/write head. The relationship of these elements is shown in figure 1.14.

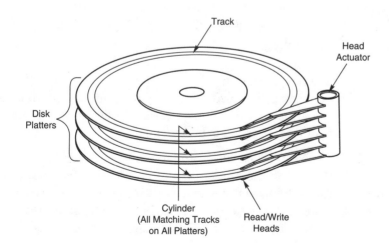

Track

Head
Actuator

Disk
Platters

Cylinder
(All Matching Tracks
on All Platters)

Read/Write
Heads

Figure 1.14

Structure of a
hard disk.

Each disk surface is formatted into tracks and sectors, although hard drives have many more tracks and sectors per disk than is possible with floppies. This is because the rigid disks are manufactured to extreme precision, and the magnetic coating is of very high quality. Because floppy disks flex, you cannot rely on them to the degree possible with hard disks.

The tracks of a hard disk are organized into *cylinders* (see fig. 1.14). A cylinder consists of all matching tracks on all the disk platters. All the tracks numbered 1 make up cylinder 1. When configuring storage volumes in NetWare, you frequently are asked to specify the volume size in cylinders.

Hard disks are also referred to as *fixed disks* by IBM because the disks are not removable. Whereas a floppy disk can be removed from the disk drive and stored off-site, a hard disk usually resides inside the PC and is seldom removed unless for repairs. Removable hard drives are available, but are costly and frequently slower than other hard drives.

Hard drives give you more space to save information than do floppies. A capacity of several gigabytes is now available. Because hard disks spin at much higher rates (between 2,400 and 3,600 rpm) than floppies, they also provide faster access time for faster data transfer.

 Explain what is meant by the random access time of a hard disk.

The speed of the disk is measured in *random access time*, the amount of time it takes the hard disk drive to locate the requested data. If an application requires many reads and writes to the hard disk drive, a faster access time is beneficial.

The hard drive uses read/write heads to magnetize and read the iron particles found on the magnetic platters. As the disk platters spin, the heads float above the surface at a microscopic distance. The closer the heads come to the disk surface, the more densely data can be stored. Because of these close tolerances, the read/

write heads and the magnetic media are enclosed in a sealed, dust-free housing. Each platter has two read/write heads, and the platters spin at speeds from 2,400–3,600 rpm.

Partitioning Hard Drives

Hard drives require *partitioning* before they can be formatted.

 Explain the purpose of partitioning a hard disk.

Partitioning enables you to reserve different portions of the hard disk for different operating systems. Partitioning also may be required for large hard disks.

If you are using DOS 3.30 or below, the maximum partition size is 32 MB. If your hard drive is larger than that, you must partition the drive into multiple 32 MB partitions, each of which is formatted like a separate drive.

DOS 4, 5, and 6 can create partitions with sizes up to 2 GB. The BIOS in most PCs, however, prevents partition sizes from exceeding 512 MB.

Multiple operating systems also can be placed on one drive. When you place different operating systems on one drive, such as DOS and OS/2, you must format each partition differently.

NetWare 2.2 ordinarily partitions the entire hard drive as a NetWare partition.

Servers for NetWare 3.11 are generally configured with a small DOS partition (5 MB is typical) for booting and starting NetWare OS, with the remainder of the drive partitioned for NetWare.

Hard Disk Drive Interfaces

The *interface* is the physical connection between the hard drive and the CPU. The connection is established through the use of a drive controller. Four popular interfaces for hard disk drives are as follows:

◆ ST506/412 interface

◆ *Enhanced Small Device Interface* (ESDI)

◆ *Small Computer System Interface* (SCSI)

◆ *Integrated Drive Electronics interface* (IDE)

ST506/412

The ST506/412 interface was developed by Seagate Technology and is commonly referred to as simply the ST506 interface. ST506 is the interface used on the original IBM PC, and has largely been supplanted by higher performance systems.

The ST506 supports two encoding methods: *Modified Frequency Modulation* (MFM) and *Run Length Limited* (RLL). These methods are defined as follows:

◆ MFM encoding enables data to be transferred at rates up to 5 *megabits per second* (Mbps).

◆ RLL encoding increases the data transfer rate to 7.5 Mbps and also increases the drive capacity by 50 percent.

ESDI

ESDI is an improved version of the ST506. ESDI has been accepted into the *American National Standards Institute* (ANSI). Both ST506 and ESDI transfer data in serial format. ESDI provides increased disk storage capacity and transfers data from 10 Mbps to 15 Mbps in some instances.

Small Computer System Interface (SCSI)

Small Computer System Interface (SCSI—pronounced "scuzzy") is a popular high-speed parallel interface. Because SCSI is parallel, it can transfer eight bits of data at a time, as opposed to a serial interface, which only transfers one bit at a time.

In addition to hard drives, SCSI also can handle devices such as CD-ROM controllers and tape drives. Up to seven devices can be connected to a single SCSI interface card. In fact, SCSI functions like a bus; each device is assigned a number that functions like the slot on the expansion bus of a motherboard.

SCSI is a system-level interface, meaning that the inner workings of the data storage devices are hidden from the interface. The computer sees only data transferred in blocks, not sectors, tracks, or clusters.

Embedded SCSI drives have a controller board built right onto the hard drive itself. If the drive does not have an embedded device, it is connected to an interface board that sits in an expansion slot. The SCSI hard drives can exist in a box external to the computer. This is called a *disk subsystem*.

SCSI interface cards are available for use with PC compatibles and are popular choices for connecting server-based hard drives. Apple built the SCSI interface into its Macintosh line of computers.

Integrated Drive Electronics (IDE)

Integrated Drive Electronics (IDE) integrates the popular Western Digital drive control electronics into the structure of the hard drive. Like the embedded SCSI boards, the IDE controller resides on the hard drive. The IDE interface, however, connects to the computer via a 40-pin connector separate from the regular expansion slots on the motherboard. (Expansion slot interface cards are available also.)

IDE has the following advantages:

◆ IDE uses the RLL encoding introduced with the ST506 to achieve denser disk storage and faster data rates.

◆ A single manufacturer designs both the controller and the hard disk and can ensure that they work together for optimal performance.

75

Understanding Ports

Ports are a computer's way of interfacing with the world. Ports are input/output interfaces that allow your computer to communicate with peripherals. *Peripherals* are devices external to the computer. Modems, printers, mice, scanners, and plotters are a few of the peripherals that can be connected via computer ports.

Two types of ports are found on most computers: parallel and serial. Parallel ports transfer data a byte at a time, whereas serial ports transfer data one bit at a time.

Parallel Ports

Parallel ports are commonly used for printers and other devices where the communications flow from the computer to the peripheral. Parallel ports are considered the easiest port to configure because they do not have complex options for configuration. Printers that use a parallel cable can usually be plugged into the parallel port on a computer without any configuration.

At the time the IBM PC was being designed, Centronics was a prominent printer manufacturer; consequently, the Centronics printer interface was selected as the printer interface for the PC. The Centronics interface has become a nearly universal de facto standard.

IBM PCs can have up to three parallel ports. By convention, these ports are identified as LPT1, LPT2, and LPT3.

In most cases, parallel printer cables are round so that they can be shielded to prevent emission of electronic noise. Flat "ribbon" also can be used, but can radiate radio frequency noise that interferes with nearby equipment. IBM established the convention of configuring printer cables with a 25-pin D-connector at the computer end and a 36-pin Centronics connector at the printer end.

 Describe how the parallel port transmits data.

Parallel cables are equipped with eight wires to transmit data, and nine to carry control signals. Parallel ports transfer data eight bits at a time—one bit over each data line wire in the cable. The remaining wires are connected to ground.

To be transferred correctly, the bits must travel at the same speed so that they reach the other end of the cable at the same time. Errors occur when the bits arrive at uneven rates.

Table 1.9 shows the pinout (what each wire should be doing) for the 25-pin connector "talking" to a printer.

Table 1.9
Pinouts for 25-Pin Parallel Connector

25-Pin Connector	Function	Direction
Pin 1	Strobe	
Pin 2	Data line 0	->
Pin 3	Data line 1	->
Pin 4	Data line 2	->
Pin 5	Data line 3	->
Pin 6	Data line 4	->
Pin 7	Data line 5	->
Pin 8	Data line 6	->
Pin 9	Data line 7	->
Pin 10	Acknowledge	<-
Pin 11	Busy	<-
Pin 12	Out of paper	<-
Pin 13	Select	<-
Pin 14	Auto feed	->
Pin 15	Error	<-
Pin 16	Initialize	->
Pin 17	Select input	->
Pins 18–25	Ground	

Parallel communication has several advantages. Virtually no configuration is required for the Centronics interface standard. Parallel communication is fast and can keep up with all but the speediest peripherals. Finally, circuitry for parallel ports is fast, relatively simple, and inexpensive.

Parallel communication has some important disadvantages, however. Probably the most important disadvantage has to do with distance limitations.

 Explain why parallel transmissions do not travel very far.

As parallel cables get longer, signals can deteriorate due to *crosstalk*. You probably have heard crosstalk on your telephone when another person's conversation interferes with yours. This can happen when the magnetic fields of nearby wires induce currents in each other. Because of crosstalk and other effects, the useful maximum distance for parallel communication is 10–50 feet, with 10 feet the maximum recommended by most manufacturers. Finally, Centronics cables can be expensive and complex to troubleshoot when cable problems occur.

Serial Ports

Serial ports are commonly used for modems and input devices, such as a mouse, trackball, or joystick.

 Describe how the serial port transmits data.

Serial ports communicate by dividing bytes into eight bits, arranging them in a series, and transmitting them one at a time. Serial ports have several other names as follows:

♦ **Comm port** refers to the most common use of a serial port—data communication.

♦ **RS-232 port** refers to the *Electronics Industry Association* (EIA) standard that defines the configuration of the port. This standard is named RS-232C.

IBM PCs can support four serial ports, labeled COM1, COM2, COM3, and COM4.

One problem in serial communication is that the receiving computer needs a mechanism to determine what bit signals the start of a communication. If the receiver starts listening in the middle of a character, for example, it is certain to receive erroneous data. Two methods of communications on serial ports resolve such communication difficulties: synchronous and asynchronous.

Synchronous communication is very fast. Data is grouped together and sent with control codes that signify the beginning and end of the block of data. The term "synchronous" is used because a mechanism called *clocking* synchronizes the sending and receiving devices so that they know exactly where the current bit is in the full message. Clocking is often accomplished by sending timing signals on an extra wire in addition to the wires used to carry data. Synchronous communication is used on mainframes and in specialized modem communication.

Asynchronous communication is slower. Each byte of data is marked with a start and stop bit that tells the receiving peripheral when to start and stop reading the bits. Because no clocking is required, asynchronous is simpler and less expensive than synchronous communication. Asynchronous communication, however, is also slower than synchronous communications. Because of low equipment costs, asynchronous equipment is used for most communication with PCs.

 Explain what is meant by baud rate.

Serial communication involves sending data across the line one bit at a time. The speed at which information travels across the line is measured in *bits per second* (BPS). A bit is represented during serial transmission as a frequency change on the line. While BPS represents the number of bits that can be transferred across the line in a single second, baud rate refers to the number of frequency changes per second. Therefore, baud rate refers to the number of frequency changes in one second, while BPS refers to the actual number of bits sent across the line in a single second.

Section Review Questions

17. Which statement is false?

    a. Input devices include keyboards and network boards.

    b. The CPU is a single chip called a microprocessor.

    c. RAM and ROM are different types of memory.

    d. Storage is limited to hard disks and floppy disks.

18. Which hard disk drive interface was used on the original IBM PC?

    a. ST506

    b. ESDI

    c. SCSI

    d. IDE

19. Signals across parallel cables do not travel well across long distances because of:

    a. Uneven baud rates

    b. Crosstalk

    c. No parity checking

    d. Troubleshooting expenses make it impractical

20. Random access time can best be described as:

    a. The amount of time it takes the hard disk drive to locate data

    b. The matching of tracks on all disk platters

    c. The division of hard disks into separate logical units

    d. The length of time required to fill a buffer for CPU access

21. Reserving different portions of the hard disk for different operating systems is called:

    a. Tracking

    b. Formatting

    c. Partitioning

    d. Defragmenting

Answers

17. d

18. a

19. b

20. a

21. c

Examining Displays

Up to this point, you have learned about the internal components of the computer. One of the external components you need to know about is the *video display*. The video display is the most common output device on a personal computer and enables the user to view applications and data. Several different types of video displays are available, each with different specifications.

Describe the common types of video monitors available.

Most computer displays are video monitors that function like a television set—both use a *cathode ray tube* (CRT). Computer monitors are not limited to this method, however. The most common alternative is the *liquid crystal display* (LCD), which is flat and well-suited to the power requirements of battery-powered portable computers. Gas-plasma displays function like grids of tiny neon lights and also are flat; however, power requirements for gas-plasma displays restrict their use to computers plugged into AC power sources.

The screen of a computer display is made up of small dots called *pixels*. Pixels is short for picture elements. The computer illuminates these pixels in different patterns to generate text or graphic displays. The more pixels per square inch of screen, the better the resolution is. High resolution displays appear less grainy and can better display smooth graphic shapes.

Resolution is generally expressed in terms of the pixels that can be displayed on the full width and height of the screen. A 640 × 480 screen can display 640 pixels on a horizontal line and 480 pixels on a vertical line.

Color Displays

Screens (*monitors*) come in monochrome, meaning black and one other color (amber, green, or white), or color. Color displays vary in degree of quality.

RGB

Red Green Blue (RGB) was the first display for the IBM PC. The name derives from the fact that an RGB monitor receives red, green, and blue signals, each on a separate wire. These monitors use a digital signal.

    Define CGA.

CGA

Color Graphics Adapter (CGA) became the first standard in color monitors. They can display 16 colors in text and graphics, but can function with suitable monochrome monitors. At 320 × 240 pixels, however, the screen resolution is poor, especially for text displays.

When CGA monitors display 80 characters of text on a line, the results are generally unacceptable for long-term use. In fact, CGA has a special 40 character-per-line text mode to improve text displays.

CGA can display four colors at a time, chosen from a palette of 16 colors.

Because most early PC applications operated in text mode, many early users preferred monochrome monitors optimized for text display. It was not uncommon for users who required both text and graphics to have two monitors on their PCs.

 Define EGA.

EGA

The *Enhanced Graphics Adapter* (EGA) was introduced in 1984 to overcome the shortcomings of the CGA display. EGA operates using RGB digital technologies. The EGA standard increased resolution to 640 × 350 pixels in both text and graphic mode. Text displays, therefore, were improved to such a level that EGA became an alternative to monochrome text monitors.

The display routines built into the PC's BIOS are quite rudimentary. The EGA display augmented the built-in BIOS with new BIOS display routines of its own. At any given time, the EGA monitor can display 16 colors from a 64-color palette. The EGA adapter also can be adapted to display graphics and text on IBM monochrome displays. In addition, the EGA system is compatible with programs written for CGA and can display both graphics and text in CGA mode.

Define VGA.

VGA

The *Video Graphics Array* (VGA) was introduced with the IBM PS/
2 line of computers and is now the most popular color graphics
monitor standard for PC compatibles. VGA adapters can display
all earlier IBM text and graphics modes. In addition, the same
adapter automatically can adapt to color or monochrome VGA
monitors.

VGA uses an analog signal instead of digital. This change allows
VGA to display gradual changes in colors instead of just turning
color pixels on and off. The two standard VGA resolution modes
are as follows:

◆ At 320 × 200 pixel resolution, VGA can display up to 256
   colors at a time from a palette of 262,144 colors.

◆ At 640 × 480 pixel resolution, VGA can display 16 colors.

In addition, a widely implemented *Super VGA* (SVGA) system can
display 256 colors at 800 × 600 pixel resolution.

Multiscanning Color Displays

IBM display technologies have relied on a wide variety of technologies. Each technology requires investment in a new type of
monitor. Multiscanning monitors can adapt automatically to these
many technologies, and can function with many different standards. This means that if you have an application designed for 16
colors at 640 × 480 resolution and another program made for 256
colors at 320 × 200 resolution, you do not have to reconfigure the
video and reboot the computer to switch between applications.

The best known example of the multiscanning color display is the
NEC Multisync monitor. Other manufacturers have competing
monitor models.

Monochrome Displays

At one time, monochrome displays were chosen for the highest resolution display, whether graphics or text. Monochrome displays also have been preferred by many users for text-intensive tasks—early color monitors were unsuitable for intense use over long periods of time. Monochrome still can be preferable for applications such as desktop publishing, where an extremely high-quality display is desired or the final product is black and white.

A variety of monochrome displays are available for PC compatibles.

TTL

The earliest displays for the IBM PC were monochrome and designed primarily to display what was then considered high-quality text. The common amber and green phosphor displays are usually TTL.

The term TTL derives from the type of circuits used to control the monitor displays. These circuits use a system called *Transistor-Transistor Logic*.

Composite Monochrome

A composite display combines all signals to the monitor on a single pair of wires, usually a coaxial cable. You can recognize a composite display if it uses a single, round, plug-type connector. The capability of a single wire pair to carry a video signal is quite limited, and composite monitors are not of high quality.

VGA Monochrome

As mentioned earlier, VGA was the first standard to support color and monochrome monitors smoothly. The VGA display adapter can detect whether the monitor is color or monochrome, and modify its operation accordingly. In monochrome mode, the VGA adapter transmits only the green signal in 64 shades of gray. The result is not perfect, but is a significant improvement over earlier display standards.

Multiscanning Monochrome

Multiscanning monochrome monitors function on the same principle as the color monitors mentioned earlier.

Section Review Questions

22. Which statement about video is false?

   a. CGA text display includes 16 colors and is very poor.

   b. Monochrome monitors are normally green, amber, or white.

   c. VGA can display 262,144 colors at a time.

   d. If you have a wide variety of technologies, you should use a multiscanning color display.

23. Which of the following is NOT a common video display technology?

   a. Laser

   b. Cathode ray tube

   c. Liquid crystal display

   d. Gas-plasma

24. The first standard in color monitors was:

   a. RGB

   b. CGA

   c. EGA

   d. VGA

25. Introduced with the IBM PS/2, the _____ monitor uses analog instead of digital signals.

    a. RGB

    b. CGA

    c. EGA

    d. VGA

26. Which color display standard became an alternative to monochrome text monitors when it was introduced?

    a. RGB

    b. CGA

    c. EGA

    d. VGA

Answers

22. c

23. a

24. b

25. d

26. c

Exploring IBM PC Setup Issues

Before an IBM-compatible computer can be used, its hardware must be configured and the system must be booted. System setup involves installing the hardware and configuring the system's setup memory for the equipment that has been installed. The system's ROM BIOS can then execute its boot routines when the PC is powered up. During boot up, the startup routines can load device drivers that enable the operating system to interface with some peripherals.

Describe how the settings on the system board are made.

System Setup

Every PC since, and including, the IBM AT has a memory device called CMOS on its motherboard, which can remember setup data when powered by a battery. The CMOS draws little current from the battery, which usually can be used for a year.

Many PCs are shipped with a disk that is booted to start setup routines. After you enter configuration data, you instruct the setup routines to store these values in CMOS. The following are examples of information that can be entered:

◆ Number and type of floppy and hard disk drives

◆ Primary monitor type

◆ Amount of memory

◆ System time and date

◆ Presence or absence of a math coprocessor

Many recent PCs build these routines into the system's ROM. Setup routines can be entered by pressing a key combination as the PC boots.

Describe the computer (initializing) boot process.

Booting the Computer

This is a complex process controlled by programs in the PC's ROM. The primary steps are discussed in the following three sections.

Power-On Self Test

When power is first applied, the PC executes programs stored in its ROM. During this step, the PC tests its circuitry in a procedure called the *power-on self test* (POST) that tests all critical systems. During this procedure, the ROM routines can consult the configuration data stored in CMOS to set up the machine.

After the POST, the ROM routines locate the operating system startup files and start the operating system's boot process. In most cases, the system first looks for the operating system on drive A, followed by B, and then C. If no operating system is found, the boot process fails and produces an error message.

Operating System Boot Process

With MS-DOS, several hidden files are stored in Track 0 of the boot drive. For MS-DOS, these files are MSDOS.SYS and IO.SYS. For IBM's PC DOS, the files are IBMBIO.COM and IBMDOS.COM. After executing, these files turn control over to the DOS command processor, which is called COMMAND.COM.

Explain the difference between a bootable and a nonbootable disk.

A *bootable disk* is a disk that contains at least the three required files, MSDOS.SYS, IO.SYS (or IBMBIO.COM and IBMDOS.COM), and COMMAND.COM. These files must be installed in a particular location by using the DOS SYS command or by formatting the disk with the /S option.

System Configuration

During execution of the boot programs, DOS reads configuration instructions from a file named CONFIG.SYS. This file is discussed in Chapter 2. CONFIG.SYS can contain configuration commands or commands to load device drivers.

Finally, COMMAND.COM is loaded, and commands in the AUTOEXEC.BAT file are executed. This file is also explained in Chapter 2.

Section Review Questions

27. The *two* hidden boot files for MS-DOS are:

    a. IBMBIO.COM, IBMDOS.COM

    b. MSDOS.SYS, IO.SYS

    c. IBMDOS.COM, IO.COM

    d. IBMBIO.SYS, MSDOS.SYS

28. CMOS is used to:

    a. Store system board settings

    b. Load device drivers

    c. Run COMMAND.COM if used with the /S parameter

    d. Execute bootup routines after a power failure

29. Which of the following describes the correct order of the primary steps involved in booting the computer?

    a. Execute DOS hidden files, perform the POST, run AUTOEXEC.BAT

    b. Perform the POST, execute DOS hidden files, run AUTOEXEC.BAT

    c. Run AUTOEXEC.BAT, perform POST, execute DOS hidden files

    d. None of the above are correct because they do not load the COMMAND.COM file

30. DOS reads configuration information from a file called:

    a. AUTOEXEC.BAT

    b. IBMBIO.COM

    c. COMMAND.COM

    d. CONFIG.SYS

31. The main difference between a bootable and a nonbootable disk is:

    a. Track 0 is not used on a nonbootable disk.

    b. COMMAND.COM and two other hidden files are stored on track 0 of a bootable disk.

    c. A nonbootable disk has been formatted using the /S parameter.

    d. You must purchase bootable disks when you purchase the PC, but nonbootable disks can be purchased anytime.

Answers

27. b

28. a

29. b

30. d

31. a

Understanding Networking

Networking is becoming more widely used everyday. Networking puts at your fingertips the advanced capabilities of computers that were previously available only to those who could afford to use large, expensive mainframes or minicomputers.

Today, networking software is more sophisticated than ever before. It is capable of connecting PCs around the world. It can even connect PCs to mainframes and microcomputers. Networking is a versatile and useful tool in today's business climate. Part of the versatility and usefulness of networking can be directly attributed to the complexity of the design of the software that controls it.

Because of its complexity, understanding at least the basics of networking is important in order for you to get the most out of working with a network. Therefore, in this section you learn the basics of networking, including information about:

- An introduction to networking
- The importance of networking
- The different types of networks
- Network communication basics

An Introduction to Networking

Networking is the ability to physically connect two or more PCs so that they can share various computing resources. Connection is made using special equipment (hardware) and programs (software). The hardware required for connecting PCs includes:

- Network Interface Cards
- Cabling

As shown in figure 1.15, a *Network Interface Card* (NIC) is added to each PC in the network. The individual NICs are then connected together using a special cabling system so that the different PCs can communicate on the network.

A network can be also be defined in terms of its ability to perform basic communication and the equipment required to accomplish that communication. This communication can be described in terms of a communications model. A basic data communication model for networking is shown in figure 1.16.

Basic data communications includes four parts:

- Sender
- Receiver
- Information
- Channel

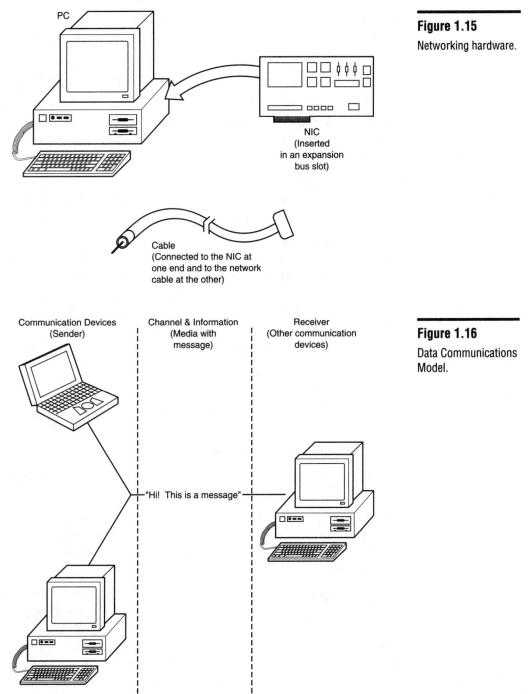

Figure 1.15
Networking hardware.

PC

NIC
(Inserted
in an expansion
bus slot)

Cable
(Connected to the NIC at
one end and to the network
cable at the other)

Communication Devices
(Sender)

Channel & Information
(Media with
message)

Receiver
(Other communication
devices)

Figure 1.16
Data Communications
Model.

"Hi! This is a message"

A *sender* is usually a PC, but can be any device that is capable of sending a signal (communication) across the media to a receiver on the other end.

A *receiver* is a device that is capable of accepting and processing (as needed) the signal that has been sent.

The *information* is the data that has been sent. It may be a request for services, actual data such as a letter to a friend, or something of a similar nature.

The *channel* is the media across which the information is sent. Different types of media channels are available, including telephone lines, cable, or in the case of microwaves, just plain air.

In addition to the physical aspects of network communications, there are also specific software requirements. Specialized software is necessary to control the communication that must occur between connected PCs in order to truly have a network. For example, if you want to send an e-mail message to another individual, you must have specialized software to create that message, and then to format and transfer it across the media to the receiver.

The software that enables you to network PCs (see figure 1.17) can be grouped into three broad categories:

◆ **Network Operating System software**—software programs that control the primary functions of networking, such as communication and data transfer

◆ **Network utilities**—software programs that let you access and control the available network resources

◆ **Workstation Communication software**—software that lets the PC access the network operating system software and utilities, including network application programs, on the network server

The PCs, together with their special hardware and software, once connected and properly installed and set up, can form a network that ranges in size from two PCs to several thousand PCs. In addition, the network can include other devices besides PCs. Some other devices that you may find in a network can include such things as modems, printers, and scanners.

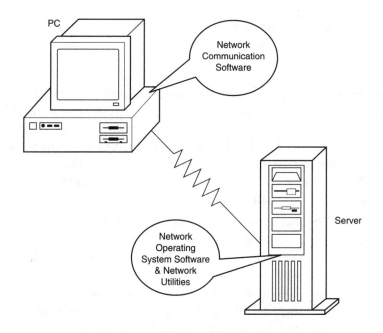

Figure 1.17
Networking software.

Proper setup involves not only the installation of the computers but also the cabling method (*topology*) used to connect them. Furthermore, proper setup should take into consideration the method used by individual PCs to access the network after the physical connection is established. (Topology and access methods are discussed later.)

Regardless of what devices are included in the network, why create and use a network to begin with?

The Importance of Networking

Resource sharing capabilities is the main reason individuals and companies decide to network their PCs. Shareable computer resources may include such things as:

◆ PCs and the data storage and data processing capabilities that they provide

◆ Application programs such as WordPerfect, Lotus 123, and so on

95

- Other equipment such as modems, fax machines, CD-ROM devices, and so on

- Information and data

Sharing resources of all types can greatly reduce the cost of doing business. Cost control/savings is a primary reason for networking. Cost savings can be accomplished because networked information is generally quicker to access. In addition, networking can reduce redundancy. One file can be stored in a central location for access by several users, instead of having to make available several copies of the same file.

Of course, with cost savings come other benefits as well. For example, keeping one copy of a file is not only less expensive than keeping several copies of that file, but it also ensures that the latest copy of that file is always available. If you have 100 copies of a file distributed onto 100 different PCs, you are less likely to get around to updating all of them as frequently as necessary than you are if you have just one copy to update.

The Different Types of Networks

The size of the network depends on the needs of those who will use it, and the location or geographic area that the network occupies. Based on these factors, there are three defined types of networks:

- *Local Area Networks* (LANs)

- *Metropolitan Area Networks* (MANs)

- *Wide Area Networks* (WANs)

LAN

A LAN is just what its name implies: local in its geographic region. A LAN is usually confined to a single business and its one or more adjacent buildings. Therefore, a LAN is also usually privately owned. However, some exceptions might include a LAN in a school or university. In these instances, unless the school or university is a private institution, the LAN might be considered to be owned by the taxpayers or the state.

The primary purpose of most LANs is sharing physical devices, such as printers and modems. They may share various software as well, particularly application programs.

LANs are often described as being capable of transferring data at high speeds because of the limited distance that the data must travel. In addition, LANs also generally experience few errors, and can take advantage of inexpensive communication media, such as telephone lines, because of the limited distance that communications must travel.

MAN

A *Metropolitan Area Network's* (MANs) geographical coverage is more extensive than that of a LAN, often encompassing entire cities, as in the case of networking several city offices all located in different regions of the city.

MANs are generally more sophisticated than LANs, and are a newer entity than WANs. MANs are often capable of sending video and audio transmissions across the network, in addition to standard data transmission.

MANs are also capable of handling greater distances than LANs, though not as great as WANS. In addition, one of the primary purposes of a MAN is that of internetworking various LANs. As in the case of several city offices in different locations mentioned previously, each of the city offices probably has a LAN of its own. The MAN is the interconnection of all of these city LANs.

WAN

A *Wide Area Network* (WAN) is just what its name implies—stretched over a very wide area. WANs can run across states or across countries. As MANs often connect several LANs, WANs may also connect several MANs and several LANs.

The major drawback associated with WANs is the fact that their speed often makes them more prone to errors than either LANs or MANs. Distance is a major factor, of course, but so is technology. WANs often encompass a wide variety of technologies. Making all possible technologies capable of working with all other technologies is a major task that has not yet been totally accomplished. Therefore, even though improvements are being made almost daily, there will continue to be problems and subsequently errors on WANs.

Network Communication Basics

To better understand networks and networking, you need a basic understanding of network communication. Physically connecting PCs to create a network is of little benefit if communication between those PCs cannot be accomplished. Therefore, communication and how it is affected is an important aspect of understanding networks.

There are three basic factors that affect network communication:

◆ Transmission medium

◆ Topology

◆ Medium access methods

Transmission Medium

Regardless of the type of computer you are using, the information and instructions that are transmitted across the network are sent as electric or electromagnetic signals. Therefore, the physical transmission medium (*channel*) across which these signals are sent, is limited to media that is capable of transmitting electric or electromagnetic signals. There are two types of such medium:

◆ Bounded media

◆ Unbounded media

Bounded Media

Bounded media has its benefits and drawbacks, as discussed with each type of bounded media.

Most people are familiar with the bounded type of media, although they may not know that it is called bounded media. Bounded media is media that is constrained by a physical conductor. Examples include shielded twisted pair wiring (such as that used in your telephone system), coaxial cable, and optical fiber. (See figure 1.18.)

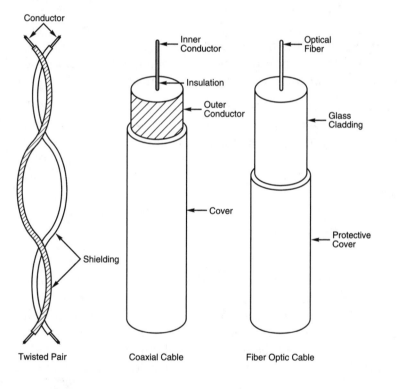

Figure 1.18

Types of Bounded Media.

Shielded Twisted-Pair Cable

Twisted-pair media consists of two strands of conducting material, usually wire. Each strand of wire is wrapped in a protective covering to insulate and shield the conductor. The two strips are then twisted around each other. Insulative materials used for the cover can vary from manufacturer to manufacturer. However, the most common material used is *Poly Vinyl Chloride* (PVC), a toxic material.

Some twisted-pair cables are unshielded. However, those are not usually used for LAN connections. Shielded cable is more common. In addition, some twisted-pair shielded cables have an extra layer of insulating foil between the wire conductor and the exterior insulation cover. This helps reduce electrical interference.

The benefit of this type of bounded media is found primarily in its cost. Shielded twisted-pair cabling is relatively inexpensive, partially because it is so common and not very expensive to produce. One other benefit is that so much of this cabling is already installed in buildings that, when it is possible to use it for networking, installation becomes an almost non-existent expense.

One of the major drawbacks of twisted-pair cabling comes from the repeated and close proximity of the two conducting cables. Because they are so close together, *electromagnetic interference* (EMI), or noise, can be a problem. In addition. This type of cabling system is easy to wire tap, thus reducing the security of your network.

Coaxial Cable

Coaxial cable consists of an inner conductor, also wire, surrounded by an insulating material. Plastic foam is often used for this purpose. Around the insulation is a layer of conducting material that resembles a wire mesh tube. This conductive layer is used as shielding rather than to conduct network transmissions. The final layer is a tube of thick, insulating plastic. This helps to further insulate the conductor as well as to protect it from damage.

You may also have seen this type of bounded media as one type of coaxial cable that is used for bringing cable TV signals into your house.

A major benefit of coaxial cable is that, while it is a little more expensive to use than shielded twisted-pair cable, it is not the most expensive option. It is also less susceptible to electromagnetic interference. In addition, it is much harder to wire tap than is shielded twisted-pair.

The drawbacks include increased complexity of installation, fewer pre-cabled sites, and distance limitations.

Fiber Optic Cable

Fiber optic cable is made with a glass or plastic center conducting core surrounded by protective cladding. The entire cable is then enclosed in a thick, outer jacket.

The more expensive fiber optic cables are made from glass, while the less expensive ones might be made from plastic. The main drawback of using plastic fiber optic is that the quality of transmission over a plastic cable does suffer from loss over great distances.

The main benefits of using fiber optic cable include the fact that many more cables can be encompassed in the same space as either a single shielded twisted-pair or coaxial cable. In addition, because the transmission is made of light pulses rather than electric pulses, fiber optic cable is not subject to either electromagnetic interference or wire tapping.

One drawback to this cable is its sensitivity to damage. A damaged fiber optic cable that lets light in will interfere with the correct transmission of information. A shielded twisted-pair or coaxial cable that has a damaged outer cover may not be noticeable, as long as the conductor is not damaged.

The biggest drawback to fiber optic cable, however, is its cost. It is very expensive to install compared to shielded twisted-pair and coaxial cable.

Unbounded Media

Unbounded media is media that does not have physical restrictions. There are four types of unbounded media—microwave, radio, laser, and infrared.

Microwave

Microwave communication is currently of two types: terrestrial and satellite.

Terrestrial

Terrestrial microwave communication consists of microwave signals that are beamed between two antennas: a transmitter and a receiver. This type of microwave communication is very effective when the transmissions involve long distances and multiple channels.

Satellite

Satellite microwave communication consists of signals sent between directional parabolic antennas located on the earth and on the satellite. As with terrestrial communication. Satellite communication is most effective when transmissions involve very long distances and use multiple channels.

The primary benefit of both types of microwave communication is their ability to support high data rates over great distances, regardless of the terrain over which they must travel.

The drawbacks include cost and a high susceptibility to external interference and jamming. Sometimes something as relatively simple as rain or fog can interfere with transmissions being sent over great distances.

Radio

Radio uses electromagnetic waves in a specific frequency—3 to 300 MHz. Transmission is accomplished by sending the signals through the air between antenna. Omnidirectional transmitting antennas are used to send the signals. Receivers are used to receive the signal. While transmitters and receivers can operate within the frequency of 3 to 300 MHz, they are usually restricted to a small frequency range so as not to interfere with each other.

Laser

A *laser* communication device sends light waves between transmitters. Separate transmitting and receiving lasers are used.

The major problem with laser transmission is that it is restricted to line of site. Anything that interrupts the line of site, including bad weather, can interfere with the transmission of information via laser.

Infrared

An *infrared* communication device sends infrared signals between transmitters and receivers. Infrared is relatively inexpensive, however, and is commonly found in use in TV and VCR remote controls.

Infrared systems are relatively cost effective. However, they are good only for short distances; they too can be effected by bad weather.

Topology

Another important factor in networks is the design of the physical layout of the network itself. This design or configuration is referred to as the network's *topology*. Several topologies are commonly used with networks, including:

◆ Star

◆ Bus

◆ Ring

Star Topology

Star topology is physically designed, as its name implies, in a star shape, with a central connecting point making up the center of the star. This connecting point is often a device such as a hub, a repeater, or a concentrator. All PCs in the network connect directly to the hub, repeater, or concentrator, as shown in figure 1.19.

103

Figure 1.19
Star Topology.

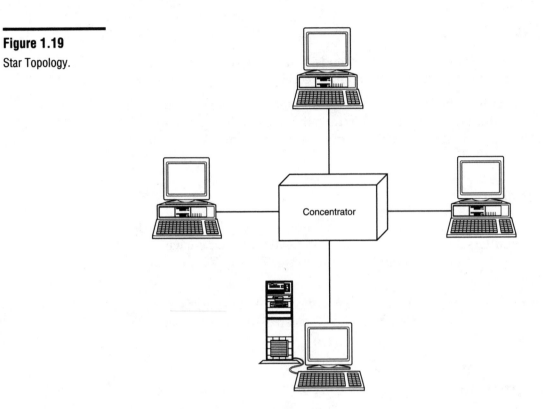

Bus Topology

In the *bus topology*, all devices are attached directly to one main cable, often referred to as *the backbone*. In a bus topology, it is important to remember that both ends of the cable must be terminated to prevent the signal from attempting to locate a device that is not there. (See figure 1.20.)

Ring Topology

In a *ring topology*, the main cable forms a ring or continuous, closed loop. Devices can be connected to the ring at any point along the loop, as shown in figure 1.21.

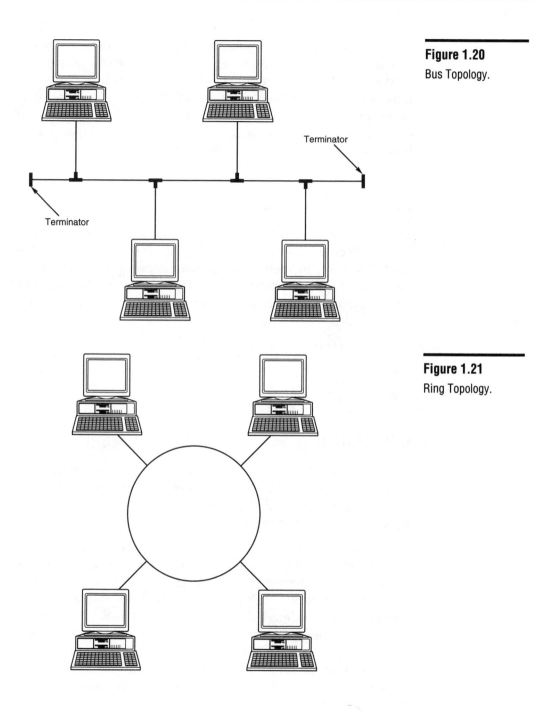

Figure 1.20
Bus Topology.

Terminator

Terminator

Figure 1.21
Ring Topology.

The star, bus, and ring topologies are not the only topologies available to someone designing a network. In fact, many networks take advantage of one topology on part of its network, and another topology elsewhere on its network. Networks of this nature are commonly referred to as *hybrid topologies*. With the expansion of networks from LAN, to MAN, to WAN, hybrid topologies are becoming more widely used and accepted.

Access Methods

How the PCs are arranged and connected to the network is an important consideration. However, once they are connected, how the PC accesses the network is also an important consideration. There are three basic network access methods that PCs can use to ensure their ability to transmit and receive (access). These methods include:

♦ Contention

♦ Polling

♦ Token Passing

Contention

Contention access involves letting the PC access the communication media whenever it needs to access it. Unfortunately, this often results in transmission from one PC colliding with the transmission of another PC.

To reduce the problems associated with this method, primarily the loss of important information, a PC that wants to transmit first senses whether or not there is another signal already on the network. If there is, the PC waits, then resenses the network. Once no other signal is detected, the PC sends out a short test signal. That way, if the PC incorrectly sensed the network, or if another PC sent a transmission in the meantime, the collision that occurs will have minimal impact on data transmission. If, however, all goes well, the PC then sends out its real transmission.

Contention access is one of the most common access methods used today. It is the method used by Ethernet networks.

Polling

Polling access is done through an Administrator. One of the devices on the network is designated as the Administrator. As such, it periodically asks (polls) each PC whether or not it needs to access the channel. If the PC's response is negative, the Administrator polls the next PC. If the PC's response is positive, the Administrator gives the PC access to the channel.

Because the Administrator must constantly poll devices on the network, the channel is busier under this type of access method than it is under the contention method. However, collisions on the channel are eliminated.

The network arranged in a star topology commonly uses the polling access method, as do many mainframes and minicomputers.

Token Passing

Token passing works much like polling does. The main difference is that instead of having an Administrator that queries each PC, the channel circulates a token (a special entity that authorizes entry into and use of the channel by the PC in possession of the token) that can be used by a PC to access the channel.

The major disadvantage of token passing is that each device on the network must be intelligent enough to accept and use the token when it is needed. This mandates that only intelligent workstations (PCs with a microprocessor) can be connected to a channel that uses token passing.

Token ring networks, introduced by IBM, use token passing to control the channel.

Section Review Questions

32. Which of the following is NOT a basic factor that affects network communication?

    a. Transmission medium

    b. Topology

    c. Medium access methods

    d. Cost of the PC

33. All of the following are types of networks except:

    a. LAN

    b. CAN

    c. WAN

    d. MAN

34. In the _____ topology, all devices are attached directly to one main cable.

    a. Star

    b. Ring

    c. Bus

    d. Poll

35. The communication device that sends light waves between transmitters is:

    a. Laser

    b. Infrared

    c. Radio

    d. Satellite

36. Which bus standard is NOT compatible with Pentium processors?

   a. ISA

   b. EISA

   c. VL-Bus

   d. PCI

Answers

32. d

33. b

34. c

35. a

36. c

Summary

In this chapter, you examined networking and the microcomputers that have made networking possible. You also discovered the details of digital computers and how they function. In addition, you examined how digital computers use bits to store and transfer information.

In the next chapter, you learn about DOS—the set of programs responsible for controlling and running the microcomputer.

Using DOS on the Network

2

CHAPTER

Chapter 1 described computer *hardware*—the part of the computer you can touch. This chapter discusses *software*—the instructions and logic that enable the hardware in your PC to execute tasks. Until software and hardware come together, a PC is useless.

Define DOS.

Disk Operating System (DOS) is probably the most understated term you will encounter when working with NetWare LANs. DOS does much more than "operate the disks" on a PC. DOS is the logical heart of the PC. Without DOS, your PC is a useless lump of plastic, metal, and silicon. Turn on a computer that does not have DOS installed, and all you get is a pathetic message:

```
DOS BOOT ERROR
Insert boot disk in A:
```

DOS wakes up your PC; it enables the parts of the PC to work together, and enables your PC to run applications. The microprocessor may be the "brain" of a PC, but DOS teaches that brain to manage the PC's resources.

Describe the basic functions of DOS.

DOS enables your computer to do the following:

◆ Read and write data to and from files on floppy and hard disks

◆ Print to a printer

◆ Manage the file systems on your disks, including moving or copying files

◆ Run application programs

◆ Display information on the computer monitor

◆ Receive information from the keyboard

◆ Control how your computer operates

As you can see, managing file resources is only a part of DOS's expertise.

DOS is actually an abbreviated name for two products: PC DOS and MS-DOS. When IBM developed the original PC, Microsoft was contracted to write the operating system software. IBM was licensed to market the software as PC DOS, whereas Microsoft sold a similar product under the trademark MS-DOS. These two versions of DOS have never been identical, but always have retained the capability to run the same applications.

Exploring the Components of DOS

DOS consists of the following three main components:

◆ **System files.** In MS-DOS, these files are named MSDOS.SYS and IO.SYS. The comparable files in PC DOS are IBMDOS.COM and IBMBIO.COM. The boot process looks for and executes these files after performing the initial hardware configuration. See Chapter 1, "Exploring Networks and Network Workstation Hardware," for more details.

 Explain the importance of the COMMAND.COM file.

◆ **COMMAND.COM.** This is the command processor, which provides the primary interface to the user. The command processor accepts commands from the keyboard (or other sources) and has the capability of directly executing many of the most common DOS functions—known as *internal commands*. When asked to perform a command that is not an internal command, the command processor has the capability of calling auxiliary DOS commands.

◆ **Auxiliary commands.** These commands, such as FORMAT, SYS, and DISKCOPY, are also called *external commands* because they are not part of the command processor. These commands are actually independent, executable command files that can be called by the command processor.

113

In Chapter 1, you learned the multistep process that boots your computer. This process has the following three goals:

◆ Testing the hardware

◆ Determining the system configuration

◆ Starting DOS

Review this process before you proceed with this chapter.

Exploring the Features of the DOS File System

In Chapter 1, you learned that files are stored on floppy disks or hard disks. These disks are organized in tracks, which are in turn organized in sectors.

DOS's task is to store data in these tracks and sectors in an organized way so that the data can be retrieved. Fortunately, most of the work DOS does is invisible. DOS performs a complex job as it breaks files into sector-sized chunks, stores them in sectors, and then makes a record of the file so that it can be retrieved at a later time. Under most circumstances, however, the user need not be aware of how this process takes place.

You must understand, however, the fundamental units of storage: files and directories.

Files

Files are the fundamental units for storing programs and data under DOS. Think of files in terms of file folders, each folder holding a related set of information. DOS keeps track of the following information for each file:

◆ The name of the file with the name extension

◆ The size of the file in bytes

◆ The date and time the file was last modified—called the date and time stamps

◆ The file attributes (more about them later)

◆ The location of the file on the disk

File Names

Files are identified by a file specification that must be in a specific format, commonly referred to as eight-dot-three. This means that the file name consists of two parts. The first part is a file name that can have up to eight characters. The second part is the file extension that can have three characters. The parts are separated by a dot or period.

Explain the proper DOS file-naming rules.

File names can contain most characters, including all letters and numbers. The following can appear in file names:

◆ Any alphanumeric character (A-Z or 0-9)

◆ The symbols ! @ # $ % ^ & ( ) ' { } ~ - _

◆ Any 8-bit character above ASCII 127 from the IBM character set; see Chapter 3, "Moving Around NetWare Directory Structures," for information about this character set

The following cannot be used in file names:

◆ The symbols * ? + = / \ ; : " , < > [ ]

◆ Spaces

◆ Names DOS reserves for device names, such as AUX, COM1, COM2, COM3, CON, LPT1, LPT2, LPT3, NUL, PRN, or CLOCKS

Identify acceptable DOS file names.

Some valid file names are as follows:

COMMAND.COM	AUTOEXEC.BAT CONFIG.SYS
REPORT.DOC	MY_FILE.TXT FILE#99.DAT
@DATA.FIL	#23.99 XCOPY.CO_

Some invalid file names, along with rules they violate, are as follows:

HOWMANY?.DAT	(Invalid character ?)
AUX.FIL	(AUX is reserved)
MY FILE.DOC	(No spaces are allowed)
AUXILIARY.RPT	(Too many characters)

Define the reserved and industry-accepted DOS file name extensions.

Some of the forbidden DOS characters are reserved for other purposes. The following list identifies the reserved characters, along with their uses:

.	Separates file names from extensions
* and ?	DOS wildcard characters
:	Identifies disk drives
/	Identifies a switch after a command
\	Identifies subdirectories
< and >	Control command redirection

You learn about the use of each reserved character later in this chapter.

File Types

Generally speaking, files fall into two categories: executable and data files.

Executable files are programs—applications such as word processors, utilities such as NetWare's SYSCON, or DOS commands such as XCOPY. A *program* is a set of instructions for the computer. When you enter the name of the program, DOS locates the file and executes the program in the file. Such programs are identified by their extensions, which are either EXE (for "executable") or COM (for "command"). Therefore, XCOPY.EXE is the program file that contains the program for the XCOPY command. Usually, a NetWare Administrator does not create program files; they are created by programmers and are turned into EXE or COM files so that you need not worry about how they work.

You will probably be required to create one type of executable file, however. *Batch files* are files that contain lists of commands, and are identified by the extension BAT. If you frequently execute a task that takes ten steps, you can place those steps in a batch file. The batch file can then be executed by typing its name. DOS then executes the command's steps stored in the batch file. You learn more about batch files in a later section of this chapter.

Data files can include word processing documents, databases, spreadsheets, and any data programs you need to store that cannot be put into RAM. Some data files are fairly permanent, such as documents you create on your word processor. Some files, however, can be created just for the duration of a specific task. Suppose that a program needs to set up a table too big to fit into the 640 KB DOS RAM allocation. The programmer might have the program set up the table in a file. When the data is no longer required, the file is erased. The user may not even be aware that the file ever existed.

117

Elsewhere in your studies, you have learned about assigning user rights. The practice of creating temporary files explains why a user might need to have Write and Create rights to a directory in which only program files are located. When executing a program creates temporary files in the directory, the program cannot create the temporary files and will fail unless the NetWare user has Write and Create rights in that directory.

The extensions for data files have no rules, although some conventions have been established. Word processing files often have the extension DOC, for example. Files containing plain text may have the extension TXT. The actual extension is entirely up to the person or program that creates the file.

 Define the DOS reserved and industry accepted DOS file name extensions.

Some examples of common file extensions are as follows:

♦ EXE—Executable DOS files (reserved by DOS)

♦ COM—DOS command files (also reserved by DOS)

♦ SYS—System driver files (see the later section on configuring DOS)

♦ BAT—DOS batch files (reserved by DOS)

♦ DOC—Document files

♦ TXT—Text files that contain only ASCII text characters

♦ OVL—Overlay files that contain extra program information for programs that cannot fit entirely into 640 KB

♦ DAT—Data files

♦ BAS—Programs written in the BASIC programming language

File Attributes

DOS files can be assigned attributes that affect how the file can be manipulated. Later you learn how to use the ATTRIB command to change file attributes. Attributes are either set, meaning that the attribute has been assigned to the file, or cleared, meaning that the attribute has been removed.

DOS file attributes are as follows:

◆ **A.** When a file is modified, it is given the A attribute, indicating that the file is to be archived. When files are backed up, the backup program can be instructed to look only for the files that have been modified. After the file has been backed up, the A attribute is removed.

◆ **H.** Files with the H attribute are hidden, meaning that they are not displayed in file directories. Such files are effectively invisible to users. This is done to simplify directories or to add a limited degree of security.

◆ **R.** These files are read-only. They cannot be modified or deleted. The information in the files, however, can be read.

◆ **S.** System files are hidden from directory displays and read-only files. Ordinarily, users do not flag files as S files. When boot files are installed on a disk, however, the files will be marked as System files. If the System attribute is set, the other attributes of the file cannot be modified.

 When DOS files are stored on a NetWare server, the files can be assigned NetWare file attributes, but not DOS attributes. NetWare attributes are assigned with NetWare's FLAG utility or with FILER.

Starting DOS on a PC

The process of turning on a PC and starting DOS is called *booting* (discussed in Chapter 1). The two methods of booting are cold and warm boots.

Cold Boot

A *cold boot* takes place when a PC is off, and the power is switched on. (Most PCs that have reset buttons also perform cold boots when reset is pressed.) During a cold boot, the system performs a *power-on self test* (POST) before DOS is started. The steps are as follows:

1a. If you are booting a floppy-only PC, make sure that a bootable DOS disk is inserted in drive A, or

1b. If you are booting a system with a hard drive, make sure that no floppy disks are in the disk drives.

2. Turn on the power.

3. Wait for the prompt to be displayed.

Explain the use of the Ctrl+Alt+Del key combination.

Warm Boot

A *warm boot* restarts DOS without turning off the power. A warm boot does not perform a POST, but does clear memory and restart DOS. Warm boots can be used to recover from hung applications and other system problems. Follow these steps:

1a. If you are booting a floppy-only PC, make sure that a bootable DOS disk is inserted in drive A, or

1b. If you are booting a system with a hard drive, make sure that no floppy disks are in the disk drives.

2. Press Ctrl+Alt+Del.

3. Wait for the prompt to be displayed.

Section Review Questions

1. Which is NOT a valid file name?

    a. DATA+TXT.FIL

    b. @TUES.1

    c. $JULY.###

    d. ^^.!!

2. DOS enables your computer to perform all of the following tasks except:

    a. Read and write data to disk

    b. Print to a file

    c. Create application programs

    d. Control how the computer operates

3. Which character is NOT an extension for an executable file?

    a. COM

    b. SYS

    c. EXE

    d. BAT

4. Without the COMMAND.COM file loaded into the PC's memory, you could NOT:

    a. Execute internal commands

    b. Write an application program

    c. Implement NetWare security

    d. Write a letter to your best friend

5. Which of the following is an allowable DOS file name character?

    a. *

    b. ?

    c. :

    d. #

Answers

1. a

2. c

3. b

4. a

5. d

Using DOS Commands

DOS provides dozens of commands. The remainder of this chapter introduces you to the most important ones.

The DOS Command Environment

The DOS command environment is provided by the command interpreter, which is a program named COMMAND.COM. When DOS boots, it installs the command interpreter, which is then ready to receive your keyboard input.

When the command interpreter is active, the screen displays the DOS prompt to notify users that DOS is prepared to accept a typed command. Normally, the prompt is either A> or C> followed by a flashing underscore where typed characters will be displayed.

The A> or C> prompt indicates the current drive. Floppy and hard disks are identified by drive letters followed by a colon (:). These drive letters are assigned as follows:

◆ **A:**—This prompt represents the first floppy disk drive. If the computer has two floppy drives, drive A is usually the top drive.

◆ **B:**—This prompt represents the second floppy disk drive, if present. If your system has only one floppy drive, both A: and B: can be used to refer to the same drive.

◆ **C:**—This prompt indicates the first hard disk drive partition. (You learn about partitions in the section about installing DOS.)

◆ **D:**—D: through **Z:** are additional hard drive partitions.

After your computer boots, the command prompt is set to the letter of the drive that contains the DOS boot files.

At any given time, your command environment can be associated with a default drive letter and a default directory. Directories are described in the next section. Normally, when you type a command, DOS expects the file associated with the command to reside in the current default drive and directory. If the command file is not in that location, DOS cannot locate it and execute the command.

Because it is usually inconvenient to constantly change the default drive and directory, DOS has a PATH option that instructs DOS to look for command files in other directories. You learn about PATH in the section about installing and configuring DOS.

To execute a command that DOS recognizes, simply type the name of the command at the cursor and press Enter. DOS locates the program associated with the command and carries it out.

 Note DOS is not case-sensitive; you can enter commands in upper- or lowercase letters.

DOS has two types of commands: internal and external. Before you learn about them, the following sections give you some guidelines about special keys that can be used when working with DOS commands.

Typing Commands

In addition to the character keys, several special keys on the keyboard can be used when working with DOS. These keys include the following:

◆ **Enter.** Pressing this key completes every command and turns it over to DOS.

◆ **Ctrl.** Pressing this key generates control codes when pressed with other keys; to type a Control+Z character (see Chapter 3, "Moving Around NetWare Directory Structures," for a discussion of the ASCII control keys), press Ctrl and type **Z**. Ctrl+C aborts some DOS processes.

◆ **Alt.** This key is used in keystroke combinations. In DOS, the primary use is in the Ctrl+Alt+Del key combination used to perform a warm boot.

◆ **Cursor keys** (left and right arrow keys). These keys are used in some DOS command-line editing. All four arrow keys can be used in some DOS utilities, such as the EDIT utility that accompanies DOS 5.0 and 6.0.

◆ **F1–F12.** These keys are used by some utilities for special purposes.

Differentiate between internal and external DOS commands.

Internal Commands

The programs required to execute internal commands are contained in the COMMAND.COM program file. Internal commands, therefore, are always available whenever the DOS command interpreter is active. You do not need to change directories or establish DOS paths to enable DOS to find an internal command.

Internal commands were made internal for convenience because many are commonly used. You learn how the commands are used in later sections of this chapter. Some examples of internal commands are as follows:

◆ **DIR.** This command displays a list of the files in the current directory, along with their sizes, date, and time stamps.

◆ **TYPE.** This command displays the contents of a text file on a screen.

◆ **COPY.** This command makes a copy of a file in another directory or on another disk.

◆ **DEL.** This command deletes a file from the disk; functions the same as ERASE.

◆ **REN.** This command renames a file.

◆ **CLS.** This command clears any text displayed on the screen.

External Commands

External commands are stored in executable files with the extensions EXE or COM. When you type a command, DOS first determines whether the command is internal. If not, DOS searches for

125

an EXE or COM file that matches the name. If, for example, you type the command **DISKCOPY**, DOS locates the file named DISKCOPY.COM and executes the program in that file.

Because external DOS commands are packaged in EXE and COM files, they actually work just like application command files. They are considered DOS commands because they are packaged with DOS, but they function more like applications than built-in DOS features.

DOS also treats batch files, identified with a BAT extension, as commands. You will learn about batch files later in this chapter.

If DOS cannot locate a COM, EXE, or BAT file to match your typed input, it responds with the message Bad command or file name.

The command files for external commands must be located in the current directory or in the directory path. See the section "Installing and Configuring DOS" for information about the DOS path. DOS external command files are usually stored in a directory named \DOS.

Some common external commands are as follows:

◆ **FDISK.** This command configures hard disk partitions.

◆ **FORMAT.** This command formats a DOS partition.

◆ **BACKUP.** This command backs up files to a floppy disk. (BACKUP has been replaced in DOS 6.0 with a more powerful backup utility.)

◆ **LABEL.** This command assigns a label of up to eleven characters to a DOS disk.

◆ **XCOPY.** This command copies files (a copy utility more powerful than the internal COPY command).

◆ **DISKCOPY.** This command duplicates floppy disks.

Note
As a NetWare Administrator, you should be aware of some characteristics of internal commands.

You are not required to map search drives to enable users to access internal commands. If a user has a properly functioning COMMAND.COM running a command interpreter, the internal commands are available.

About the only time internal commands cause difficulty is in login scripts. The # command can be used to execute program files, including DOS external commands. Internal commands, however, are not stored in program files. You therefore cannot delete a file by putting a #DEL command in a login script. Rather, you must run a new command processor.

COMMAND.COM is actually a DOS external command that creates a DOS command processor and optionally executes a command. You can pass a command to a command processor by using the /C switch. For example, the following line in a login script deletes a file from the user's C drive:

```
#COMMAND /C DEL C:\NETWARE\NETFILE.TXT
```

Command Parameters

Most DOS commands require that you provide some information as to how they are to operate. The COPY command cannot copy files unless you specify which files to copy. This information is usually provided in the form of parameters that follow the command. The following command copies all the files on the A: floppy to the B: floppy:

```
COPY A:*.* B:
```

127

All items following the COPY command name are parameters.

 Explain the use of command line switches.

Command Switches

Many DOS commands have options. These options are specified by typing switches following the commands. For example, you can use a switch if you want to view a directory that contains more than 25 files. Normally, the files scroll up the screen, and some are lost from the top. You can add the /W switch to the DIR command, however, to instruct DOS to display a wide directory with many names displayed in columns.

Switches follow the command. DOS frequently indicates a switch with a / character. The wide directory command is typed like this:

```
DIR /W
```

Case Insensitivity

DOS does not distinguish between upper- or lowercase letters. Commands, directory names, file names, and switches all can be entered in any case or even in mixed case.

Error Messages

DOS can produce a wide variety of error messages if a command you enter contains an error. If you enter a non-existent command, DOS provides one of its most common error messages. The following example is a dialog. The user has typed the text shown in bold type:

```
CPOY A:*.* B:
Bad command or file name
```

Another common error is attempting to access a floppy disk drive that does not contain a disk. The following example illustrates this:

```
DIR A:
Not ready error reading drive A
Abort, Retry, Fail?
```

This is such a common error that you should know how to cope with it. You can make the following responses:

◆ **A**—Attempts to abort the current operation. If DOS can recover and establish itself on a valid drive, it will do so and redisplay a prompt.

◆ **R**—Attempts the operation again. Suppose that you try an operation on drive A, but forget to insert a floppy. You can put your floppy disk into the drive and retry the operation without reentering the command.

◆ **F**—Fails, and prompts you to enter the drive letter for a valid and available disk drive. You can then specify a drive, such as C, that DOS can use as a default.

Section Review Questions

6. Which character is used as a command switch?

    a. /

    b. \

    c. >

    d. <

7. The DIR, TYPE, and COPY commands are:

    a. Internal DOS commands

    b. External DOS commands

    c. Stored in executable files with EXE or COM extensions

    d. All used to access the hard disk

129

8. What does the following error message mean?

   ```
   Not ready error reading drive A:
   ```

   ```
   Abort, Retry, Fail?
   ```

   a. The disk in drive A is not formatted.

   b. Drive A does not exist.

   c. There is no disk in drive A.

   d. a and c

9. The /W switch used with the DIR command:

   a. Indicates that the directory listing should be shown with additional file information

   b. Tells the computer to display the directory in a wide format without additional file information

   c. Tells the computer to widen its search for the specified files

   d. Has no effect on the DIR command, although it used to

10. External DOS commands are called external because:

    a. All external DOS commands must be installed after the internal DOS commands have been loaded.

    b. Microsoft could not think of any better way to describe them.

    c. They are never copied to RAM, an internal DOS storage area.

    d. They are packaged with DOS, but function more like applications than built-in features.

Answers

6. a

7. a

8. c

9. b

10. d

Managing Disks

In Chapter 1, you learned about the floppy disks and hard disks used to store most DOS files. You learned that these disks must be formatted into tracks and sectors before they can be used with DOS. You also learned that disk drives are identified by their letters.

This section reviews the essential tools you need to manage disk drives.

 You might want to try some of the commands in the remainder of this chapter as you read the book. It will be helpful if you type the following command before you do so:

```
PROMPT $P$G
```

The PROMPT command is explained in the "Managing Directories" section of this chapter. After you type this command, your command interpreter prompt is modified to show your default drive and directory. You will discover that this is handy information to have available.

Formatting Floppy Disks

Although you can purchase floppy disks that are factory formatted, most floppies are purchased unformatted. You need to know how to format these disks. You also may need to know how to create a system floppy that can be booted.

In Chapter 1, you learned that floppy disks are available in several different sizes and densities. You may want to review that information at this time because disk formatting requires you to use the correct commands for each drive/disk combination.

 Demonstrate the proper use of the FORMAT, LABEL, and VOL DOS commands.

Standard Formatting

If your floppy disk exactly matches the standard capacity of your disk drive, formatting is quite simple. To format a floppy in drive A, just type the following:

```
FORMAT A:
```

DOS responds with the following message:

```
Insert new diskette for drive A: and press ENTER when ready.
```

When you press Enter, the format proceeds.

Every floppy disk or hard disk partition can be assigned a label of up to 11 characters. After the format has been applied, you are asked for a label for the new disk. You can enter an eleven-character volume label or press Enter if you do not want the disk to have a label. DOS then prompts you with the following message:

```
Volume label (11 characters, ENTER for none)?
```

Enter a label name and press Enter, or press Enter alone to leave the disk unlabeled.

If the format is successful, DOS produces a report similar to the following:

```
1457664 bytes total disk space
1457664 bytes available on disk

Format another (Y/N)?
```

You can format another disk with the same capacity, or press **N** to exit the format utility.

Labels are more important on hard disks than on floppies because labels provide a double-check against accidentally formatting a hard disk. When you format a previously formatted hard disk, you must enter the volume label to confirm that formatting should proceed.

You can format a floppy disk in drive B by simply changing the drive letter. In fact, you can format a partition on your hard drive by substituting the drive letter in the FORMAT parameter. Because hard drives are a bit more involved, however, read the section "Installing and Configuring DOS" later in this chapter before you format your hard drive.

 Match floppy disk size, density, and format capacity.

You can use FORMAT without any command switches when you are formatting disks under the following conditions:

- A 3 1/2-inch double-density (720 KB) disk is in a 3 1/2-inch double-density drive.

- A 3 1/2-inch high-density (1.44 MB) disk is in a 3 1/2-inch high-density drive.

- A 5 1/4-inch double-density (1.2 MB) disk is in a 5 1/4-inch double-density drive.

- A 5 1/4-inch high-density (360 KB) disk is in a 5 1/4-inch high-density drive.

Formatting with Other Floppy Drive Combinations

If your disk does not exactly match the standard characteristics of your floppy drive, you must add switches to the FORMAT command.

To format a 5 1/4-inch double-density (360 KB) disk in a 5 1/4-inch high-density (1.2 MB) drive, use this command format:

```
FORMAT A: /4
```

 The heads on a high-density 5 1/4-inch disk drive are narrower than those of a double-density drive because the high-density drive records on more tracks. Therefore, disks formatted on a 5 1/4-inch high-density drive cannot be used on a double-density drive; the wide heads of the double-density drive read beyond the width of the track and probably pick up erroneous data.

You, therefore, should use this procedure only if the double-density disk is to be used exclusively with high-density drives. No reliable method is available for exchanging disks between 5 1/4-inch double-density and high-density drives.

To format a 3 1/2-inch double-density (720 KB) disk in a 3 1/2-inch high-density (1.44 MB) disk drive, use this command:

```
FORMAT A: /N:9/T:80
```

This command instructs FORMAT to format the disk with 80 tracks and 9 sectors per track.

When using DOS 5.0 and 6.0, the /F: switch makes it possible to format by directly specifying the desired density, rather than the tracks and sectors. The density you specify must be valid for the combination of floppy disk and disk drive you are using.

To format a 5 1/4-inch double-density (360 KB) floppy in a 5 1/4-inch high-density drive, use this command with DOS 5.0 or 6.0:

```
FORMAT A: /F:360
```

To format a 3 1/2-inch double-density (720 KB) floppy in a 3 1/2-inch high-density drive, use this command with DOS 5.0 or 6.0:

```
FORMAT A: /F:720
```

Understanding What Formatting Does

Formatting a disk accomplishes the following things:

◆ Defines the tracks and sectors on the disk, each of which is numbered

◆ Creates a *file allocation table* (FAT), used to record the location of each file along with a record of all sectors used to store each file

◆ Creates a root directory

◆ Optionally adds the required system files to make the disk bootable

 Explain the purpose of formatting a disk.

Before a disk can be used for storage, it is formatted—divided into small units, each of which can hold a fixed amount of data. These units, called *sectors*, are indexed so that they can be located easily by DOS.

How Files Are Stored on Disks

DOS organizes floppy disks in clusters of one or more sectors. Most files are larger than a single cluster, so DOS must be capable of fragmenting the file into cluster-size chunks, and then reassembling the chunks when the data or program in the file is required. When DOS stores a file, the following events take place:

◆ A directory entry is created containing the file name and extension, any file attributes, the date and time stamps, and the file size in bytes.

◆ The FAT is updated to show which sectors are being reserved for the file.

◆ The location of the file by sector and track is recorded so the file can be located.

135

DOS writes files by looking for the first available cluster starting on Track 1, and then proceeding to the next available cluster, which might be nearby or on an entirely different track. When a disk is freshly formatted, DOS can store files in contiguous sectors.

As files are erased, however, the clusters they occupied are released for reuse. This can create a gap in a track between the clusters in use by two other files. When new files are written, DOS begins to store them in these gaps. A file that might fit in a single track can be spread across several tracks because DOS could not find a contiguous block of clusters large enough to hold the file.

When large numbers of files are stored in this disorganized way, the disk is said to be *fragmented*. To retrieve fragmented files, DOS must move the read/write head to each track that contains part of the file. This slows disk performance considerably.

Especially with hard drives, it is a good idea to defragment the drive occasionally. A variety of commercial defragmentation utilities are available. DOS 6.0 includes a utility called DEFRAG.

Demonstrate the proper use of the FORMAT, LABEL, and VOL DOS commands.

Changing a Disk Volume Label

To change the label of a volume, use the LABEL command. For example, to change the label of a floppy disk in drive A to NEWLABEL, enter the following command:

```
LABEL A: NEWLABEL
```

To view the label of a disk, type **LABEL** followed by the desired disk drive, as in the following example:

```
LABEL A:
```

DOS displays the label and gives you the option of entering a new label or pressing Enter to leave the label unchanged. You can also display the label of a volume by typing **VOL** only to see the label for the default drive. If you type VOL followed by the drive letter, you can see the volume label of that drive letter, drive D for example, as in the following example:

```
VOL D:
```

Creating Boot Disks

In Chapter 1, you learned that certain files must be on a floppy disk in order to boot a PC. These files must be installed in a specific location on the disk, and in one of two ways. Later in the chapter, you learn about the SYS command, which is used to install the system files on a previously formatted disk. However, an option for FORMAT also installs the system files after the disk is formatted.

To format and create a system disk, use the /S switch with FORMAT, as in the following command:

```
FORMAT A: /S
```

After the disk is formatted, FORMAT copies the system files from the disk used to boot the computer. It is most convenient if the computer is booted from drive C because the system files are always available. Depending on whether you use MS-DOS or PC DOS, FORMAT copies MSDOS.SYS and IO.SYS, or IBMDOS.COM and IBMBIO.COM. Additionally, the COMMAND.COM file is copied to the disk. These three files enable the floppy disk to boot the PC and start a command processor.

Adding System Files to a Formatted Disk

You need not reformat a disk to make it a system disk. You do, however, need to remove the files because they probably occupy the system file area. After you delete the files from a floppy in drive A, you can add the system files with the following command:

    SYS A:

SYS copies the system files from the boot disk.

Changing the Default Disk

You always have a disk assigned as your default disk. Immediately after booting, the default disk is the drive used to boot, usually A or C. When you type a command, DOS assumes that the associated command file is located on the default disk, unless you add another drive letter to the command.

To change the default drive, type the letter of the desired drive followed by a colon:

    B:

Your prompt then indicates that B is the new default drive.

Remember that even though COMMAND.COM is on the boot drive, all the internal commands are always available, regardless of which drive is the default drive.

 Demonstrate the proper use of the FORMAT, LABEL, and VOL DOS commands.

Executing Commands on Other Drives

If you are only going to execute a single command on another drive, you can add the drive letter to the command. You change the volume label of a disk with the LABEL command. If drive A is your default drive, and LABEL.EXE is on C, you can relabel the disk in A with the following command:

```
C:LABEL ARCHIVE
```

You also can use a drive letter to indicate that a command is to process a file on another disk. If C is your default drive, you can easily view the contents of a file on A with a command such as the following:

```
TYPE A:MYFILE.TXT
```

Volume Names

As you have learned, every disk can be assigned an 11-character label. You can do this when the disk is formatted, or you can add or change the label on a formatted disk using the LABEL command. To change the label of the floppy in B to ACCOUNTS, type the following:

```
LABEL B: ACCOUNTS
```

If you are relabeling the current drive, you can leave out the drive letter as follows:

```
LABEL BACKUPS
```

Copying Disks

You can duplicate disks using the DISKCOPY command. The disk that receives the copy must be identical to the original—you cannot duplicate a 1.44 MB disk to a 1.2 MB disk, for example. If you want to copy files between different types of floppy disks, you must use the COPY command discussed in the "Managing Files" section of this chapter. Also, DISKCOPY works only for floppy disks. You cannot use it to copy a hard disk.

If you have two identical disk drives, you can duplicate directly between them. To duplicate the disk in drive A to a disk in drive B, enter the following command:

DISKCOPY A: B:

DISKCOPY refers to the floppy disks as source and destination (also called the target) disks. The first letter is the *source disk*; the second letter is the *destination disk*.

You are prompted to insert the disks in the appropriate drives and press Enter. DISKCOPY duplicates the disk in A in one operation. If the target disk has not been formatted, DISKCOPY formats it with the same format as the source disk.

 Note If you only buy one type of floppy disk, it is a good idea to have two identical floppy disk drives. They are not that expensive, and then you can easily make archive backup copies of any software you buy. Otherwise, this task is so inconvenient that it is routinely not performed.

Few PCs have two identical disk drives, however. Usually you duplicate a disk using a single drive. To do this, enter the drive letter in the command twice:

DISKCOPY A: A:

DISKCOPY duplicates the disk by reading as much data into memory as possible, and then asking you to insert the target disk. DOS writes the data in memory to the target disk, and then asks you to reinsert the source disk. You will need to swap disks several times to complete the copying operation.

Section Review Questions

11. If you have only a high-density 5 1/4-inch floppy drive and you need to format a double-density disk, type:

    a. **FORMAT A: /4**

   b. **FDISK A: /4**

   c. **FORMAT A: /D**

   d. **FORMAT A/4**

12. To perform a DISKCOPY from a 1.2 MB disk to a 1.44 MB disk, type:

   a. **DISKCOPY A: B:**

   b. **DISKCOPY A: B: /4**

   c. **DISKCOPY A: B: /N:9/T:80**

   d. This cannot be done

13. A 3 1/2-inch double-density disk can hold _____ of information.

   a. 360 KB

   b. 720 KB

   c. 1.2 MB

   d. 1.44 MB

14. Which of the following is NOT a proper use of the VOL DOS command?

   a. LABEL *Newlable* A:

   b. LABEL A:

   c. A: LABEL

   d. None of these are valid uses of this command

15. Which of the following statements about the DISKCOPY command is true?

   a. Requires two separate disk drives of the same type in order to work

   b. Duplicates the disk by reading as much data into memory as it can from one disk, then copying it to the next disk

141

    c. Requires that the target disk be formatted before it can be used

    d. Can only be used with disks that have not yet been formatted

Answers

11. a

12. d

13. b

14. c

15. b

Managing Directories

Floppy disks generally hold only a few dozen files, but hard disks can hold thousands. If all those files were stored in the same place, the result would be like a file cabinet with thousands of pieces of paper but no way to organize them into categories.

Directories are like adding index tabs to a file cabinet. They enable you to group files into meaningful collections. For example, all the DOS external commands, along with some other DOS files, are usually installed in a directory named DOS.

In this section, you learn about directories and subdirectories. You also learn the commands and procedures for managing DOS directories.

Directories and Subdirectories

When any disk is formatted, an initial directory is created. This directory is named the *root directory* for reasons that will become clear in a moment.

Directory names are identified with backslashes (\). The root directory is simply named \.

New directories can be created in the root directory. A directory named DOS is usually created. To show that the DOS directory is located just inside the root directory, it can be prefaced with a backslash: \DOS.

Explain the use of subdirectories.

Directories can contain other directories, which are called *subdirectories*. Suppose that you have a directory named \DOCS to hold your word processing documents. You can subdivide your documents by adding subdirectories for categories of documents. You can have a subdirectory named MEMOS, for example. To show that this is a subdirectory of \DOCS, its full name appears like this:

    \DOCS\MEMOS

This full notation is a directory path. The path shows a subdirectory along with all the directories between it and the root.

Now for an explanation of the term *root*.

Explain the DOS directory structure.

The directories on a disk are frequently drawn in a diagram like an inverted tree, called a *directory tree*. If you turn the diagram in figure 2.1 upside down, you see that the root directory is at the root of the tree.

Directories can be created and removed. You can also move around the directory structure (change the default directory). The next three sections explain the three related commands.

143

Figure 2.1

A directory tree.

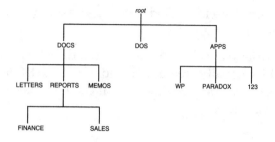

 Demonstrate the proper use of the *CHDIR* (CD), *MKDIR* (MD), and *RMDIR* (RD) commands.

Creating Directories

Directories must be created one subdirectory level at a time. A new directory is created with the *Make Directory* (MD) command. To create part of the tree in figure 2.1, enter the following sequence of commands:

```
MD \DOCS
MD \DOCS\REPORTS
MD \DOCS\REPORTS\FINANCE
```

Deleting Directories

Directories are deleted with the *Remove Directory* (RD) command. To be deleted, a directory must be empty—that is, it must not contain any subdirectories or files. In addition, you cannot remove your default directory (see the next section). The directories created in the preceding discussion can be erased with the following commands:

```
RD \DOCS\REPORTS\FINANCE
RD \DOCS\REPORTS
RD \DOCS
```

Changing the Default Directory

Just as you always have a default disk, you also always have a default—or current—directory. When you execute a command, DOS looks for the command file on the default disk in the current directory.

You can change your default directory by using the *Change Directory* (CD) command.

If you enter the following command, your default directory changes to \DOCS\REPORTS:

```
CD \DOCS\REPORTS
```

Viewing Directories

You can see a list of directories, subdirectories, and files on a disk by using the DOS DIR command.

 Demonstrate the proper use of the DIR command.

The DIR command has switches, two of which are particularly useful: the /P and the /W switches. Using the /P switch causes only a single screen of directory and file information to be displayed at one time. Using the /W switch causes file and directory names only to be displayed across the screen.

The /P and /W switches can be used separately or together in the same command, such as:

```
DIR /P /W
```

The DIR command can also be used with wildcards, such as the asterisk (*), to see a list of all available directories and files. The proper syntax for using this wildcard is:

```
DIR * or DIR *.*
```

145

Using DIR * shows files and directories. Using DIR *.* shows only files.

Using Directory Names in Commands

You can include directory paths if you need to work with other directories. To display the \DOS directory file, enter the following command:

DIR \DOS

You can combine drive letters with directory paths. To type a file on drive A, use this command:

TYPE A:\DOCS\MYFILE.TXT

Relative Path Names

Until now you have seen only fully qualified path names. These names always begin with a backslash (\), indicating that the path originates at the root directory.

You also can use relative path names that begin at the current directory. Refer to the directory tree in figure 2.1. Suppose that your default directory is \DOCS, and that you want to type a file in the REPORTS subdirectory. You can do so easily by using the following command:

TYPE REPORTS\EXPENSE.TXT

Notice that no \ appears before REPORTS. This indicates that the path begins with the current directory, not with the root. This path is relative to the \DOCS directory.

If, instead, the command is entered as:

TYPE \REPORTS\EXPENSE.TXT

DOS looks for a \REPORTS directory just under the root directory.

You can tell DOS to search directories in a specific order by using the PATH command. You can also display the current search order by using this command.

 Demonstrate the proper use of the PATH command.

Setting the Path

To specify drive letters and path names every time a command is executed is inconvenient. The DOS command PATH enables you to specify directories that DOS is to search to locate command files.

Creating the Path

The command to create a DOS path is as follows:

```
PATH C:\DOS;C:\123;D:\WORDPERF;C:\UTILITY
```

This PATH command specifies four directories, separated by semicolons. When you enter a command, DOS first examines your current directory for the appropriate command file. If the file is not found in the current directory, DOS begins to search for the command in the directories specified in the path, starting with the first directory and working toward the last.

Displaying the Current Path

You can display the current path by typing **PATH** without any parameters.

You will almost always want to have a path that specifies at least the \DOS directory on your boot drive.

147

Guidelines for Paths

Notice in the preceding example that all the directories specify a disk drive. When a drive is not specified, DOS assumes that the directory in the path is on the default disk. Suppose that your path command looks like the following:

```
PATH \DOS;\123;\WORDPERF;\UTILITY
```

If you execute the following commands, DOS produces an error message:

```
A:\
DISKCOPY A: A:
```

DOS responds with the Bad command or file name message because DOS only looks for the \DOS directory on drive A. Therefore, it is always a good idea to specify a drive letter for each directory in your PATH command.

 Do not include floppy disk directories in your path because a disk may not be in the disk drive when the command is executed. Suppose that you have the following path:

```
PATH C:\DOS;A:
```

And then you execute a command that DOS cannot find. DOS searches drive A. If no disk is in A, you see the following message:

```
Not ready reading drive A:
Abort, Retry, Fail?
```

Summary of DOS Command Searches

 Explain the DOS command search order.

When a command is entered for DOS, the following steps occur:

1. DOS looks for a matching internal command.

2. DOS looks for a COM, EXE, or BAT file (in that order) in the current directory.

3. DOS looks for a COM, EXE, or BAT file (in that order) in the directories in the path, starting with the first directory of the path and working toward the last directory.

4. If DOS still cannot find a corresponding command file, the message Bad command or file name is displayed.

Section Review Questions

16. What is the order in which the PC looks for an executable command?

    a. Current directory, path, internal command, error

    b. Internal command, current directory, path, error

    c. Path, internal command, current directory, error

    d. Path, current directory, error

17. Typing **DIR *.TXT** shows you:

    a. The entire contents of the directory

    b. Only files with an extension of TXT

    c. Any file with TXT in it

    d. Nothing

18. Subdirectories are used to:

    a. Subdivide documents

    b. Eliminate all files from root

    c. Provide an upside-down directory structure

    d. None of the above

19. Which definition describes the appearance of the DOS directory structure?

    a. Group of files

    b. Series of directories

    c. Inverted tree

    d. None of the above

20. Which command will create a directory called DOCS under the root directory?

    a. CD C;\DOCS

    b. RD C:\DOCS

    c. DD C:\DOCS

    d. MD C:\DOCS

Answers

16. b

17. b

18. a

19. c

20. d

Managing Files

All data and programs stored on disks are stored in files. Disk management is concerned with making sure that the right files are in the right places and accessible in the right way.

DOS has a wide variety of operations related to files. These operations are reviewed in this section.

Demonstrate the proper use of the COPY, XCOPY, DISKCOPY, TYPE, DEL, ATTRIB, and REN commands.

Copying Input to a File

In Chapter 1, you learned that PCs have a number of devices, such as COM ports and LPT ports. One such device is CON, which stands for console. As an input device, CON is the device that accepts your keyboard input.

In DOS, most devices can be used as if they were files. You soon will use the COPY command to copy disk files. In this section, however, you use COPY to copy typed information from the console (keyboard) to a file. This is a quick way to create simple text files.

The remainder of this discussion about managing files is an exercise. If you work at a PC and enter every command in the following exercise, you will gain some valuable experience using the DOS commands discussed.

When you see a dialog, the boldface text corresponds to the text that you enter on the keyboard.

To try this out, enter the following. Every keystroke is indicated:

```
MD \DIR1 Enter
CD \DIR1 Enter
COPY CON TEST1.TXT Enter
This is test file one Enter
F6 Enter
```

The first command creates a new directory named \DIR1. You then use CD to make this your default directory. The next three lines create a new file named TEST1.TXT.

In the following examples, it is assumed that \DIR1 was created on drive C.

The COPY command instructs DOS to copy the input from the keyboard (the console or CON device) to a file named TEST1.TXT. When you press Enter after typing this command, DOS creates the file, and then waits for your keystrokes.

In the next line, you type some text to be stored in the file. When you press Enter, you actually insert some special characters that mark the end of a line in a text file.

In the last line, you press F6 to insert a Control+Z character (ASCII 26) into the file. Control+Z is used by DOS to mark the end of a text file. (You can accomplish the same thing by pressing both Ctrl and Z at that point, but F6 is used for convenience.) After you press F6, the copy process ends, and you are returned to a DOS prompt.

Viewing File Directories

You can display a list of all the files in a directory with the DIR command as shown in the following example:

```
DIR
Directory of C:\DIR1
    .            <DIR>        05-25-93   1:00p
    ..           <DIR>        05-25-93   1:00p
    TEST1   TXT       23 05-25-93   1:00p
          3 file(s)              23 bytes
                      68546560 bytes free
```

Notice that the result indicates that three files are in the directory \DIR1. One is the file TEST1.TXT that was just created.

Notice that two other entries in the preceding file are flagged with the <DIR> label. The single . entry refers to the current directory. The double .. entry refers to the parent directory—the directory of which \DIR1 is a subdirectory, in this case the root directory.

When directories become long, you have two options to make them more manageable to read on the screen:

◆ The /P switch causes DOS to pause and wait for a keypress after each full screen of directory data.

◆ The /W switch lists directory names in columns, but without the file size, attributes, or date/time stamps.

Viewing the Contents of a Text File

You can use the TYPE command to display the contents of any text file. To view the file you just created, enter this command:

```
TYPE TEST1.TXT
This is test file one
```

If a file is longer than a single screen can display, you can pause the scrolling display by pressing Ctrl+S. Press Ctrl+Q to resume scrolling.

Copying Files

Two commands are used for copying files. You learn about XCOPY later. For now, you need to know about the basic COPY command.

Copying to a File with a New Name

COPY is used to create a duplicate of a file. The duplicate must either have a new name, be in a new location, or both. The following example creates a copy of a file with a new name:

```
COPY TEST1.TXT ANOTHER.TXT
```

Demonstrate the proper use of the COPY, XCOPY, DISKCOPY, TYPE, DEL, ATTRIB, and REN commands.

If you issue the TYPE command on ANOTHER.TXT, you see that it has the same content as TEST1.TXT.

153

DOS does not allow two files with the same name to reside in the same directory. When you copy a file, the destination file specification must differ from the source in at least one of the following ways:

◆ The destination file must be in a different directory.

◆ The destination file must have a different name.

The following example shows what happens if you try to copy a file without changing its name or directory:

```
COPY TEST1.TXT TEST1.TXT

File cannot be copied onto itself
    0 file(s) copied
```

Copying to a Different Directory

To copy a file to another directory, the directory path must be included with one or both file names. The following example shows you how to create a new subdirectory and copy a file to it:

```
MD \DIR2
COPY \DIR1\TEST1.TXT \DIR2
```

If you now type **DIR \DIR2**, you will notice that the file was copied to that directory using its original name. Because no name was specified with the destination, COPY retained the original file's name.

Copying to the Current Directory

If you do not specify a destination, the COPY command copies files to the current directory. The following commands illustrate this:

```
CD \DIR2
COPY \DIR1
```

All the files in \DIR1 are copied to the current directory, which is \DIR2. Notice that it is not necessary to specify *.* (you learn about wildcards later) as the source files. When you specify a directory alone as the source, COPY duplicates all the files in the directory.

Copying to a Different Disk

Copying between disks can be simple or complicated depending on the number of files being copied and the configuration of your PC. Before you try the next two examples, format a disk for your drive A. Insert a disk and type the following:

```
FORMAT A:
```

Leave this disk in the drive for the next few examples.

Copying with Two Disk Drives

Copying between disk drives is a simple matter of specifying the drive letters, as in the following examples:

```
COPY C:\DIR1\TEST1.TXT A:
```

```
COPY A:TEST1.TXT C:\DIR2\NEWFILE.TXT
```

If you fail to specify a disk drive letter for the source or the destination, COPY assumes that you intend to use the current drive.

Copying with One Floppy Disk Drive

Remember that if you have only a single floppy disk drive, DOS recognizes that drive as either A or B.

If you want to copy files to a different floppy disk and you have only one disk drive, you need to take advantage of this feature. The following command does the trick:

```
COPY A:TEST1.TXT B:
```

COPY reads the file into memory, and then prompts you with the following message:

```
Insert diskette for drive B: and press any key when ready
```

155

After you change disks and press a key, the file is written to the destination disk.

Later you learn how to copy large numbers of files using wild-cards. If you copy a large number of files using this procedure, you are asked to swap disks for each file. If you have a hard drive, you should copy all the files into a temporary directory on the hard drive, and then change disks and copy all the files from the hard drive to the destination disk.

 Demonstrate the proper use of the COPY, XCOPY, DISKCOPY, TYPE, DEL, ATTRIB, and REN commands.

Erasing Files

DEL and ERASE can both be used to erase files. To delete ANOTHER.TXT, enter one of the following commands:

```
DEL ANOTHER.TXT
```

```
ERASE ANOTHER.TXT
```

Renaming Files

Assign a new name to a file with the REN command. The following example changes the name of the TEST1.TXT file:

```
REN TEST1.TXT MYFILE.TXT
```

Using Wildcards

 Explain the DOS wildcard characters and how they are used.

Wildcards are special characters that make it easier to manipulate groups of files. After all, if you are copying 20 files, it would be a nuisance to have to enter a separate COPY command for each file.

The two wildcard characters are as follows:

◆ *—Matches any series of characters of any length

◆ ?—Matches any single character

To see how wildcards work, enter the following commands (press Enter after each command line has been typed):

```
CD \DIR1
COPY CON FILE1.TXT
This is file one
F6
COPY CON FILE11.TXT
This is file eleven
F6
COPY CON FILE2.TXT
This is file two
F6
COPY CON FILE22.TXT
This is file twenty-two
F6
```

Now you can try some wildcard options in the following example:

```
COPY *.* \DIR2
FILE1.TXT
FILE11.TXT
FILE2.TXT
FILE22n.TXT
    4 file(s) copied
```

The expression *.* (often called "star dot star") matches any file name with any extension. This copy command, therefore, copies any file in the current directory to \DIR2. COPY reports the name of each file that it duplicates.

The wildcard combination *.* is extremely useful. To erase all files in \DIR2, issue the following command:

```
DEL \DIR2\*.*
```

After you enter the command, you are asked to confirm your command to delete all files in the directory. DEL always asks you to confirm a delete that involves wildcards.

Using *.* is easy, but it also can get you into trouble. Make sure that you use the command on the correct files in the correct directory. Many users have lost valuable files because of incautious use of wildcards, especially *.*!

 When files are deleted, they are not really removed from the disk. If you have not saved anything to the disk since the file was erased, a variety of commercial tools are available that can undelete the file. If you have saved any files, there is a good chance that the old data has been overwritten and that the file cannot be undeleted.

The ? can also be useful. Try the following command and see which files are copied:

```
COPY FILE?.TXT
```

You see that FILE1.TXT and FILE2.TXT are copied, whereas the other two files are ignored.

Unfortunately, the ? is a bit unpredictable as the following command illustrates:

```
COPY FILE1?.TXT
```

The file FILE11.TXT is copied, as you should expect by now. However, FILE1.TXT also is copied, even though the ? does not correspond in position to a character.

Another problem with wildcards is illustrated in the following example. Suppose that you want to copy any file with a name ending in two. You might be tempted to try this command:

```
COPY *2.* \DIR2
```

If you try this command on the sample files, however, all the files in the directory are copied, regardless of whether they end in two. An initial * matches any file name, and characters following the * have no effect.

Given the wildcard inconsistencies discussed in this section, it is useful to have a way to test wildcard patterns before you issue a potentially disastrous command. This is easy to do with DIR. If you issue the DIR command with the wildcard pattern, DIR lists all the files that will be affected. If you are uncertain, use DIR to make a trial run, especially before issuing the DEL command.

Rules for File Specifications

The parameter for a command that specifies a file or group of files is called a *file specification* or *file spec*. Many rules about file specifications have been distributed throughout this chapter; these rules, and a few new ones, are listed here:

1. DOS assumes the current disk drive unless a drive letter appears as part of the file specification.

2. DOS assumes the current directory unless a directory specification appears as part of the file specification.

3. If a directory path begins with a \, the path begins at the root directory. This is called an *absolute path*.

4. If a directory path does not begin with a \, the path begins with the current directory. This is called a *relative path*. Single-level relative paths can easily be confused with files, so caution is advised.

5. A * in a directory or a file name is a wildcard character that matches zero, one, or more characters.

6. A ? in a directory or a file spec is a wildcard character that matches one (or occasionally no) character.

7. In some cases, specifying a directory without a file specification causes a command to act on all files in the directory. For example, DEL \DIR1 attempts to delete all files in the directory (after asking the user to confirm). COPY \DIR1 \DIR2 copies the entire contents of \DIR1, even though *.* is not specified.

Setting File Attributes

Earlier in this chapter, you were introduced to the following file attributes:

◆ **A**—Indicates that a file has been modified and needs to be archived

◆ **H**—Hides files from the DIR command

◆ **R**—Makes files read-only so that they cannot be modified or deleted

◆ **S**—Marks the files as system files which are both hidden and read-only

 Demonstrate the proper use of the COPY, XCOPY, DISKCOPY, TYPE, DEL, ATTRIB, and REN commands.

Adding an Attribute to a File

You can modify the attributes of a file by using the ATTRIB command, as in the following example:

```
ATTRIB +H FILE1.TXT
```

If you enter this command and then a DIR command, FILE1.TXT does not appear in the directory.

Displaying File Attributes

You can see a hidden file and the attributes of files by issuing the ATTRIB command without any attributes, as follows:

```
ATTRIB *.*

A   H      C:\DIR1\FILE1.TXT
A          C:\DIR1\FILE2.TXT
A          C:\DIR1\FILE11.TXT
A          C:\DIR1\FILE22.TXT
```

FILE1.TXT appears in this list, and you can see that it has the H attribute. Also, all the files you have created in this chapter have been assigned the A attribute.

Removing Attributes

To unhide a file, use the following command:

```
ATTRIB -H FILE1.TXT
```

FILE1.TXT will again show up in a directory.

The Read-Only Attribute

The R attribute can protect you from accidentally deleting files. To demonstrate, try the following commands:

```
ATTRIB +R FILE2.TXT
DEL FILE2.TXT
Access denied
```

Because the file was read-only, you cannot delete it. DOS responds with the message Access denied. To delete the file, you must first remove the R attribute with this command:

```
ATTRIB -R FILE2.TXT
```

161

Rules for Adding and Removing Attributes

The rules for using the ATTRIB command are as follows:

◆ The S attribute has precedence. Before you can make any
  other modifications to a file, you must remove the S attribute.

◆ If a file is marked as R, its attributes cannot be changed until
  the R attribute is removed.

◆ Multiple attributes can be changed in the same command by
  combining them before the file specification. The following
  example unhides a file and makes it read-only:

```
ATTRIB -H +R FILE1.TXT
```

 ATTRIB is the one way you can easily see the
system files that FORMAT puts on a bootable disk.
If you issue the ATTRIB command in the root
directory of your boot disk, among the items you
will see are the following:

```
SHR              C:\IO.SYS
SHR              C:\MSDOS.SYS
```

If you are using PC DOS, you see the PC DOS boot
files instead.

Using XCOPY

The COPY command dates back to the earliest versions of DOS
and is rather limited. The following problems exist with the COPY
command:

◆ If multiple files are copied, COPY does so one file at a time.
  This is a nuisance when copying in a single floppy disk drive
  because of the number of required disk swaps.

162

◆ COPY does not copy files in subdirectories or duplicate the subdirectories.

◆ COPY does not recognize the A attribute, so it cannot be used to back up modified files.

The newer XCOPY command corrects all these problems.

Using XCOPY with Wildcards

The XCOPY command is much more efficient than COPY when it performs a wildcard copy. XCOPY reads as many files into memory as possible prior to writing the duplicate files.

If you have a floppy disk handy, try the following series of commands:

```
XCOPY C:\DIR1\*.* A:
Reading source file(s)
FILE1.TXT
FILE2.TXT
FILE11.TXT
FILE22.TXT
      4 file(s) copied
```

Notice that the floppy disk does not start to turn until XCOPY has read all four files into memory. If the files to be copied do not all fit into memory, then XCOPY performs as few disk swap operations as possible.

Explain the functions of the /S, /E, and /W switches of the XCOPY command.

Copying Directories with XCOPY

Sometimes you want to copy both files and the directories in which they reside. XCOPY can accommodate you, as in the following example:

163

```
XCOPY C:\DIR1 A:\DIR1
Does DIR1 specify a file name
or directory name on the target
(F = file, D = directory)?D
Reading source file(s)
\DIR1\FILE1.TXT
\DIR1\FILE2.TXT
\DIR1\FILE11.TXT
\DIR1\FILE22.TXT
        4 file(s) copied
```

To make this work, you must specify a directory name in the destination specification. If the requested directory does not exist, XCOPY asks you to clarify whether the destination is a file or a directory. After you respond with D, the directory is created, and the files are copied into it.

If you include an /S switch, XCOPY copies all files and subdirectories that reside under the source directory.

If any subdirectories are empty but should be copied into the destination directory structure, you must include the /E switch with the /S switch to copy empty directories.

 If you are booting from a floppy disk, you must use the /W switch with XCOPY. Otherwise, XCOPY copies the files on your boot DOS disk. With /W, XCOPY waits and prompts you to enter the disks that contain the files to be copied.

Copying Modified Files

The /M switch instructs XCOPY to copy only files that have the A attribute assigned. These files have been modified without having been backed up.

The following commands illustrate the /M switch:

```
CD \DIR1
DEL \DIR2
All files in this directory will be deleted!
Are you sure?Y
```

```
XCOPY \DIR1 \DIR2 /M
Reading source file(s)
\DIR1\FILE1.TXT
\DIR1\FILE2.TXT
\DIR1\FILE11.TXT
\DIR1\FILE22.TXT
    4 file(s) copied
COPY FILE1.TXT NEWFILE.TXT
XCOPY \DIR1 \DIR2 /M
Reading source file(s)
\DIR1\NEWFILE.TXT
    1 file(s) copied
```

The first XCOPY copies all the files because none have been backed up. After copying them, the /M switch instructs XCOPY to clear the A archive attribute.

The COPY command creates a new file. Because it is new, its A attribute will be set.

Finally, the second XCOPY command copies only one file—the one that was newly created—because it is the only file with an A attribute.

 You can use the /M feature of XCOPY to easily archive modified files to floppy disks. Just occasionally execute XCOPY with /M to back up any files that have been updated recently.

Section Review Questions

21. After typing **COPY TEST.TXT ANOTHER.TXT**:

   a. Only ANOTHER.TXT exists

   b. ANOTHER.TXT exists as an empty file

   c. An error message appears

   d. Both TEXT.TXT and ANOTHER.TXT exist in the directory, and the contents are identical

165

22. After typing REN TEST.TXT OTHER.TXT:

    a. Only OTHER.TXT exists

    b. OTHER.TXT exists as an empty file

    c. An error message appears

    d. Both TEXT.TXT and OTHER.TXT exist in the directory, and the contents are identical

23. Which of the following commands create a text file called MY.TXT?

    a. COPY C:\MY.TXT A:

    b. COPY CON MY.TXT

    c. DISKCOPY A:MY.TXT B:MY.TXTS

    d. MAKEFILE C:\MY.TXT

24. Which command lets you copy a file from one disk to another on a single floppy disk drive system?

    a. COPY CON B:TEST.TXT A;

    b. DISKCOPY CON B: A:

    c. COPY A:TEST.TXT B:

    d. COPY A:TEST.TXT C:;B:

25. Which of the following is a DOS wildcard character?

    a. ?

    b. \

    c. |

    d. .

Answers

21. d

22. a

23. b

24. c

25. a

Understanding Utility Commands

This section discusses some useful utility commands available in DOS.

Demonstrate the proper use of the DATE, TIME, VER, PROMPT, and CLS commands.

DATE and TIME

Your PC has a clock/calendar that keeps track of the date and time. Data from this device is used to create the date and time stamps for the directory entries of your files.

The DATE and TIME commands can be used to display or temporarily modify these settings.

If you enter the DATE command, DOS responds with the following message:

```
Current date is Wed 06-22-1994
Enter new date (mm-dd-yy):
```

Press Enter if you do not want to change the date, or you can enter a new date to change the clock's current date. If you enter a date, you can separate the month, day, and year with hyphens (-) or slashes (/). Leading zeros are not required, but can be included. The century for the year entry is optional. The following examples are acceptable date entries:

```
6/22/94
06-22-1994
6/22-94
```

You also can set the time by entering the TIME command. DOS responds like this:

```
Current time is 18:09:08.55a
Enter new time:
```

Press Enter to leave the time unchanged, or enter a new time to update the clock. DOS uses a 24-hour clock—18 represents 6 p.m. If you change the time, you must enter the time in 24-hour format. Separate the entries for hour, minute, and second with colons (:).

These changes do not update the date and time in your PC's system clock, and the date and time will be set in accordance with the system clock the next time you reboot. You must use your PC's configuration utility if you want to permanently change the date and time in the system clock.

VER

DOS is available in many different versions. As a network Administrator, you frequently need to know which DOS version is on a particular workstation. Some applications require specific DOS versions, and some NetWare shell programs are specifically tailored to particular DOS versions.

To display the DOS version on a machine, simply type **VER**. DOS responds with a display similar to the following:

```
MS-DOS Version 6.00
```

PROMPT

Early in this chapter, it was suggested that you use the PROMPT command so that your prompt would display your current directory. You used the following command:

```
PROMPT $P$G
```

Although the directory path is perhaps the most useful thing you can show in a prompt, other items are available. You can insert text messages, and these messages can be mixed with special symbols that display system information. Here is a list of the symbols that can appear in the parameters of a PROMPT command:

- **$P**—The current drive and directory path
- **$N**—The default drive
- **$D**—The current date
- **$T**—The current time
- **$V**—The DOS version number
- **$G**—A greater-than sign (>)
- **$L**—A less-than sign (<)
- **$Q**—An equal sign (=)
- **$B**—A vertical bar character (|)
- **$$**—A dollar sign ($)

This following command combines text with special PROMPT characters:

```
PROMPT The time is $T. The directory is $N. $B$G
```

Although this is probably more verbose than you want to use, it illustrates the flexibility of the PROMPT command.

CLS

This is an easy command. To clear the screen and display just the prompt, enter the CLS command.

PRINT

If you need to print a text file, use the PRINT command as follows:

```
PRINT MYFILE.DOC
```

You are asked to specify a printer port to receive the file. Press Enter for PRN:, which is the default port. Output to PRN: goes to the LPT1 parallel printer port.

Redirection

It occasionally is useful to capture DOS command dialogs in file form. Suppose that you want to create a text file containing the output of all your batch files. This can be accomplished with the following command:

```
DIR *.BAT > DIRLIST.TXT
```

After the file is built, you can type the file with the following command:

```
TYPE DIRLIST.TXT
```

This file can be used in word processing or in other document files.

The > character is the DOS redirection operator. It channels the output of the preceding command to the specified file name.

The redirection operator also can work with devices. You will recall that DOS devices such as LPT1 can be used like files in many cases. If you want to print the output of a command, you can simply redirect the output to the PRN: device (PRN: and LPT1 both point to your first parallel printer port), as in the following example:

```
DIR *.* > PRN:
```

If you use redirection with an interactive command, you will not see any prompts when it is time for you to provide input. Your system will appear to "hang" until you enter the required keystrokes.

Section Review Questions

26. After typing the commands **PROMPT PG** and **CD DATA**, your prompt looks like:

    a. DATA>

    b. \DATA>

    c. C:DATA>

    d. C:\DATA>

27. The proper command to change the current date is:

    a. CHDATE

    b. DATE

    c. DATE MM-DD-YY

    d. None of the above

28. The command that displays the current version of DOS running on the PC is:

    a. DOS VERSION

    b. VERSION DOS

    c. VER

    d. VER DOS

29. Which of the following PROMPT switches adds the greater-than sign to the prompt?

    a. $G

    b. /G

    c. $>

    d. />

30. To capture a listing of directory files to a text file, use this command:

    a. DIR | FILES.TXT

    b. DIR > *.* C:\DIRTXT

    c. DIR *.* C:\DIRTXT

    d. DIR *.* > DIRTXT C:

Answers

26. d

27. b

28. c

29. a

30. d

Understanding Batch Files

Sometimes you are required to enter the same set of commands repeatedly. You might be entering the following commands to start a modem communications program named QCOM, for example:

```
CD \PROGRAMS\QCOM
QCOM
CD \
```

After you enter these three commands a few times, you will be looking for a shortcut.

 Explain the purpose of batch files.

Batch files are text files that contain DOS commands. When DOS executes a batch file, it executes the commands in the file in the order in which they appear.

You can create batch files with the COPY CON technique mentioned earlier in this chapter, but you probably will want to use a text editor. A useful editor named EDIT is packaged with DOS 5.0 and higher. Earlier DOS versions used a program called EDLIN, which is somewhat harder to use than the EDIT program.

Any command you type at the keyboard can be put in a batch file. All batch files must have the extension BAT. A useful name for the hypothetical batch file in the preceding example might be QC.BAT. To execute the commands in the batch file, type **qc**.

 DOS must be able to find your batch files. It is useful to create a directory specifically for batch files and to include that directory in your PATH command. If your batch files are stored in \BAT, your PATH command might look like the following:

```
PATH C:\DOS;C:\BAT
```

Many users are tempted to add every application directory to their path, but this can result in extremely long PATH commands. A QC.BAT file that changes to the appropriate directory and runs the QCOM application eliminates the need to have a PATH entry for the QCOM directory.

Stop a Batch File During Execution

If necessary, you can stop a batch file from running before it has executed all of its DOS commands.

Identify the key sequence that terminates a batch program during execution.

To halt a batch file during execution, press Ctrl+C, and answer Yes when prompted with Halt batch process?(Y/N).

Useful Batch File Commands

Several DOS commands are specifically intended for use in batch files. The following sections discuss some of them.

Explain the use of the REM, ECHO, and PAUSE batch file commands.

REM

The REM command places a remark in your file. A *remark* consists of text that is ignored when the batch file is executed. Use remarks to explain what your batch file is doing. An example of a remark in a batch file is as follows:

```
REM Copy modified files to a floppy disk
XCOPY *.* A: /M
```

ECHO

ECHO displays a message on the screen, as in the following example:

```
ECHO Insert the archive floppy in A:
REM Copy modified files to a floppy disk
XCOPY *.* A: /M
```

ECHO also instructs DOS if it should display the commands in a batch file as they are executed. The command ECHO ON activates command display. ECHO OFF turns off command display. Ordinarily, you use ECHO ON while you are testing a new batch file so that you can see what is going on. When the batch file works properly, change the line to ECHO OFF to suppress commands and have a cleaner screen display.

PAUSE

PAUSE causes the batch file to wait for the user to press a key. When PAUSE is executed, DOS displays the message Press any key to continue, as in the following example:

```
ECHO OFF
ECHO Insert the archive floppy in A:
PAUSE
REM Copy modified files to a floppy disk
XCOPY *.* A: /M
```

Try the preceding batch file with ECHO ON and ECHO OFF to see the difference.

AUTOEXEC.BAT

After your PC boots and starts COMMAND.COM, the command processor looks for a batch file named AUTOEXEC.BAT in the boot drive's root directory.

Explain the purpose of the AUTOEXEC.BAT file.

The AUTOEXEC.BAT file can contain any commands you want executed whenever your PC is booted.

Create a batch file.

The following example is of an AUTOEXEC.BAT file that uses several of the commands introduced in this chapter. It also includes an example of a command to start a common utility, in this case, a mouse driver. Finally, it contains the commands to start a NetWare shell and log in to a server.

```
ECHO OFF
CLS
PROMPT $P$G
PATH C:\DOS;C:\BAT

REM Start the mouse driver
C:\MOUSE\MOUSE

REM Attach to a server and log in
CD \NETWARE

IPX
NETX
F:
CLS

LOGIN
```

Section Review Questions

31. Batch files are:

    a. Text files containing DOS commands

    b. Any text file with a BAT ending

c. Created using the BATCH application program

d. None of the above

32. Terminate a batch file by pressing:

a. Ctrl+Pause

b. Ctrl+T

c. Ctrl+C

d. Ctrl+Alt+Shift

33. Use PAUSE in a batch file to:

a. Allow and instruct the user to do something

b. Prevent information from displaying to the screen

c. Add a remark to a file

d. None of the above

34. The purpose of the AUTOEXEC.BAT file is to:

a. Load device drivers

b. Hold commands to run when the PC is booted

c. Expand available memory on older PCs

d. Cause other programs to start automatically

35. Which of the following statements about batch file creation is true?

a. Batch files can only be created by System Administrators.

b. All PCs require at least an AUTOEXEC.BAT file.

c. They must be modified using the DOS EDIT utility.

d. REM can be used when creating the file to annotate its contents.

Answers

31. a

32. c

33. a

34. b

35. d

Installing and Configuring DOS

All current versions of DOS are distributed with a program named SETUP that configures the computer's boot disk and installs DOS. Consult your DOS manual for the correct installation procedure.

The exact process differs depending on what version of DOS is being used, but the following things must be accomplished to install DOS:

1. Partition the hard drive.

2. Set an active partition.

3. Format the boot drive.

4. Install the DOS files, which involves the following:

   ◆ Putting the system files in the proper location

   ◆ Placing COMMAND.COM on the boot drive

   ◆ Installing the DOS auxiliary files in a suitable directory

5. Configure the CONFIG.SYS and AUTOEXEC.BAT files as required.

Each of these steps is described in the following sections.

Partitioning Hard Drives

To boot DOS, your first hard drive must have one *primary partition*. This partition will be formatted for DOS, after which the required files will be installed to enable the drive to boot. The bootable DOS partition also must be marked as the active partition.

 Any change to a hard disk partition erases all files in the partition! Do not experiment or make changes unless you have made a complete backup of the affected files.

The disk can have two other types of partitions. *Extended DOS partitions* can be configured as additional DOS drives starting with the letter D. DOS primary and extended partitions may be created and formatted on additional hard drives. However, additional primary partitions cannot be made bootable.

Non-DOS partitions are created by other operating systems, such as UNIX or OS/2. A *NetWare partition* also is a non-DOS partition. You can have several operating systems on the same hard drive. In fact, this is normally done when NetWare 3.11 is installed. The hard drive will have a small (about 5 MB) DOS primary partition, but the rest of the drive will be partitioned for use by NetWare.

 Explain the purpose of a hard disk partition.

Hard drive partitions enable you to divide one physical hard disk into one or more smaller, logical disks.

 Explain the function of the FDISK command.

Hard drive partitions are created and managed by the DOS FDISK utility.

Running FDISK

When you execute the FDISK command, the first thing displayed is the FDISK menu, as shown in figure 2.2. This menu has four options.

Figure 2.2

The FDISK main menu.

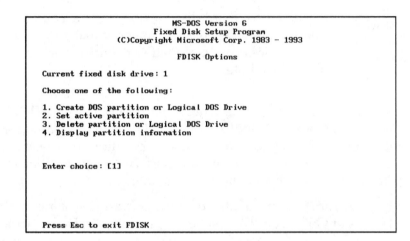

```
                        MS-DOS Version 6
                     Fixed Disk Setup Program
              (C)Copyright Microsoft Corp. 1983 - 1993

                          FDISK Options

    Current fixed disk drive: 1

    Choose one of the following:

      1. Create DOS partition or Logical DOS Drive
      2. Set active partition
      3. Delete partition or Logical DOS Drive
      4. Display partition information




    Enter choice: [1]




    Press Esc to exit FDISK
```

Displaying the Partition Information

To display the current partition information, select option 4. You see a display similar to figure 2.3. Figure 2.3 shows a hard drive with three partitions: a DOS primary partition, a non-DOS partition, and a DOS extended partition.

Notice that the DOS primary partition shows an A below Status. This is the active partition, and is the one DOS uses to boot the PC. You also can see the sizes of the three partitions.

Extended DOS partitions can contain logical drives. If you have more drives than C on your hard drive, drives D and higher will be logical drives in extended partitions.

```
                   Display Partition Information

Current fixed disk drive: 1

Partition  Status    Type    Volume Label  Mbytes  System  Usage
  C: 1       A     PRI DOS    DOS_NT         250    FAT16    49%
     2              Non-DOS                  159             31%
     3              EXT DOS                  100             20%


Total disk space is  509 Mbytes (1 Mbyte = 1048576 bytes)


The Extended DOS Partition contains Logical DOS Drives.
Do you want to display the logical drive information (Y/N)......?[Y]



Press Esc to return to FDISK Options
```

Figure 2.3

FDISK displaying current partition information.

Creating Partitions

If you select option 1 from the FDISK Options menu, you see the menu shown in figure 2.4.

```
             Create DOS Partition or Logical DOS Drive

Current fixed disk drive: 1

Choose one of the following:

1. Create Primary DOS Partition
2. Create Extended DOS Partition
3. Create Logical DOS Drive(s) in the Extended DOS Partition


Enter choice: [1]



Press Esc to return to FDISK Options
```

Figure 2.4

Creating a DOS partition with FDISK.

Every hard drive must have a primary partition. Only a primary partition can be made active and can be formatted to be bootable.

With DOS 4.0 and above, you will probably select option 1, Create Primary DOS Partition. After you create the partition, you are asked whether or not it should occupy the entire hard drive. If you answer Yes, the partition is made as large as possible.

If you answer No, you must specify a size for the newly created drive. Any remaining space can be allocated to other operating systems or to extended DOS partitions.

 If you are installing a NetWare 3.11 server, use FDISK to create a small primary DOS drive to boot the server and start NetWare 3.11's SERVER.EXE program to start the server. Your primary partition will be about 5 MB in size.

If you create extended DOS partitions, you need to create logical DOS drives in the extended partition. Logical DOS drives have drive letters, but cannot be made bootable. You can have only one extended DOS partition, but that partition can be divided into multiple logical drives.

Setting the Active Partition

The active partition is the one your PC attempts to boot during the boot process. Normally, your active partition is the DOS primary partition. If you have installed other operating systems in non-DOS partitions on your hard drive, you can make them bootable by using option 2 of the FDISK Options menu to make the appropriate partition active.

Deleting Partitions and Logical DOS Drives

Option 3 in the FDISK Options menu enables you to delete partitions and logical DOS drives. Before you delete an extended DOS partition, you must delete all logical drives in that partition.

Formatting the Boot Drive

Any partition that will contain DOS files must be formatted with the FORMAT command. You must also make sure that the system files are installed on the drive in the primary DOS partition.

You can choose to create and format the partition yourself by creating a bootable floppy disk on another PC. Install FDISK.EXE and FORMAT.EXE on this disk.

You can then boot your PC with this bootable floppy disk, use FDISK to partition the hard drive, and use the command FORMAT c: /s to format the C drive and install the partition. Finally, you must copy all the DOS files to a \DOS directory on drive C.

With most recent versions of DOS, however, you will use a SETUP program provided with your copy of DOS. This SETUP program ensures that the disk is suitably partitioned, formatted, and configured with DOS. It is difficult to explain this process in detail because several versions of DOS are currently in widespread use.

Configuring CONFIG.SYS and AUTOEXEC.BAT

AUTOEXEC.BAT was explained in the earlier section on batch files.

CONFIG.SYS also is a text file, but contains commands executed prior to running COMMAND.COM. The commands used in CONFIG.SYS are specific to that file and cannot be entered from the keyboard.

Explain the function of the CONFIG.SYS file.

The two major purposes of CONFIG.SYS are as follows:

◆ Sets up your DOS operating characteristics

◆ Loads device drivers

183

Before these two categories are examined, take a look at a typical CONFIG.SYS file:

```
BUFFERS=30
FILES=20
LASTDRIVE=F
DEVICE=C:\DOS\ANSI.SYS
DEVICE=C:\MOUSE\MOUSE.SYS
DEVICE=C:\DOS\HIMEM.SYS
DEVICE=C:\DOS\EMM386.EXE
```

Setting DOS Operating Characteristics

A wide variety of CONFIG.SYS options are used to configure DOS. The preceding sample CONFIG.SYS file contains three examples discussed in the following sections.

Explain the purpose of the CONFIG.SYS file commands: DEVICE, FILES, BUFFERS, and LASTDRIVE.

BUFFERS

BUFFERS determines how many 512 KB buffers DOS configures in your RAM to buffer disk access. When DOS reads from a hard disk, it takes time to move the head to the proper track and spin the disk to the proper sector. DOS stores the data most recently read from the disk in buffers. If this data is needed again, DOS can find it in the buffers without going through the time-consuming process of finding it on disk.

The default number of buffers is seldom enough. By setting BUFFERS=20 or 30 in CONFIG.SYS, you can usually improve your system's performance. Setting the value too high robs valuable DOS memory and can actually slow your system down.

FILES

This parameter determines how many files DOS can open at one time. The default value is 8, but many applications require you to set this value higher. WordPerfect, for example, requires that FILES be set to at least 20. Consult your program documentation for specific requirements.

LASTDRIVE

When a workstation is attached to a NetWare server, users access files on the server by mapping drive letters to server directories. LASTDRIVE= tells DOS how many drive letters to reserve for use on the local disk drive.

Normally, DOS reserves drives A through E for local use. You can change this by changing the parameter of LASTDRIVE.

 When you start the workstation shell commands and attach to a server, the server's SYS:LOGIN directory is assigned the drive letter following the LASTDRIVE parameter. If no LASTDRIVE command appears in CONFIG.SYS, the LOGIN directory is assigned to drive F.

Loading Device Drivers

The example CONFIG.SYS file loads four device drivers using the DEVICE= command. Notice that this command must be given a complete path to the command file, including the complete directory path. After all, AUTOEXEC.BAT has not been executed yet, and no PATH command has established a directory search path.

The drivers that were chosen as examples are fairly common ones. Except for the MOUSE.SYS driver, the example drivers are shipped with DOS.

List the purpose of device drivers.

ANSI.SYS installs an ANSI screen driver. Some applications use ANSI screen control characters to draw lines, change character colors, and affect other screen display features. If you are using an application that uses ANSI screen control characters, you need to install this driver. You see very strange characters on the screen if you do not.

MOUSE.SYS is an example of a mouse driver. Some mouse drivers are installed as CONFIG.SYS device drivers. Some are EXE files executed in AUTOEXEC.BAT. Consult your mouse documentation for specifics.

HIMEM.SYS and EMM386.EXE work together to establish extended and expanded memory on PCs equipped with 80386 and 80486 microprocessors. You can read about extended and expanded memory in Chapter 1. These drivers (EMM386.EXE is a system driver despite the EXE extension) require your PC to be equipped with memory above the 1 MB line.

Configuring DOS Memory for NetWare

In Chapter 1, you learned that DOS makes only 640 KB of conventional memory available for use by programs. Of this, portions are reserved for the use of DOS. The remaining memory is in short supply and is extremely precious.

To illustrate, try booting a PC with minimum CONFIG.SYS and AUTOEXEC.BAT files like these:

```
(CONFIG.SYS is empty)

rem AUTOEXEC.BAT@echo off
PROMPT $p$g
PATH C:\DOS
```

Boot a PC with these files. Then use a utility such as MEM, which ships with MS-DOS 6.*x*, to determine how much conventional memory is available. You will probably get a figure close to 578 KB of free memory.

A PC can't connect to the network without running network software, however. Here is an AUTOEXEC.BAT file that runs ODI drivers and a NETX.EXE command shell:

```
@echo off
PROMPT $p$g
PATH C:\DOS
cd \nwclient
lsl
3c509
ipxodi
netx
```

If you boot a PC using this file to load network drivers, you will find that you have only about 511 KB of free conventional memory. Just connecting to the network has cost you 67 KB, over 10 percent of your RAM.

In Chapter 1, you learned that some 80286 and all 80386 PCs are capable of utilizing memory above 640 KB if they run special memory-driver programs. These drivers work best with 80386 and higher PCs, so this discussion will focus on that class of equipment.

Two programs work together to manage memory with MS-DOS— HIMEM.SYS makes memory up to 1 MB available, and EMM386.SYS manages the rest of system memory and provides other services as well. Once these programs are loaded, programs can be loaded high into *upper memory blocks* (UMBs)—the memory blocks between 640 KB and 1 MB.

These programs also permit one program at a time to run in the *high memory area* (HMA), a block of 64 KB (minus 16 bytes) just above 1 MB.

Configuring EMM386 and deciding which commands to load high can be extremely complex and time consuming. Fortunately, most current memory managers now are equipped with automatic configuration programs that can do a surprisingly good job of configuring for best memory usage.

The memory manager configuration program for MS-DOS 6.2 is called MEMMAKER, which has an automatic setting that tries all available combinations of the programs you wish to load and selects the best configuration it can find. The following sample CONFIG.SYS and AUTOEXEC.BAT files occur after MEMMAKER has been run:

```
rem CONFIG.SYS
DEVICE=C:\DOS\HIMEM.SYS
DEVICE=C:\DOS\EMM386.EXE NOEMS
BUFFERS=15,0
FILES=8
DOS=UMB
LASTDRIVE=E
FCBS=4,0

rem AUTOEXEC.BAT
@echo off
PROMPT $p$g
PATH C:\DOS
cd \nwclient
LH /L:2,9296 lsl
LH /L:1,32688 3c509
LH /L:1,30576 ipxodi
netx
```

MEMMAKER has added numerous statements to CONFIG.SYS to optimize performance. HIMEM.SYS and EMM386.SYS were installed. EMM386.SYS was configured with the NOEMS parameter so that it would not tie up extended memory by emulating expanded memory (see Chapter 1). This configuration makes the maximum amount of memory available for programs like Windows that do not require expanded memory but do need lots of extended memory.

MEMMAKER also added several commands to optimize DOS performance such as FILES= and BUFFERS=.

The command DOS=UMB instructs DOS to load itself into upper memory blocks. Beginning with DOS version 6.0, it became possible to load DOS itself into upper memory. DOS is a large program, and this is one of the best ways to conserve conventional memory.

MEMMAKER configured several command lines in AUTOEXEC.BAT with LH commands to load the programs into UMBs. NETX.EXE was not configured to load high because it won't run in that mode. As automatically configured by MEMMAKER, this PC now has 536 KB of conventional DOS memory available.

Incidentally, device drivers in CONFIG.SYS can also be loaded high with the DEVICEHIGH command. However, no device drivers were present in this example for MEMMAKER to operate on.

As mentioned, NETX.EXE will not run in high memory. Two different possibilities can be examined:

◆ XMSNETX.EXE is a version of NETX that loads itself into extended memory. Substituting XMSNETX for NETX increased available DOS memory to 562 KB.

◆ VLM.EXE is the latest version of workstation network interface, and is included with NetWare 3.12 and 4.01. Substituting VLM for NETX increased available DOS memory to 567 KB.

Table 2.1 summarizes the memory availability for the various DOS configurations that have been discussed.

Table 2.1
DOS Memory Available for Various Configurations

Available Configuration	DOS Memory
No programs or memory management	578 KB

continues

Table 2.1, Continued
DOS Memory Available for Various Configurations

Available Configuration	DOS Memory
Network drivers, no memory management	511 KB
Extended memory manager with NETX	536 KB
Extended memory manager with XMSNETX	562 KB
Extended memory manager with VLM	567 KB

It is almost essential to use extended memory utilities on DOS workstations. Windows requires the use of an extended memory manager. Few DOS workstations can afford to give up the memory that network drivers require. Many DOS programs require 512 KB of memory to run.

Section Review Questions

36. Which command configures hard disk partitions?

   a. FORMAT

   b. FDISK

   c. SYSTEM

   d. PARTITION

37. Which statement about hard disk formatting is false?

   a. Every bootable DOS hard drive must have a primary DOS partition.

   b. The active partition is normally the primary DOS partition.

   c. The bootable partition must be the entire disk size.

   d. FDISK enables you to delete partitions.

38. LASTDRIVE=:

    a. Should be placed in CONFIG.SYS

    b. Should be set if you want more than A: through E: to point to the hard drive

    c. L means that the first network drive is M:

    d. All of the above

39. The ANSI.SYS device driver is used to:

    a. Provide HIMEM.SYS with conventional memory access

    b. Load other device drivers

    c. Establish a SYSTEM search path

    d. Provide some applications with special screen control characters, such as lines

40. The BUFFERS command:

    a. Determines how many 512 KB buffers will be set up

    b. Establishes a maximum number of files to be buffered

    c. Moves data from the hard disk to a ROM buffer

    d. Improves system performance if set at 10 over the maximum needed

Answers

36. b

37. c

38. d

39. d

40. a

Summary

This chapter introduced you to DOS—the Disk Operating System used on IBM PCs and compatibles. From this chapter, you learned about the various components of DOS, file-naming conventions used in DOS, how to load and run DOS, the difference between internal and external DOS commands, and other related information, such as how files are stored on disk.

In the next chapter, you will begin to learn about NetWare. Chapter 3 teaches you about the NetWare directory structure, and shows you how it is similar to the DOS directory structure. It also examines how the NetWare directory structure is different from the DOS directory structure.

NetWare Basics

Moving Around NetWare Directory Structures

CHAPTER 3

In this chapter, you become familiar with the basic structure of a Novell NetWare network from the viewpoint of a *System Administrator* (an individual who is responsible for managing a NetWare network). You learn to do the following:

◆ Describe the basic function and services of a network

◆ Identify the levels of a NetWare directory structure

◆ Name the required NetWare volume and the system-created directories, their contents, and their location in the directory structure

◆ Organize an efficient directory structure

◆ Write a NetWare directory path using the proper syntax

◆ Identify the DOS and NetWare command functions related to directory structures

◆ Identify default drive pointers

◆ Differentiate between network drive mappings and search drive mappings

◆ Identify all MAP parameters and syntax

At the end of each section, you find review questions. At the end of this chapter, you also find case studies. Both the review questions and the case studies are designed to help you reexamine the information presented in this chapter.

The most basic element common to all NetWare versions through 3.1x is the directory structure. NetWare enables DOS directory structures to exist on the network much as they would on a stand-alone computer running DOS. Most of the commands available in DOS to manipulate and manage the directory structure also are available in NetWare.

There are a few other things that you should know about the directory structure before learning the basics about file servers, *volumes* (the highest directory structure level on a file server), and so on. Those items of information are discussed first. In addition, NetWare includes many utilities to control the directory structure and provide greater functionality.

Describing Network Functions and Services

Networks provide access to computer software, particularly to application programs, and to computer equipment, including hard disk storage, printers, modems, facsimile machines, and so on, as well as to network services. Networks enable users to share those resources so that every user does not have to have his or her own. Sharing network resources can provide substantial cost savings to small and large businesses alike.

 Describe the basic functions and services of a network.

Providing access to shared hardware, software, and network services is the basic function of a network. The types of shared services that NetWare provides include:

- ◆ File storage and retrieval

- ◆ Distributed, as well as centralized, processing

- ◆ Network security

- ◆ Printing

- ◆ Backup and other methods of data protection

- ◆ Communication among various offices, departments, companies, and so on

- ◆ Connectivity

The last item on the list—connectivity—is provided by networking software, as well as by physical equipment.

Client Types

The access to the network is made by PCs. These PCs are also called *workstations*. Workstations can be of different client types.

 Identify the client types that are supported in NetWare 3.12.

NetWare most commonly supports the DOS client. However, there are three other client types that NetWare supports as well. They include:

- ◆ OS/2

- ◆ Macintosh

- ◆ UNIX

Some of these clients, the Macintosh AppleTalk Filing Protocol in particular, require that you purchase additional Novell software to provide NetWare file, print, and routing services, however.

Regardless of the client you choose to use in order to access a NetWare network, communication is an important aspect of working in a NetWare environment.

197

Network Communication

As mentioned previously, network communication requires special hardware—a network board and cabling—in addition to the PC and special software.

 Describe workstation communications with the network, and list the files required to connect a DOS workstation to the network.

To connect a workstation to the network, several files must be loaded into memory at the workstation. These files include:

- ◆ LSL.COM
- ◆ LAN Driver (such as NE2000.COM)
- ◆ IPXODI.COM
- ◆ VLM.EXE

When these files are loaded into workstation memory, the DOS-based workstation can then send and receive information and instructions on the network.

 Describe the function of the software necessary to connect a workstation to the network, including local operating systems, NetWare DOS Requester, communication protocols, and network board.

Special software is required for network communication. This special software includes not only the PC's local operating system (DOS-based machines use DOS as their local operating system), but several other software files, including:

- ◆ The NetWare DOS Requester
- ◆ A communications protocol
- ◆ The Link Support Layer
- ◆ A LAN driver

Because DOS cannot communicate directly with the network, the NetWare DOS Requester is provided with NetWare to let you connect DOS-based workstations to the network. The NetWare DOS Requester acts as a connections point between the workstation's local operating system and the network.

The NetWare DOS Request consists of a series of files called *Virtual Loadable Module*s (VLMs). Typing VLM at the DOS prompt, or inserting it into a startup file, loads the NetWare DOS Requester.

In addition to loading the NetWare DOS Requester, a *communications protocol* (set of rules that determine how the network and workstation will communicate) is needed for a workstation to communicate with the network. The communications protocol used with NetWare 3.12 is one that follows the *Open Data-Link Interface* (ODI) specification. To load the communications protocol, type **IPXODI** at the DOS prompt, or insert the command into a startup file.

ODI is implemented through the *Link Support Layer* (LSL). The LSL takes incoming network information and sends it on to IPXODI so it can communicate with the PC. Load the LSL.COM file by typing **LSL** at the DOS prompt, or inserting the command into a startup file.

The final piece of communication software is the LAN driver. This is a file that activates and controls your PC's network board (NIC). You must load the LAN driver that matches the NIC installed in your PC. For example, if you have an NE2000 card installed in your PC, you would load the NE2000.COM file as your LAN driver.

Load the LAN driver by typing the name of the corresponding LAN driver file at the DOS prompt, or putting it into a startup file.

It is important to note that some LAN drivers support the ODI specification. These LAN drivers are known as *Multiple Link Interface Driver*s (MLIDs). MLIDs are required for NetWare 3.12 access.

All of these files are important to network communication. The order in which these files are loaded is important as well; some files cannot load if one or more of the other files has not first been loaded into memory.

 Connect a workstation to the network by loading the appropriate DOS workstation files.

After the NIC has been installed into the PC and the cabling has been attached, you can boot the PC using its local operating system. The connection software must then be loaded, in the following order:

1. LSL.COM

2. MLID (such as NE2000.COM)

3. IPXODI.COM

4. VLM.EXE

Once these files are loaded into the PC's workstation memory in the listed order, the PC can then communicate with the network. However, you as a user cannot access the network until you log in to the network.

 Explain and perform the login procedure.

The first step to logging in to the network is to change the default directory drive to the first available network drive. Most commonly, this is drive F:.

Once you have changed the default drive, type **Login** followed by a space, the name of the file server, a forward slash, and your assigned user identification name—also called the user login ID. An individual user login ID is assigned by the network Administrator to each user on the network. Using separate IDs for different users helps to ensure the security of the network, and to maintain the integrity of the network's data. Typing **Login** runs a file called LOGIN.EXE. This file is the software that completes the login process.

After you have entered your user ID, you are prompted to enter a password. The password can be anything you want; this helps to ensure that you are the network user that you claim to be. In addition, it also causes basic setup to occur specifically for you. For example, if you have a network login script set up for you, then logging in under your user login ID runs the login script.

As noted in the login instructions, you type in a file server name in order to log in to the network. Of course, before you can type in a file server name, a named file server must exist.

In DOS, you can name a storage device, whether it is a hard drive or a floppy disk. NetWare requires you to name storage device portions: the file server and its volumes. The next section discusses file server names and volumes.

Creating File Server Names

File servers must have unique names to "talk" to other file servers. Computers do not recognize nonverbal communication. If you are in a room full of people named Chris, for example, you can expect some confusion. Gestures and eye contact can help you single out one of the individuals with little difficulty. Computers do not have the capability to see and interpret visual clues. If you try to access two computers with the same name, the system locks up, because NetWare cannot figure out which system you want.

Before you name a file server, consider its intended use and how easily you want users to access it. In most NetWare training classes, the first generic file server is referred to as FS1 and the second as FS2. Some NetWare students are so comfortable with these file server names that they use them in their offices. However, such names do not provide network users with any clue as to what the file server might contain, where it is located, or anything that might help the user select the correct file server when they need something specific. Therefore, more descriptive names are recommended.

You can give files server names from two to 45 characters in length. For this reason, most companies use some form of their names or department names for their file servers. Some examples of useful file server names include:

- ACCTSERVER

- PAYROLL

- SERVER_NEAR_PRINTER

As with DOS file naming conventions, there are some characters that you should not use with file server names. You cannot use the hyphen (-), although you can use the underline (_) character. You also cannot use the forward (/) or backward (\) slash, or the period (.), comma (,), colon (:), or semicolon (;). Some examples of incorrect file server names include:

- ACCT-SERVER

- PAYROLL:1

- SERVER/NEAR/PRINTER

The file server name is important because a NetWare file server's structure begins with the file server name, which launches the full directory path. The shorter the name, the easier the users can move among file servers. File server names resemble DOS labels for hard drives or floppy disks, and like drives or floppy disks, file server names usually indicate the type of information the drive contains.

A full directory path in NetWare uses the following *syntax* (rules that specify how commands must be typed in order for the computer to recognize and respond to them):

```
FILESERVER\VOLUME:DIRECTORY\SUBDIRECTORY
```

Syntax specifically defines what information you must give the computer, and in what order you must give it, in order for the computer to understand what it is you are requesting it to do. Both DOS and NetWare *command utilities* (utilities that are activated by typing the command and associated parameters at the prompt, and which do not bring up a menu from which you can make selections) have syntax specific to the utility. For example, the syntax for the NDIR command is:

```
NDIR [path] [/option...]
```

The NDIR syntax, as shown, tells you that to use the NDIR command, you must first type **NDIR** followed by a space, and then type the directory path where you want NDIR to begin searching. This is then followed by another space and by any options you want to include—each preceded by a forward slash (/). For example, typing the following NDIR command results in displaying a list of all files and subdirectories starting from the C:\DOS7 path:

```
NDIR C:\DOS7 /SUB
```

When using the appropriate syntax for a command, note that any portion of the syntax enclosed in square brackets ([]) indicates that it is optional. You may use the optional syntax if you choose. For example, both the path and options in the preceding NDIR example are optional. If you type only **NDIR** without either specifying a path or adding options, NDIR gives you a list of files only on the default drive.

The directory path CDI\SYS:PROGRAMS\DATABASE, for example, begins with a file server name (CDI) and then a volume name (SYS:). The file server name and the volume name are separated with a backslash (\). The volume name always is followed by a colon (:). After the volume name, the first-level directory, or *parent* directory (named PROGRAMS), appears, followed by a secondary directory, or *subdirectory*, called DATABASE. The full directory path indicates your location on a network or your desired location. If your network plans do not include connecting to another file server, you can name your server anything you want.

In a single server environment, you can leave the file server name out of the directory path. Because you did not specify another server, the system assumes that you want to address this file server. That assumption, however, does not mean that you can leave the file server unnamed after you install it. All file servers require a server name, even in a single-server environment.

Accessing NetWare Volumes

Volumes are the next level in a full directory path. Unlike file server names, volumes are essential to the full directory path.

 Describe a volume and its technical specifications.

Volumes, NetWare, and DOS

Volumes are to NetWare what root drives are to DOS. In a DOS directory tree, the highest level you can access is the root drive. On a NetWare 3.1*x* file server, the highest level that you can access is the volume. NetWare 3.1*x* volumes have specific technical requirements, including:

- ◆ Multiple segments that span multiple hard disks

- ◆ A volume that has a maximum of 32 segments

- ◆ A hard disk that has a maximum of 8 segments

- ◆ No more than 64 volumes existing on a single server

Regardless of the technical specifications, root drives are identified by a backslash after the drive indicator. The root drive of C is shown as C:\. To get to this directory structure level, tell the system to change the directory to the root by typing **CD**.

One of the most common mistakes users make when they change directories is to improperly use the backslash. After you type the backslash directly after the CD command, as in **CD**, the system is instructed to find the root directory. If the directory to which you want to change is really the current directory's subdirectory, insert a space rather than the backslash after the CD command, followed by the subdirectory name. For example, to change to the subdirectory called DBASE1 from your current path of CDI\SYS:PROGRAMS\DATABASE, type **CD DBASE1**. A directory beginning with a backslash is located below the root; a directory without a backslash is located below the current directory. In the following example, the directory DATABASE is represented by the following directory structure:

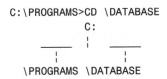

```
C:\PROGRAMS>CD \DATABASE
                C:
      _____    |   _____
            |        |
      \PROGRAMS \DATABASE
```

In the next example, DATABASE is a subdirectory of PRO-GRAMS. The directory structure that applies to this example is as follows:

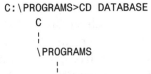

```
C:\PROGRAMS>CD DATABASE
         C
         |
         \PROGRAMS
            |
            \DATABASE
```

This information on DOS applies to both a stand-alone DOS workstation and DOS used on a network. Keep the directory structure in mind when changing directories.

 Note   NetWare 2.2 can have up to 32 volumes, and NetWare 3.1*x* can have up to 64 volumes.

Naming and Setting Up Volumes

When you create and name volumes in NetWare, remember that the volume name must follow certain conventions. The following rules apply to all NetWare volume names:

◆ You can assign volume names of one to 15 characters.

◆ Except for the characters *, /, \, ?, and @, you can use almost any keyboard character for volume names. The @ sign is new to the unavailable characters list and is reserved for designations made by the *NetWare Naming Service* (NNS) product, which came out with 3.1. Novell offers this product for simplifying the login process in multiple-server environments.

◆ You can use a period (.) in a file server name as long as the period is not the first character.

◆ The first volume on the first drive always is called SYS:.

◆ Volume names always are followed by a colon (:).

 In NetWare 2.2, the largest volume that you can access is 255 MB. If you have a drive larger than 255 MB, use the remaining space for additional volumes. If you have a 650 MB drive, for example, one option is to break the drive into three volumes—two volumes that contain 255 MB and another volume that contains 140 MB.

NetWare 3.1*x* breaks the 256 MB limitation, enabling you to create a single volume of up to 32 terabytes. A *terabyte* (TB) is a number that has 12 zeros after it (1 TB equals 1,099,511,627,776).

Understanding Directories

Both DOS and NetWare use directories to organize files. A basic understanding of directories is helpful to understanding NetWare's required directories.

 Describe a directory, including its main function, hierarchical structure, directory name, and directory path.

The highest level of a DOS directory structure is the root. The highest level of a NetWare directory structure is the volume, with directories underneath the volume. Directories can hold both files and other directories, often referred to as subdirectories. Both DOS and NetWare directory structures are hierarchical. (See fig. 3.1).

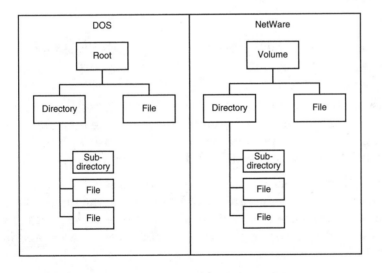

Figure 3.1

DOS and NetWare directory structures.

The main function of both the DOS and NetWare directory structure is to organize files and subdirectories. In order to do that, each directory must have its own name, because directories are accessed by name.

NetWare's directory structure uses a specific path. That path starts with the file server name, followed by a volume name, a directory, and then subdirectories, if applicable. The typical NetWare directory structure looks like this:

JJSERVER/SYS:USERS/JOHN

JJSERVER is the server name and must be followed by a slash in the directory path. SYS is the volume name and must be followed by a colon; USERS is a directory name and is followed by a slash. JOHN is a subdirectory name, and has no characters following it. If you wanted to access another subdirectory within the JOHN subdirectory, then you would follow the JOHN subdirectory name with a slash, and follow it by the name of the next subdirectory.

Now that you know how the directory is structured and understand its main function, understanding how network file storage works is the next important aspect of NetWare networks with which you should become familiar.

 Explain the basic concepts of network file storage, including volume and directory structures.

Network file storage allows multiple users to access and use data, as well as application files from the network. The network's file storage design is important to the speed and ease with which network users can access data and application files.

To keep the network file storage system organized, network volumes and directories are used. Volumes are the highest level on a NetWare file server. Volumes contain directories. Files are not stored directly at the volume level, but are instead stored in directories on volumes.

A better understanding of the NetWare file system can be obtained by understanding both the required NetWare directories and the suggested NetWare directories, discussed in the following sections.

Understanding Required Directories

When you install NetWare, five directories are created that are essential to an efficient and reliable system. The PUBLIC, SYSTEM, MAIL, LOGIN, and ETC directories are established in the SYS: volume. (See fig. 3.2.) These directories are very important to network functionality and should never be deleted. The next few sections describe these directories and show you the way they work within the NetWare environment.

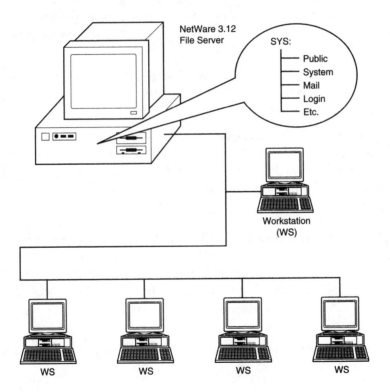

Figure 3.2

NetWare required directories.

209

SYS:LOGIN

LOGIN is the first directory you can access on a network. It contains the SLIST.EXE and LOGIN.EXE files. SLIST.EXE displays all the file server names of which the routing table is aware.

Figure 3.2 illustrates one network's response to the SLIST command. As you can see, servers are listed in alphabetical order by server name. Each server's network, node address, and status also are shown.

A status appears for each listed file server. Three status types are displayed: Blank, Default, and Attached. The status field displays the workstation's relationship (status) to the listed file server. It does not reflect the actual status of the server itself, as is commonly first assumed.

A *Blank* status means that this workstation has no relationship established with the server other than the fact that it can see that server on the network.

The *Default* status means that after the workstation loaded the files necessary to communicate with the network, this server was the first server on which it found a LOGIN directory containing files with which it could log in to the network.

 If you have a PREFERRED SERVER = statement in your workstation's NET.CFG file, the default server is the same as the server named in the PREFERRED SERVER = statement, unless the preferred server could not be found on the network.

The *Attached* status means that this workstation has logged in to or attached to this file server.

 Little difference exists between logging in to a server and attaching to a server. The two processes' results, however, can differ substantially.

After you log in to a server (by typing the LOGIN command), available system and user login scripts are run. If no system or user login script is found, a default login script runs instead.

After you attach to a server, no login script of any type is run. Because you can establish or change drive mappings, attachments to other servers, batch files, and other elements of your networking environment using login scripts, the result of a login can differ substantially from that of an attachment.

The other main difference between logging in to a server and attaching to a server can have significant consequences as well. If you attach to a server after having previously logged in to another server, existing drive mappings and other workstation configuration information remains unchanged. After you log in to a server, however, a log out of all other connected servers is assumed and run. Your workstation, therefore, loses all its previously set connections and drive mappings.

As noted previously, by entering **SLIST** from a workstation, you can see a list of file servers from which you can select. SLIST is particularly useful for three reasons.

First, if you attempt to log in to the network without typing the exact name of the file server to which you want to log in, the system attempts to log you into the first available server. If you do not have a user identification on that server, you are prompted for a password, then denied access. NetWare's security system does not tell you that you are not a user on the server. You might not, therefore, immediately realize what went wrong.

Second, you can see at a glance to which servers you already are attached. This command is a quick way to find out this type of information.

Third, if you cannot remember the exact name of a file server, you can use the SLIST command with a wildcard character. Using the servers listed in figure 3.2, for example, to see all servers that begin with the letter B, type **SLIST B***, and press Enter. Only servers B386, BILL, and BRIAN appear.

Before you can attach to a file server and access the LOGIN directory, you must load some client files on your workstation. These files announce your presence on the cable system and communicate to NetWare that you want to connect to the server. The file server returns a response similar to, "I recognize you as a node. You can use this directory to attempt logging in to a server in the server list." At this point, changing to the F drive or to the first available network drive specified in your workstation's NET.CFG file points you to the SYS:LOGIN directory. You then can view and read any file in this directory.

If your workstation is a *diskless* workstation (one without a hard disk or a floppy disk drive), your workstation can now access the boot image file it requires to log in to the network. The boot image file for logging a diskless workstation into the network resides in this directory. If you have multiple file servers, place this image file in each server's login directory so that each workstation can find its proper boot file in any server to which you attach. You can learn more about this process in *NetWare Training Guide: Networking Technologies*, the companion volume to this book.

 Use caution after you place files in the SYS:LOGIN directory. Anyone who has access to the SYS:LOGIN directory can use files placed here. A user can get access to SYS:LOGIN after loading the necessary client files.

SYS:MAIL

This directory takes its name from a simple mail program that Novell provided with previous versions of NetWare. This program introduced users to electronic mail by saving messages in each user's ID directory. NetWare no longer includes this program. The SYS:MAIL directory is still used, however.

Each user has a MAIL_ID directory, as NetWare refers to the user's MAIL directory, which is created after the user is added to the network. These directories hold the user's personal login script. They also contain the PRINTCON.DAT file if the user has print jobs created through PRINTCON.

The MAIL_ID directories reside under the SYS:MAIL directory. The MAIL_ID directory names are up to eight hexadecimal digits long.

The system SUPERVISOR ID has the distinct name of SYS:MAIL\1.

Two screens in NetWare enable you to view MAIL directories and their corresponding users. Both screens are options in the SYSCON menu utility—a user and Administrator utility that lets you perform such tasks as:

- ◆ Setup or change file server accounting
- ◆ View file server specification information
- ◆ Work with groups and users
- ◆ Perform Supervisor functions such as setting default time restrictions, and creating and modifying system login scripts

If you select the User Information option in the SYSCON menu and then specify a user, two menu options enable you to view ID information. The first option, the Other Information Option, shows a User ID number. The User ID number is the same as the name of the user's mail directory, but with the preceding zeros deleted.

Another place that lists ID information is in the Trustee Directory Assignments list, illustrated in figure 3.3. After you become a new user on the network, you automatically are granted all rights by NetWare under your USER_ID directory, except for Access Control in 2.2 and Supervisory in 3.1*x*. Use this option to see the directory under SYS:MAIL in which you have rights. Notice the manner in which the system automatically truncates the preceding zeros as SYSCON displays this information.

Figure 3.3

SYSCON, User
Names, and Trustee
Directory
Assignments
windows.

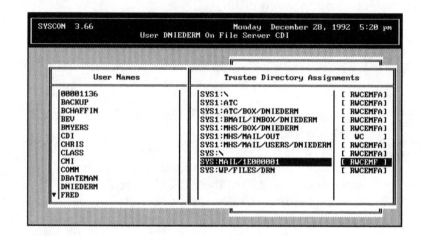

Users have rights to their own MAIL_ID directories, and system managers also have rights to user MAIL_ID directories. By default, System Supervisors have rights to all directories. This privilege enables Supervisors to create personal login scripts and PRINTCON printing jobs for users.

SYS:PUBLIC

The SYS:PUBLIC directory contains all the network management command files that network users need to access. Each menu utility and the command-line utilities available to network users appear in this directory. *Printer definition files* (PDF) and *overlay* (OVL) files reside in the SYS:PUBLIC directory. These overlay files are NetWare Operating System subroutines brought in and out of file server memory as needed. The *help* (HLP) files for utilities stored in this directory also appear in the directory, and provide you with an online reference guide to NetWare.

Although NetWare creates the SYS:PUBLIC directory for NetWare utilities, the System Administrator should create a directory structure beneath this directory for COMMAND.COM files used on DOS machines. Follow the procedure described in Chapter 7 to ensure that each workstation is capable of finding the appropriate COMMAND.COM files.

This directory also contains other subdirectories, such as the NLS subdirectory used to hold the *unicode tables* (files that accommodate different language versions of NetWare).

SYS:SYSTEM

This directory contains the command-line utilities that only network Supervisors and users with Supervisor rights (privileges) can access. A few of the most frequently used utilities put into the SYS:SYSTEM directory are accessed by using the following commands:

◆ **ATOTAL**—Computes the aggregate totals for the system if you are using NetWare's accounting feature. These totals are shown as per day and per week values. Figure 3.4 illustrates the result of running this command.

```
[RUBY_3] F:\SYSTEM>atotal

Accounting Services Total Utility

12/06/1993:
    Connect time:       97    Server requests:    8112
    Blocks read:       388    Blocks written:
    Blocks/day:


12/07/1993:
    Connect time:       11    Server requests:     356
    Blocks read:        18    Blocks written:
    Blocks/day:


Totals for week:
    Connect time:      108    Server requests:    8468
    Blocks read:       406    Blocks written:
    Blocks/day:


[RUBY_3] F:\SYSTEM>
```

Figure 3.4

The ATOTAL accounting screen.

◆ **PAUDIT**—Lists individual entries for each user who logs in to or out of the system. Figure 3.5 illustrates the result of running this command.

Figure 3.5

The PAUDIT
accounting screen.

```
[RUBY_3] F:\SYSTEM>paudit

12/6/93 17:59:23  File Server TSARINA
   CHARGE: 220 to User SUPERVISOR for File Server services.
   Connected 97 min.; 8112 requests; 1590016 bytes read; 0 bytes written.
12/6/93 17:59:23  File Server TSARINA
   NOTE: about User SUPERVISOR during File Server services.
   Logout from address 01D0C300:00001B045C70.
12/7/93 8:40:34  File Server TSARINA
   NOTE: about User SUPERVISOR during File Server services.
   Login from address 01D0C300:00001B045C70.
12/7/93 8:51:57  File Server TSARINA
   CHARGE: 9 to User SUPERVISOR for File Server services.
   Connected 11 min.; 356 requests; 73008 bytes read; 0 bytes written.
12/7/93 8:51:57  File Server TSARINA
   NOTE: about User SUPERVISOR during File Server services.
   Logout from address 01D0C300:00001B045C70.
12/7/93 9:25:55  File Server TSARINA
   NOTE: about User SUPERVISOR during File Server services.
   Login from address 01D0C300:00001B045C70.
[RUBY_3] F:\SYSTEM>
```

◆ **SECURITY**—Compares your system to the NetWare recommendations for securing a system (see fig. 3.6). SECURITY displays System Supervisor, manager accounts, and user accounts that have not been used recently.

Figure 3.6

A sample report from
SECURITY.

```
SECURITY EVALUATION UTILITY, Version 2.23

Group NFSGROUP
   No Full Name specified


Group NOGROUP
   No Full Name specified


User NFSDEMO
   Has [ R    F ] rights in SYS:SYSTEM (maximum should be [        ])
   Has [ R    F ] rights in SYS:MAIL (maximum should be [   C    ])
   Has no login script
   Is not required to change passwords periodically
   Can have passwords that are too short (less than 5)
   No Full Name specified


User NOBODY
   Has [ R    F ] rights in SYS:SYSTEM (maximum should be [        ])
   Has [ R    F ] rights in SYS:MAIL (maximum should be [   C    ])
   Has no login script
Press any key to continue ... ('C' for continuous)
```

◆ **BINDFIX**—Attempts to repair bindery problems. This utility creates new bindery files and renames the previous files with OLD extensions. Use BINDFIX if you suspect bindery file corruption.

◆ **BINDREST**—Deletes the newly created binderies created by BINDFIX, renames the OLD files to SYS files, hides the new files, and then makes them system files. Use BINDREST if the BINDFIX command does not fix corrupted files and you need to put the binderies back to their original state.

> **Note**
>
> Bindery files contain security information regarding users and groups on the system. This security information includes password requirements, station and time restrictions, trustee rights, and security equivalencies. If these files are corrupted, random portions of the user and group accounts cannot be modified.
>
> NetWare 2.2 contains two bindery files: NET$BIND.SYS and NET$BVAL.SYS. NetWare 3.1x contains three bindery files: NET$OBJ.SYS, NET$PROP.SYS, and NET$VAL.SYS. These files are hidden system files that reside in the SYS:SYSTEM directory.

In addition, the SYS:SYSTEM directory contains various *NetWare Loadable Modules* (NLMs) that the System Administrator might use. For example, this directory contains the UPS.NLM which lets the network Administrator run software that activates *Uninterruptible Power Supply* (UPS) services, and then notifies the network Administrator and users to log out when the power has been interrupted.

This directory also contains:

◆ The MAC.NAM file which lets Macintosh name spaces be used on this file server

◆ Files with the LAN extension which provide LAN driver support for various network boards

◆ Help files for the utilities kept in this directory

217

SYS:ETC

SYS:ETC is also a required NetWare directory. This directory contains files for use with TCP/IP connectivity. In particular, it contains a series of text files that provide connectivity information such as IP addresses for other network devices.

Here is an easy way to remember the required directories. It is SiMPLE!

> **S**YSTEM
>
> i
>
> **M**AIL
>
> **P**UBLIC
>
> **L**OGIN
>
> **E**TC

Managing Required Directories

When you work with NetWare directories, remember that these directories are created by the NetWare installation procedure. In other words, DOS plays no part in their creation. After NetWare networks are installed, the operating system sets up these directories for its own use. If a user tries to delete or rename these directories within DOS, the results can produce difficulties for the network. For this reason, follow these guidelines when you work with NetWare directories:

◆ Keep these directories clean. Leave these directories for the network. Do not add programs and data files to the default NetWare directories; instead, place program and data directories elsewhere on the system. Even though you might find it convenient to place program directories in the SYS:PUBLIC directory, you do not gain any performance advantage by doing so.

◆ Do not modify the installed NetWare directories. If you change a NetWare MAIL ID directory name, the directory becomes unusable because NetWare uses hexadecimal names, not logical names. Although you might find it inconvenient to try and match hexadecimal-named subdirectories with logical names in the MAIL program, the system uses these different naming methods to match user names and directories. For this reason, do not change the subdirectory names in NetWare or they might not work.

◆ Do not move default NetWare directories. NetWare looks in only one place for the four installed directories. The place for these directories is SYS:.

In addition, do not modify or move the PUBLIC, SYSTEM, MAIL, LOGIN, and ETC directories. You can effectively improve network performance if these directories are left alone—NetWare does not need to sort through data to find the information it seeks.

If an application insists on installing itself in one of the essential directories, however, you can leave the program in the directory. Whenever possible, load the application in something other than an essential directory.

In some instances, you can successfully install a program that requires installation at the root directory. You might have to install it from a workstation rather than directly from a DOS prompt at the file server console, using a drive that has been mapped using the MAP ROOT command. To see the exact syntax for using this command, log in to a NetWare server from a workstation, type **MAP /?**, and press Enter.

Do not be afraid to create directories. A good directory structure tells a story about your network. A well-constructed directory tree enables anyone who views it to know instantly the location of utilities, programs, and data directories for each program.

 When you create directories in NetWare, remember a rule applied to creating DOS directories: not too deep and not too wide. In other words, do not

continues

219

create directories that have too many subdirectories or files. Network users notice that the system slows down when more than 500 files exist in a directory. Backup programs have been known to choke and fail if a directory has more than 1,000 files.

For easier security administration, create categories of directories. The following section examines some categories for directories.

Using Recommended Directories

NetWare supplies the directories it needs for proper operation. The System Administrator must decide the manner in which she wants to manage programs and data directories. This section examines several options to help you determine where to place new directories.

The preceding section discussed the directories that NetWare needs to operate. This section examines other directory types not mandatory to NetWare operation. The following three categories of directories can help you organize your system: HOME directories, application directories, and data directories.

HOME Directories

Network structures that include HOME directories for end users can help you monitor network usage. Although they are optional, Novell recommends the use of HOME directories to help keep your network running smoothly. HOME directories are useful on your network for other reasons as well.

HOME directories are set up for the user to store personal files. Users can, for example, determine if any of their files should be shared with others and control access within their own directories.

Many companies set up a directory off SYS: called \USERS. Each user has a directory with a login name. Users usually have all privileges at their HOME directory level. This type of setup works well if user names are eight characters or less, because DOS sets an eight-character limit for directory names.

You can thus create user names that are a maximum of eight characters, which then ensures that users' HOME directory names are no longer than eight characters. Companies use different approaches to solving this problem.

Some companies, for example, assign user names based on the employees' first and last names. A user is assigned a network identification name using the first initial of the user's first name and the first seven characters of the user's last name.

Another option is to use only the first eight characters of a user's first or last name. This approach is only effective when the company has a limited number of employees and no one has the same last or first name.

If the company is too large for either of these options, use a variation of one or more of these approaches. For duplicate names, you can add a user's middle initial, thus limiting the first or last name characters to a maximum of seven.

If your network has a user named John C. Smith and one named Jane R. Smith, using JSMITH as a user name can cause a conflict. You can, however, use JCSMITH and JRSMITH successfully, as well as JOHN and JANE, or JOHNS and JANES.

Note In 3.1*x*, you can limit directory structure branches to a specific amount of file server disk space allowed for the users. In other words, System Administrators can decide the amount of space each user can have for his own work. In both 2.2 and 3.1*x*, you can limit space per user for the entire volume. Both features enable System Administrators to monitor file server disk consumption.

Network protection provides another reason to give users their own separate HOME directories. Supplied with their own directories on the file server, users can control their files and subdirectories. Given a structural branch that they can modify, users are less likely to cause system damage. If you provide directories that users can manipulate, they tend to stay in those directories rather than wander around the system.

From an Administrator's point of view, knowing where to look for expendable files saves time. If the System Supervisor instructs users to place only nonessential data in HOME directories, he can delete files easily and safely in the event that the system runs out of storage space.

Application Directories

The placement of *application directories* (directories required by an application) depends on where the program designers want the program to be located. The installation procedure for an application largely dictates the placement of its directories in the NetWare directory tree. Other applications can be placed anywhere. The designer of your system's security structure ultimately determines where application directories are installed on the network.

You can locate application directories in any volume on the network, which provides you, the System Administrator, with several options. If a volume is going to be used primarily by the accounting department, and the accounting programs are used only by the accounting staff, for example, then place the application among directories that pertain to those users. In other words, place applications within the directory for the department that uses the programs. Figure 3.7 shows this type of directory structure.

Another option is to place application directories under the SYS: volume—everyone has rights to these directories.

You can put application directories anywhere. The placement of application directories, however, factors into any security plans for a network. Whichever method you select, remember that the best planned systems always clearly label the directory's contents.

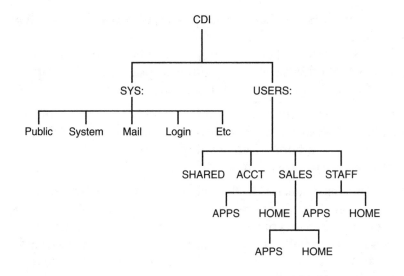

Figure 3.7
Structure for applications on the network.

Data Directories

Never mix applications and data in the same directory. The main responsibility of the System Administrator is to ensure that end users can work without a system failure. The extra burden of determining which files are data and which contain applications is a task that can and should be solved early in the network's life.

If a program needs to be deleted or upgraded, a well-planned directory structure prevents wasting the Administrator's time sorting through directories for data files. By placing data in a separate directory, Administrators easily can update the application without losing data.

Numerous options are available for data directories. One option, called a *shared data directory*, places the data directory with the program. This method enables anyone who uses the program to place the data files in a common directory.

Another possibility for organizing data is to create *departmental directories*. Each member of a department then has a place to put his data files. Departmental directories often are used when departments work mostly on their own.

223

One other popular method for organizing network data is to have users place their data files in their own HOME directories. This method usually includes a single shared directory in which users place files that other users need. Many corporations that employ tight security use this method for their data directories.

Finally, creating a separate volume for data is a practical solution if you have disk drives with large amounts of memory storage. This method maintains a high level of security, but also requires that users have more system knowledge.

The directories discussed in this section are only suggestions to help you organize your network—you cannot use every option on every system. Before you configure a network structure, try it on paper so you can better understand what your structure should look like. Your network users will let you know quickly what needs to be changed. Fortunately, you can move most applications and modify the system without many problems.

In the next section, you are introduced to several commands used both in DOS and NetWare. You also are shown several commands used in NetWare to manipulate the DOS directory structure and to view statistics about the directories.

Section Review Questions

1. File servers must have unique names.

   a. This is required at all times.

   b. This is required only when communicating with another file server.

   c. This is optional.

   d. This cannot be done.

2. NetWare 3.1x can have ___ volumes.

   a. 16

   b. 32

    c. 64

    d. 128

3. Which of the following is a legal volume name?

    a. TAX.VOL:

    b. SYS\VOL:

    c. VOL@COM:

    d. *STARCOM:

4. Which of the following is NOT a required directory?

    a. LOGIN

    b. HOME

    c. SYSTEM

    d. MAIL

5. Which directory belongs to the user SUPERVISOR?

    a. SYS:SYSTEM\1

    b. SYS:MAIL\1

    c. SYS:LOGIN\SUPERVISOR

    d. SYS:MAIL\00000001

6. What can the Supervisor put into a user's MAIL_ID directory?

    a. PRINTCON.DAT and LOGIN

    b. PRINT.CON and QUEUE.DAT

    c. PRINTCON.DAT and LOGIN.EXE

    d. PRINT.LOG and INFO.LOG

7. Which of the following is a true statement?

    a. The required directories must appear in every volume.

    b. You should not move the required directories because the operating system depends on their location.

    c. Because Novell no longer includes an electronic mail package, you can delete the SYS:MAIL directory.

    d. To make it easier to spot the MAIL_ID directories, you can change the hexadecimal name to the user's login name.

8. Which of the following portion of a path name does NOT have to be used in a single-server network?

    a. SERVER

    b. VOLUME

    c. DIRECTORY

    d. SUBDIRECTORY

9. The NetWare directory structure's volume level is equivalent to which of the following?

    a. A NetWare search drive

    b. The root directory of a DOS directory structure

    c. A mapped root drive in a local DOS directory

    d. No equivalent exists

Answers

1. b
2. c
3. a
4. b
5. b
6. a
7. b
8. a
9. b

Using DOS Commands in NetWare

NetWare enables many commands created for DOS to be used on the network. The following list contains the most common commands used by the average network user.

- ◆ **COPY CON.** This command enables the user to create a file on the network when this command is followed by a file name. The F6 function key, or Ctrl+Z, quits and saves the file. In the following example, a simple file called DATA.TXT is created with a row of Xs.

```
>copy con DATA.TXT
xxxxxxxxxxxxxxxxxxxxxxxxxx
^Z
        1 file(s) copied
C:>
```

- ◆ **CD.** Change Directory. This command enables you to change from one directory to another.

Perform directory management tasks, such as creating, deleting, and renaming directories.

- ◆ **RD.** Remove Directory. You also can use RMDIR. This command enables you to get rid of empty directories.

- ◆ **MD.** Make Directory. You also can use MKDIR. This command enables you to create new directories.

- ◆ **RENDIR.** Rename Directory. This command enables you to rename a directory.

- ◆ **DEL.** Delete. This command enables you to remove files from a directory.

- ◆ **COPY.** This command enables you to copy a file to another location. See the next section to learn the difference between using DOS's COPY command and NetWare's NCOPY command.

227

Using NetWare Commands on the Directory Structure

This section discusses several commands that can help you learn about and manage an existing directory structure.

CHKDIR

CHKDIR is used to view information about a volume or directory. CHKDIR displays space limitations for a particular file server, volume, and directory.

Display and modify the display of file system information on volumes, directories, and files.

This command displays the maximum storage capacity of a volume or directory if a space limitation has been placed on it. CHKDIR is useful to determine the amount of free space a directory has.

If space limitations have been placed on users, the CHKDIR utility enables them to keep track of the amount of space they have left. To use CHKDIR, simply enter the command by itself, or enter the command plus the path of the directory you are checking. Figure 3.8 shows a CHKDIR command example.

Figure 3.8

Displaying CHKDIR information.

```
[RUBY_3] Z:\PUBLIC>chkdir

Directory Space Limitation Information For:
TSARINA\SYS:PUBLIC

     Maximum        In Use      Available
     30,888 K       18,372 K       12,516 K    Volume Size
                     9,828 K       12,516 K    \PUBLIC

[RUBY_3] Z:\PUBLIC>
```

CHKVOL

The CHKVOL utility displays total volume space. This space includes total space used by files, deleted files, FATs, and directories. All CHKVOL information is presented in kilobytes and is useful when complete volume information is required.

The information provided by CHKVOL is presented in a simple, two-column format. CHKVOL displays the following information:

◆ File server name

◆ Volume name

◆ Total volume space

◆ Total space used by files, FATS, and directory tables

◆ Space in use by deleted files

◆ Space available from deleted files

◆ Space remaining on volume

◆ Space available to user

As with CHKDIR, you can use CHKVOL with or without a directory path. You also can use the standard DOS wildcards (* and ?) with CHKVOL. The command CHKVOL *, for example, displays information for all volumes, and CHKVOL */* displays information for all volumes on all the file servers to which you are attached. Figure 3.9 is a sample of the information available by using CHKVOL.

```
F:\>chkvol

Statistics for fixed volume CDI/SYS:

Total volume space:                    628,120   K Bytes
Space used by files:                   505,292   K Bytes
Space in use by deleted files:          44,636   K Bytes
Space available from deleted files:     44,636   K Bytes
Space remaining on volume:             122,828   K Bytes
Space available to DNIEDERM:           122,828   K Bytes

F:\>
```

Figure 3.9

Displaying CHKVOL information.

LISTDIR

LISTDIR is similar to the DOS TREE command. As shown in figure 3.10, each subsequent subdirectory is indented to show the hierarchy. You can use this command to view your directory structure:

```
LISTDIR /S
```

Figure 3.10

A sample SYS1: volume directory tree.

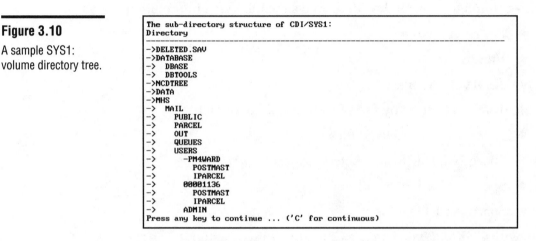

```
The sub-directory structure of CDI/SYS1:
Directory
-------------------------------------------------------------------
->DELETED.SAV
->DATABASE
->   DBASE
->   DBTOOLS
->NCDTREE
->DATA
->MHS
->   MAIL
->      PUBLIC
->      PARCEL
->      OUT
->      QUEUES
->      USERS
->         -PM4WARD
->            POSTMAST
->            IPARCEL
->         00001136
->            POSTMAST
->            IPARCEL
->      ADMIN
Press any key to continue ... ('C' for continuous)
```

The LISTDIR command has other options that you can use:

```
LISTDIR path option
```

Remember to use a backslash (\) for path names and a forward slash (/) for options.

Options

LISTDIR also can use several command-line switches. The following switches are available. Be sure to place a space after LISTDIR and the switch.

◆ **/R**—Lists directory rights and inherited rights masks.

◆ **/E**—Lists effective rights.

◆ **/D** or **/T**—Lists both creation date and time.

- ◆ **/S**—Lists all subdirectories. Subdirectories show up as indented line items.

- ◆ **/A**—Lists all available information.

NCOPY

The NCOPY command is similar to the DOS COPY and XCOPY commands. NCOPY has two advantages over the DOS command speed and source and destination directory listings.

 Perform file management tasks, such as copying, moving, deleting, salvaging, and purging files.

The first advantage is that NCOPY is faster. If you want to copy all the files from the path of P:\DATA\NEW to M:\DATA\OLD using the DOS command, enter the following:

    COPY P:*.* M:

The command first passes to the file server and grabs the necessary tables from memory. These tables then are downloaded to the workstation (pass 2), and the changes in file placement are written to the tables. The tables then go back to the file server (pass 3). Finally, the token returns to the workstation for further instructions (pass 4). The DOS COPY command takes four passes on the cable to complete the action.

Token is a file server process that tells a workstation to transmit information to the network. The process of sending a token from one *node*, either a workstation or a file server, to another is called a *pass*.

If you want to transfer files, use the same syntax, but add the letter N in front of the copy command, as follows:

    NCOPY P:*.* M:

NCOPY goes straight to the file server to manipulate its memory tables rather than the workstation's. This process takes only two passes, one to the file server and one back to the workstation. The result is two passes less than the DOS COPY procedure. The difference between COPY and NCOPY is minimal for small amounts of files, but the time saved is substantial when copying large directory structures.

The second advantage to using NCOPY rather than COPY or XCOPY is that NCOPY displays the source and destination directories. This information is helpful if you often use shortcuts when you copy files, and you mistakenly copy dozens of files to the wrong place. Figure 3.11 shows the NCOPY command that copies all files with the OVL extension in the U:\PROGRAMS\UTILS directory to the directory to which G points, SYS1:\STORE. You see the destination directory because of the way NCOPY works. DOS does not give you this information.

Figure 3.11

An example of using the NCOPY command.

```
G:\STORE>ncopy u:*.ovl g:
From CDI/SYS:\PROGRAMS/UTILS
To    CDI/SYS1:\STORE
      IBM$RUN.OVL    to IBM$RUN.OVL
      $RUN.OVL       to $RUN.OVL
      NDOS.OVL       to NDOS.OVL

      3 files copied.

G:\STORE>
```

NDIR

The *Network Directory Search* (NDIR) command is used to search the network for file or directory parameters.

Display and modify the display of file system information on volumes, directories, and files.

Figure 3.12 shows available information about files and subdirectories in the G:\STORE directory. This information includes file name, file size, last update (the last time the file was modified), flags (attributes), and owner (who created the file). In addition, you see the subdirectory name, inherited and effective rights, and the date and time it was created or copied. Finally, you see the number of files NDIR found and the amount of space they occupy.

```
G:\STORE>ndir
CDI/SYS1:STORE

Files:                 Size    Last Updated      Flags          Owner
-------------------   --------  -------------   -------------   --------
$RUN        OVL        2,288   3-27-86  9:38a  [RoS----------DR] DNIEDERM
IBM$RUN     OVL        2,288   3-27-86  9:38a  [RoS----------DR] DNIEDERM
NDOS        OVL       73,510   8-05-91  6:01a  [RoS----------DR] DNIEDERM

        78,086 bytes in    3 files
        81,920 bytes in   20 blocks

G:\STORE>
```

Figure 3.12

An example of using the NDIR command.

You also can use NDIR to search for specific information. The syntax for the NDIR command is as follows:

    NDIR *path* /*options*

Path

You can replace this option with a directory path, wildcards, or up to 16 file names. Use a backslash to specify path names and a forward slash for the options.

Sort Parameters

Sort parameters alter the order in which files and subdirectories are displayed to the user.

- ◆ **/SORT** *(parameter)*—Enables you to sort the directory on selected parameters by using the parameters described in the following section. The parameter you specify is substituted into the parameter variable after you type the SORT option.

- ◆ **/REV /SORT** *(parameter)*—Reverses the SORT according to the parameters you specify after the SORT option.

- ◆ **/UN**—Leaves the list unsorted.

Parameters

A complete list of parameters for the NDIR command is given in this section. You can use these parameters to gather specific information about files and subdirectories.

233

Parameter	Description
OW	Owner
SI	Size
UP	Update (Last Modified Date)
CR	Created Date
AC	Last Accessed Date
AR	Last Archived Date

Display Formats

NDIR displays whatever you request. The following switches describe specific conditions that you can meet by using NDIR.

- **/FO**—Displays file names only

- **/DO**—Displays directories only

- **/SUB**—Searches all subdirectories

- **/DATES**—Lists last modified, last archived, last accessed, and created dates

- **/RIGHTS**—Lists inherited and effective rights

- **/MAC**—Lists Macintosh files and subdirectories

- **/LONG**—Lists the long file names for Macintosh, OS/2, and NFS

- **/HELP**—Lists NDIR options

Attribute Searches

If you need to look for files flagged with specific attributes, the following list shows each switch and the attribute it represents.

Attribute Search	Limitation
/A	Archive Needed
/CI	Copy Inhibit
/DI	Delete Inhibit
/H	Hidden
/I	Indexed
/N	Normal
/P	Purge
/RI	Rename Inhibit
/RA	Read Audit
/RO	Read Only
/S	Shareable
/Sy	System
/T	Transactional
/WA	Write Audit
/X	Execute Only

To search for select attributes, place the /NOT option before the attribute.

Restricted Displays

NDIR enables you to restrict displays according to specified conditions.

◆ **/OW EQ** *name.* Enables you to search for files or directories created by the user's name.

◆ **/OW NOT EQ** *name.* Enables you to search for file and directory owners, not the user name specified.

235

◆ **/SI operator** *nnn.* Finds all files of a certain size. The *nnn* parameter specifies the number of bytes in a file.

◆ **/SI NOT** *operator nnn.* Finds all files that do not fall into the category of requested information. To look for files no bigger than 10 KB, for example, type **NDIR /SI NOT GR10**.

◆ **/UP** *operator mm-dd-yy.* Finds all files updated before, after, or on a certain date.

◆ **/UP NOT** *operator mm-dd-yy.* Finds all files not updated before, after, or on a certain date.

◆ **/CR** *operator mm-dd-yy.* Finds all files created before, after, or on a certain date.

◆ **/CR NOT** *operator mm-dd-yy.* Finds all files not created before, after, or on a certain date.

◆ **/AC** *operator mm-dd-yy.* Finds all files accessed before, after, or on a certain date.

◆ **/AC NOT** *operator mm-dd-yy.* Finds all files not accessed before, after, or on a certain date.

◆ **/AR** *operator mm-dd-yy.* Finds all files archived before, after, or on a certain date.

◆ **/AR NOT** *operator mm-dd-yy.* Finds all files not archived before, after, or on a certain date.

Operators

Operators, or basic math concepts, are available when using the NDIR command. NDIR does not accept the > or < characters. These operators are used to connect parameters to form specific conditions for NDIR to search.

Operator	Description
GR	Greater Than
LE	Less Than

Operator	Description
EQ or =	Equal To
BEF	Before
AFT	After

RENDIR

The RENDIR command enables you to rename a network subdirectory without affecting users' rights to that directory.

In the following example, the SYS:APPS directory is renamed to SYS:PROGRAMS.

```
F:\>RENDIR APPS PROGRAMS
```

 Note RENDIR works only in the Parent directory when renaming. You cannot include a path.

VOLINFO

The *Volume Information* (VOLINFO) utility is probably the Administrator's most commonly used command. The VOLINFO utility presents in table form the total space, free space, and directory entries in all volumes (see fig. 3.13). The VOLINFO command is the simplest way to view volume free space.

You can change how frequently the information on this screen is updated as well.

To change the update frequency, choose Update Interval from the Available Options menu, and then type in the update interval (in seconds) that you prefer. You can enter anything from 1 to 3,600 seconds.

237

Figure 3.13

The Volume Information main screen.

```
Volume Information  3.54                Monday  December 28, 1992  5:31 pm
                        User DNIEDERM On File Server CDI

     Page 1/1         Total    Free     Total    Free     Total    Free

     Volume name        SYS               SYS1
     KiloBytes      628,120  122,800   315,024   18,672
     Directories     39,264   15,051    55,264   43,709

     Volume name
     KiloBytes
     Directories


                                 Available Options
                                 Change Servers
                                 Update Interval
```

Novell also has made available a Windows version of VOLINFO. Figure 3.14 is an example of VOLINFO for Windows. This utility is part of the NetWare tools program provided by Novell. It provides a standard Microsoft Windows interface and enables space to be presented in megabytes or kilobytes.

Figure 3.14

Windows 3.1 Volume Information screen.

```
                              Program Manager
  File   Options   Window   Help

                              NetWare Tools

                             Volume Information
    Volume Information on Server   CDI

    Name          Total Dir.   Free Dir.        Total Mb   Free Mb
    SYS              27360       11438             280         71
    SYS1             29504       10861             307        132



    Update Interval:  5      ┌Display Format────────────────┐       Close
         (Seconds)           │ ● Megabytes   ○ Kilobytes    │
    Games       Accessories      Main      Windows Apps    LANTern
```

In the next section, you learn about mapping drives and their uses on the network.

Section Review Questions

10. Which utilities give you statistical information about the volumes?

    a. LISTDIR, VOLINFO, CHKDSK

    b. VOLINFO, CHKVOL, VOLDIR

    c. VOLINFO, CHKDIR, CHKINFO

    d. VOLINFO, CHKVOL, CHKDIR

11. Which of the following is NOT a valid option?

    a. LISTDIR /T

    b. NDIR SYS:*.dat /OW=SUPERVISOR /SUB

    c. LISTDIR /O

    d. NDIR \may.?? /FO /AC NOT BEF 2/5/92

12. Which utility is most closely related to the DOS TREE command?

    a. DIR /S

    b. LIST /A

    c. DIRLIST /S

    d. LISTDIR /A

13. Which statement about using DOS commands on the network is NOT true?

    a. DOS commands must never be used on the network.

    b. You can use DOS commands on the network to access DOS system files.

    c. You can use DOS commands from drives A through E without affecting network drive mappings.

    d. DOS commands, such as CD, can be used to reestablish a drive mapping when it has been accidentally changed and NetWare commands cannot be accessed.

239

Answers

10. d

11. c

12. d

13. a

Mastering Drive Mappings

NetWare uses drive mappings to enable users to quickly access commonly used directories. Drive mappings are necessary for all NetWare networks. This section discusses the following types of mappings available in NetWare and ways you can use them to customize your network:

◆ Mappings to local drives

◆ Mappings to network data directories

◆ Search mappings to network program directories

You can think of drive mappings as bookmarks in NetWare. If you are reading a textbook or reference manual, for example, the easiest way to access useful data quickly is to mark the pages with bookmarks. Then, whenever you need to access this information, you can easily flip to the pages by using the bookmarks. Drive mappings in NetWare enable the user to quickly find the needed directory.

Networks and Drive Mappings

Networks have 26 available mappings. By pointing these bookmarks to frequently used directories, you can move to any directory in three keystrokes.

Navigate volumes and directories by using network drives.

Suppose, for example, that the directory structure shown in figure 3.15 is on the hard drive of a PC shared by several part-time employees. The morning-shift user, USERAM, needs to access several directories, marked A, B, and C.

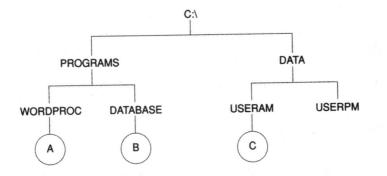

Figure 3.15

A sample directory structure.

Now, suppose that USERAM boots the PC and begins the workday. First, USERAM needs to go to the word processing directory. At the DOS prompt, he types **CD PROGRAMS\WORDPROC**. If you include typing the space and pressing Enter, 21 keystrokes are used.

Next, USERAM needs to go to his HOME directory. From the C:\PROGRAMS\WORDPROC directory, USERAM types **CD\DATA\USERAM**. This takes a total of 15 keystrokes. USERAM'S manager now asks USERAM to print a database report, so USERAM must type **CD\PROGRAMS\DATABASE**, which again is 21 keystrokes. These procedures can add up to a substantial number of keystrokes typed during the workday.

By using the same directory on a network, C:\ becomes the volume level. By assigning drive letters to each directory, USERAM can get to any of the directories in three keystrokes. Suppose, for example, that drive letter W is assigned to the \PROGRAMS\WORDPROC directory, drive letter X is assigned to the \PROGRAMS\DATABASE directory, and drive letter H is assigned to the \DATA\USERAM directory. To get to any directory, USERAM simply types **H:** , **W:** , or **X:** and presses Enter—just three keystrokes each time. Later in this chapter, you learn the requirements for setting up drive mappings on your network.

Networks and Search Drives

To make finding files in directories even easier, you can use *search drives.* These drive mappings enable you to place yourself in a directory created to store data and call the program from the searched drive. Most programs, unless otherwise configured, dump data into the same directory from which they were called. In NetWare, you can use search drives to help you locate certain files. NetWare performs the following basic steps whenever you ask for a file: the system searches for the file in the current directory; if the system fails to find the file in the current directory, the system then searches each established search drive in order.

In NetWare, a maximum of 16 search drives are available, out of a possible 26 drive mappings. Because of the method used for searching for files, the more search drives you use, the longer searches can take. Suppose, for example, that you have 16 search drives and are currently in a directory not set up as searchable. If you request a file that does not exist in any directory, the system searches through 17 directories before you receive a File not found error message. Another problem is that the system allocates file server RAM for search drives. The more search drives users have on the system, the more memory is taken away from the server.

Note   Each user can create and use his or her own set of up to 26 drive mappings. The drive mappings that USERAM sets up, for example, have no effect on the mappings that USERPM creates. Figure 3.16 shows the way you can map all 26 drive mappings in NetWare. NetWare offers several options for assigning drive letters to a directory. These options are discussed later in this chapter.

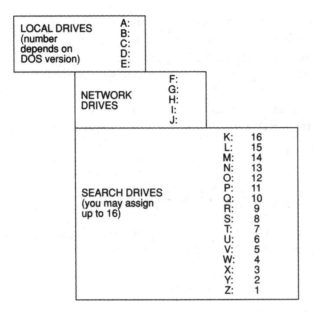

Figure 3.16

NetWare's default
drive mappings.

Setting Up Drive Mappings

You can set up drive mappings in several places on the network.
Two places are considered temporary; three places are permanent.
To set up drive mappings temporarily, type the command at the
DOS prompt or from a menu called Session. Whenever you log
out, these mappings are discarded. To set up drive mappings
always available for use, use a system login script, user login
script, or menu option.

With the exception of using SESSION and NWUSER, the syntax
for defining drive mappings is the same. The syntax for drive
mappings is discussed in the next few sections.

Using Local Drive Mappings

NetWare automatically allocates the letters A through E for local
hardware. The drive letter A refers to the first floppy drive, and B
refers to the second floppy drive. The drive letters C, D, and E

refer to local hard drives. Even if your workstations do not have all this local hardware, these drive letters are reserved. You can, however, redirect any drive letter to refer to a network drive. If a local drive is remapped to a network drive and then deleted, the drive letter reverts back to referring to the local drive. The following example shows a way you can redirect the local drive E to the network drive SYS:DATA:

```
MAP E:=SYS:DATA
```

Using Network Drive Mappings

You usually use network drive mappings with data directories. Several parameters are used when you map to a directory on the network.

 Access file systems by mapping network drives to application directories.

The following is the syntax for mapping network drives:

```
MAP options A-Z: = fileserver/volume:path
```

You can use the following options in the preceding syntax:

◆ **NEXT.** This option enables you to map the next available network drive letter. You can use this option when you are not sure which drive letters are not being used. End users using the DOS LAST DRIVE command can use this option to find the next open drive letter. When using this option, you do not specify a drive letter. To map the next available network drive to file server CDI, PUBLIC directory, APPS subdirectory, type the following:

```
MAP NEXT CDI\SYS:PUBLIC\APPS
```

This option also helps to prevent mapping over a drive letter that already has been mapped. When you map a drive letter that has been mapped previously, the original mapping is scrapped without an error message. By using the NEXT option, you preserve any existing mappings.

◆ ***#:.** This option is used only in login scripts and works in the same way as the NEXT option. *#: searches for the next unused drive letter and maps it to the directory.

◆ **ROOT.** Some older programs and many single-user programs require all rights in the root directory, which is an unacceptable request. To get around this, NetWare enables you to specify a false root drive. A false root drive appears to be a real root directory to the user and the computer. A *false root drive* displays as a drive letter with a backslash, indicating that it is a root drive. When you use the CD\ command, you return to the false root, not the real root. To return to the real root, the user must type **CD** *volume:*, which returns the user to the volume's true root. To map drive K as a root drive to the APPS directory in the PUBLIC directory on file server CDI, type the following:

```
MAP ROOT K:=CDI\SYS:PUBLIC\APPS
```

Note

Using the DOS CD\ command takes the user to the false root, not the real root. To get back to the real root directory, type **CD** *volume:*.

False root drives appear differently when you use the MAP command to display the drives. In figure 3.17, for example, S: is mapped to the false root of \APPS\SS. The user sees only part of the directory, in this case \DATA.

```
S:\DATA>MAP

Drive  A:   maps to a local disk.
Drive  B:   maps to a local disk.
Drive  C:   maps to a local disk.
Drive  D:   maps to a local disk.
Drive  E:   maps to a local disk.
Drive  F: = CDI286\SYS:   \SHELLS
Drive  G: = CDI286\SYS:   \USERS\DAVE
Drive  S: = CDI286\SYS:APPS\SS   \DATA
       ----
SEARCH1:   = Z:. [CDI286\SYS:   \PUBLIC]
SEARCH2:   = Y:. [CDI286\SYS:   \PUBLIC\IBM_PC\MSDOS\V3.30]
SEARCH3:   = X:. [CDI286\SYS:   \APPS\SS]

S:\DATA>
```

Figure 3.17

An example of a MAP screen.

The choice of letters is up to you. Generally, a letter that mne-
monically represents the directory path is chosen. This type of
drive mapping should be done with directories that hold data.
Program directories should be search drives. You might, for
example, map the drive letter M: to point to the \MENUS directory, as discussed in the following section. The following is an
example syntax of this mapping:

```
MAP M:=SYS:MENUS
```

If you are logged in to only one file server, you can skip the MAP
command's portion that refers to the file server name. Using the
volume name is always recommended.

Using Search Drive Mappings

Search drive mappings are used with program directories to
enable users to access programs while actually being at a data
directory.

Access network applications by mapping search
drives to application directories.

The syntax for mapping search drives follows:

```
MAP options S1-16: = fileserver/volume:path
```

You can use the following options in the preceding syntax:

◆ **INSERT.** This option puts a search drive mapping into a
specific slot. INSERT ensures that an existing drive is not
overwritten and that the new drive is put in the order specified.

If you require path statements to your local drives,
always use INSERT for search drives. This procedure ensures that previous path statements to local
drives are not overwritten.

246

By using this method, you can retain your DOS PATH statement when you log out of the network.

◆ **ROOT.** This option is the same as the ROOT option used for network data drive mappings. This option enables you to set false root directories. The command CD\ returns the user to the false root. To return to the real root, the user needs to type **CD** *volume:*, which returns the user to the volume's true root.

When mapping a search drive, specify S*n*, in which *n* is replaced by the desired search drive number, and NetWare automatically assigns the next available drive letter beginning at Z and working up the alphabet. You also can insert a search drive, if you need that drive to be searched in a particular order. If, for example, you set up a root search drive to a directory that contains a quirky application, and it requires that it be the first search drive, you can accommodate the program by entering the following:

```
MAP INS S1:=CDI\SYS:PUBLIC\APPS
```

In the preceding example, the first existing search drive becomes the second search drive, the second becomes the third search drive, and so on. The search drive you inserted becomes the first search drive. No search drive mappings are lost. Their order simply is changed.

Deleting Drive Mappings

You might find that you are not using all your current drive mappings. By eliminating these excess drive mappings, you can increase your file server performance by returning memory used for tracking search drives to the file server. Also, when a user exits an application and does not need access to a directory, you can maintain system security by deleting the drive mapping. This makes it more difficult to get to the directory through an existing mapping.

To delete a mapped data drive, use the following syntax:

    MAP DEL drive letter:

To delete a mapped search drive, use the following syntax:

    MAP DEL Sdrive number:

These commands remove the mapping from the list. You do not need to specify the full path to delete the drive mappings. NetWare is concerned only with the label, or drive letter.

If you MAP DEL a search drive by using the letter rather than the S#:, the following message appears:

    This is a SEARCH DRIVE, are you sure you want to
    Delete? (Y/N)

If you make it a habit to delete all drive mappings by drive letter, including search drive mappings, you are less likely to accidentally delete a search drive mapping that you really need, such as the drive mapped to SYS:PUBLIC.

If you accidentally delete the SYS:PUBLIC drive mapping, you cannot run network commands. You must use DOS to CD through the directory structure until you again have a drive mapping to SYS:PUBLIC. Then you can use the MAP command to remap the deleted search drive.

Using the DOS CD Command on Drive Mappings

Drive mappings are *dynamic*, which means that they change. When you use the DOS CD command, drive mappings follow you around. As you learned in the previous sections, the MAP command establishes a drive letter and where that letter initially points. After the letter is initially set, you can determine where the letter points. To do this, use the CD command. This makes the mapping point to the new location. Drive mappings match the DOS prompt path; if it changes, the mapping reflects the change. Consider the following drive mapping shown when **MAP** is entered at the DOS prompt:

```
Drive M: = CDI386\SYS: \UTILS\MENUS
```

This mapping uses the following syntax:

```
MAP M: = SYS:UTILS\MENUS
```

By entering **M:** at the DOS prompt, you are taken to the UTILS/ MENUS directory. If you type **CD\LOGIN** at this directory, you are taken to the LOGIN directory. If you type **MAP** again, you see the following entry for M:

```
Drive M: = CDI386\SYS: \LOGIN
```

Changing directories using CD changes the location shown to you using MAP.

 You might find that using the CD command is a disadvantage if you issue it to a search drive. Possible inconveniences include searching a drive that does not need to be searched, or losing the path to a directory needed to run a program. If you find that you are lost, simply log in again. This procedure resets your mappings to the way they were set up in the login scripts.

Figure 3.18 shows the screen Windows provides for doing your mappings. Novell's Windows utilities follow the traditional point-and-shoot method of choosing a directory.

Figure 3.18

The Windows
mapping screen.

Section Review Questions

14. Which of the following is the correct syntax for a path
    pointing to the server B386, volume APPS, and subdirectory
    PROGRAMS under directory DATA?

    a. B386:SYS\PROGRAMS\DATA

    b. B386\SYS:APPS\PROGRAMS

    c. B386\APPS:DATA\PROGRAMS

    d. B386\DATA:PROGRAMS\DATA

15. Which command should you use to map a drive to the
    PROGRAM directory on the server NORTH386 on the SYS:
    volume?

    a. MAP INSERT S3:=NORTH386:\SYS\PROGRAM

    b. MAP INSERT S3:NORTH386\SYS:PROGRAM

    c. MAP INSERT 3:=NORTH386\SYS:PROGRAM

    d. MAP INSERT S3:=NORTH386\SYS:PROGRAM

16. Where are you NOT allowed to map a drive?

    a. At the DOS prompt

    b. In FILER

    c. In a menu

    d. In a login script

17. Which command is added to the MAP statement to map a false root?

    a. DEL

    b. FALSEROOT

    c. ROOT

    d. NEXT

18. DOS reserves certain drive letters to use for local devices. Which of the following is a reserved drive letter for the local disk?

    a. E

    b. F

    c. S1

    d. Z

19. How many search drives are available for each user as the default?

    a. 26

    b. 16

    c. 13

    d. 5

20. When a first search drive exists, which command should you use to add a new first search drive?

    a. MAP NEXT

    b. MAP BEFORE

    c. MAP S1

    d. MAP INSERT

Answers

14. c
15. d
16. b
17. c
18. a
19. b
20. d

Case Study

Create a network environment for the following scenario.

You are setting up a network for the BDHOME company. They have two servers and 60 users. They use the following applications:

◆ Accounting

◆ Inventory

◆ Word Processing

◆ Spreadsheet

◆ Name and Address Database

The key people, listed by login name, are as follows:

◆ BD, the owner

◆ MYERS, the System Administrator

◆ KMURPHY, the controller

◆ GDALL, quality-control Supervisor

◆ TERESA, the administrative assistant

The file servers each have one 650 MB drive.

Based on this information, answer the following questions.

1. Create a directory structure for the BDHOME company, keeping the following points in mind:

    ◆ The Inventory and Accounting databases are the largest.

    ◆ The key people want their own directories.

    ◆ Accounting wants to make certain that their people are the only ones with access to the accounting software.

    ◆ Everyone can access the Inventory database.

    ◆ The programs and the data must be kept separate from each other.

2. Discuss the difference between using NetWare 2.2 and 3.1x for this installation.

Understanding NetWare Security

NetWare 3.1*x* has substantially improved the way passwords are handled. Passwords are now encrypted at the workstation before they go onto the cable. This procedure prevents anyone from tapping into the cable, extracting a packet, and viewing an unencrypted password.

NetWare Core Protocol (NCP) *Packet Signature* also has been added to NetWare 3.1*x*. NCP Packet Signature is a security enhancement for NetWare 3.1*x* servers and clients that prevents users from forging packet identifications. NCP Packet Signature is built into the NetWare 3.12 operating system and client software. Chapter 7, "Customizing the User's Environment," discusses NCP Packet Signature in more detail.

 Note NetWare 3.1*x* also adds the following features:

- ◆ Trustee rights that can be granted to files as well as to directories.

- ◆ Attributes that can be applied to directories as well as to files.

In this chapter, you learn about not only the newer NetWare 3.1*x* security elements , but also about NetWare security in general. The items covered in this chapter include the following:

- ◆ User types and what they can accomplish
- ◆ Levels of NetWare security
- ◆ Security functions at each level
- ◆ Security attributes
- ◆ Command-line utilities that affect security
- ◆ NetWare NCP Packet Signature security

Defining Security Levels

NetWare has seven different types of network users. You can combine many of these types with other types to fine-tune what a user can do on the system. The following list shows the different NetWare user types, ranging from the highest level to the lowest level:

- ◆ Supervisor
- ◆ Supervisor equivalents
- ◆ FCONSOLE operators
- ◆ Workgroup managers
- ◆ PCONSOLE operators
- ◆ Account managers
- ◆ End users

 The user Supervisor is an actual login account, while a Supervisor equivalent is a user account that can perform all the same functions as the Supervisor.

Workgroup managers have the power to create users and are, therefore, more authoritative than account managers.

Most users can be managed by a different type of user. By combining user types, you can create the Administrators and users to fully utilize your network. Figure 4.1 illustrates the hierarchy of network administration.

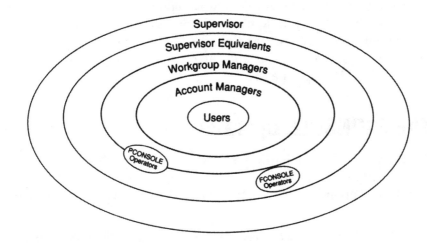

Figure 4.1

NetWare's subsets of the security divisions and their domains.

The Supervisor

The *Supervisor*, who has rights to every utility and file on the network, is the highest-level network user. Only one user named Supervisor is permitted on the network. This user is given all rights and privileges. The Supervisor can be viewed as having a "back door" into the network, meaning that he or she can get into the network in case of an emergency. Because of the Supervisor's high status, he or she is exempt from deletion by other users on the network. This capability does not, however, give the Supervisor full rights to all files on the network. If, for example, a file is marked as read-only, the Supervisor cannot delete the file until the attribute is changed to Read/Write.

The Supervisor password can be changed by the Supervisor or by the Supervisor equivalents (discussed in the following section). Many third-party network management programs that have system security still require the login ID of the Supervisor and do not function for the Supervisor-equivalent users.

The Supervisor Equivalent

The *Supervisor-equivalent* user is a regular end user who has the same authority on the system as the Supervisor. Supervisor-equivalent users have the capability to create other Supervisor-equivalent users and can change the Supervisor account, including the password.

The FCONSOLE Operator

NetWare's FCONSOLE utility enables you to view certain information about the network. FCONSOLE operators have certain privileges depending on whether they also are Supervisor equivalents.

FCONSOLE operators who have Supervisor equivalence can use all options available in FCONSOLE. FCONSOLE operators who do not have Supervisor equivalence, however, cannot clear connections or down the file server from FCONSOLE. Users who are not FCONSOLE operators or Supervisor equivalents can use FCONSOLE, but are severely limited in the types of information they can see.

 Novell often refers to FCONSOLE operators as CONSOLE operators.

Chapters 8 and 11 walk you through all the FCONSOLE options and point out the features of FCONSOLE that are limited to FCONSOLE operators.

The Workgroup Manager

Workgroup managers can be individual users or a group of users. Workgroup managers can create, delete, and manage user accounts. They also can change passwords, account restrictions, and login scripts for users. Workgroup managers, however, can manage only those users and groups assigned to them or that they create. They cannot modify users or groups not in their list of managed users and groups.

The User Account Manager

User account managers can be users or groups. User account managers can manage and delete accounts assigned to them. Unlike workgroup managers, user account managers cannot create users and groups.

The PCONSOLE Operator

NetWare has two types of PCONSOLE operators. One type, the *print queue operator*, manages and deletes print queues. The print queue operator cannot be assigned to a group. It must be assigned to individual users. The other type, the *print server operator*, manages and deletes print servers. The only type of user that can create print servers and queues, however, is the Supervisor.

Table 4.1 lists the functions that Administrators and end users can use on the network, and helps you visualize which types of users on the network can accomplish different management tasks.

Table 4.1
Security Domains

	Create/Delete Supervisor Equivalent	Create/Delete Workgroup Managers	Create Account Managers	Create/Delete Users	Inherits All Rights To Network	Create/Delete Print Queues and Servers	Manage Print Queues (by default)	Manage Print Servers (by default)	Use FCONSOLE (LIMITED) Access	Use FCONSOLE (UNLIMMITED) Access
Supervisor	●	●	●	●	●	●	●	●		●
Supervisor Equivalent	●	●	●	●	●	●	●			●
Workgroup Manager			●	●					●	
User Account Manager			●						●	
Print Queue Operator							●			
Print Server Operator								●		
FCONSOLE Operator									●	

The End User

End users make up the majority of NetWare users. End users can perform only the functions given to them by the other six categories of users.

Section Review Questions

1. Who can change the Supervisor's password?

    a. Supervisor

    b. Supervisor and all Supervisor equivalents

    c. Supervisor, Supervisor equivalents, and workgroup managers

    d. Supervisor and FCONSOLE operators

2. Can an account manager delete a user?

    a. Yes

    b. No

    c. Only if he or she manages that user

    d. Only if he or she created that user

3. Which of the following CANNOT be assigned to a group of users?

    a. Workgroup manager

    b. Account manager

    c. Print queue operator

    d. Supervisor equivalent

4. Who can create a workgroup manager?

    a. Supervisor only

    b. Supervisor and Supervisor equivalents

    c. Supervisor, Supervisor equivalents, and account managers

    d. Account managers

5. Which of the following is NOT a type of NetWare operator?

    a. Print queue operator

    b. Print server operator

    c. Console operator

    d. Account operator

6. Which user is most commonly found on an average network?

    a. The end user

    b. The Supervisor equivalent

    c. The print server operator

    d. The FCONSOLE operator

Answers

1. b
2. c
3. d
4. b
5. d
6. a

Exploring NetWare Security Levels

This section examines the various layers of NetWare security. In the process, you learn why NetWare can reliably provide the right level of protection for any company.

Identify the levels and functions of network security.

Four levels of network security exist. The following list ranks these levels in order from lowest to highest:

- ◆ Login/Password

- ◆ Rights

- ◆ Attributes

- ◆ File server

Login/Password-Level Security

NetWare enables you to use passwords as a measure of security. At least a dozen parameters are available for this feature; each parameter can be set for individual users or as a default for all users.

Describe login security, including user account restrictions, time restrictions, station restrictions, and intruder detection.

NetWare offers a defense measure before the password ever comes into play. Suppose, for example, that you want to log in to a network. Because most small to mid-sized companies use first names for login names, you might assume that a login name is "Ann" and try to log in with that name. The system responds to this request by asking for a password. You try using common passwords, but the network denies access each time.

You can try different passwords continually, but NetWare never tells you whether a user named Ann is on that system. This feature is NetWare's first line of defense against *hackers* (unauthorized users). Instead of responding with a message that Ann is not a valid user name, NetWare simply asks you for a password.

User Account Restrictions

User Account restrictions permit the network Administrator to control how, when, and where a user accesses the network. User account restrictions are implemented by accessing the Supervisor Options menu of SYSCON. From this menu, network Administrators can initiate intruder detection, set time restrictions, and perform other network administrative (user Supervisor) tasks.

The first two items in the Supervisor Options menu affect only future users added to the system:

◆ Default Account Balance/Restrictions

◆ Default Time Restrictions

Default Account Balance/Restrictions and Default Time Restrictions have no effect on current users. As you add new users to the network, the parameters defined in these two options automatically are added to the new user's account.

When you create new user accounts on the network, you can set user account restrictions that are automatically implemented for each new user account. The account restrictions that you can set include:

◆ Whether or not the account has an expiration date

◆ The date the account expires

◆ Whether the user can have more than one network connection at a time

◆ The largest number of simultaneous network connections the user is allowed to have

◆ If a home directory for the user should be automatically created

◆ If the user is required to have a password

◆ What the minimum password length must be

◆ Whether or not the user is going to be required to change his or her password at specified intervals

- How many days are allowed between password changes

- Whether or not the user will be limited as to the number of times they can log in after their password has expired and has not been changed, also called *grace logins*

- How many grace logins the user is allowed

- Whether or not the user can reuse the same password or if they must supply a different password when changing their password

- If accounting is turned on, the maximum number of charges the user will be allowed on this server

- Whether or not the user will be allowed to use accounting credit

- If accounting is set on the server, what the lowest allowed balance will be on his or her account

Time Restrictions

This option is also part of the SYSCON utility. To access it, choose Default Time Restrictions from the Supervisor Options menu. When you choose this option, you can specify which days of the week and which times of the day (in half-hour increments) the new users are allowed to log in to the network.

Station Restrictions

Station restrictions can be set for new users as well. They are set to define whether or not a new user is restricted in the number of network connections they can have; if so, the user must also specify the maximum number of allowed connections.

In addition to setting station restrictions for new user accounts, you can set them for existing users as well. This is also done using the SYSCON utility. However, instead of choosing Supervisor Options from the SYSCON Available Topics menu, you choose User Information from this same menu, then choose the user whose account you want to restrict. When the User Information menu appears, choose Account Restrictions and modify the user's account restrictions as needed.

Intruder Detection

Another security feature of NetWare is the capability of the network operating system to lock out a user account if the user attempts too many unsuccessful logins. This is known as *intruder detection lockout*. The Supervisor user (or a Supervisor-equivalent user) must set intruder detection lockout in order for it to work.

Intruder detection lockout is set using the SYSCON utility. To set intruder detection lockout, choose Supervisor Options from the Available Options menu, and then choose Intruder Detection/ Lockout. You can now set the following intruder detection lockout specifications:

- ◆ Whether intruder detection is on or off

- ◆ The number of incorrect login attempts allowed, after which the user will be prevented from logging in to the network

- ◆ The length of time (in days, hours, and/or minutes) that the number of bad login attempts will be kept

- ◆ Whether or not the user is to be locked out after intruder detection has met its preset criteria indicating that an intruder is trying to access the network

- ◆ The length of time (in days, hours, and/or minutes) that the user is locked out if *Lock Account After Detection* is set to Yes

Chapter 5, "Working with User Utilities," contains additional information on using the SYSCON utility to implement network security.

Describe NetWare 3.12 file system security, including the concepts of trustees, directory and file rights, inheritance, Inherited Rights Mask, and effective rights.

User Rights

The rights a user or group has in a directory or on a file are called *trustee rights*. Eight trustee rights exist in NetWare 3.1x. Trustee rights are the keys each user has for a directory or file.

NetWare 3.1x also has replaced the concept of NetWare 2.2's Maximum Rights Mask with the *Inherited Rights Mask* (IRM). The IRM is a filter. Each directory has an IRM that allows all rights to flow through to subdirectories. The System Administrator can change the IRM to allow only certain rights to flow down to subsequent subdirectories. This change can be made by using the ALLOW command or the FILER menu utility, which are discussed later in this chapter.

You must remember the following rules when figuring the results of setting up an IRM:

1. IRMs only affect the rights that flow down from the directory above. If you are granted rights specifically through the GRANT command, FILER, or SYSCON, the IRM has no effect, because these rights do not flow down.

2. *Effective rights* equal trustee rights when the user has been given the rights explicitly in a directory. In other words, when you give the user rights in a directory, those rights become her effective rights, and the IRM has no effect.

3. When the user has the Supervisory right, the IRM has no effect. The *Supervisory right*, described in the next section, gives the user all rights to all subdirectories under the directory in which it was granted.

4. Every directory has a full set of rights in its IRM by default. When you change a directory's IRM, you do not affect the IRMs of any of that directory's subdirectories.

5. IRMs cannot add rights back for the user; the IRM can state only what rights are not allowed to flow from a parent directory.

Note NetWare security measures, from lowest to highest security, include the following:

◆ Log in name

◆ Password

◆ Directory rights

◆ File rights

◆ Directory attributes

◆ File attributes

If a file is flagged Read Only and the directory or the file has the Erase right, the file cannot be deleted until the Read Only file attribute is changed to Read/Write.

Table 4.2 lists the rights common to both NetWare 2.2 and 3.1x.

Table 4.2
Rights Common to NetWare 2.2 and 3.1x

Right	Function
Read	Enables the user to see the contents of a file and to use the file.
Write	Enables the user to alter the contents of a file.
Create	Enables the user to make new files and directories.
Erase	Enables the user to delete existing files and directories.
File Scan	Enables the user to view files and subdirectories in a directory; without this right, you cannot see files.
Modify	Enables the user to change the attributes of a file; the user can change a file from Read/Write to Read-Only or from Nonshareable to Shareable.

Right	Function
Access Control	Enables the user to give any of the preceding rights to other users on the network.

In NetWare 2.2, you still can see subdirectories, even if you are denied rights; 3.1*x* hides subdirectories from the user.

In NetWare 3.1*x*, Modify also enables the user to change the attributes for directories; 2.2 does not enable you to set attributes for directories.

NetWare 3.1*x* has an eighth right, Supervisory, which gives all the other rights to the user or group. This right makes the user a *directory Supervisor*—someone who has control over what happens to a directory structure's branch. NetWare 2.2 only has seven rights.

The following rights are available to users:

◆ **Read.** When assigned to a directory, Read enables the user to see the contents of the files in the directory. The user can use or execute files in the directory.

When assigned to a file, Read enables the user to see the contents of a closed file and to use or execute the file, even if the directory does not allow the Read privilege.

◆ **Write.** When assigned to a directory, Write enables the user to alter the contents of files in the directory.

When assigned to a file, Write enables the user to alter the contents of the file even when the Write privilege is not given to the directory.

In either case, the file must be flagged Read/Write for the Write privilege to have any effect.

269

♦ **Create.** When assigned to a directory, Create enables the user to make new files and directories.

When assigned to a file, Create enables the user to salvage the file if it has been deleted.

♦ **Erase.** When assigned to a directory, Erase enables the user to delete existing files and directories.

When assigned to a file, Erase allows the file to be deleted even if the directory does not have the Erase right.

Files flagged as Read Only cannot be erased until they are flagged Read/Write.

♦ **File Scan.** When assigned to the directory, File Scan enables the user to view files and subdirectories in a directory. Without this right, you cannot see files.

NetWare 3.1*x* hides subdirectories from the user when he does not possess this right.

When assigned to a file, File Scan enables the user to view the file by using DIR. If the user does not have File Scan rights to other files, these files do not appear when the DIR command is issued.

 If you grant the File Scan right to a file, users can see subdirectories all the way back to the root directory. They cannot see any files in these directories, however, unless they have rights to them.

♦ **Modify.** When assigned to the directory, Modify enables the user to change the attributes and names of subdirectories.

When assigned to a file, Modify enables the user to change the attributes and the name of a file. This right enables the user to change a file from Read/Write to Read Only or from Nonshareable to Shareable.

♦ **Access Control.** When assigned to the directory, Access Control enables the user to give any of the preceding rights to other users on the network.

When assigned to a file, Access Control enables the user to give any of the preceding rights to another network user.

> **Note** Access Control does not enable you to assign the Supervisory right. You must be the Supervisor, a Supervisor equivalent, or a workgroup manager with the Supervisory right to the directory in which rights are assigned.

◆ **Supervisory.** When assigned to a directory, Supervisory gives all the other rights to the user or group. This right makes the user a *directory Supervisor*, someone who has control over what happens to a branch of the directory structure.

When assigned to a file, Supervisory enables the user to have all rights to that file.

Combining IRMs and Trustee Rights

Now that you understand what trustee rights can accomplish and how the IRM affects the outcome of flow-through, the next step is to take a look at combining trustee rights and IRMs.

The following example uses this directory structure:

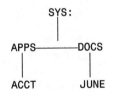

```
              SYS:
               |
   APPS————————DOCS
    |           |
   ACCT        JUNE
```

The following IRMs and rights have been assigned:

IRMs:

SYS:	[SRWCEMFA]
SYS:APPS	[SR F]

```
SYS:APPS\ACCT              [SRWCEMFA]

SYS:DOCS                   [SRWC  F ]

SYS:DOCS\JUNE              [SRWCE F ]
```

DAVE has the following rights:

```
SYS:APPS\ACCT              [ RWCE F ]

SYS:DOCS                   [S       ]
```

BEV has the following rights:

```
SYS:                       [ R    F ]

SYS:DOCS                   [ RWCEMFA]
```

PAULETTE has the following rights:

```
SYS:                       [S       ]
```

The following is a list of the rights of each user, based on the rules stated in the preceding section on IRMs.

DAVE

```
SYS:                       [        ]
                           Rule #1

SYS:APPS                   [        ]
                           Rule #1

SYS:APPS\ACCT              [ RWCE F ]
                           Rule #2

SYS:DOCS                   [SRWCEMFA]
                           Rule #3

SYS:DOCS\JUNE              [SRWCEMFA]
                           Rule #3
```

BEV

```
SYS:                       [ R    F ]
                           Rule #2

SYS:APPS                   [ R    F ]
                           Rule #1
```

```
    SYS:APPS\ACCT              [ R   F ]
                               Rule #5

    SYS:DOCS                   [ RWCEMFA]
                               Rule #2

    SYS:DOCS\JUNE              [ RWCE F ]
                               Rule #1
```

PAULETTE

```
    SYS:                       [SRWCEMFA]
                               Rule #3

    SYS:APPS                   [SRWCEMFA]
                               Rule #3

    SYS:APPS\ACCT              [SRWCEMFA]
                               Rule #3

    SYS:DOCS                   [SRWCEMFA]
                               Rule #3

    SYS:DOCS\JUNE              [SRWCEMFA]
                               Rule #3
```

Effective Rights

You can think of *directory rights* as locks that every directory has on your system. NetWare gives each directory a full set of locks by default.

Trustee rights act as keys that fit the directory locks. Each user can have his or her own set of unique keys. As an example, think of your own key ring. You have your own house key, car key, and so on. Chances are that no one has the same keys as you. Everyone has different locks that need to be opened. The same concept applies to networks. You have specific needs in directories. Some users have the same needs; others have different needs. Each user can have his or her own set of keys, or rights.

Calculate effective rights.

Effective rights are the trustee rights (keys) that actually match available directory rights (locks). If a lock exists and you do not have a key, you cannot perform the function. The only way you can use a right is to have matching locks and keys.

Trustee rights include all the rights you have been given individually, combined with all the rights given to any groups to which you belong, as well as any you have been granted through security equivalency.

Effective rights are the trustee rights' results after they have been filtered by the *Maximum Rights Mask* (MRM) in NetWare 2.2 or the *Inherited Rights Mask* (IRM) in NetWare 3.1*x*. See Chapter 10 for more information on MRM.

NetWare automatically calculates your effective rights. You can view those effective rights by using SYSCON, FILER, or the command-line command RIGHTS. However, even though NetWare can calculate the effective rights for you, you still need to know how to manually calculate those rights.

Calculate effective rights by first looking at the directory for which you are calculating the rights. Any rights granted to you at that directory level are your effective rights for that directory. Rights granted at levels above that specific directory are subject to being filtered through the IRM. For example, if you are granted rights to the directory called TEST in the following example, your effective rights in directory TESTFILES will be R (Read) and W (Write) because the IRM at directory FILES filters out those rights you were granted at the directory called TEST (see fig. 4.2).

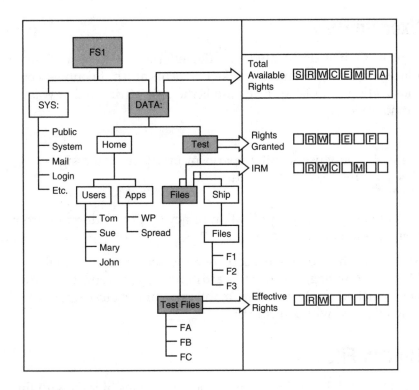

Figure 4.2
Effective Rights.

File Attributes

On the network, files are secured by the use of *attributes*, conditions placed on the files. These conditions help to control what can be done to the files and the ways in which the files can be used on the network. Many combinations of attributes are attached to files and directories. This section discusses NetWare attributes and how you can use them on your network.

Archive Needed

NetWare uses the letter A to signify files that have been altered since the last backup. The Archive Needed attribute also is assigned to files that have been copied into another directory. Archive Needed looks for the DOS Archive Bit flag on a file.

Execute Only

Execute Only is designated with the letter X. After this attribute is placed on a file, it cannot be taken off. This attribute only affects files ending in COM or EXE, and is the only attribute that you cannot reverse.

 Only users with Supervisor privileges can assign the Execute Only attribute.

Execute Only hinders application piracy by preventing files from being copied or downloaded.

Make sure that you have a copy of a file before you attach the Execute Only flag, because this attribute also prevents files from being backed up. In addition, many programs cannot operate when flagged with Execute Only.

Hidden File

The Hidden File attribute uses the letter H. Files hidden with this attribute do not show up when you use the DOS DIR command. If a user has the File Scan right, files hidden with this attribute appear after using NDIR.

Read Audit and Write Audit

NetWare is still in the process of perfecting a built-in audit trail on files. Currently, you can flag files with Ra for Read Audit and Wa for Write Audit, but they have no effect.

Read Only and Read/Write

You cannot write to, delete, or rename a read-only file. The Read Only attribute enables users to read and use files. Program files are most often flagged with Ro for read-only.

A Read/Write file attribute enables users to read from the file and write back to the file. This attribute is designated with Rw and is the default on newly created files. Flagging a file with Read Only deletes the Read/Write attribute. Data files are usually flagged with Read/Write.

When Read Only is used in NetWare 3.1*x*, the attributes of Delete Inhibit and Rename Inhibit also are included.

Shareable and Nonshareable

NetWare uses the letter S to designate shareable files. This attribute enables several users to access a single file at the same time. This flag is used most often with read-only files and database files.

Nonshareable, or Normal, is the system default. If you flag a file with N, you set the attributes as Nonshareable Read/Write. Nonshareable files normally are assigned to program files that are single-user applications. This attribute ensures that only one person can use the file at any one time.

System File

System files, flagged with Sy, are not listed after you use the DOS DIR command. These files cannot be deleted or copied. If you have the File Scan right, you can see these files by using the NDIR command.

Transactional

Files marked with T can be tracked using the *Transaction Tracking System* (TTS). TTS is a method the file server uses to track the integrity of database files during database file updates. For more information about TTS, see Chapter 10, "Understanding NetWare 2.2 System Manager Functions." All database files that need to be tracked while being modified must have this attribute.

Copy Inhibit

Marked as a C, Copy Inhibit prevents files from being copied to another directory. This attribute is used only with Macintosh files.

Delete Inhibit

The Delete Inhibit attribute is one half of the Read Only file designation. Rename Inhibit represents the other half of Read Only. The Delete Inhibit flag, marked as a D, prevents files from being deleted.

Rename Inhibit

Along with Delete Inhibit, Rename Inhibit is the second Read Only attribute. Marked as an R, Rename Inhibit prevents users from renaming files.

Purge

Purge uses the letter P to show files considered purged when deleted. If you mark a file with the P flag, you ensure that it cannot be restored after it is deleted.

Using Directory Attributes

You also can use attributes on directories. The attributes discussed in the following sections can be used on directories in NetWare.

Hidden Directory

The Hidden Directory attribute uses the letter H. Directories hidden with this attribute do not show up when you use the DOS DIR command. If a user has the File Scan right, files hidden with this attribute appear.

System Directory

System directories, designated with Sy, are hidden from the DOS DIR command. These directories cannot be deleted or copied. If a user has the File Scan right, these directories appear when using the NDIR utility.

Purge Directory

This attribute uses the letter P to show directories in which all files are considered purged when deleted. This flag ensures that after the directory is deleted, no files in the directory can be restored.

Section Review Questions

7. Which is NOT a level of NetWare security?

    a. Login/Password

    b. File server

    c. Menus

    d. Attributes

8. Which is the correct order of NetWare security from highest to lowest?

    a. File server, rights, attributes, password

    b. File server, attributes, rights, password

    c. Attributes, rights, password, file server

    d. Password, attributes, rights, file server

9. Which rights are necessary to use an executable file?

    a. Read, Write, and File Scan

    b. Read and File Scan

    c. Read

    d. Read and Access Control

10. Which right enables you to assign the Shareable attribute to a file?

    a. Access Control

    b. Access Control and Modify

    c. Modify

    d. File Scan and Modify

11. Effective rights include:

    a. All the rights you have, plus the rights of any groups to which you belong

    b. All of the rights assigned to your user account

    c. The rights assigned to the Supervisor

    d. All of your rights, minus the rights of any group to which you belong

12. Which attribute enables you to change the contents of a file?

    a. Modify

    b. Access Control

    c. Read/Write

    d. Read Audit

13. Which of the following is NOT a feature of NetWare 3.1x Security?

    a. Trustee rights

    b. File rights

    c. Directory attributes

    d. Maximum Rights Mask

14. Which statement about rights is incorrect?

    a. The C right enables you to create files and directories.

    b. The C right enables you to salvage a file.

    c. The M right enables you to rename a directory.

    d. The A right enables you to change a file from Ro to Rw.

15. Which of the following is the only attribute that CANNOT be revoked after it is granted?

    a. X

    b. H

    c. E

    d. SY

16. Which statement about attributes is false?

    a. The A attribute is assigned to files that are new or have just been copied to a new directory.

    b. Ra and Wa are not currently being used.

    c. Workgroup managers can assign the X attribute if they have the S right.

    d. C is used only with Macintosh.

17. To make sure that files are removed from the file server's disk when they are deleted, place this flag on the file or directory.

    a. P

    b. C

    c. M

    d. X

Answers

7. c

8. b

9. b

10. d

11. a

12. c

13. d

14. d

15. a

16. c

17. a

Using Command-Line Security Utilities

This section discusses the command-line utilities available in NetWare that Administrators and managers can use to implement security by manipulating user accounts. Command-line utilities are used from the DOS prompt.

The RIGHTS Command

The RIGHTS command shows the user which rights he or she has in any given directory. If you seem to have more rights in one directory than you were granted originally, then rights have flowed down from a higher directory. This event is referred to as flow-through. *Flow-through* automatically occurs to all subdirectories beneath the directory in which rights have been granted.

The following syntax is used for the RIGHTS command:

```
RIGHTS path
```

In the example shown in figure 4.3, the RIGHTS command is entered from the O prompt to see the available rights in that directory.

```
O:\OFFICE>rights
B386\SYS:OFFICE
Your Effective Rights for this directory are [SRWCEMFA]
      You have Supervisor Rights to Directory.    (S)
    * May Read from File.                          (R)
    * May Write to File.                           (W)
      May Create Subdirectories and Files.         (C)
      May Erase Directory.                         (E)
      May Modify Directory.                        (M)
      May Scan for Files.                          (F)
      May Change Access Control.                   (A)

  * Has no effect on directory.

      Entries in Directory May Inherit [SRWCEMFA] rights.
      You have ALL RIGHTS to Directory Entry.

O:\OFFICE>
```

Figure 4.3

The RIGHTS command lists and explains each available right.

The TLIST Command

The TLIST command displays the users that have been given explicit rights in a specific directory. Flow-through does not occur in TLIST. The TLIST command is typed in the following manner:

TLIST *path*

In figure 4.4, the TLIST command shows that the user DBATEMAN and the group TECHS have all rights except Supervisory.

```
O:\OFFICE>tlist

B386\SYS:OFFICE
User trustees:
  DBATEMAN                                  [ RWCEMFA]
  _____
Group trustees:
  TECHS                                     [ RWCEMFA]

O:\OFFICE>
```

Figure 4.4

TLIST displays the rights granted to users and groups.

The GRANT Command

The GRANT command grants rights to users or groups. You also can use menu items in the User Information menu in SYSCON to grant rights. Any information changed by using the GRANT command is permanent and appears in the user's trustee information screens in SYSCON. The GRANT command is typed in the following manner:

GRANT *rightslist* [FOR *path*] TO [USER¦GROUP] *name*

In figure 4.5, for example, the user DBATEMAN requests Read and File Scan rights in the SYS:SERVICE directory. The Supervisor uses the GRANT command and a shortcut to give him the rights. Instead of spelling out the full path name, the system needs only the drive letter that points to the proper path. The TLIST command is used after GRANT to verify that the rights are granted.

Figure 4.5

The GRANT command gives rights to a user for a specific directory.

```
O:\SERVICE>grant r f for o: to dbateman

B386/SYS:SERVICE
SERVICE                              Rights set to [ R    F ]


O:\SERVICE>tlist

B386\SYS:SERVICE
User trustees:
   BACKUP                                        [ R    F ]
   DBATEMAN                                      [ R    F ]
   ────────
Group trustees:
   ACCOUNTING                                    [ RWCEMFA]

O:\SERVICE>
```

The REVOKE Command

The REVOKE command takes away rights from a user in either directories or files. REVOKE uses the following syntax:

REVOKE *rightslist* [FOR *path*] FROM [USER¦GROUP] *name*

Figure 4.6, for example, shows that the user DBATEMAN has more rights than necessary in the SYS:PUBLIC directory. The excess rights are removed by using the REVOKE command; the TLIST command is used to verify the process.

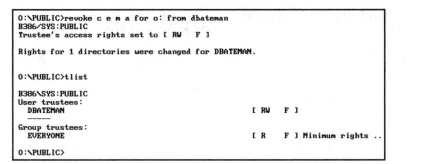

```
O:\PUBLIC>revoke c e m a for o: from dbateman
B386/SYS:PUBLIC
Trustee's access rights set to [ RW   F ]

Rights for 1 directories were changed for DBATEMAN.


O:\PUBLIC>tlist

B386\SYS:PUBLIC
User trustees:
  DBATEMAN                                  [ RW   F ]
  --------
Group trustees:
  EVERYONE                                  [ R    F ] Minimum rights ..

O:\PUBLIC>
```

Figure 4.6

The REVOKE command is used to deny rights from a user for a specific directory.

The REMOVE Command

The REMOVE command removes the user from the trustee list. REMOVE uses the following syntax:

    REMOVE [USER¦GROUP] *name* [FROM *path*]

In figure 4.7, the user DBATEMAN is removed from the O directory by using the REMOVE command. The TLIST command then confirms the results.

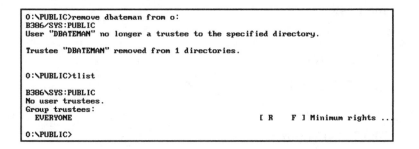

```
O:\PUBLIC>remove dbateman from o:
B386/SYS:PUBLIC
User "DBATEMAN" no longer a trustee to the specified directory.

Trustee "DBATEMAN" removed from 1 directories.


O:\PUBLIC>tlist

B386\SYS:PUBLIC
No user trustees.
Group trustees:
  EVERYONE                                  [ R    F ] Minimum rights ...

O:\PUBLIC>
```

Figure 4.7

The REMOVE command is used to remove a user from a trustee list.

285

Section Review Questions

18. Which command-line utility shows the effective rights of a user?

    a. RIGHTS

    b. TLIST

    c. GRANT

    d. ERIGHTS

19. Which statement takes the Access Control and Modify rights away from the user JOE for the file called DATA.FIL?

    a. REMOVE JOE FROM DATA.FIL

    b. REVOKE A M FOR JOE FROM DATA.FIL

    c. REMOVE A M FOR DATA.FIL FROM JOE

    d. REVOKE A M FOR DATA.FIL FROM JOE

20. Which of the following does NOT display the proper command syntax

    a. RIGHTS path

    b. GRANT path

    c. TLIST path

    d. None of the above

21. The TLIST command:

    a. Displays users with explicit rights in a given directory

    b. Transfers rights to a user or group

    c. Cannot be used to view a user's rights

    d. None of the above

22. Which of the following commands requires that the list of rights be included?

    a. RIGHTS

    b. TLIST

    c. REMOVE

    d. GRANT

23. To take rights away from a user, issue the following command:

    a. `REMOVE [user]` *name* `[FROM` *path*`]`

    b. `REMOVE [rights]`

    c. `REVOKE [username]` `[`*rightslist*`]`

    d. `REVOKE` *rightslist* `[FOR` *path*`] FROM [user]` *name*

24. Which of the following statements is true?

    a. The REVOKE command can be used to take away a list of specific rights from either a user or a group.

    b. TLIST cannot display the new rights for a user until he or she exits SYSCON and restarts this command-line utility.

    c. If you seem to have more rights in a directory than you were originally granted, rights have flowed down from another directory.

    d. None of the above statements are true.

25. Regarding the statement "REMOVE or REVOKE can be used interchangeably:"

    a. This is a true statement.

    b. This statement is only true for users, not groups.

    c. Both commands have a net effect of changing the user's rights to a given directory.

    d. Both commands are menu-based utilities that allow the Supervisor to change a user or group rights.

Answers

18. a

19. d

20. b

21. a

22. d

23. d

24. c

25. c

Making Trustee Assignments

Trustees can be either users or groups. A trustee may be assigned to directories or to files. Once a user or group becomes a trustee, access rights are assigned for the directories or files to which they were assigned as a trustee.

There is more than one way to receive rights. Rights can be granted to a user directly, or might be given to a user from a direct trustee assignment. Rights also can be passed along to a user because of their membership in a group that has been given trustee rights to directories or files. In addition, a user can gain rights through a security equivalence.

Users with Supervisor or Supervisor-equivalent rights can grant rights to other users. When implementing and managing file system security needs to be easy, the best method to use when granting rights is to assign the trustee rights to a group; those users who should be given trustee rights are thus put into that group.

The previous section discussed command-line commands that can be used to give rights to a user or a group. Both SYSCON and FILER—NetWare menu utilities—can also be used to assign or delete trustees.

Make a trustee assignment and apply rights in
SYSCON and FILER.

To make a user a trustee of a directory or file, run SYSCON.
Choose User Information from the Available Topics menu, then
choose the user to be made a trustee. Next, choose either Trustee
Directory Assignments or Trustee File Assignments from the User
Information menu.

If you select the Trustee Directory Assignments option in the User
Information menu, you can grant rights to the user you chose as a
trustee. To add rights, press Ins and enter the full path name, or
press Ins again to select the path. Grant rights by pressing Ins and
choosing the rights that you want to grant.

You can also modify the rights assignments on any directory by
completing the following steps:

1. Press Enter on the directory whose trustee rights you want
   to change.

2. When the list of trustee rights granted appears, press Ins to
   see the list of trustee rights that have not been granted.

3. Press F5 to mark each right that you want to grant to the
   user, then press Enter. (To delete marked rights, press Del
   rather than Enter.)

Press Esc to return to the new rights. The list then is updated in
the Trustee Directory Assignments window. Figure 4.8 shows the
screens for modifying trustee directory rights.

Trustees can also be assigned using the FILER program. To grant a
trustee assignment using this method, type **FILER** at the DOS
prompt to open the FILER utility. Change to the directory that is
to have a trustee assignment. Then return to the Available Topics
Menu and choose Current Directory Information. When the
Directory Information screen opens, choose Trustees. From the
Trustee Name screen, press Ins to see a list of available users and
groups. Choose the user or group to whom you want to grant
trustee rights for this directory. You can then modify that user's or

group's rights by choosing the user or group name from the Trustee Name list, then pressing Ins and choosing the rights to be granted. Both File Scan and Read From File rights are granted automatically.

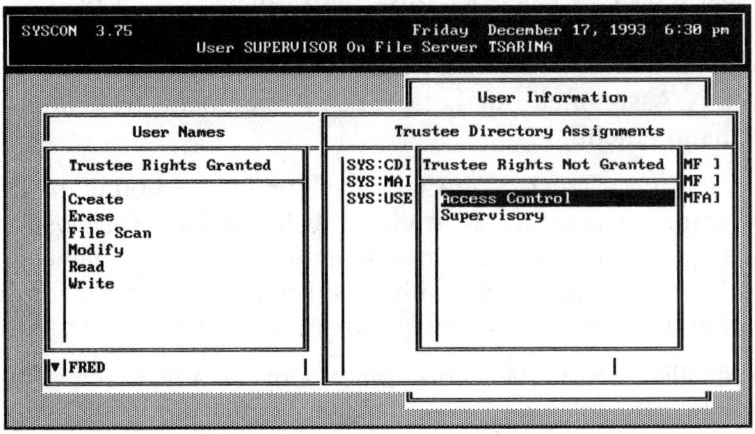

Figure 4.8

Screens for Granting Trustee Rights Using SYSCON.

Section Review Questions

26. Which of the following statements about trustees is false?

    a. Trustees can be either users or groups.

    b. Users with Supervisor or equivalent rights can make trustee assignments.

    c. SYSCON and FILER can be used to make a trustee assignment and apply rights.

    d. None of the above statements about trustees are false.

27. Rights can be given using all except:

    a. FILER

    b. TLIST

    c. SYSCON

    d. GRANT

28. One of the best ways to simplify system security is to:

   a. Give Supervisor equivalency to all users and groups

   b. Give all rights except Supervisor and Access Control to groups

   c. Assign trustee rights to groups, then put the appropriate users into those groups

   d. There is no best method for granting rights in order to simplify the process

29. Which is NOT a way that a user can receive rights?

   a. Granting rights directly to the user

   b. Making the user a Supervisor equivalent

   c. Putting the user into a group that has no rights

   d. Granting rights to a group to which the user belongs

30. The proper function key to use in order to mark multiple rights to be granted is:

   a. F5

   b. F1

   c. F3

   d. Ins

Answers

26. d

27. b

28. c

29. c

30. a

Understanding NCP Packet Signature

The server and the client on a NetWare network communicate by sending packets back and forth between them. A *packet* contains the data or request for a network service, as well as information that identifies such things as the following:

◆ Where the packet originated

◆ Where the packet is to be delivered

◆ Information that authenticates the user to the network

Identifying the client and its right to access the network services or information being requested is an important aspect of each packet. It provides a certain level of network security. In the fall of 1992, however, students working in a laboratory at Lieden University in the Netherlands discovered a way to defeat this security. Using a very complex procedure, they were able to forge a packet's identification, giving a client greater security privileges than originally authorized.

This problem, however, is not just a NetWare problem. All networking products have the same problem inherent in their design. To correct the problem in NetWare, Novell developed a security enhancement. This enhancement became an operating system component for NetWare 3.12 shortly after the problem was discovered. The enhancement is called *NCP Packet Signature*.

 Describe NCP Packet Signature.

The NCP Packet Signature Process

To remedy this security problem, Novell developed a process of identifying packets. If the set level of NCP packet signature requires it, when a client logs into a NetWare 3.12 server, the server and client agree upon a single, shared identification key called the *session key*. Each client that logs into the server has a unique session key.

After the client is logged into the server, the client adds its unique signature to the packet each time the client requests services. The server checks the packet signature to ensure its correctness for this client. Correctly signed packets are processed.

Packets without the correct signature, or with no signature at all, are discarded. The server console then reports the offending client by placing an alert message in the server error log and then reporting it to the server console.

The client is notified that an error occurred during server attachment, but is not warned or told the type of error or reason for it. This distinction also provides a certain amount of security. If someone at the client is trying to gain greater security rights than he or she is permitted, the server does not tell the client that an illegal request is being made.

Figure 4.9 shows the NCP Packet Signature process from client to server.

NCP Packet Signature Security Levels

The NCP packet signature enables the network Administrator to determine the level of security implementation on the network. Although many networking sites need the highest level of security provided by the NCP packet signature process, not all networks require as high a level of security.

Identify the performance implications associated with the NCP Packet Signature.

293

Figure 4.9

The NCP Packet
Signature process.

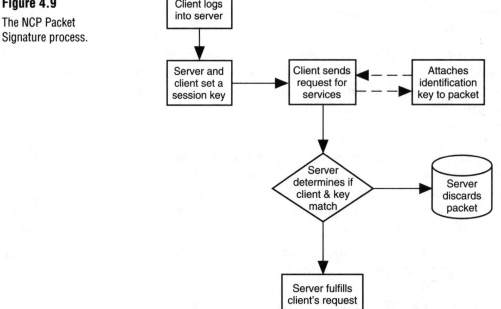

Because network performance is affected to a certain extent by the NCP packet signature process, network Administrators might want to adjust the level of NCP packet signature used on their network.

Consider the following example. In a network on which a single server can contain highly sensitive information, such as patient health records in a medical facility, the NCP packet signature can be set at the highest level—level 3—at the server and at each client.

At server level 3, all packets sent from the server contain an NCP packet signature. This level requires that all packets received by the server from clients be correctly signed.

At client level 3, all packets are signed before they are sent to the server. This level requires that anything received by the client from the server be correctly signed.

Network Administrators set the level of NCP packet signature security by choosing from one of four levels at both the server and the client. Each combination of client and server level settings affects the overall security of packets on the network.

Table 4.3 lists the security levels available for clients and servers and shows the net effect that each combination of server and client level settings has on the network's overall security. The default is marked with an asterisk (*).

Table 4.3
NCP Packet Signature Levels

Server Level	Effect on Server +	Client Level	Effect on Client =	Effective Level
0	Packets not signed	0	Packets not signed	No packet signature
0	Packets not signed	1	Signed if server asks	No packet signature
0	Packets not signed	2	Signs if server can sign	No packet signature
0	Packets not signed	3	Always signs and requires server to sign	Failed login
1	Signs only if client asks	0	Packets not signed	No packet signature
1	Signs only if client asks	1	Signed if server asks	No packet signature
1	Signs only if client asks	2	Signs if server can sign	Packet signature
1	Signs only if client asks	3	Always signs and requires server to sign	Packet signature
2	Signs if client can	0	Packets not signed	No packet signature

continues

295

Table 4.3, Continued
NCP Packet Signature Levels

Server Level	Effect on Server +	Client Level	Effect on Client =	Effective Level
2*	Signs if client can	1*	Signed if server asks	Packet signature
2	Signs if client can	2	Signs if server can	Packet signature
2	Signs if client can	3	Always signs and requires server to sign	Packet signature
3	Always signs and requires client to sign	0	Packets not signed	No packet signature
3	Always signs and requires client to sign	1	Signed if server asks	Packet signature
3	Always signs and requires client to sign	2	Signs if server can sign	Packet signature
3	Always signs and requires client to sign	3	Always signs and requires server to sign	Packet Signature

After the network Administrator has determined the level of packet security needed, he or she must then set that level on each affected server and client. If the default settings of level 2 for the server and level 1 for each client is sufficient, the network Administrator does not need to change these levels. If changes are warranted, however, or if the network Administrator decides that no packet signing is necessary, he or she can make changes to the appropriate server and client files.

Change or Disable Packet Signing

NCP packet signature levels are set at both the server and the client. As previously noted, level 2 is the default setting for the server, and level 1 is the default setting for each client. You can, however, modify both settings.

To change the server's default packet signature setting, type the following statement at the server console and press Enter, or edit the server's AUTOEXEC.NCF file to include the following statement:

```
SET NCP PACKET SIGNATURE OPTION = number
```

If you add the statement to the server's AUTOEXEC.NCF file, it does not take effect until the next time that the AUTOEXEC.NCF file is run, at server startup.

Figure 4.10 shows a server's AUTOEXEC.NCF file with the SET NCP PACKET SIGNATURE OPTION line included.

```
NetWare Server Installation V3.12          NetWare 386 Loadable Module

  Inst              File Server STARTUP.NCF File

  Dis  load ISADISK port=1F0 int=E
  Vo   SET NCP PACKET SIGNATURE OPTION = 3
  Sy
  Pr
  Ex




          Edit the file as needed.  Press <ESCAPE> when done.
```

Figure 4.10

Server AUTOEXEC.NCF file with the NCP Packet Option line.

To change a client's default packet signature, modify the client's NET.CFG file to add the following statement as an indented line under the NetWare DOS Requester heading:

```
SIGNATURE LEVEL = number
```

297

Like the AUTOEXEC.NCF file, the change to the NET.CFG file does not take effect until the NET.CFG file is reloaded at client bootup.

Figure 4.11 shows a client's NET.CFG file with the SIGNATURE LEVEL line included.

Figure 4.11

Client NET.CFG file with the Signature Level line.

```
[RUBY_1] C:\>TYPE NET.CFG
Link driver NE2000
    INT 5
    PORT 340
    MEM D0000
    FRAME Ethernet_802.3

Netware DOS Requester
    FIRST NETWORK DRIVE = F
    PREFERRED SERVER = JOHN
    SIGNATURE LEVEL = 1
    SHOW DOTS = ON
    VLM = NMR.VLM

Protocol IPX
        IPX SOCKETS 45
[RUBY_1] C:\>
```

Section Review Questions

31. Which of the following is the correct name for the NetWare security enhancement that prevents packet forgery?

    a. NCP Packet Signature

    b. NCP Packet Signing Process

    c. NCP Security Packet Process

    d. NCP Security Packet Signing Process

32. Where should security level be assigned in order to prevent packet forgery?

    a. At the file server only

    b. At the client only

    c. At all file servers and clients

    d. At only file servers and clients that need it

33. How many effective levels of security can the network Administrator set?

    a. 1

    b. 4

    c. 8

    d. 16

34. What is the default setting for packet security?

    a. Server 1, Client 2

    b. Server 2, Client 1

    c. Server 2, Client 2

    d. No default setting exists

35. Which packet security levels should the network Administrator set if the server contains sensitive information, such as patient files?

    a. Server 1, Client 3

    b. Server 3, Client 1

    c. Server 2, Client 1

    d. Server 3, Client 3

36. What security levels should the network Administrator set if the server contains some sensitive information, but users share clients for accessing that information?

    a. Server 1, Client 3

    b. Server 2, Client 2

    c. Server 3, Client 1

    d. Server 3, Client 3

Answers

31. a

32. d

33. d

34. b

35. d

36. c

Case Study

1. Refer back to the directory structure you created in Chapter 3. Assign security to the directory structure, keeping the following points in mind.

   ◆ BD and KMURPHY are the only users permitted into the accounting package.

   ◆ MYERS is the only Supervisor equivalent, but wants GDALL and KMURPHY to be able to create and assign rights for future personnel.

   ◆ TERESA needs access to run all programs, but not to modify the programs. She needs the ability to change data for all programs except payroll.

   ◆ GDALL only needs access to the Inventory and Name and Address databases.

   ◆ All users need to print, but MYERS needs to control the print server.

2. Program files need to be protected from deletion.

   ◆ By using the preceding information, determine the user type for the following users. Decide who should be Supervisor equivalent users, workgroup managers, or network users:

BD, the owner
MYERS, the System Administrator
KMURPHY, the controller
GDALL, the quality control Supervisor
TERESA, the administrative assistant

◆ Using the following chart, determine the rights each user needs in each directory.

	Directories	BD	MYERS	KMURPHY	GDALL	TERESA	Attributes
NetWare	SYS: Mail						
	SYS: Public						
	SYS: Mail \ Mail_ID						
Applications							

3. Using the directory structure, IRM assignments, rights assignments, and attribute assignments previously described, answer the following questions.

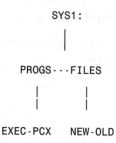

```
              SYS1:
                |
                |
         PROGS---FILES
            |       |
            |       |

        EXEC-PCX   NEW-OLD
```

IRM Assignments:

```
SYS1:                    [S      ]
SYS1:PROGS               [SR   F ]
SYS1:FILES               [SRWC F ]
SYS1:FILES\NEW           [SRWCE F ]
SYS1:FILES\OLD           [SR   F ]
```

TRUSTEE Assignments:

CHRIS

```
SYS1:                    [S      ]
```

JOE

```
SYS1:FILES               [ R    F ]
SYS1:PROGS               [ RWCEMFA]
```

TERESA

```
SYS1:FILES               [ RWCEMFA]
SYS1:FILES\OLD           [ R  E F ]
```

ATTRIBUTE Assignments:

SYS1:PROGS has been flagged DI and RI

♦ Fill in the following form, listing each user's effective rights in each directory.

	Sys1:	Sys1:Prog	Sys1:Prog/Exec	Sys1:Prog/PCX	Sys1:Files	Sys1:Files/New	Sys1:Files/Old
Chris							
Joe							
Teresa							

◆ Who can delete files from the SYS1:PROGS directory? The SYS1:PROGS\PCX directory? The SYS1:FILES\OLD directory?

Working with User Utilities

This chapter teaches you about the menu utilities NetWare offers to help you manage the network. These utilities include the following:

- ◆ SYSCON
- ◆ ATOTAL and PAUDIT
- ◆ FILER
- ◆ MAKEUSER and USERDEF
- ◆ SBACKUP
- ◆ SESSION
- ◆ WSUPDATE

In this chapter, you examine all the options in the menu utilities in the preceding list. You also discover how to create a MAKEUSER script and use USERDEF to make a script. In addition, you learn about the utilities associated with the Accounting option of SYSCON, and become familiar with backing up files by using the SBACKUP Utility.

Navigating the Menus

Before you learn the different menus and submenus of the utilities, you need to become familiar with the keys that enable you to navigate the various menus in the utilities. Following is a list of these keys:

◆ **Enter**—Moves you to the next level in the menu or accepts an item from the list.

◆ **Esc**—Takes you back to a previous level or stops the selecting process.

◆ **F1**—Shows you the definition of a highlighted item.

◆ **F1,F1**—Shows you a list of function key definitions.

◆ **F3**—Enables you to change the name of the object or path when the object or path is highlighted.

◆ **F5**—Enables you to select multiple items from a list, then press Enter to bring the selected item into the current list. When you select an item, the item blinks on-screen. To deselect an item, press F5 again.

◆ **F6**—Enables you to mark a pattern of items.

◆ **F7**—Enables you to unmark all marked items.

◆ **F8**—Enables you to unmark a pattern of items.

When you select or mark an item, NetWare places a marker on the object, causing it to blink. You then can delete or copy marked items. Some of these keys do not work in all menu items. F6, F7, and F8, for example, work best in FILER (discussed later in this chapter), but do not work in SYSCON (discussed in the next section).

Other ways to select an item in a list include highlighting the desired item by pressing the up or down arrow keys, or typing the name of the item. Repeat this process until the desired item is highlighted.

When you are in a menu that contains a list of many items, you can go directly to the item you want by typing in one letter at a time. If you want to go to a group called SUPERS, for example, simply type the letter **S**. If no other group exists with the letter S, you go directly to SUPERS. If, on the other hand, a group called SALES exists, you would jump to SALES. In this case, you need to type **SU** to go to SUPERS.

Exploring SYSCON

This section discusses the role of SYSCON. The SYSCON menu, which stands for SYStem CONfiguration, enables you to set up NetWare's accounting feature, change to a different file server, check file server information, create groups, perform administrative network functions, and create users. These functions are set up by using the options listed in the Available Topics menu, as shown in figure 5.1. Each option is described in more detail in the following sections.

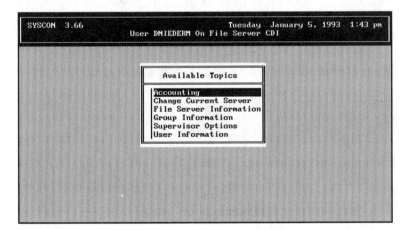

Figure 5.1

The Available Topics menu in SYSCON.

The SYSCON Accounting Option

The first option on the SYSCON menu is Accounting. The Accounting option enables you to charge users for use of the network, based on the following five areas:

◆ Blocks read

◆ Blocks written

◆ Connect time

◆ Disk storage

◆ Service requests

Large installations can cover several departments. In many businesses that have networks, departments must pay for part of the network. NetWare's accounting feature enables the System Administrator to charge each department for its portion of the total network usage. Users in each department are charged only for what they do on the network.

To set up accounting on your network, you need to decide which charge rates you want to use and in what combinations. These areas, which appear on-screen on the Accounting menu (see fig. 5.2), can be joined in any combination to charge different users. NetWare automatically tracks user logins and logouts.

Figure 5.2

Accounting options in the SYSCON menu.

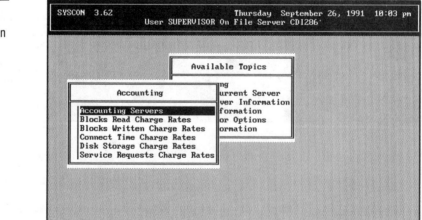

Note The accounting information is stored in SYS:SYSTEM in a file named NET$ACCT.DAT.

Each Accounting option is described in the following list:

◆ **Blocks Read Charge Rates.** This option determines the amount of information users request from the file server. Users are charged for each block of information read from the file server. A *block* is the minimum size of a piece of information that NetWare can read and write. The default block size in NetWare is 4 KB. When you select this option, the Blocks Read Charge Rates screen appears (see fig. 5.3). This screen enables Administrators to configure the accounting charge rates.

```
 SYSCON   3.68                      Tuesday  January 5, 1993   3:11 pm
                      User SUPERVISOR On File Server B386

                                      Sun   Mon   Tue   Wed   Thu   Fri   Sat
         Blocks Read Charge Rates   8:00am   1     1     1     1     1     1     1
                                    8:30am   1     1     1     1     1     1     1
                                    9:00am   1     1     1     1     1     1     1
 Sunday                             9:30am   1     1     1     1     1     1     1
 8:00 am To 8:29 am                10:00am   1     1     1     1     1     1     1
                                   10:30am   1     1     1     1     1     1     1
 Rate   Charge      Rate   Charge  11:00am   1     1     1     1     1     1     1
  1   No Charge      11             11:30am   1     1     1     1     1     1     1
  2                  12             12:00pm   1     1     1     1     1     1     1
  3                  13             12:30pm   1     1     1     1     1     1     1
  4                  14              1:00pm   1     1     1     1     1     1     1
  5                  15              1:30pm   1     1     1     1     1     1     1
  6                  16              2:00pm   1     1     1     1     1     1     1
  7                  17              2:30pm   1     1     1     1     1     1     1
  8                  18              3:00pm   1     1     1     1     1     1     1
  9                  19              3:30pm   1     1     1     1     1     1     1
 10                  20              4:00pm   1     1     1     1     1     1     1
         (Charge is per block)       4:30pm   1     1     1     1     1     1     1
```

Figure 5.3

An example of the Blocks Read Charge Rates screen.

◆ **Blocks Written Charge Rates.** This option determines the amount of information being written back to the file server. Users are charged for each full block of information written to the server.

◆ **Connect Time Charge Rates.** This option determines the amount of time a user is logged in to the network. Users are charged for each minute they are attached to the network.

◆ **Disk Storage Charge Rates.** This option determines the amount of disk space each user takes up on the file server. Users are charged for space occupied by files they own.

◆ **Service Requests Charge Rates.** This option determines the amount of network traffic a user generates. Users are charged for each request they make to the file server.

Setting Up a Network Account

When you set up accounting on your network, the *charge rates* specify the amount each user's account is to be debited when using the network. A charge rate appears as a fractional number, such as 1/4. The *multiplier*, or top portion of the fraction, specifies the amount of monetary units debited against an account. The *divisor*, or lower portion of the fraction, determines the number of units that must accumulate before the charge is made. The most common unit of measure is one cent.

A charge of 1/4, for example, means that one cent is charged for every four units of measure. A unit of measure can equal one minute, one read, one write, one server request, or one block of disk storage.

Before you set the charge rates, you need to know the times during the week that you want to use those rates. You might, for example, want to charge different rates for different days of the week. NetWare enables you to set different rates for different times and different days. When you select a charge rate from the Accounting menu, a grid appears that divides each day, including Saturday and Sunday, into half-hour increments (see fig. 5.3). Each increment has a number that corresponds to the Rate column in the lower left corner of the screen. The numbers in the Rate column, in turn, correspond to the rate shown in the Charge column. Each half hour on the grid is set to charge rate number 1 (no-charge rate) by default. To see the times before 8:00 a.m. and after 4:30 p.m., use the up and down arrows and the PgUp and PgDn keys to scroll the screen.

To change the charge rate of a particular time, highlight the desired time or block of time and press Enter. To highlight a block of time, use the cursor arrows to move the cursor to the desired time and press F5. This action marks the upper left corner of the time you want to change. Next, use the right- and down-arrow keys to position the lower right corner of the highlight box. This action highlights the block of time that you want to set. Press Enter and a menu appears that enables you to define the charge rate. You can establish up to 20 charge rates by using this method of blocking time periods (see fig. 5.4 and fig. 5.5).

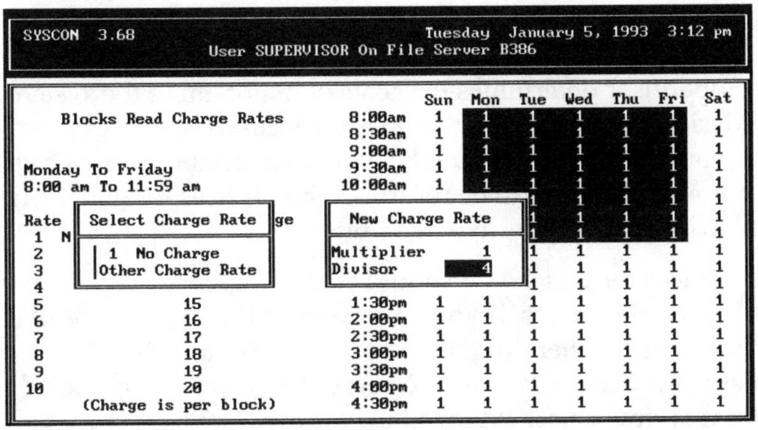

Figure 5.4

Creating a new charge rate.

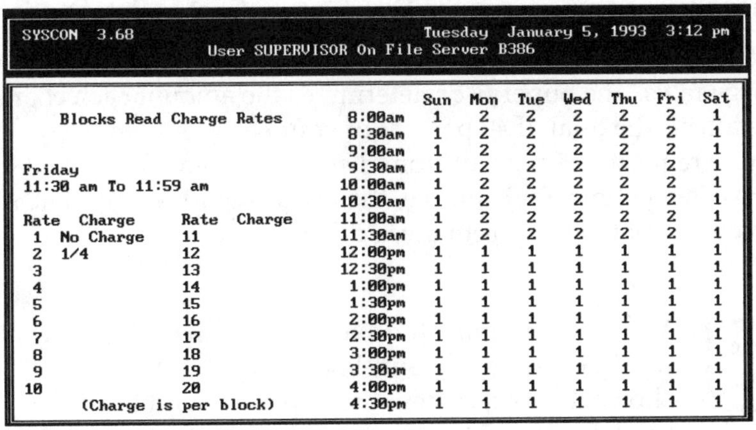

Figure 5.5

Viewing multiple charge rates.

Figure 5.4 shows a block of time marked using F5 (from Monday 8:00 a.m. to Friday 11:30 a.m.). The Select Charge Rates screen appears. To choose another charge rate, select the Other Charge Rates option and press Enter. The New Charge Rate screen appears. NetWare prompts you for the multiplier and divisor. This formula becomes the charge rate. After you enter the charge rate, press Esc to save your entries. In the example shown in figure 5.4, the charge rate is set to one monetary unit for four network usage units used. Figure 5.5 shows that the time period marked in figure 5.4 is now set to a charge rate of two, which is set to 1/4.

Determining Charge Rates

The Supervisor determines the costs of maintaining the system and decides how much to charge for system usage. To determine what your charge rate should be, you must establish three factors: the amount of dollars to be returned, the services for which you want to charge, and the average units used.

The services for which you should charge depend on the way you want to monitor users. If you are concerned with the amount of traffic a user is generating, then you should charge for the service by using the Service Requests Charge Rates option. To track the amount of time a user is logged in, use the Connect Time Charge Rates option. If you want to determine the amount of hard drive space a user occupies, use the Disk Storage Charge Rates option.

NetWare also enables you to charge for combinations of the five charge rates. The Supervisor determines the amount each charge rate affects the total. If 40 percent of your charges stem from service requests, 35 percent from disk storage, and 25 percent from connect time, for example, then you should recoup that percentage of the total from these different areas.

 Note You can determine the average units used by using the ATOTAL command-line utility. ATOTAL shows the total system usage per day and for the week (see fig. 5.6). You should run Accounting for

three to four weeks after you set the ratios as 1:1 in
the services for which you are planning to charge.
The one-to-one ratio gives an accurate usage accounting.

```
      Blocks read:           0   Blocks written:         0
      Blocks days:           0

Totals for week:
      Connect time:        386   Server requests:      109
      Blocks read:           0   Blocks written:         0
      Blocks days:           0

01/04/1993:
      Connect time:        145   Server requests:     4625
      Blocks read:         423   Blocks written:         0
      Blocks days:           0

01/05/1993:
      Connect time:        400   Server requests:     2745
      Blocks read:         230   Blocks written:         0
      Blocks days:           0

Totals for week:
      Connect time:        545   Server requests:     7370
      Blocks read:         653   Blocks written:         0
      Blocks days:           0

F:\SYSTEM>
```

Figure 5.6

An example of
ATOTAL results.

Note Run ATOTAL from the SYS:SYSTEM directory;
ATOTAL does not require any command-line
switches.

An ATOTAL report can be lengthy if Accounting has been installed for a long time. The output can be redirected to a printer or
to a file to be printed at another time. Redirect the printout by
means of the DOS > command. To redirect the output to a file
called ACCT.RPT, for example, type the following statement at
the SYS:SYSTEM directory:

```
ATOTAL > ACCT.RPT.
```

Note Accounting information is kept in a file called
NET$ACCT.DAT. This file grows automatically as
data accumulates. NetWare enables you to delete
the data in this file; however, as the accounting
program gathers new information, this file is re-
created.

continues

The second file associated with accounting in
NetWare is NET$REC.DAT. This file translates the
compressed binary information kept in the
NET$ACCT.DAT file. Do not delete this file.

After determining the factors for accounting and running the
ATOTAL command for several weeks, replace the 1:1 ratio with a
ratio that enables you to calculate accounting charges for each
user. To determine what your new ratio should be, use the following formula:

Amount to charge for total system use per week

Estimated average amount of charge used per week

You might, for example, want to receive $600 per week for the
time twenty users spend logged in to the network. All twenty
users work 40 hours a week. In NetWare, the connect time is
calculated in minutes that a user is logged in to the network. In
this case, 40 hours is 2,400 minutes. Multiply the minutes by the
number of users (2,400 x 20) to get the number of minutes on the
network per week (48,000 minutes) for the twenty users.

You now need to calculate the amount of money you want to
charge each user. In this case, the unit of measure is one cent. To
recoup or get back the $600 per week for the use of the network,
calculate the number of pennies in $600, which is 60,000. This
makes the numerator 60,000, or the amount to be charged for total
system use per week. The ratio before reducing is 60000/48000
(60000 for the charge rate and 48000 for the minutes used on the
network). Reduced, this ratio is 5/4, or five cents charged for
every four minutes a user is logged in to the network.

Establishing Account Balances

One more step is required before you can begin to charge users for
use of the network. (Time is only one of five things to be tracked.)
You must establish an account balance for each user. When you
open a checking account at your local bank, for example, you

must give the bank a sum of money before you can debit the account. This banking procedure is the same for NetWare accounting. The beginning balance is arbitrary. The system uses the balance to establish an account that is depleted as the user works on the system. If the balance is not limited, the account acts as an odometer by tracking the amount of units used. The maximum number of units for an account balance is 99999999.

Limiting NetWare account balances is useful when you want users to be aware of the amount of time they spend on a network. When a user's account reaches the low balance limit, they are asked to log out of the system. If they do not log out, the system does it for them. To prevent this inconvenience, set the Low Balance Limit to a negative number. If you set a user's balance to -1000, for example, the message You have exceeded your credit limit for this server warns the user of a low account balance when the account reaches zero. The user now has 1000 units to use to finish and exit the network properly. The system tracks the way the user consumes certain network resources. As the user's account reaches zero, the counter starts using negative numbers.

Every time the user logs out of the system, NetWare accounting updates the account. You can use the PAUDIT file, illustrated in figure 5.7, to view login, logout, and system usage information for every user.

```
   Logout from address 00000003:00000000000E.
1/5/93 10:16:10  File Server CDI286
   NOTE: about User CBT4 during File Server services.
   Login from address 00000CDC:00001B1EC81A.
1/5/93 10:16:21  File Server CDI286
   NOTE: about User CBT2 during File Server services.
   Login from address 00000CDC:00001B1ECA96.
1/5/93 13:36:18  File Server CDI286
   CHARGE: 200 to User CBT4 for File Server services.
   Connected 200 min.; 506 requests; 000000000237508  bytes read;
   000000000000000 bytes written.
1/5/93 13:36:18  File Server CDI286
   NOTE: about User CBT4 during File Server services.
   Logout from address 00000CDC:00001B1EC81A.
1/5/93 13:36:33  File Server CDI286
   CHARGE: 200 to User CBT2 for File Server services.
   Connected 200 min.; 2239 requests; 000000001152034  bytes read;
   000000000000000 bytes written.
1/5/93 13:36:33  File Server CDI286
   NOTE: about User CBT2 during File Server services.
   Logout from address 00000CDC:00001B1ECA96.
1/5/93 13:55:56  File Server CDI286
   NOTE: about User SUPERVISOR during File Server services.
   Login from address 00000005:00001B191D38.
F:\SYSTEM>
```

Figure 5.7

An example of using the PAUDIT command.

The Change Current Server Option

The Change Current Server option in the Available Topics menu lists options for attaching to and logging out of a server. If you select the SYSCON Change Current Servers option, a menu appears that lists the file servers you are currently logged in or attached to (see fig. 5.8). Press Ins at this menu to list available servers to which you can log in. NetWare asks you for a valid user name and a password before it attaches you to the new server.

Figure 5.8

The Change Current Server screen.

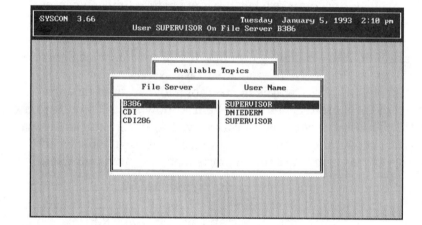

The File Server Information Option

The File Server Information option in the SYSCON Available Topics menu enables you to view information about the operating system for each server on the network. To view information on a specific server, highlight the server name and press Enter in the Known NetWare Servers screen. This displays the File Server Information screen for the specified server (see fig. 5.9). You cannot change any information on this screen. If you are a Supervisor or if you have Supervisor privileges, the serial and application numbers for that server appear on this screen. Figure 5.9, for example, shows information about the file server named TSARINA that is important for the System Administrator to know if it becomes necessary to contact an outside support person for assistance.

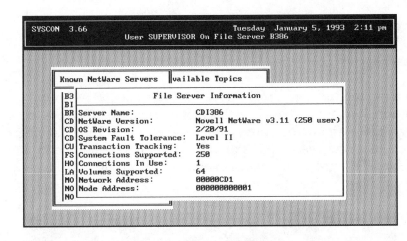

Figure 5.9

An example of the File Server information screen.

The Group Information Option

In NetWare, groups are designed to save you time and work when privileges are granted to users. If you select the Group Information option in the SYSCON Available Topics menu, a list of existing groups appears in the Group Names Screen (see fig. 5.10). When NetWare is installed, the only group created by the system is the group EVERYONE. Every user added to the system is automatically added to this group so that global rights can be issued.

```
SYSCON  3.66                          Tuesday  January 5, 1993  2:11 pm
                       User SUPERVISOR On File Server B386

            ┌──────────────────┐ ┌──────────────────────┐
            │    Group Names    │ │vailable Topics       │
            │ ╔══════════════╗  │ │                      │
            │ ║ACCOUNTING    ║  │ │ounting               │
            │ ║CU            ║  │ │nge Current Server    │
            │ ║EVERYONE      ║  │ │e Server Information  │
            │ ║MICHAELS      ║  │ │up Information        │
            │ ║STUDENTS      ║  │ │ervisor Options       │
            │ ║TECHS         ║  │ │r Information         │
            │ ╚══════════════╝  │ └──────────────────────┘
            │                   │
            └──────────────────┘
```

Figure 5.10

The Group Names screen.

Set up group accounts and user account management.

You can modify a group in several ways by using the Group Information menu. To access this menu, use the arrow keys to highlight a group, then press Enter (see fig. 5.11). The following sections discuss each option of the Group Information menu. To create a new group, press Ins, then name the group in the New Group Name screen (see fig. 5.12).

Figure 5.11

The Group Information menu.

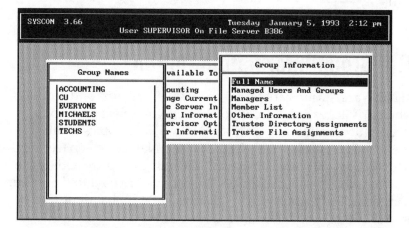

Figure 5.12

Adding a new group by using the New Group Name screen.

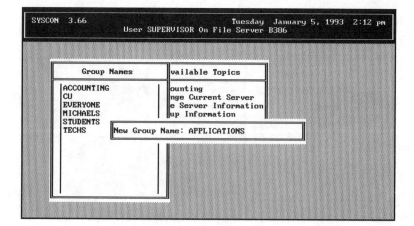

Note In every NetWare version up to 3.1*x*, the installation of the operating system creates the group EVERYONE; all users are automatically added to this group.

Full Name

If you select a group in the Group Names screen and press Enter, the Group Information menu appears. The Full Name option in this menu enables you to give a more descriptive name to the selected group.

Managed Users and Groups

This option lists users and groups for which the group selected in the Group Names screen can grant and revoke rights, assuming that your login name was chosen as a group manager or a workgroup manager. This option does not give you rights over the individual user accounts, but does enable you to modify member list and trustee assignments.

Managers

Select the Managers option in the Group Information menu to list the managers of the group you selected in the Group Names screen. You cannot modify this menu item unless you are a manager.

Member List

If you highlight this option and press Enter, members of the selected group are listed in the Group Members screen. When a group is created, it initially has no members (see fig. 5.13). To add users to a group, follow these steps:

1. Highlight the Member List option and press Enter.

2. Press Ins to list users who do not belong to the group.

3. For each user you want to add to the new group, highlight the user in the Not Group Members screen and press F5. Use F5 to mark each of the users you want to add to the group and press Enter.

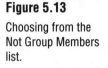

Figure 5.13

Choosing from the Not Group Members list.

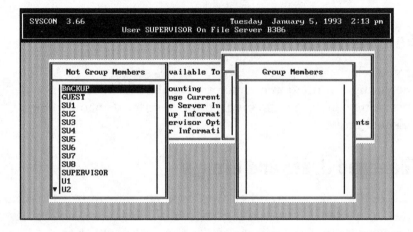

After you press Enter, the chosen user is added to the selected group.

Trustee Directory Assignments

Select this menu item to add rights to a group. If you highlight this item and press Enter, the currently assigned rights for the group are listed. As shown in figure 5.14, a new group has no assigned rights. To add rights, press Ins and enter the full path name.

If you are not sure of the directory structure, press Ins a second time to have the network prompt you for information about the path. The File Servers menu appears. In this menu, NetWare prompts you to select the server for which you want to assign rights (see fig. 5.15). The server you select becomes the first part of the full path name.

After you select a server and press Enter, the Volumes menu prompts you for the volume (see fig. 5.16).

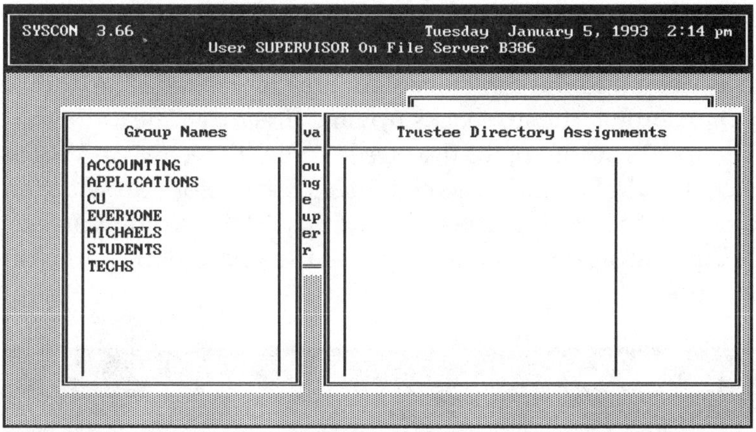

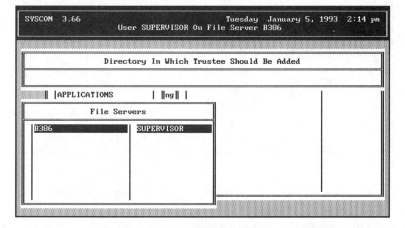

Figure 5.14

Viewing the Trustee Directory Assignments menu.

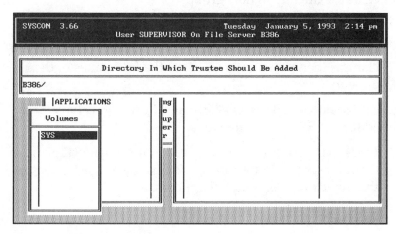

Figure 5.15

Choosing a file server for the path.

Figure 5.16

Choosing a volume for the path.

The last prompt asks for the directory for which you want to grant rights (see fig. 5.17). The Network Directories menu enables you to go as deep into the directory structure as needed. The double dot (..) prompt at the top backs up one directory. The path you select appears at the top of the screen in the Directory In Which Trustee Should Be Added screen. Press Esc to stop the selection process and to return to the top window. At this point, you can press Enter to accept the path or press Esc to erase the path you have chosen.

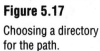

Figure 5.17

Choosing a directory for the path.

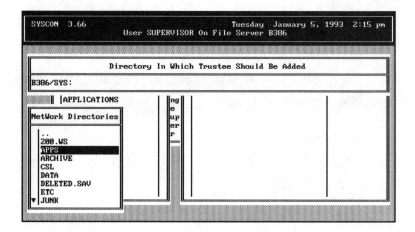

After you select a path, the Trustee Rights Granted screen appears. As shown in figure 5.18, File Scan and Read privileges are granted automatically to new groups.

To modify the rights assigned to a group, follow these steps:

1. Use the cursor keys to highlight the option that you want to change, then press Enter. A list of the full names of the rights appears.

Figure 5.18 shows that the File Scan and Read rights have been granted for the SYS:APPS directory.

2. Press Ins to list rights not granted in the Trustee Rights Not Granted screen. In figure 5.19, for example, a list of rights that have not been granted appears.

3. Use F5 to mark each right you want to grant to the group, then press Enter.

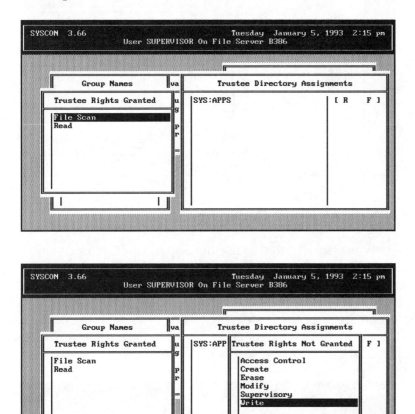

Figure 5.18

Assigning rights to a directory.

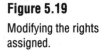

Figure 5.19

Modifying the rights assigned.

To delete rights in a group, mark the rights by using F5, then press Del.

After you mark the rights you want to assign or delete, the new rights list is updated in the Trustee Directory Assignments screen (see fig. 5.20).

Figure 5.20

Viewing the
modified rights.

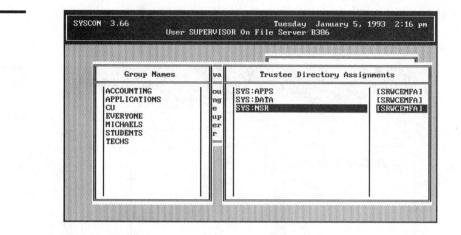

The Supervisor Options

The only users permitted to use the Supervisor Options menu of
SYSCON are the Supervisor and Supervisor equivalents. In this
menu, Supervisors can specify system defaults, set up FCONSOLE
operators, manage server-configuration files, initiate intruder
detection, manage the system login scripts, view the error log, and
create workgroup managers (see fig. 5.21). Each of these options is
outlined in the following sections.

Figure 5.21

The Supervisor
Options menu in
SYSCON.

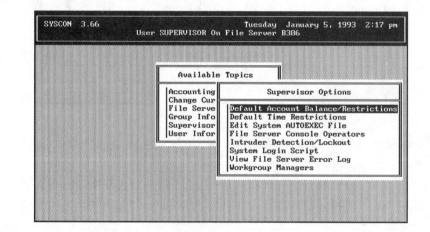

Default Account Balance/Restrictions and Default Time Restrictions

The first two items in the Supervisor Options menu affect only future users added to the system:

◆ Default Account Balance/Restrictions

◆ Default Time Restrictions

These options are the same ones listed in individual user accounts. Default Account Balance/Restrictions and Default Time Restrictions have no effect on current users. As you add new users to the network, the parameters defined in these two options automatically are added to the new users' account.

Edit System AUTOEXEC File

The Edit System AUTOEXEC File option enables you to modify the file with which the file server boots up. Please see Chapters 8, "Administering NetWare 3.1x Networks," and 10, "Understanding NetWare 2.2 System Manager Functions," for specific information about each operating system.

File Server Console Operators

In the File Server Console Operators Options menu, FCONSOLE, operator status can be given to individual users or to groups. *FCONSOLE* is a menu utility used for monitoring the file server. Users who are Supervisor equivalents can use all the options in FCONSOLE. Regular users whose names appear in this screen cannot clear connections or down the server from FCONSOLE. Users whose names do not appear in this list can use FCONSOLE, but are severely limited as to what information they can see. For more information on FCONSOLE, see Chapter 8.

Intruder Detection/Lockout

Intruder detection is designed to alert the network when someone tries to log in to the system using an invalid password. The Intruder Detection/Lockout option has several configurable parameters, because users often make a mistake when they enter a password.

The network enables you to track incorrect login attempts. An incorrect login attempt is considered to be the number of times in a specific number of minutes that a user can try to log in using an incorrect password. In figure 5.22, for example, users can attempt to log in to the network seven times in 59 minutes before intruder detection locks them out. The length of the lockout also is configurable. The Length Of Account Lockout line in figure 5.22 shows the maximum allowable lockout time—40 days, 23 hours, and 59 minutes.

Figure 5.22

The Intruder
Detection/Lockout
option.

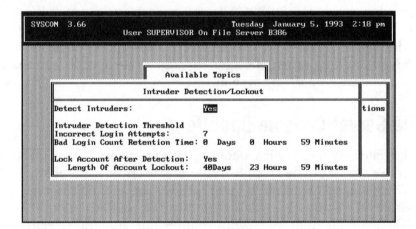

To unlock an account, you must select the User Information option in the Available Topics menu, then select the Intruder Lockout Status option under the name of the user who has been disabled.

System Login Script

The System Login Script option is designed to configure the network environment for all users. This file is created and maintained by the System Supervisor. For more information on the system login script, see Chapter 7, "Customizing the User's Environment."

View File Server Error Log

To view the File Server Error Log file, press Enter on the View File Server Error Log entry in the Supervisor Options menu. Then use the arrow, PgUp, and PgDn keys to move around the File Server Error Log screen (see fig. 5.23).

```
SYSCON  3.66                          Tuesday  January 5, 1993  2:20 pm
                   User SUPERVISOR On File Server B386

                          File Server Error Log

  12/28/92 10:30:59 am  Severity = 0.
  1.1.60 Bindery open requested by the SERVER

  12/28/92 10:32:49 am  Severity = 0.
  1.1.62 Bindery close requested by the SERVER

  12/28/92 10:32:49 am  Severity = 4.
  1.1.72 B386 TTS shut down
     because backout volume SYS was dismounted

  12/28/92 10:33:33 am  Severity = 0.
  1.1.60 Bindery open requested by the SERVER

  12/28/92 10:48:30 am  Severity = 0.
  0.0.0 Remote Console Connection Granted for 00000CDB:00001B196662
```

Figure 5.23

The File Server Error Log screen.

 Note   The information shown in the error log is stored in a file called NET$LOG.ERR.

The *error log* contains system errors and other information not serious enough to crash a file server, but still important to the Administrator. Press Esc to exit this screen. Before the error log exits, you are prompted with Clear Error Log. If you select Yes,

NetWare deletes the current information. If you need to review this information in the future, save the error log to a file before deleting it.

Workgroup Managers

The Workgroup Managers option in the Supervisor Options menu enables you to define workgroup managers. As you learned earlier in this chapter, *workgroup managers* are users or groups that can add, delete, and manage other user accounts. Workgroup managers, however, cannot create other workgroup managers or use the Supervisor Options in SYSCON. Press Enter to see the names of potential workgroup managers for users and groups on your network (see fig. 5.24). Press Ins to select other network users and groups to be workgroup managers.

Figure 5.24

The Workgroup Managers screen.

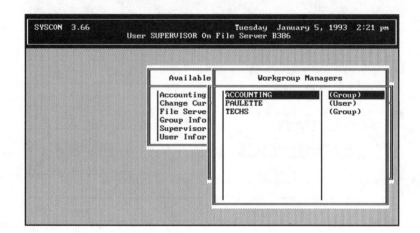

The User Information Option

The User Information option in the Available Topics menu enables you to set up individual user accounts. Highlight this option and press Enter to display every user who has an account on the network. Figure 5.25 shows the User Names screen that lists the names of users established on the network.

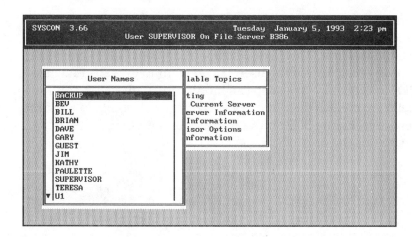

Figure 5.25
The User Names
screen.

Set up network user accounts and apply account restrictions.

To create a new user, press Ins and use the User Name window to name the new user. Figure 5.26, for example, shows the user USERAM being added to the network.

Figure 5.26
Adding a user to
the network.

After you enter a name for a new user, the network prompts you to select whether you want a HOME directory created for the new user on volume SYS:. Press Esc if you do not want to create a HOME directory for the user. If you want to give the new user a HOME directory, you also can modify the path. After you finish, NetWare creates the directory and assigns all rights to it for the new user. Figure 5.27 shows the default path that the network creates for the user USERAM.

Figure 5.27

Creating a HOME directory.

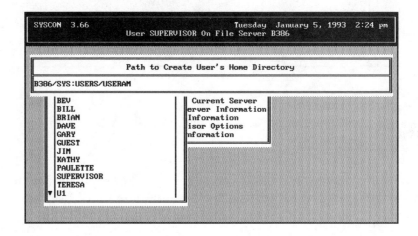

After you create the new user, highlight the user's name and press Enter. The User Information screen appears, enabling you to modify the user's account (see fig. 5.28). This screen shows the information that a system manager can modify for a specific user's account. Each option in the User Information menu is described in the following sections.

Account Balance

The Account Balance option enables Supervisors to set up and monitor the user's account balance. When you select this option, the Account Balance For User screen appears on-screen. If the Accounting option has not been installed on the network, the Account Balance option does not appear. In the example shown in figure 5.29, the user BRIAN has been given an account balance of 500,000. This amount decreases as BRIAN uses the accounting services.

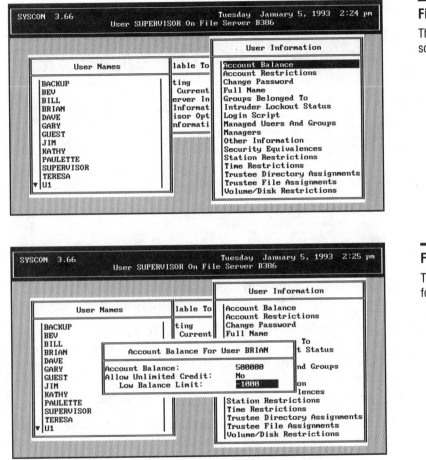

Figure 5.28

The User Information screen.

Figure 5.29

The Account Balance for User screen.

Account Restrictions

Describe login security, including user account restrictions, time restrictions, station restrictions, and intruder detection.

Supervisors can use the Account Restrictions option of the User Information menu to set up the password and connection parameters for a user. Figure 5.30 lists the account restrictions for the user BRIAN. Each parameter in this menu is discussed in the following list.

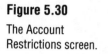

Figure 5.30

The Account Restrictions screen.

```
SYSCON  3.66                              Tuesday  January 5, 1993  2:25 pm
                         User SUPERVISOR On File Server B386

          ┌──────────────── Account Restrictions For User BRIAN ────────────────┐
          │Account Disabled:                          No                         │
     BACK │Account Has Expiration Date:               No                         │
     BEV  │    Date Account Expires:                                             │
     BILL │Limit Concurrent Connections:              No                         │
     BRIA │    Maximum Connections:                                          s   │
     DAVE │Allow User To Change Password:             No                         │
     GARY │Require Password:                          Yes                    ps  │
     GUES │    Minimum Password Length:               5                          │
     JIM  │Force Periodic Password Changes:                                      │
     KATH │    Days Between Forced Changes:                                      │
     PAUL │    Date Password Expires:                                            │
     SUPE │    Limit Grace Logins:                                               │
     TERE │        Grace Logins Allowed:                                 gnments  │
   ▼ U1   │        Remaining Grace Logins:                               ts       │
          │Require Unique Passwords:                  Yes                ns       │
          └──────────────────────────────────────────────────────────────────────┘
```

Supervisors can change the following items in the Account Restrictions screen to configure a new or existing user's account:

◆ **Account Disabled.** This line is set to Yes if any of the following conditions occur: the user's expiration date has passed, the grace logins have run out, or a Supervisor does not want this user logging in to the network. If Account Disabled is set to No, the user can log in to the network.

◆ **Account Has Expiration Date.** If you want a new user to have only temporary access to the network, set an expiration date for his account. The user cannot log in to the network after the date set in this field. If you do not want to set an expiration date, set this line to No.

◆ **Limit Concurrent Connections.** The Supervisor can use this field to specify the number of workstations a new user can log in to using the same login name. The default enables the user to log in from all nodes on the network simultaneously.

Note

You might want to limit the number of allowable logins for Supervisors and users with Supervisor privileges. A limited number of connections prevents privileged users from leaving a trail of workstations logged in with Supervisory rights.

◆ **Allow User To Change Password.** If this field is set to Yes, the user can change his password whenever he wants. If this field is set to No, only the System Supervisor can change the user's password.

◆ **Require Password.** If you want to require a password, set this field to Yes. You also need to specify the minimum length for the password. If you set this field to No, the user is not required to have a password. Even if Require Password is set to No, the user still can have a password.

◆ **Force Periodic Password Changes.** If you set this parameter to Yes, specify the number of days between forced changes and the next date that the password expires. The network default is 40 days.

Note

One of Murphy's laws states that whenever something must be done immediately, it is always the worst possible time to do it. This "law" also applies to network users. The morning a user logs in to the network to find that his password has expired, for example, probably will be the same morning that a record number of crises occur. This problem is the reason for grace logins. *Grace logins* tell the network that you are too busy at the moment to think of a new password, but to ask for a new password the next time you log in.

The default for grace logins is six. In other words, you can answer No to a new password request six times before the network locks your account.

continues

333

Only a Supervisor equivalent or workgroup manager can unlock the account after grace logins have run out.

♦ **Require Unique Passwords.** This option requires that you do not repeat the most recent passwords when your current password expires.

This option for 2.2 requires each user to create up to eight new passwords before he can repeat the first password. In 3.1*x*, users must create ten new passwords before they can repeat the first password. In addition, these passwords must be in effect for 24 hours.

♦ **Limit Server Disk Space.** If this option is set to Yes, you must specify the maximum amount of disk space in kilobytes that the user is permitted. When you limit a user's disk space, make sure that the user knows that if he runs out of space while he saves or prints a file, he might lose the information. The network needs to store print files as temporary files on the network. If his memory space runs out while he prints a large job, the job is lost.

Change Password

The Change Password option in the User Information menu adds or changes passwords. The DOS command for this task is SETPASS.

Users cannot see the password, but are asked to repeat the new password to make sure that it is typed correctly. Supervisors do not need to know the old password, but regular users need to put in the old password before they can change it.

Full Name

The Full Name option in the User Information menu enables you to give a more descriptive name to the user. This requirement is optional and is used with the identifier variable FULL_NAME in login scripts.

Groups Belonged To

The Groups Belonged To option in the User Information menu provides an opposite view of the Group Information option in the Available Topics menu. In the Groups Belonged To option, you can view the groups to which the highlighted user belongs. Press Ins to view the groups to which the user does not belong (see fig. 5.31).

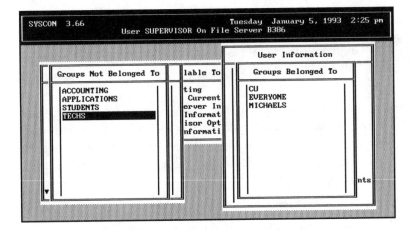

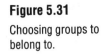

Figure 5.31
Choosing groups to belong to.

The system manager can pick from this list the groups to which he wants a user to belong. To add a user to a group, such as TECHS, highlight the group and press Enter. The Groups Belonged To screen then shows the updated groups list (see fig. 5.32).

Figure 5.32

The modified
groups list.

```
SYSCON  3.66                              Tuesday  January 5, 1993  2:26 pm
                     User SUPERVISOR On File Server B386

                                          ┌──── User Information ────┐
        ┌───────── User Names ─────────┐lable To│   Groups Belonged To   │
        │ BACKUP                        │ting    │ CU                     │
        │ BEV                           │ Current│ EVERYONE               │
        │ BILL                          │erver In│ MICHAELS               │
        │ BRIAN                         │Informat│ TECHS                  │
        │ DAVE                          │isor Opt│                        │
        │ GARY                          │nformati│                        │
        │ GUEST                         │        │                        │
        │ JIM                           │        │                        │
        │ KATHY                         │        │                        │
        │ PAULETTE                      │        │                        │
        │ SUPERVISOR                    │        │                        │
        │ TERESA                        │        │                    nts  │
      ▼ │ U1                            │        │                        │
        └───────────────────────────────┘        └────────────────────────┘
```

Intruder Lockout Status

Describe login security, including user account
restrictions, time restrictions, station restrictions,
and intruder detection.

Intruder Lockout Status displays the network and workstation
address out of which a selected user is locked and the time remaining until the lockout is reset. When the user tries to log in
and activates the Intruder Detection/Lockout feature, the following message appears:

```
Intruder Detection/Lockout has disabled this account.
```

If the user is not currently locked out, you can view only the
system. As a user with Supervisor rights, you can see the Intruder
Detection/Lockout option in the User Information list for the
specific user, only if Intruder Detection/Lockout has been set for
this server. If you are a system manager and the user is locked out,
the border for this menu becomes a double line. You can unlock
the account if you have Supervisor rights.

Figure 5.33 shows an active lockout for user CHRIS.

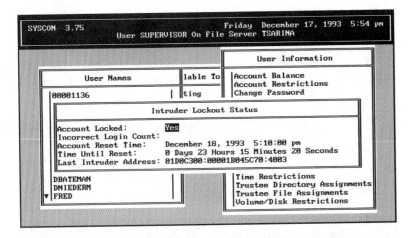

Figure 5.33

The Intruder Lockout Status screen.

Under the address portion of the Intruder Lockout Status screen, the first portion of the address is the network address (shown as 01DOC300 in figure 5.33). The second part is the workstation address (shown as 00001B045C70), and the third number is a network socket number (shown as 4003).

Socket numbers provide a type of mail slot for processes that occur within a workstation. These mail slots exist so that each process can identify itself to IPX. Whenever a workstation needs to access the *NetWare Core Protocol* (NCP—the heart of the operating system), the workstation uses socket 45lh, for example.

Login Script

The Login Script option in the User Information menu enables the user or a system manager to add or manage the login script for a selected user. In addition, login scripts can be copied from other users, but only if no existing login script exists for the current user. If a login script exists, and you want to assign another user's login script, perform the following steps:

1. Highlight the existing login script by pressing F5 and using the arrow keys to mark it.

2. Press Del.

337

3. Press Esc to exit, then save the changes.

4. Press Enter to return to the login script screen. When you go back into this option, the system tells you that a login script does not exist. You now can read the login script from another user.

5. Replace the current user's name in the screen with the user's name from which a login script is copied. Figure 5.34, for example, shows that the user BRIAN does not have a login script. To copy one from the user JIM, use Backspace to delete BRIAN, then enter **JIM**.

Figure 5.34

An example of copying login scripts in SYSCON.

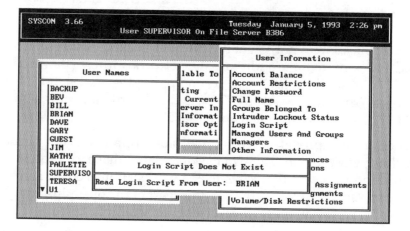

Managed Users And Groups

The Managed Users And Groups option in the User Information menu lists the users and groups that can be granted rights and that can have rights revoked by the selected user. In addition, this category designates the users whose accounts are managed by the selected user. You can use this option to modify member lists and trustee assignments.

In figure 5.35, the classification Direct means that the selected user is assigned specific users and groups to manage. Indirect-managed users and groups are assigned by the network so that the manager can change rights to the group EVERYONE. Although EVERYONE is created by NetWare, the system managers can add and delete rights for this group.

Managers

The Manager options in the User Information menu item lists the manager or manager of a selected user (see fig. 5.36). You can modify this option only if you are a manager.

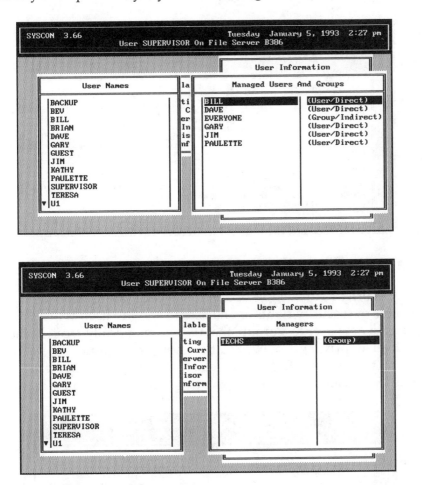

Figure 5.35

Examples of managed users and groups.

Figure 5.36

Account managers for the selected user.

Other Information

The Other Information option in the User Information menu shows you when a selected user last logged in to the network (see fig. 5.37). If this is a new user, the message Not known appears. This screen also shows if this user is an FCONSOLE operator.

The Maximum Server Disk Usage setting in the Account Restrictions option also appears here, including information about the amount of disk space the user currently is using on the network. The final field is the User ID, which is the same as the directory under SYS:MAIL that belongs to this user.

Figure 5.37

The Other Information option.

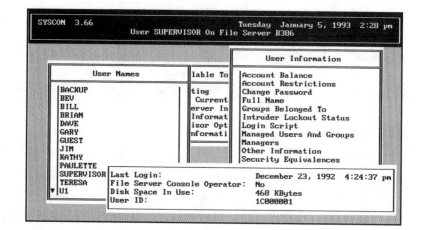

Security Equivalences

The Security Equivalences option in the User Information menu assigns the security rights of one user to another user. When you assign a new user to a group, that user automatically receives the equivalent privileges of every other user in that group. Figure 5.38 shows that the user BRIAN belongs to the groups EVERYONE and TECHS and has the same security rights as the groups listed.

Figure 5.38

The Security Equivalences option screen.

```
SYSCON  3.66                        Tuesday  January 5, 1993  2:29 pm
                   User SUPERVISOR On File Server B386

                                        ┌─────────────────────────────┐
                                        │      User  Information       │
            ┌────────────────────┐┌─────┤─────────────────────────────┤
            │     User Names     ││lable│   Security Equivalences     │
            │ ┌────────────────┐ ││ting ││ ┌─────────────┬──────────┐ │
            │ │BACKUP          │ ││ Curr││ │EVERYONE     │(Group)   │ │
            │ │BEV             │ ││erver││ │TECHS        │(Group)   │ │
            │ │BILL            │ ││Infor││ │             │          │ │
            │ │BRIAN           │ ││isor ││ │             │          │ │
            │ │DAVE            │ ││nform││ │             │          │ │
            │ │GARY            │ ││     ││ │             │          │ │
            │ │GUEST           │ ││     ││ │             │          │ │
            │ │JIM             │ ││     ││ │             │          │ │
            │ │KATHY           │ ││     ││ │             │          │ │
            │ │PAULETTE        │ ││     ││ │             │          │ │
            │ │SUPERVISOR      │ ││     ││ │             │          │ │
            │ │TERESA          │ ││     ││ │             │          │ │
            │ ▼│U1             │ │└─────┘│ └─────────────┴──────────┘ │
            │ └────────────────┘ │       └─────────────────────────────┘
            └────────────────────┘
```

The following steps show you ways to assign Supervisor privileges to a user. Figure 5.39 shows that SUPERVISOR has been added to the Security Equivalences option screen. This setting makes the new user BRIAN a Supervisor-equivalent user. To assign Supervisor privileges, select Security Equivalences in the User Information menu and perform the following steps:

1. Press Ins at the Security Equivalences menu to display a list of other users and groups.

2. From the list, find the heading SUPERVISOR (User).

3. Highlight SUPERVISOR and press Enter. The selected user now is a Supervisor equivalent (see fig 5.39).

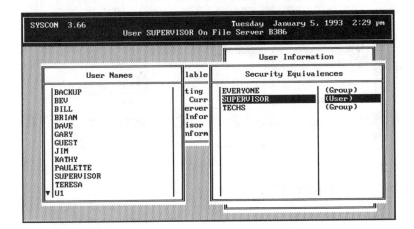

Figure 5.39

Creating a Supervisor-equivalent user.

This process is the only way to make a Supervisor-equivalent user.

Station Restrictions

Describe login security, including user account restrictions, time restrictions, station restrictions, and intruder detection.

By default, NetWare enables a user to log in to any workstation attached to the network. Through the Station Restrictions option in the User Information menu, the System Administrator can create a list of networks and workstations to which a user can log in. The user cannot log in to any network or workstation whose address does not appear on this list. Figure 5.40 shows the list of node addresses and network addresses of the workstations from which a selected user is permitted to log in.

Figure 5.40

A list of login addresses.

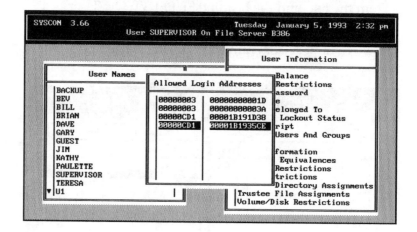

Time Restrictions

The Time Restrictions option in the User Information menu enables you to restrict individual users to network use at specific times. In figure 5.41, asterisks denote half-hour time increments during which a user can be logged in to the network. Every empty space represents one half hour of time that a user is denied access. To set restrictions on times when users can log in, use the following steps:

1. Open the Allowed Login Times For User screen.

2. Use the arrow keys to move the cursor to the day and time when the time restriction is to start.

3. Press F5.

4. Use the arrow keys to move the cursor to the day and time when the time restriction is to end.

5. Press Enter.

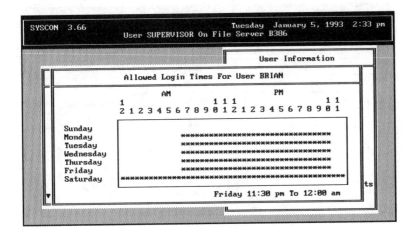

Figure 5.41

Setting time restrictions for a user.

Trustee Directory Assignments

Select the Trustee Directory Assignments option in the User Information menu to view the rights assigned to a user and to add rights that a user needs. A new user automatically has rights to his HOME directory and to his SYS:MAIL/USER_ID directory. To add rights, press Ins and enter the full path name, or press Ins again to select the path. See the section on adding rights to groups for more information about entering full path names.

NetWare grants the File Scan and Read privileges automatically. To modify the rights assignments on any directory, use the following steps:

1. Press Enter on the directory whose trustee rights you want to change.

2. When the list of trustee rights granted appears, press Ins to see the list of trustee rights that have not been granted.

3. Press F5 to mark each right that you want to grant to the user, then press Enter. (To delete marked rights, press Del rather than Enter.)

343

Press Esc to return to the new rights. The list then is updated in the Trustee Directory Assignments window. Figure 5.42 shows the screens for modifying trustee directory rights.

Figure 5.42

Screens for modifying trustee directory rights.

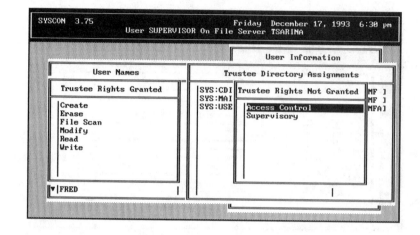

 Note   In 3.1*x*, you also can grant rights to specific files. Please see Chapter 8 for more information on this option.

Volume/Disk Restrictions

The User Volume/Disk Restrictions option in the User Information menu enables you to limit the disk space available to the user. This option appears in 2.2 only if the Limit Server Disk Space option is selected during installation. Figure 5.43 shows that the user can use 10240 KB, or about 10 MB of space. The Administrator can check this number to see the amount of space a user has taken up on the system. The Volume Space In Use field shown in figure 5.43, for example, shows that the user currently has used 468 KB of disk space.

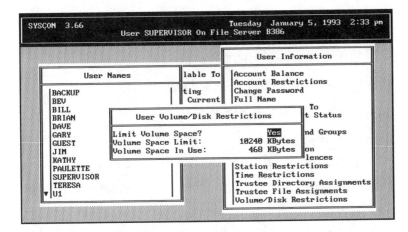

Figure 5.43

The User Volume/Disk Restrictions screen.

 The following command-line utilities also can be accomplished by using SYSCON:

- ATTACH
- GRANT
- REMOVE
- REVOKE
- RIGHTS
- SETPASS
- SLIST
- TLIST

Section Review Questions

1. Which function key enables you to change a file's name?

   a. F1

   b. F3

   c. F5

   d. F6

345

2. What is the name and location of the file that stores accounting information?

   a. SYS:SYSTEM\NET$REC.DAT

   b. SYS:PUBLIC\NET$REC.DAT

   c. SYS:SYSTEM\NET$ACCT.DAT

   d. SYS:PUBLIC\NET$ACCT.DAT

3. The Accounting ratio 6/5 in Disk Storage means:

   a. Six cents is charged for every five files stored on the network

   b. Six cents is charged for every five blocks of data stored

   c. Five cents is charged for every six blocks of data stored

   d. Five cents is charged for every six files stored on the network

4. Where can you view the File Server Error log?

   a. SYSCON, SUPERVISOR OPTIONS

   b. FILER, FILE SERVER INFORMATION

   c. SYSCON, FILE SERVER INFORMATION

   d. FILER, VIEW ERROR LOG

5. What best describes a workgroup manager?

   a. Created in SYSCON under user information, these users can create and manage other users.

   b. Created in SYSCON under group information, these groups of users control the network administration.

   c. Created in SYSCON under Supervisor options, these users cannot create users, but can manage existing users.

   d. Created in SYSCON under Supervisor options, these users can create and manage other users.

6. Which key do you use to insert a new user in SYSCON?

    a. F3

    b. Ins

    c. F5

    d. Ctrl+Home

7. When does intruder detection protect the system?

    a. Whenever a user logs out of the network

    b. Whenever the SECURITY program is run

    c. Whenever someone uses a login name that does not exist on the network

    d. Whenever a user does not use the correct password

8. Which of the following statements about Intruder Detection/Lockout is true?

    a. It is turned on by default during installation.

    b. It can be set for just one user.

    c. It always shows as an option in the User Information menu.

    d. It displays a message telling the user they have been locked out when it activates.

9. How can you create a Supervisor-equivalent user for an existing user?

    a. SYSCON, user information, select user account, security equivalences, add Supervisor

    b. SYSCON, user information, select Supervisor, security equivalences, add user account

    c. SYSCON, Supervisor options, security equivalences, add user account

    d. SYSCON, Supervisor options, select Supervisors, add user account

10. What rights are granted by default when you add a user as a trustee to a directory?

    a. F and R

    b. F, W, and R

    c. C, W, F, S

    d. No rights are granted by default

Answers

1. b
2. c
3. b
4. a
5. d
6. b
7. d
8. d
9. a
10. a

Exploring the FILER Menu Utility

This section describes *FILER*, a menu utility that you can use to manipulate directories and files. The utilities discussed in this section are used differently, depending on your security status. System Supervisors can use all the functions, but the typical end user might be limited to only certain functions. This section describes all the options for FILER.

FILER can be used as an alternative to DOS commands when you manage directories. The main screen in FILER enables you to view a specific directory or a directory's contents, specify search options, or look at volume information (see fig. 5.44).

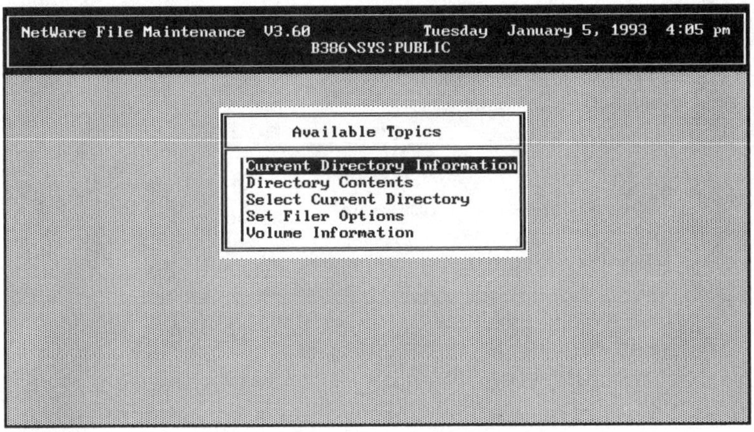

Figure 5.44

The FILER main menu.

Current Directory Information Menu

The first menu item in FILER, Current Directory Information, enables you to see and assign the following information (see fig. 5.45):

♦ Who created, or owns, a specific directory

♦ When a directory was created

♦ The setting of the directory attributes

♦ The setting of the Maximum Rights Mask in 2.2

♦ The setting of the Inherited Rights Mask in 3.1*x*

♦ Who has specifically been granted rights to this directory

The Current Effective Rights line, shown in figure 5.45, lists current rights for the user; the Inherited Rights Mask line lists the allowable rights. The Inherited Rights field cannot be changed directly. It reflects what you are able to do currently in a directory.

349

Figure 5.45

Current directory information.

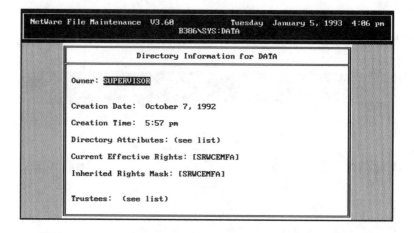

Figure 5.45

Current directory information.

At the DOS prompt, you can change directory attributes by using the FLAGDIR command. Inside FILER, you add attributes by pressing Ins, then choosing from the available list, shown in figure 5.46. You can delete attributes just as easily by highlighting the attribute, then pressing Del.

Figure 5.46

Choosing directory attributes.

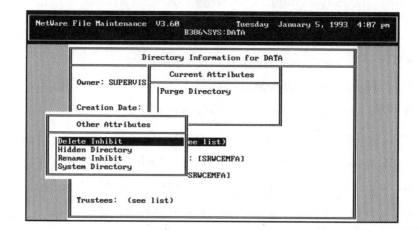

Figure 5.46 shows directory information for the \DATA directory. The current attributes show that this directory was flagged by using the FLAG command to immediately purge any files deleted from the directory. By pressing Ins, another menu appears that

displays all other available flags that can be assigned to this directory.

You can assign and manage trustees by choosing the Trustees option from Current Directory Information in FILER. At the DOS prompt, trustees are managed by using the GRANT, REMOVE, and REVOKE commands. Figure 5.47 shows that two groups are given rights to the directory SYS:DATA. Rights are discussed in depth in Chapter 7. By giving groups rights, you make them the directory's trustees.

```
NetWare File Maintenance  V3.60          Tuesday   January 5, 1993  4:07 pm
                              B386\SYS:DATA

                       Directory Information for DATA

        Trustee Name           Type              Rights

       APPLICATIONS        (Group)           [SRWCEMFA]
       STUDENTS            (Group)           [ RW    F ]
       U1                  (User)            [ RWCEMF ]




       Trustees:   (see list)
```

Figure 5.47

Viewing trustee assignments from FILER.

Directory Contents Menu

The next FILER main menu option, Directory Contents, enables you to perform the following tasks after choosing Directory Contents (see fig. 5.48):

◆ Create and delete subdirectories (press Ins)

◆ Copy subdirectory structures (press Enter on a subdirectory)

Perform file management tasks such as copying, moving, deleting, salvaging, and purging files.

◆ Move file and subdirectory structures (press Enter on a file or subdirectory). This option applies to 3.1*x* only.

◆ Copy files (press Enter on a file or subdirectory).

◆ View and set directory information (press Enter on a subdirectory—see fig. 5.49).

◆ View and set file information (press Enter on a file—see fig. 5.50).

◆ Change directories (select a subdirectory, parent, or root).

Figure 5.46 shows two subdirectories and two files in the directory SYS:DATA. After you highlight a directory and press Enter, you see the menu options shown in figure 5.47. Highlighting a file and pressing Enter shows you the menu options displayed in figure 5.48.

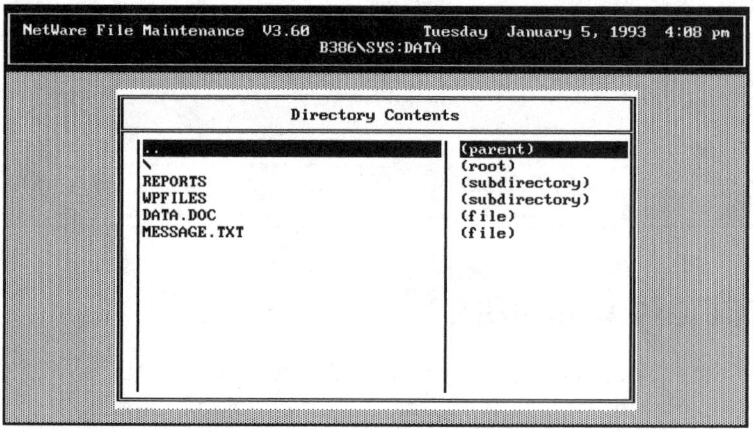

Figure 5.48

Directory Contents with subdirectories and files.

To create directories from the Directory Contents screen, press Ins. A box appears, in which you type the new directory name, then press Enter. The *Make Directory* (MD) command at the DOS prompt follows the same procedure.

To delete a directory, highlight the directory to be deleted and press Del. Another menu appears that enables you to select between deleting files only from this directory and any subdirectories under it, or deleting the complete directory structure beneath the highlighted directory.

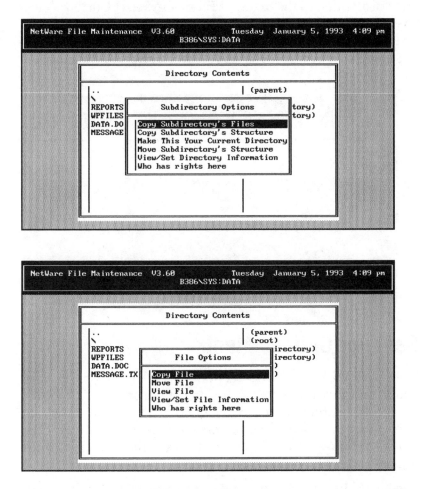

Figure 5.49

NetWare 3.1x Subdirectory Options in Directory Contents.

Figure 5.50

NetWare 3.1x File Options in Directory Contents.

Files also can be deleted by highlighting the file and pressing Del. Other function keys work to mark multiple files. See the beginning of this chapter for more information on function keys.

When you work in DOS, you often need to delete several directories at once. If you delete directories in DOS, you must specify the directory and the files you want to delete, which can be a tedious process—especially if the directories contain read-only or hidden files. If you use FILER instead, you can delete an entire directory structure, all files in a directory structure, or specific files.

353

Select Current Directory Menu

The third option in the main FILER menu, Select Current Directory, enables you to change the directory being viewed (see fig. 5.51). If you are not sure of the exact directory path, press Ins to call up a list of available file servers, volumes, and directories.

Figure 5.51

Setting a directory path for viewing.

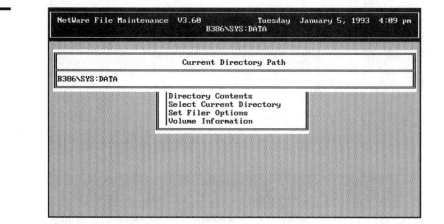

Set Filer Options Menu

The fourth FILER main menu option, Set Filer Options, enables you to set the parameters for viewing and manipulating the directory structure (see fig. 5.52). In FILER, under Set Filer Options, you can specify letter patterns to view directories or files. You also can search for hidden and system files and directories under the Search Attributes.

The Notify Extended Attributes/Long Name Lost line in the Filer Settings box applies to OS/2 attributes (see figs. 5.53 and 5.54). These two figures are examples of help screens that Novell provides in all the menu utilities; the screens can be accessed by pressing F1 whenever you need additional information about a current screen.

Any options set in FILER under Filer Settings apply only to that FILER session. (Figure 5.52 shows the default settings.) The settings have no effect at the DOS prompt.

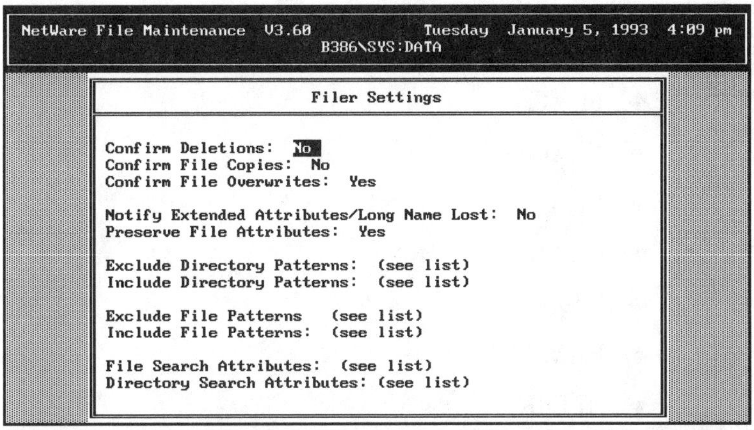

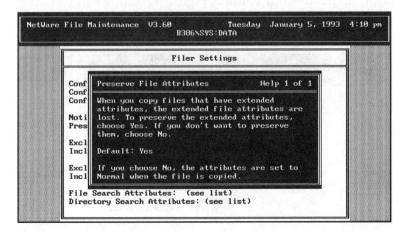

Figure 5.52
Filer Settings options.

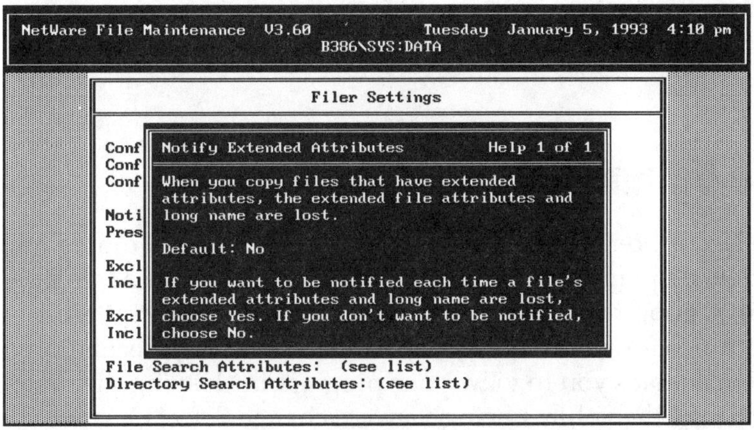

Figure 5.53
A Filer Settings
sample help screen.

Figure 5.54
Another Filer Settings
sample help screen.

The following command-line utilities also can be accomplished by using FILER:

- FLAG
- FLAGDIR
- LISTDIR
- NCOPY
- NDIR
- REMOVE
- REDIR
- REVOKE
- TLIST

The Volume Information Menu

The last option in FILER's Available Topics menu, Volume Information, displays information about network volumes (see fig. 5.55). A good reason for using FILER is to clean up cluttered directories for increased disk space. The Volume Information option enables you to view your progress in cleaning the system. To change the volume being viewed, change Select Current Directory to the desired volume. Figure 5.55 shows information on the current volume SYS: on a file server called B386.

Figure 5.55

Viewing volume information.

```
NetWare File Maintenance  V3.60              Tuesday  January 5, 1993  4:11 pm
                                  B386\SYS:DATA


                        ┌──────────────────────┐
                        │    Available Topics   │
                        ├──────────────────────┤
                        │Current Direc          │
                        │Directory Con  ┌─────────────────────────────────┐
                        │Select Curren  │      Volume  Information         │
                        │Set Filer Opt  │Server Name:              B386    │
                        │Volume Inform  │Volume Name:              SYS     │
                        └─────────────  │Volume Type:              fixed   │
                                        │Total KBytes:             112,688 │
                                        │Kilobytes Available:       23,296 │
                                        │Maximum Directory Entries: 12,704 │
                                        │Directory Entries Available: 8,086│
                                        └─────────────────────────────────┘
```

Section Review Questions

11. Which utility enables you to find out when a directory was created?

    a. SYSCON, Trustee Information

    b. FILER, Directory Contents

    c. SYSCON, User Information, Account Balance

    d. FILER, File Server Information

12. Which of the following tasks CANNOT be performed using the FILER utility?

    a. Create and delete subdirectories

    b. Copy files

    c. Assign trustee rights

    d. Change directories

13. Which utility has FLAG, NCOPY, NDIR, and REVOKE as command-line utility equivalents?

    a. FILER

    b. SESSION

    c. NBACKUP

    d. SYSCON

14. Which FILER menu option would you choose in order to see when the current directory was created?

    a. Directory Contents

    b. Current Directory Information

    c. Select Current Directory

    d. Set FILER Options

15. The command-line command that lets you set or change directory attributes is:

    a. FLAGDIR

    b. NDIR

357

   c. REMOVE

   d. REDIR

16. Which *two* statements about the FILER utility are true?

   a. Any options set in FILER under Filer Settings apply only to that FILER session.

   b. FILER's Notify Extended Attributes/Long Name Lost line in the FILER Settings box applies to OS/2 attributes.

   c. REDIR and NDIR are NOT command-line equivalent features of FILER.

   d. Only DIRDEL allows you to delete an entire directory structure, an option not available in FILER.

17. Pressing INS while inside the Select Current Directory option of FILER:

   a. Lets you type in a new directory path

   b. Requires that you select a subdirectory from directories above the current level

   c. Lets you view a list of subdirectories from which to choose

   d. Does not function within this FILER option

18. Which FILER option lets you search for hidden and system files according to those attributes?

   a. Directory Contents

   b. Current Directory Information

   c. Select Current Directory

   d. Set FILER options

19. Which FILER option should you choose if you need to perform the NetWare equivalent to the DOS MD command?

   a. Directory Contents

   b. Current Directory Information

358

    c. Select Current Directory

    d. Set FILER Options

20. Which key shows you Help when inside the FILER utility?

    a. Ctrl+H

    b. F3

    c. F1

    d. Shift+H

Answers

11. b

12. c

13. a

14. b

15. a

16. a and b

17. c

18. d

19. a

20. c

Exploring the MAKEUSER and USERDEF Utilities

The MAKEUSER and USERDEF utilities are designed to help simplify setting up large numbers of users on the network. MAKEUSER can also be used to remove users from the network. This section discusses these two utilities.

MAKEUSER

MAKEUSER is a utility you can use to create, edit, and process a script that adds users to the network (see fig. 5.56).

Figure 5.56

The MAKEUSER utility options.

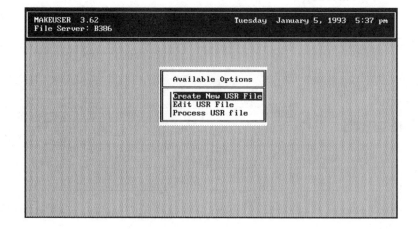

The following rules help you develop a MAKEUSER script:

- ◆ All keywords must be uppercase and must be preceded by a pound sign (#).

- ◆ If you want to use any keywords concerned with passwords, you must type **#PASSWORD_REQUIRED**.

- ◆ The flow of events is always upward. #CREATE always refers to the commands preceding it to determine the user's parameters.

- ◆ MAKEUSER files are saved with a USR extension in the directory from which the MAKEUSER utility is accessed.

- ◆ After the file is processed, MAKEUSER leaves a report file with the same file name, but with an RPT extension. This file shows if the users have been created.

You can use a MAKEUSER file as computerized notes for adding users to the network. All that is necessary for reprocessing this file is to change the user's name on the CREATE statement.

Figure 5.57 shows an example of a MAKEUSER file. In this example, two users are added to the system. Each user has several unique restrictions and shared parameters. Because of the way MAKEUSER interprets keywords, the user DIANA is affected only by the keywords listed before the #CREATE DIANA statement. The user HENRY, on the other hand, is affected by all the keywords in this file.

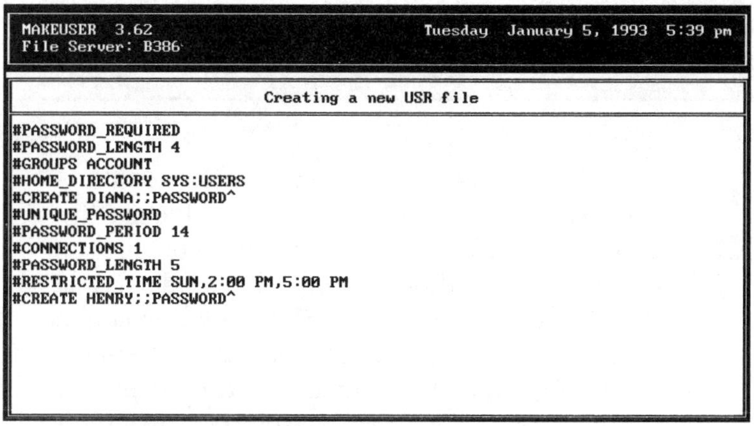

```
MAKEUSER  3.62                    Tuesday  January 5, 1993  5:39 pm
File Server: B386

                      Creating a new USR file
#PASSWORD_REQUIRED
#PASSWORD_LENGTH 4
#GROUPS ACCOUNT
#HOME_DIRECTORY SYS:USERS
#CREATE DIANA;;PASSWORD^
#UNIQUE_PASSWORD
#PASSWORD_PERIOD 14
#CONNECTIONS 1
#PASSWORD_LENGTH 5
#RESTRICTED_TIME SUN,2:00 PM,5:00 PM
#CREATE HENRY;;PASSWORD^
```

Figure 5.57

An example of a MAKEUSER script.

After you fill in the Creating a New USR file and press Esc, NetWare prompts you to save and name the USR file. Do not give the file a dot extension—it is added automatically. The extension is always USR. You name the file TEST.USR, for example, by typing **TEST**.

After you create a USR file, you must process it. Processing it tells you what syntax errors you have made. If there are no syntax errors, processing the file runs the file's commands. If errors appear, you must correct the errors, then reprocess the file to run the commands.

Edit the USR file by selecting the Edit USR File option. Figure 5.58 shows the error report that results from processing the TEST.USR file with errors.

Figure 5.58

The USR error report.

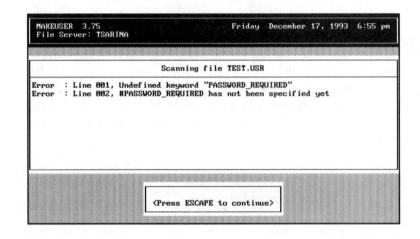

```
MAKEUSER  3.75                        Friday  December 17, 1993  6:55 pm
File Server: TSARINA
```

```
                         Scanning file TEST.USR

Error  : Line 001, Undefined keyword "PASSWORD_REQUIRED"
Error  : Line 002, #PASSWORD_REQUIRED has not been specified yet
```

```
                         <Press ESCAPE to continue>
```

Note   Figure 5.58 shows two errors in this file. In truth, however, only one error exists. Because the line that contains the error must run correctly before the line that includes the second error, both lines display an error. Fix the errors in your USR file—therefore, from the top down. Fixing one error can correct several subsequent errors. You might, in fact, want to reprocess the file after you fix each error to see the number of other errors it cleared up.

MAKEUSER Keywords

The following list contains the available MAKEUSER commands and syntax:

◆ **#ACCOUNT_EXPIRATION** *month, day, year.* The account no longer permits access after the date specified.

◆ **#ACCOUNTING** *balance, lowlimit.* The account is given an account balance with which to start, and a low limit below which it cannot go. Both parameters are required.

- **#CLEAR or #RESET.** These commands act as stop markers. When the script is processed, a #CREATE or #DELETE statement processes all keywords until it encounters a #CLEAR or #RESET.

- **#CONNECTIONS *number*.** The account is limited as to the number of workstations it can log in to at one time.

- **#CREATE *username;fullname;password;groups;rights*.** Establishes a user ID. The only required field is username; if #PASSWORD_REQUIRED is used, the password field also is required. You must leave a blank space between semicolons if you do not intend to use a field. Use the carat (^) to end the #CREATE field if you do not plan to use all fields.

- **#DEFAULT_PROFILE *profile*.** If NetWare Name Service is used, this keyword enables the account to access a preassigned profile name.

- **#DELETE *username*.** If you use MAKEUSER to clean up user accounts no longer active, this keyword wipes out old accounts.

- **#GROUPS *group*.** This keyword adds to the listed groups any user defined by the #CREATE statement.

- **#HOME_DIRECTORY *path*.** MAKEUSER creates a HOME directory for each user defined by the #CREATE keyword. The default HOME directory is off the root of SYS:. This keyword enables you to redirect the HOME directory path.

- **#HOME_SERVER *server*.** NetWare Name Services utilizes this keyword, which enables you to specify the file server in which the HOME Directory is created. This keyword is used in conjunction with #HOME_DIRECTORY. If you use the #MAX_DISK_SPACE keyword, the #HOME_SERVER keyword must come first.

- **#LOGIN_SCRIPT *path\filename*.** This keyword copies the specified text file into the user account's MAIL_ID directory as the LOGIN file.

- **#MAX_DISK_SPACE *vol:,number*.** This keyword enables you to specify the maximum disk space allowed to the user for the volume specified.

◆ **#NO_HOME_DIRECTORY.** This keyword disables MAKEUSER's function of creating a HOME directory for the user.

◆ **#PASSWORD_LENGTH** *length.* This keyword defines the minimum length of a password.

◆ **#PASSWORD_PERIOD** *days.* This keyword specifies the number of days a password is valid.

◆ **#PASSWORD_REQUIRED.** Use this keyword if you require users to have passwords. This keyword must come before all other password-related keywords.

◆ **#PROFILES** *profile.* This keyword enables you to assign existing profiles to users. This keyword is new for NetWare Naming Services.

◆ **#PURGE_USER_DIRECTORY.** When using MAKEUSER to delete users, this keyword deletes all the files and subdirectories under the specified user's HOME directory. Use #HOME_DIRECTORY to specify where to find the user's HOME directory if it is not off SYS:.

◆ **#REM or REM.** These keywords enable you to keep notes in the MAKEUSER file. Anything typed on the same line as #REM or REM is not processed.

◆ **#RESTRICTED_TIME** *day,start,end.* Use this option to specify when a user cannot be logged in to the network.

◆ **#STATIONS** *network,station#,station#.* The #STATIONS keyword enables you to specify the network and node addresses to which the user can log in. The first number after #STATIONS is the network address followed by a comma; then a list follows of all the node addresses on that network to which the user can log in. Separate each node address with a comma.

◆ **#UNIQUE_PASSWORD.** This keyword requires that users cannot repeat the most recent passwords.

USERDEF

The USERDEF utility enables you to add, create, and edit templates, then use those templates to process users. Figure 5.59 shows the Available Options menu for USERDEF. Instead of creating and managing several files from MAKEUSER, you can use templates available in USERDEF by using different user parameters. Figure 5.60, for example, shows three templates created by the System Administrator.

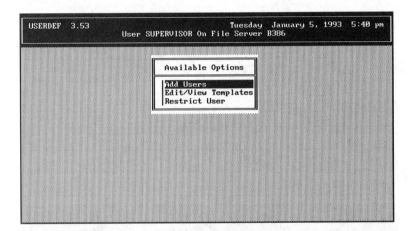

Figure 5.59

The Available Options menu in the USERDEF utility.

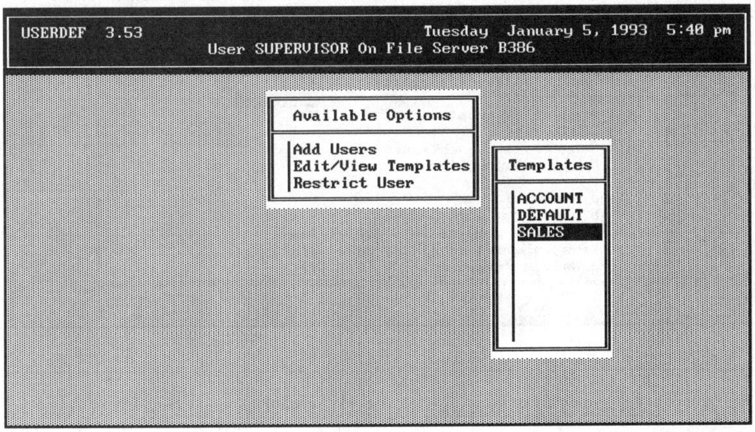

Figure 5.60

Examples of USERDEF templates.

Each template enables you to create or edit login scripts and other parameters (see fig. 5.61). The parameters you can use include setting up default directories, copying PRINTCON jobs from other users, determining to which groups users should belong, and creating account restrictions. Figure 5.62 shows all the available parameters for configuring a template.

Figure 5.61

USERDEF template options.

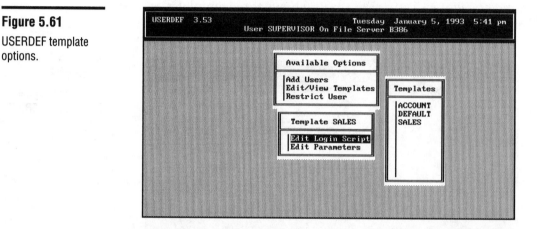

When you add users, a list appears that shows users that already exist on the network and those that have not yet been added. If you press Ins, the USERDEF utility asks for the user's full name.

Figure 5.62

USERDEF template parameters.

In figure 5.63, for example, a new user named PM – Afternoon Shift is added to the list of users by using the Account template.

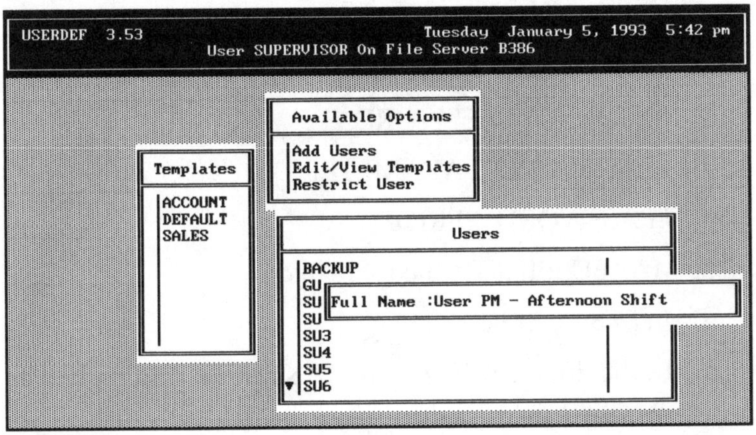

Figure 5.63

Adding a new user in the USERDEF Account template.

After you add the user, USERDEF uses the first name as the login name. If you press Esc, USERDEF asks if you want to create the user by using the specified template. Figure 5.64 shows the confirmation menu for the Sales template when you add a new user to the sales list. After you confirm that you want to create a new user using that template, NetWare compiles and processes a USR file.

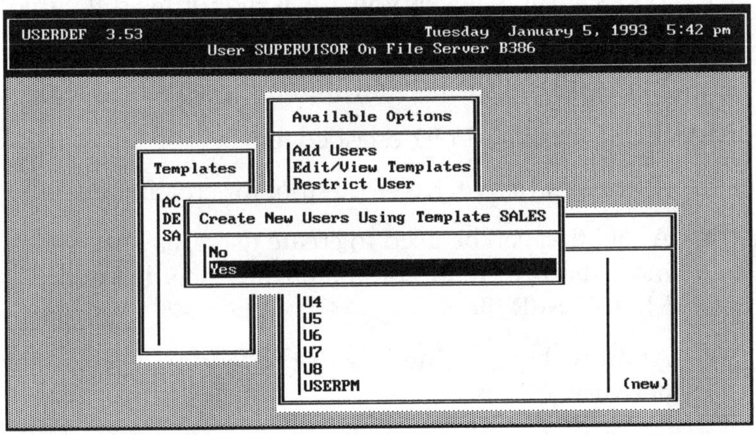

Figure 5.64

Confirming a new user in the Sales template.

Section Review Questions

21. Which keyword is necessary in the MAKEUSER utility to enable you to set password parameters?

    a. #PASSWORD_REQUIRED

    b. #REQUIRE_PASSWORD

    c. #PASSWORD_PARAMETERS

    d. #PASSWORD_PERIOD

22. The MAKEUSER .RPT file is created:

    a. In SYS:PUBLIC

    b. In the directory in which MAKEUSER originally was executed

    c. In the user's HOME directory

    d. In SYS:SYSTEM

23. Which statement about USERDEF is correct?

    a. You can make someone a Supervisor equivalent using USERDEF.

    b. You can create a PRINTCON job for the new user.

    c. When adding a user, you are asked for his full name, then for his login name.

    d. You can limit the user's volume space using a template.

24. MAKEUSER can best be described as:

    a. A non-restrictive, free-form tool for creating users

    b. A tool that can be used to create users, as long as no more than 10 create commands are included in the MAKEUSER file

    c. A utility that provides a script for adding users to the network

    d. A utility that can be used in place of USERDEF because there are no differences between the two

25. All files created with the MAKEUSER utility have a _____ extension.

    a. SCP

    b. MKU

    c. COM

    d. USR

26. Which of the following is NOT a true statement?

    a. After creating a USR file you must process it.

    b. USR files must be correct the first time because they can only be processed once.

    c. All USR files create users when processed.

    d. Processing a USR file tells you what syntax errors have been found in the file.

27. When correcting errors in the USR file:

    a. Only syntax errors must be corrected

    b. Make certain all keywords are lowercase and preceded by a pound sign (#)

    c. Work from the top down because correcting one error may correct several errors on lines below it

    d. Remember that the flow of events is always downward

28. The following MAKEUSER keyword requires a user name, but considers information such as password and rights to be optional:

    a. GROUPS

    b. DELETE

    c. CLEAR

    d. CREATE

29. The keyword in a MAKEUSER script that enables an account to access a preassigned profile name when NetWare Name Services is used is:

    a. DEFAULT_PROFILE

    b. GROUPS

    c. CREATE

    d. PROFILE

30. To specify when a user CANNOT be logged into the network, create user accounts with a MAKEUSER file containing this command:

    a. LOGIN_SCRIPT

    b. PROFILES

    c. RESTRICTED_TIME

    d. STATIONS

31. Which of the following statements is true?

    a. LOGIN_SCRIPT must be used if NO_HOME_DIRECTORY is not used.

    b. REM is used to put non-processed statements into a USR file.

    c. NO_HOME_DIRECTORY sends the user's data files to SYS:PUBLIC for storage.

    d. None of these statements are true.

32. Which *two* MAKEUSER commands should be used together?

    a. PASSWORD_LENGTH

    b. PASSWORD_PERIOD

    c. RESTRICTED_TIME

    d. STATIONS

33. Which MAKEUSER command must be used on a network requiring strict access control?

    a. UNIQUE_PASSWORD

    b. PASSWORD_LENGTH

    c. PASSWORD_PERIOD

    d. PASSWORD_REQUIRED

Answers

21. a

22. b

23. c

24. c

25. d

26. b

27. c

28. d

29. a

30. c

31. b

32. a and b

33. d

Performing Backups Using SBACKUP

Storage Management Services (SMS) are included with NetWare 3.12 in the form of SBACKUP. SBACKUP is included with NetWare 3.12 to provide backup and restoration of data independent of the operating system or file system version. SBACKUP can be used to back up NetWare file systems and also lets Btrieve (SQL) databases, DOS workstations, and OS/2 workstations take advantage of backup capabilities.

Back up and restore a server bindery and trustee assignments using SBACKUP.

SBACKUP functions by using files called *Target Service Agents* (TSA). A TSA called TSA_DOS.NLM is loaded at the host server, along with the SBACKUP.NLM. (A *host server* is the one from which the backup capability is being run.)

A host server has the storage device and storage controller attached to it. All *targets* (devices being backed up) are backed up to the host.

Another TSA, called TSA_SMS, is loaded at the DOS client (target). When the TSAs are loaded with parameters correctly set, the client is able to specify drives to back up, the server to attach to in order to backup and restore, buffer size for faster access, and other options.

The backup software determines which files to back up based on the *modify bit*. Whenever a file is added or changed, the file is flagged with a modify bit so that the backup software knows it was added or changed.

Backup Options

 Describe SMS and strategies for implementing successful storage management.

SBACKUP is Novell's implementation of SMS on NetWare 3.12. As such, it provides four strategies (options) for backing up your server. These four options include the following:

◆ **Full backup**—Backs up all files on the target. It does not take into consideration whether these files were backed up previously and have not changed since. The modify bit is cleared when a full backup is performed.

♦ **Incremental backup**—Backs up all files that are new or that have been modified in some way since the last backup. The modify bit is cleared when an incremental backup is performed.

♦ **Differential backup**—Backs up all data that has changed since the last time a full backup was done, even if the changed files were previously backed up using an incremental backup. The modify bit is not cleared when a differential backup is performed. By not clearing this bit, the backup software "knows" to back up this file again during the incremental backup.

♦ **Custom backup**—Backs up what you specify. The status of the modify bit on changed or added files depends on what you decide to back up.

SMS provides these backup options so that you can reduce the amount of time spent doing a backup. If you perform a full backup on Friday, for example, you can do an incremental backup on Monday through Thursday. Depending on the amount of work done during the week, each of your incremental backups should take just a few minutes.

If you have to restore your backup files at any time during the week, you will have to restore Friday's full backup as well as each day's incremental backup.

Assuming you performed a full backup on Friday, and then performed a differential backup each day that week, restoring your files is much quicker. You only need to restore Friday's full backup, as well as the differential backup for the day before you lost your files. The differential backup is cumulative, meaning that it backs up all files that were modified or added since the last full backup.

A differential backup takes longer than an incremental backup, but is quicker to restore—you only have to restore the full backup and the single differential backup. The incremental backup method requires that you restore the full backup and each of the incremental backups that have been run since the last full backup.

373

Running SBACKUP

SBACKUP can be used to back up and restore NetWare servers. In addition, the SBACKUP NLM can be loaded onto a NetWare server and be used to backup a network client. This section discusses backing up and restoring a NetWare server, as well as backing up a NetWare client.

Backing Up and Restoring a NetWare Server

 Use SBACKUP, NetWare's utility for implementing SMS, to perform a simple backup and restore.

To perform a backup using NetWare's SBACKUP utility, first load the required TSAs on the clients and servers. The TSAs will then automatically load any needed support files. Once the TSAs and support files are loaded, load the SBACKUP NLM (type **load SBACKUP** at the file server console and press Enter). Next, choose the device to be backed up (*the target*), and choose a working directory to hold the session log and error files. Now you can decide what is to be backed up.

 Backup and restore a server bindery and trustee assignments using SBACKUP.

For example, choose the NetWare Server when prompted with what to back up. Choosing this option backs up the server bindery files, which includes the user's trustee assignment information.

The next step in the process is to set the *archive bit* (a file attribute which indicates the file was backed up), and choose to append this backup to a previous one if appropriate. Then provide a title for this session. Once the backup device is set up, complete the backup.

You can restore backed-up files using the SBACKUP NLM. Choose to restore, however, instead of backing up files, and follow the instructions. They are very similar to the original backup instructions.

Besides backing up NetWare servers, you can also back up clients using the SBACKUP NLM.

Backing Up a NetWare Client

Load the components needed to perform a client backup using SBACKUP.

To back up a NetWare DOS client, load TSA_DOS at the server. At the client, setup the AUTOEXEC.BAT file to load the TSA_SMS.COM file, then reboot the client so the file will be loaded.

Once the TSA is loaded on the client, choose the client to be backed up from the server. When prompted for a user name, enter *user identification* (user ID) for a user who has Supervisor or Supervisor-equivalent rights. Then, complete the backup by following the prompts; the client backup is similar to the NetWare server backup.

Section Review Questions

34. Which SBACKUP option backs up only those files that have changed since the last backup, even if it was NOT a full backup?

    a. Full

    b. Incremental

    c. Differential

    d. Custom

35. Which SBACKUP option backs up only those files that have changed since the last full backup was performed?

    a. Full

    b. Incremental

    c. Differential

    d. Custom

36. Which files must be loaded in order to run the SBACKUP utility?

    a. SBACKUP.EXE and SBACKUP.NLM

    b. SBACKUP.NLM and TSA_DOS.NLM

    c. SBACKUP.NLM, TSA_DOS.NLM, and TSA.EXE

    d. SBACKUP.NLM, TSA_DOS.NLM, and TSA_SMS

37. The computer that has the storage device and storage controller attached to it is called:

    a. Target

    b. Host

    c. Server

    d. Storage Device

38. The backup software determines which files to back up based on the _____.

    a. Modify bit

    b. Backup flag

    c. Restore attribute

    d. Date file

39. In order to back up a NetWare client:

    a. You must load the SMS_TSA.COM file at the server

    b. Load all TSA support files by listing them individually in the server's AUTOEXEC.NCF file

   c. You must choose the server as the target device

   d. You must load the SBACKUP NLM at the file server

40. Which option must you choose in order to backup a server's bindery and trustee assignments?

   a. Target Service Agent

   b. Archive Bit

   c. NetWare Server

   d. Backup Host Device

Answers

34. b

35. c

36. d

37. b

38. a

39. d

40. c

Using NetWare HELP

 Activate and navigate Help for each type of utility.

NetWare provides two online help facilities:

◆ Novell ElectroText

◆ F1 Help

Novell ElectroText contains an electronic copy of the entire
NetWare 3.12 manual set, while the F1 help (also known as
contact-sensitive help) is provided at the point of contact with a
utility menu or option. Both Novell ElectroText and F1 Help are
discussed in this section.

Novell ElectroText

ElectroText is Novell's online help utility that provides access to
the online equivalent of Novell's manual set. It uses a search
engine and the online set of manuals, referred to as a *bookshelf*, to
find the information that you request.

There are three specific benefits to using Novell's ElectroText.
First, you can search the entire bookshelf, or search only a single
book using ElectroText. If you do not know in which Novell book
the information that you are seeking can be found, ElectroText can
find the correct book for you.

Second, if the network Administrator sets up ElectroText with
appropriate access rights for the group EVERYONE, each user on
the network can access ElectroText. Contrast this to the single set
of manuals that ship with the product and are often locked in the
network Administrator's office.

Third, if a printed copy of specific information is needed, Novell's
ElectroText allows you to print small or large portions of the
electronic documentation.

The main drawback of Novell ElectroText is that it requires about
30 MB of extra disk space to install the documentation. In addition, the search engine and the bookshelf work only on a
Microsoft Windows client. You cannot run it from DOS.

When you open Novell's ElectroText documentation, you notice
that it looks similar to the pages of a book, pasted inside a
Microsoft Windows' window. This was done by design to simplify its use.

Novell's ElectroText contains three components:

- ◆ Library window
- ◆ Book window
- ◆ Search windows

The Library window lets you choose the book from which you want to conduct your search and then read the desired information. The Book window displays the book's table of contents, as well as the page of the book that you are reading. The Search window lets you choose a word or a phrase for which to search.

During installation, Novell's ElectroText executable file—ET.EXE—is copied into the SYS:PUBLIC directory. This allows access by all users with rights to the PUBLIC directory. The documentation itself is copied to a directory called DOC. To provide Microsoft Windows support, the ET.INI file is copied into the Windows directory on each client.

F1 Help

Help is also provided from within DOS-based menu utilities. To activate help in these utilities, start the utility by typing the name of the utility at the DOS prompt, such as SESSION. Once the main menu is open, you can get help by pressing F1. To see help on any particular item of information in the utility, choose the item and then press F1.

Section Review Questions

41. Which function key shows you help screens?

    a. F1

    b. F3

    c. F5

    d. F6

42. Which of the following is NOT a window component of Novell's ElectroText documentation?

    a. Library

    b. Find

    c. Book

    d. Search

43. The file which starts ElectroText is called:

    a. ET.EXE

    b. BOOK.EXE

    c. ET.COM

    d. STARTBK.EXE

44. The files which contain the ElectroText manuals are stored in:

    a. PUBLIC

    b. DOC

    c. BOOK

    d. LOGIN

45. The main drawback of Novell ElectroText is:

    a. Its documentation cannot be printed

    b. It is only available to people with Supervisor rights

    c. Its files take up 30 MB of disk storage space

    d. It can only be installed on a stand-alone PC

Answers

41. a

42. b

43. a

44. b

45. c

Understanding the SESSION Menu Utility

NetWare includes a utility that is more useful for novice users than it is for System Administrators. This utility is called SESSION. In the SESSION utility, you can map drives, send messages to users and groups, and view your effective rights.

Figure 5.65 shows the main SESSION menu screen. From this menu, you can perform the tasks discussed in the following sections.

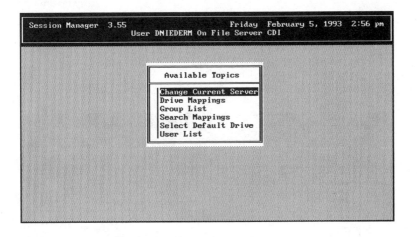

Figure 5.65

The SESSION main menu.

Change Current Server

This option enables you to attach to another server and perform SESSION functions on another server.

Drive Mappings

From this option, you can add and delete regular drive mappings. Figure 5.66 shows a currently mapped drive. To add a drive mapping, press Ins, type an available drive letter, and press Enter. You then can enter the path or press Ins a second time and select the path through menus. Both methods were previously explained in the section on SYSCON.

381

Figure 5.66

Current Drive
Mappings in
SESSION.

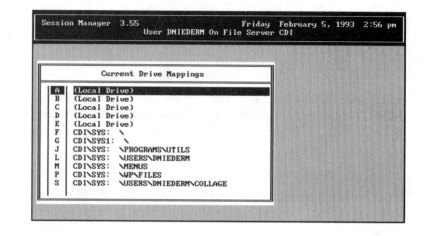

You also can view your effective rights in any of the mapped
drives by highlighting the mapping and pressing Enter. Figure
5.67 shows a listing of Effective Rights for the
\PROGRAMS\UTILS mapping.

Figure 5.67

Viewing Effective
Rights in SESSION.

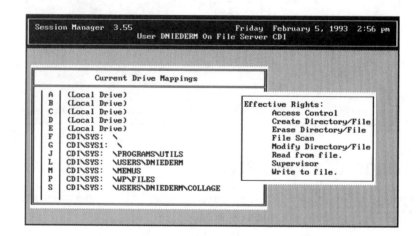

Note

In figure 5.67, notice that the Current Drive Mappings menu has a double-line border. The Effective
Rights menu has only a single-line border.

The double-line border is NetWare's notation that
items from this menu can be chosen or changed.

The single-line border means that the information can only be viewed, that there are no submenus, and the information cannot be changed from that location.

Figure 5.68 reminds you that you cannot set Effective Rights for local drives.

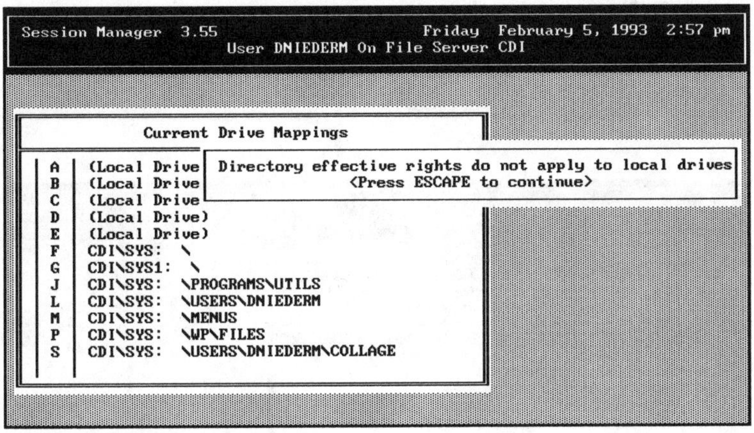

```
Session Manager  3.55                    Friday  February 5, 1993  2:57 pm
                      User DNIEDERM On File Server CDI

          Current Drive Mappings

     A   (Local Drive  Directory effective rights do not apply to local drives
     B   (Local Drive          <Press ESCAPE to continue>
     C   (Local Drive
     D   (Local Drive)
     E   (Local Drive)
     F   CDI\SYS:   \
     G   CDI\SYS1:  \
     J   CDI\SYS:   \PROGRAMS\UTILS
     L   CDI\SYS:   \USERS\DNIEDERM
     M   CDI\SYS:   \MENUS
     P   CDI\SYS:   \WP\FILES
     S   CDI\SYS:   \USERS\DNIEDERM\COLLAGE
```

Figure 5.68

Reminder that you cannot assign rights to local drives.

Group List

This option displays all the groups that have been created in SYSCON. You can highlight a group and press Enter to send a message to any user who is logged in and belongs to this group. Figure 5.69 shows a message sent to anyone belonging to the CASTELLE group.

Search Mappings

The Search Mappings option enables you to view your current search drive mappings, as shown in figure 5.70, and to create and delete search mappings. This option works the same way as Drive Mappings, except that you select a search drive number rather than a letter when creating a search drive mapping.

383

Figure 5.69

Sending a message
through SESSION.

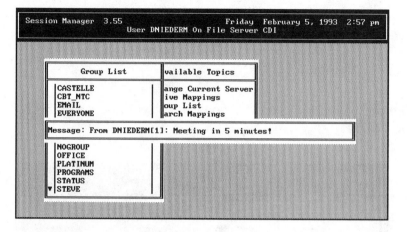

Figure 5.70

Viewing search
mappings in
SESSION.

Select Default Drive

This option displays all your currently mapped drives. When you
highlight a drive and press Enter, the SESSION menu sets the
drive letter to which you exit when you leave SESSION.

User List

This option shows you all the users currently logged in to the
network. After you highlight a user and press Enter, you see a

menu with two options: Display User Information and Send Message.

From this menu, you can view user information, as shown in figure 5.71, or you can send a menu.

```
Session Manager  3.55                  Friday  February 5, 1993  2:58 pm
                    User DNIEDERM On File Server CDI


    Current Users        Station  ble Topics

   00001136               013    Current Server
   BCHAFFIN               011    appings
   CMI
   CMI                 Full Name:        Brian Chaffins
   COMM                Object Type:      User
   DNIEDERM            Login Time:       Friday  February 5, 1993   12:52 pm
   FRED                Network Address:  00000005
   GDALL               Network Node:     191f02706301
   GUEST
   JWEYAND               024
   LORI                  023
   MHS                   002
 ▼ NOT-LOGGED-IN         003
```

Figure 5.71

Viewing information about a user in SESSION.

Section Review Questions

46. Which of the following is NOT a task that can be performed using the SESSION utility?

    a. Change servers

    b. View your effective rights

    c. Create users

    d. View users currently logged in

47. A double-line border in a utility indicates:

    a. Items in this menu can be chosen or changed

    b. Items in this menu require Supervisor rights

    c. Items in this menu are flagged as read-only

    d. Items in this menu apply only to users, not groups

385

48. Which of the following statements is true?

  a. You can only make a temporary change in the default drive assignment using the SESSION utility.

  b. The SESSION utility was designed primarily for network Administrators.

  c. Choose Select Default Drive to send a message to a user with a drive mapped to that letter.

  d. You cannot set effective rights for local drives.

49. The *two* options found in the User List menu include:

  a. Select Default Drive

  b. Display User Information

  c. Send Message

  d. Set Effective Rights

50. To view, create, or delete drive numbers that are to be used when looking for executable files, choose the _____ option from the SESSION menu.

  a. Change Current Server

  b. Search Mappings

  c. Drive Mappings

  d. Select Default Drive

Answers

46. c

47. a

48. d

49. b and c

50. b

Using WSUPDATE

WSUPDATE is a command-line utility that enables you to update workstation files from newer files located on the file server. This utility is useful for updating DOS Requester files. By using the WSUPDATE utility, you can have the workstation compare the date stamp on a file located on the workstation's hard drive or floppy drive to a version of the file in a specified directory on the file server. If the version on the file server is newer than the one on the workstation, you can have the file on the workstation overwritten or copied to a file with an OLD extension and updated.

Use the following syntax for WSUPDATE:

```
WSUPDATE source destination options
```

or

```
WSUPDATE /F=scriptfile
```

In the preceding syntax, *source* is the location and name of the file on the network that other files are checked against, *destination* is the location and name of the file to be replaced or updated, and *scriptfile* is a file you create that contains a list of source and destination pairs for automatic execution.

To update the workstation files easily, copy the updated files into one of the search drives on the network and type the following on a workstation using the regular DOS Requester file:

```
WSUPDATE V:\UPDATE\VLM.EXE C:\NWCLIENT\VLM.EXE
```

You can update the workstation DOS Requester files when the user logs on to the network by creating a WSUPDATE configuration file for each user's workstation, and executing the WSUPDATE program from the user's login script. If the user's WSUPDATE script is named WSUPD.CFG, for example, type the following into the login script:

```
IF DAY_OF_WEEK = 2 #WSUPDATE /F=WSUP.CFG
```

The script WSUPD.CFG resembles the following:

```
F:XMSNETX.COM C:XMSNETX.COM
F:CONFIG.SYS C:CONFIG.SYS
```

387

Be cautious about globally updating files using WSUPDATE, particularly IPX.COM or NET.CFG files. Not all workstations use the same configuration files; replacing a good configuration file with a generic file can cause the workstation to fail to connect to the network.

The WSUPDATE utility enables you to use the following options:

- ◆ **/I.** Prompts the user to input whether the file should be overwritten, renamed, or ignored (the default option).

- ◆ **/C.** Copies the new file over an existing one automatically.

- ◆ **/R.** Renames the old file with the OLD extension automatically.

- ◆ **/S.** Searches all subdirectories on the workstation for outdated files.

- ◆ **/O.** Updates read-only files.

- ◆ **/L=*path/filename*.** Creates a log file that tracks WSUPDATE activity.

 The source path must be the full directory path, including the file name.

The destination must be a specific drive; paths are not permitted. You also can use ALL or ALL_LOCAL in place of the drive letter. ALL searches *each* network drive.

Section Review Questions

51. One recommended use of WSUPDATE is:

    a. To update DOS Requester files

    b. To update WordPerfect Office shell files

c. To update bindery files

d. To update application programs

52. What does the WSUPDATE utility use to determine whether the client or the server file is the newest?

    a. Directory date

    b. Current date and time

    c. File date

    d. Server backup date

53. What additional information must file the /F option of the WSUPDATE utility?

    a. Name of a specific file to be updated

    b. The fixed time the update is to start

    c. The first file to be found and updated

    d. Name of the script file that contains source and destination pairs

54. To update the DOS Requester files on a client at the time the user logs in to the network:

    a. Send a broadcast message asking them to notify you of their login

    b. Execute the user's specific WSUPDATE file from within their login script

    c. Set the /U option of WSUPDATE to activate whenever the LOGIN.EXE file is run

    d. None of the above will automatically update files at a user's login

55. Which of the following is NOT a WSUPDATE option?

    a. /I

    b. /C

    c. /U

    d. /O

Answers

51. a

52. c

53. d

54. b

55. c

Case Study

1. Correct the following MAKEUSER file.

The file is called NEWUSER.TXT.

```
#Account_Expiration December 31, 1994
#CONNECTION 2
#GROUPS ACCOUNT,TECHS
#HOME_DIRECTORY SYS:USERS
#LOGIN_SCRIPT SYS:SCRIPTS\LOGIN.NEW
#NO_HOME_DIRECTORY
#PASSWORD_LENGTH 6
#PASSWORD_REQUIRED
#UNIQUE_PASSWORD YES
#CREATE TOM;TOM WEYAND;;TECHS
```

2. Several items must exist on the network before the corrected script will work. Please list them in the following spaces.

   a.

   b.

   c.

   d.

3. Create a MAKEUSER script that does the following:

   a. Deletes the users Lori, Fred, and Marie.

   b. Deletes each user's HOME directory under SYS:USERS.

Printing on a
Novell Network

Chapters 4 and 5 showed you ways to set up directory structures, add users and groups to the network, control and manage the system by using command-line utilities, and navigate the menu utilities. The next factor common to all current versions of NetWare is printing. Frequently, users need to print hard copies of their work on a network, much as they do on stand-alone PCs. Through NetWare you can set up printing on your network so that any networked user can access the printer needed to get the job done.

In this chapter, you learn to do the following tasks:

- ◆ Define queues by using PCONSOLE
- ◆ Install print servers
- ◆ Direct the output
- ◆ Control the print server
- ◆ Customize the printers by using PRINTDEF
- ◆ Create print jobs by using PRINTCON
- ◆ Use related print commands
- ◆ Print from an OS/2 workstation

Keep in mind that this chapter explains the common features of printing. Core printing and the PSERVER VAP are explained in Chapter 10, "Understanding NetWare 2.2 System Manager Functions," and the PSERVER *NetWare Loadable Module* (NLM) is discussed in Chapter 9, "Learning NetWare 3.1*x* Advanced Administration Skills."

Understanding Network Printing

When you print from a stand-alone computer, the job goes through the cable directly to the printer's buffer. Only after the entire print job has been printed or is in the printer's buffer is the computer free to perform other tasks.

When you print on a network, however, the job is sent from your workstation out through the network cable to the file server. The job then is directed into a queue, which is assigned a hexadecimally named directory under SYS:SYSTEM. A *queue* assigns printer jobs in the specific order in which they are printed. Queues can have English names to help you remember them, and are created through the PCONSOLE menu utility.

 In 2.2, you can create a queue at the file server console. You cannot create a queue at the 3.12 file server console.

All print jobs are kept in the queues until the designated printer is available. The file server is in charge of polling the printers and queues to make sure that jobs are getting to the printers.

 Novell provides four basic methods of printing in the network environment:

- ◆ Core printing services
- ◆ VAP or NLM print servers
- ◆ Dedicated print servers
- ◆ Remote workstation printing

In this chapter, you learn about dedicated print servers and remote workstation printers, as well as the command-line utilities involved with printing.

The printing methods discussed in this section require a dedicated workstation to be used as the print server. The PSERVER.EXE program supplies the same functionality as the PSERVER.VAP and the PSERVER.NLM that run on the file server, but adds the benefit of printer service dedication. This solution is best for heavy production printing. The capability to use computers as print servers—from the 8088 to the current 80486 series—enables you to tailor this configuration to your needs.

PSERVER.EXE runs on a workstation.
PSERVER.VAP runs on 2.2 file servers.
PSERVER.NLM runs on 3.1*x* file servers.

Older 8086 and 8088 PCs are considerably slower than the newer processors. For optimum performance, consider using an 80386 or 80486.

Novell also offers the capability to share a locally attached printer. To enable the RPRINTER.EXE command to function, you must set up a remote printer definition on a print server. The RPRINTER.EXE loads as a background task that uses approximately 5 KB to 9 KB of memory. Because of this background operation, do not use this method for heavy printing.

The NetWare RPRINTER.EXE command is selective regarding the hardware with which it works. If you experience problems with a particular computer port using this type of shared printing, use a different port.

Describe the basic components of network printing and how they interrelate in processing a print job. Describe the general steps necessary for setting up the components.

Novell's NetWare printing environment consists of three primary components:

◆ Print queues

◆ Print servers

◆ Printers

The next three sections of this chapter discuss each of these components.

Section Review Questions

1. When you print on a network, where does a print job go first after leaving the workstation that printed the job?

    a. To the print server

    b. To the printer

    c. To a network queue

    d. To RPRINTER

2. Which of the following is not a method of printing?

    a. Print server

    b. Nondedicated print server

    c. Remote workstation

    d. Core printing

3. Which of the following programs activate printing when loaded on a workstation?

    a. PSERVER.EXE

    b. PSERVER.VAP

    c. RPRINTER.EXE

    d. PSERVER.NLM

4. Of the following, which *two* programs provide printing services from a file server?

    a. PSERVER.VAP

    b. PSERVER.EXE

    c. RPRINTER.EXE

    d. PSERVER.NLM

5. Which printing program is best for light production printing?

    a. PSERVER.EXE

    b. PSERVER.VAP

    c. RPRINTER.EXE

    d. PSERVER.NLM

6. The main difference between printing on a stand-alone computer and printing on a network computer is:

    a. Hexadecimal names are used instead of English names for print jobs on the network.

    b. A stand-alone computer sends the print job to a printer buffer, but the print job on the network goes to a queue on the file server.

    c. File server queues must have the same name as a printer or the print job cannot be stored in a print buffer.

    d. You can send only one print job at a time to be printed on the network, but you can send several jobs simultaneously to a stand-alone printer.

7. The PSERVER.EXE program runs:

    a. On the 2.2 file server

    b. On the 3.1x file server

    c. On a print server attached to the network

    d. On the workstation

Answers

1. a

2. b

3. a

4. a and d

5. c

6. b

7. d

Examining and Defining Queues Using PCONSOLE

The PCONSOLE menu utility enables System Supervisors to create and define queues and print servers. Queue operators and print server operators can manage queues and print servers from this menu, while users can place jobs into queues and manage their own print jobs from this menu.

The first PCONSOLE menu, the Available Options menu (see fig. 6.1), enables you to select from the following three options: Change Current File Server, Print Queue Information, and Print Server Information.

Perform basic network printing maintenance tasks, such as viewing and modifying printing information in PCONSOLE.

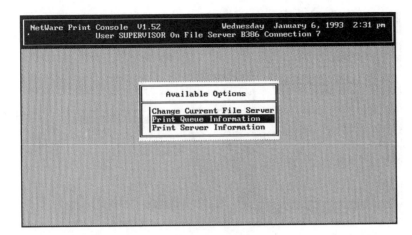

Figure 6.1

PCONSOLE's main menu.

After you select the Print Queue Information option, a list of print queues appears on-screen (see fig. 6.2). If you are a Supervisor equivalent, you can create a new queue in this option by pressing Ins and entering the new queue.

Figure 6.2

PCONSOLE's print queue information.

After highlighting a queue and pressing Enter, the Print Queue Information menu appears (see fig. 6.3). This menu has seven options, which are described in the following sections.

397

Figure 6.3

PCONSOLE's specific queue information.

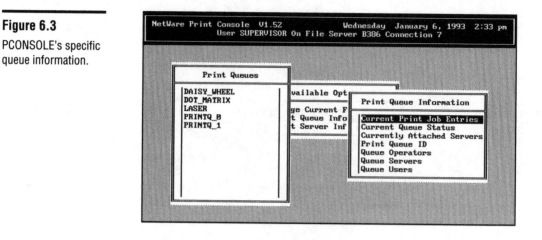

Current Print Job Entries

The Current Print Job Entries option in the Print Queue Information menu shows you all the jobs in a queue. Once you understand the information it provides, you can then access the options to manage print jobs.

 Manage print jobs in the print queue by viewing their properties, pausing, rushing, delaying, printing, and deleting jobs in the queue.

The information is arranged in six columns, as illustrated in figure 6.4. The first column, Seq, which stands for *Sequence*, shows the order in which the jobs will be printed. The second column, Banner Name, is the name of the user sending the print job. Description, the third column, lists the file names. If the job is sent through a DOS command, such as PRINT, or a print screen, or is directed to a print device, this column shows the logical port from which the job was captured, and the word CATCH, as shown in the third job in figure 6.4. The Form column shows the form that has been mounted for this queue.

```
NetWare Print Console  V1.52           Wednesday  January 6, 1993  2:44 pm
                  User SUPERVISOR On File Server CDI286 Connection 2

   Seq Banner Name  Description                        Form Status  Job
       1 SUPERVISOR   ADMINS.MNU                          0 Ready      1
       2 SUPERVISOR   NEW.TXT                             0 Held       2
       3 DNIEDERM     LPT1 Catch                          0 Waiting    4
       4 SUPERVISOR   AUDIT.LOG                           0 Adding     5
       5 SUPERVISOR   FTPSERV.CFG                         0 Ready      6
```

Figure 6.4

An example of PCONSOLE's active jobs.

The fifth column, Status, displays one of five possible conditions: Active, Held, Adding, Waiting, and Ready.

> The Active condition designates the job currently printing. No parameters can be changed for this job.

The only thing you can do to a job marked Active is delete it. Place the highlight bar on the desired print job and press Del. You also can use F5 to mark several jobs, then press Del. You are asked for confirmation if you attempt to delete the active job. The active job's deletion does not stop the printer. Before you can delete the active job and clear the job from the printer buffer, however, you must abort the job from the print server. Refer to the section on print servers later in this chapter.

Any jobs marked with the Held condition are not printed until the hold flag is removed. Two different hold flags can be placed on a job that has been queued to print. A User Hold can be placed on the file by pressing Enter on the job and changing the User Hold to Yes. The job owner and the queue operators can place and remove this flag. The Operator Hold flag can be placed or removed only by the queue operator. To set this flag, select the job to be held by pressing Enter, and set the Operator Hold to Yes.

399

The Adding condition designates a job that is in the process of being sent by a user. If the user has exited an application and the job still says ADDING, the user should type

ENDCAP, which forces the job into the Ready mode.

The Waiting condition is shown when a print job has been told to wait until a specific date and time before printing. To set deferred printing, press Enter on the queued job and set Deferred Printing to Yes. You can define the Target Date and Time for that file to be printed.

 Note The Ready condition is put on any job available for printing.

The sixth column, Job, keeps track of the number of print jobs that have gone through the queue since it was created.

 Note All 3.1*x* copies of NetWare currently do not show a valid number in the Job field.

Highlight any queued job and press Enter to display additional information about print jobs. Figure 6.5, for example, shows the information you can obtain and the parameters you can set for each queued job after pressing Enter.

Figure 6.5

Job entry information in PCONSOLE.

```
NetWare Print Console  V1.52              Wednesday  January 6, 1993  2:45 pm
              User SUPERVISOR On File Server CDI286 Connection 2

                          Print Queue Entry Information

Print job:          4               File size:          2052
Client:             SUPERVISOR[2]
Description:        LPT1 Catch
Status:             Waiting for Target Execution Date and Time

User Hold:          No
Operator Hold:      No              Job Entry Date:     January 6, 1993
Service Sequence:   3               Job Entry Time:     2:42:36 pm

Number of copies:   1               Form:               LETTERHEAD
File contents:      Byte stream     Print banner:       No
Tab size:                           Name:
Suppress form feed: No              Banner name:
Notify when done:   No
                                    Defer printing:     Yes
Target server:      (Any Server)    Target date:        January 7, 1993
                                    Target time:        2:00:00 am
```

Table 6.1 explains what some of the terms stand for in the Print Queue Entry Information screen.

Table 6.1
Print Queue Entry Information

Item	Description
Print Job	Specifies the job number in the queue.
File Size	Specifies the size of the print job.
Client	Specifies who sent the print job.
Description	Specifies the name of the job.
Status	Denotes the condition of the job.
User Hold	Denotes the print jobs that are placed or removed by the job owner or queue operator. Held jobs are not printed.
Operator Hold	Denotes the print jobs that are placed or removed by the queue operator. Held jobs are not printed.
Service Sequence	Specifies the order in which the job is to be printed.
Job Entry Date	Shows the date that the queue received the print job. This field cannot be altered.
Job Entry Time	Shows the time that the queue received the print job. This field cannot be altered.
Number of Copies	Specifies the number of copies of the file to be printed. This number can be set from 1 to 65,000.
File Contents	Specifies text or byte stream print jobs. Text converts indents to spaces. Byte stream enables the application to determine the printer codes.

continues

Table 6.1, Continued
Print Queue Entry Information

Item	Description
Tab Size	Specifies the number of spaces to convert indents if File contents line is set to Text.
Suppress Form Feed	Sets the form feed to On or Off.
Notify When Done	Turns on or off notification of job completion.
Form	Sets the form number to use for the print job.
Print Banner	Sets the banner to On or Off.
Name	Displays the name printed on the banner. The sender's login name is the default.
Banner Name	Displays the file name by default.
Target Server	Displays the print servers that can service the current print job.
Defer Printing	Enables you to defer printing. Set to Yes or No.
Target Date & Time	Enables you to set the time and day. Default is set to the following day at 2:00 a.m.

Print a document using print job configurations that have been created in PRINTCON.

You can add jobs at the Current Print Job Entries screen. Press Ins to bring up the current directory. Change to the directory that contains the file to be printed and press Enter. The next screen is a list of all files in the directory (see fig. 6.6).

```
NetWare Print Console  V1.52        Wednesday  January 6, 1993  2:46 pm
                  User SUPERVISOR On File Server CDI286 Connection 2

                        Select Directory to Print From

CDI286/SYS:MENUS

                                 Available Files
                            ┌──────────────────────┐
                            │▲│NEW.TXT             │
                            │ │S.BAT               │
                            │ │SALES.MNU           │
                            │ │STUDENT.BAT         │
                            │ │SYS.MNU             │
                            │ │TEST.MNU            │
                            │ │TG.MNU              │
                            │ │WAIT.COM            │
                            │ │WIN.BAK             │
                            │ │WORK.MNU            │
                            └──────────────────────┘
```

Figure 6.6

Selecting a file to print in PCONSOLE.

After you highlight the file in this list to be printed, press Enter. If you want to print several files, use F5 to mark each file, and then press Enter.

Perform printing maintenance tasks with PCONSOLE and PSC.

The Print Job Configurations screen displays the list of printer configurations that you can use (see fig. 6.7). Highlight the desired configuration and press Enter.

```
NetWare Print Console  V1.51       Wednesday  February 3, 1993  2:20 pm
                  User SUPERVISOR On File Server B286 Connection 5

                        Select Directory to Print From

B286/SYS:MENUS           Print Job Configurations
                    ┌─────────────────────────────────┐
                    │(PConsole Defaults)              │
                    │daisywheel                       │
                    │dotmatrix                        │
                    │laser                            │
                    │laser_landscape                  │
                    │                                 │
                    │                                 │
                    │                                 │
                    │                                 │
                    └─────────────────────────────────┘
                         │WIN.BAK              │
                         │WORK.MNU             │
```

Figure 6.7

The Print Job Configurations screen in PCONSOLE.

403

PCONSOLE then displays configuration options. It uses options set in PRINTCON, but enables you to modify any fields. After changing any necessary fields, press Esc and save the job. This job now appears in the queue to be printed.

Current Queue Status

The Current Queue Status option of the Print Queue Information menu has the following five items (see fig. 6.8):

◆ **Number of entries in queue**—Displays the number of print jobs currently in a queue.

◆ **Number of servers attached**—Displays the number of file servers that have this queue defined.

◆ **Users can place entries in queue**—Enables users to place jobs (Yes) or not place jobs (No) in this queue.

◆ **Servers can service entries in queue**—Enables you to have jobs printed (Yes) or not printed (No) in this queue.

◆ **New servers can attach to queue**—Enables users on other file servers to use this queue (Yes) or denies users on other file servers access to this queue (No).

Figure 6.8

PCONSOLE's Current Queue Status option.

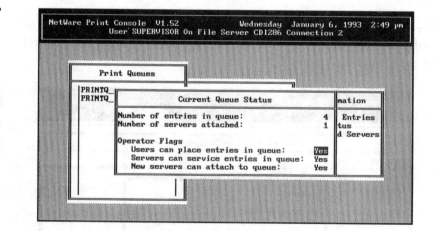

Currently Attached Servers

The Currently Attached Servers option of the Print Queue Information menu shows a list of all servers using this queue. This option can be used to see which file servers currently are putting jobs into the queue.

 Note All PCONSOLE screens are viewed in *real time*. As jobs are added and deleted, servers attached, or print servers activated, you see the screens change.

Print Queue ID

The Print Queue ID option of the Print Queue Information menu indicates the name of the hexadecimally named subdirectory under SYS:SYSTEM with the QDR extension. Jobs printed to this queue are held in the subdirectory until printed.

Queue Operators

The Queue Operators option of the Print Queue Information menu lists all users who can manage the selected queue. *Queue operators* manage the queue and all jobs going through the queue. Supervisor equivalent users automatically are queue operators. Queue operators can rearrange the order in which jobs print. They also can mark print jobs as Held so that they do not print. To add users or groups to this list, press Ins and select the users or groups that you want to manage this queue. Press Enter to accept your choices.

Queue Servers

The Queue Servers option of the Print Queue Information menu lists all the print servers that can service the selected queue.

To add servers to this list, press Ins and select the desired servers. Press Enter to accept your choices. After a printer is defined and attached to the selected queue, the print server for which the printer was configured appears on this list.

Queue Users

The Queue Users option of the Print Queue Information menu lists all the users and groups that can add jobs to this queue.

 The group labeled EVERYONE automatically becomes a queue user.

To modify this list, delete the group EVERYONE. You then can add users or groups to this list by pressing Ins and choosing the users or groups that can use this queue. Press Enter to accept your choices.

Section Review Questions

8. How do you defer printing a file?

   a. Use PRINTDEF, DEVICE

   b. Use PRINTCON, QUEUE CONTENTS

   c. Use PSC HOLD

   d. Use PRINTCON, CURRENT PRINT JOB ENTRIES

9. Which entry in PCONSOLE do you use to stop a queue from printing, but still enable users to place jobs in the queue?

   a. Servers can service entries in queue: Yes

   b. New servers can attach to queue: No

   c. New servers can attach to queue: Yes

   d. Servers can service entries in queue: No

10. Who can modify the print server by default?

    a. Supervisor

    b. Supervisor-equivalent users

    c. Print queue operators

    d. The group EVERYONE

11. Who can modify a print queue by default?

    a. Supervisor

    b. Supervisor-equivalent users

    c. Print queue operators

    d. The group EVERYONE

12. Which of the following statements is most true regarding PCONSOLE?

    a. Queue operators can manage print servers from this menu.

    b. Only print queue managers can place jobs in queues using this utility.

    c. Users can place jobs into queues, but cannot manage jobs from this menu.

    d. Users and print server operators must have Supervisor-equivalent rights to add jobs to queues.

13. If you are the Supervisor or a Supervisor equivalent, you can insert a job into a print queue using the PCONSOLE menu utility from which Print Queue Information menu option?

    a. Current Print Job Entries

    b. Current Queue Status

    c. Queue Operator

    d. Queue Servers

14. Which of the following is NOT a PCONSOLE print job status condition?

    a. Active

    b. Adding

    c. Held

    d. Ready

15. Which of the following is the status for any job available for printing?

    a. Active

    b. Adding

    c. Held

    d. Ready

16. Which of the following PCONSOLE print job parameters can you use to print your documents after you leave the office?

    a. Status

    b. Target time

    c. Job entry time

    d. Suppress form feed

17. Which of the following tasks CANNOT be done by a print queue operator?

    a. Reorder print jobs

    b. Mark print jobs to be held

    c. Add users as print queue operators

    d. Delete print jobs

Answers

8. b

9. d

10. a

11. a and b

12. a

13. a

14. c

15. d

16. b

17. c

Installing Print Servers

 Print servers can be file servers or dedicated PCs. PSERVER.VAP files are used on a router or 2.2 server; PSERVER.NLM files are used on a 3.1*x* server; and PSERVER.EXE files are loaded onto a PC designated as a dedicated print server.

A NetWare print server can manage up to 16 printers. Up to five of those printers can be attached to the print server, and the rest can be remote printers. A *remote printer* is any printer hooked up to a workstation that is attached to the network and can share its printer with other network users.

The following procedure shows how to set up a basic print server that has two printers—one local and one remote. This setup can be modified to fit your networking needs.

1. Type **PCONSOLE**.

2. Select the Print Queue Information option from the Available Options menu.

3. Press Ins and add the new queue name, then press Enter. Repeat this step for every queue.

One Printer Servicing Multiple Queues

Figure 6.9 shows an example of one printer serviced by three queues. Determining whether or not one printer servicing multiple queues, or multiple queues servicing one printer is best for your network's organization is one of the decisions that must be made as part of advanced setup.

Figure 6.9

One printer serviced by multiple queues.

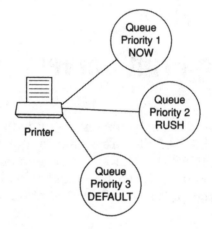

Printer

Queue
Priority 1
NOW

Queue
Priority 2
RUSH

Queue
Priority 3
DEFAULT

 Identify advanced printing setup and management design considerations.

Other advanced printing setup and management design considerations include such tasks as:

- ◆ Rearranging print queue users into workgroups
- ◆ Setting priorities for print queues
- ◆ Adding or renaming print queues as needed
- ◆ Assigning individual users to be print queue operators
- ◆ Adding or removing print servers

Each queue shown in this example (fig. 6.9) is set at a different priority. The DEFAULT queue is set at priority 3, RUSH is set at priority 2, and NOW is set at priority 1. By setting up system defaults, users print to the DEFAULT queue. If a rush job comes in, it goes to the RUSH queue. In the event of a super-high priority job coming in while jobs are in the RUSH queue, the print job is sent to the NOW queue. Jobs currently printing are allowed to finish before priority queues are serviced.

One Queue Using Identical Printers

In the example shown in figure 6.10, one queue is used to service three printers. This setup requires identical printers. When a job enters the queue, the queue polls the printers to find the next available one and sends the job there. Jobs are processed quickly using this arrangement.

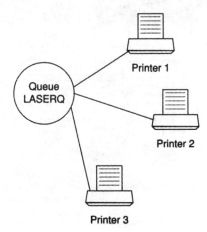

Figure 6.10

One printer queue servicing multiple printers.

1. Press Esc to return to the Available Options menu.

2. Select the Print Server Information option.

3. Press Ins to add the new print server name, type the new print server name, and press Enter (see fig. 6.11).

4. Select the Print Server Configuration option (see fig. 6.12).

411

5. Select the Printer Configuration option in the Print Server Configuration Menu (see fig. 6.13).

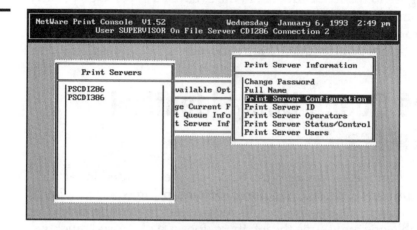

Figure 6.11

PCONSOLE's Print
Server Information
option.

Figure 6.11

PCONSOLE's Print
Server Information
option.

Figure 6.12

PCONSOLE's Print
Server Configuration
Menu.

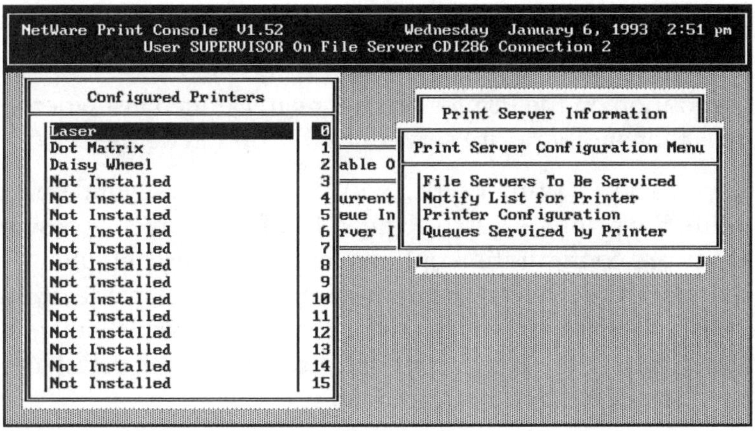

```
NetWare Print Console  V1.52          Wednesday  January 6, 1993  2:51 pm
              User SUPERVISOR On File Server CDI286 Connection 2

        Configured Printers
   ┌──────────────────────────┐        ┌────────────────────────────┐
   │ Laser                  0 │        │   Print Server Information │
   │ Dot Matrix             1 │   ┌────┤────────────────────────────┤
   │ Daisy Wheel            2 │able O│ Print Server Configuration Menu │
   │ Not Installed          3 │   ┌──┤──────────────────────────────┤
   │ Not Installed          4 │urrent│ File Servers To Be Serviced  │
   │ Not Installed          5 │eue In│ Notify List for Printer      │
   │ Not Installed          6 │rver I│ Printer Configuration        │
   │ Not Installed          7 │      │ Queues Serviced by Printer   │
   │ Not Installed          8 │      └──────────────────────────────┘
   │ Not Installed          9 │
   │ Not Installed         10 │
   │ Not Installed         11 │
   │ Not Installed         12 │
   │ Not Installed         13 │
   │ Not Installed         14 │
   │ Not Installed         15 │
   └──────────────────────────┘
```

Figure 6.13

Choosing configured printers in PCONSOLE.

You now need to set up printers for local or remote ports. Select a printer number that you want to configure and press Enter. Add a logical name for the printer and press Enter. Next, press Enter on the Type field. This action displays the Printer types screen. The first seven options in this screen enable you to hook up a printer to the print server (see fig. 6.14). The next eight remote options in this screen are for remote printers.

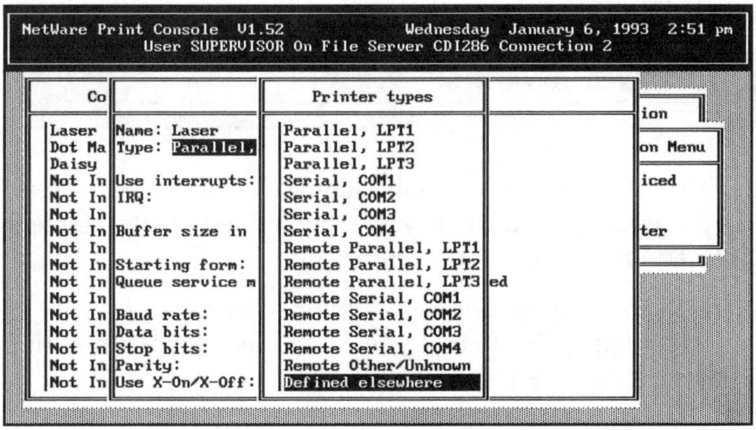

```
NetWare Print Console  V1.52          Wednesday  January 6, 1993  2:51 pm
              User SUPERVISOR On File Server CDI286 Connection 2

   ┌──────┬─────────────────┬──────────────────────────┬──────────────┐
   │  Co  │                 │      Printer types       │          ion │
   ├──────┤─────────────────┼──────────────────────────┤    ┌─────────┤
   │Laser │Name: Laser      │ Parallel, LPT1           │    │on Menu  │
   │Dot Ma│Type: Parallel,  │ Parallel, LPT2           │    ├─────────┤
   │Daisy │                 │ Parallel, LPT3           │    │iced     │
   │Not In│Use interrupts:  │ Serial, COM1             │    │         │
   │Not In│IRQ:             │ Serial, COM2             │    │         │
   │Not In│                 │ Serial, COM3             │    │ter      │
   │Not In│Buffer size in   │ Serial, COM4             │    └─────────┤
   │Not In│                 │ Remote Parallel, LPT1    │             │
   │Not In│Starting form:   │ Remote Parallel, LPT2    │             │
   │Not In│Queue service m  │ Remote Parallel, LPT3 ed │
   │Not In│                 │ Remote Serial, COM1      │
   │Not In│Baud rate:       │ Remote Serial, COM2      │
   │Not In│Data bits:       │ Remote Serial, COM3      │
   │Not In│Stop bits:       │ Remote Serial, COM4      │
   │Not In│Parity:          │ Remote Other/Unknown     │
   │Not In│Use X-On/X-Off:  │ Defined elsewhere        │
   └──────┴─────────────────┴──────────────────────────┘
```

Figure 6.14

Selecting printer types in PCONSOLE.

Remote Other/Unknown has two functions in NetWare:

1. Enables printer setup for a workstation without definition of the printer port from PCONSOLE.

2. Enables you to attach printing devices that connect directly to the LAN, bypassing a workstation.

The last option on the Printer types screen, Defined elsewhere, assumes that another print server has this option defined.

When you select a printer type, NetWare displays several screens to modify the printer setup (see fig. 6.15). These screens present all the hardware configuration options for the printer; defaults usually work fine. If your printer requires special consideration, however, use these screens to customize the printer. When you are finished defining the printer options, press Esc. Then select Yes from the Save Changes menu and press Esc.

Figure 6.15

PCONSOLE's Printer Configuration menu.

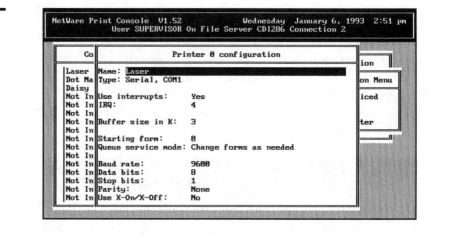

In the Print Server Configuration menu, select the Queues Serviced by Printer option. Next, select the defined printer name in the Defined Printers screen (see fig. 6.16).

Press Ins to add a queue for each printer configured. Priority 1 is the highest queue priority that you can define, as shown in figure 6.17. Press Esc twice when finished.

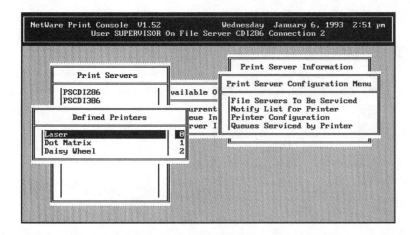

Figure 6.16

Choosing a defined printer.

Figure 6.17

Adding a queue to a printer.

> **Note**
> Queue priority enables a queue with higher priority to print all queued jobs before it looks to see if lower-priority queues have jobs waiting.

Next, select the Notify List for Printer option on the Print Server Configuration menu. Then press Ins to add users or groups who should be notified if problems arise, such as if the printer is offline or out of paper. At the top of the list of potential users and groups, the option labeled (Job Owner) (Unknown Type) appears (see fig. 6.18). This option reports any messages back to the job originator.

415

Figure 6.18

The Notify Candidates
screen for printer
problems.

```
NetWare Print Console  V1.52            Wednesday  January 6, 1993  2:53 pm
             User SUPERVISOR On File Server CDI286 Connection 2

                                                  Print Server Information

                Notify Candidates                    Notify Type    First  Next

        (Job Owner)       (Unknown Type)
        BACKUP            (User)
        CBT               (Group)
        CBT1              (User)
        CBT2              (User)
        CBT3              (User)
        CBT4              (User)
        CBT5              (User)
        CBT6              (User)
        CBT7              (User)
        CBT8              (User)
      ▼ CLASS             (Group)
```

After you select users or groups to be notified, the system
prompts you for information about when they are to be notified
and how often. By default, the persons in the notify list are first
told of printer problems in 30 seconds and again every 60 seconds
until the problem is solved (see fig. 6.19). Press Esc three times
when you are finished making your selections.

Figure 6.19

The list of users to be
notified in case of a
printer problem.

```
NetWare Print Console  V1.52            Wednesday  January 6, 1993  2:53 pm
             User SUPERVISOR On File Server CDI286 Connection 2

                                                  Print Server Information

        File Server      Notify Name           Notify Type    First  Next

        CDI286           (Job Owner)            (Unknown Type)   30     60
```

Note   The default Queue Operator is the group EVERY-
ONE.

The default Print Server Operator is the user
SUPERVISOR.

416

Select the Print Server Operators option in the Print Server Information menu. Then press Ins to add any users or groups that need to support the print server. After you make your selections, press Alt+F10 to return to DOS.

At the file server, type the following to launch the print server. You should spool printer 0:

S *nn* TO *queuename*

The S *nn* TO *queuename* command enables the Administrator to accomplish the following:

◆ **Create a path for a default queue.** This procedure helps when a user issues a CAPTURE or NPRINT statement without any flags. If a default queue is not chosen with the spool statement, the user receives an error message.

◆ **Route jobs from applications that print to printer numbers.** Many older applications are hard-coded to print to printer numbers. NetWare no longer enables the user to specify a printer number. To ensure that the file prints, a spool statement also enables Administrators to designate to which queue a job goes if the application sends it to a printer number.

◆ **Print on a 2.2 system.** NetWare 2.0a uses the SPOOL statement rather than the CAPTURE statement. This option enables 2.0a system users to print on both 2.0a and 2.2 operating systems.

Set up network printing hardware by bringing up a print server on a dedicated workstation or NetWare server, and connecting a printer to the network through a NetWare server on a DOS workstation.

At the workstation designated as the dedicated print server, log in

417

as a user who has Read and File Scan rights to the SYS:PUBLIC directory. Type the following command to launch the print server:

```
PSERVER printservername
```

Any workstation used as a print server must have the number of its *sequenced packet exchange* (SPX) connections increased. Create a text file called NET.CFG. Older versions of NetWare had you create a SHELL.CFG file, which also can be used. Place the line SPX=60 in this file. This file needs to be in the directory from which IPX.COM is called when attaching to the file server (see fig. 6.20).

Figure 6.20

The SHELL.CFG file and its contents.

```
A:\SHELLS>dir

 Volume in drive A is SYS
 Directory of  A:\SHELLS

SHELL    CFG        8  11-08-91   6:32p
TEMP     FIL        7   7-31-91   6:42p
IPX      COM    29919  10-10-91   6:38p
AUTOEXEC BAT       13   8-01-91   9:35a
NET3     COM    49198   2-06-91   4:44p
NET4     COM    49625   2-06-91   4:39p
NETBIOS  EXE    21506  11-15-90   3:48p
         7 File(s)  60473344 bytes free

A:\SHELLS>type shell.cfg
SPX=60

A:\SHELLS>
```

No matter where the print server is activated—at a dedicated print server or at the file server—the print server screen looks the same. Figure 6.21 provides an example of a typical print server screen. When you press the spacebar, you can see the next group of printers—8 through 15.

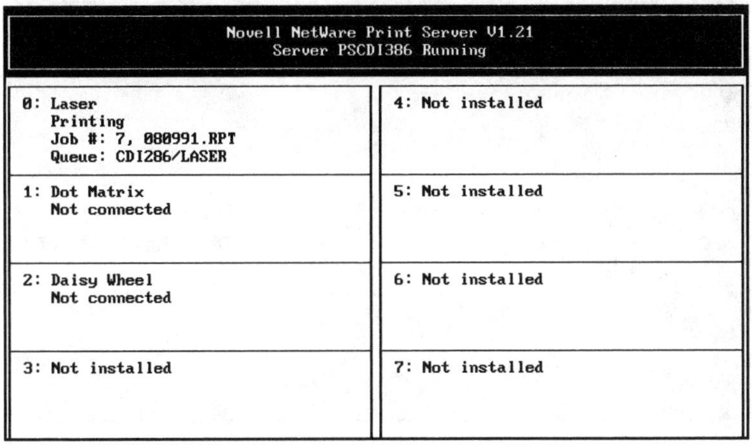

```
         Novell NetWare Print Server V1.21
              Server PSCDI386 Running
┌─────────────────────────────┬──────────────────────────┐
│ 0: Laser                    │ 4: Not installed         │
│    Printing                 │                          │
│    Job #: 7, 080991.RPT     │                          │
│    Queue: CDI286/LASER      │                          │
├─────────────────────────────┼──────────────────────────┤
│ 1: Dot Matrix               │ 5: Not installed         │
│    Not connected            │                          │
├─────────────────────────────┼──────────────────────────┤
│ 2: Daisy Wheel              │ 6: Not installed         │
│    Not connected            │                          │
├─────────────────────────────┼──────────────────────────┤
│ 3: Not installed            │ 7: Not installed         │
│                             │                          │
└─────────────────────────────┴──────────────────────────┘
```

Figure 6.21

An example of the print server information screen.

The final step in installing a print server to host a remote printer is to type **RPRINTER** at each of the Remote Stations. A list of print servers then appears (see fig. 6.22). After choosing the print server, all available remote printer setups appear (see fig. 6.23). Select the workstation that you want, and NetWare displays a message telling you that a successful installation has occurred (see fig. 6.24).

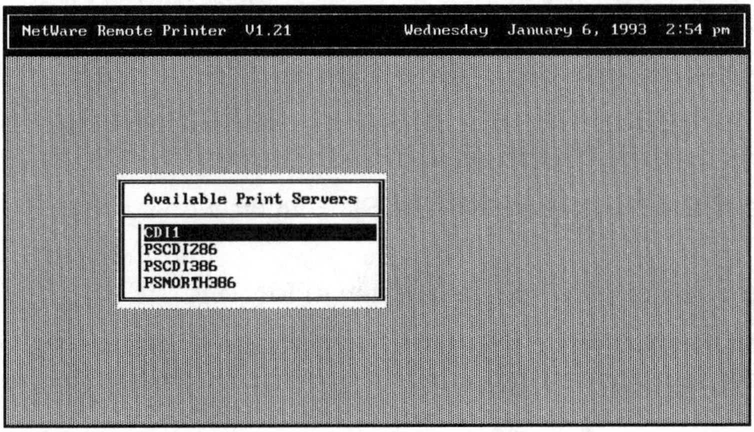

```
┌──────────────────────────────────────────────────────────────────┐
│ NetWare Remote Printer  V1.21        Wednesday  January 6, 1993  2:54 pm │
│                                                                    │
│                                                                    │
│              ┌─────────────────────────────┐                      │
│              │  Available Print Servers    │                      │
│              ├─────────────────────────────┤                      │
│              │ CDI1                        │                      │
│              │ PSCDI286                    │                      │
│              │ PSCDI386                    │                      │
│              │ PSNORTH386                  │                      │
│              └─────────────────────────────┘                      │
│                                                                    │
└──────────────────────────────────────────────────────────────────┘
```

Figure 6.22

RPRINTER's main menu selections.

Figure 6.23

RPRINTER's remote
printer choices.

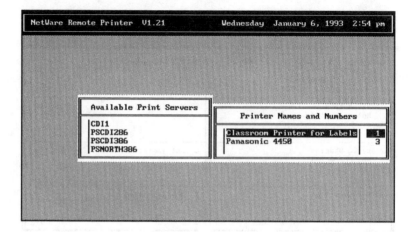

Figure 6.24

RPRINTER's
installation
confirmation.

```
*** Remote Printer "PRINTQ_1 printer" (printer 1) installed ***
F:\SHELLS>
```

RPRINTER

The RPRINTER command has several options. The full syntax line
for this command is as follows:

    RPRINTER *printservername printernumber flag*

By placing the print server name and printer number in the
command line, you can avoid using the menu.

The -R flag removes the RPRINTER from the workstation's
memory.

The -S flag displays the status of the RPRINTER.

After the print server is installed, workstations can send jobs to
network printers by indicating the queue name attached to those
printers. The next section describes this process.

Section Review Questions

18. When running RPRINTER, what needs to be set in the configuration file?

    a. IPX=40

    b. IPX=60

    c. SPX=60

    d. SPX=40

19. The PSERVER.VAP program runs on:

    a. A router or 2.2 file server

    b. A 3.1*x* file server

    c. A remote printer

    d. A client

20. Using PCONSOLE, which of the following is NOT true?

    a. You can set up one printer to serve multiple print queues.

    b. You can set up one queue to serve multiple identical printers.

    c. Both of the above are true.

    d. None of the above are true.

21. Which flag displays the status of RPRINTER?

    a. -D

    b. -S

    c. -R

    d. -P

22. Which *two* are functions of the Remote Other/Unknown Option of PCONSOLE?

    a. Allows adding printers to all attached clients

421

    b. Allows printer set up for a client without first defining the printer port

    c. Allows direct LAN attachment of printers, bypassing workstations

    d. Allows printing without using PCONSOLE

Answers

18. c

19. a

20. c

21. b

22. b and c

Directing Printer Output

If you are using an application written to run on a Novell NetWare network, chances are that the program knows the way to "talk" to a network printer. Many newer programs enable you to define a queue name as a print device. In these instances, the user is not required to define the printing environment before entering the application.

A significant number of programs, however, still need help to print on a network. For these programs, the user must set up the printing environment before entering the program.

CAPTURE and NPRINT are two commands that enable you to print on the network. Figure 6.25 shows the way each command is filtered to the printer. CAPTURE sets up a printing environment for the user. This command dictates the way all print jobs sent by that user are directed, and does not change unless the user reissues a CAPTURE command or logs out. NPRINT is used outside of an application to send a file to a printer. This command is intended specifically for a set of files and does not reset previous CAPTURE commands.

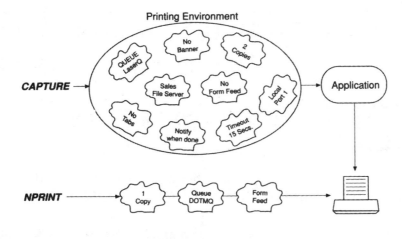

Figure 6.25

Directing printer output by using the CAPTURE and NPRINT commands.

Note Remember that NPRINT *always* requires a file name. CAPTURE does not.

The CAPTURE Command

CAPTURE sets up the printing environment for a user. Before using a print screen, the user must first execute a CAPTURE statement.

Figure 6.26 shows an example of a CAPTURE statement directed to the queue called LASER, with no banners, no form feed, no tabs, and a timeout of 5 seconds.

The CAPTURE command is not used to print existing files; CAPTURE sets up the way in which a file is printed. The generic syntax when using CAPTURE is the following:

```
CAPTURE flags
```

The ENDCAP Command

If the CAPTURE command is set up for No Autoendcap, then ENDCAP must be specified at the DOS prompt before anything is printed. When used by itself, the ENDCAP command ends the CAPTURE statement to LPT1.

423

Figure 6.26

An example of using the CAPTURE command.

```
F:\DATA>capture q=laser nb nff ti=5 nt
Device LPT1: re-routed to queue LASER on server CDI286.

F:\DATA>
```

•Note You can also use ENDCAP to return the workstation ports to local use.

Table 6.2 lists the various flags that you can use to direct the ENDCAP statement.

Table 6.2
ENDCAP Flags

Flag	Description
ALL	Ends the CAPTURE statement on all ports, such as ENDCAP ALL.
L=*n*	Stops the CAPTURE statement to a specified port. Replaces *n* with the logical port number, such as ENDCAP L=1.
C	Ends the CAPTURE statement to LPT1 and abandons any data without printing it, such as ENDCAP C.
CL=*n*	Ends the CAPTURE statement for a specific port and discards the data to be printed, such as ENDCAP CL=2.
C ALL	Ends the CAPTURE statement for all ports and abandons all data to be printed.

424

The NPRINT Command

The NPRINT command is used to print data files or files that have been formatted for a specific printer. The syntax for NPRINT is the following:

```
NPRINT filenames flags
```

 Note   Wildcards are acceptable when indicating file names.

A file name must be specified directly after the NPRINT statement and before indicating which flags to use.

Figure 6.27 shows an NPRINT statement that prints all files that end in RPT and sends the job to the LASER queue.

```
F:\DATA>nprint *.rpt j=laser
Queuing data to Server CDI286, Queue LASER.
CDI286\SYS:DATA
        Queuing file 092491.RPT
        Queuing file 092691.RPT
        Queuing file 092791.RPT
        Queuing file 092591.RPT

F:\DATA>
```

Figure 6.27

An example of using the NPRINT command.

CAPTURE and NPRINT Flags

This section discusses each flag that you can use with the CAPTURE and NPRINT commands. See table 6.3 for a complete list and description of flags.

When you use the NOTI flag, NetWare notifies the user after the job is printed. When several jobs are *buffered* (temporarily stored in memory) in the printer, you might want to know when the job is ready for the user to pick up. The normal default is not to notify the user when the job has been printed. Both NOTI and NNOTI work with CAPTURE and NPRINT. Use the following syntax lines for each flag:

425

```
CAPTURE NOTI
```

The preceding command requests notification.

```
CAPTURE NNOTI
```

The preceding command prevents notification.

You can designate exactly where the job is to be printed by using the Server and Queue flags to specify the queue name and file server. If neither of these is specified, the system relies on the SPOOL statement for printer 0 as the default. As mentioned earlier, you should spool printer 0. The S and Q flags work with both CAPTURE and NPRINT. Use the following syntax for these flags:

```
CAPTURE S=CDI386 Q=LASER
```

Table 6.3
CAPTURE and NPRINT Flags

Flag	Description
Flags that work with CAPTURE and NPRINT:	
NOTI	NOTIfies when the job is done
NNOTI	Does Not NOTIfy when the job is done
S	Specifies the Server
Q	Specifies the Queue
J	Specifies the Job configuration
F	Specifies the Form name
C	Specifies the number of Copies to print
T	Specifies the Tabs (TEXT)
NT	Specifies when No Tabs (BYTE STREAM) are used
B	Specifies when the Banner name is printed
NB	Specifies when No Banner is printed
NAM	Specifies the NAMe

Flag	Description
FF	Specifies the Form Feed from the printer
NFF	Specifies No Form Feed from the printer
D	Deletes the file after it is printed (NPRINT only)

Flags that work only with *CAPTURE*:

Flag	Description
TI	Specifies the TImeout period before printing
AU	Denotes AUtoendcap
NA	Denotes No Autoendcap
L	Specifies the Local port
CR	CReates a file
K	Keeps the received portion of the job in the file server and prints it
SH	SHows the current CAPTURE settings
?	Lists the available flags

The PRINTCON menu utility enables the System Administrator or user to create print jobs with parameters similar to the CAPTURE flags. The Job flag enables the user to call on one of the jobs that have been created. The J flag works with both CAPTURE and NPRINT. Use the following syntax with this flag:

```
CAPTURE J=LASER_LANDSCAPE
```

By using the PRINTDEF menu utility, the System Supervisor can create forms. *Forms* in NetWare force a user to verify that the proper form is in the printer before printing begins. At the command line, the user can specify which form to use for a particular job. The default is form 0. The Form flag works with both CAPTURE and NPRINT. Use the following syntax with this flag:

```
CAPTURE  F=14
```

At the DOS prompt, you can specify between one and 999 copies of a particular job. The system default is one copy. The Copies flag works with both CAPTURE and NPRINT. Use the following syntax with this flag:

```
CAPTURE  C=3
```

When sending a print job to the printer as a text file, the Tabs flag is the fastest method of printing. Formatting codes are interpreted by the printer and text is printed. NetWare enables you to set the number of spaces between tabs at the command line. The default is 8.

 Remember that the following pairs of terms are often interchanged in NetWare menus and documentation:

Tabs and Text

No Tabs and Byte Stream

When you use the No Tabs flag, all control characters are interpreted by the sending application. This also is called *byte-stream printing*. This method is slightly slower than text.

If an application is sending simple text, such as a nongraphics spreadsheet, send the job as Tabs. If the application sends more complex text, such as text created by a desktop publisher, send the job as No Tabs.

 If the printer adds miscellaneous characters on the page, switch printing methods. If you print the file by using the Tabs flag (text), then resend the print job and use the No Tabs flag (byte stream). The problem can occur when codes are being misinterpreted; the alternative method usually clears up any problems. No Tabs is a good default.

The T and NT flags work with both CAPTURE and NPRINT. Use the following syntax with these flags:

```
CAPTURE T=5
```

The preceding command requests a tab of five characters. The following command requests printing in byte stream:

```
CAPTURE NT
```

The network, by default, sets up a banner page before each job is printed. This page contains information about who sent the job, the name of the file, and when and where it was printed. The banner page is separated into three sections. The top section is information about the job and sender and cannot be modified. The second section is the name of the sender by default, and you can change it by using NAM=n (up to 12 characters). The third section, by default, is the name of the file; you can change it by using B=n (up to 12 characters).

If you do not have a need for a banner page, use the No Banner flag after the CAPTURE statement.

The Banner, No Banner, and NAMe flags work with both CAPTURE and NPRINT. Use the following syntax with these flags:

```
CAPTURE NAM=GARY B=JUNERPT
```

The preceding command sets the top of the banner to read GARY and the bottom of the banner to read JUNERPT.

 Note   Banners do not work with PostScript printers.

The following command does not print a banner:

```
CAPTURE NB
```

Sometimes printers give you more or less paper than you really need. The Form Feed and No Form Feed flags help you tell the printer what you are expecting. Many laser printers kick out extra sheets of paper after printing a job. Use the NFF switch to tell the printer not to send out the extra sheet after the job is done.

Dot-matrix printers often stop and reset the Top of Form if you send only a half-page of data. To make sure that the printer returns to the true top of the page, use FF to issue a form feed after the print job.

The FF and NFF flags work with both CAPTURE and NPRINT. Use the following syntax with this flag:

```
CAPTURE NFF
```

The Delete flag only works with NPRINT. When the print job is finished, the file automatically is deleted from the system. Use the following syntax with this flag:

```
NPRINT SYS:DATA\*.RPT D
```

The system default requires you to exit, or *shell out*, to DOS before the job is printed. This requirement is considered Autoendcap. Nothing prints until the user exits the program.

Most of the time, a user wants the job to print before exiting an application. The Timeout flag helps the user print immediately, and you can set it from zero to 1,000 seconds. This feature tells the system the amount of time to wait for new information to be sent to the printer before considering the job closed and beginning to print. Fifteen seconds is an average timeout period, but some applications might require more time.

Occasionally, you might find that neither the Timeout flag nor the Autoendcap flag produces the desired results. Some printers that contain downloadable fonts in combination with graphical interfaces cannot work with an automatic ENDCAP. In such cases, you can use the No Autoendcap flag to enable the printer to work.

 Before the job prints, the user first must type **ENDCAP** at the DOS prompt. LOGIN, LOGOUT, NPRINT, and CAPTURE also force an ENDCAP statement.

The Autoendcap, No Autoendcap, and Timeout flags work only with CAPTURE. Use the following syntax with these flags:

```
CAPTURE TI=15
```

The preceding command requests a timeout of 15 seconds. The following command requires the capture statement to be terminated manually:

```
CAPTURE NA
```

NetWare enables the user to specify CAPTURE statements for up to three logical LPT ports. If you need two or three different CAPTURE statements, depending on the application you are using, the user can run CAPTURE each time he or she accesses the program. An alternative method is to issue different CAPTURE statements for each logical port and to tell the application which LPT port to use.

The Local Port flag works only with CAPTURE. Use the following syntax with this flag:

```
CAPTURE L=1 Q=LASER NFF
CAPTURE L=2 Q=LASER FF NT
CAPTURE L=3 Q=DOTMATRIX
```

You can capture print jobs to a file rather than a printer. This method imports screen captures to an editor or accumulates data from multiple programs. When using the Create flag, you must include the path and file name. By default, if you capture to a file that previously was used, the existing contents are overwritten with the new print job. To append information to a CAPTURE CR= file, use NA after the file name.

The CR flag works only with CAPTURE. Use the following syntax with this flag:

```
CAPTURE CR=SYS:DATA\SAVE.SCR NA
```

If there is a risk of your workstation hanging up or disconnecting during the printing process, use the Keep flag. This flag ensures that the server knows to accept as much of the job as possible and print it. The default environment permits the file server to discard print jobs if the sending workstation is disconnected during the print job.

The K flag works only with CAPTURE. Use the following syntax with this flag:

```
CAPTURE K
```

NetWare displays the current CAPTURE settings for a user. Figure 6.28 shows the CAPTURE statement issued and the result shown by using the SHow flag.

Figure 6.28

Displaying current CAPTURE settings by using the SHow flag.

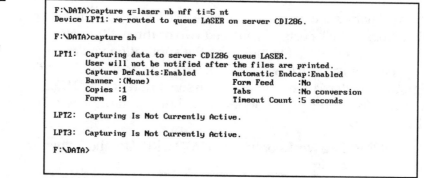

```
F:\DATA>capture q=laser nb nff ti=5 nt
Device LPT1: re-routed to queue LASER on server CDI286.

F:\DATA>capture sh

LPT1:  Capturing data to server CDI286 queue LASER.
       User will not be notified after the files are printed.
       Capture Defaults:Enabled        Automatic Endcap:Enabled
       Banner :(None)                   Form Feed      :No
       Copies :1                        Tabs           :No conversion
       Form   :0                        Timeout Count :5 seconds

LPT2:  Capturing Is Not Currently Active.

LPT3:  Capturing Is Not Currently Active.

F:\DATA>
```

The ? flag lists all the available flags. SH and ? work only with CAPTURE. Use the following syntax with these flags:

```
CAPTURE SH
CAPTURE ?
```

Section Review Questions

23. Which CAPTURE statement produces an error?

    a. `CAPTURE NB NA CR=SYS:TEMP.PRN`

    b. `CAPTURE NB NFF TI=15 D NT`

    c. `CAPTURE /TI=15 /NB`

    d. `CAPTURE /C=5 /FF /NOTI`

24. Which NPRINT statement produces an error when printing the file SYS:\INFO\DATA.TXT to the queue LASER?

    a. `NPRINT D SYS:\INFO\DATA.TXT Q=LASER`

    b. `NPRINT SYS:\INFO\DATA.TXT Q=LASER`

```
c.  NPRINT SYS:\INFO\DATA.TXT Q=LASER T=5

d.  NPRINT SYS:\INFO\DATA.TXT NB Q=LASER
```

25. The _____ command is used to set up the printing environment for a user.

    a. ENDCAP

    b. CAPTURE

    c. NPRINT

    d. ENDPRINT

26. The _____ command is used to print files that have been formatted for a specific printer.

    a. ENDCAP

    b. CAPTURE

    c. NPRINT

    d. ENDPRINT

27. When all control characters sent to the printer are interpreted by the sending application, this is also called:

    a. Tabbed printing

    b. Captured printing

    c. Text printing

    d. Byte-stream printing

Answers

23. b

24. a

25. b

26. c

27. d

Controlling the Print Server

After you get the print server up and running, a new option appears in the Print Server Information menu (see fig. 6.29). This option, Print Server Status/Control, enables a print server operator to manage the print server (see fig. 6.30).

Figure 6.29

The Print Server Information menu.

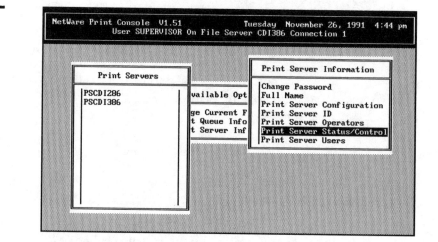

Under Printer Status, a print server operator can view information about the job currently being serviced. Figure 6.31 shows a job that has just entered the queue.

Figure 6.30

The Print Server Status and Control menu.

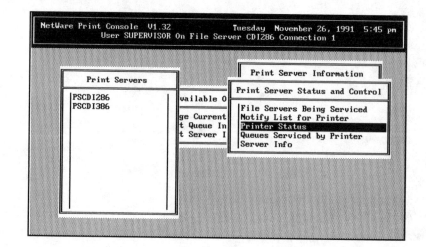

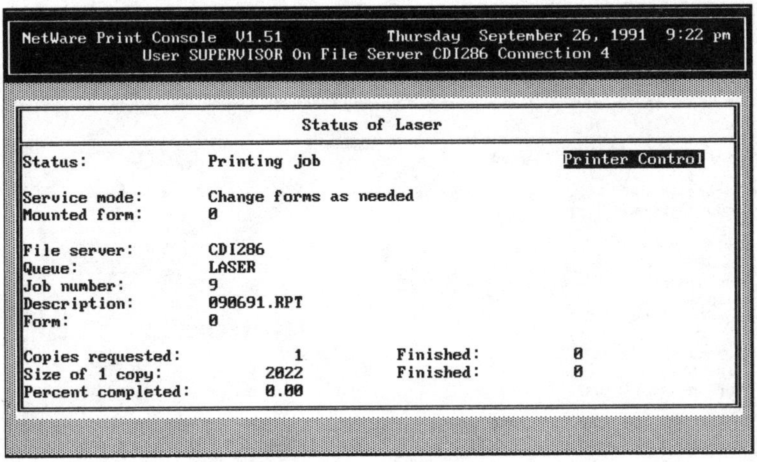

```
NetWare Print Console  V1.51          Thursday  September 26, 1991  9:22 pm
                User SUPERVISOR On File Server CDI286 Connection 4

                             Status of Laser

Status:              Printing job                      Printer Control

Service mode:        Change forms as needed
Mounted form:        0

File server:         CDI286
Queue:               LASER
Job number:          9
Description:         090691.RPT
Form:                0

Copies requested:            1      Finished:         0
Size of 1 copy:           2022      Finished:         0
Percent completed:        0.00
```

Figure 6.31

An example of a print job status.

The status line shows that this job is being sent to the printer. The following service modes are available:

◆ **Change forms as needed.** This mode prompts the user to change forms each time a different form is encountered.

◆ **Minimize form changes across queues.** This mode specifies that the printer prints all jobs with the same form number before proceeding to the next highest form number. This procedure is done for all queues, regardless of queue priorities.

◆ **Minimize form changes within queue.** This mode specifies that the printer prints all jobs within a high-priority queue that share similar form numbers before servicing lower-priority queues.

◆ **Service only currently mounted form.** This mode prints only the jobs that have the current form number.

When the printer status screen appears, the Printer Control field is highlighted. Press Enter to display the next options menu (see fig. 6.32). The following options enable you to modify the print job currently printing. These options are not available from the Print Queue options, which enable you to modify only those print jobs not currently printing.

435

Figure 6.32

The Printer Control
menu.

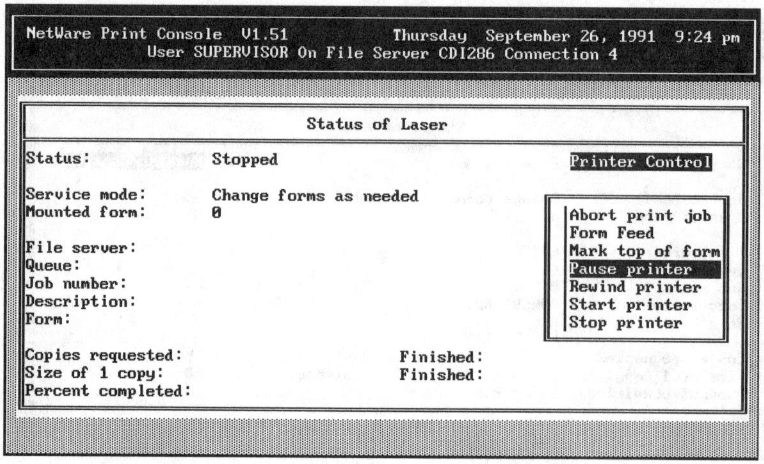

```
┌─────────────────────────────────────────────────────────────────┐
│ NetWare Print Console  V1.51          Thursday  September 26, 1991  9:24 pm │
│               User SUPERVISOR On File Server CDI286 Connection 4   │
└─────────────────────────────────────────────────────────────────┘

       ┌──────────────────────────────────────────────────────┐
       │                    Status of Laser                   │
       │ Status:          Stopped                ┌Printer Control┐│
       │                                                        │
       │ Service mode:    Change forms as needed               │
       │ Mounted form:    0                      ┌────────────────┐
       │                                         │Abort print job │
       │ File server:                            │Form Feed       │
       │ Queue:                                  │Mark top of form│
       │ Job number:                             │Pause printer   │
       │ Description:                            │Rewind printer  │
       │ Form:                                   │Start printer   │
       │                                         │Stop printer    │
       │ Copies requested:              Finished:└────────────────┘
       │ Size of 1 copy:                Finished:              │
       │ Percent completed:                                    │
       └──────────────────────────────────────────────────────┘
```

◆ **Abort print job.** This mode enables the printer to abandon
   the current job. The job then is deleted from the queue. This
   method is the best way to stop a print job, because it clears
   the job from the print buffer.

◆ **Form feed.** This mode specifies that the printer advance to
   the top of the next page.

◆ **Mark top of form.** This mode prints a row of asterisks (*)
   across the top of the page to check form alignment.

◆ **Pause printer.** This mode temporarily pauses the printer. To
   restart the printer, select the Start Printer option.

◆ **Rewind printer.** This mode enables the printer to rewind a
   specific number of bytes or advance a specific number of
   bytes. This line also enables you to specify which copy to
   print if multiple copies are specified at the time of printing.

◆ **Start printer.** This mode starts the printer if stopped or
   paused.

◆ **Stop printer.** This mode stops the printer and returns the
   print job to the queue. Printing is stopped until the printer is
   started again by using the Start Printer option.

You now can select the Server Info item of the Print Server Status
and Control menu.

Compare the steps required to set permanent and temporary settings for print queues and notification lists.

You can make both permanent and temporary changes to print queues or printers using PCONSOLE.

Permanent changes are made using the regular PCONSOLE menus. To make a change permanent using this method, you must first bring the print server down and then reload it.

Temporary changes do not require that the print server be first downed to take effect. Temporary changes are made in the Print Server Status and Control screen of the PCONSOLE utility.

After selecting the Server Info item of the Print Server Status and Control menu, the Print Server Info/Status screen (see fig. 6.33) displays the following information about the print server:

◆ **Print server version**—Specifies that the print server version is 1.2.1.

◆ **Print server type**—Specifies that the print server is running on a dedicated DOS machine rather than on the file server.

◆ **Number of printers**—Specifies that the print server is hosting three printers.

◆ **Queue service modes**—Denotes the number of service modes available.

◆ **Current server status**—Specifies that the print server is currently running.

437

Figure 6.33

An example of the
Print Server Info/
Status screen.

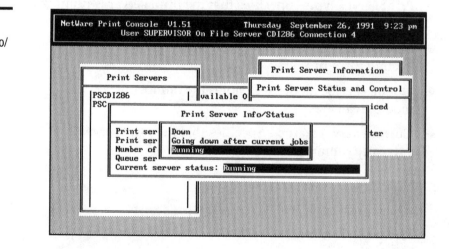

When you select the Current server status option, a screen appears
(see fig. 6.34) that enables the server operator to do the following
three things:

- ◆ Down the print server immediately.

- ◆ Down the print server after the last job is printed.

- ◆ Enable the server to continue running.

Figure 6.34

The Print Server Info/
Status menu.

Customizing the Printers Using PRINTDEF

NetWare's PRINTDEF menu utility enables a System Administrator to create forms and define printers (see fig. 6.35).

```
Printer Definition Utility  V1.51      Thursday  September 26, 1991   9:29 pm
                    User SUPERVISOR On File Server CDI286

                            PrintDef Options
                           ┌──────────────────┐
                           │ Print Devices    │
                           │ Forms            │
                           └──────────────────┘
```

Figure 6.35
PRINTDEF's main menu.

Print Devices

If you have a printer capable of advanced features and fonts and you are using a program that does not know how to make full use of the printer's capabilities, you can solve this problem by using PRINTDEF. Perhaps you want to print a document sideways from a spreadsheet program using condensed print. This type of printing can be difficult to set up internally in the spreadsheet program. By using PRINTDEF, however, you can define a mode that has the functions necessary for the printer to print condensed and sideways.

Describe how you use PRINTDEF to customize print jobs.

To edit, import, or export print devices, select the Print Devices option in the PRINTDEF Options menu. The Print Device Options screen appears (see fig. 6.36).

Figure 6.36

PRINTDEF's Print
Device Options menu.

```
┌──────────────────────────────────────────────────────────────────┐
│ Printer Definition Utility  V1.51     Thursday  September 26, 1991  9:29 pm │
│                User SUPERVISOR On File Server CDI286                │
└──────────────────────────────────────────────────────────────────┘

                              ┌─────────────────────┐
                              │  PrintDef Options   │
                              ├─────────────────────┤
                              │ Print Devices       │
                              │ Forms               │
          ┌──────────────────────┐                  │
          │  Print Device Options │                  │
          ├──────────────────────┤
          │ Edit Print Devices    │
          │ Import Print Device   │
          │ Export Print Device   │
          └──────────────────────┘
```

The PRINTDEF command contains a database of information about printers. Each printer has an entry in this database. If you create a print device and want it to be used on another network, you can select the Export Print Device option. This option enables you to create a file with a *printer definition file* (PDF) extension that you can copy and import into another network.

Importing is done when an Administrator wants to use a PDF file that someone else has created. A large list of printer definition files are included with NetWare. These files are copied into the SYS:PUBLIC directory.

> **Note** By default, the PDF are kept in SYS:PUBLIC.

To see a list of PDFs in the SYS:PUBLIC directory (or whatever directory contains the files), select the Import Print Device option in the Print Device Options menu. Press Enter again and NetWare displays a list of PDF files (see fig. 6.37). To import a PDF file into the list of editable items, highlight the file and press Enter.

440

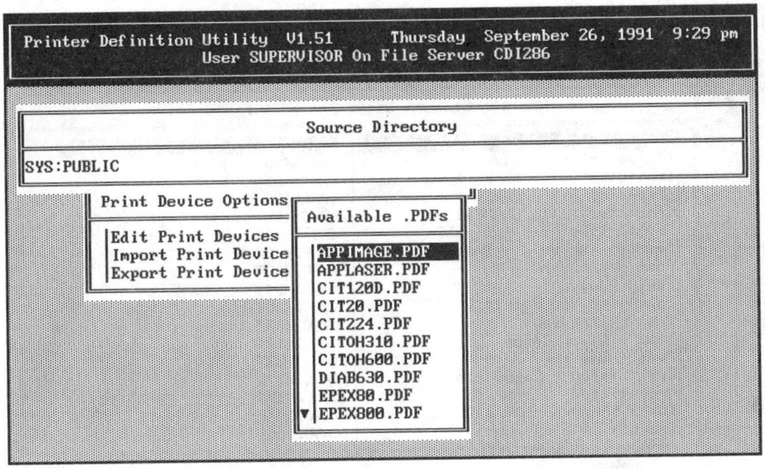

Figure 6.37
PRINTDEF's available files.

If you activate the Edit Print Devices option, a submenu appears that enables you to edit device modes or device functions (see fig. 6.38). A *device mode* is a list of functions that produce a desired output.

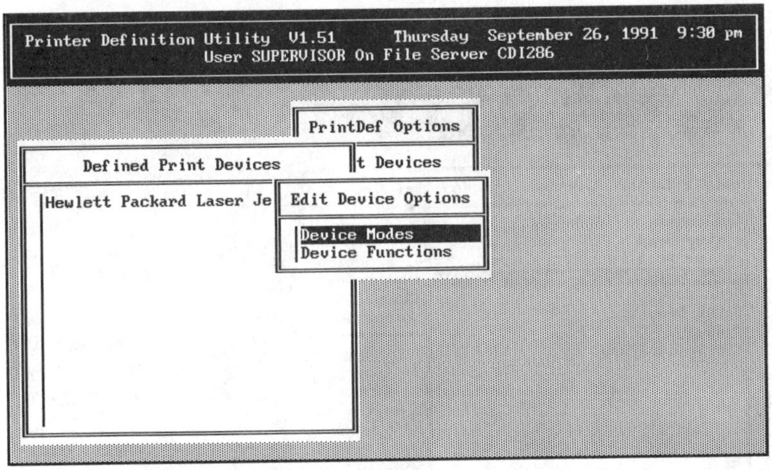

Figure 6.38
PRINTDEF's Edit Device Options menu.

You must begin this editing process by activating the Device Functions choice. When you press Enter after highlighting the Device Functions option, NetWare displays a screen that shows all the escape sequences necessary for a specific printer (see fig. 6.39). To add new functions, press Ins and input the escape codes. You can input the codes in ASCII or hexadecimal format.

Figure 6.39

PRINTDEF's printer escape codes.

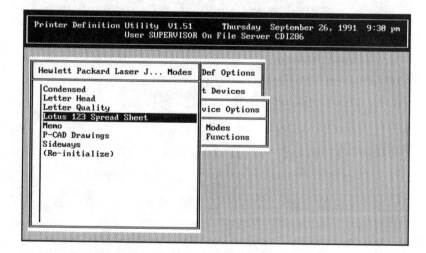

The other Edit Device option, Device Modes, enables you to combine print functions to customize the printer output. As illustrated in figure 6.40, this example shows a Hewlett-Packard LaserJet with the following possible settings: Condensed, Letter Head, Letter Quality, Lotus 123 SpreadSheet, Memo, P-CAD Drawings, Sideways, and Re-initialize.

Figure 6.40

PRINTDEF's Device Modes screen.

Figure 6.41 shows the suggested functions to print a Lotus 1-2-3 spreadsheet sideways.

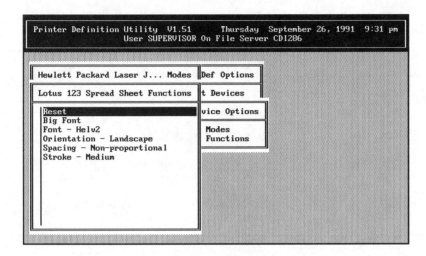

Figure 6.41

The device mode for a spreadsheet.

To use the modes and devices defined here, you need to set up print job configurations in PRINTCON, discussed in the next section.

Forms

The second choice under the PRINTDEF Options menu is Forms. Some businesses need to share one printer for several different types of forms. By creating jobs that use different forms, you can control the printer's use. Each time the printer encounters a change of form, it waits until either a statement is typed at the file server (such as **PRINTER** *printernumber* **MOUNT** *formnumber*) or the Print Server Command is issued (such as **PSC PS=**_printserver_ **P=**_printer_ **MO=2**). You can replace *formnumber* with *formname* when mounting a form with PSC.

After you select the Forms option, NetWare displays the Forms and Form Definition screen. Table 6.4 describes the four items that you need to fill in to define a form, as shown in figure 6.42.

Table 6.4
Form Definitions

Item	Definition
Name	Specifies the form's name, up to 12 characters
Number	Specifies the form number, from 0 to 255
Length	Indicates the number of lines in the form, between 1 and 255
Width	Indicates the number of columns in the form, between 1 and 999

 The form's length and width are there to help the Administrator keep track of the form's use. Neither the network nor the printer are affected by these numbers.

Figure 6.42

Defining a form in PRINTDEF.

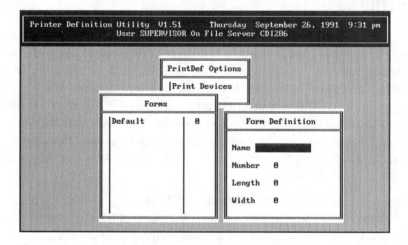

Section Review Questions

28. Which of the following statements about PRINTDEF is most true?

    a. The forms option lets you define a database of print devices.

    b. You can use the forms option in this utility to control the printer so that different users with different types of documents to be printed can share one printer.

    c. Print device definitions must be created from scratch using the forms option.

29. By default, the printer definition files are kept in:

    a. SYS:PUBLIC

    b. SYS:SYSTEM

    c. SYS:MAIL

    d. SYS:ETC

30. To use an existing print device on another network, choose:

    a. Create PDF

    b. Import Print Device

    c. Export Print Device

    d. Move PDF

31. Which of the following is NOT one of the items you need to fill in when defining a form?

    a. Length

    b. Width

    c. Name

    d. Size

32. When you choose Current Server Status Option in PCONSOLE, which three functions can you perform?

   a. Create Server Print Configuration

   b. Down Print Server immediately

   c. Down Print Server after last job is printed

   d. Enable server to continue running

Answers

28. b

29. a

30. c

31. d

32. b, c, and d

Creating Print Jobs Using PRINTCON

The PRINTCON command enables Administrators and users to create print configurations. This capability means the difference between a user needing to know each of the CAPTURE flags or learning the name of a print job that uses all the same flags. Jobs work as shortcuts. You usually can remember job names easier than you can all the flags that make up the job name.

 Describe how you use PRINTCON to customize print jobs.

The main menu in PRINTCON displays three options for Supervisors (see fig. 6.43). Regular network users see only the first two options. Only Supervisors can copy print job configurations.

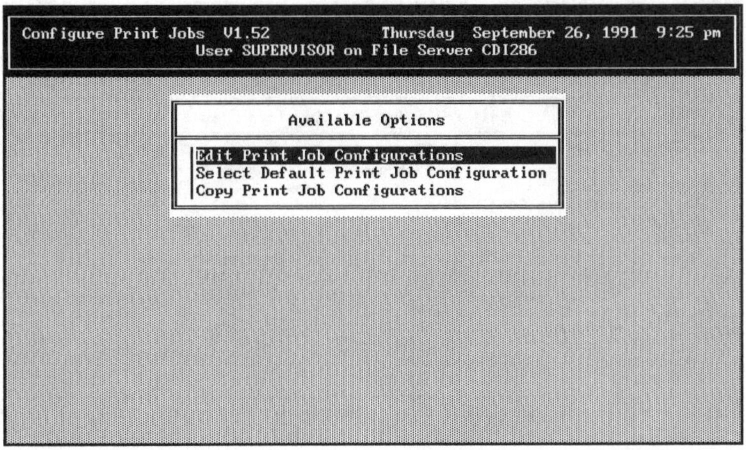

```
Configure Print Jobs  V1.52        Thursday  September 26, 1991  9:25 pm
                   User SUPERVISOR on File Server CDI286

                          Available Options
                Edit Print Job Configurations
                Select Default Print Job Configuration
                Copy Print Job Configurations
```

Figure 6.43

PRINTCON's main menu.

To display a list of jobs, select the Edit Print Job Configurations option in the Available Options menu (see fig. 6.44). You then can add a new job by pressing Ins, or modify a current job by pressing Enter.

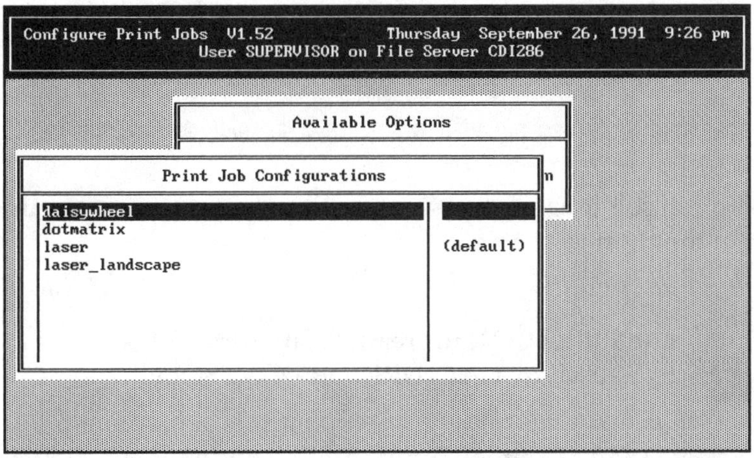

```
Configure Print Jobs  V1.52        Thursday  September 26, 1991  9:26 pm
                   User SUPERVISOR on File Server CDI286

                          Available Options

                    Print Job Configurations
            daisywheel
            dotmatrix
            laser                       (default)
            laser_landscape
```

Figure 6.44

An example of PRINTCON's available jobs.

You can set up many of the CAPTURE and NPRINT flags in the Print Job Configuration screen, as shown in figure 6.45. The bottom half of the screen also enables you to use the Device and Modes set up in PRINTDEF.

447

Figure 6.45

PRINTCON's Edit Print
Job Configuration
menu.

```
Configure Print Jobs  V1.52          Thursday  September 26, 1991  9:27 pm
                  User SUPERVISOR on File Server CDI286

              ┌──────────────────────────────────────────────┐
              │         Edit Print Job Configuration "laser"  │
    ┌──       │                                              │
    │         │ Number of copies:   1         Form name:     Default   │
    │         │ File contents:      Byte stream  Print banner:  Yes      │
    │         │ Tab size:                     Name:         SUPERVISOR │
  dai│        │ Suppress form feed: No        Banner name:             │
  dot│        │ Notify when done:   No                                 │
  las│        │                                                        │
  las│        │ Local printer:      1         Enable timeout:  Yes     │
    │         │ Auto endcap:        Yes       Timeout count:   5       │
    │         │                                                        │
    │         │ File server:        CDI286                             │
    │         │ Print queue:        LASER                              │
    │         │ Print server:       PSCDI386                           │
    │         │ Device:             (None)                             │
    │         │ Mode:               (None)                             │
              └──────────────────────────────────────────────┘
```

In the example shown in figure 6.45, the print job named "laser"
sends the printout to the queue named LASER. Before she can use
this job, the user needs only to type the following command:

```
CAPTURE J=LASER
```

If the user does not set up this printer job to include all the parameters in figure 6.45, she needs to type the following rather than the
preceding syntax:

```
CAPTURE S=CDI386 Q=LASER C=1 NT F=0 FF NAM=SUPERVISOR NNOTI
_L=1 AU TI=5
```

As you can see, it is much easier to set up the print job once, then
type in the short job name.

Use PRINTCON to create default print job settings
to be used by CAPTURE and PCONSOLE.

The Select Default Print Job Configuration option in the Available
Options menu enables you to select which job is the default. If you
issue a CAPTURE or NPRINT command without specifying any
commands, the parameters of the default job are used.

Note

The Copy Print Job Configurations option in the Available Options menu enables Supervisors to copy PRINTCON jobs to other users. The personalized PRINTCON file is called PRINTCON.DAT and is kept in the user's ID directory under SYS:MAIL.

When you select the Copy Print Job Configurations option, NetWare displays the Source User prompt (see fig. 6.46). At this prompt, enter the name of the user (the *source user*) whose job you want to copy. NetWare then asks you for the name of the user, called the *target user*, to copy the selected file to (see fig. 6.47). The PRINTCON.DAT file then is copied from the source user to the target user. You must perform this procedure separately for each user who needs the selected file.

```
Configure Print Jobs  V1.52          Thursday  September 26, 1991  9:27 pm
                     User SUPERVISOR on File Server CDI286

                 ┌─────────────────────────────────────┐
                 │         Available Options            │
                 ├─────────────────────────────────────┤
                 │Edit Print Job Configurations         │
                 │Select Default Print Job Configuration│
                 │Copy Print Job Configurations         │
                 └─────────────────────────────────────┘

         ┌───────────────────────────────────────────────┐
         │Source User:                                    │
         └───────────────────────────────────────────────┘
```

Figure 6.46

The Source User prompt.

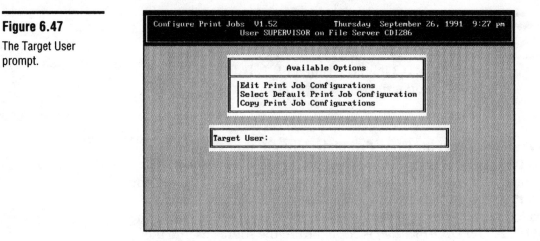

The following steps enable you to make use of a common
PRINTCON.DAT file that uses your files, if defined, or uses a file
kept in SYS:PUBLIC, if undefined.

1. Copy the desired PRINTCON.DAT file into the SYS:PUBLIC
   directory.

2. Execute the following commands from the SYS:SYSTEM
   directory while logged in as a Supervisor, and have drive Z
   mapped to SYS:PUBLIC.

```
SMODE Z:PCONSOLE.EXE 5
SMODE Z:CAPTURE.EXE 5
SMODE Z:NPRINT.EXE 5
```

After you modify the search mode, the network uses this method
to search for the specified file unless you issue another SMODE
statement.

The PSC Command

The *Print Server Command* (PSC) is used to control and view the
status of print servers. Many of the functions that you can control
with PSC you can also do from within PCONSOLE. Sometimes,
though, you might find that issuing a command at the DOS
prompt is quicker than accessing a menu utility.

Perform printer maintenance tasks with
PCONSOLE and PSC.

Table 6.5 lists the various flags available in the PSC command. The
flags are discussed in more detail following the table.

Table 6.5
PSC Flags

Flag	Description
AB	ABorts the print job
CD	Cancels a Down server
FF	Advances (Form Feeds) the printer to the top of the next page
K	Keeps the received portion of the job in the file server and prints it
MA	MArks an asterisk (*) at the printer head
MO	Specifies a different MOunt form
PAU	PAUses the printer
PRI	Specifies that the printer is PRIvate
SH	Enables the printer to be SHared
STAR	STARts the print job
STAT	Shows the STATus of the connected printers
STO	STOps the print job

The ABort flag stops the current job from printing. The job is
deleted from the queue. The following command tells print server
PS1 to abort the job going to printer 2:

```
PSC PS=PS1 P=2 AB
```

The Cancel Down flag enables print server operators to override
the PCONSOLE command after the Going down after current jobs

option in PCONSOLE is selected to down the print server. Use the following syntax when issuing this flag:

```
PSC PS=PS1 CD
```

The Form Feed flag is used to advance the printer to the top of the next page. The user must stop or pause the printer before she can issue a form feed. Use the following syntax when issuing this flag:

```
PSC PS=PS1 P=2 FF
```

The MArk flag is used to position the form in the printer. The MArk flag places an asterisk (*) at the position of the printer head. The user can use any character to mark the form by placing that character after the MArk flag. When issuing this flag, use the following syntax:

```
PSC PS=PS1 P=1 MA ?
```

The MOunt Form flag is used if you select a form number different from the one currently mounted. The correct syntax is MO=formnumber. Use the following example when issuing this flag:

```
PSC PS=PS1 P=0 MO=2
```

The PAUse flag temporarily pauses a printer. Use the following syntax when issuing the PAUse flag:

```
PSC PS=PS1 P=3 PAU
```

Use the STARt flag to resume printing.

The PRIvate flag is used when you are at a remote printer and want to prevent others from using the attached printer. This flag removes the printer from the print server list. When issuing this flag, use the following syntax:

```
PSC PS=PS1 P=2 PRI
```

The SHared flag is used after issuing the PRIvate flag. This flag enables the remote printer to be used as a network printer again. Use the following syntax when using this flag:

```
PSC PS=PS1 P=2 SH
```

The STARt flag is used to resume printing if the STOp or PAUse flags are issued. The syntax for this flag is the following:

```
PSC PS=PS1 P=2 STAR
```

Use the STATus flag to show the status of printers connected to a specific print server (see fig. 6.48).

```
F:\>psc ps=pscdi286 stat
Printer 0: PRINTQ_0 Printer
Printing job
Off-line

Printer 1: PRINTQ_1 printer
Not connected


F:\>
```

Figure 6.48

An example of a PSC status.

STAT can display the following messages:

```
In private mode

Mark/Form feed

Mount Form n

Not Connected

Not installed

Offline

Out of paper

Paused

Printing Job

Ready to go down

Stopped

Waiting for a job
```

The STOp flag is used to stop the printer. If the print job needs to be resubmitted from the beginning, then the Keep flag also should

453

be used. Otherwise, the job is deleted from the queue. When issuing this flag, use the following syntax:

```
PSC PS=PS1 P=3 STO K
```

Printing Under OS/2

The latest version of the NetWare 3.1*x* operating system, NetWare 3.12, provides enhanced support for printing from an OS/2 client.

The enhanced printing features of NetWare 3.12 support extended attributes for OS/2. The support changes come mostly from the updated client software. To take advantage of the increased OS/2 printing support, therefore, workstations running OS/2 need to be updated with the OS/2 Requester 2.01.

OS/2 remote printing also is supported. It uses NPRINTER.EXE rather than RPRINTER.EXE.

If you want more information on NPRINTER.EXE, you can refer to the OS/2 Requester 2.01 manual. You also can refer to the NetWare 4.0 manual set, because NPRINTER.EXE also ships with NetWare 4.0.

Section Review Questions

33. Which of the following commands do you use to stop a printer?

    a. PSTAT

    b. PSC

    c. PRINTDEF

    d. CAPTURE

34. Which of the following statements marks the top of a form with an asterisk (*)?

    a. `PSC PS=PSCDI386 P=1 MA`

    b. `PSC PS=PSCDI386 MA`

c. `PSC PS=PSCDI386 MARK`

d. `PSC PS=PSCDI386 P=1 MARK`

35. Supervisors can copy print jobs to other users by choosing the _____ option from the PRINTCON menu.

    a. Edit Print Job Configurations

    b. Select Default Print Job Configurations

    c. Copy Print Job Configurations

    d. Import Print Devices

36. Which PSC flag advances the printer to the top of the next page?

    a. AB

    b. MA

    c. PRI

    d. FF

37. Remote printing for OS/2 clients is supported by:

    a. NPRINTER.EXE

    b. RPRINTER.EXE

    c. CAPTURE.EXE

    d. NPRINT.EXE

Answers

33. b

34. a

35. c

36. d

37. a

Case Study

1. List the steps, in order, that you must follow to create a print server.

2. Create a CAPTURE statement that captures to two ports on the same machine, each with different parameters.

3. Create CAPTURE statements that accomplish the same things as shown in the following PRINTCON screens.

```
Configure Print Jobs  V1.52              Wednesday  January 6, 1993  4:40 pm
                      User DNIEDERM on File Server CDI


                         Edit Print Job Configuration "123"

       Number of copies:    1             Form name:      DEFAULTCDI
       File contents:       Byte stream   Print banner:   No
       Tab size:                          Name:
   123 Suppress form feed:  No            Banner name:
   bro Notify when done:    Yes
   cmi
   DEB Local printer:       1             Enable timeout: Yes
   hps Auto endcap:         Yes           Timeout count:  15
   lab
   lot File server:         CDI
   new Print queue:         PRINTQ_0
 ▼ pan Print server:        (Any)
       Device:              (None)
       Mode:                (None)
```

a. CAPTURE _____

```
Configure Print Jobs  V1.52              Wednesday  January 6, 1993  4:41 pm
                       User DNIEDERM on File Server CDI


                  ┌──────── Edit Print Job Configuration "new" ────────┐
          │   │   Number of copies:     4          Form name:      DEFAULTCDI
          │   │   File contents:        Text       Print banner:   Yes
      123 │   Tab size:             12         Name:           DEB
      bro │   Suppress form feed:   Yes        Banner name:
      cmi │   Notify when done:     No
      DEB │
      hps │   Local printer:        2          Enable timeout: No
      lab │   Auto endcap:          No         Timeout count:
      lot │
      new │   File server:          CDI
   ▼  pan │   Print queue:          HP
              Print server:         (Any)
              Device:               (None)
              Mode:                 (None)
```

b. CAPTURE _____

```
Configure Print Jobs  V1.52              Wednesday  January 6, 1993  4:42 pm
                       User DNIEDERM on File Server CDI


                  ┌──────── Edit Print Job Configuration "pana_12" ────────┐
          │   │   Number of copies:     1          Form name:      default
          │   │   File contents:        Text       Print banner:   No
      bro │   Tab size:             8          Name:
      cmi │   Suppress form feed:   Yes        Banner name:
      DEB │   Notify when done:     Yes
      hps │
      lab │   Local printer:        1          Enable timeout: Yes
      lot │   Auto endcap:          Yes        Timeout count:  25
      new │
      pan │   File server:          B386
      pan │   Print queue:          PRINTQ_0
              Print server:         (Any)
              Device:               (None)
              Mode:                 (None)
```

c. CAPTURE _____

457

Customizing the User's Environment

7
CHAPTER

This chapter is the final one that deals with the NetWare utilities common in 2.2 and 3.x systems. In this chapter, you learn about the following topics:

- ◆ Choosing and installing application software
- ◆ Developing login scripts
- ◆ Creating custom menus
- ◆ Using workstation files

In the first section of the chapter, you are introduced to the concepts involved in loading any software application. Included in this discussion are the steps you must take to allow a network user to have access to the new application.

Next, you learn to create and manage login scripts. These scripts are useful in streamlining the login process for all users. You learn all the commands that can be used in the login scripts.

You then learn to create a menu. NetWare provides a convenient mechanism for automating the user's interface to the network through menus.

The menuing system used in NetWare 3.12 is not the same menuing system used in NetWare 2.2. The NetWare 2.2 version of the menuing system is discussed in Chapter 10, "Understanding NetWare 2.2 System Manager Functions."

Finally, you learn to understand and use the necessary files so a user can gain access to the network. You also learn about the NetWare DOS Requester.

Choosing and Installing an Application

In this section, you learn what to look for when choosing an application for the network. You also discover some basic rules to help you install the programs, and the methods available for securing the executable and data files.

 Identify basic guidelines for selecting application software.

Six essential steps are involved in choosing an application and installing it onto the network. You must do the following:

1. Verify network compatibility.

2. Ascertain if the software is meant for a single user or for multiple users.

3. Make a directory structure for the files.

4. Install the application.

5. Flag the files.

6. Grant access rights to the users.

Ascertaining Software Network Support

Four types of software packages are currently on the market: stand-alone, single-user, network-compatible, and NetWare-aware. These four types are discussed in the following sections.

Stand-Alone Applications

Stand-alone applications are written to run on computers not attached to a network. These applications can cause two types of problems:

◆ The application might not run properly while the user is logged in to the network. This problem can manifest itself in many different forms: the application might not load, might hang the workstation, might create garbage data, or might not print to a network queue.

◆ The application might be written to look for signs that the workstation is attached to a network; if found, the application will not run. Most applications written in this way give error messages indicating that they do not run if the workstation has a network connection.

Stand-alone applications are not written to work on networks; as a result, these programs often are incapable of efficiently using NetWare resources.

Single-User Applications

A *single-user* application is an application that can run on a network, but is intended to be used by only one person at a time. The main problem with using a single-user application on the network is that everyone must share configuration files. Users cannot customize the program for their own needs without customizing the program identically for everyone.

Single-user applications are protected by law against multiple users using the program simultaneously. Although these programs might not give you problems, they are not the most

461

desirable type of network applications. Site licensing, which calls for one entire software package per concurrent user, can become costly.

Network-Compatible Applications

Network-compatible applications are written specifically to run on a network. The problem is that you must determine whether the network it was written for was a NetWare network. Not all networks are the same. A product written for networks needs to provide information about whether it works with your version of NetWare.

Many applications that claim to be network-compatible require you to set rights to root directories and also need CAPTURE statements to run properly. You also might need special software to make the application function as you need it to.

NetWare-Aware Applications

A *NetWare-aware* application is guaranteed to run well on your NetWare network. Applications written to know about NetWare normally provide optimum use of NetWare resources.

Most vendors are proud of the fact that these applications were written with NetWare in mind, and normally boast that fact. Look for applications that claim to run with the same versions of NetWare as you currently are running.

While you are looking at applications, also find out about telephone and on-site support. The more accessible the software-support people are, the easier it is to solve problems you might encounter. Find out also if the software company uses the same version of NetWare. This parallelism helps if they need to re-create any problems you are having.

You can obtain information about a program's NetWare compatibility from a variety of locations:

◆ Your local Novell office

- ◆ NetWire, Novell's electronic bulletin board
- ◆ The software vendor
- ◆ Novell Support Encyclopedia
- ◆ Most high-quality NetWare vendors

Creating a Directory Structure

At a minimum, you need to make a directory for the executable files and a directory for the data files. You might find that you need to make even more directories. The basic concept to keep in mind is that the executable files and the data files should be kept in separate areas. This arrangement makes managing the files easier, because you do not have to sort through data files to find the application files. Keeping these files separate also helps prevent accidental deletion of program files.

 Whenever possible, use directories to categorize specific groups of files. If, for example, you have word-processing files that everyone in the sales office shares, label a portion of the directory structure SYS:\WORDPROC\SALESDOCS.

Installing the Application

You can install an application in the following two ways:

- ◆ Use an installation option included with the application. This method is the preferred way to install a program; not all programs offer this option, however.
- ◆ Use NCOPY to copy the files from the floppy disks onto the network drives.

Flagging the Files

Application files, unless otherwise noted in the installation documentation, should be flagged as Shareable Read Only. To assign these flags, change to the directory that contains the files and issue the following command:

```
FLAG *.* SRO
```

This entry flags all files in the directory Shareable and Read Only. If you need to flag only some of the files, replace the wildcards with the correct file names.

The necessary attributes for all other application files should be documented in the application's installation guide.

Granting Access to Users

To grant users access to the files, you must map drives and assign rights to users or groups. Drive mapping can be done using login scripts, menus, or batch files.

 Create search drive mappings to program directories and regular drive mappings to data directories.

 List basic steps to be completed when loading applications.

Grant the users or groups rights to the application as specified in the installation manual. The rule of thumb in granting rights is that the user needs only Read and File Scan rights to the application files.

Remember these six steps in the following order:

1. Verify network compatibility.

2. Ascertain if the software is meant for a single user or for multiple users.

3. Make a directory structure for the files.

4. Install the application.

5. Flag the files.

6. Grant access rights to the users.

The final step, which is not required in all cases, involves updating CONFIG.SYS for each workstation to make use of environmental variables. Some programs require memory managers that must be loaded and configured in the CONFIG.SYS file.

Some programs also require you to load software at the file server.

In NetWare 2.*x*, you must copy any required VAP files into the SYS:SYSTEM directory and reboot the file server.

In 3.*x*, you need to copy any required NLM files into the SYS:SYSTEM directory, or any directory that the server searches for NLM files, and use the LOAD command from the server console to start the NLM.

Section Review Questions

1. Which of the following statements is false?

   You can find out about an application's compatibility with NetWare by contacting:

    a. NetWire, Novell's electronic bulletin board

    b. Your local Novell office

    c. NetWare Buyers Guide

    d. The software vendor

2. What needs to be done to enable multiuser access to an application?

    a. Flag executable file SRO, grant rights to users, map drives to application files

    b. Flag data files RO, grant rights to groups, map drives to data files

    c. Flag executable files RO, flag data files N

    d. Grant rights to users and groups

3. Which of the following statements is false?

    a. Application files need to be in a directory that is separate from data files.

    b. Multiuser applications require that the application files be flagged as Shareable.

    c. The Fake Root feature of the MAP command works to fool unruly applications that require the program to execute from a root directory.

    d. All network applications run on NetWare networks.

4. Where are NLM files copied when NetWare 3.1x is installed?

    a. SYS:PUBLIC

    b. SYS:SYSTEM

    c. SYS:MAIL

    d. SYS:ETC

5. Which of the following is NOT used to map drives?

    a. Login scripts

    b. Menus

c. Batch files

d. PCONSOLE

Answers

1. c

2. a

3. d

4. b

5. d

Developing Login Scripts

A successful network is planned first and implemented later. Login scripts play an important part in building and executing a successful network plan.

Build and execute a plan using system and user login scripts.

Login scripts enable system managers and users to customize the network environment. *Map commands*, discussed in Chapter 3, "Moving Around NetWare Directory Structures," are used in login scripts to establish paths to commonly used directories.

Describe the types of login scripts and how they coordinate at login.

This section discusses the three types of login scripts and the command options that can be placed in login scripts.

The order of login script execution is as follows:

1. System login script

2. User login script

3. Default login script (only if a user login script does *not* exist)

System Login Scripts

The system login script is designed to service all users on the network. When a user logs in to the network, the system executes this login script. The system login script includes drive mappings intended for all system users, global DOS set variables, and greeting messages (see fig. 7.1). System login scripts contain commands that all users need, such as a search mapping to SYS:PUBLIC. For more information on these commands, see the login script commands section later in this chapter.

Figure 7.1

An example of a system login script.

```
SYSCON   3.62                        Friday  September 27, 1991  7:29 pm
                    User JIM On File Server CDI286

                           System Login Script

map display off

** Please keep search mappings in system login script to a minimum - Thanks**

map s1:=sys:public
map s2:=sys:public\dos\%os_version
map s3:=sys:email

** Global Mappings **

comspec=s2:command.com

map f:=sys:
Map S:=sys:system
map m:=sys:menus
```

The system login script is a text file called NET$LOG.DAT, stored in the SYS:PUBLIC directory. This file is created and maintained by the System Supervisor in the SYSCON menu utility, under Supervisor options.

468

User Login Scripts

User login scripts are created and maintained by System Administrators or by individual users for themselves.

 The user login script file, called LOGIN, is held in the user ID directory under SYS:MAIL.

User login scripts contain commands that personalize the network environment for the user. The section on login script commands discusses the commands that you can use with these scripts.

Default Login Scripts

Default login scripts set up basic mappings on the network if a valid user login script does not exist or if no readable characters are in the user login script.

 The commands found in the default login script are established as part of the LOGIN.EXE file and cannot be altered.

For more information on default login scripts, see the 2.2 *Concepts Manual* or the 3.11 *Installation Manual*.

Script Parameters

NetWare offers a variety of script parameters. One parameter is called identifier variables. *Identifier variables* force the network to return information such as the time of day or a workstation address.

469

Note Identifier variables need to be presented in upper-case characters when enclosed in quotation marks.

Although many commands are not case-sensitive, less debugging is necessary if you present items in uppercase characters.

Each login script command requires its own line. The maximum is 150 characters per line, but 78 characters per line is recommended. Make sure that the line wraps naturally when it is longer than the width of the screen. Hard returns are interpreted as new lines. You also can use blank lines. Blank lines have no effect on the execution of the script, but help to break up its appearance.

 Note A cut-and-paste feature also is available in the login script screens. Use F5 to mark items and the arrow keys to highlight a block of data. By pressing Del, you can remove the block. You can return the information to the screen by pressing Ins; you can use Ins as many times as needed as long as you do not exit SYSCON. Each time you use the blocking-and-deleting process, you replace previous data.

Login Script Commands

You can use all the login script commands in system or user login scripts. Keep in mind that everyone needs to go through the system login script; personalization can be done through variables or user login scripts. The following commands show you a variety of ways to make a login script "personal."

 Explain each login script command, propose standard procedures that are executed through login scripts, and plan a system of login scripts for user login.

The MAP Command

The MAP command can be placed in login scripts. In regular drive mappings, the syntax is as follows:

```
MAP options A-Z: = fileserver/volume:path
```

The options you can use are ROOT and *#:.

In search drive mappings, the syntax is as follows:

```
MAP options S1-16: = fileserver/volume:path
```

The options you can use are ROOT and INSERT.

NetWare also enables you to turn on and off what users see when they log in to the network. The DISPLAY statement functions like the DOS ECHO OFF command. MAP DISPLAY ON, which is the default, enables the user to see all commands as they are executed. MAP DISPLAY OFF does not display the login commands. The syntax for each switch follows:

```
MAP DISPLAY ON
MAP DISPLAY OFF
```

NetWare also provides many identifier variables, described previously. You can use identifier variables in several ways in the login scripts. When you use them with the MAP command, a corresponding directory that matches the result of the variable must exist. See the section on identifier variables for a complete list of these variables.

When you use identifier variables in a MAP statement, the variables must be in uppercase characters and preceded by a percent sign (%).

Note To map a network drive letter to the next available drive letter in a login script, use %# in place of the drive letter. %1 maps to the first available network drive, and %2 maps to the next available letter after %1.

The same function at the DOS prompt or in a menu uses MAP NEXT rather than MAP %#.

Some examples of the MAP command and identifier variables follow:

◆ When mapping a HOME directory that changes depending on who logs in, NetWare assumes that a directory matching the user's login name is on the system. The following syntax shows you the way to map the H drive to a user's HOME directory:

```
MAP H:=SYS:USERS\%LOGIN_NAME
```

This mapping requires a directory called SYS:USERS\TWEYAND for the user TWEYAND.

◆ If you want to map a directory based on the current year and month, use the following map statement to check the file server for dates:

```
MAP G:=SYS:%YEAR\%MONTH
```

This mapping requires a directory called SYS:1994\01 if you logged in during January, 1994.

◆ You should have a mapping for each different COMMAND.COM that your workstations use to boot. Depending on the number of different versions you have, the MAP statements that follow ensure that workstations find the appropriate files.

The following MAP statement assumes that the only differences are the DOS version numbers:

```
MAP S2:=SYS:PUBLIC\DOS\%OS_VERSION
```

This mapping requires a directory called SYS:PUBLIC\DOS\V3.30 for any users who have booted their PCs on DOS 3.3.

The following MAP statement assumes that you might have different DOS types, such as DR-DOS, MS-DOS, and PC-DOS, as well as different version numbers:

```
MAP S2:=SYS:PUBLIC\%OS\%OS_VERSION
```

This mapping requires a directory called SYS:PUBLIC\MSDOS\V5.00 for any users who have booted their PCs on MS-DOS 5.0.

Occasionally, DOS versions might be recognized as other types, due to similarities in size, dates, and signatures. In these cases, two different COMMAND.COMs might register as the same version, which means that some users might receive an `Invalid COMMAND.COM` or `COMMAND.COM Not Found` message. The following MAP statement solves this problem:

```
MAP S2:=SYS:PUBLIC\%MACHINE\%OS\%OS_VERSION
```

This mapping requires a directory called SYS:PUBLIC\XYZ\PCDOS\V3.30 for any users who have booted their PCs on PC-DOS 3.30 and have a statement in their SHELL.CFG or NET.CFG that says `LONG MACHINE TYPE = "XYZ"`. (See the section on required commands later in this chapter for more information on this procedure.)

The WRITE Command

The WRITE command enables you to print information to the screen. To use this statement, observe the following conditions:

◆ Enclose in quotation marks the text you want to write to the screen.

◆ Type variables inside of quotation marks in uppercase characters.

◆ Precede the variables with a percent sign (%).

Figure 7.2 shows three statements in a user's login script. Figure 7.3 shows the results if the user, James Weyand, logs in to the network at 4:30 p.m. with the login name JIM.

Figure 7.2

Examples of login
script commands.

```
SYSCON  3.62                          Friday  September 27, 1991  7:27 pm
                        User JIM On File Server CDI286

                         Login Script For User JIM
WRITE "GOOD MORNING, BOSS!"
WRITE ""
WRITE "Good %GREETING_TIME, %LOGIN_NAME"
WRITE ""
WRITE "Good ";GREETING_TIME; ", ";FULL_NAME
WRITE ""
PAUSE
```

Figure 7.3

The results of the
login script
statements.

```
F:\>LOGIN JIM
GOOD MORNING, BOSS!

Good evening, JIM

Good evening, James T. Weyand

Strike any key when ready . . .
```

The PAUSE Command

The PAUSE command, when placed in a login script, issues the
message Press any key when ready. The system waits until the user
presses a key before continuing.

The FIRE PHASERS Command

The FIRE PHASERS command produces a "bloop" noise for every
number placed after the command. The resultant noise is designed
to draw attention to the screen without startling the user. This
command is useful if you want to display a message to the user.
Use the following syntax for FIRE PHASERS:

```
FIRE nn
```

The IF-THEN-ELSE Statement

IF-THEN-ELSE statements are conditional statements that enable a parameter to be issued if a condition exists. In an IF-THEN-ELSE statement, the basic idea is "If the condition is true, then do something."

If you want the system to do only one thing, you can specify the command on one line. On the first line in figure 7.4, the system is checking whether today is Friday. If today is Friday, then the system writes TGIF!!!! on-screen. If today is any other day of the week, the system skips over this conditional statement.

If you need more than one thing to happen, BEGIN and END statements are necessary. Examples of these conditions are shown in figure 7.4. BEGIN appears before any executable statements, and END completes the entire statement.

```
SYSCON   3.62                      Friday  September 27, 1991  9:56 am
                    User SUPERVISOR On File Server CDI286

                        Login Script For User DAVE

IF DAY_OF_WEEK = "FRIDAY" THEN WRITE "TGIF!!!!"

IF HOUR24 > "08" AND HOUR24 > "10" THEN BEGIN
     FIRE 9
     WRITE "%FULL_NAME, YOU ARE LATE!!!!"
     PAUSE
ELSE
     WRITE "ON TIME AGAIN, %LOGIN_NAME"
END
```

Figure 7.4

An example of an IF-THEN-ELSE statement.

 Note You must always end an IF-THEN-ELSE statement with an END.

In the second IF-THEN statement in figure 7.4, the condition is true if the time is between 9:00 a.m. and 9:59 a.m. If the file server time is in this range when a user logs in, then the workstation

475

issues an attention-getting sound. The FIRE 9 command tells the user by name that he or she is late, and then pauses, as shown in figure 7.5. If the condition is false, then the ELSE statement is executed; in this example, the statement complements the user's timeliness (see fig. 7.6).

Figure 7.5

The result if both conditional statements are true.

```
F:\>LOGIN CHRIS
TGIF!!!!
Christopher Winslow Bell, YOU ARE LATE!!!!
Strike any key when ready . . .
```

Figure 7.6

The result if only the first conditional statement is true.

```
F:\>LOGIN DAVE
TGIF!!!!
ON TIME AGAIN, DAVE

F:\>
```

In this example, hours before or after 9:00 a.m., such as 8:00 a.m. and 10:00 a.m., force the statement about being on time, which might not be the intended result. You cannot embed IF-THEN statements, so the best solution is to use two separate state-ments—one for hours before 9:00 a.m. and one as shown in figure 7.4.

The BREAK ON/OFF Command

The BREAK ON/OFF command determines whether you can interrupt the login script by using Ctrl+Break or Ctrl+C.

The DISPLAY and FDISPLAY Commands

The DISPLAY and FDISPLAY commands enable you to display a text file on the user's screen as she logs in. If the file is an ASCII file, the DISPLAY command presents the file's contents. If the file was created using another program and extra characters appear, FDISPLAY filters out all control characters and displays only text. Use the following syntax for the DISPLAY command:

```
DISPLAY volume:path/filename
```

In figure 7.7, the system is looking for the date to be July 4. If the date is July 4, the screen shown in figure 7.8 is displayed.

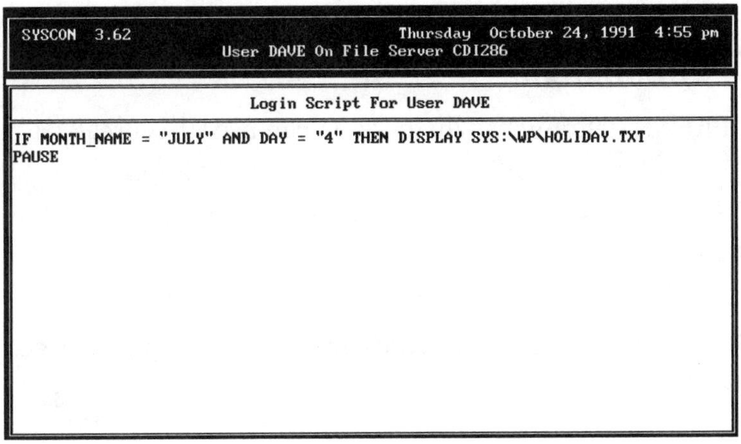
SYSCON 3.62
Thursday October 24, 1991 4:55 pm
User DAVE On File Server CDI286
Login Script For User DAVE
IF MONTH_NAME = "JULY" AND DAY = "4" THEN DISPLAY SYS:\WP\HOLIDAY.TXT
PAUSE

Figure 7.7
A DISPLAY command in a login script.

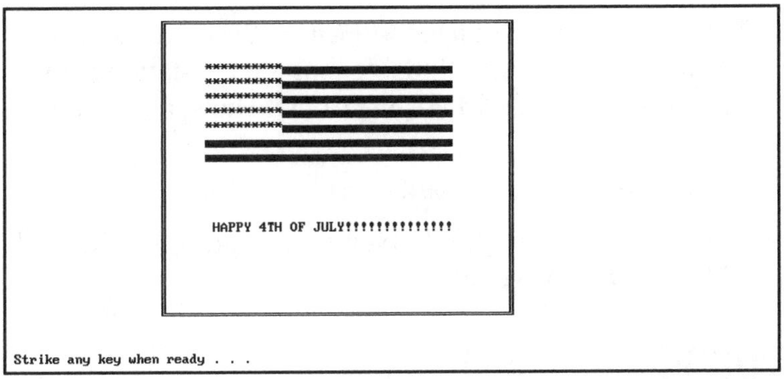
HAPPY 4TH OF JULY!!!!!!!!!!!!!!!
Strike any key when ready . . .

Figure 7.8
The result if the date is July 4.

The INCLUDE Command

The INCLUDE command enables the System Administrator to control changes to the login scripts from a common text file. INCLUDE works like a subroutine in a login script. This text file can be created by any text editor and should contain only valid login script commands. All the commands listed in this section qualify. INCLUDE's syntax is as follows:

`INCLUDE` *`volume:path/filename`*

If you have several users who share common scripts, placing an INCLUDE statement in their existing login scripts is convenient. Any changes can then be made to the text file.

DOS Commands

DOS BREAK determines whether you can use Ctrl+Break or Ctrl+C at the DOS prompt to interrupt programs.

DOS SET enables you to set DOS variables to a specified value. The syntax is as follows:

```
DOS SET variable name = "value"
```

DOS VERIFY enables you to verify that files are copied correctly to a local drive.

The COMSPEC Command

COMSPEC stands for *COMmand SPECifier*. You can use this command to specify the search drive that a workstation is to use to find the appropriate COMMAND.COM. The syntax is as follows:

```
COMSPEC = search drive:COMMAND.COM
```

The search drive variable should be replaced with the search drive assigned to the DOS directory.

The DRIVE Command

The DRIVE command specifies exiting to a previously mapped drive letter from a login script. The syntax is as follows:

```
DRIVE drive letter:
```

The GOTO Command

You use the GOTO command in the same way you do in a DOS batch file. Do not use GOTO within a BEGIN-END conditional statement. For easy debugging, you also should use the

BREAK ON command. For more information on the GOTO command, see your DOS manuals.

Exit Commands

This section discusses the various ways in which you can exit a login script. When you use the EXIT command by itself in the system login script, NetWare exits to DOS without going to the user login script.

In a user login script, EXIT takes the user to the DOS prompt, which usually is the default drive. To execute a DOS command, use the following syntax:

```
EXIT filename
```

The file name in the EXIT statement can be any file ending in EXE, COM, or BAT.

When you use the EXIT filename command, the system takes you to DOS, closes the login script, and executes the command.

You are limited to 14 characters inside the quotation marks.

If no EXIT statement is called in the system login script, the user login script is executed. If no EXIT statement is called in the user login script, the user is taken to the default directory DOS prompt.

Using the # With a Command

If you type the following syntax, for example, you can execute a command at the DOS prompt, then return to the login script to complete further commands.

```
#filename
```

This command only works with EXE or COM files.

479

If you have an internal DOS command, such as CLS, or you want to execute a batch file, you must use the following syntax:

```
#COMMAND /C command
```

This command loads an additional DOS environment to execute the command. If you want to clear a screen from the login script, for example, type the following:

```
#COMMAND /C CLS
```

If workstations frequently run out of memory with the programs you use, using # in login scripts is not advisable. The memory needed to execute the command at the workstation is not released back to the workstation until it is rebooted.

Remark Statements

Remark statements are used to leave notes for the Administrator. Remark statements enable you to document what you have done in a login script; these remarks are not executed. Three parameters are available for creating a remark statement in a login script.

 REM, *, and ; all are valid remark parameters. They must be the first characters on a line.

Command-Line Parameters

NetWare also enables you to use parameters in the login statement to customize your login even further. The available parameters are %0 through %9. Parameters %2 through %9 are user-definable.

 %0 is the file server name
%1 is the user's login name

The example that follows enables a user named DIANA to exit to DOS, thereby skipping any additional login script commands, if she types **OUT** after her name on the login line.

First, the following line must be placed in the login script:

```
IF "%2" = "OUT" THEN EXIT
```

Then, at the DOS prompt, Diana can type the following to exit to DOS:

```
LOGIN DIANA OUT
```

In the preceding syntax, OUT is considered to be the %2 variable.

ATTACH Command

By using the ATTACH command, users can attach to other file servers from within the login script. The syntax is as follows:

```
ATTACH fileserver/username;password
```

A password placed in the login script file can be a security breach. NetWare prompts you for all information if you choose not to include the password, user name, or file server.

The PCCOMPATIBLE or COMPATIBLE Commands

Use the PCCOMPATIBLE or the shorthand COMPATIBLE command if you have set the LONG MACHINE TYPE variable. These commands tell the network that your machine is an IBM-compatible PC.

Required Commands

Novell requires the following three statements in the system login script:

```
MAP S1:=SYS:PUBLIC
MAP S2:=SYS:PUBLIC\%MACHINE\%OS\%OS_VERSION
COMSPEC=S2:COMMAND.COM
```

By placing the search mapping to PUBLIC first, you ensure that all commands kept there are executed with priority. You can alter the mapping to the DOS path to match your directory structure. In figure 7.9, you see a small network with five workstations that all use a different COMMAND.COM.

Figure 7.9

An example of automatic mapping to the proper COMMAND.COM.

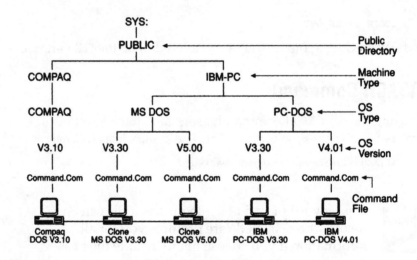

 Novell uses the phrases *essential environmental components* and *essential system login script commands* to describe the following three statements:

```
MAP S1:=SYS:PUBLIC
MAP S2:=SYS:PUBLIC\%MACHINE\%OS\%OS_VERSION
COMSPEC=S2:COMMAND.COM
```

The network queries the workstation at bootup to fill in the variable values. By default, NetWare recognizes all workstations as IBM PCs. If you need to use another directory at this level, you must create a SHELL.CFG or NET.CFG text file wherever you call your IPXODI.COM file. In that file is one line that should read as follows:

```
LONG MACHINE TYPE = directoryname
```

Standards help you to regulate the way systems are set up. They also help you to avoid conflicts. The previous three statements attempt to standardize the operating system environment. You can use other options, but these lines guarantee that you do not get Invalid or Missing COMMAND.COM messages that lock workstations when you are exiting programs.

Identifier Variables

Table 7.1 lists the identifier variables and their definitions. You can use these variables in login scripts.

Table 7.1
Identifier Variables

Conditional Items	Screen Display
ACCESS_SERVER	Displays TRUE if access server is functional; displays FALSE if not functional
ERROR_LEVEL	Displays the number of errors, if no errors are found
MEMBER OF group	Displays TRUE if the user is a member of a specified group; displays FALSE if the user is not a member of a specified group

Date	Screen Display
DAY	Displays the day from 01 to 31
DAY_OF_WEEK	Displays the day of the week
MONTH	Displays the month from 01 to 12
MONTH_NAME	Displays the name of the month
NDAY_OF_WEEK	Displays the number of the week-day

continues

483

Table 7.1, Continued
Identifier Variables

Date	Screen Display
SHORT_YEAR	Displays the year in short format, such as 92, 93, and so on
YEAR	Displays the year in full format, such as 1992, 1993, and so on
DOS Environment	Uses any DOS environment variable as a string

Network	Screen Display
NETWORK_ADDRESS	Displays the network number of the cabling system in eight hex digits
FILE_SERVER	Displays the name of the file server

Time	Screen Display
AM_PM	Displays the time as day or night, by using a.m. or p.m.
GREETING_TIME	Displays the time of day as morning, afternoon, or evening
HOUR	Displays the time of day in hours, from 1 to 12
HOUR24	Displays the hour in 24-hour time, from 00 to 23
MINUTE	Displays the minutes from 00 to 59
SECOND	Displays the seconds from 00 to 59

User	Screen Display
FULL_NAME	Displays the full name of the user by using SYSCON information
LOGIN_NAME	Displays the user's login name
USER_ID	Displays the ID number of each user

Workstation	Screen Display
MACHINE	Displays the machine for which the shell was written, such as IBM PC
OS	Displays the workstation's operating system, such as MS-DOS
OS_VERSION	Displays the DOS version of the workstation
P_STATION	Displays the station address or node address in 12 hex digits
SMACHINE	Displays the name of the machine in short format, such as IBM
STATION	Displays the connection number

Section Review Questions

6. Which login script is used after the system login script?

    a. The user's login script

    b. The default login script, if the user's login script does not exist

    c. The default login script

    d. The system login script is loaded last

7. Which of the following statements about login scripts is true?

    a. 80 characters per line is recommended.

    b. Identifier variables always are preceded with a %.

    c. Blank lines and remark statements are not a good idea.

    d. Putting all commands in uppercase cuts down on debugging.

8. If the following statement is in the system login script, which directory must exist for a user whose workstation booted with MS-DOS 5.0?

   ```
   MAP S2:=SYS:PUBLIC\%MACHINE\%OS\%OS_VERSION
   ```

   a. SYSPUBLIC\IBMPC\MSDOS\V5.00

   b. SYS:PUBLIC\IBM_PC\MSDOS\V5.0

   c. SYS:PUBLIC\IBM_PC\MSDOS\V5.00

   d. SYS:PUBLIC\IBM_PC\MS_DOS\V5.00

9. Which of the following statements is false?

   a. The INCLUDE command enables you to display a text file.

   b. The DRIVE command is the same as typing in a drive letter and a colon at the DOS prompt.

   c. If you put an EXIT command into the system login script, the user login script will not be executed.

   d. Use the command #COMMAND /C CLS to clear the screen for the user from the login script.

10. What would the following login script lines accomplish?

    ```
    IF "%2" = "EXIT" THEN BEGIN
        #COMMAND /C CLS
            EXIT
    END
    ```

    a. If the user issues the command **ATTACH EXIT**, the screen clears and he exits the login script.

    b. If the user BMYERS issues the command **LOGIN BMYERS EXIT**, his screen clears, and he quits the login script.

    c. If the user issues the command **LOGIN %2 EXIT**, his screen clears, and a batch file called EXIT.BAT starts.

    d. If the user BMYERS issues the command **LOGIN BMYERS EXIT**, the screen clears, all other script commands are skipped, and the user proceeds directly to his user login script.

486

Answers

6. a

7. d

8. c

9. a

10. b

Creating Custom Menus

Menus make access to applications easy for end users. By using menus, users never have to learn what drives a program. Instead, they can focus their efforts in more productive areas. Many third-party menu programs are available, but few have the simplicity and network compatibility that the menus in NetWare offer. One of the most appealing features of NetWare menus is the cost: they are free with the NetWare operating system.

NetWare 3.12 uses a newer menuing system than was used with previous versions of NetWare. It is a simplified version of Saber's menuing system. This section discusses NetWare 3.12's menuing system, and shows you how to convert menus created with the earlier version of NetWare's menuing system.

 The older version of the NetWare menuing system is discussed in detail in Chapter 10, "Understanding NetWare 2.2 System Manager Functions."

NetWare 3.12 Menuing System

NetWare 3.12's new menuing system is a scaled-down version of the Saber menu system. The biggest advantage that this NetWare menu utility has over the menuing system used in earlier versions of NetWare is that it does not remain resident in RAM while it is executing applications. Thus, more RAM is available for the application itself.

 Describe the components of a user menu system.

Three primary files are used with the new menuing system. These files include the following:

- **NMENU.BAT**—Runs a menu. To start a menu, type **NMEMU.BAT**, then type the name of the menu and press Enter.

- **MENUCNVT.EXE**—Converts menus created in the older menuing system into menus that run under the new menuing system. To convert an older menu, type **MENUCNVT.EXE** followed by the menu file name, then press Enter.

- **MENUMAKE.EXE**—Compiles the menu you create following the conventions required by the new menuing system into a file that can be run. To compile the menu, type **MENUMAKE.EXE** followed by the name of the menu and press Enter.

Creating a Menu

The NetWare 3.12 menuing system has its own command language and method for creating menus.

 Describe NetWare 3.12 menu command language, and plan a simple user menu.

The new menuing system, like the older version, has a title on every menu. It also uses Options (the menu item that the user can choose) that are set to the left margin. Under each option is a command that will execute or a submenu title that opens another menu window.

Unlike the old menuing system, when you create a menu using this new system, you cannot specify where the menu window displays. The modified Saber menuing system uses a series of sideways-cascading menu windows that are controlled by the program itself.

The modified Saber menuing system also uses two types of commands: organizational commands and control commands. *Organizational commands* determine what the menu program looks like when it appears on the screen. *Control commands* tell the NMENU.BAT program how to run the menu, process information, and execute commands.

The menuing system includes two organizational commands (MENU and ITEM) and six control commands (EXEC, LOAD, SHOW, GETO, GETR, and GETP). Table 7.2 shows these commands, as well as the commands that you can use with them. (These commands are indented under each of the organizational and control commands.)

Note
Commands shown with braces ({}) are commands that are put into the menu with the braces around them, as shown in the examples included in the table. The BATCH command, for example, is shown as {BATCH}. Type it into the menu *with* the braces around it.

Also note in the table that sometimes a number is shown with a karat (^) in front of it. The karat is entered to cause the menu to display the number that follows it as part of the menu option. The entry **^1 Utilities**, for example, is displayed as option 1 Utilities on the menu that appears on the screen. This format enables the user to select this option by choosing the number 1 instead of the letter U.

Table 7.2
New Menuing System Commands

Command	Purpose/Use	Example of its use in a menu
MENU	Starts menu	MENU *menunumber,* *menuname* MENU 1, Utilities
ITEM	Defines options	ITEM *itemname option option* ITEM ^2NetWare Utilities
BATCH	Remove menu from memory while running	MENU 1 Utilities {BATCH} memory
CHDIR	Return to default menu. (Automatic when BATCH is used. Can use without BATCH)	MENU 1 Utilities {BATCH} MENU 1 Utilities {CHDIR}
PAUSE	Like DOS Pause, shows a Press any key message	MENU 1 Utilities {PAUSE}
SHOW	Shows DOS command if one is being run	MENU 1 Utilities {Pause}
EXEC	Runs executable or DOS commands	EXEC *executable* or *command* EXEC WP.EXE or EXEC LOGOUT
LOAD	Loads a separate submenu, by name	LOAD *menu_name* LOAD *Batch_files*
SHOW	Loads a separate submenu, by number	LOAD *menu_number* LOAD 2
GET*x*	Prompts for user input, then F10	GET*x command_* *format/parameters*

Command	Purpose/Use	Example of its use in a menu
GETO	Input from user is optional	GETO Enter path: { }40,,P{}
GETR	Input from user is required	GETR Type name: { }25,,{}
GETP	Input from user is stored	GETP Enter source: {}40,,{} GETP Enter target: {}40,,{}

Table 7.2 shows the available options for the menu utility. One of the options it shows is the GETx option. You can use three parameters in place of the x in this menu entry. In addition, you must follow this specific command format:

```
GETx instruction{prepend}length,prefill,SECURE{append}
```

Replace each of the above format options according to these explanations:

instruction Enter the message you want the user to see.

{*prepend*} Enter information you want to be attached before the user types in his or her information. You *must* use the braces even if you have no information typed in between them.

length Specify the maximum number of characters the user can enter in response to the instruction.

prefill Enter any default response you want to appear.

SECURE Use this option to make the user's response appear as only asterisks. This feature is helpful for protecting passwords and other security-related input.

append Enter information you want to attach to the end of the response typed by the user.

Compiling a Menu

Creating a menu is only part of the menu-making process.

 Build and execute a NetWare 3.12 menu.

After you create a menu, you must save it as a file with a dot extension name of **SRC**. You also must compile the menu before it can be used. Compiling a menu is easy. Simply type the command for compiling a menu (**MENUMAKE**), followed by the path and name of the menu file. To compile a menu called MAINMENU.SRC saved to the MISC directory on drive C, for example, type the following at the system prompt, then press Enter:

```
MENUMAKE C:\MISC\MAINMENU.SRC
```

After you compile the menu, it is saved as a file with a dot extension of DAT. In the preceding example, the compiled menu name is *not* MAINMENU.DAT—the DAT version is run to start the menu.

To start the MAINMENU, type **NMAKE C:\MISC\MAINMENU.**

For more information on this new menuing system, refer to the ElectroText documentation that comes with NetWare 3.12.

Converting NetWare 3.11 and Earlier Menus

Because many menus created with Novell's earlier version of the menuing system are still valid, Novell provides a program that lets you convert these menus to the new menuing system. This section explains the process to follow in order to convert the older *.MNU menu files to the newer *.SRC files.

 Convert menu files from earlier versions of NetWare into the new menu utility.

The conversion process is simple. Type the following and press Enter:

```
MENUCNVT menuname
```

Replace **menuname** with the name of the menu you are converting. For example, if you are converting a menu called FIRST.MNU, type **MENUCNVT first** and press Enter. This process reformats the commands within the old menu to commands used in the new menuing system.

Once you have run the MENUCNVT program, compile the new file using MENUMAKE.EXE. The menu now is usable on a NetWare 3.12 network.

Section Review Questions

11. Which of the following is NOT one of the primary files used with the NetWare 3.12 primary files?

    a. NMENU.BAT

    b. CREATMNU.EXE

    c. MENUCNVT.EXE

    d. MENUMAKE.EXE

12. The *two* types of commands used by the Saber menuing system are:

    a. Organizational and Control

    b. Edit and Create

    c. Control and Create

    d. Organizational and Edit

13. Which character must be placed in front of the Saber menu option in order to make it possible for the user to choose a number to select a menu option?

    a. @

    b. #

c. *

d. ^

14. The Saber menu command {BATCH} has what effect when used?

    a. Executes a separate batch file

    b. Lists other files in a BATCH directory

    c. Automatically executes the PAUSE command

    d. Removes the menu from memory while running

15. Which of the following Saber menu commands runs a DOS command?

    a. BATCH

    b. CHDIR

    c. EXEC

    d. SHOW

16. Which of the following Saber menu commands loads a separate submenu by number?

    a. SHOW

    b. GETx

    c. CHDIR

    d. EXEC

17. Which dot extension must you use on your Saber menu file before you can compile it?

    a. DAT

    b. EXE

    c. SRC

    d. MNU

Answers

11. b
12. a
13. d
14. d
15. c
16. a
17. c

Logging In to the Network

This section teaches you to log in to the network from a DOS workstation. In this section, you get hands-on practice with logging in through the NetWare DOS Requester

Once your workstation files are copied to your boot disk and loaded into RAM on the client, you are ready to attach to the NetWare file server.

You can issue the following commands manually or place them in a batch file in the order listed:

```
LSL
LAN Driver (such as NE2000)
IPXODI
VLM
F:
LOGIN fileserver name/username
```

 Note The drive letter F might not be available on some workstations. Therefore, replace F with the first available network drive, depending on the number of locally attached hard drives or on the CONFIG.SYS file's LASTDRIVE setting. The login drive is the first available unused drive letter.

495

Logging in to the network involves the use of *Open Data-link Interface* (ODI) drivers, as part of the NetWare DOS Requester (IPXODI). The NetWare DOS Requester is the key to accessing Novell NetWare 3.12 file servers from a workstation. Therefore, it is important for you to understand some basic information about the NetWare DOS Requester.

 The NetWare DOS Requester replaces the SHELL files used in earlier versions of NetWare. The SHELL files are discussed in Chapter 10, "Understanding NetWare 2.2 System Manager Functions."

The NetWare DOS Requester

Because DOS and most DOS-based applications are not able to directly access the network and utilize the resources that it supplies, networking software must fill in the hole. The NetWare DOS Requester fills that hole with several files that are loaded into the client's memory by running the Requester's executable file—VLM.EXE. When VLM.EXE is run, the related files called *Virtual Loadable Module*s (VLMs) are loaded into client memory.

 Identify the options available to load the NetWare DOS Requester.

VLMs can be loaded into conventional, extended, or expanded memory. You choose which type of memory to load these files into by using the related command switch, /M, followed by a character that designates which type of memory to load the files into. The available options are:

◆ **C**—Conventional

◆ **X**—Extended

◆ **E**—Expanded

For example, to load the NetWare DOS Requester into conventional memory, type **VLM /MC** and press Enter. This loads the VLMs found in the default directory (current directory path) into conventional memory.

The VLM.EXE and the associated VLMs are not the only files that have to be loaded in order for client-to-network communication to be successful. The other required files must be loaded into the workstation's memory in the following order:

- LSL.COM
- LAN Driver
- IPXODI.COM
- VLM.EXE

LSL.COM program loads the Link Support Layer of the ODI specification, thus making it possible for network information to be routed between the LAN driver and the software.

The LAN driver activates the network board so it can connect the client software to the physical components of the network.

The IPXODI.COM program loads the NetWare IPX protocol used to process network requests when appropriate, or to pass the information between the NetWare DOS Requester and the Link Support Layer.

VLM.EXE loads the NetWare DOS Requester into the PC's memory to provide a connection point between the client's DOS and DOS-based applications, and the services provided by the network.

Once these files are executed and the related information is stored in the client's memory, you can log in to the network from this client.

Implementing ODI Drivers

Implementing ODI drivers requires no generation or linking process. You can control the ODI files' custom configuration by

497

creating a NET.CFG file. Loading the ODI files is a simple process when you understand what each file supplies.

The ODI drivers are configured in layers that correspond somewhat to the lower layers of the OSI reference model. A comparison of the ODI drivers to the OSI reference model is shown in figure 7.10.

Figure 7.10

Relationship of the ODI drivers to the OSI reference model.

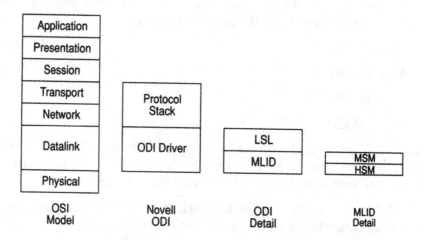

The *Link Support Layer* (LSL) is the first program loaded (see fig. 7.11). This program acts as a switchboard between the network interface driver and the protocol stack. LSL also handles traffic between multiple stacks when they are present.

Figure 7.11

The Link Support Layer (LSL) driver.

```
[DR DOS] C:\NET>lsl
NetWare Link Support Layer  v1.10 (910625)
(C) Copyright 1991 Novell, Inc.  All Rights Reserved.

[DR DOS] C:\NET>
```

Note A *protocol stack* is the process that controls the type of communication taking place. If your PC workstation requires access to both the NetWare file server and your SUN UNIX server, for example, you need to install a Novell IPX and TCP/IP protocol stack.

After the LSL.COM program is loaded, the network interface driver, or *Multiple Link Interface Driver* (MLID), is loaded (see fig. 7.12). This program, provided by the manufacturer, supplies the hardware support for the individual interface cards. ODI drivers are available for the vast majority of network interface cards intended for use with NetWare.

```
[DR DOS] C:\NET>ne2000
Novell NE2000 Ethernet MLID  v1.34 (910603)
(C) Copyright 1991 Novell, Inc.  All Rights Reserved.

Int 5, Port 320, Node Address 1B34C5BE
Max Frame 1514 bytes, Line Speed 10 Mbps
Board 1, Frame ETHERNET_802.3

[DR DOS] C:\NET>
```

Figure 7.12

The Multiple Link Interface Driver (MLID).

After the MLID is loaded, the protocol stack and shell are loaded to complete the attachment to a NetWare file server. A typical ODI driver loading sequence uses the following commands in this order:

LSL

NE2000

IPXODI

VLM

Here, ODI drivers have the advantage over the standard IPX drivers used in earlier versions of NetWare client files. At this point, you might have loaded a TCP protocol stack if your company uses UNIX hosts. With ODI drivers, however, you can load the IPX and the TCP stacks to provide both protocols at the same time.

The preceding list of commands loads the LSL file and then the MLID required for a Novell NE2000 Ethernet card. Next, the standard IPX protocol stack is loaded (see fig. 7.13). Finally, a shell (NetWare 2.2) or requester (NetWare 3.1*x*) must be loaded. If any nonstandard hardware settings are required, the NE2000 module reads them from the NET.CFG file. A simple example of a NET.CFG file follows:

```
Link Driver NE2000
INT 5
PORT 300
```

The NET.CFG file supports many configuration options for each layer of the ODI drivers. At this time, you only need to be concerned with changing the network interface hardware settings. Further instructions usually are provided with hardware that might need special settings.

Figure 7.13

The IPX protocol stack.

```
[DR DOS] C:\NET>ipxodi
NetWare IPX/SPX Protocol  v1.10 (910625)
(C) Copyright 1991 Novell, Inc.  All Rights Reserved.

IPX protocol bound to NE2000 MLID Board #1.

[DR DOS] C:\NET>
```

Any statements used in a SHELL.CFG file simply can be added to the front of NET.CFG in a left-justified manner.

Modify the NET.CFG file to configure the ODI environment.

You must follow a few simple rules when creating the NET.CFG file. The heading statement must be left-justified, and the configuration entries must be tabbed at least one space. If any commands were used previously in a SHELL.CFG file, add them to the beginning of the NET.CFG file.

Each ODI module provides command-line switches for unloading and for memory-saving loads.

Use /U to unload LSL, MLID, IPXODI, and VLM in reverse order of the way in which they originally were loaded.

The IPXODI module provides two extra switches that enable memory savings if full functionality is not needed. Use /D to load IPX/SPX protocols only without any diagnostic capability; this switch provides a memory savings of 4 KB. Use /A to load the

IPX protocol only; this switch provides a memory savings of 8 KB. Use /? to display information about any ODI module.

Novell has approved all ODI modules to operate in high memory.

Figure 7.14 shows the display during an unload, in which the program module is being unloaded in the wrong order; this type of error results in a *fatal unload*.

```
C:\NET>ipxodi /u

NetWare IPX/SPX Protocol  v2.12 (930625) BETA 1
(C) Copyright 1990-1993 Novell, Inc.  All Rights Reserved.

IPXODI-212-16: Cannot unload IPXODI because another program has been loaded
above it.  Unload the other program or programs and try again.

C:\NET>
```

Figure 7.14

An unsuccessful unload of IPXODI.

When you understand the flow of the modules, you should find that changing a driver's configuration by editing a text file is remarkably convenient.

Using the NetWare VLMs

Newer versions of Novell's NetWare Shell (the DOS Requester) use VLMs to provide advanced functionality and support in a modular fashion.

 Summarize the capabilities of the NetWare DOS Requester.

VLMs are a series of files that are loaded in place of the NETX file. Several VLMs are loaded when the VLM command is entered in the following example:

```
LSL
NE2000
IPXODI
VLM
```

When VLM is run, it starts a program called VLM.EXE. This program is a manager for the other files (all with dot extensions of

501

VLM) that load into memory and control the workstation environment and its ability to access network resources.

Running the DOS Requester in place of the old NETX command provides many advantages:

◆ It takes advantage of memory swapping and DOS redirection capabilities to handle requests.

◆ It includes Packet Burst and LIP (described later).

◆ It provides backward compatibility with applications that still require the functions of the NETX shell.

◆ It supports Microsoft Windows drivers that are included with the client software but do not work with the NETX shell.

When the DOS Requester loads, a series of items appears on your workstation's screen. That screen should look similar to the one shown in figure 7.15.

Figure 7.15

Display of DOS Requester loading.

```
(C) Copyright 1990-1993 Novell, Inc.  All Rights Reserved.

Configuration File "C:\NWCLIENT\NET.CFG" used.

Max Boards 4, Max Stacks 4

Novell NE2000 Ethernet MLID  v1.53 (930730)
(C) Copyright 1991 - 1993 Novell, Inc.  All Rights Reserved.

Int 5, Port 340, Mem D0000, Node Address 1B1ED82D L
Max Frame 1514 bytes, Line Speed 10 Mbps
Board 1, Frame ETHERNET_802.2, LSB Mode

NetWare IPX/SPX Protocol  v2.12 (931007)
(C) Copyright 1990-1993 Novell, Inc.  All Rights Reserved.

IPX SOCKETS 45
Bound to logical board 1 (NE2000) : Protocol ID E0
VLM.EXE      - NetWare virtual loadable module manager  v1.10 (931209)
(C) Copyright 1993 Novell, Inc.  All Rights Reserved.
Patent pending.

The VLM.EXE file is pre-initializing the VLMs..............
The VLM.EXE file is using extended memory (XMS).
```

Four of the VLMs are of particular importance in a mixed networking NetWare environment. If you are running NetWare Lite, Personal NetWare, and/or NetWare 2.*x*, NetWare 3.*x*, or NetWare 4.*x* in a network environment, these VLMs enable you to access all three types of NetWare networks without conflict. The VLMs include the following:

- ◆ **NDS.VLM**—Enables you to access NetWare 4 NetWare Directory Services.

- ◆ **BIND.VLM**—Enables you to access NetWare bindery service (NetWare 2x and 3x servers provide bindery services).

- ◆ **LITE.VLM**—Enables you to access services provided by NetWare Lite servers.

- ◆ **PNW.VLM**—Enables you to access services provided by Novell Personal NetWare servers.

VLMs fall into three categories, depending on the service they perform:

- ◆ **DOS redirection**—Responsible for requesting file and print services from a server.

- ◆ **Service protocols**—Handle requests for several specific services, including establishing connection with servers, sending broadcast messages across the network, servicing file reads and writes, and redirecting printing requests.

- ◆ **Transport protocols**—Responsible for two very important functions: maintaining connections to servers and providing various services related to the transport of network packets.

Note

If you upgrade your client (workstation) to run the new DOS Requester, be sure to remove any calls to the NETX.EXE file. This file conflicts with the REDIR.VLM. Both the NETX.EXE file and the REDIR.VLM work with DOS to handle redirection tasks. Both must not be loaded.

To prevent any conflicts, delete the NETX.EXE line from your workstation's NET.CFG file and replace it with the VLM.EXE command.

You should consider some other reasons to upgrade to the DOS Requester in addition to those already mentioned.

◆ The NetWare 3.*x* shell only supports eight connections to the network, but the DOS Requester supports from 2 to 50 connections.

◆ The DOS Requester supports DOS 3.1 and above; the NetWare 3.*x* shell supports DOS 2.*x* and above. You do not need to continue to support DOS 2.*x* if you are not using it on your network.

◆ The DOS Requester supports nine LPT ports; the shell supports only three LPT ports.

◆ The DOS Requester helps to overcome some of the memory limitations of the NetWare 3.*x* shell. The shell is subject to a memory limitation of 64 KB; the DOS Requester requires memory for background processing and can have a large portion of itself loaded into extended or expanded memory as well as conventional memory.

If you upgrade to the NetWare DOS Requester, your configuration files are updated by the client installation, as follows:

◆ **CONFIG.SYS.** The following line is added:

```
LASTDRIVE=Z
```

◆ **AUTOEXEC.BAT.** A call to another file that is created during the installation of the client:

```
@CALL C:\NWCLIENT\STARTNET
```

◆ **STARTNET.BAT.** This file is added, and includes the following lines:

```
@ECHO OFF
C:
CD\ NWCLIENT
SET NWLANGUAGE=ENGLISH
LSL
NE2000
IPXODI
VLM
```

 Customize the NET.CFG file with parameters that affect the NetWare DOS Requester.

◆ **NET.CFG.** A new heading and a line are added to this file if the heading did not exist before. It is added after the Link Driver commands.

```
NetWare DOS Requester
FIRST NETWORK DRIVE = F
```

The NET.CFG file can have other modifications as well. Because the default frame type for the client is now Ethernet_802.3, the Link Driver section of your NET.CFG file needs to have the following line added to it:

```
FRAME Ethernet_802.3
```

If your NET.CFG file currently has a line that says FRAME Ethernet_802.2, change this line to 802.3.

Because Packet Burst is available with NetWare 3.12, if you are running 3.12, the following line can be added to your NET.CFG file under the (left-justified) heading of NETWARE DOS REQUESTER:

```
PB BUFFERS = number
```

In this syntax, number represents either Packet Burst off, if set to 0, or specifies the number of buffers set aside for Packet Burst, with 1 through 10 being available.

If you are running Windows as well as the DOS Requester, add the following line to your NET.CFG file:

```
SHOW DOTS = ON
```

This entry enables you to see dots appear across the screen as the VLM modules load into your workstation's memory.

Update existing client files using WSUPDATE, and describe the procedures and login script commands used to automate the process.

505

You can update client files using Novell's WSUPDATE software. WSUPDATE is a command-line utility that enables you to update workstation files from newer files located on the file server. This utility is useful for updating DOS Requester files. By using the WSUPDATE utility, you can have the workstation compare the date stamp on a file located on the workstation's hard drive or floppy drive to a version of the file in a specified directory on the file server. If the version on the file server is newer than the one on the workstation, you can have the file on the workstation overwritten or copied to a file with an OLD extension and updated.

Use the following syntax for WSUPDATE:

```
WSUPDATE source destination options
```

or

```
WSUPDATE /F=scriptfile
```

In the preceding syntax, *source* is the location and name of the file on the network that other files are checked against, *destination* is the location and name of the file to be replaced or updated, and *scriptfile* is a file you create that contains a list of source and destination pairs for automatic execution.

To update the workstation files easily, copy the updated files into one of the search drives on the network and type the following on a workstation using the regular DOS Requester file:

```
WSUPDATE V:\UPDATE\VLM.EXE C:\NWCLIENT\VLM.EXE
```

You can update the workstation DOS Requester files when the user logs on to the network, by creating a WSUPDATE configuration file for each user's workstation and executing the WSUPDATE program from the user's login script. If the user's WSUPDATE script is named WSUPD.CFG, for example, type the following into the login script:

```
IF DAY_OF_WEEK = 2 #WSUPDATE /F=WSUP.CFG
```

The script WSUPD.CFG resembles the following:

```
F:XMSNETX.COM C:XMSNETX.COM
F:CONFIG.SYS C:CONFIG.SYS
```

The WSUPDATE utility enables you to use the following options:

◆ **/I**—Prompts the user to input whether the file should be overwritten, renamed, or ignored (the default option).

◆ **/C**—Copies the new file over an existing one automatically.

◆ **/R**—Renames the old file with the OLD extension automatically.

◆ **/S**—Searches all subdirectories on the workstation for outdated files.

◆ **/O**—Updates read-only files.

◆ **/L=path/filename**—Creates a log file that tracks WSUPDATE activity.

Using the ATTACH Command

The ATTACH command enables users to attach to additional file servers while they are logged in to the default server. ATTACH accepts two command-line parameters: fileserver and loginname. At the F:\> prompt, for example, type the following:

```
ATTACH ACCOUNTING\TOM
```

If no parameters are specified, the user is prompted for each one. ATTACH does not provide drive mapping, because the system login script is not executed. To map network drives, simply use the MAP command after a successful server attachment.

Using the LOGOUT Command

Use the LOGOUT command to log out of all file servers. LOGOUT terminates your access privileges and removes all drive mapping that was set up while you were logged in.

You can log out of a specific file server by typing the name of the file server after the LOGOUT command. At the prompt, enter the following, for example:

```
LOGOUT SALES
```

This command terminates the access privileges and removes drive mapping to the SALES file server, but maintains all other file-server connections.

 Logging out of all file servers before shutting down for the day is important. If you do not log out of a workstation, some files might not be backed up properly, because most tape drives cannot back up open data files.

Section Review Questions

18. Which file replaces the NETX file in the NetWare 3.12 client?

    a. LSL.COM

    b. VLM.EXE

    c. IPXODI.COM

    d. EMSNETX.EXE

19. The NetWare DOS Requester includes Packet Burst and

    _____.

    a. Large Internet Packet

    b. NETX Shell

    c. Drivers that work with MS Windows and NETX

    d. Added memory

20. Which of the following VLMs, when loaded, supports NetWare Directory Services?

    a. BIND.VLM

    b. VLM.EXE

    c. NDS.VLM

    d. LITE.VLM

21. The VLM.EXE file is primarily responsible for:

    a. Swapping memory

    b. Managing the other VLMs

    c. Accessing NetWare Directory Services

    d. Preventing conflicts with NETX

22. Which protocol is responsible for establishing connections with servers?

    a. Service

    b. Transport

    c. Redirection

    d. Connections

23. Which startup file loads the DOS Requester if you do NOT specify otherwise?

    a. CONFIG.SYS

    b. AUTOEXEC.BAT

    c. NET.CFG

    d. STARTNET.BAT

24. Which NET.CFG command accurately specifies a number of Packet Burst buffers?

    a. PB = 3

    b. Packet Burst = 3

    c. PB Buffers = 3

    d. Packet Buffers = 3

Answers

    18. b

    19. a

20. c

21. b

22. a

23. d

24. c

NetWare 3.12 Environment Enhancements

As mentioned earlier, Packet Burst has been added as an enhancement to the NetWare 3.12 environment. One additional enhancement has been added as well—*Large Internet Packet* (LIP). In addition, NetWare 3.12 supports Microsoft Windows, considered a key feature of NetWare 3.12. NetWare 3.12 also supports diskless workstations. These features are discussed in the following section.

Packet Burst

Packet Burst is a communication protocol that enables clients and servers to communicate more efficiently. It speeds up the transfer of multiple *NetWare Core Protocol* (NCP) packets across the network connection. This protocol is built into the NetWare 3.12 operating system code as well as the client-connection software.

Conceptually, Packet Burst is quite simple. Whenever you need a file or request a service on the network, a packet is sent across the network connection. This packet then is accepted by the server, and an acknowledgment of its receipt is sent back across the network connection. Each packet sent receives an acknowledgment. Although this procedure helps ensure that packets are received and processed, it increases the traffic across the network connection.

Describe how the LIP and Packet Burst protocol affect network performance.

Packet Burst enables the responding server to hold its acknowledgment of a packet until it receives several packets. It then sends a "burst" across the network connection that contains acknowledgment of all packets it received. Instead of a one-to-one relationship of request to acknowledgment, the server now can operate under a one-to-many relationship. This process substantially reduces network traffic.

For Packet Burst to function, it must be enabled at the server and the client.

Packet Burst increases the speed of packets distributed on the network. It also supports high transmission speeds such as those provided by T1 (fast links). In addition, Packet Burst allows a packet to travel over many routes if the network is using X.25. These packets also can make several hops over routers and bridges. A *router* is a workstation or file server running software that allows information exchange between different network cabling systems, and sends it the most efficient possible route. A *bridge* is also a router, but it does not have the capability to determine the most efficient route to send the packet.

Packet Burst also is included with NetWare 3.11, but it is loaded as an NLM (PBURST.NLM) at the 3.11 server, and as a COM file (BNETX.COM) at the workstation. In NetWare 3.12, Packet Burst is enabled at the server and workstation by default.

Large Internet Packet (LIP)

NetWare 3.12 also supports LIP. A router has limitations on the size of a packet it can handle. In NetWare 3.11, whenever a router exists between the server and the client, the maximum packet size that can be sent is 512 bytes, including 64 bytes of packet header information. This limitation can have a substantial effect on the performance of your network.

To get around that limitation, LIP was added to NetWare 3.12 at the server and in the client-connection software. LIP enables the server and the client to negotiate the size of the packet when it has to be sent through a router. If the router is capable of handling it (some are not; LIP is not effective for those routers), a packet size as large as 4202 bytes can be sent through the router.

In NetWare 3.12, LIP is part of the server and client code. In NetWare 3.11, LIP is supported through the BNETX shell at the client.

Microsoft Windows Support

Support of Microsoft Windows is provided in NetWare 3.12 when a NetWare 3.12 client is installed. The installation copies several files to the WINDOWS directory and to the WINDOWS/SYSTEM directory of the client. In addition, the installation modifies three of the MS Windows files.

Describe the changes made to a client station during the client installation for *Microsoft* (MS) Windows.

The following files are copied to the WINDOWS directory:

- ♦ NWADMIN.INI
- ♦ NETWARE.INI
- ♦ ET.INI
- ♦ NWUSER.EXE
- ♦ NWUTILS.GRP

The following files are copied to the WINDOWS/SYSTEM directory:

- ♦ NETWARE.DRV
- ♦ NETWARE.HLP

- ◆ NWPOPUP.EXE
- ◆ VIPX.386
- ◆ VNETWARE.386

The following Microsoft Windows files are modified during the client installation:

- ◆ SYSTEM.INI
- ◆ WIN.INI
- ◆ PROGMAN.INI

Diskless Workstation Setup

If your network contains diskless workstations, NetWare 3.12 file servers can be set up to support those diskless workstations.

 Describe the method used to support diskless client stations, and identify the files used with the method.

To support diskless clients on a NetWare 3.12 network, you must install RPL.NLM on the NetWare server, bind RPL.NLM to the network server board, load the bootstrap program files into the file server's SYS:LOGIN directory, and create remote boot disk image files for each diskless client in the SYS:LOGIN directory of the NetWare 3.12 file server.

If the diskless client does not already have a remote boot *Programmable Read Only Memory* (PROM) chip installed, you may also have to install that chip.

Section Review Questions

25. The main benefit of LIP is:

    a. It is part of the OS in NetWare 3.12

    b. It improves performance across routers

    c. It limits the size of packets going across bridges

    d. It lets networks communicate without routers

26. LIP stands for:

    a. Large Interrouter Packet

    b. Listening International Packet

    c. Large Internet Packet

    d. Listening Interrupt Packet

27. Which statement best describes Packet Burst?

    a. A client-server communication protocol

    b. Router to handle large packets

    c. Solution to memory limitations

    d. None of the above

28. For Packet Burst to function:

    a. It must be enabled at the client and server

    b. It can be enabled only at the server

    c. It can be enabled only at the client

    d. None of the above

29. Which file is NOT copied to the WINDOWS directory when the client Microsoft files are installed?

    a. NWADMIN.INI

    b. NETWARE.INI

    c. ET.INI

    d. SYSTEM.INI

30. To support diskless clients on a NetWare 3.12 network, you must install:

    a. RPROM.NLM

    b. ET.INI

    c. RPL.NLM

    d. NWUSER.EXE

Answers

    25. b

    26. c

    27. a

    28. a

    29. d

    30. c

Case Study

1. Debug the following system login script:

```
COMSPEC = S2:COMMAND COM
MAP NEXT SYS:USERS\THASSELL\REPORTS93
IF %LOGIN_NAME <> "SUPERVISOR" THEN
DOS SET USERNAME = "%LOGIN_NAME"
DRIVE K:
STOP
IF MEMBER_OF_TECHS THEN BEGIN WRITE "CHECK YOUR EMAIL"
```

2. Create a user login script that accomplishes the following items:

    ◆ Checks for the day of week and, if it is Tuesday, has a message telling the user about a meeting the next day at 10 a.m.

◆ Maps a drive to a spreadsheet application and has the user change to that drive letter when he or she exits.

◆ Maps a drive to a data directory that corresponds to the current month and year.

◆ Checks for the user named BACKUP and has him exit to a batch file that starts the nightly backup. (This user can only log in between 7:00 p.m. and 11:00 p.m.)

◆ Makes sure that only people belonging to the group ACCOUNTING can log in to the workstation whose address is 7E.

3. Create a menu with the following parameters:

◆ Provides access to three applications—one for spreadsheets, one for accounting, and one for word processing. Use applications with which you are familiar.

◆ Has a submenu with several NetWare menu utilities.

◆ Has a submenu with SEND, NCOPY, and NDIR.

PART 3

NetWare 3.1x

Administering NetWare 3.1*x* Networks

8 CHAPTER

To help you understand things specific to NetWare 3.12, Chapter 8 first reviews some basics about NetWare 3.1*x* and NetWare file servers, then focuses on information specific to the basic NetWare 3.1*x* operating system. This chapter provides information about NetWare 3.1*x* from the perspective of the System Administrator. The following items are discussed:

- ◆ NetWare 3.1*x* file servers
- ◆ Hardware and software features
- ◆ Workstation utilities
- ◆ Console commands
- ◆ NetWare loadable modules
- ◆ Remote console management

Understanding NetWare 3.1*x* File Servers

NetWare 3.1*x* networks use file servers to perform the basic duties of networking, and to provide file and storage services. File servers require basic components in order to accomplish their assigned tasks. Most of these components have been discussed in detail in other chapters; therefore they are only listed here.

Identify and describe the server components.

Basic file server components include:

◆ Hardware components, including an Intel microprocessor, adequate RAM, sufficient disk storage, and network board and cabling

◆ Software components, including SERVER.EXE, a disk driver, and a LAN driver

Each file server must also be assigned unique network addresses. Unique identification numbers are required for the file server, the network board, and the communication protocol.

Once the basics have been put into place, a file server must be started before it can provide network services.

Perform a server startup procedure.

To start a NetWare 3.1*x* file server, complete the following steps:

1. Run SERVER.EXE.

2. LOAD the appropriate disk driver.

3. MOUNT the file server's volume(s).

4. LOAD the LAN driver appropriate for the installed NIC.

5. Bind the communication protocol to the LAN driver.

While completing many of these steps, you may be prompted to provide additional information. The file server startup/configuration files can be used to automate this process.

 Identify and describe server configuration files.

Server startup/configuration files that can be used to automate this process include:

◆ STARTUP.NCF

◆ AUTOEXEC.NCF

STARTUP.NCF can be used to automatically issue commands to load disk drivers. The STARTUP.NCF file can be generated for you automatically at the time you run the NetWare 3.1*x* installation program.

AUTOEXEC.NCF is used to provide information to the server as to what it should do during the bootup process.

 Identify commands and options used to customize the appropriate server configuration file.

For example, the STARTUP.NCF file can also be used to provide the configuration parameters necessary for loading disk drivers, as well as for configuring other aspects of the server. To load disk drivers, you would use this command:

```
LOAD ISADISK port=1F0 int=D
```

The AUTOEXEC.NCF file can contain information such as the name of the file server and its internal network (IPX) number. In addition, this file can contain instructions for loading and binding the LAN driver, and for loading NLMs, such as those used for

521

remote access (RSPX.NLM and REMOTE.NLM) or for monitoring network performance (MONITOR.NLM). An example of some lines that are used in an AUTOEXEC.NCF file include:

```
FILE SERVER NAME LEE_SERVER
IPX INTERNAL NET 1D0D1994
LOAD MONITOR
```

As mentioned previously, server configuration files are generated automatically when you install the NetWare 3.1*x* server. However, you may have need to later edit one or more of these files.

Select the appropriate utility and edit the server configuration files.

If you need to edit these files, you must edit them using the INSTALL.NLM. After typing **LOAD INSTALL** at the file server keyboard, press Enter. Then, choose the Available System Options menu. Next, choose either Edit AUTOEXEC.NCF File or Edit STARTUP.NCF File. You then can edit and save these files.

If these two startup/configuration files are not sufficient for your needs, you can automate other server processes by creating server batch files.

Create server batch files that perform specific tasks, such as remotely downing the server.

NetWare 3.1*x* provides an NLM, called EDIT, that you can use to create or modify batch files. To use this NLM, type **LOAD EDIT** at the file server keyboard, and press Enter. Add or change commands in the file as needed and exit this NLM. Then, whenever you need to run this batch file, you can run it either at the file server console or remotely. If you want, you can create a batch file that downs the file server when you run it. The batch file must contain the following lines in order to remotely down the server:

```
REMOVE DOS
DOWN
EXIT
```

To run this batch file, use RCONSOLE to access the file server's console from your client, then type the name of the batch file and press Enter.

Now that you have reviewed both basic and more advanced information about NetWare 3.1x file servers, you can learn about software and hardware requirements for these file servers.

Section Review Questions

1. Which file server configuration file provides information during bootup?

   a. STARTUP.NCF

   b. INSTALL.NLM

   c. SERVER.EXE

   d. AUTOEXEC.NCF

2. The last step needed to start a 3.1x file server is:

   a. Bind protocol to LAN driver

   b. Load disk driver

   c. Mount volume

   d. Run SERVER.EXE

3. Which information is NOT saved in the AUTOEXEC.NCF file?

   a. File server name

   b. Load disk_driver

   c. IPX Internal Net number

   d. Load Monitor

4. To edit the STARTUP.NCF file, you must load:

   a. INSTALL.NLM

   b. EDIT.NLM

    c. MONITOR.NLM

    d. CREATE.NLM

5. The NLM you can use to create batch files is called:

    a. CREATE

    b. BATCH

    c. EDIT

    d. MAKE

Answers

1. d

2. a

3. b

4. a

5. c

Software and Hardware Requirements

In order to set up a Novell NetWare 3.1*x* network, you must understand something about NetWare 3.1*x* and its requirements. As you know from having read previous chapters in this book, Novell's NetWare *Operating System* (OS) provides network services to clients.

Describe the function of a server, its interface, and its communication with the network.

The basic services provided by a NetWare file server include, but are not limited to:

◆ File storage

◆ System and data security

◆ Printing

◆ File storage and retrieval

◆ Network and media management

◆ Server monitoring

NetWare Loadable Modules (NLMs) are used to interface with a file server. Communication is provided using various protocols (as discussed in Chapter 9, "Learning NetWare 3.1*x* Advanced Administration Skills") and by loading the NetWare DOS Requester (as discussed in Chapter 7, "Customizing the User's Environment") on each network client.

NetWare 3.12 requires minimum hardware configurations in order to load NetWare's OS. File server requirements for NetWare 3.1*x* include the following:

◆ 80386- or 80486-compatible computer

◆ 4 MB of RAM (more for drives larger than 80 MB)

◆ 20 MB hard disk (minimum)

◆ 1.2 MB floppy drive

NetWare 3.1*x* offers the following five different user quantities:

◆ 5-user version

◆ 10-user version

◆ 20-user version (in NetWare 3.11)

◆ 25-user version (in NetWare 3.12)

◆ 50-user version

◆ 100-user version

525

◆ 250-user version

◆ 500-user version (NetWare 3.11 only)

◆ 1000-user version (NetWare 3.11 only)

 The only difference in functionality between the user versions of 3.1*x* is the number of users that can access the file server at one time. This number is different from 2.15, in which connections such as VAPs stole available connections.

NetWare 3.1*x* enables you to use any 8086-compatible or better PC as a workstation. Keep in mind that 486 and 386 systems currently are the best for local processing, upon which NetWare relies heavily.

One major advantage to networking with 3.1*x* is the capability to communicate with multivendor computers.

 TCP/IP and NFS connections are not possible with 2.2. This means that the 2.2 system is severely limited in the methods available to communicate with other computer systems.

NetWare 3.1*x* provides the means to communicate with diverse single- and multiple-user systems. 3.1*x* is a corporate solution; its networking features work for the entire company, as opposed to a single workgroup within the company.

 NetWare 3.1*x* supports the following operating systems and environments:

◆ DOS

◆ OS/2

◆ Windows

- ◆ Macintosh
- ◆ UNIX
- ◆ OSI

NetWare 3.1*x* is far more advanced than 2.2 in its maximum limitations for hardware and services. Table 8.1 is a list of specifications.

Note Several of these numbers are theoretical—you reach hardware limitations before NetWare limitations. As soon as hardware vendors catch up and can provide more slots, more unique hardware addresses, and more storage capabilities, these maximums will become practical instead of theoretical.

Table 8.1
NetWare 3.1x Specification List

Specification	Maximum
User connections per server	Up to 1,000 depending on version
Simultaneous open files per server	100,000
Simultaneous TTS transactions	10,000
Hard drives per server	2,048
Maximum disk storage	32 TB
Hard drives per volume	32
Volumes per file server	64
Largest volume	32 TB
Directory entries per volume	2,097,152
Largest file	4 GB
Maximum RAM on file server	4 GB

NetWare provides *System Fault Tolerance* (SFT) features in NetWare 3.1x as well as 2.2. Each of these processes, however, has been improved in NetWare 3.1x.

Explain System Fault Tolerance and describe how to implement it.

NetWare 3.1x provides the following methods of improving system reliability:

♦ **Read-After-Write Verification and Hot Fix.** These features ensure that data is not written to bad blocks and tracks statistics when bad blocks are found. When you install NetWare, a portion of the disk—two percent by default—is set aside for dynamic bad block remapping. Every time a block of data is written to the hard drive, the server compares what was written to disk to what is in memory. If these things match, the server goes on to the next task. If any discrepancy exists, the server writes the block again to the area set aside during installation. This area is tracked as *hot fix*. The block to which the data is originally written is marked as a bad block so it is not reused. Using FCONSOLE, you can view the number of hot fix blocks used. Each used hot fix block represents a server-detected bad block.

♦ **Duplicate File Allocation Tables and Directory Entry Tables.** *File Allocation Tables* (FATs) and *Directory Entry Tables* (DETs) store information that the server uses to save and retrieve data on the hard disk. If the original tables become corrupt, NetWare can retrieve and use the backup copies because they are stored on separate areas of the disk.

♦ **Disk Mirroring and Disk Duplexing.** NetWare allows certain pieces of equipment to be duplicated—if the original piece fails, the secondary device can be used. *Disk mirroring* enables you to attach two drives on the same controller. *Disk duplexing* requires that you duplicate the disk interface board, the cable connection, the drive controllers, and the hard disks. This method is more secure than disk mirroring.

◆ **Transaction Tracking System.** The *Transaction Tracking System* (TTS) is used with databases. TTS is provided for application developers so database files can be rolled back to their original state if a failure occurs during processing. This protection must be built into the application for you to take advantage of this feature. NetWare 2.2 uses TTS for some of its system files.

◆ **Uninterruptible Power Supply.** *Uninterruptible Power Supply* (UPS) protection prevents power loss from causing the server to crash. The UPS contains a battery capable of maintaining power to the file server for a short period of time. By using a configuration file, the UPS can be configured to tell the server to issue the DOWN command after a specified time.

The file you use to configure the UPS is called CONFIG.UPS and needs to be placed into the SYS:SYSTEM directory. You can set the following parameters:

   ◆ Type of hardware

   ◆ I/O address

   ◆ UPS down time

   ◆ UPS wait time

NetWare 3.1x also uses directory caching and hashing. *Directory caching* can reduce the response time of disk I/O by 30 percent. *File caching* can be up to 100 times faster than accessing a file on hard disk.

In NetWare 3.12, file access speed has been increased by the addition of a feature called *cache read ahead*, which reads more information into memory at a single time than could be read in NetWare 3.11.

529

Elevator seeking has been improved for performance. UPS monitoring is done by loading an NLM and is configured by using the LOAD UPS and UPS TIME console commands.

Elevator seeking is used because data is not stored sequentially on a hard drive. *Elevator seeking* is an algorithm that eliminates disk thrashing and excessive seeks.

An additional enhancement is the capability for the server to dynamically configure memory. NetWare 3.1x does not require the installer to allocate memory for different services. The NetWare operating system can allocate memory for a process and, in many cases, release it back to the server when the memory is no longer needed. This process is covered in greater detail in Chapter 9.

Directory and file attributes are another important feature that NetWare 3.1x provides. Network Administrators can take advantage of this feature when planning their networks.

Describe directory and file attributes and their use in a file system security plan.

Basic file attributes provided in NetWare 3.1x include:

◆ **A**. Archive Needed signifies files that have been altered since the last backup.

◆ **X**. Execute Only prevents files ending in COM or EXE from being copied, and is an attribute that cannot be reversed.

◆ **H**. Hidden File hides files so they do not show up when you use the DOS DIR command.

◆ **RA**. Read Audit was intended to provide a built-in audit trail on files, but currently has no effect.

◆ **WA**. Write Audit was intended to provide a built-in audit trail on files, but currently has no effect.

◆ **RO**. Read Only enables user to only read and use files, but not to change or modify them.

◆ **RW**. Read/Write enables users to read from the file and write back to it.

◆ **S**. Shareable enables several users to access a single file at the same time.

◆ **N**. Nonshareable ensures that only one person is allowed to use the file at a time.

◆ **Sy**. System file marks a file as being a system-related file, and prevents it from being listed when a DOS DIR command is executed.

◆ **T**. Transactional allows files to be tracked with the Transactional Tracking System feature of NetWare.

◆ **C**. Copy Inhibit prevents Macintosh files from being copied to another directory.

◆ **D**. Delete Inhibit prevents files from being deleted.

◆ **R**. Rename Inhibit prevents users from renaming a file.

◆ **P**. Purge ensures that a file cannot be restored once it has been deleted.

Directory attributes provided in NetWare 3.1x include:

◆ **H**. Hidden Directory prevents directories from showing up when the DOS DIR command is run.

◆ **Sy**. System Directory hides directories from the DOS DIR command by marking them as directories that contain system files.

◆ **P**. Purge Directory ensures that after a directory is deleted, no files in the directory can be restored.

Any system security plan should be designed to take advantage of file and directory attributes available in NetWare 3.1x.

Note You can read more about network security, including attributes, in Chapter 4, "Understanding NetWare Security."

Section Review Questions

6. Which statement about NetWare 3.1x is false?

   a. NetWare 3.1x requires a minimum of 4 MB memory on the file server.

   b. NetWare 3.1x can run on an 80286 or better computer.

   c. You can have a hard drive as small as 20 MB for volume SYS.

   d. Workstations can be XTs.

7. Which workstation operating system is not available on NetWare 3.1x?

   a. UNIX

   b. OS/2

   c. CTOS

   d. Macintosh

8. Which statement about NetWare 3.1x maximums is true?

   a. NetWare 3.1x allows hard disk storage of up to 32 TB.

   b. The maximum amount of RAM on the file server is 16 MB.

   c. The maximum amount of open files is 1,000,000.

   d. The largest file allowed is 2.2 GB.

9. What feature of NetWare 3.12 increases access speed?

   a. Cache read ahead

   b. File buffers

   c. Disk hashing

   d. Maximum Rights Mask

10. Which of the following is NOT part of SFT?

   a. Read-after-write verification

   b. Duplicate FAT and DET

   c. UPS

   d. Removable disk drives

Answers

6. b

7. c

8. a

9. a

10. d

Using NetWare 3.1*x* Documentation

As a System Administrator, you need to know where to find information about the NetWare 3.1*x* operating system. Novell provides many manuals with NetWare 3.1*x*. You should be familiar with the following five books and with Novell's ElectroText. The five books include:

◆ *NetWare Concepts.* This book contains definitions and examples of the key features in NetWare 3.1*x*.

◆ *Utilities Reference.* This book contains information about the NetWare 3.1*x* command-line utilities and menu utilities provided with the operating system.

◆ *Installation.* This book describes the process of installing and upgrading to a NetWare 3.1*x* network. You also find information about setting up the network for users and login script commands.

◆ *System Administration.* This book contains information about file server utilities, troubleshooting, and maintenance.

◆ *Print Server.* This book covers network printing utilities, setting up a print server, and troubleshooting network printing.

 Activate and navigate Novell Electrotext.

Novell ElectroText is an electronic method of distributing Novell's documentation. ElectroText is available with NetWare 3.12, and is distributed on CD-ROM. ElectroText is graphical-based and runs only on MS Windows clients. During installation, a file called ET.INI is copied to the Windows client directory in order to support ElectroText.

ElectroText consists of a *search engine* that enables you to search for and find information, and also an electronic set of manuals called a "bookshelf."

Novell's NetWare 3.12 ElectroText includes three components:

◆ **Library Window.** This window enables you to choose the book that you want to read.

◆ **Book Window.** This window shows you the table of contents and text for the book you choose.

◆ **Search Window.** This window enables you to select a word or phrase to search for within the book.

To install the ElectroText, you need a minimum of 30 MB of extra disk space. The program that runs ElectroText, ET.EXT, is installed to the SYS:PUBLIC directory, and the books are installed into a directory called DOC.

Section Review Questions

11. Electrotext is NOT:

     a. Available with NetWare versions earlier than 3.12

     b. Novell's electronic manual set

     c. Provided on CD-ROM

     d. Graphical-based, running only on MS-Windows

12. Which of the following is NOT one of the ElectroText windows:

     a. SEARCH

     b. BOOK

     c. BOOKCASE

     d. LIBRARY

13. All except the _____ book are provided on Electrotext.

     a. Print Server

     b. System Maintenance

     c. NetWare Concepts

     d. Utilities Reference

14. Which window enables you to choose a book to read?

     a. Library

     b. Book

     c. Search

     d. None of the above

15. Which book must be installed in the SYS:SYSTEM directory?

     a. Library

     b. Book

     c. Search

     d. None of the above

Answers

11. a

12. c

13. b

14. a

15. d

Understanding Workstation Utilities

Workstation utilities are programs that run on a Network client to accomplish different tasks. Some workstation utilities are straight DOS command-line utilities. Some are menu-based utilities, while some are graphic-based utilities. Most DOS text and graphic-based utilities also have command-line equivalent commands.

Identify, navigate, and perform similar basic functions using a DOS text utility, a command-line utility, and a graphical utility.

SYSCON is a good example. SYSCON is a text utility that lets you perform many network security tasks. Some equivalent command-line utilities include GRANT, REVOKE, and ALLOW. Experiment with these and other NetWare utilities to see how to accomplish the same task using different types of NetWare utilities.

NetWare 3.1*x* does not use some utilities found in many previous versions of NetWare. Several new utilities were added, but the bulk of the utilities remain the same in NetWare 3.1*x*.

The following utilities (defined in more detail in Chapter 11, "Understanding NetWare 2.2 Advanced System Manager Functions") can be found in earlier versions of NetWare, but are not included in NetWare 3.1*x*:

HIDEFILE, SHOWFILE

HOLDON, HOLDOFF

LARCHIVE, LRESTORE

NARCHIVE, NRESTORE

MACBACK

MAIL

NSNIPES

PSTAT

The following sections outline the utilities added to NetWare 3.1*x*. Some of these utilities are particularly useful in implementing network security. The ALLOW utility is one example.

 Implement a file system security plan using command line and menu utilities.

The ALLOW utility, along with other utilities discussed in Chapter 4, "Understanding NetWare Security," can help you when planning and implementing security on your NetWare network.

ALLOW

The ALLOW command enables the System Administrator to modify an IRM. The following example illustrates the way in which this command is used:

```
ALLOW path\filename rightslist
```

The *rightslist* is a list of the first initials of each right. If, for example, you want to set the IRM to allow only Read and File Scan for the directory SYS:APPS\ACCT, you type the following:

```
F:>ALLOW SYS:APPS\ACCT R F
```

You also can use the parameters ALL or N for No rights in place of the rightslist.

 Remember that you cannot add the Supervisory right with the ALL command, nor can you deny the Supervisory command by using the N flag. The Supervisory right always is in place.

ACONSOLE

This command is part of the remote management provided by NetWare 3.1*x*. ACONSOLE is used for an asynchronous link to a remote server. You learn more about this feature in Chapter 11.

ADMIN

The ADMIN utility is used to add and manage mail user accounts and to maintain mail distribution lists. This utility is part of the Basic *Message Handling Service* (MHS) that Novell has added to NetWare 3.12 to provide an entry-level mail solution for small (single-server) networks.

 Before running ADMIN.EXE at the workstation, run the Btrieve Requester (BREQUEST.EXE). The Btrieve Requester is an important requirement for running ADMIN.

If your network has 25 or fewer users, Basic MHS is an effective way to establish communication among users across the network. As your network grows, Basic MHS can be upgraded to Global MHS.

When you start ADMIN.EXE, the first screen that appears is the Admin Functions screen. The ADMIN utility enables you to accomplish the following tasks:

- Create new users. If you use the ADMIN utility to create new users, however, a HOME data directory is not created for them.

- Modify or delete existing user accounts.

- Create, modify, or delete mail distribution lists.

- Register e-mail applications that are allowed to use Basic MHS.

- Modify the Basic MHS system configuration.

Describe NetWare Basic *Message Handling Service* (MHS).

Although Basic MHS provides the background functionality of mail services in a small network environment, the actual interface is called First Mail.

Describe the steps required to install Basic MHS on a NetWare server.

Installing MHS is the first step to using MHS. You can install MHS by following a few simple steps:

1. Type **LOAD INSTALL** at the NetWare 3.12 file server console.

2. Choose the Installation Options menu.

3. Choose **Product Options**.

4. Press Insert and type in the path to the Basic MHS installation files.

5. Accept the default workgroup name by typing **Y**, or type **N** and create a workgroup name.

6. Accept the default SYS:MHS path for installing MHS by typing **Y**, or type **N** and enter a different path.

7. Type **Y** to let the install program add all existing users to the MHS list of users.

8. Update the AUTOEXEC.NCF file automatically by typing **Y** twice.

To start First Mail, type **MAIL** at a DOS prompt, and press Enter. First Mail enables you to do the following:

◆ Send messages to users

◆ Send messages to a list for distribution

◆ Add an attachment to the message you are sending

◆ Read your messages

Basic MHS provides two utilities that let you perform these user tasks and other administrative tasks. Any of these user tasks are accessed from the Mail Options menu.

Send, read, and file mail in First Mail

For example, you can send mail by choosing *Send a mail message* from the Mail Options menu, and following the prompts. You can read your mail messages by choosing *Browse mail messages* from the Mail Options menu. You also can edit and save file messages by choosing *Edit a file* from the Mail Options menu.

Perform administrative tasks, such as adding a user and creating a distribution list, using the Basic MHS Administration software.

If you are a network Administrator, you run the ADMIN.EXE administrative utility to create new users, modify or delete user accounts, create and modify or delete distribution lists, register e-mail applications and modify Basic MHS configuration information.

To accomplish any of these tasks, run ADMIN.EXE and choose one of the following options:

- Users
- Distribution Lists
- Applications
- Configuration

Choosing any of these options allows you to perform the administrative tasks previously described. While working with Basic MHS, additional information on any step or menu item is available by pressing the F1 help key.

CHKDIR

CHKDIR is used to view information about a volume or directory. CHKDIR displays space limitations for the file server, volume, and directory you are checking.

This command displays the maximum storage capacity of a volume or directory if a space limitation has been placed on it. CHKDIR is a useful utility for determining the amount of free space available in a directory.

If space limitations are placed on users, the CHKDIR utility enables them to keep track of the amount of space they have left. To use CHKDIR, simply enter the command by itself or enter the command and the path of the directory you want to check.

DSPACE

NetWare's DSPACE utility enables System Administrators to place limits on the amount of disk space a particular user can use. DSPACE is designed to limit a user's personal use of disk space. Many network users assume that the file server has unlimited storage capacity. A knowledgeable computer user easily can use a large amount of disk space. When used properly, DSPACE can limit a user's available space without jeopardizing normal network operations. Figure 8.1 shows the opening screen of the DSPACE utility.

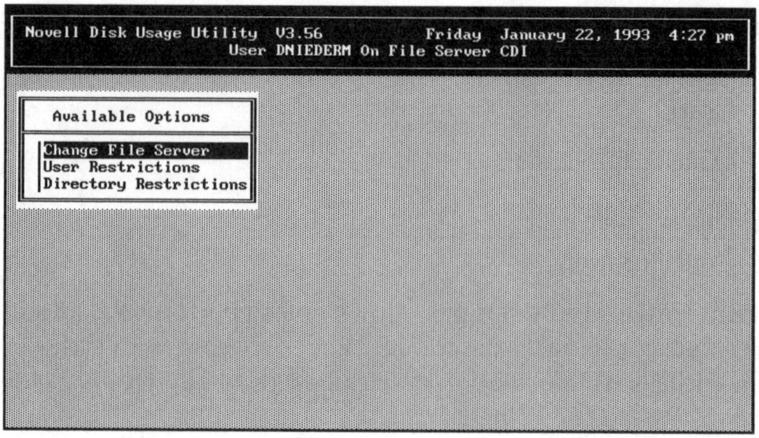

Figure 8.1

The DSPACE utility's opening screen.

Figure 8.1

The DSPACE utility's opening screen.

```
Novell Disk Usage Utility  V3.56         Friday  January 22, 1993  4:27 pm
                     User DNIEDERM On File Server CDI

        ┌──────────────────────────┐
        │    Available Options     │
        ├──────────────────────────┤
        │ Change File Server       │
        │ User Restrictions        │
        │ Directory Restrictions   │
        └──────────────────────────┘
```

The DSPACE utility provides the following options:

◆ Limit users' disk space

◆ Limit disk and directory space

◆ Change current file server

To limit disk space in a volume directory, select the Directory Restrictions option from the menu. Then select a directory and modify the field presented in the Directory Disk Space Limitation Information data entry box (see fig. 8.2). If you do not have rights to modify this directory area, the DSPACE utility does not provide you with modifiable fields.

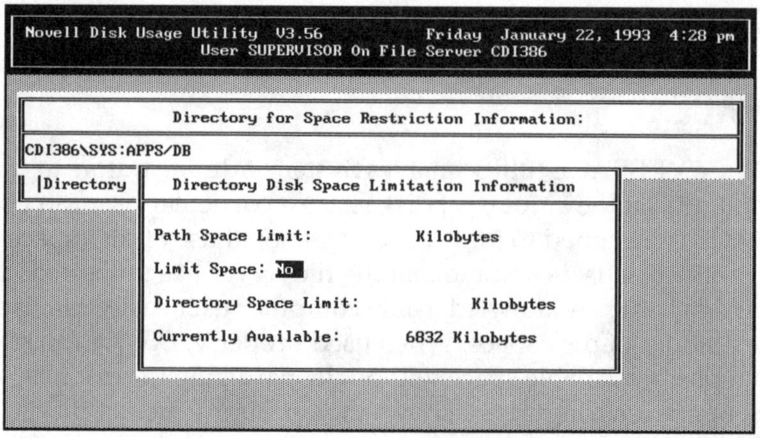

Figure 8.2

The Directory Disk Space Limitation Information data entry box.

```
Novell Disk Usage Utility  V3.56         Friday  January 22, 1993  4:28 pm
                   User SUPERVISOR On File Server CDI386

   ┌────────────────────────────────────────────────────────────┐
   │        Directory for Space Restriction Information:         │
   ├────────────────────────────────────────────────────────────┤
   │ CDI386\SYS:APPS/DB                                          │
   │ ┌─────────┬──────────────────────────────────────────────┐ │
   │ │Directory│ Directory Disk Space Limitation Information   │ │
   │ │         │                                              │ │
   │ │         │ Path Space Limit:          Kilobytes         │ │
   │ │         │ Limit Space: No                              │ │
   │ │         │ Directory Space Limit:     Kilobytes         │ │
   │ │         │ Currently Available:    6832 Kilobytes       │ │
   │ └─────────┴──────────────────────────────────────────────┘ │
   └────────────────────────────────────────────────────────────┘
```

To limit a user's space on a disk drive, select the User Restrictions option from the DSPACE main menu (see fig. 8.1). After selecting a user, a list of available volumes appears. You are presented with the User Disk Space Limitation Information screen if you have the proper rights (see fig. 8.3).

In figures 8.2 and 8.3, the user SUPERVISOR has no restrictions. To limit disk space, you must answer Yes to Limit Space, then fill in the memory limit.

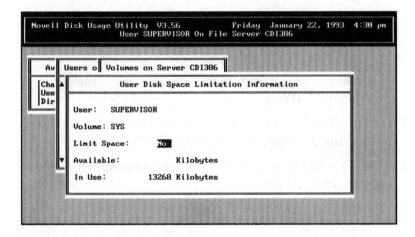

Figure 8.3

The User Disk Space Limitation Information screen.

MIGRATE

NetWare 3.12 includes the MIGRATE.EXE utility, which enables you to upgrade an existing NetWare network to NetWare 3.12. It is run from a client attached to a network.

By using the MIGRATE utility, you can perform an *across-the-wire* migration (which upgrades a NetWare server running an earlier version of NetWare from another NetWare server running NetWare 3.12) or a *same-server* migration (which updates the existing pre-NetWare 3.12 server to a NetWare 3.12 server).

If you run the across-the-wire version of the MIGRATE utility, you must have an existing NetWare 3.12 server. An across-the-wire migration follows these general steps:

1. The old bindery information on the *source server* (the server running the previous version of NetWare) is copied to a DOS client.

543

2. At the DOS client, the old bindery information is updated to 3.12.

3. NetWare 3.12 is installed on another server (the *destination server*).

4. The updated bindery information is migrated from the DOS client to the NetWare 3.12 server.

With an across-the-wire migration, users' trustee assignments also can be migrated to the new NetWare 3.12 server.

If you run the same-server version of the MIGRATE utility, you upgrade the bindery and related files. A same-server migration follows these general steps:

1. A backup is performed on the server running the older version of NetWare.

2. MIGRATE.EXE is run to migrate the bindery information to a working directory on a network client.

3. NetWare 3.12 is installed on the server running the older version of NetWare.

4. The backup is restored to the server that now is a NetWare 3.12 server.

5. The MIGRATE utility is run and the bindery information that was restored to the new NetWare 3.12 server is migrated.

NMENU

NMENU.BAT is the file that executes the menu program that is new to NetWare 3.12. This utility is a modified version of the Saber menuing utility. As such, it provides many enhancements in menu design and creation. One of the best reasons for using this newer menu utility, however, is its capability to be unloaded from memory while it is executing a menu option, thus leaving more memory for application execution.

More information about the new NetWare 3.12 menuing system is provided in Chapter 7, "Customizing the User's Environment."

RCONSOLE

Although many of the familiar FCONSOLE functions are no longer available when used on the 3.1x file server, Novell provides a workstation connection through RCONSOLE that enables System Administrators to access the MONITOR and other console utilities. RCONSOLE enables system utilities and CONSOLE operations that normally require direct console access from the workstation.

The RCONSOLE utility requires two NLMs to be loaded at the file server. Both REMOTE.NLM and RSPX.NLM must be loaded on any 3.1x file server that requires access by the RCONSOLE utility. After selecting the file server from the list provided and typing in your password, you are presented with a connection to the file server console. You learn more about RCONSOLE in Chapter 11.

UPGRADE

The UPGRADE utility enables the installer to upgrade versions of NetWare from 2.0a to 2.2 to 3.1x.

In NetWare 3.12, an in-place upgrade is provided that upgrades a NetWare 3.1x server to a NetWare 3.12 server. The *in-place upgrade* upgrades the current file system, then installs the new operating system. VAPs, core printing services, and volume and disk restrictions, however, are not upgraded to NetWare 3.12 with the in-place upgrade.

Modified Utilities

The following utilities exist in previous NetWare versions, but have changed noticeably in NetWare 3.1x.

SALVAGE

In 3.1x, SALVAGE is much more sophisticated than in previous versions. From the main menu, users can view or recover files, choose a directory, or set the viewing options (see fig. 8.4). Users must have the Create right before they can retrieve a file by using SALVAGE.

545

Figure 8.4

The 3.1*x* SALVAGE
Main Menu Options
screen.

```
NetWare File Salvage Utility  V3.56       Friday  January 22, 1993  4:32 pm
                      DNIEDERM on CDI/SYS:OFFICE


                   ┌──────────────────────────────────┐
                   │         Main Menu Options         │
                   ├──────────────────────────────────┤
                   │ Salvage From Deleted Directories  │
                   │ Select Current Directory          │
                   │ Set Salvage Options               │
                   │ View/Recover Deleted Files        │
                   └──────────────────────────────────┘
```

 Perform file management tasks such as copying, moving, deleting, salvaging, and purging files.

Files retrieved using SALVAGE are placed back into the directory from which they were deleted. If a file with the same name already exists, the system prompts you to rename the file being salvaged. Files are tracked by date and time, so several versions of the same file name can accumulate. NetWare does not keep track of deleted directories, but the program does track the files in deleted directories. When you are salvaging files from a deleted directory, the files are restored to a hidden directory called DELETED.SAV. Although you do not see this directory, one exists on every volume. Supervisors can use the DOS CD command to make DELETED.SAV the current directory.

SALVAGE also enables the user to choose specific file names to view (see fig. 8.5). Each file shown in the resulting list has been deleted, but the directories still exist. The directories display so you can change directories from this screen. If you press Enter with a file highlighted, you are shown when the file was deleted, when it was modified prior to deletion, who owned it, and who deleted it. At this time, you can restore the file by answering Yes at the Recover This File menu (see fig. 8.6).

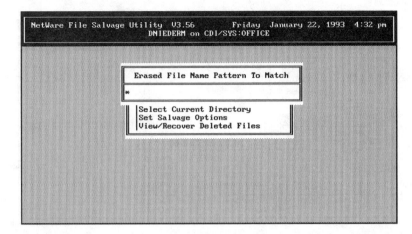

Figure 8.5

Specifying the files to view.

Figure 8.6

Preparing to restore a deleted file.

You can use F5, F6, F7, and F8 to mark and unmark patterns of files for restoring or purging. When you press Del with a file highlighted, NetWare purges the file from the list (see fig. 8.7). When you purge a file, it cannot be retrieved under any circumstances.

When preparing to view a list of files that can be salvaged, you can sort by deletion date, deletor, file size, or file name (the default). These options are on the Salvage Options menu (see fig. 8.8).

Figure 8.7

Purging a deleted file.

```
NetWare File Salvage Utility  V3.56        Friday  January 22, 1993  4:33 pm
                         DNIEDERM on CDI/SYS:OFFICE

┌                                          ┌──able Files────────────────┐
│ Deletion Date  :  1-18-93 12:51:22pm     │          0  THASSELL       │
│ Modify Date    :  1-18-93 12:50:56pm     │          0  THASSELL       │
│ Deletor        :  THASSELL               │          0  THASSELL       │
│ Owner          :  THASSELL               │          0  THASSELL       │
│ TEH)NB.CHK         1-19-93   2:┌─────────────────┐ASSELL             │
│ TEH)NB.CHK         1-19-93   1:│ Purge This File │ASSELL             │
│ TEH)NB.CHK         1-19-93  11:└─────────────────┘ASSELL             │
│ TEH)NB.CHK         1-19-93  11: │No              │ASSELL             │
│ TEH)NB.CHK         1-19-93   9: │Yes             │ASSELL             │
│ TEH)NB.CHK         1-18-93   3:└────────────────┘ ASSELL             │
│ TEH)NB.CHK         1-18-93   2:15:50pm    0  THASSELL               │
│ TEH)NB.CHK         1-18-93   2:13:32pm    0  THASSELL               │
│ TEH)NB.CHK         1-18-93   2:10:06pm    0  THASSELL               │
│ TEH)NB.CHK         1-18-93   2:07:10pm    0  THASSELL               │
│ TEH)NB.CHK         1-18-93   2:05:52pm    0  THASSELL               │
│ TEH)NB.CHK         1-18-93   2:04:34pm    0  THASSELL               │
▼ TEH)NB.CHK         1-18-93  12:51:22pm    0  THASSELL               │
```

Figure 8.8

The Salvage Options menu.

```
NetWare File Salvage Utility  V3.56        Friday  January 22, 1993  4:33 pm
                         DNIEDERM on CDI/SYS:OFFICE




              ┌────────────────────────────────┐
              │        Main Menu Options        │
              ├──────┌────────────────────────────┐es─┤
              │      │       Salvage Options       │   │
              │      ├─────────────────────────────┤   │
              │      │ Sort List by Deletion Date  │   │
              │      │ Sort List by Deletor        │   │
              │      │ Sort List by File Size      │   │
              │      │ Sort List by Filename       │   │
              │      └─────────────────────────────┘   │
              └────────────────────────────────┘
```

Files can be salvaged as long as the files and the directory are not marked with a P (for Purge), and the system has enough room. As room is needed on the server's hard drive, the oldest files are removed from SALVAGE.

The DOS PURGE /ALL command also clears out all salvageable files from a volume.

Section Review Questions

16. Which of the following utilities registers e-mail applications for use with Basic MHS?

    a. BREQUEST

    b. ADMIN

    c. MAIL

    d. EMAIL

17. If your network has 25 or fewer users, which of the following mail packages is recommended?

    a. ADMIN.EXE

    b. GLOBAL MHS

    c. ADMIN EMAIL

    d. BASIC MHS

18. Which of the following CANNOT be done using ADMIN.EXE?

    a. Modify Basic MHS configuration

    b. Delete user accounts

    c. Register e-mail applications

    d. Send e-mail messages

19. Which of the following programs enables you to send messages to other users?

    a. First Mail

    b. ADMIN.EXE

    c. BASICMHS.EXE

    d. GLOBLMHS.EXE

20. Which program enables you to upgrade an existing NetWare network to NetWare 3.1*x*?

    a. INSTALL.NLM

    b. MIGRATE.EXE

    c. BINDUPD.EXE

    d. UPGRADE.NLM

21. What is the main benefit of updating your existing NetWare menus to the new Saber-based menuing system?

    a. Menus have a better look.

    b. Menus can have more options.

    c. Menus can be unloaded from memory when running other menus.

    d. Menus can be limited to a single user.

22. Which of the following statements about NetWare 3.12 is NOT true about the in-place upgrade?

    a. Volume disk restrictions are upgraded.

    b. Printing services are not upgraded.

    c. The current file system is upgraded.

    d. A new version of the operating system is installed.

23. Which command displays the maximum storage capacity of a volume?

    a. CHKDIR

    b. CHKVOL

    c. DIRCHK

    d. VOLCHK

Answers

16. b

17. d

18. d

19. a

20. b

21. c

22. a

23. a

Learning File Server Console Commands

Console commands are instructions entered at the file server console.

 Describe console commands and identify the functions of commands commonly used by Administrators.

Console commands perform many network maintenance and management tasks. NetWare 3.1*x* has more console commands than 2.2. In this section, you are introduced to several commands that work at the file server's prompt—the colon (:). Many of these commands are explored in depth in Chapter 9, "Learning NetWare 3.1*x* Advanced Administration Skills."

ABORT REMIRROR

This NetWare 3.12 console command enables you to stop the remirroring of a logical disk partition.

ADD NAME SPACE *name* TO VOLUME *volume*

This command enables you to store non-DOS files on a NetWare volume. The following name spaces are available: MAC, OS2, NFS, and FTAM.

BIND, UNBIND

The BIND command attaches the desired protocol to the network board through which it is expected to communicate. The protocol is usually IPX for pure Novell Networks, but other protocols, such as IP, can be bound to the board. The parameters are used to tell the network about the hardware and configuration settings for each board. If you do not state the driver or protocol parameters when binding the board, you are prompted for the necessary information.

The UNBIND statement releases the protocol from the board, and memory used by this process is returned to the server.

Use the following syntax for these commands:

```
BIND protocol TO board_name parameters
BIND protocol TO LAN_driver [driver_parameters] protocol
    parameters
UNBIND protocol FROM LAN_driver or board_name
```

CD-ROM

Describe the utility used to support read-only devices.

CD-ROM is an NLM that supports read-only network volumes. After loading this NLM on a NetWare 3.1x file server, you can use related console commands to change media, view the root directory of the volume, list, mount, and dismount volumes, and list devices.

CLS

This command, as well as OFF, clears the screen of any accrued messages.

ENABLE TTS, DISABLE TTS

These commands tell the network to start or stop using the Transaction Tracking System.

DISPLAY NETWORKS

This command shows all known network numbers, including cable numbers, as well as 3.x internal IPX numbers.

Internal IPX numbers are used only with NetWare 3.x. This number is set when installing NetWare and should be unique for all file servers. The internal IPX number allows multiple NLMs to communicate within a single server.

You also see a fractional number displayed after the network address. This number signifies the number of hops and ticks necessary to reach that board.

Hops are the number of network boards that must be crossed to reach the destination from the server where the command was issued.

continues

553

Ticks are the amount of time it takes a packet to reach the destination. One tick is equal to 1/18th of a second.

Figure 8.9 shows 24 unique network addresses on the internetwork. The addresses CDA, CDA386, and BAC all have a hop and tick count of 0/1. These addresses are for the server on which DISPLAY NETWORKS was executed. This server is running NetWare 3.1*x*, so you can deduce that this server is displaying numbers for two network boards and an internal IPX number.

Figure 8.9

Viewing the effects of
DISPLAY SERVERS
and DISPLAY
NETWORKS.

```
:display servers
    A386            0   A386            1   A386            1   A40             1
    A40             1   B386            1   B386            2   B386            2
    B40             1   B40             1   BART            1   BART            1
    BART            1   CBT             2   CBT             3   CDADS_____    1
    CDADS_____    1   CDADS_____    1   CDBF            2   CDBF            2
    CDI             2   CDI             3   CDI             3   CDI1            3
    CDI_ACCESS__    1   CDI_NACS        1   CPNETAV_8295    2   CPNETAV_8295    3
    CPNETAV_8295    2   CPNETAV_8295    2   CPNETAV_8295    2   CRIS_____     2
    CRIS_____     2   D386            1   D386            2   D386            2
    FAX1            2   MASTER_CPNET    2   MERLIN          1   MERLIN          2
    MERLIN          2   MHS_____      3   NORTH386        1   NORTH386        2
    NORTH386        2   PS-B40          1   PSB386          2   PSD386          2
    PSNORTH386      2   merlin          2
There are 50 known servers
:display networks
    00000003   2/3      00000005   1/2      00000020   2/3      00000022   2/3
    000000AB   1/2      000000FE   2/3      00000100   2/3      000000ACE  2/3
    000000BAC  0/1      00000CDA   0/1      00000CDC   1/2      00000CDD   1/2
    00002EE2   1/2      0000CDBA   1/2      0000CDDA   1/2      00BAC802   1/2
    00CDA386   0/1      00CDB802   1/2      00CDC802   1/2      00CDD802   1/2
    2BEE6B8C   1/2      2C7D2AFB   1/2      A1100001   1/2      FEFEFEFE   1/2
There are 24 known networks
:
```

DISPLAY SERVERS

This command displays the names of any file server processes that the network is aware of, as well as a hop count. File server processes are services that various file servers on the network have to offer. Print servers show up as server processes, as do some third-party NLMs.

 Note If volume SYS: is not mounted, the file server does not appear in the DISPLAY NETWORKS list.

EXIT

The EXIT command takes the file server back to the DOS prompt after the DOWN command has been issued.

DOWN

The DOWN command ensures that all files have been properly closed and everything stored in memory is written to the hard drive. When the server is rebooted, FAT and DET tables are replaced in memory.

LIST DEVICES

This NetWare 3.12 console command displays information about devices loaded on the server.

LOAD *path* NLM *parameter*

This command is used to initiate an NLM. The path is necessary only if the NLM does not appear in the SYS:SYSTEM directory, and you have not used the SEARCH command to direct the system to look in the directory where the NLM resides.

UNLOAD releases the NLM, and memory used by the NLM is returned to the server.

MAGAZINE

This NetWare 3.12 console command is used to verify that magazine requests from the server have been satisfied or to see that they have not been satisfied, if that is the case.

MEDIA

This NetWare 3.12 console command is used to verify whether media requests made by the server have been met.

MEMORY

This command displays the total amount of memory in the file server.

MIRROR STATUS

This NetWare 3.12 console command is used to display all mirrored logical partitions and to see the status of each of these partitions.

MODULES

This command displays all the currently active NLMs that have been loaded onto the file server.

PROTOCOL

This command lists each protocol loaded onto the server along with the packet frame type the protocol uses.

REGISTER MEMORY

This command is used on ISA machine architectures that have more than 16 MB of RAM in the file server. Microchannel and EISA computers do this automatically.

REMIRROR PARTITION

This NetWare 3.12 command starts the remirroring of a logical partition that has been stopped with the ABORT REMIRROR command.

REMOVE DOS

This command prevents the file server from returning to the DOS prompt after the DOWN command is typed. A small amount of memory is returned back to the file server. This command also forces a reboot after DOWN is issued.

RESET ROUTER

This command forces the internal routing table to be updated in the file server.

SCAN FOR NEW DEVICES

This NetWare 3.12 command checks for hardware that has been added since the server was last booted. Running this command lets the server recognize any newly added disk hardware without having to reboot the server. Rebooting the server automatically performs a scan for devices.

SEARCH

The SEARCH ADD *number path* and the SEARCH DEL *number* commands add and delete paths that the file server uses when looking for NLMs. The number is used to set priority levels for searching. Search #1 is the first path searched, #2 is the second path searched, and so on. The path must include the volume name.

SECURE CONSOLE

This command is used to protect your file server from sabotage. Five security measures are taken when SECURE CONSOLE is used at the file server. These measures include the following:

1. REMOVE DOS is executed so that when the file server is downed, the DOS prompt is not available, which protects the DOS partition.

2. All users except FCONSOLE operators are prevented from changing the time and date on the file server, which protects the integrity of Intruder Detection Lockout.

3. Entry into the OS debugger is prevented. The OS debugger is useful if the server crashes. It enables you to dump the contents of the memory registers to evaluate what was happening when the server crashed.

4. The SEARCH command is disabled so that NLMs only run from the SYS:SYSTEM directory.

5. The copying of NLMs into the SYS:SYSTEM directory is limited only to those who have rights to the SYS:SYSEM directory.

 The only way to remove the effects of SECURE CONSOLE is to down the file server and reboot. Make sure that SECURE CONSOLE is not in the AUTOEXEC.NCF configuration file. This file is explored further in Chapter 9.

SET

This command is used to display and change tunable file server parameters. In Chapter 11, you learn about several of the SET variables.

Describe the utilities used to set time and time zone support.

SET TIME

This command sets the time and the date on the file server. You can use this command without date and time parameters to view the current date and time, or include the appropriate parameters and change either or both the date and time.

SET TIME ZONE

This parameter is used to synchronize internetworked servers that reside in different time zones.

SPEED

This parameter represents the relative speed of the file server. This number is useful only when comparing servers running the same version of NetWare.

TRACK ON

This utility displays the Router Tracking Screen. The Router Tracking Screen then displays all server and network advertising packets that this server has either sent or received.

Display and explain routing information with the TRACK ON utility.

In order for network file servers to see each other, they must let each other know that they are there. This is done by advertising themselves to the network. To do this, they send packets of information out on to the network that provide the following information about themselves:

- ◆ The network number of the file server sending/receiving the packet

- ◆ The node address of the file server sending/receiving the packet

- ◆ Notification that a message is either incoming or outgoing

TRACK ON is issued at the file server console to activate this utility. You can then view the resulting information and determine which file servers are currently up and running on the network.

VERSION

This command tells you what version of NetWare the file server is using and the copyright information.

VOLUMES

This command displays all mounted volumes on the file server.

Section Review Questions

24. Which console command enables you to interrupt remirroring?

　　a. REMIRROR INTERRUPT

　　b. ABORT REMIRROR

　　c. REMIRROR STOP

　　d. STOP REMIRROR

25. Which console command enables you to restart remirroring?

    a. MIRROR STATUS

    b. REMIRROR PARTITION

    c. RESTART REMIRROR

    d. SET REMIRROR RESTART

26. Which console command do you use to get the cable addresses of all known networks?

    a. DISPLAY ADDRESSES

    b. DISPLAY SERVERS

    c. DISPLAY NETWORKS

    d. DISPLAY NETNUMBER

27. Which console command prevents access into the OS debugger?

    a. REMOVE DOS

    b. REMOVE SERVER

    c. SECURE SERVER

    d. SECURE CONSOLE

Answers

24. b

25. b

26. c

27. d

Understanding NetWare Loadable Modules

NetWare Loadable Modules (NLMs) are key NetWare features.

Describe NLMs, explain how they are loaded, and identify their types.

NLMs are loaded into memory on NetWare 3.1*x* file servers. They can be loaded manually by using the LOAD NLM_name command at the file server prompt, or by placing the LOAD commands into a file server startup file.

There are four different types of NLMs used. These modules, listed by their extensions, include the following:

◆ **NLM.** These modules usually are menu utilities and services that can be added to the file server. MONITOR.NLM, VREPAIR.NLM, and INSTALL.NLM are examples.

◆ **DSK.** These NLMs are disk drivers; they provide communication with the disk drives. DCB.DSK, ISADISK.DKS, and PS2ESDI.DSK are a few examples.

◆ **LAN.** These NLMs are LAN drivers. Loading one of these NLMs provides communication with the network boards. NE2000.LAN, TOKEN.LAN, and TRXNET.LAN are examples of LAN Driver NLMs.

Identify the components and requirements involved in name space support.

◆ **NAM.** These NLMs add name space to a volume. There are four of these NLMs: MAC.NAM, OS2.NAM, NFS.NAM, and FTAM.NAM. Load the MAC.NAM and OS2.NAM NLMs to provide OS/2 and Macintosh name space support.

Identify the purpose and function of the major NLMs, such as INSTALL, MONITOR, and UPS.

Several NLMs are commonly used on NetWare 3.1*x* file servers. Three of the more common ones include:

- **INSTALL**—Used to modify configuration information for a currently installed file server.

- **MONITOR**—Used to see who is accessing the network, as well as view other important network information. Chapter 9, "Learning NetWare 3.1*x* Advanced Administration Skills," provides details on using this NLM.

- **UPS**—Used to define what happens when an attached Uninterruptible Power Supply is activated.

Section Review Questions

28. Which of the following is NOT a type of NLM?

    a. DSK

    b. NAM

    c. NIC

    d. NLM

29. Which type of NLM provides communication with drivers?

    a. DSK

    b. NAM

    c. NIC

    d. NLM

30. Which NLM provides support for Macintosh files?

    a. DSK

    b. NAM

    c. NIC

    d. NLM

Answers

28. c

29. a

30. b

Understanding Remote Console Management

This section discusses remote console management, and helps you learn how to administer a NetWare 3.1x file server from a client functioning as a remote console.

 Describe remote console management, and list the steps necessary to set up a server for both SPX and asynchronous remote connections.

If your network is small, with only a single NetWare 3.1x server that is readily accessible, you may not need to use Novell's remote console management features. On the other hand, unless that single server is sitting at your workstation, you may still be able to take advantage of remote console.

Remote console lets you access the NetWare server using your client, and make your client look and act just like the file server.

However, in order to run remote console from your client, you must load the required NLMs at the file server. The required NLMs include:

♦ RSPX.NLM

♦ REMOTE.NLM

Loading these two modules at the file server provides you with a direct network connection.

 Use RCONSOLE.EXE to connect remotely to the server, and describe the purpose and function of the available options in RCONSOLE.

From your client that is attached to the network, you can type **RCONSOLE**, follow the prompts, and access the file server as if you were sitting at the file server console. This type of a connection is know as an *SPX connection*.

You can also make an asynchronous connection to a network file server. *Asynchronous connections* use an RCONSOLE-equivalent utility called ACONSOLE. ACONSOLE is used to access a file server over a modem. When running ACONSOLE, you choose to *Connect to Remote Location*, and when prompted, enter the password.

Running RCONSOLE lets you choose from the following Available Options:

♦ Select a Screen to View

♦ Directory Scan

♦ Transfer Files To Server

♦ Copy System And Public Files

♦ End Remote Session With Server (Shift+Esc)

♦ Resume Remote Session With Server (Esc)

RCONSOLE and ACONSOLE let you access the server from any client. This could be a security problem, but is not because both utilities require a password. Accessing a file server console directly, without using remote console, could also be a security problem. However, this problem is solved by putting a console password on all file server consoles.

 Implement console security features on the server by assigning a console password and placing the server in a secure location.

You should secure your file server console in a locked room as the first level of network protection. If this is not possible, or if you want to add an additional level of security, you can put a password on each file server's console by issuing the SECURE CONSOLE command at the file server console. This command removes the DOS COMMAND.COM file from the file server's memory. No one can then access the file server's hard disk using DOS, from the file server console. Your other option is to LOAD MONITOR and choose the Lock Server Console option. This option prompts you for a password and prevents people who do not know the password from accessing the file server from the file server's keyboard.

Section Review Questions

31. The TWO NLMs required for remote console use are:

    a. RSPX.NLM

    b. REMOTE.NLM

    c. ASYNC.NLM

    d. SYNC.NLM

32. To end a remote session with a server, you can press:

    a. Enter

    b. Esc+Esc

    c. Shift+Esc

    d. Shift+Ctrl

33. The asynchronous connection utility equivalent to RCONSOLE is:

    a. REMOTE

    b. ASYNCH

    c. ACONSOLE

    d. ACONNECT

34. The first level of file server console security is:

    a. Assigning only one Supervisor-equivalent user

    b. Locking the file server in a separate room

    c. Giving the file server console a password

    d. Giving remote console a password

35. The SECURE CONSOLE command:

    a. Locks the file server keyboard

    b. Is NOT recommended in small installations

    c. Prompts you for a remote console password

    d. Removes the DOS COMMAND.COM file from RAM

Answers

31. a and b

32. c

33. c

34. b

35. d

Case Study

Load the necessary NLMs at the file server. Next, log into the server from a client. Run RCONSOLE. Run the TRACK ON utility and count the number of active servers.

Learning NetWare 3.1*x* Advanced Administration Skills

9 CHAPTER

This chapter focuses on advanced NetWare 3.1*x* features. In this chapter, you learn about the following topics:

◆ Protocol support

◆ ODI configuration files

◆ SBACKUP

◆ BINDFIX, BINDREST, and VREPAIR

◆ Memory management

◆ Remote capabilities

◆ NetWare Name Service

◆ NetWare 3.12 server and client installation and upgrade

Providing Protocol Support in NetWare 3.1*x*

Chapter 7, "Customizing the User's Environment," introduced you to the *Open Data Link Interface* (ODI), which provides a flexible, multiprotocol interface between the workstation and the Novell network. The Open Data Link puzzle has five pieces. These five pieces make up the capability to support multiple protocols, because you can change the pieces to fit your system's unique requirements.

◆ LAN adapter (Network Interface Board)

◆ LAN driver (Software driver for LAN Adapter)

◆ *Link support layer* (LSL)

◆ Protocol stack layer

◆ Protocol-independent services

In Chapter 7's discussion on loading the workstation ODI files, you learned that the first file loaded is LSL.COM. This file enables the network board to communicate with the desired protocol.

Describe the communication and name space protocols supported by a NetWare server.

For more information on communication protocols, refer to Chapter 7, "Customizing the User's Environment."

The next file loaded is a LAN driver or *Multiple Link Interface Driver* (MLID). The MLID reads the NET.CFG for configuration information. This step takes care of pieces one and two.

Next, load the protocol stack files, such as IPXODI.COM or TCPIP.EXE. This step is piece number four.

Piece number five is the most diverse and represents utilities that can speak to the network boards regardless of which protocols are used. Examples of protocol-independent services are NETX for IPX networks, *Apple FileTalk Protocol* (AFP) for AppleTalk networks, or *File Transport Protocol* (FTP) for TCP/IP networks. NetWare 3.1*x* is considered a protocol-independent service.

Discovering Other Protocol Options

NetWare supports IPX as well as other protocols. NetWare provides the capability to communicate with many protocols other than IPX. NetWare also supports SPX, RIP, SAP, NCP, and Packet Burst.

Describe the services provided by the NetWare protocol suite, including IPX, SPX, RIP, SAP, NCP, and Packet Burst.

Chapter 7 provides information about the NetWare protocol suite. Also refer to the NET.CFG Driver Configuration Options section later in this chapter.

The following section discusses supported protocols and the methods used to implement them.

NetWare Requester for OS/2

OS/2 uses the *High-Performance File System* (HPFS) rather than FAT tables. OS/2 also uses long file names of up to 255 bytes and extended attributes that describe file names and values. NetWare Requester provides the support for OS/2 files on the NetWare network.

Transport Control Protocol/Internet Protocol (TCP/IP) and Network File System (NFS)

NetWare includes the capability to bind the *Internet Protocol* (IP) to network boards to communicate with UNIX client-host machines. Support files for TCP/IP are kept in the SYS:ETC directory. NetWare also includes *Transport Control Protocol/Internet Protocol* (TCP/IP) *Network Loadable Modules* (NLMs).

 Install TCP/IP support on a server.

To install NetWare support for TCP/IP, load the related NLM.

The *Network File System* (NFS) is another protocol used in conjunction with TCP/IP. Novell's NFS product allows full implementation of Sun Microsystems' NFS.

NetWare for Macintosh

NetWare 3.1*x* supports Macintosh workstations through NLMs that support AppleTalk Filing Protocol. This support allows Macintosh workstations to print, save files, and route through a NetWare 3.1*x* server.

Exploring the ODI Configuration Files

With standard NetWare protocols, two files are used to control the configurations of network software that runs on the PC. NET.CFG is the primary ODI configuration file.

Identify the ODI support architecture and related files that are used at a NetWare server.

If you have a SHELL.CFG file for your workstation, it is used to configure non-ODI drivers, but many of the SHELL.CFG parameters are applicable to ODI workstations as well. You can leave these parameters in the SHELL.CFG file or move them to NET.CFG.

These files are created by a text editor and must be located in the current directory when the network drivers are started.

NET.CFG Driver Configuration Options

When using ODI drivers, the driver configurations are controlled by entries in the NET.CFG file. This section outlines the LAN Driver parameters and their options in the NET.CFG file.

The NET.CFG file contains three major sections:

◆ The Link Driver section is used to configure the drivers associated with the network interface cards in the workstation. Some of these parameters control hardware functions; others control software functions.

◆ The Link Support section configures the link support layer of the network protocols. This layer is controlled by the ODI LSL program.

◆ The Protocol section determines which protocols are associated with each network interface card.

In addition, NET.CFG can contain any parameters that earlier driver versions placed in SHELL.CFG.

Table 9.1 shows the Link Driver hardware parameters. Each option is explained in detail after the table.

573

Table 9.1
Link Driver Hardware Options

Option
Link Driver *drivername*
CONNECTOR DIX
DMA *channel number*
INT *interrupt request number*
MEM *hex starting address [hex length]*
PORT *hex starting address [hex number of ports]*
NODE ADDRESS *hex address*
SLOT *number*

Link Driver *drivername*. This heading should start at the left margin in the NET.CFG file. The drivername is the name of the driver you are using. If you are using the NE2000.COM driver, for example, then your drivername is NE2000 and the Link Driver section looks like the following:

```
Link Driver NE2000
```

The following list defines the hardware options that you can use to configure the shell to the hardware settings on the network board. These options must be indented underneath the Link Driver statement.

◆ **CONNECTOR DIX.** This option is used only with 3Com's 3C503 network board for 3Com EtherLink Series II to change the connector type from thinnet BNC to thicknet DIX. The following example demonstrates the way to set a 3C503 board to use the DIX connector.

```
Link Driver 3C503
    CONNECTOR DIX
```

◆ **DMA** *channel number.* If the network board you are using needs to be configured for *Direct Memory Access* (DMA), use this option. In the following example, a 3Com 3C505 card is configured to use channel 3.

```
Link Driver 3C505
    DMA 3
```

◆ **INT** *interrupt request number.* This option is used to state the interrupt—often seen stated as IRQ or INT—that the network board uses. The following example shows the way to set an ARCnet board to interrupt 5 using the TRXNET driver.

```
Link Driver TRXNET
    INT 5
```

◆ **MEM** *hex starting address.* This option is used to specify the memory range that the network board is configured to use. This number should be entered as a hex value. The following example demonstrates the way to set an ARCnet board to use the hex memory address of D000.

```
Link Driver TRXNET
    MEM D000
```

◆ **PORT** *hex starting address.* This option is used to specify the I/O port address that the network board is configured to use. This number should be entered as a hex value. The following example shows the way to set an Ethernet board to use the hex port address of 300.

```
Link Driver NE1000
    PORT 300
```

◆ **NODE ADDRESS** *hex address.* Some network boards allow the hardware address to be set in the NET.CFG file. The NODE ADDRESS option enables you to define the hex address. The following example shows the way to set a Novell Ethernet NE2100 board to use the address of 22A31.

```
Link Driver NE2100
    NODE ADDRESS 22A31
```

◆ **SLOT** *number*. When using a network board in a slot-based machine, the driver attempts to locate boards by scanning the slots from the lowest to highest. This option speeds up the process by telling the driver in which slot to look for the board. In the following example, you learn to set a Novell Ethernet NE/2 board to use slot 3.

```
Link Driver NE2
    SLOT 3
```

Table 9.2 shows the Link Driver software parameters and the default options. These options are used to configure the shell to the hardware settings on the network board. Each option is explained in detail after the chart. These options must be indented beneath the Link Driver statement.

Table 9.2
Link Driver Software Options

Option	Defaults
ALTERNATE	
FRAME *frame type*	
LINK STATIONS *number*	1
MAX FRAME SIZE *number*	
PROTOCOL *name hex protocol ID frame type*	
SAPS *number*	1

◆ **ALTERNATE.** This option is used only with the LANSUP driver for IBM LAN Support, the TOKEN driver for IBM Token-Ring, or the PCN2L driver for the IBM PC Network II and II/A. It is used when you want the driver to use a network board other than the primary network board. The following example shows the PCN2L driver configured to use the secondary board.

```
Link Driver PCN2l
    ALTERNATE
```

Identify the default Ethernet frame type and match the appropriate frame type to the communication protocol supported.

◆ **FRAME** *frame type.* This option is used to enable multiple frame types for network boards. This option works only if the network board supports multiple frame types. Ethernet drivers default to ETHERNET_802.3 frames. Other options include: ETHERNET_802.2, ETHERNET_II, and ETHERNET_SNAP. Token-Ring drivers default to TOKEN-RING frames, but can support TOKEN-RING_SNAP as well. ARCnet supports only one frame type, NOVELL_RX-NET. The following example shows the way to use both the ETHERNET_II and the ETHERNET_802.3 frames with an NE2000 driver.

```
Link Driver NE2000
    FRAME ETHERNET_II
    FRAME ETHERNET_802.3
```

◆ **LINK STATIONS** *number.* This option is only used with the LANSUP driver for IBM LAN support. Set LINK STATIONS to allow for all applications using the IBM LAN Support Program.

◆ **MAX FRAME SIZE** *number.* This option enables you to set the maximum number of bytes that the LAN driver can put onto the network cable at one time. This option is used only with the LANSUP driver for IBM LAN Support or the TOKEN driver for IBM Token-Ring. The default size for TOKEN is 4216 bytes; however, if the board has 8 KB of shared RAM available, the default size is 2168. Use the following formula to figure the number:

> number of bytes for the data packet (1, 2, 4, or 8 KB)
>
> plus 6 bytes for adapter overhead
>
> plus the largest possible header (currently 114 bytes)

This number needs to be a multiple of eight. If 4 KB packets are used, this number is 4096+6+114, or 4216. To set the maximum size to 4216 using the TOKEN Link Driver, place the following lines in your NET.CFG.

```
Link Driver TOKEN
        MAX FRAME SIZE 4216
```

If you are using TBMI2 or TASKID, this option is not available.

◆ **PROTOCOL** *name hexprotocol frametype.* This option is used to allow existing LAN drivers to handle network protocols. The name of the new protocol is *name*, the protocol ID stated in hex is *hexprotocol*, and *frametype* is the name of the frame that the protocol uses.

◆ **SAPS** *number.* This option is used only with the LANSUP driver for IBM LAN Support. This option enables you to define the number of *Service Access Points* (SAPs) needed. Set this number to allow for all applications using the IBM LAN Support Program.

Table 9.3 shows the Link Support options and their defaults in NET.CFG. Each option is explained in detail after the chart.

Table 9.3
Link Support Options

Option	Default
Link Support	
BUFFERS *number [size]*	0 [1130]
MAX BOARDS *number*	4
MAX STACKS *number*	4
MEMPOOL *number*	

Link Support. This heading should be placed at the left margin in the NET.CFG file. The following are the definitions for the Link Support options that you can use to configure the shell. These options must be indented beneath the Link Support statement:

◆ **BUFFERS** *number [size]*. This option enables you to configure the number and size of the receive buffers. This number must take into account enough room to hold all headers, as well as the maximum data size. Using the size parameter is optional. The minimum is 618 bytes, and the total buffer space must fit into 59 KB.

◆ **MAX BOARDS** *number*. This option enables you to specify the maximum number of logical boards the LSL can handle. The range is from 1 to 16, and the default is 4. If you load all possible frame types for Ethernet, you would load four frames. Your MAX BOARDS number must be set for at least four protocols.

◆ **MAX STACKS** *number*. Because each protocol stack uses one or more resources, you need to define a sufficient amount of stacks or you receive Out of resource errors. The range is from 1 to 16, and the default is 4.

◆ **MEMPOOL** *number*. The IPXODI protocol stack does not use this option; however, other protocol stacks might require the size of the memory pool buffers to be adjusted. See the documentation supplied with the protocol for recommended settings.

Table 9.4 lists the Protocol Selection parameters and their options in NET.CFG. Each option is explained in detail after the table.

Table 9.4
Protocol Selection Options

Option
Protocol *protocol name*
BIND *board name*

Protocol *protocol name*. This heading should start at the left margin in the NET.CFG file. The *protocol name* is the actual protocol you choose for the LAN board.

The following is the definition for the Protocol Selection option that you can use to configure the shell. This option must be indented beneath the Protocol Selection statement.

◆ **BIND** *board name*. This option binds the protocol to the appropriate LAN board. In the following example, the IPXODI protocol is bound to a Novell Ethernet NE2000 board.

```
Protocol IPXODI
    BIND NE2000
```

The file used before NET.CFG is SHELL.CFG. You can use the options listed in table 9.5 in SHELL.CFG as well as NET.CFG. If they are used in NET.CFG, they should come before any parameters used in tables 9.1 through 9.4.

SHELL.CFG Parameters

SHELL.CFG is used to configure non-ODI drivers. Many of these parameters are applicable to ODI and might be included in NET.CFG. ODI drivers, however, look for configuration parameters in the SHELL.CFG and the NET.CFG files.

 If a SHELL.CFG exists, you might choose to leave it alone and place only new information into the NET.CFG. Alternatively, you can add the SHELL.CFG information to the beginning of the NET.CFG file.

If neither file exists, create only the NET.CFG file.

Table 9.5 contains the definitions for the options that you can use to configure the shell. These options must be placed at the left margin in NET.CFG. The options are discussed in detail after the table.

Table 9.5
Shell Options

Option	Default
INT64=on/off	ON
INT7A=on/off	ON
IPX RETRY COUNT=*n*	20 retries

Option	Default
SPX ABORT TIMEOUT=*n*	540 ticks
SPX CONNECTIONS=*n*	15 connections
CACHE BUFFERS=*n*	5 cache blocks
FILE HANDLES=*n*	40 open files
LOCAL PRINTERS=*n*	# of ports
LONG MACHINE TYPE=*name*	IBM_PC
MAX TASKS=*n*	31
PREFERRED SERVER=*name*	
PRINT HEADER=*n*	64 bytes
PRINT TAIL=*n*	16 bytes
SHOW DOTS=on/off	OFF

◆ **INT64.** Certain applications, including earlier versions of
NetWare, use this interrupt to access IPX services. Set this
option to OFF if an application requests interrupt 64h, or if
you have an application that works with NetWare 2.0a but
locks up the workstation when using 3.*x*. The default is ON.

◆ **INT7A.** Certain applications, including earlier versions of
NetWare, used this interrupt to access IPX services. Set this
option to OFF if an application requests interrupt 7Ah or if
you have an application that works with NetWare 2.0a but
locks up the workstation with 3.*x*. The default is ON.

◆ **IPX RETRY COUNT.** This option enables you to specify the
number of times a packet can be resent. Use this option if
you are losing many packets. The default is 20 retries.

Note Increase IPX RETRY COUNT when users need to
cross a router to access a printer on a remote workstation running RPRINTER. Increase it also if the
network supports heavy traffic and long distances.

581

◆ **SPX CONNECTIONS.** This option sets the maximum number of SPX connections a workstation can use at one time. If the workstation uses RPRINTER, set this number to 60. The default is 15 connections.

◆ **SPX ABORT TIMEOUT.** This option sets the amount of time in ticks that SPX waits for a response before ending the session. The default is 540 ticks.

◆ **CACHE BUFFERS.** You can use this option to speed up the processing of sequential reads/writes. The option enables you to set the number of 512 byte buffers available for local caching of non-TTS, nonshared files. The default is five cache buffers.

◆ **FILE HANDLES.** This option indicates the number of files the workstation is allowed to have open on the network at one time. Set the number of open local files in CONFIG.SYS. The default is 40 open files on the network.

Note

CACHE BUFFERS in NET.CFG corresponds to BUFFERS in CONFIG.SYS.

FILE HANDLES in NET.CFG corresponds to FILES in CONFIG.SYS.

◆ **LOCAL PRINTERS.** This option is used to override the number of local printer ports on the workstation. If you set this option to 0, the workstation does not hang when Shift+PrntScrn is pressed, and the workstation does not have a local printer or a CAPTURE statement was not issued.

◆ **LONG MACHINE TYPE.** This option tells the network what type of machine is being used. This option works in conjunction with the %MACHINE login script variable. Because the default for all machines is IBM_PC, this option is used to correctly identify the machine type.

◆ **MAX TASKS.** This option sets the maximum number of active tasks. Programs like Microsoft Windows or DESQview allow multiple active tasks. Increase this number if you are unable to open additional tasks.

◆ **PREFERRED SERVER.** Use this option to force a connection to a specific server. The shell polls up to five servers for available connections.

◆ **PRINT HEADER.** This option enables you to set the buffer size for the print header. The information held in this buffer is used to initialize a printer. Increase this buffer if the printer is not receiving all the requested attributes. The default is 64 bytes, and the range is from 0 to 255.

◆ **PRINT TAIL.** This option enables you to set the buffer size for the print tail. The information held in this buffer is used to reset the printer after issuing a print job. If the printer fails to reset, increase this buffer. The default is 16 bytes, and the range is from 0 to 255.

◆ **SHOW DOTS.** The NetWare file server does not have directory entries for . and .. as DOS does. If you are using an application that requires the use of . and .., such as Windows, you must set this option to ON. The default is OFF.

Section Review Questions

1. Which of the following statements is true about NET.CFG?

   a. Link Driver Options should be at the top of the file and Cache Options should be at the end of the file.

   b. NET.CFG and SHELL.CFG are interchangeable.

   c. You need to define every option under the headings.

   d. Headings need to be left-justified; options need to be indented.

2. Which of the following statements about Shell options is false?

   a. INT64 and INT7A both default to ON.

   b. You should increase the number of IPX RETRY COUNT if the workstation is running PCONSOLE.

    c. SPX CONNECTIONS only needs to be increased to 60 if the workstation is running PSERVER.EXE.

    d. CACHE BUFFERS=*n* and FILE HANDLES=*n* belong in NET.CFG; BUFFERS=*n* and FILES=*n* belong in CONFIG.SYS.

3. Which SET parameter should be increased if the network is large and traffic is heavy or RPRINTER is used over routers?

    a. IPX RETRY COUNT

    b. SPX ABORT TIMEOUT

    c. SPX RETRY COUNT

    d. a and b

4. Which of the following statements is correct for making certain that a workstation without a printer does not lock up if the user presses Shift+PrntScr?

    a. LOCAL PRINTERS=0

    b. LOCAL PRINTERS=NO

    c. CAPTURE

    d. a and c

5. If the print job you are sending to the printer contains an unusually high amount of initialization codes for the printer, which of the following statements should you increase?

    a. PRINT HEADER=*n*

    b. PRINT TAIL=*n*

    c. LOCAL PRINTER=*n*

    d. PRINTER INITIALIZE=*n*

Answers

1. d
2. b
3. d
4. d
5. a

Protecting Your Network

When it comes to protecting your network data, most companies feel that an occasional backup is all they need. After all, the system runs fine—why should it crash? You might be surprised by the number of companies, large and small, that do not own a reliable backup device or maintain a reliable backup schedule. If the same data was located on a minicomputer or a mainframe, a reliable system of backing up data would be a requirement.

To effectively determine a data-protection system, you first need to evaluate the importance of your data in relation to the impact of losing it. Can your company or department operate without your system data for one hour, four hours, eight hours, 24 hours, or longer? Can you continue to operate with the total loss of your system data? Most companies cannot afford to experience these losses. A study performed by the University of Texas reports some alarming statistics: 43 percent of all companies that did not plan for a total system failure never reopened after the failure occurred. And 90 percent of those unprepared companies that did reopen after a total system failure went out of business within two years.

Data backup on a shared data-storage device is critical, yet this area seems to be the first place the budget is cut. Data can be lost or damaged in many ways. A user can cause accidental damage, and although this type of data loss can be controlled by system security, it is still one of the most common occurrences. Software bugs or improper setups can cause data loss. Hardware failures vary from drive or controller failure to a workstation hanging or the file server itself failing. The computer virus is becoming more common in the workplace and also should be a concern when designing a protection plan. Sooner or later, all computer equipment fails. Data loss or data corruption might require files to be restored from an earlier copy. Investing in an adequate and reliable backup system minimizes the inconvenience and cost of downtime.

You might find it difficult to choose the backup device right for you from among all the backup devices on the market today. Both

585

hardware and software are required to create a complete backup system, but also a motivated individual is required to make the backup system work.

SBACKUP

Identify the purpose and procedures of server maintenance utilities, such as BINDFIX, BINDREST, VREPAIR, and SBACKUP.

The SBACKUP utility is actually a 3.1*x NetWare Loadable Module* (NLM) that enables a tape drive to be attached directly to the file server. The SBACKUP system implements a technology that uses a host and a target. The target technology allows multiple file servers located on the LAN to be selected for backup as long as the target file server is running the TSA.NLM.

A *host* is a file server that has a backup device attached. A *target* is a file server being backed up. A *parent* is anything backed up that has a subordinate data set. A directory, for example, has a subordinate data set of subdirectories and files. A *child* has no subordinates—a file.

Remember four terms dealing with the SBACKUP utility:

◆ **HOST.** Where the backup device is attached

◆ **TARGET.** Each server that is backed up

◆ **PARENT.** Directories, subdirectories, and binderies

◆ **CHILD.** Files

Load the components needed to perform a client backup using SBACKUP.

The SBACKUP system is made up of five modules—three host modules and two target modules. These modules are provided by Novell and are included with NetWare 3.1x.

The host modules include the following:

◆ **SBACKUP.NLM.** The main user interface.

◆ **SIDR.NLM.** The data requester. This module passes data to and from the host and target NLM by using Novell's *Storage Management Services Protocol* (SMSP).

◆ *driver***.NLM.** The actual device driver required for interface. The module name varies for different interface cards.

The target modules include the following:

◆ **TSA.NLM.** The link between the data requester and the target.

◆ **TSA-311.NLM.** The target module for NetWare 3.1x.

In addition to the minimum memory needed to operate NetWare, the host file server requires approximately 3 MB to operate the backup device properly.

Together the five SBACKUP modules make a system that enables you to back up data from any target on the network to the host. Figure 9.1 depicts a network of four file servers, all using the SBACKUP system with one acting as host and three acting as targets.

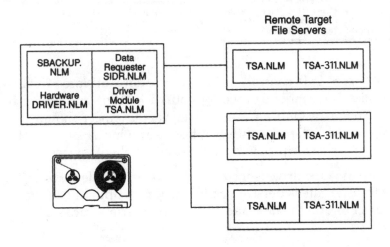

Figure 9.1

Host/target communications.

Novell has licensed the use of ArcServe from Cheyenne Software to enable SBACKUP to support a reasonable range of devices. This support is only at the hardware device driver level—SBACKUP and Cheyenne's ArcServe product are not the same.

Novell supplies drivers that support approximately 50 tape drives currently being sold by various manufacturers. These drives, along with a SCSI controller, enable you to back up the complete file server at speeds generally not possible on the workstation.

The SBACKUP system is made up of a hardware NLM, a target NLM, and the SBACKUP NLM itself. The Adaptec driver pictured in figure 9.2 is included with NetWare 3.1x. This driver supports the common 16-bit 154x series SCSI controller that supports many popular SCSI tape drives.

Figure 9.2

The Adaptec driver.

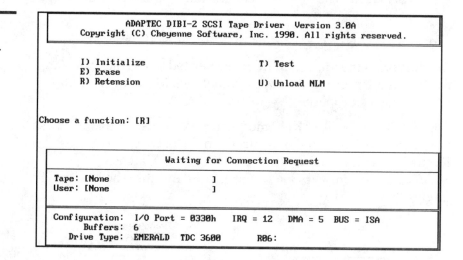

```
        ADAPTEC DIBI-2 SCSI Tape Driver   Version 3.0A
     Copyright (C) Cheyenne Software, Inc. 1990. All rights reserved.


    I) Initialize                    T) Test
    E) Erase
    R) Retension                     U) Unload NLM



Choose a function: [R]



                  Waiting for Connection Request

  Tape: [None                    ]
  User: [None                    ]


  Configuration:  I/O Port = 0330h   IRQ = 12   DMA = 5  BUS = ISA
        Buffers:  6
     Drive Type:  EMERALD  TDC 3600       R06:
```

The Adaptec 154x controller also is a popular NetWare SCSI disk controller, but cannot be used for both disk drives and tape drives simultaneously. Only a Certified NetWare Engineer should configure the Adaptec controller, because an incorrectly installed interface can cause problems with other installed devices.

Because the tape drive is installed directly in the file server, the data transfer rate is determined by the throughput rate of the file server's bus and the tape and hard drive interface cards. This arrangement provides high performance when backing up the locally attached server. When backing up a remote target file server located on the LAN, however, the data throughput drops drastically due to performance limits of the network cable and possible bridge hops required to reach the data.

Back up and restore a server bindery and trustee assignments using SBACKUP.

The operation of SBACKUP is similar to NetWare's NBACKUP. After loading the hardware driver with the console LOAD command, you can check your hardware operation directly with the driver, which provides the erase, initialize, and retention options. At this point, you can load the TSA.NLM and SBACKUP. Because you are not normally logged in at the file server, SBACKUP prompts for a login name and password, as figure 9.3 illustrates.

```
NetWare Server Backup Utility   v3.11        NetWare 386 Loadable Module



                        Enter user name for CDI
            User:


```

Figure 9.3
The SBACKUP user login prompt.

The main menu option Select Target to Backup/Restore displays a menu of all file servers currently running the TSA target NLM. After selecting a target, you are prompted again to log in to the selected file server. After your target selection, you return to the main menu to select the Backup or Restore option. At this time, you see a Backup menu similar to the one in the NBACKUP utility. The screens in SBACKUP have been altered slightly from those in NBACKUP, but still provide the necessary session configuration options. Figures 9.4 and 9.5 show the additional submenus that make up the SBACKUP configuration screens.

Figure 9.4

The Backup Options main menu.

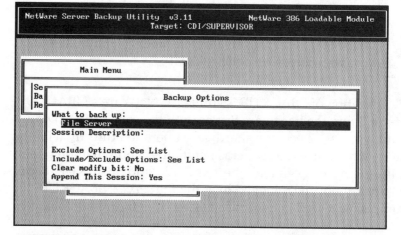

Figure 9.5

The Exclude Options submenu.

In figure 9.4, you are presented with a menu that asks what you want to back up and if any special configuration options are to be used. The first item asks what to back up—the file server, a directory, or a list of files. By making use of the available options under the exclude and include selections, as shown in figure 9.5, you can customize the backup session. These options generally default to the most commonly used settings. Changing these parameters requires you to understand the way in which your system is structured and, in most cases, which defaults are safe to use.

The SBACKUP utility provides a high-speed solution to data backup, but can be cumbersome on the file server. The SBACKUP system is a limited version of some of the full backup systems available.

The tape cartridge data format used by SBACKUP is not the same as that used by NBACKUP. Data sets, therefore, cannot be read from one utility to the other.

Backup Hardware

The only thing constant in the computer industry is change. Hardware and software evolve so quickly that most companies cannot keep up with the constant changes. Rather than keeping up with technology, however, you should be taking advantage of it. Not all new products are right for everyone. As technology makes advances, it provides the user with a wider range of products. If selected carefully, new products can provide efficient and economical solutions for your computer needs.

The most commonly used backup devices use floppy disks, hard drives, tapes, and optical drives. Floppy drives do not provide an efficient means to back up a file server because of their size. Some systems use nonremovable disk drives as the backup media. These devices should only be considered as temporary or secondary backup devices, because they are susceptible to the same defects as the original hard drive. Likewise, because hard drives generally are not kept off-site to protect against hazards such as fire, they are a poor choice as a primary backup device. This section discusses the technology available in tape and optical drives.

Interface Adapters

Any backup device, whether a tape drive or a disk drive, requires an interface card. Currently, three popular interface standards are available: the floppy controller, SCSI Host Adapter, and *Quarter-Inch Cartridge* (QIC) interfaces. All these interfaces can provide adequate data throughput in the right environment.

The floppy interface is used by many popular personal tape systems and provides an acceptable level of data transfer on small systems and personal computers. This interface, however, generally cannot handle the data transfer of a larger company's file server. The floppy controller can supply throughput from 250 Kbps on an XT class computer to 500 Kbps on the AT class computer. The floppy controller also is limited to a single tape drive and is not expandable beyond the initial installation.

The QIC interface was developed primarily for the DC6*xxx* tape systems providing a capacity of 60 MB and larger. This interface provides backup rates of up to 5 megabytes-per-minute in a properly designed system. This standard, although early technology, still can provide an adequate backup system with a properly designed software system. The QIC standard at this time consists of many variations that provide standards for the DC6*xxx* and DC2*xxx* series of data cartridges.

For any corporation with a wide variety of computer equipment and needs, standards might be the key to a successful future. When multivendor communication is important, following standards is almost a requirement. Without standards in a complex system, you cannot ensure functionality and support in the future.

Although support of industry standards always should be a concern when you design a system, many good networking solutions are not necessarily standards. Most network hardware manufacturers support Novell NetWare, and many manufacturers provide small companies with low-cost, highly reliable solutions that might not follow a standard.

Using standards is not always the best approach when you implement a system. In cases that require connectivity to larger systems, standards might offer the highest degree of reliability and service-ability, but not the performance of alternative methods. In these cases, you must weigh the values of performance, reliability, and serviceability before making a decision.

The *Small Computer System Interface* (SCSI) was designed as a general-purpose interface for mass-storage devices. The SCSI interface is a standard maintained by the *American National Standards Institute* (ANSI). The SCSI standard allows up to eight devices to be placed on the interface. This design provides expandability for future system growth and the capability to transfer data at much higher speeds than a floppy controller or the QIC interface, which makes SCSI the interface of choice for current and future technology.

The SCSI adapter is actually a *Host Bus Adapter* (HBA). SCSI is a bus system standard just as the *Industry Standard Architecture* (ISA) and *Micro Channel Adapter* (MCA) are IBM bus standards. The SCSI interface is a converter that enables the different buses to communicate.

Media and Drive Types

Manufacturers supply many different media and recording methods. The most common methods are explained here to give you some general knowledge of the different types available.

QIC and cassette tapes are recorded in a back-and-forth manner. This method, as illustrated in figure 9.6, is called the *serpentine recording method* and enables multiple tracks to be recorded on the tape by moving the tape across a stationary recording head. These tapes can provide from 15 MB to 320 MB storage on a single tape depending on the tape type.

Helical scan technology is probably the most commonly used recording method today. This technology has been used in video equipment since the mid-1950s and is used in the common VCR. Helical scan tapes are available in 4 mm and 8 mm size, providing from 1.3 GB to 5 GB on a single tape cartridge. In this recording method, both the tape and the recording head move. The recording head is constructed as a drum and is placed at a five- to six-degree angle to the tape surface (see fig. 9.7). This positioning allows the recording head to write diagonal stripes on the tape.

Figure 9.6

Serpentine recording method.

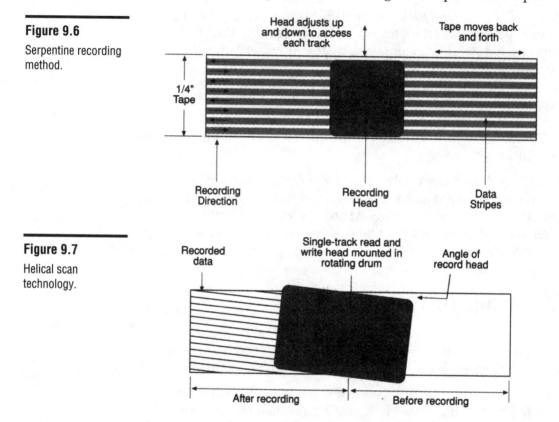

Figure 9.7

Helical scan technology.

The 8 mm tape cartridges are similar to those used in today's 8 mm video camcorders, but with an important difference. The recording surface of videotape normally has some flaking of the oxide. In the video environment, this flaking might show up as a single speck of snow on the screen that might not even be visible to the viewer. But in the data environment, a single flake of oxide can represent extensive loss of data. To prevent oxide flaking, the data-specific tapes are manufactured to more stringent specifications, and the cost of these tapes generally reflects this higher quality. Currently, this technology is supplied by the Exabyte Corporation, which offers a 2.2 GB and a 5 GB version.

The 4 mm or *Digital Audio Tape* (DAT), offering 1.2 GB and 2.0 GB storage, also is making its way into the technologically sophisticated tape-drive market. This tape format is similar to the 8mm technology. Both the 4 mm and the 8 mm tape systems provide high throughput and reliability along with a convenient, compact tape size.

Optical Drives

The family of optical disk drives includes the *Compact Disk-Read Only Media* (CD-ROM), *Write Once Read Many* (WORM), and *Magnetic Optical* (MO)—erasable optical disks. These removable drives provide very fast data access in a reliable format, if implemented properly.

Although the CD-ROM is a read-only device and is, therefore, not a backup device, it is rapidly becoming popular for fixed data storage.

This technology is reliable and is used as a storage device for large databases that do not change, but often are used as reference. CD-ROMs use a solid-state laser beam to read the surface.

WORM is similar to CD-ROM technology except that, although the CD-ROM information is written on the surface by the manufacturer, the WORM drive can write data to the disk. After this data has been added, however, it cannot be erased. The WORM disk is not susceptible to mechanical head crashes experienced by normal hard drives, because WORM disks have no read/write heads that come in contact with the surface. These disks also are not magnetic and, therefore, do not suffer from degradation due to electrical, magnetic disturbances. Figure 9.8 illustrates the CD-ROM and WORM technology.

The MO disk is actually two technologies working together to provide an optically erasable disk that gives the performance of a low-end hard drive. As illustrated by figure 9.9, the magnetic optical disk operates by using a solid-state laser beam to heat the surface of the disk to allow a magnetic field to change the phase of the metallic structure of the coating on the disk's surface. The phase changes are then interpreted as digital 1s and 0s.

Figure 9.8

CD-ROM and WORM technology.

Figure 9.9

Magnetic optical technology.

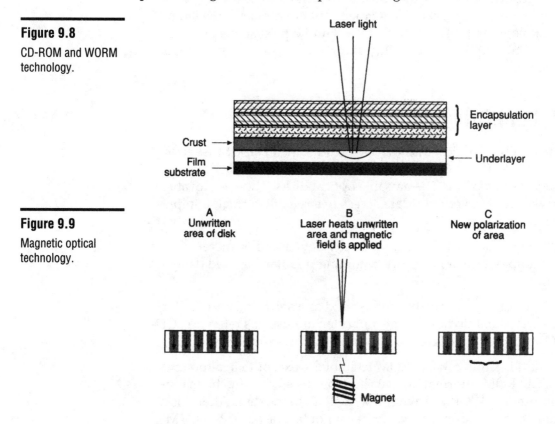

Optical drives also are available in automatic disk changers referred to as *jukeboxes*. These jukeboxes can provide many gigabytes of data, but require special software to manage the robotic movements needed to perform the disk-change operations.

Software

Many high-quality tape and optical drives currently are available, but without good software, these drives are worthless.

The software, not the hardware, directs the backup and manages the data. Ask the following questions when putting together the backup system to determine if it is right for you:

- Does it back up all NetWare security information?

- Does it allow password protection on the backup media?

- In what way does it handle a selective backup and restore?

- Can I redirect the data on a restore?

- Can it back up open files?

- What type of backup media management does it provide?

- In what way does the system handle backup media or tape spanning?

- In what way does it handle automatic or unattended back-ups?

- What method of reporting is used?

These questions are important when selecting a backup system. It also is important to add any questions that might be required to service your company's special needs.

When considering a backup system for a NetWare network, make sure that the system can back up all the NetWare bindery files and trustee information. Smaller software systems might not be able to do this backup because they require the capability to close, back up, and reopen special invisible system files located on the file server.

Novell provides special API function calls to the programmer. The following calls back up the bindery files:

- CloseBindery

- OpenBindery

To back up Novell directory trustees, the function calls include the following:

- ScanDirectoryForTrustees

- AddTrusteeToDirectory

To maintain file attributes, the function calls are as follows:

♦ ScanFileInformation

♦ SetFileInformation

Novell API programming function-call information is available from Novell vendors in OS/2, NLM, and DOS assembly and C libraries.

Security should be considered when selecting your tape-backup system. If your server has sensitive information, an unprotected tape can be a security hole. Some tape software systems have the capability of adding a password to the tape, which disarms the restore function without the proper password. The password, if used, is important, because most tape software packages cannot read the tape without it.

You also should consider the method used to back up files. Some tape software programs provide image, file-by-file, or both methods of backing up data. The *image method* is fast and can provide an efficient means of restoring the system in the event of a total failure, but the image method generally is cumbersome—it is sometimes impossible to restore a single file when needed. Most systems today use the *file-by-file* method of backup. This method reads each and every file separately while performing the backup, unlike the image method, which reads the disk partition from beginning to end.

The capability to redirect data during a restore can be a convenient feature. This capability can save many hours when replacing data to a different drive. Although most systems provide this feature, it might be worth your while to confirm that the system you are considering does.

Open files have always been a problem with tape software, because files open during backup do not get backed up. The usual way to deal with this problem is to skip the file, add an entry into the error log, and proceed. Some systems make use of the error report and attempt to back up open files after the main backup has finished. This feature works in some cases, as long as the files are not open due to an improperly logged-out workstation. Recently, a software package has come on the market that backs up open files. This software makes a "best attempt" service and is dependent on the way in which the file was opened. The integrity of these files is uncertain.

The capability to span tape is no longer as great a concern as it used to be. *Spanning* allows a backup to fill one tape and to continue on another. Many of the older technology systems did not provide this service. Current technology does provide spanning; make sure that the system you are considering does.

Currently, some backup software programs have trouble backing up large files or traversing large directory structures. If your system maintains a large database, avoid backup software that cannot back up large files. Traversing large directory structures also can be a problem, but can be resolved by restructuring the directories. Large directory structures can cause a performance problem, and large files sometimes can prevent correct operation.

A little-known problem with DOS can occur on file servers or large DOS drives. DOS begins to experience performance problems with more than 500 files or directories at a single level. This problem can be attributed to the sequential manner in which DOS starts at the top of the *File Allocation Table* (FAT) and scans to the end in search of a file. More than 500 files in a subdirectory, or more than 500 subdirectories under a single directory, causes the problem. If this number reaches 1000, the problem becomes visible to the user; when the number reaches 2000 or more, serious performance problems occur when backing up these files or directories.

If the backup software builds a temporary table in memory, a large directory structure also can cause problems by running out of memory.

Another area of concern is documentation and the user interface. Any well-written program should include properly written user and Administrator manuals. Both the manual and user interface should be clear and easy to understand.

599

The interface should have a system of double-checks and confirmations to prevent accidental damage to files. A functional online help system can be a great time-saver and, over time, is worth every dollar spent.

Although a well-written user interface with online help makes a system easy to use and understand, the capability to execute the backup from a command line also is important in some cases. The command line provides the inventive System Administrator with the capability to implement various methods of starting and automating the backup procedure.

Some systems provide batch or macro functionality in place of command-line utilities. This functionality also can be beneficial if the macro system is not overly complicated. You also should confirm that both the command-line and macro options provide a full set of functions available through the normal user interface.

Most backup software provides a scheme for starting the backup at a later time. These scheduling schemes vary greatly in their functionality; you should, however, make sure that the system you use maintains a level of security while waiting for the scheduled time to perform the backup. Some systems simply sit at the DOS prompt, logged in with Supervisor rights, until backup time. This scheme can be a major security problem in some environments.

Some server-based backup systems currently are available. These systems enable the backup device to be connected directly to the file server and run as a *value-added process* (VAP) or *NetWare Loadable Module* (NLM). Evaluate these systems as thoroughly as you would any standard workstation-based software.

Most server-based systems provide backup services without the use of a workstation, and can supply high data throughput because the data does not travel through the network cable. These functions are not automatic, however. One server-based system, for instance, requires a Windows application running on a workstation to perform a backup. This system transmits the data from the server to the workstation and back to the server, effectively eliminating most of the advantages of a server-based system, because it doubles network traffic rather than reduces it.

All backup software uses some kind of reporting method. Errors commonly occur during an unattended backup. Without a status report, these problems can go undetected and cause problems later.

Most backup software written today includes the capability to generate status reports. These reports vary in their level of detail, but most are more than adequate for tracking errors.

Novell provides a certification program for manufacturers who want to have their products tested as Novell-approved. This testing procedure confirms that products provide an adequate level of performance and are compatible with the Novell NetWare environment.

Copies of the *Independent Product Testing* (IPT) bulletins are available from any Novell vendor or CompuServe NetWire.

Backup Plans

After locating a suitable backup software and hardware system, you must develop a plan that effectively uses the equipment to obtain the level of protection required. This plan should at least answer the following questions:

◆ Who is responsible for the backup?

◆ When and how often do you back up?

◆ What method of rotating the backup media should be used?

◆ Which backup media should be taken off-site, and when?

◆ When and how often should backup media be tested?

◆ What type of plan do you need for a disaster?

An adequate backup system should account for these questions, and although each item might vary slightly in importance depending on your situation, none should be bypassed.

Your company also might require additional steps to be taken to ensure total protection. No one set plan fits everyone. Each company has different priorities and resources. A properly designed plan should provide a standard procedure and an alternative that does not allow the level of required protection to fail.

Responsibility

The person chosen to be responsible for maintaining the backup system must be sufficiently motivated to back up when planned. Inconsistent backups allow periods of time when files might not be retrievable and can prove costly under the wrong circumstances.

Frequency

Because most backup software requires users to be logged out of the system, the most common time to perform backup is after business hours. This schedule generally requires an unattended backup system that provides adequate error reporting.

The frequency of the backup should be determined by the amount of data changed and the cost to reconstruct the data if lost. Most companies find that a backup once a day is adequate. Those companies that require more frequent backups usually do so because they have large systems that would require many hours of data entry to rebuild. The cost of this reconstruction should be calculated on a worst-case basis to determine if backups are required more often or if a dedicated backup device might be required.

Rotation Methods

Rotating the backup media is important to provide proper protection. Rotating the media provides multiple copies of data in the event of a natural disaster, such as a fire, or in the case of a physical backup media failure. You can rotate tapes in many ways. The following examples are the most commonly used and proven methods. Note that most of these methods assume your network is used primarily Monday through Friday, with little to no activity on Saturday or Sunday.

Grandfather Method

The grandfather method is fairly simple and provides an adequate level of protection to a small-to-midsize file server. This method requires 20 tape sets. A *tape set* is a set of tapes required to perform a backup. The grandfather method is simple to control if the total disk volumes can fit on a single tape and if the backup system can transfer all the data in an acceptable amount of time.

In the grandfather system, four daily tapes (or other media) are labeled Monday through Thursday, four Friday tapes are labeled to be used on Friday, and 12 monthly tapes are labeled January through December. The four daily tapes are used on the designated day with the weekly Friday1, Friday2, Friday3, or Friday4 tape being used on that week. The 12 monthly tapes are used on the last day of each month as labeled. This method provides current files Monday through Thursday and a weekly and monthly archive tape set.

If the file server to be backed up is larger than the maximum tape capacity, the number of tapes and the need to exchange tapes halfway through the backup become difficult to manage.

10-Tape Rotation

The *10-tape method* rotates all tapes evenly and provides a backup history of about 12 weeks. This system also becomes cumbersome if the data requires more than one tape to perform the backup.

Many companies only back up modified files on a daily basis to overcome the problem of the tape drive being too small. Most tape software can check the DOS Modified Attribute (the +A parameter sets the archive bit) to determine if the file has been changed since the last backup. This flag greatly reduces the number of files that require backup on a daily basis.

Managing this type of rotation can be complicated and possibly hazardous if a mistake occurs. This method of backup also can increase greatly the time required to restore a system in the case of

603

a failure. To restore more than a single file from this type of rotation might require all tapes to be restored. This restoration can take many hours using some software systems.

The 10-tape method uses a series of four-week cycles during a 40-week period. During a given four-week cycle, the same four tapes are used Monday through Thursday. This technique starts out much like the grandfather method. Each Friday of a four-week cycle, however, the number of the tape is increased by one. Also, at the start of each new four-week cycle, the Monday through Thursday tape numbers are increased.

The following example shows the different tape sets as they are used during the complete 40-week period. As you can see, this method can become confusing if multiple tapes are required for each backup session.

> 1-2-3-4-**5**-1-2-3-4-**6**-1-2-3-4-**7**-1-2-3-4-**8**
>
> 2-3-4-5-**6**-2-3-4-5-**7**-2-3-4-5-**8**-2-3-4-5-**9**
>
> 3-4-5-6-**7**-3-4-5-6-**8**-3-4-5-6-**9**-3-4-5-6-**10**
>
> 4-5-6-7-**8**-4-5-6-7-**9**-4-5-6-7-**10**-4-5-6-7-**1**
>
> 5-6-7-8-**9**-5-6-7-8-**10**-5-6-7-8-**1**-5-6-7-8-**2**
>
> 6-7-8-9-**10**-6-7-8-9-**1**-6-7-8-9-**2**-6-7-8-9-**3**
>
> 7-8-9-10-**1**-7-8-9-10-**2**-7-8-9-10-**3**-7-8-9-10-**4**
>
> 8-9-10-1-**2**-8-9-10-1-**3**-8-9-10-1-**4**-8-9-10-1-**5**
>
> 9-10-1-2-**3**-9-10-1-2-**4**-9-10-1-2-**5**-9-10-1-2-**6**
>
> 10-1-2-3-**4**-10-1-2-3-**5**-10-1-2-3-**6**-10-1-2-3-**7**

Tower of Hanoi Method

This method is named after a mathematical game in which the player must move a stack of different-sized rings in the proper order.

The tape sets are labeled A, B, C, and so on. A tape set generally has between five to eight tapes. The following example shows a typical rotation. The bold letters show the first use of a tape set.

A-**B**-A-C-A-B-A-**D**-A-B-A-C-A-B-A-**E**

A-B-A-C-A-B-A-D-A-B-A-C-A-B-A-**F**

A-B-A-C-A-B-A-D-A-B-A-C-A-B-A-E

A-B-A-C-A-B-A-D-A-B-A-C-A-B-A-**G**

This rotation method is one of the most difficult to maintain manually, but can offer a wide range of file histories. The window of available files doubles each time a new tape set is introduced. A set of five tapes, for example, provides files up to 16 days old, six tapes 32 days, and seven tapes 64 days. You also can implement this system using a single tape for a whole week, which extends the window to 16 weeks, 32 weeks, and 64 weeks, respectively.

This rotation method recently has been implemented in a backup system that maintains a full database and handles the task of rotating tapes when needed. This system is one of the few that provides a full archive of file histories and enables the System Administrator to restore from a list of versions in the archive. This particular system enables a spreadsheet or database to be restored as it was weeks or months ago.

Off-Site Backups

When examining the backup systems and rotation methods available, plan for multitape sets so that you have a complete set you can store off-site. A moderately current data set off-site protects you in the event of a building disaster, such as a fire or flood. A log book should be set so that others know where you last were in the rotation. This practice helps to keep the backup as consistent as possible. Tape sets should be scheduled to be stored off-site with plenty of time provided to retrieve them before needed. These off-site sets also should be second- or third-level copies that enable the most recent sets to remain on-site for immediate access, if needed. Generally, sets are moved on- and off-site every one to two weeks. This rotation might be done more frequently on a large system.

As networks become more complex and require a higher level of protection, backup systems need to be more versatile. Automatic expert systems are already starting to appear, providing full, intelligent solutions. One current system is not just a tape backup but a fully automated storage-management product. Providing fully automatic on- and off-site tape rotation schedules, these systems require a high level of knowledge to totally understand their flow of events.

Testing

It is critical that a backup system be tested from time to time. Many systems have experienced permanent data loss simply because the backup system was never tested. A backup is no good if you cannot restore it.

A simple way to test the backup is to create a dummy test directory that contains a few executable programs backed up at all times. This approach enables you to delete the directory structure and to restore from the backup media without losing important data. This restore test should be done after the initial system install and after any system change that can affect the operation of the backup device. Workstation hardware changes or DOS upgrades easily can cause a backup system to malfunction.

Disaster Recovery

A disaster-recovery plan should be a complete solution. This solution should include a backup system and a company plan to follow in the event of a total system failure. In most cases, disaster recovery is simply an afterthought, something that would have been handy. A backup system is required to maintain a complete set of data, as complete and current as possible. This data sometimes is required to re-create the system as it was after a major hardware problem.

A backup device is only a single part of what is generally needed to be properly protected. The following sections are intended as a guide to aid you in planning the proper system for your needs. Disaster-recovery systems or plans should be taken seriously if your company's data has any value. A written list of procedures, a list of support personnel, or a tape backup can make an adequate disaster recovery plan if it covers all your needs. Although most plans include some or all of these items, the key is to create a plan that provides your company with the necessary insurance.

Proper Preplanning

Proper preplanning of a recovery system easily can become overly complicated. The best plan is one that can be followed, fits the needs of your company, and provides an acceptable end result. A well-designed plan should have a backup schedule or log and a documented list of steps to take in the event of a problem, and should include more than one responsible person.

Needed Equipment

Novell provides safety mechanisms for a first level of protection. NetWare's disk mirroring or disk duplexing can greatly reduce the cost of downtime in the event of a hard drive failure. NetWare provides a hot backup drive or complete disk channel that takes over in the event of a primary drive failure.

Many companies do not take advantage of this feature simply because of the cost of an additional hard drive. In most cases, the mere cost of a second hard drive is much less than the cost of downtime that might be experienced during a drive failure.

If implemented properly, Novell NetWare's disk duplexing can add as much as 50 percent to the disk-read performance. This additional performance alone can offset the cost of the extra hard drive and controller required.

By using disk mirroring or duplexing, you can schedule a failed hard disk for repair after normal business hours, eliminating user downtime completely.

Power Protection

A major source of file server data corruption is power loss. NetWare increases its performance by reading large amounts of data into a special portion of memory called a *cache*. The cache enables data to be read many times faster than if it were being read directly from the hard disk. The cache, however, is vulnerable to poor power conditions. If a power line spike or surge passes through the file server, data reliability is affected.

Many NetWare Administrators are familiar with the *General Protection Interrupt* (GPI) or *Non-Maskable Interrupt* (NMI) errors at the file server console. These errors are displayed by an operating system task that constantly checks the integrity of the system memory. Both errors generally are traced to power or memory problems. And in most cases, a power-related problem makes the memory appear bad.

Power protection is important to the integrity of data on a file server. The minimum protection is a good surge strip to guard against spikes and surges.

A good quality *Uninterruptible Power Supply* (UPS) should be installed to prevent any unnecessary problems. A UPS that has Novell communications capability can save many hours by making it unnecessary to repair data in the event of a power failure. Many vendors offer an interface that informs the file server when commercial power has been lost. When properly installed, these units can shut down the file server correctly, minimizing damaged data.

Available Utilities

The computer *virus* (vital information resources under siege) appears to be a growing problem. The first virus-like programs started out as a game, a battlefield between a few young geniuses writing self-repairing, roaming code. These programs had a mission to seek out and destroy the opponent. From these first amazing programs, the virus has developed into a special program designed to interfere with the normal operations of a computer. This interference varies from a simple message informing the user of its presence to the destruction of as much data as possible. Currently, more than 400 virus programs are known to exist, and more are added to the list daily.

Describe the procedures used to protect against virus intrusion.

Most viruses found today multiply by attaching to executable (EXE and COM) files and becoming memory-resident.

This spread of infectious programs prompted the growth of vaccine or virus detection and repair software. The capability of these programs to seek out and destroy the virus enables the System Administrator to breathe more easily.

Although antivirus software has proven useful in the battle against viruses, do not think of it as an alternative to a properly designed network security system. Currently, no well-designed and properly administered Novell security system has been infected. The most dangerous and most common access point of a virus is through the user Supervisor.

The special user Supervisor and Supervisor equivalents should be reserved for administrative tasks only. A user does not need the rights of the System Supervisor to execute normal applications.

If a user has the right to change the read-only flag on all executable files, most new virus programs attack those files. If the user does not have the right to modify the flag, the file is protected.

Currently, the quality and methods of antivirus programs vary from one system to another. The best means of selecting a detection system is to follow trade magazines' software reviews or to contact a reputable software retailer.

Support Issues

Though network service persons are everywhere, an experienced and knowledgeable network service person is difficult to find.

A good, reputable service organization that can provide quality service and support is probably the most important key to a successful operation. Whether you are self-sufficient or totally dependent, you need a reliable source for replacement parts and assistance occasionally.

As part of your plan, a carefully planned service contract or agreement should be set up to supply the level of support your company might need in the event of a system failure. Include in the contract such items as on-site service, software, and hardware. The amount of on-hand parts and a reasonable time period should be specified as well. The service organization should be able to supply suitable replacement parts within the agreed time period and handle the problem with a suitable level of knowledge.

If your network is large, it might require an internal support staff. If so, Novell offers a *Network Support Encyclopedia* that can supply answers to a majority of your technical questions. This extensive database is available on floppy disk and CD-ROM. Novell provides a yearly subscription service that supplies updates.

Each main menu option offers submenus that enable Administrators to narrow the search field or perform global searches on the complete database. The NSE database provides useful information that can be obtained quickly and is a practical addition to the NetWare toolbag.

Novell's *NetWire,* a special-interest group located on CompuServe, also is a good source of information. Through NetWire, you can communicate with other users, System Administrators, and Novell technical persons. It is not uncommon to post a question in the evening and have a suggested solution waiting for you in the morning.

Training

As demonstrated in the industry, successful Novell networks are administered and run by highly competent people using Novell NetWare. The most cost-effective way to become familiar with the system is to receive professional training from an organization that can supply a working, hands-on environment. An experienced instructor can help you with both application and procedural issues. You can compensate for the cost of this training many times over by your improved ability to handle normal administrative issues internally.

Today's NetWare networks are not just an office of personal computers sharing printers. These networks have replaced many large, expensive corporate systems and have proven their capability to supply office automation.

Common problems are most often created by untrained employees and Administrators. A simple, time-consuming problem like "My data was there before lunch" easily can be avoided by a knowledgeable Administrator. A well-designed security system with a functional menu can prevent most accidental problems. In most cases, missing data files and programs are products of untrained users allowed to roam the system. These accidents usually stem from good intentions and can be prevented with proper user and Administrator training.

Consultants

The network industry can supply professional consultants for any technical and administrative area needed. Many consultants are extremely good at what they do; some are not. As with selecting a service organization, a consultant should be selected based on experience and knowledge. You can train your staff to operate and administer your network. You should not be required to train your consultant to obtain the level of service you require.

Fixing Volumes Using BINDFIX, BINDREST, and VREPAIR

Bindery files contain security information regarding users and groups on the system. This security information includes password requirements, station and time restrictions, trustee rights, and security equivalencies. If these files are corrupted, random portions of the user and group accounts cannot be modified.

Repair the server bindery using BINDFIX and BINDREST.

NetWare 3.1*x* contains three bindery files: NET$OBJ.SYS, NET$PROP.SYS, and NET$VAL.SYS. These files are hidden system files that reside in the SYS:SYSTEM directory.

Identify the purpose and procedures of server maintenance utilities, such as BINDFIX, BINDREST, VREPAIR, and SBACKUP.

The **BINDFIX** utility attempts to repair bindery problems. This utility creates new bindery files and renames the previous files with OLD extensions. Use BINDFIX if you suspect bindery file corruption.

The **BINDREST** utility deletes the newly created binderies created by BINDFIX, renames the OLD files to SYS files, hides the new files, and then makes them system files. Use BINDREST if the BINDFIX command does not fix corrupted files and you need to put the binderies back to their original state.

Describe the reasons you would use VREPAIR.

VREPAIR enables an Administrator to attempt a software repair of a volume that appears to have problems. The most common use of VREPAIR is when the power to the file server has been cut off, causing data mirror mismatches or *File Allocation Table* (FAT) errors that prevent the server from booting.

In 3.1*x*, type **LOAD VREPAIR** and repair the dismounted volume.

Use VREPAIR with discretion and always make sure that you have a current backup. When run on a good disk having FAT errors, VREPAIR is effective. If, however, the disk has hard-to-detect defects, VREPAIR might destroy data.

The VREPAIR NLM enables you to choose a volume to repair or set the VREPAIR options (see fig. 9.10).

```
Current Urepair Configuration:

    Quit If A Required URepair Name Space Support NLM Is Not Loaded

    Write Only Changed Directory And FAT Entries Out To Disk

    Keep Changes In Memory For Later Update

Options:

    1. Remove Name Space support from the volume

    2. Write All Directory And FAT Entries Out To Disk

    3. Write Changes Immediately To Disk

    0. Return To Main Menu

    Enter your choice:
```

Figure 9.10
The VREPAIR options screen.

Use VREPAIR to remove name space support from a volume.

The options that you can set are as follows:

◆ Remove name space support

◆ Write the DET and FAT tables to disk

◆ Write changes at once to disk

613

VREPAIR checks the volume and attempts to repair file discrepancies with a valid File Allocation Table. Figure 9.11 shows the VREPAIR prompts. VREPAIR takes a considerable length of time if problems exist with the files. Avoid interrupting the VREPAIR process to allow sufficient time for the utility to complete the repair procedure.

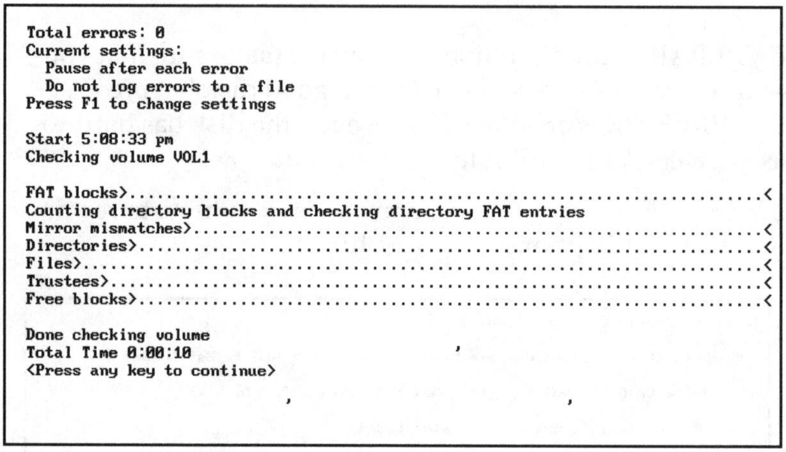

Figure 9.11

VREPAIR on VOL1.

```
Total errors: 0
Current settings:
  Pause after each error
  Do not log errors to a file
Press F1 to change settings

Start 5:08:33 pm
Checking volume VOL1

FAT blocks>...........................................................<
Counting directory blocks and checking directory FAT entries
Mirror mismatches>...................................................<
Directories>.........................................................<
Files>...............................................................<
Trustees>............................................................<
Free blocks>.........................................................<

Done checking volume
Total Time 0:00:10
<Press any key to continue>
```

Section Review Questions

6. Which of the following statements about SBACKUP terminology is false?

    a. A host also can be a target.

    b. A parent is a bindery or a directory.

    c. A child can be a file or an empty subdirectory.

    d. A target is any server backed up with SBACKUP.

7. Which of the following statements about SBACKUP NLMs is false?

    a. SBACKUP is comprised of three target modules and two host modules.

    b. SIDR is the data requester and uses SMSP.

    c. TSA links the data requester and the target.

    d. SBACKUP.NLM is the user interface.

8. Which rotation method is the easiest to maintain?

    a. Two-Week Inverted

    b. Tower of Hanoi

    c. Ten-Tape Rotation

    d. Grandfather Rotation Method

9. How many tapes does the Grandfather Rotation Method require?

    a. 19, plus one fresh tape a month

    b. 20 for the year

    c. 10 tapes for the year

    d. 5 to 8 tapes a year

10. Which of the following statements about VREPAIR is true?

    a. You must run VREPAIR to remove name space support.

    b. VREPAIR enables you to write the DET and FAT tables to floppy disk.

    c. VREPAIR should be run occasionally to fix problems on the hard drive.

    d. VREPAIR should be run on a downed file server.

Answers

6. c

7. a

8. d

9. b

10. a

Exploring the NetWare 3.1*x* Memory Model

NetWare 3.1*x* manages memory differently. NetWare 3.1*x* is dynamic and can vary or reallocate its memory as needed. NetWare 3.1*x* divides memory into memory pools. (A *memory pool* is an area of the file server's memory set aside for the server's use in processing request for services or for recording status of the server's various resources.)

A 3.1*x* file server requires at least 4 MB of system memory, providing the disk drive is not larger than 80 MB, although it can address up to 4 GB of memory. These memory pools are divided into pools according to the way in which the memory is used.

Identify NetWare 3.12 memory pools and describe the features, content, resource use, and effect of each.

The pools as defined by NetWare are as follows:

- File Cache Buffer
- Cache Movable
- Cache Non-Movable
- Permanent
- Semi-Permanent
- Alloc Short Term

You must have an understanding of these memory pools to understand the many performance features available in NetWare 3.1*x*.

Describe the tables, blocks, and buffers that are important to the workings of server memory.

File Cache Buffer Memory Pool

All versions of NetWare make use of much of the system memory allocated as cache. This *cache memory* greatly speeds up the access time to the file server. Workstations can access information held in cache memory much faster than directly reading it from the system disk. When the NetWare 3.1x file server boots, any free memory is allocated as cache memory—the main memory pool used by NetWare 3.1x.

NetWare makes use of this cache memory in many ways. Cache memory is reallocated as system demands increase and memory is needed in other areas. The NetWare operating system uses memory from this pool to provide buffer resources to other areas when needed. The file cache buffer memory might be called upon to temporarily loan memory to the following processes:

◆ Cache buffers required by other applications (NLMs). This memory is returned to the Cache Buffer Pool after the NLM is unloaded.

◆ Cache buffers as needed to service user requests to access disk data.

◆ Cache buffers to build disk hash tables, *file allocation tables* (FATs), Turbo FATs, and *directory entry tables* (DETs).

All other pools obtain memory when needed in the file cache buffer memory pool. As memory is taken from this pool, the amount of memory available as file cache reduces. This process might result in some loss of performance, depending on the amount of total memory available to the system.

Cache Movable and Non-Movable Memory Pools

Both the Cache Movable Memory Pool and Cache Non-Movable Memory Pool give and take memory directly from the File Cache Memory Pool. These pools differ in that the movable pool moves or relocates itself to prevent memory fragmentation. Memory fragmentation, if excessive, can reduce overall file server performance.

The Cache Movable Memory Pool supplies memory to system tables such as FATs, DETs, and hash tables. Because of their dynamic nature, the size of these tables can grow and shrink quickly, resulting in memory fragmentation. (These tables are explained in the next section.) The Movable Memory Pool relocates itself when needed to minimize any fragmentation and, therefore, maintains optimum memory performance. Because of this feature, all tables maintained in cache movable memory are in a contiguous format. The tables maintained by this pool are relatively small in size and are dynamically expandable.

The Cache Non-Movable Memory Pool is used for larger memory buffers and tables as needed by NLMs. The memory used here is primarily for the loading and unloading of NLMs and is generally a short-term usage. The memory used from this pool is returned to the file cache buffer pool when no longer needed but is not relocated to prevent memory fragmentation. The tables and buffers that make use of the cache non-movable memory are not expandable and are held in noncontiguous memory blocks. An example of the usage of this pool is with the MONITOR and INSTALL NLMs. Each of these NLMs allocates memory from the Cache Non-Movable Memory Pool when loaded.

If cache non-movable memory is allocated and deallocated often by the loading and unloading of NLMs, memory can be fragmented to the point of appearing to be out of memory. Non-movable memory does not eliminate memory fragmentation and can become so bad that no contiguous block of memory is large enough to load NLMs. This problem generally only occurs with a file server short on system memory.

Permanent Memory Pool

The Permanent Memory Pool is the source drawn from by both the Semi-Permanent Pool and the Alloc Short Term Memory Pool. The Permanent Memory Pool is used for long-term necessities, such as permanent tables and packet-receive buffers. NLMs cannot make use of the memory in this pool. The Permanent Memory Pool takes additional memory from the File Cache Memory Pool, if necessary, but does not return it. This memory, however, is returned when the file server is brought down and back up.

Semi-Permanent Memory Pool

The Semi-Permanent Memory Pool is a secondary pool of the permanent pool. The Semi-Permanent Memory Pool is used by loadable modules, such as disk and LAN card drivers, when they are expected to make use of this resource for long periods. This memory is returned to the Permanent Memory Pool when no longer needed, but is not returned to the File Cache Buffer Memory Pool.

Alloc Short Term Memory Pool

The Alloc Short Term Memory Pool is used by many procedures and NLMs when memory is needed for short periods. This memory also is taken from the permanent pool when more resources are needed, but is not returned.

The Alloc Short Term Memory pool defaults to a minimum value of 2 MB in NetWare 3.11, but has a default value of 8 MB for NetWare 3.12. The maximum value is 32 MB in NetWare 3.12, an increase from NetWare 3.11. You can temporarily change the minimum value by entering a SET command at the server console command line or change it permanently by placing a SET command in the server's STARTUP.NCF or AUTOEXEC.NCF file as follows:

```
SET MAXIMUM ALLOC SHORTTERM MEMORY = value
```

Replace value with any value in the range of 50000 to 33554432 (32 MB).

After you change the Alloc Short Term Memory Pool size, allow the server to run for a few days, then check the server to see if sufficient memory has been allocated or if you allocated too much memory to this pool. If memory pool information is set too low, you see messages indicating that an operation could not be completed because the memory pool has reached its allocated limit.

Use MONITOR to view server memory statistics.

To check the memory, complete the following steps:

1. Load MONITOR.NLM at the server console.

2. Choose the Resource Utilization option.

3. View the Server Memory Statistics screen that appears.

4. Check the Alloc Memory Pool line. It tells you the number of bytes set for this memory pool. It also tells you the number of bytes in use. Compare the two figures.

The Alloc Short Term Memory Pool increases its size when needed but does not return the memory to the permanent memory pool or the file cache memory pool. After the Alloc Short Term Memory Pool increases in size, that memory remains in that pool until the server is rebooted. Thus, increase the Alloc Short Term Memory Pool if the comparison that you made in step 4 indicates that a high percentage (75 percent or more) of the Alloc Short Term Memory Pool is being used. This setup prevents requests for services from not being completed due to an insufficient amount of space in the memory pool.

Examples of processes or items that make use of the Alloc Short Term Memory Pool are as follows:

♦ Drive mappings

♦ Service requests

♦ File locks and open requests

◆ Service advertising and requests (SAPs and RIPs)

◆ User connection information

◆ Queue manager and NLM tables

◆ Message broadcasts pending

Now that you have a basic understanding of each memory pool, you can learn the way in which the pools are handled internally. This information is for those interested and is not a necessity.

When a 3.1x file server is first booted, the operating system allocates as much memory as possible to the file cache buffers pool. It allocates the minimum amounts of memory for all others. You can adjust this allocation by using the console SET commands, but adjustment rarely is required. After the file server has been up and running, and as users and applications make requests of the server, memory is allocated as needed. If the server is up for longer periods, you might notice that the total free cache blocks as shown on the MONITOR main screen changes. This change is a result of the dynamic allocation process.

Memory pools are allocated in one of two ways. Movable memory, or the Cache Movable Pool, is allocated from the bottom up, but the Cache Non-Movable, Permanent, and Alloc Short Term memory are allocated from the top down. The center of these areas is the File Cache Buffer Pool. NetWare maintains a minimum number of cache buffers (default of 20); without any, the file system cannot function.

Understanding NetWare 3.1x Memory Configuration

This section discusses ways in which you can determine the amount of memory your file server needs to perform properly by identifying the memory considerations particular to your installation. The issues to be considered are as follows:

◆ Minimum amount of memory to run NetWare

◆ Memory required by NLMs, including all drivers, name spaces, and communications devices

◆ Total hard disk and volume sizes

◆ Number of *directory entry tables* (DETs)

◆ Total memory required to properly cache volumes

Most NLMs require just enough memory to load; the memory needed is generally the size of the NLM. But many NLMs require the support of additional NLMs to operate. This requirement most often is true with communications NLMs, because they require buffer space. If so, the total size of all required NLMs must be considered. Some NLMs allocate additional memory as they are running. A simple method to determine memory requirements is to check memory before and after loading the NLM in the Resource Utilization option in the console MONITOR utility.

Determine NetWare 3.12 server memory requirements for given cases.

You can calculate estimated basic 3.1*x* file server memory requirements by using the following formulas. These numbers are estimated; each system has a different set of requirements because of the loads and expectations placed on the file server by its users.

    M = .023 × VOLUME SIZE / BLOCK SIZE

The letter "M" is the memory required in megabytes.

If name space is added to a volume, then use the following:

    M = .032 × VOLUME SIZE / BLOCK SIZE

To determine the total memory, add the memory requirements of all volumes together with 2 MB for the operating system, as follows:

    TOTAL MEMORY = M1 + M2 + M3 + 2 MB (ROUNDED TO THE HIGHEST M)

M1, M2, M3, and so on refer to each volume on the server.

If your file server has a 600 MB hard drive and you are setting it up to use the default of 4 KB blocks, for example, the following is true:

```
(600 × .023) / 4 = 3.45 + 2 = 5.45 or 6.0 MB
```

This number is rounded up to 6 MB, although most current PCs require you to go up in standard memory blocks of 4 MB, resulting in a server with 8 MB. With NetWare 3.1*x*, you should never be overly concerned with too much file cache as in NetWare 2.2. The memory concerns of NetWare 2.2 do not pertain to NetWare 3.1*x*. As a rule, in NetWare 3.1*x*, the more memory the merrier.

NetWare Tables and Buffers

NetWare makes use of tables and buffers to manage the attached disk drives. These tables and buffers enable NetWare to provide the high level of performance necessary to service many simultaneous users.

Each volume connected to a NetWare file server has two tables associated with it. The *Directory Entry Table* (DET) and *File Allocation Table* (FAT) both reside on the individual volumes and are loaded into cache buffers while running or mounted. NetWare 3.1*x* caches only the most recently used block of the DET. In earlier versions, the entire DET was cached.

Directory Entry Table (DET)

The DET contains all the directory entries for that particular volume. A *directory entry table* consists of data made up of items such as file and directory entries that include information on file name, owner, last date of update, and file location. The DET also contains entries for file trustees and directory trustees. Because NetWare 3.1*x* can span multiple hard disks, a disk might contain more than one DET. Directory Entry Blocks are always 4 KB, regardless of the FAT blocks' settings. When a volume is first installed, six DET blocks are allocated. Each block can support 32 128-byte entries. The maximum number of DET blocks per volume is 65,536, which also reflects the maximum number of files per volume of 2,097,152. DET blocks are allocated automatically as needed.

623

File Allocation Table (FAT)

The FAT contains information corresponding to the location of disk blocks required to retrieve a file. This table is accessed from the DET. NetWare divides each volume into blocks or disk allocation blocks. You can configure these blocks during the installation process to have a block size of 4, 8, 16, 32, or 64 KB (the default is 4 KB). Each file stored on the volume has an entry in the FAT that lists all the blocks used to store the file.

File cache buffers are also an important feature of NetWare's performance. File cache buffers are blocks of memory where files are stored when being used.

 You can configure the size of these cache buffers, as in the FAT blocks, but never make them larger than the smallest disk allocation block.

These file cache buffers are the main memory used in the file server, and make up the file cache buffer memory pool.

Directory Cache Buffers

Directory cache buffers are blocks of file server memory used to cache the DET blocks. NetWare allocates directory cache buffers as needed, taking them from the file cache buffer memory pool.

Packet Receive Buffers

Packet receive buffers are made up of file server memory areas set up as temporary holding areas for communications data coming in through the LAN interface. Data packets are held here until the file server can service them. During periods of heavy activity, data would be ignored and lost without this buffer area.

You can control these buffers by using a console SET command, and the MONITOR utility shows the number of buffers available for use.

Optimizing Memory and Performance

This section presents some of the more common concerns when configuring your file server memory and fine-tuning for performance. NetWare 3.1*x* provides many console SET commands to enable you to manually fine-tune your system. You should be aware, however, that in many cases simply adding file server memory eliminates the need to fine-tune or make adjustments. Novell has provided, as a default, a good set of rules if your file server is configured with the proper amount of memory.

NetWare 3.1*x* can support up to 4 GB of system memory. Resources are dynamically allocated as needed, and the system is designed to return memory no longer being used to the appropriate pools whenever possible.

Describe server console commands related to memory.

Novell provides a basic tool to enable you to monitor the individual functions of the 3.1*x* file server. The MONITOR NLM provides many options and menus in which you can find performance-tuning information. The main information screen (statistics screen) of MONITOR displays some of the more important information when evaluating the performance of a file server.

The information, as shown in figure 9.12, is informative when evaluating the basic condition of a file server.

Identify components that affect server and network performance.

The following items are important to a properly operating file server. A basic understanding of these items is critical to understanding why a file server might be performing poorly.

- ◆ Total cache buffers
- ◆ Dirty cache buffers
- ◆ Packet receive buffers
- ◆ Service processes

Figure 9.12

The 3.1x Server Information screen.

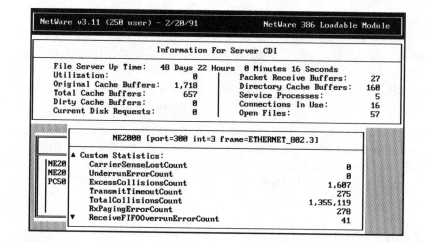

```
NetWare v3.11 (250 user) - 2/20/91          NetWare 386 Loadable Module

                        Information For Server CDI

   File Server Up Time:    48 Days 22 Hours  0 Minutes 16 Seconds
   Utilization:                      0      Packet Receive Buffers:     27
   Original Cache Buffers:       1,718      Directory Cache Buffers:   160
   Total Cache Buffers:            657      Service Processes:           5
   Dirty Cache Buffers:              0      Connections In Use:         16
   Current Disk Requests:            0      Open Files:                 57

              NE2000 [port=300 int=3 frame=ETHERNET_802.3]

 NE20   ▲ Custom Statistics:
 NE20       CarrierSenseLostCount                              0
 PC50       UnderrunErrorCount                                 0
            ExcessCollisionsCount                          1,607
            TransmitTimeoutCount                             275
            TotalCollisionsCount                       1,355,119
            RxPagingErrorCount                               278
          ▼ ReceiveFIFOOverrunErrorCount                       41
```

Use MONITOR to verify server and network performance, and to view resource and processor utilization.

Total Cache Buffers

The Total Cache Buffers field displays the total number of cache buffers currently available for use by the system. This number varies both up and down as NLMs and other processes require memory from the File Cache Memory Pool. If cache available buffers become too low, performance suffers. To determine the amount of memory available for cache buffers, check the Server Memory Statistics window found under the Resource Utilization option.

If the Total Cache Buffers level gets to 20 percent or lower, add memory as soon as possible. An ideal level is 50 percent or better.

Dirty Cache Buffers

This field indicates the number of cache buffers that contain changed information and are waiting to be written to disk.

 The number of dirty cache buffers should not reach more than 70 percent of the total cache buffers available.

If dirty cache buffers consistently exceed 70 percent, you can obtain some relief by setting the Maximum Concurrent Disk Cache Writes to a high number using the console SET command.

Packet Receive Buffers

This field shows the number of buffers configured to handle workstation requests. You also can configure this option by using the console SET commands. The SET commands are discussed later.

Directory Cache Buffers

This number indicates the number of cache buffers allocated to handle directory entries. You can modify this number as needed. If you have more than 100 buffers in use, you need to increase the minimum setting.

Service Processes

Service processes are "task handlers" configured to service work-station requests. These are dynamically configured as the load on the file server increases. You can configure the total maximum service processes with the appropriate console SET command.

File Server Statistics

You can monitor file server memory by selecting the Resource Utilization option from the main MONITOR screen. Here you are shown the way in which your file server's memory is allocated among the different pools. The two most important memory pools to monitor are the Alloc Memory Pool (the Alloc Short Term Memory Pool discussed earlier) and the cache buffers. If the Alloc Memory Pool reaches 2 MB, use the SET command to increase it by 1 MB. If this situation occurs, it can indicate a problem, and any third-party NLM developers should be contacted. The cache buffers should never fall below the level of 20 percent. If so, additional memory is required. Rebooting the server to recover memory from the permanent pools and unloading unnecessary NLM might provide temporary relief.

Many other options and resources can be monitored using NetWare's MONITOR utility. A few of the more important options are as follows:

- Resource Tags
- System Module Information
- Resource Utilization
- Processor Utilization

These options not only enable you to track your file server memory utilization, but also to provide information on processes running on the server.

Resource Tags

This option displays a list of modules and tracked resources. This tool is helpful in determining if a particular NLM is not behaving properly. All NLMs are required to request resources from the operating system when they load. These resources should be returned after use. You can check this process by using this option.

System Module Information

System modules are NLMs. Selecting this option enables you to view the resources currently being used by a module.

Resource Utilization

The Resource Utilization option enables you to view the actual amount of memory being used in a pool by each resource. This option is useful in determining if a particular resource is consuming too much of the file server's memory.

Processor Utilization

This option of the MONITOR utility is only available when you load it using the -P command-line switch (LOAD MONITOR -P, for example). After you load MONITOR, select Processor Utilization from the main menu. You then are presented with a list of the currently loaded processes and interrupts being served by the CPU. To view a process or group of processes, simply use the NetWare standard function keys—F5 to mark and F3 to mark all. You then are shown a chart of the selected processes with information on Time, Count, and Load statistics. When viewing this screen, note that the Polling Process should represent most of the load.

Note   If any NLM displays more than a 60-percent load, you should suspect a problem. NLMs that impose such a high load on the system can result in poor performance to all other users.

An example of the Resource Utilization screen appears in figure 9.13. Notice the load used by the polling process, which is normal.

Figure 9.13

The Resource Utilization screen.

```
NetWare v3.11 (250 user) - 2/20/91          NetWare 386 Loadable Module

┌────────────────────────────────────────────────────────────────────┐
│                      Server Memory Statistics                        │
│                                                                      │
│    Permanent Memory Pool:        1,368,732 Bytes  19%  1,353,844 In Use │
│    Alloc Memory Pool:              364,864 Bytes   5%    163,296 In Use │
│    Cache Buffers:                2,772,540 Bytes  38%                 │
│    Cache Movable Memory:         1,704,880 Bytes  23%                 │
│    Cache Non-Movable Memory:     1,135,180 Bytes  15%                 │
│    Total Server Work Memory:     7,346,196 Bytes                     │
└────────────────────────────────────────────────────────────────────┘

                    ┌──────────────────────────────────┐ ions
                    │        Tracked Resources         │ ation
                    │ ▛ AES Process Call-Backs         │
                    │   Alloc Short Term Memory (Bytes) │
                    │   Alternate Debugger Handlers    │ ormation
                    │   C Library BSD Sockets          │ Console
                    │   Cache Memory Below 16 Meg (Bytes) │ Activity
                    │ ▼ Cache Movable Memory (Bytes)   │ ion
                    └──────────────────────────────────┘
```

Section Review Questions

11. Which memory pool is responsible for pop-up menus like MONITOR?

    a. File Cache Buffer

    b. Cache Movable

    c. Cache Non-Movable

    d. Alloc Short Term

12. Which memory pool is responsible for FATs and DETs?

    a. File Cache Buffer

    b. Cache Movable

    c. Cache Non-Movable

    d. Permanent

    e. Semi-Permanent

    f. Alloc Short Term

13. From which memory pool are all other pools taken?

    a. File Cache Buffer

    b. Cache Movable

    c. Cache Non-Movable

    d. Permanent

    e. Semi-Permanent

    f. Alloc Short Term

14. Which memory pool is used to load and unload NLMs?

    a. File Cache Buffer

    b. Cache Movable

    c. Cache Non-Movable

    d. Permanent

    e. Semi-Permanent

15. Which memory pool can be reduced by limiting the number of network drive mappings users have?

    a. File Cache Buffer

    b. Cache Movable

    c. Cache Non-Movable

    d. Permanent

    e. Semi-Permanent

    f. Alloc Short Term

16. Which memory pool cannot be used by NLMs?

    a. File Cache Buffer

    b. Cache Movable

631

    c. Cache Non-Movable

    d. Permanent

    e. Semi-Permanent

17. Which memory pool is used when loading LAN and disk drivers?

    a. File Cache Buffer

    b. Cache Movable

    c. Cache Non-Movable

    d. Permanent

    e. Semi-Permanent

Answers

11. d

12. b

13. a

14. c

15. f

16. d

17. e

Using Console SET Parameters

This section discusses some of the more common SET parameters used to adjust a 3.1*x* file server's performance. You can enter most of the parameters discussed here directly at the console prompt or place them in the AUTOEXEC.NCF and STARTUP.NCF files.

List interactions between various SET parameters and the considerations for changing settings.

The parameters covered in this section are grouped into the following categories:

◆ Communications

◆ Memory

◆ File caching

◆ Directory caching

◆ Miscellaneous

Many more SET parameters are supported by NetWare, but this book covers only the most important ones used in general system maintenance.

Communications

The following SET parameters pertain to network communications.

Maximum Packet Receive Buffers

This option enables you to configure the maximum number of packet receive buffers that the server can allocate.

Select and implement the appropriate SET parameter needed to alter network performance based on a given case.

Many SET parameters can be used to alter system performance. Maximum Packet Receive Buffers is one of them.

Uses

If the current number of packet receive buffers is at the maximum, increase this number (in multiples of 10) until you have one buffer per workstation.

If you are using EISA or microchannel bus master boards in the file server, increase this number at least five buffers per board.

If you are receiving No ECB available count errors, increase this number at least 10 buffers per board.

Range

50 to 2000

Default

100

Placement

This option can be placed in the AUTOEXEC.NCF or entered at the console prompt.

Minimum Packet Receive Buffers

This parameter sets the minimum number of buffers the server immediately allocates upon booting.

Uses

Increase this number if the server is slow to respond immediately after booting.

If you are using EISA or microchannel bus master boards in the file server, and you are receiving No ECB available count errors, increase this number at least five buffers per board.

Range

10 to 1000

Default

10

Placement

This option must be set in the STARTUP.NCF file.

Memory

The next few sections discuss SET parameters that pertain to memory.

 Identify the relationships and balances needed between server memory components to maintain optimum server performance.

Maximum Alloc Short Term Memory

This option enables you to set the amount of memory given to Alloc Short Term Memory.

Uses

Alloc Short Term Memory is responsible for drive mappings, NLM tables, user connection information, request buffers, open and locked files, and messages waiting to be broadcast.

Decrease this value if the server is allocating too much memory because of some temporary condition.

Increase this value if you receive error messages indicating that operations are not completed because this memory pool has reached its maximum.

Range

50000 to 16777216

Default

2097152

Placement

Place this option in the AUTOEXEC.NCF or type it at the console prompt.

Auto Register Memory Above 16 Megabytes

You can set this option to automatically see memory above 16 MB on an EISA bus machine.

Uses

Leave this option set to ON if you want the server to find memory above 16 MB.

Set this option to OFF if you have a network board that uses DMA or AT bus mastering. Leaving this option set to ON under these conditions corrupts file server memory.

Range

ON and OFF

Default

ON

Placement

This option must be set in the STARTUP.NCF file.

Cache Buffer Size

Use this option to set the size of the cache buffers.

Uses

If you are using block sizes greater than 4 KB, increasing the cache buffer size can improve performance.

If your volumes vary in size, set the cache buffer so that it is not larger than the smallest block size.

 The file server does not mount any volumes in which the block allocation size is smaller than the cache buffer size.

Range

4096, 8192, and 16384

Default

4096

Placement

This option must be set in the STARTUP.NCF file.

File Caching

The following SET parameter deals with file caching.

Minimum File Cache Buffers

All memory not being used by other processes is used for file caching. This option enables you to set the minimum number of file cache buffers needed on your system, thereby limiting the amount of memory given to requesting services.

Uses

If this number is set too high, you might have trouble loading additional NLMs into memory. Increase this value only when you need more memory for file caching.

Range

20 to 1000

Default

20

Placement

You can place this option in the AUTOEXEC.NCF or enter it at the console prompt.

Directory Caching

The next two SET parameters deal with directory caching.

Maximum Directory Cache Buffers

This option sets the maximum number of directory cache buffers the operating system is allowed to create.

Directory cache buffers are allocated permanently until the server is rebooted. This option helps to keep the number of unnecessary blocks down.

Uses

Increase this number if the file server is responding slowly when performing directory searches.

Decrease this number if you receive messages that the server is low on memory or if too much memory is being allocated to directory caching.

Range

20 to 4000

Default

500

Minimum Directory Cache Buffers

This option is set to allow a minimum number of directory cache buffers to be allocated for directory searches.

Uses

This number should be increased slightly when directory searches are slow immediately after booting the server. You must have enough buffers to perform searches quickly; you do not, however, want to over-allocate these buffers, because they do not go back into the memory pool. Unused directory cache buffers simply remain unused.

Range

10 to 2000

Default

20

Placement

You can set this option in the AUTOEXEC.NCF or STARTUP.NCF file or enter it at the console prompt.

Defining NetWare Name Service (NNS)

NetWare Name Service (NNS) is an item that you can purchase from Novell. Although it does not come automatically with NetWare 3.1x, it is worth mentioning.

The first step to learning about NNS is defining the terms. The following sections define the words and phrases you encounter when exploring the potential benefits of NNS.

Domains

A *domain* is a group of servers networked together. Each domain can have up to a maximum of 400 file servers.

Profiles

A *profile* is a group of up to eight file servers in a domain. Because users can attach to a maximum of only eight servers (a universal NetWare limitation), *profiles* designate specific file server connections within a domain.

Synchronization

Each server in a domain has its bindery files and queues duplicated on all other servers. This process is called *synchronization* and is the engine by which NNS functions. A user can log in to any server in the domain with the same password. Because queues also are duplicated, the user does not have to specify a file server when printing, only the queue name. Logical queues are created on all servers in the domain, and print jobs are routed to the correct printer.

Filling in the Full Name field for each user is important. If two users have the same login name, synchronization is alerted if the full name is used.

Name Service Database

The Name Service Database is part of the binderies and contains information about users authorized to use the domain, their passwords, and their profile information.

Remember the following about NNS:

Domains

- ◆ Domains have a maximum of 400 file servers.

- ◆ A single file server can belong only to one domain.

- ◆ The domain login script replaces the system login script.

- ◆ User information and print queues are identical on all domain servers.

- ◆ Logical queues are created from the original on all other file servers in the domain.

- ◆ If all servers on the domain are NetWare 3.x, you can have up to 16 million users.

- ◆ If you have a mix of NetWare 2.x and NetWare 3.x servers, you can have only 5,000 users.

continues

641

Profiles

◆ Each profile has a name.

◆ Each profile lists its members, which can be both users and groups.

◆ Profile login scripts are similar to user login scripts, but do not replace user login scripts.

◆ Each profile specifies up to eight fileservers.

NETCON

When using NNS, the NETCON utility replaces SYSCON. The two utilities are similar.

 For a workstation to run NETCON, you must have at least 640 KB of memory in the workstation.

Three major items have been added to NETCON, as follows:

◆ **Change Current Domain.** This option is similar to Change Current Server in SYSCON. Change Current Domain enables you, if you have the appropriate rights, to look at information about another domain.

◆ **Domain Administration.** This option enables you to add and delete domain servers, to synchronize the user accounts and queues on the domain, and to edit the domain login script.

◆ **Profile Information.** This option enables you to set a full name for the profile, specify the domain managers, add members, modify the profile script, and designate up to eight servers for attachment.

When you purchase NNS, you receive several revised utilities. Do not replace these utilities with other versions after NNS is in place. The Name Service Database can become corrupt if non-NNS utilities are used. SYSCON is aware of NNS and alerts users that they should use NETCON.

Modified Utilities

The following sections discuss utilities and their parameters changed by NNS.

Printing Utilities

CAPTURE and NPRINT have added DO=*domain name* to specify a domain other than the default.

PCONSOLE now creates logical queues on all other servers whenever a new queue is added to the domain.

Connection Utilities

ATTACH, LOGIN, and LOGOUT have added @ *domain name* to specify which domain to attach to or log out of.

LOGIN has added /PRO=*profile* to specify which profile to use.

Examples of ways to use these files are as follows:

In the first example, INSTRUCT is the user attempting to attach to the domain CDI:

```
ATTACH INSTRUCT @ CDI
```

The next example logs in the user INSTRUCT to the domain CDI by using the profile EDUCATION. The profile designates to which file servers INSTRUCT attaches and executes the user's Profile Script.

```
LOGIN /PRO-EDUCATION INSTRUCT @ CDI
```

643

This following example logs the user out of the CDI domain.

```
LOGOUT @ CDI
```

User Utilities

SLIST and WHOAMI have added a /D parameter that specifies the domains available.

SETPASS has added the @ DOMAIN parameter to set your password on a domain.

MAKEUSER has added #DEFAULT_PROFILE to use when creating new users.

USERDEF now offers a Default Profile option.

The First NNS Server

The first server to utilize NNS becomes the template for all other servers and is considered the default server. For easy administration, the first server should be the one with the most users.

Passwords are set to expire automatically on the first domain server. Users must enter new passwords to maintain encrypted passwords. If you add more servers to the domain before users change their passwords, a random password is assigned to each user with an old password.

These items are not synchronized between domain servers:

- ◆ Directories and subdirectories
- ◆ Files
- ◆ Volume or disk space restrictions
- ◆ NetWare accounting
- ◆ Intruder detection
- ◆ Grace logins

Domain servers take up two grace logins whenever users decline a request to change passwords.

 A file is kept of the random passwords in SYS:SYSTEM/NEW.PWD.

Section Review Questions

18. Which of the following statements about NNS is false?

   a. A file server can be in multiple domains.

   b. A file server can be in multiple profiles.

   c. A profile can include only eight servers.

   d. The domain login script replaces the system login script.

19. Which of the following statements about NNS is true?

   a. SYSCON should be used along with NETCON.

   b. NNS is not packaged with NetWare 3.11.

   c. Synchronization creates physical queues on each file server.

   d. Only one grace login is used when a user is asked to change his password and NNS is running.

20. Which utility replaces the SYSCON utility in NNS?

   a. NETCON

   b. NNSCON

   c. NNSUTIL

   d. NETUTIL

21. The SET parameter that should equal one (1) for each client on the network is:

    a. Minimum directory cache buffers

    b. Maximum alloc short term memory

    c. Auto register memory

    d. Maximum packet receive buffers

22. Console SET parameters can be entered in which *three* ways:

    a. STARTUP.NCF

    b. CONFIG.NCG

    c. AUTOEXEC.NCF

    d. File server console

Answers

18. a

19. b

20. a

21. d

22. a, c, and d

Understanding Remote Management

NetWare 3.11 offers many features for remote file server management. File server access is available to LAN Administrators connected directly to the LAN with a network interface and remotely through a modem. In this section, you are shown the different utilities supplied by Novell that allow this access.

Remote management enables you, as the System Administrator, to perform the following tasks:

- ◆ Use file server utilities (NLMs)

- ◆ Search and edit files in DOS and NetWare directories

- ◆ Transfer files to a remote file server

- ◆ Install NetWare on a remote file server

- ◆ Add an existing file server to remote management

- ◆ Reboot a file server from a remote console

The first utility discussed here is RCONSOLE. RCONSOLE requires a total of three program modules to operate. Two of these modules are NLMs and operate on the file server; the third is a normal DOS-executable program. This utility communicates to the file server's console, enabling you to use the network cabling by using the NetWare SPX protocol. RCONSOLE provides complete access to the console, enabling you to use any NLM or console command. The RCONSOLE command is stored by default in volume SYS: under the SYSTEM directory to prevent any general user access to the utility itself. As a System Administrator with Supervisor privileges, this utility is available for your use.

For RCONSOLE to operate, you must first load the appropriate NLM modules on the file server. The first NLM to be loaded is REMOTE.NLM. This module provides the actual information exchange between the file server console and the remote Administrator. The next NLM is RSPX.NLM, which supplies the communication layer that handles the actual connection through the SPX protocol and provides the advertisement of remote console capability to RCONSOLE users.

 When loading the REMOTE.NLM, you are prompted for a password. This password is required for users who want to access the console by using the RCONSOLE DOS utility. When loading this NLM in the AUTOEXEC.NCF file, simply place the password on the command line, as in the following example.

Simple AUTOEXEC.NCF statements are as follows:

```
LOAD REMOTE password
LOAD RSPX
```

The RCONSOLE utility provides complete access to the file server console along with the added features of scanning network directories and copying files to NetWare directories and DOS partitions.

Please note that the capability to copy files is in one direction only; you cannot copy from the network.

Upon executing the RCONSOLE utility, you are presented with a list of file servers advertising themselves as available for remote access. Select the file server you want to access, and you are prompted for a password. This password can be either the password selected at the time the REMOTE.NLM was loaded, or the file server's SUPERVISOR password. At this time, the standard file server console screen appears.

If the keyboard is locked through the MONITOR utility, you are prompted to supply that password also.

Press the * key on the numeric keypad to open a menu of available options.

Press Shift+Esc to exit the remote console.

You can move between console screens by using both the + and - keys, also located on the numeric keypad.

From the available options menu, you can select one of the options shown in figure 9.14.

```
Mounted Volumes              Name Spaces
   SYS                          DOS
   LAB1                         DOS
   LAB2                         DOS
   LAB3                         DOS
   LAB4                         DOS
   USERS                        DOS, NFS
1/22/93 11:27am: 0.0.0 Remote Console Connection Cleared for 00000005:00001B191D
38
:load install              ┌─────────── Available Options ────────────┐
Loading module IN          │                                          │
   NetWare 386 Ins         │ Select A Screen To View                  │
   Version 1.56            │ Directory Scan                           │
   Copyright 1991          │ Transfer Files To Server                 │
   :                       │ Copy System And Public Files             │
   :                       │ Shell To Operating System                │
1/26/93 4:10pm: 0          │ End Remote Session With Server (SHIFT-ESC)│00CDC:00001B1EE62
0                          │ Resume Remote Session With Server (ESC)   │
1/27/93 2:16am: 1          └──────────────────────────────────────────┘
1/27/93 2:17am: 1.1.60 Bindery open requested by the SERVER
:
:send hello
1/27/93 1:08pm: 0.0.0 Remote Console Connection Granted for 00000CDA:00001B198C6
5
:
```

Figure 9.14
RCONSOLE available
options.

The RCONSOLE utility allows concurrent access to the file server. Thus, more than one System Administrator can have access to the console at the same time. Although concurrent access can be beneficial when assisting a remote Administrator through a problem, it also can cause confusion. If Administrators using remote connections are working on different console screens, no conflicts arise. But if both users access the same console screen, keyboard entries can become mixed, creating confusion at first glance.

The Available Options menu of the RCONSOLE utility provides various functions that can assist you in your administrative tasks. The option Scan File Server Directories provides a way to scan or search both the DOS partition and NetWare volumes for any files about which you might be inquiring. If searching a DOS partition, make sure that you use the proper DOS drive letter, such as C. When searching NetWare volumes, make sure to use the full path including the volume label. This feature comes in handy for locating files you want to edit using the EDIT.NLM utility, described later in this section.

The Transfer Files option enables you to copy files easily from your workstation to the file server. When you select this option, a screen appears requesting that you supply both the Source Path on Workstation and Target Path on Server. Each file is listed on the remote console screen as it is copied.

649

The next option is used to load or reload the original SYSTEM and PUBLIC utility files. This function is similar to that performed by the INSTALL.NLM with the exception that you must feed the floppy disks into your remote console.

 It is strongly recommended that loading of the utility files be performed only on RCONSOLE. The ACONSOLE utility, which is explained later, does not guarantee data delivery.

The option Resume Remote Session with Server enables you to return to the console screen after using any of the available options described here.

The End Remote Session menu option terminates the session in the same manner as all other Novell NetWare menu utilities. This option is one of many ways to properly exit the remote console operation. After selecting this option, a small menu box appears, asking End Remote Console?. Selecting Yes or No determines the outcome. The remote console also can be exited by pressing Alt+F10 at the menu options. You also can press Shift+Esc, as instructed earlier, when you are in the remote console and bypass the menu options screen altogether.

ACONSOLE

ACONSOLE is NetWare's asynchronous remote console. This utility provides access to the file server through an asynchronous communications port by using a null modem cable or Hayes-compatible modem. You can use the ACONSOLE utility where support is provided over a large distance or as a redundant secondary link to the management workstation. This utility allows access to the file server even if the LAN cabling was not functional. If you intend to use ACONSOLE, the proper NLMs must be loaded at the file server. As with RCONSOLE, the REMOTE.NLM is loaded and a password is provided. Then the RS232.NLM is loaded with the parameters needed to communicate with your modem and COM port.

Please note that because of the communications speeds of asynchronous devices, file transfers are not recommended using ACONSOLE.

RSETUP.EXE

The RSETUP.EXE menu utility is designed to enable you to create a file server boot floppy. The RSETUP.EXE utility places all the required files and drivers, along with the AUTOEXEC.NCF and STARTUP.NCF, on the floppy. Although this utility is seldom used, you should be aware that it is available if needed.

EDIT.NLM

The EDIT.NLM utility is an ASCII text editor that enables you to edit files on NetWare volumes and file server DOS partitions. The EDIT command gives you the ability to modify NCF files while accessing the console. To use EDIT, simply use the console load command as in the following example:

```
LOAD EDIT oath/filename
```

This loads the EDIT utility with the specified file name. When you complete your file changes, press Esc and save your changes.

Note The Edit NLM searches directories created as search directories by using the console SEARCH command on the file server. By default, this directory is SYS:SYSTEM. You can have EDIT look to the file server's local drive as well.

You also can use the EDIT utility to create an NCF file that enables you to remotely reboot your file server. Create a file with the NCF extension and place the following command in it:

```
REMOVE DOS
DOWN
EXIT
```

Note You can use the EDIT.NLM to create various small (8 KB or smaller) files. When the file has an NCF extension, it can be used on the file server like a DOS batch file is used on a workstation.

Running this command from the file server console downs the server and automatically reboots. For this process to complete properly, you must have the server command in your AUTOEXEC.BAT file located on the C drive set up correctly.

Section Review Questions

23. Which of the following statements about Remote Management is false?

    a. The EDIT command is used to create the reboot file.

    b. RSETUP creates a bootable disk for the remote server.

    c. Typing **DOWN** reboots the server.

    d. RCONSOLE requires REMOTE.NLM and RSPX.NLM to be loaded in that order.

24. Which *three* modules does RCONSOLE require in order to operate?

    a. AUTOEXEC.NCF

    b. REMOTE.NLM

    c. RSPX.NLM

    d. RCONSOLE.EXE

25. Which of the following is NOT an RCONSOLE option?

    a. Shell to operating system

    b. Directory scan

    c. Copy system and public files

    d. Session Description

26. The purpose of the RSETUP.EXE menu utility is to:

    a. Set up remote console management

    b. Let you start an asynchronous connection

    c. Enable you to create a file server boot floppy

    d. None of the above

27. The file that lets you make changes to files on NetWare volumes and file server DOS partitions is:

    a. EDIT.NLM

    b. MODIFY.NLM

    c. RSPX.NLM

    d. MONITOR.NLM

Answers

23. c

24. b, c, and d

25. d

26. c

27. a

Installing and Upgrading NetWare 3.12 Server and Client

You can install the NetWare 3.1x server from disk or, in the case of NetWare 3.12, from CD-ROM. Installing NetWare 3.1x enables you to install a new NetWare 3.1x server.

You also have the option of upgrading an existing NetWare server to NetWare 3.1x. Two utilities for upgrading current versions of NetWare are provided: MIGRATE.EXE and 2XUPGRDE.NLM.

These utilities enable you to upgrade using three separate methods:

◆ Across-the-wire

◆ Same-server

◆ In-place

In addition to installing or upgrading your server, you also must install or upgrade clients (workstations).

An overview of server installation and upgrade, as well as client installation and upgrade, are discussed in this section.

Installing a NetWare 3.1x Server

You can run the NetWare 3.1x installation program by using the INSTALL disk or, in the case of NetWare 3.12, by running the INSTALL program from CD_ROM.

To run INSTALL from disk, place the disk in drive A of the computer on which you are installing NetWare 3.1x, then boot your computer.

To run install from CD-ROM, install the CD-ROM device and software, including the CD-ROM drivers, on to the computer. Make sure that the CD-ROM installation updated the CONFIG.SYS and AUTOEXEC.BAT files on the computer so that the CD-ROM drive is recognized on this system. Next, insert the NetWare 3.12 disc into the CD-ROM drive, and turn on the CD-ROM reader. Reboot the computer to make certain that the modified CONFIG.SYS and AUTOEXEC.BAT files are loaded. Change to the drive that represents the CD-ROM, then type **INSTALL** and press Enter.

Both of these installation startup processes load the installation interface that completes several tasks:

◆ Creating and formatting a DOS partition

◆ Copying system files for Novell DOS 6 to the created and formatted DOS partition

- ◆ Enabling you to enter a server name after the prompt

- ◆ Generating or assigning an IPX internal number

- ◆ Copying the server boot files to a server directory called SERVER.312

- ◆ Setting code page information

- ◆ Selecting to use the DOS file name format

- ◆ Creating the AUTOEXEC.NCF and STARTUP.NCF files

- ◆ Running the file that starts the server and loads it into memory—SERVER.EXE

Installation is provided through INSTALL.NLM. Figure 9.15 shows the INSTALL.NLM utility with screens open to specify a drive or directory for installing NetWare from other than drive A.

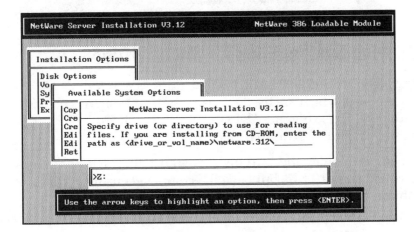

Figure 9.15

NetWare 3.12 INSTALL.NLM.

Creating and Formatting a DOS Partition

The first portion of the installation requires you to create and format a DOS partition on the hard drive of the computer onto which you are installing NetWare 3.1x. To accomplish this task, load the INSTALL NLM, choose Disk Options from the Installation Options screen, then select Format from the Available Disk Options screen. Formatting is optional; you do not need to do this step if the hard drive is already formatted.

By choosing Partition Tables from the Available Disk Options menu (see fig. 9.16), you can see if a DOS partition has already been created.

Figure 9.16

The Partition Tables Option in Available Disk Options screen.

```
┌─────────────────────────────────────────────────────────────────────┐
│ NetWare Server Installation V3.12          NetWare 386 Loadable Module│
│                                                                       │
│   ┌────────────────────────┐                                          │
│   │ Installation Options   │                                          │
│   ├────────────────────────┤                                          │
│   │ Disk Options           │                                          │
│   │ Vo┌───────────────────────────────┐                              │
│   │ Sy│ Available Disk Options         │                             │
│   │ Pr├───────────────────────────────┤                              │
│   │ Ex│ Format (optional)              │                             │
│   │   │ Partition Tables               │                             │
│   │   │ Mirroring                      │                             │
│   │   │ Surface Test (optional)        │                             │
│   │   │ Return To Main Menu            │                             │
│   │   └───────────────────────────────┘                              │
│                                                                       │
│   ┌───────────────────────────────────────────────────────────────┐  │
│   │ Use the arrow keys to highlight an option, then press <ENTER>. │  │
│   └───────────────────────────────────────────────────────────────┘  │
└─────────────────────────────────────────────────────────────────────┘
```

Copying System Files for Novell DOS 6

The NetWare 3.12 INSTALL disk includes two Novell DOS 6 system files, which are used to create partitions on the computer's hard disk. These files are FDISK.COM and FORMAT.COM. These files are included to make disk partitioning easier.

When partitioning the hard disk, you must allow a minimum DOS partition size of 2 MB, but Novell recommends using 5 MB as a minimum DOS partition size.

Naming the Server

The third main task to perform when installing NetWare 3.1x is to name the file server. Follow these rules when creating a name for the server:

◆ Give the server a name at least two characters long, but that does not exceed 47 characters.

◆ Use only legal characters, which include any alphanumeric characters plus hyphens and underscores. Periods (.) and spaces cannot be used in a server name.

Some valid server names would include SERVER_1, ACCTG-1, S1, and S00147A.

Generating or Assigning an IPX Internal Network Number

Each NetWare 3.1*x* server has its own unique network number that identifies it from other servers on the network. The install program generates a random number for you during installation. You can use your own numbering system if you want.

An internal network number must consist of hexadecimal numbers. Using base 16, you can create an internal network number that contains the numbers 0 through 9 and/or the letters A through F. The internal network number must be no longer than eight digits, but can be as few as one digit. Consider the following examples:

- ◆ DAD
- ◆ BAD1
- ◆ 11111111
- ◆ 1BADCAD9

Set Code Page Information

NetWare 3.1*x* does not support multiple client languages. The install program, however, does enable you to choose a code page to set the language in which NetWare screens appear at the file server console.

Select DOS Filename Format

NetWare 3.12 does not require you to use only the standard DOS (eight characters plus a three-character dot extension) file naming convention. You have the option during install, therefore, to select the DOS filename format that you want to use. Novell, however, recommends that you select the DOS Filename Format and that you do not use extended characters.

657

Creating AUTOEXEC.NCF and STARTUP.NCF Files

Installation also creates AUTOEXEC.NCF and STARTUP.NCF files if you select the related Create option from the Available System Options menu.

 Identify and describe server configuration files.

To open the Available System Options menu, choose System Options from the Installation Options menu.

These two files control what happens when the server is first loaded.

 Identify commands and options used to customize the appropriate server configuration file.

The AUTOEXEC.NCF file, for example, contains information that specifies in which time zone the server is located, as well as the file server's name and IPX internal net number. This file also loads various files including the LAN board, and other information.

 Select the appropriate utility and edit the server configuration files.

Once created, these files can be edited by loading INSTALL.NLM, choosing System Options, then choosing the related Edit option. Figure 9.17 shows the File Server AUTOEXEC.NCF File for a server called TSE-TSE.

Load the Server (SERVER.EXE)

SERVER.EXE is the file that, when run on the computer, loads the NetWare 3.1*x* server.

```
NetWare Server Installation V3.12                 NetWare 386 Loadable Module

Inst                    File Server AUTOEXEC.NCF File
Dis  set time zone = MST7MDT
Vo   file server name TSE-TSE
Sy   ipx internal net 1D0C32E
Pr   load streams
Ex   load clib
     load ne2000 port=300 int=3 frame=ETHERNET_802.3 Name=LabNet
     bind ipx to LabNet net=01D0C301
     load trxnet port=2e0 mem=d0000 int=2
     bind ipx to trxnet net=01D0C320
     mount all
     load remote kermit
     load rspx


       Edit the file as needed.  Press <ESCAPE> when done.
```

Figure 9.17

The File Server
AUTOEXEC.NCF File.

Perform a server startup procedure.

Loading the server causes the AUTOEXEC.NCF and the STARTUP.NCF files to run. These files, as mentioned previously, perform such tasks as loading the LAN driver, binding the communication protocol to the LAN board, and loading NLMs such as MONITOR.NLM.

Upgrading Existing NetWare Servers

If your computer currently has an earlier version of NetWare 2.*x* or NetWare 3.*x* installed on it, two utilities are provided that enable you to upgrade that server to NetWare 3.12. These utilities are MIGRATE.EXE and 2XUPGRDE.NLM.

You run MIGRATE.EXE from a client attached to the network. The network requires both a source and a destination server in order to run this utility. (A *source server* is a server from which the files are being migrated, and a *destination server* is a server to which the files are being migrated.)

You run 2XUPGRDE.NLM at the server.

MIGRATE.EXE

MIGRATE.EXE enables you to upgrade the files on a NetWare 2.*x* or 3.*x* server to NetWare 3.12. This utility enables you to run two types of migrations:

- ◆ Across-the-wire migration
- ◆ Same-server migration

An *across-the-wire* migration is run from a DOS client. It takes files from a source server to a destination server using the network cabling system.

A *same-server migration* takes the bindery information on an existing NetWare server, copies it to a working directory on a network DOS client, translates (upgrades) the bindery information so that it is usable in a NetWare 3.1*x* format, then migrates it from the DOS client to the destination (NetWare 3.1*x*) server.

The MIGRATE.EXE utility enables you to perform a standard migration or a custom migration. If you have run the migration utility several times before and are very familiar with it, then you can run the Custom migration. Otherwise, Novell recommends that you run the Standard migration. Figure 9.18 shows the screens that appear when you choose Standard migration when running MIGRATE.EXE.

Figure 9.18

The standard migration option in MIGRATE.EXE.

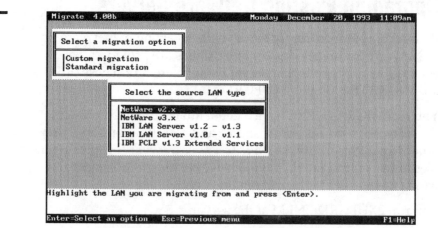

The across-the-wire migration enables you to merge multiple-source servers to create a single, customized destination server. This option is particularly useful in an environment in which you have several older computers running older versions of NetWare that would be more useful to you if you combined their bindery files into one bindery on a more powerful computer.

When migrating source servers, you can let the system assign random passwords to the users whose accounts are migrated. Figure 9.19 shows the migration window that enables you to set a working directory for the migration files, define the NetWare source and destination servers, and even choose to assign random passwords to user accounts.

```
 Migrate  4.00b                        Monday  December  20, 1993  11:11am

  1. Configure the migration utility

              Working directory:  A:\
  _____

  2. Define the NetWare source server (v2.X - v3.X)

                       Server:  TSARINA

       Source volumes to migrate:  (Volumes selected)
  _____

  3. Define the NetWare destination server (v3.X - v4.X)

                       Server:  TSARINA
          Volume destinations:  (Destinations specified)
                    Passwords:  Assign random passwords

 _____
 Choose whether or not to assign random passwords for users that are migrated to
 the destination server.
 Enter=Display options    Esc=Exit the program                      F1=Help
```

Figure 9.19

The migration configuration screen.

Regardless of whether you choose to let the system assign random passwords to user accounts, merging several source servers into one offers several other benefits. Some of those benefits include the following:

- You can establish a default account balance and account restrictions on the installed NetWare 3.1x destination server, which then is applied to the migrated accounts.

- You can set up other user restrictions on the destination server, which also are applied to the migrated accounts.

- You can preserve each user's individual account restrictions for each individual source server.

- You can merge users on different source servers into groups established on the single destination server.

- You can combine print queues and print servers to a single print queue that services multiple printers and let multiple queues service a single printer.

The across-the-wire upgrade is flexible and can help you overcome some networking restrictions. If the across-the-wire upgrade is not an option for you, however, you still can perform an in-place upgrade.

2XUPGRDE.NLM

The in-place upgrade uses the 2XUPGRDE.NLM, loaded at the server to be upgraded. The *in-place upgrade* enables you to upgrade an existing NetWare 2.1x server to a NetWare 3.1x server without the need for a second server. Your existing NetWare server must meet some minimum hardware requirements, however, including the following:

- An Intel 80386 processor

- 4 MB of RAM

- The ability to be booted as a DOS device

- The ability to load SERVER.EXE

If your existing server can meet these minimum requirements, you can perform an in-place upgrade on this server.

Before running the in-place upgrade, however, you *must* back up your current server. A power failure or upgrade interruption at the wrong moment can cause you to lose your existing server information.

Novell considers the backup of your server before upgrading to be a very important step. So important, in fact, that one of the first screens you see after loading the 2XUPGRDE.NLM is a warning screen that prompts you to answer Yes or No to whether you have a recent backup of your server (see fig. 9.20). If you answer No to this prompt, the in-place upgrade is aborted.

```
┌─────────────────────────────────────────────────────────────┐
│  ┌────────────────────────────────────────────────────────┐  │
│  │   In-Place Upgrade from NetWare v2.1x and v2.2 to NetWare v3.1x │  │
│  └────────────────────────────────────────────────────────┘  │
│                                                               │
│  This utility upgrades a NetWare v2.x file system to a NetWare v3.1x file │
│  system.  After running this utility, format the new DOS partition and then │
│  load the INSTALL NLM to place the new operating system files onto volume SYS. │
│                                                               │
│     ┌──────────┐      ┌──────────┐      ┌──────────┐          │
│     │ WARNING  │      │ WARNING  │      │ WARNING  │          │
│     └──────────┘      └──────────┘      └──────────┘          │
│                                                               │
│  You could lose all data on your server if there is a hardware failure during │
│  the upgrade.  Make sure you have a recent backup of your data.  If your │
│  NetWare v2.x server has IDE hard disks, check the warning in the README file. │
│                                                               │
│  Do you have a recent backup of your server? n                │
│                                                               │
│  ZXUPGRDE-1.10-153: The In-Place Upgrade process has been aborted by the user. │
│  The In-Place Upgrade process is now being aborted.            │
│                                                               │
│  <Press ESC to terminate or any other key to continue>        │
│                                                               │
└─────────────────────────────────────────────────────────────┘
```

Figure 9.20

The In-Place Upgrade Backup Prompt screen.

The in-place upgrade is run in four stages. First, an analysis of the system is performed to determine which disks are on the server and the amount of memory needed and available to complete an upgrade.

The second stage performs an analysis of the critical parts of the disks, looking in particular at the Hot Fix area, the File Allocation Tables, and the Directory Entry Tables. The FATs and DETs are then translated for the newer NetWare version, and directory attributes, file attributes, and Macintosh files are upgraded.

The third stage makes needed modifications to the disks, upgrades the partition table, adds the NetWare 3.1x files, and relocates data blocks as needed.

The fourth stage actually creates and updates the NetWare bindery.

The in-place upgrade has three limitations—it cannot upgrade any of the following:

◆ *Value-added processes* (VAPs)

◆ Core printing services

◆ Volume and disk restrictions

663

Figure 9.21 shows the Phase Descriptions screen of the in-place upgrade. The purpose of this screen is two-fold. First, it shows you the process that NetWare goes through to upgrade your existing server. Understanding this process is important—if problems occur during the upgrade, you might have to restore your backup and start over.

Figure 9.21

The In-Place Upgrade Phase Descriptions screen.

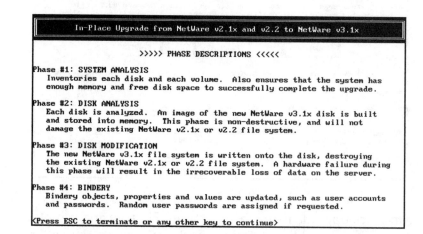

```
┌──────────────────────────────────────────────────────────────────────────┐
│       In-Place Upgrade from NetWare v2.1x and v2.2 to NetWare v3.1x        │
└──────────────────────────────────────────────────────────────────────────┘

                        >>>>> PHASE DESCRIPTIONS <<<<<
Phase #1: SYSTEM ANALYSIS
    Inventories each disk and each volume.  Also ensures that the system has
    enough memory and free disk space to successfully complete the upgrade.

Phase #2: DISK ANALYSIS
    Each disk is analyzed.  An image of the new NetWare v3.1x disk is built
    and stored into memory.  This phase is non-destructive, and will not
    damage the existing NetWare v2.1x or v2.2 file system.

Phase #3: DISK MODIFICATION
    The new NetWare v3.1x file system is written onto the disk, destroying
    the existing NetWare v2.1x or v2.2 file system.  A hardware failure during
    this phase will result in the irrecoverable loss of data on the server.

Phase #4: BINDERY
    Bindery objects, properties and values are updated, such as user accounts
    and passwords.  Random user passwords are assigned if requested.

<Press ESC to terminate or any other key to continue>
```

The second purpose of this screen is to give you another opportunity to exit the in-place upgrade before it begins—in case, after reading the Phase Descriptions screen, you realize you still need to do something before you start the in-place upgrade.

Installing a DOS Client

In addition to installing or upgrading a NetWare server, the DOS clients that use the server need to be updated as well.

Perform a DOS and MS Windows client installation using the NetWare client installation software.

The DOS client installation is quick and easy to perform. Installing the DOS client updates the CONFIG.SYS, AUTOEXEC.BAT, and

NET.CFG files for the workstation, or creates a NET.CFG file if one does not exist.

 Describe the function of the CONFIG.SYS, AUTOEXEC.BAT, and NET.CFG. configuration files.

These three client files are needed to prepare the client for use. The CONFIG.SYS file specifies the hardware that is part of this PC and loads driver files so the software and hardware can communicate. The AUTOEXEC.BAT file is run when the PC boots. It contains, among other things, commands to start common utilities such as a mouse driver, as well as commands to start a NetWare configuration file, NET.CFG, and log in to a server. The NET.CFG file contains specifics for network connection.

Five steps are needed to update the DOS client. These steps appear as questions on the initial NetWare Client Install screen. These steps include the following:

1. Enter the target directory name for Client Installation. By default, the client files are installed to a directory called C:\NWCLIENT. You can change the location of these files if you need to.

 Alter workstation configuration files such that they contain all pertinent information to automate the process of connecting to the network, loading the DOS Requester, and logging in to the network.

2. Allow changes to the CONFIG.SYS and AUTOEXEC.BAT files. One line needs to be added to each of these files. To the CONFIG.SYS file, add LASTDRIVE=Z; to AUTOEXEC.BAT, add CALL STARTNET.BAT.

   The LASTDRIVE command makes it possible for your client to access all network drives, up through and including drive Z. If this entry is set to anything other than Z, your client only sees up to and including the drive letter that was set in this file. If no LASTDRIVE line exists in the CONFIG.SYS file, your client does not see any network drives.

The CALL STARTNET.BAT line in the AUTOEXEC.BAT file calls another file that is added during the DOS client installation. This other file, STARTNET.BAT, is used to load the NetWare DOS Requester. (See Chapter 7, "Customizing the User's Environment," for more information on the NetWare DOS Requester.)

3. Choose whether to install support for Windows. If you do not run Windows on your client, choose No. If you run Windows on your client, choose Yes, then enter the path and directory name in which your Windows files are stored. Because this directory is usually C:\WINDOWS, it is the default. Change the default if the Windows files are stored elsewhere on this client.

4. Install a driver for your LAN board. If possible, the DOS client install program detects the installed LAN board and its settings, and fills in this information for you. If the DOS client install program cannot detect the type of LAN card installed in this client, you must choose the card from a list of drivers and enter the configuration information manually.

5. Start the installation by pressing Enter with step 5 highlighted.

The DOS Client Installation also enables you to upgrade ODI files and drivers. If the installation program finds an existing ODI LAN driver, it tells you that a newer version of the driver is being installed.

 Note Each update to the DOS Client Installation attempts to simplify the installation process. NetWare 3.1*x* simplifies the installation process by only requiring that you create a NET.CFG file. NetWare 3.12 does not have GENSH, SHELLGEN, or WSGEN utilities. In addition, NetWare 3.12 creates the NET.CFG file for you if one does not exist or automatically updates the one that does exist if you choose to have it do so.

If you have to upgrade several DOS clients that have similar hardware and software configurations, Novell provides two utilities to simplify that process:

- ◆ **WSUPGRD.** Upgrades IPX drivers currently using the IPX.EXE file, to make them ODI drivers.

- ◆ **WSUPDATE.** Updates workstation files such as NET.CFG and CONFIG.SYS when they already exist on your DOS clients and when the configurations set in these files are the same for many clients.

These two utilities should be used with caution, because a variety of network problems can result from incorrectly updating NET.CFG and CONFIG.SYS files in multiple clients with different configurations. (For more information about these two utilities, refer to *Workstation Basics and Installation* in the NetWare DOS Client kit documentation.)

Section Review Questions

28. Which of the following is NOT an upgrade option?

    a. Across-the-wire

    b. Same-server

    c. Workstation-to-server

    d. In-place

29. Which install option has become part of the NetWare 3.12 INSTALL?

    a. INSTALL A

    b. INSTALL C

    c. INSTALL J

    d. INSTALL U

30. Which *two* Novell DOS 6 system files are copied to the DOS partition during INSTALL?

    a. FORMAT.EXE

    b. FORMAT.COM

    c. RDISK.COM

    d. FDISK.COM

31. Which of the following is NOT a legal server name?

    a. AMADMAN

    b. 123B4FAD

    c. 00712

    d. S_123BAD

32. Which of the following CANNOT be used in server names?

    a. Hyphen (-)

    b. Underscore (_)

    c. Space

    d. Hexadecimal characters

33. INSTALL randomly generates a(n) _____ that you can change.

    a. Server name

    b. IPX internal number

    c. STARTUP.NCF

    d. SET SERVER=0

34. MIGRATE.EXE is run from:

    a. A NetWare 2.*x* server

    b. A NetWare 3.*x* server

    c. A dedicated file server

    d. A client

35. MIGRATE.EXE enables you to run which *two* types of migrations?

    a. Across-the-wire

    b. Same-server

    c. In-place

    d. DOS-client

36. Which of the following is NOT a benefit of merging several source servers into one?

    a. Default account balances can be established on the new server.

    b. Users can be merged into groups.

    c. Print queues and print servers can be combined.

    d. You can use your existing Intel 80286 server.

37. Which of the following is a minimum requirement of the destination server when running 2XUPGRDE.NLM?

    a. An 80486 Intel processor

    b. 6 MB RAM

    c. A DOS device

    d. Two different source and destination computers

38. The 2XUPGRDE.NLM can upgrade server files except (choose two):

    a. VAPs

    b. SERVER.EXE

    c. Core printing

    d. Users and groups

39. Which file is NOT updated during client install?

    a. STARTNET.BAT

    b. CONFIG.BAT

    c. AUTOEXEC.BAT

    d. CONFIG.SYS

669

40. The _____ utility upgrades IPX drivers currently using the IPX.EXE file, to make them ODI drivers.

    a. WSUPGRD

    b. WSUPDATE

    c. INSTALL

    d. CONFIG

Answers

28. c

29. c

30. b and d

31. a

32. c

33. b

34. d

35. a and b

36. d

37. c

38. a and c

39. b

40. a

Case Study

1. Create a NET.CFG file for a workstation on your network. Define each parameter.

PART 4

NetWare 2.2

Understanding NetWare 2.2 System Manager Functions

Most of the chapters in this book concentrate on the NetWare 3.1*x* product. NetWare 3.1*x* is designed with NetWare 2.*x* as its predecessor. Therefore, NetWare 2.*x* and NetWare 3.1*x* have many things in common. This chapter and the following chapter focus on the 2.2 System Manager and 2.2 Advanced System Manager objectives, which differ from the NetWare 3.1*x* Administration and Advanced Administration objectives. To make it easier for you to gain sufficient knowledge from this book to pass both the NetWare 2.2 System Manager and NetWare 2.2 Advanced System Manager tests, Appendix C, "Test Objectives," includes a list of specific test objectives for both of these tests, as well as for the NetWare 3.1*x* Administration and Advanced Administration tests.

In this chapter, you learn about the following items:

- ◆ File server requirements
- ◆ Security
- ◆ Printing
- ◆ Custom menus
- ◆ WSGEN

Exploring NetWare 2.2

If your server is equipped with a 286 processor, NetWare 2.2 is the only version of NetWare that will work on your equipment. Version 2.2 also can be used on 386- and 486-based servers, but will not take full advantage of the features offered by those more advanced processors. Four different configurations of NetWare 2.2 are available, depending on the number of connections supported.

Connections, as defined by Novell, are taken up by print servers, communications, and specialized processes. *Value-added processes* (VAPs) take up most of the connections. VAPs are programs that increase the functionality of the server.

Common VAPs include print servers and file server keyboard software locks. You learn more about VAPs later in this chapter. Depending on the functionality of the VAP, it can take up several connections. The following list outlines the different versions of 2.2 and the number of connections provided with each version.

◆ The five-user version provides up to 32 connections

◆ The 10-user version provides up to 32 connections

◆ The 50-user version provides up to 64 connections

◆ The 100-user version provides up to 116 connections

Early NetWare versions, called *entry-level solutions* (ELS), limited the functionality of the operating system. The newer versions limit only the number of users and none of the other features.

The only real limitation of features occurs when a file server runs in a nondedicated mode (functioning as a server or a workstation) rather than a dedicated mode (functioning as a server only). Dedicated file servers are SFT Level II and provide transaction tracking system services. Nondedicated file servers do not provide the capability for disk duplexing. Disk duplexing is discussed later in this chapter.

NetWare 2.2 includes Macintosh 2.0 VAPs. Version 2.2 supports AppleTalk Phase II and TokenTalk. Novell allows several Macintosh file attributes to be carried over into the NetWare environment for compatibility.

List the hardware requirements for a file server.

File server requirements for 2.2 are as follows:

◆ 80286-, 80386-, or 80486-compatible computer

◆ 2.5 MB of RAM (more for hard drives larger than 80 MB)

◆ 10 MB hard disk (minimum)

◆ 1.2 MB floppy disk drive

Create a distributed processing environment.

Workstations need to be 8086-compatible computers or better. The faster the workstation, the faster the network operates because of distributed processing. The workstation processes a large amount of information for programs, so an 80386 system always outperforms an 8086 computer.

When the workstation loads an application from the file server into its memory and downloads files from the file server to use with the application, *distributed processing* has taken place. In distributed processing, the workstation can process information without requiring the file server's processing power. This capability enables the workstation to calculate, sort, and format information, leaving the file server free to service other requests.

continues

675

NetWare 2.2 is intended to be a workgroup solution to fit the simple needs of small departments. This version works well as a specialized node in 386-based networks when a workgroup does not need connectivity to other systems.

Section Review Questions

1. Which *two* NetWare 2.2 versions provide up to 32 connections?

    a. 5

    b. 10

    c. 50

    d. 100

2. Which of the following is NOT supported by NetWare 2.2?

    a. AppleTalk Phase I

    b. AppleTalk Phase II

    c. TokenTalk

    d. SFT Level II

3. Which of the following is NOT a file server requirement for NetWare 2.2?

    a. 80286 or above PC-compatible microprocessor

    b. 2.5 MB or RAM or more

    c. Dedicated file server

    d. 10 MB hard disk minimum

4. Which *two* of the following are supported in NetWare 2.2?

   a. TokenTalk

   b. AppleTalk Phase I

   c. AppleTalk Phase II

   d. EtherTalk

5. What is the maximum number of network connections supported by NetWare 2.2?

   a. 32

   b. 64

   c. 116

   d. 128

6. Which of the following statements about NetWare 2.2 is true?

   a. No SFT Level II support is available.

   b. It runs in dedicated or nondedicated mode.

   c. TTS is not available in this version.

   d. Disk duplexing works in dedicated and nondedicated modes.

7. Which server type can run as both a file server and a workstation?

   a. Dedicated

   b. Nondedicated

   c. Either dedicated or nondedicated

   d. NetWare 2.2 servers can run only as nondedicated

8. Loading applications and files from the server into work-station memory is called:

   a. Data processing

   b. File server processing

   c. TTS

   d. Distributed processing

Answers

1. a and b

2. a

3. c

4. a and c

5. c

6. b

7. b

8. d

Exploring the NetWare 2.2 File Server

You can create two different types of NetWare 2.2 file servers: dedicated and nondedicated.

The difference between these two types is in what the file server is asked to do. A *dedicated* file server operates solely as a file server. A *nondedicated* file server runs as both a file server and a work-station.

The following list explains the benefits that the dedicated server has over the nondedicated file server:

◆ The dedicated file server is faster than a nondedicated server—the dedicated server does not have to split its time between servicing all network users and servicing the DOS process being used by the local user.

◆ The dedicated file server is more secure and reliable than a nondedicated server. If an application running on the workstation portion of the nondedicated server locks up, the entire network is affected. Rebooting the workstation also reboots the file server.

File Server Memory

The slowest function for any file server is accessing the hard drive. To improve the file server's performance, NetWare uses the RAM installed in the file server to store information accessed most often.

A more detailed discussion of NetWare 2.2 file server memory is included in Chapter 11, "Understanding NetWare 2.2 Advanced System Manager Functions."

Value-Added Processes

NetWare 2.2 uses *value-added processes*—programs the file server runs to add features that the core operating system uses to customize the network.

Note

Novell recommends a minimum of 2.5 MB RAM for the file server and 8 to 10 MB as the maximum amount of RAM.

A VAP must be placed in the SYS:SYSTEM directory. All VAPs have a VAP file extension.

To load a VAP, follow these steps:

1. Place the file with the VAP extension in the SYS:SYSTEM directory.

continues

2. Down the file server and reboot.

3. When the file server comes up, NetWare asks if you want to load the VAP. Answer any questions specific to the VAP being loaded.

To unload a VAP, follow these steps:

1. Down the file server and reboot.

2. When asked to load the VAP, answer no.

NetWare 2.2 Disk Storage

NetWare 2.2 enables you to put up to two *gigabytes* (GB) of storage onto the network. This storage capability enables you to use combinations of hard drives, CD-ROM drives, and optical disks.

You can create up to 32 volumes, each no larger than 255 MB.

System Fault Tolerance

 Use various fault tolerance features of NetWare 2.2.

NetWare 2.2 provides the following methods of system reliability:

◆ **Read-After-Write Verification and Hot Fix.** These features ensure that data is not written to bad blocks and track statistics when bad blocks are found. When you install NetWare, a portion of the disk—two percent by default—is set aside for dynamic bad-block remapping. Every time a block of data is written to the hard drive, the server compares what was written to disk to what is in memory. If these things match, the server goes on to the next task. If any discrepancy exists, the server writes the block again to the area set aside during installation. This area is tracked as *hot fix*. The block to which the data is originally written is marked as a bad block so it is not reused. Using FCONSOLE, you can view the number of hot fix blocks used. Each used hot fix block represents a server-detected bad block.

◆ *Duplicate File Allocation Tables* **(FAT)** and *Directory Entry Tables* **(DET).** These tables store information that the server uses to save and retrieve data on the hard disk. If the original tables become corrupt, NetWare can retrieve and use the backup copies because they are stored on separate areas of the disk.

◆ **Disk Mirroring and Disk Duplexing.** NetWare allows certain pieces of equipment to be duplicated so that if the original piece fails, the secondary device can be used. *Disk mirroring* enables you to attach two drives on the same controller. *Disk duplexing* requires that you duplicate the disk interface board, the cable connection, the drive controllers, and the hard disks. This method is more secure than disk mirroring.

◆ *Transaction Tracking System* **(TTS).** Transaction Tracking System is used with databases. TTS is provided to application developers so database files can be rolled back to their original state if a failure occurs during processing. This protection must be built into the application for you to take advantage of this feature. NetWare 2.2 uses TTS for some of its system files.

◆ *Uninterruptible Power Supply* **(UPS).** Uninterruptible Power Supply protection prevents power loss from causing the server to crash. The UPS contains a battery capable of maintaining power to the file server for a short period of time. By using a configuration file, the UPS can be configured to tell the server to issue the DOWN command after a specified time.

The file you use to configure the UPS is called CONFIG.UPS and needs to be placed into the SYS:SYSTEM directory.

In this file, you can set the following parameters:

- ◆ Type of hardware
- ◆ I/O address
- ◆ UPS down time
- ◆ UPS wait time

File Server Console Commands

The following is a list of commands that you can use on the NetWare 2.2 file server:

- ◆ **BROADCAST** *message.* Sends a message to all network users currently logged in to or attached to the network.

- ◆ **CLEAR MESSAGE.** Clears any messages that appear on the screen under the Monitor display.

- ◆ **CLEAR STATION** *number.* Clears a workstation that has problems. This command should be issued before you press Ctrl+Alt+Del at the workstation.

You can learn a user's station number by typing **USERLIST/A** at a workstation.

- ◆ **DISK.** Checks the status of each network drive.

- ◆ **DOWN.** Writes cache buffers to the file server hard drives and shuts down the operating system. This command must be used before you turn off power to the server.

- ◆ **MONITOR** *number.* Brings up a grid of six boxes, each containing information about a network connection.

- ◆ **SPOOL.** Lists spooled queues. See the following section on printing for other SPOOL options.

- ◆ **VAP.** Lists currently loaded VAPs.

- ◆ **WATCHDOG.** Enables monitoring of all network connections for inactivity.

Section Review Questions

9. VAP stands for:

   a. Value-Added Process

   b. Variable-Added Process

   c. Value-Aided Process

   d. Value-Added Procedure

10. Which of the following statements is true?

    a. VAPs are stored in the SYS:PUBLIC directory.

    b. VAPs can be loaded only while the server is booting.

    c. VAPs can be unloaded while the file server is up and running.

    d. VAPs are necessary if you want to print.

11. Which of the following statements is false?

    a. NetWare 2.2 creates duplicate DET and FAT tables in separate disk partitions.

    b. The CONFIG.UPS file is used to configure the length of time that the file server waits to see if the power returns.

    c. Only files written for TTS can use it.

    d. Nondedicated file servers can do disk duplexing.

12. Which command is the most appropriate to use on the workstation at connection 3 that has crashed?

    a. Ctrl+Alt+Del at workstation

    b. CLEAR STATION 3 at file server

    c. CLEAR CONNECTION 3 at file server

    d. MONITOR 3 at file server

13. Which rights would you need to create a file in the SYS:PROGRAM\DATA?

    a. C, W

    b. C

    c. W

    d. C, F, W

14. Which rights would you need to change the attributes of a file from Read/Write to Read Only?

    a. F, M

    b. M

    c. C, M

    d. A, M

15. Programs that the file server runs to add features for the core operating system to use in customizing the network are called:

    a. NLMs

    b. NNSs

    c. VLMs

    d. VAPs

16. Programs that the NetWare 2.2 file server runs to add customizing operating system features always have the extension:

    a. NLM

    b. APP

    c. VAP

    d. VLM

17. The maximum storage space available on a NetWare 2.2 server is:

    a. 3 GB

    b. 2 GB

    c. 255 MB

    d. Unlimited

18. The largest volume that a NetWare 2.2 server can address is:

    a. 3 GB

    b. 2 GB

    c. 255 MB

    d. Unlimited

19. Which of the following is NOT a method of system reliability provided by NetWare 2.2?

    a. Bad block reuse

    b. Duplicate FAT and DET

    c. TTS

    d. UPS

20. Which of the following is NOT true regarding Read-After-Write verification?

    a. Two percent of the disk is set aside at installation for Read-After-Write verification.

    b. It lets the server reuse bad blocks because it repairs them first.

    c. You can see the number of bad blocks used by running FCONSOLE.

    d. Server compares what is written to the disk with what is still in memory each time the server writes a block of data.

21. Which of the following is set when configuring the UPS?

    a. File server name

    b. UPS start time

    c. UPS name

    d. UPS down time

22. Before downing the NetWare 2.2 server, which console command should you issue?

    a. Clear Message

    b. Clear *station*

    c. Userlist/A

    d. Broadcast

23. Which command enables you to find out a user's workstation number?

    a. Broadcast

    b. Watchdog

    c. Clear *station*

    d. Userlist/A

24. Which command enables monitoring of all network connections for inactivity?

    a. Broadcast

    b. Watchdog

    c. Clear *station*

    d. Userlist/A

Answers

 9. a

10. b

11. d

12. b

13. a

14. a

15. d

16. c

17. b

18. c

19. a

20. b

21. d

22. d

23. d

24. b

Exploring Network Security

Trustee rights are the rights users or groups have in a directory. These rights also are referred to as *privileges*. Seven trustee rights exist in 2.2. Trustee rights are the "keys" each user has for a directory. These seven rights are listed and defined in table 10.1.

Table 10.1
Trustee Rights

Right	Function
Read	Enables the user to see the contents of a file and to use the file.
Write	Enables the user to alter the contents of a file.
Create	Enables the user to make new files and directories.
Erase	Enables the user to delete existing files and directories.
File Scan	Enables the user to view files and subdirectories in a directory. Without this right, you cannot see files. In 2.2, you still can see subdirectories, even if you are denied rights.
Modify	Enables the user to change the attributes of a file in 2.2. With this right, the user can change a file from Read/Write to Read Only or from Nonshareable to Shareable. In 3.1x, this right also enables the user to change the attributes for directories
Access Control	Enables the user to give any of the preceding rights to other users on the network.

Directory Rights

Directory rights, also known as the *maximum rights mask*, are the same as trustee rights, but directory rights belong to the system—not the users. Directory rights override trustee rights.

Suppose, for example, that a user has the Erase trustee right to a directory, and the directory enables the Erase right. The user then can erase files. If the directory does not enable the Erase right, however, no user can erase files in that directory—even if he or she has the Erase trustee right.

Effective Rights

You can think of directory rights as "locks" that you can put on your system. NetWare gives each directory a full set of locks by default. The trustee rights are the "keys" that fit the directory locks. Each user can have his or her own set of unique keys. As an example, think of your own key ring. You have your own house key, car key, and so on. Chances are that no one has the same keys as you. Everyone has different locks that need to be opened. The same concept applies to networks. You have specific needs in directories. Some users have the same needs, and others have different needs. Each user can have his or her own set of keys, or rights.

Effective rights are the trustee rights (keys) that actually match available directory rights (locks). If a lock exists and you do not have a key, you cannot perform the function. Likewise, if you have a key and no lock exists, you cannot perform the function. The only way you can use a right is to have matching locks and keys.

Anyone who has the Access Control right in a directory can change the Maximum Rights Mask.

Each newly created directory automatically has all seven rights available through the Maximum Rights Mask.

689

Use table 10.2 as a guideline to determine which rights are required to perform common operations to files.

Table 10.2
Required Rights for Common Operations

Action	Required Rights
Read a closed file	R
Write to a closed file	W
Create and write to a file	C & W
Delete a file flagged Read/Write	E
Rename a file	M or C & W
Change a file's attributes	F & M
See files using DIR	F
Create a directory	C
Change the Maximum Rights Mask	A
Change trustee rights	A

Section Review Questions

25. Trustee Rights are:

    a. Rights users or groups have in a directory

    b. The keys that open all locks

    c. The same as the minimum rights mask

    d. Granted to network directories

26. Which right lets you alter the contents of a file?

    a. Create

    b. Modify

    c. Access control

    d. Write

27. Another word for effective rights is:

    a. Locks

    b. Chances

    c. Access

    d. Keys

28. Which *two* rights are needed to delete a file flagged as Read/Write?

    a. R

    b. C

    c. E

    d. W

29. The one right you should NOT give to users because they can then grant rights to other users is:

    a. R

    b. W

    c. C

    d. A

Answers

25. a

26. d

27. d

28. c

29. d

Examining NBACKUP

The NetWare NBACKUP utility is used to back up and restore files on a NetWare file server and local hard drives. A user does not require full or supervisory rights to properly back up files. Any user who has the minimum rights of File Scan and Read can use NBACKUP to back up personal files.

NBACKUP enables the following devices to be used as backup media:

- ◆ Floppy drives

- ◆ Tape drives that use DOS device drivers

- ◆ Optical drives that use DOS device drivers

- ◆ Local hard drives

- ◆ Network drives

- ◆ Novell DIBI devices (Novell Wangtek Tape Drive)

To back up the complete file server, the user must have supervisor privileges to access the system security information. The first screen displayed enables the backup device type to be selected. Select the device required and continue.

If a non-DOS device is not available, you can remove this menu selection by deleting the DIBI$DRV.DAT file from the SYS:PUBLIC directory.

Select Backup Options from the NBACKUP main menu (see fig. 10.1). Next, select the Select Working Directory option. This directory is where the session and error log files are held. These files are important to determine the integrity of the backup session and to restore the session. Insert the path of the directory you want to use.

After you select your working directory, choose the Backup File Server option. You then see a Backup Options window that enables you to customize the backup session. The session parameters are configured here (see fig. 10.2).

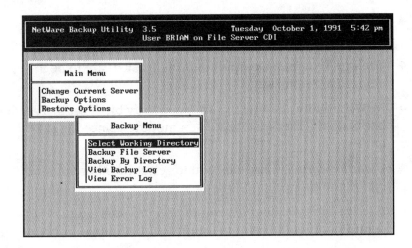

Figure 10.1
NetWare 2.2
NBACKUP menu.

NBACKUP does not back up hidden and system files on a NetWare 2.*x* file server.

Volumes that have additional name space support are not supported in NBACKUP.

Figure 10.2
Session configuration.

You tell NBACKUP what task you want it to perform by responding to the following options:

◆ **Session Description.** Provides a means to place a label on each session, making it unique.

- ◆ **Backup Bindery.** Determines if the bindery is to be backed up.

- ◆ **Backup Trustees.** Determines if the trustees are to be included in the session.

- ◆ **Modified Files Only.** Checks the modify bit; if set to Yes, backs up the files that have been modified since the last backup.

- ◆ **Clear Modify Bit.** Enables you to select whether the Modify bit will be cleared.

- ◆ **Files to Include.** Enables you to back up selected files. The default is All.

- ◆ **Files to Exclude.** Used to prevent specific files from being backed up. The default is None.

- ◆ **Directories to Exclude.** Operates the same as the Files to Exclude option but at the directory level.

- ◆ **Backup Hidden Files.** Backs up hidden files.

- ◆ **Backup System Files.** Backs up system files.

- ◆ **Source Directory.** Locates where you have chosen to back up whether it is a file server, volume, or directory.

- ◆ **Destination Directory.** Locates the DOS device to which you want to archive data; can be any DOS device to which you have access and security privileges.

When you select from the Backup menu to back up a file server or a directory structure, the Backup Options window changes; options that do not pertain to that operation are disabled.

As with NetWare utilities, the data entry fields pertaining to volumes and directories provide a point-and-shoot menu choice when you press Ins, as figures 10.3 and 10.4 illustrate.

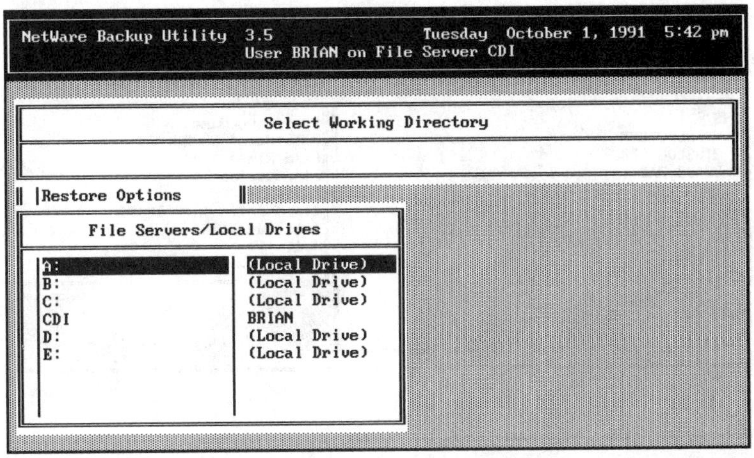

Figure 10.3
Select destination.

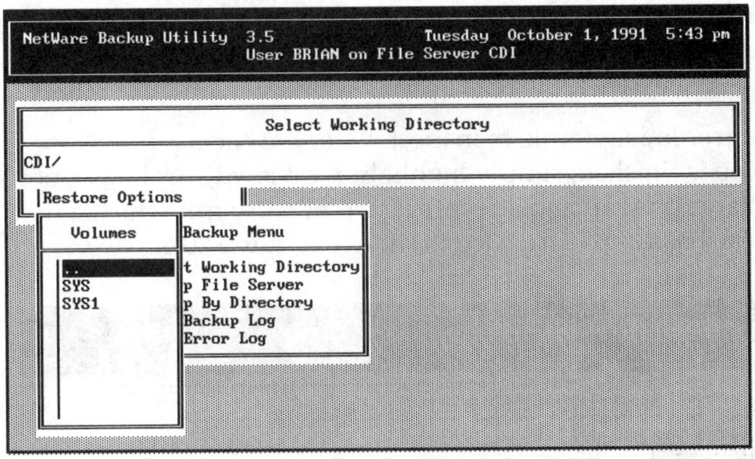

Figure 10.4
Select volume.

After completing the options window, the backup process is started by pressing Esc. You then are prompted to start the backup at that time or later. If you select to start it later, you must provide the start date and time. At this point, the workstation remains at that prompt until the desired time and date. The workstation can be interrupted simply by pressing the Esc key.

After the backup begins, the status screen displays the current activity, errors encountered, and total files and directories backed up. This screen remains active until the session is completed (see fig. 10.5).

Figure 10.5

The status screen.

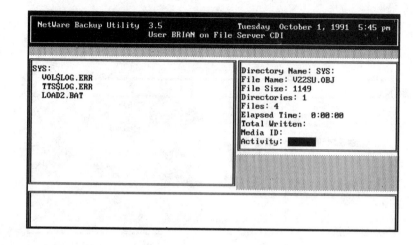

Always examine the error log after the session is complete. One of the most common problems encountered with backup systems is failure to check the log file. Most operators assume that everything is fine; when the backup is needed, they find out otherwise.

The error log is simple to inspect. After the backup or restore session is finished, simply highlight the View Error Log option of the Backup menu and select the current entry from the list that appears. A sample error log is shown in figure 10.6.

Figure 10.6

The session error log.

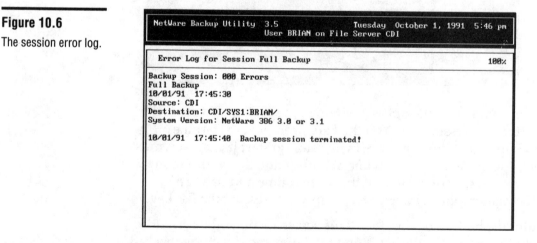

Section Review Questions

30. What can NBACKUP do?

    a. Back up to any tape drive

    b. Back up 2.2 hidden and system files

    c. Back up OS/2 files

    d. Back up to another network

31. To use NBACKUP, which *two* rights must you have?

    a. Read

    b. File Scan

    c. Write

    d. Erase

32. Which of the following CANNOT be used as an NBACKUP device?

    a. Floppy drives

    b. Tape drives using DOS device drivers

    c. Local hard disks

    d. Tape drives using non-DOS devices

33. The directory where the NBACKUP session and error logs are stored is called:

    a. Data storage directory

    b. Error log directory

    c. Working directory

    d. Backup logs directory

34. Which *two* types of files are not backed up by NBACKUP?

    a. Data

    b. Executable

    c. Hidden

    d. System

697

35. Which NBACKUP option places a label on each NBACKUP session?

    a. Source directory

    b. Session description

    c. Destination directory

    d. Backup trustees

Answers

30. d

31. a and b

32. d

33. c

34. c and d

35. b

Examining Network Printing

Identify the two printing services available.

Core printing service is the oldest method of network printing and was, at one time, the only method supplied by Novell. *Core printing* services enable you to connect printers directly to the file server. Thus, printer jobs are handled directly by the operating system. This method is supported only on NetWare 286 and has both advantages and disadvantages.

Identify parameters for choosing the right service.

If your system simply requires one or two printers in a central location, then core printing might be all that you need.

 NetWare 2.2 uses the following files for printing and print services:

CAPTURE.EXE

NPRINT.EXE

END CAP.EXE

PSC.EXE

PCONSOLE.EXE

PRINTDEF.EXE

PRINTCON.EXE

RPRINTER.EXE

PSERVER.VAP

PSERVER.EXE

Although basic, core printing can burden the file server with printing tasks that reduce file server performance. Core printing also requires downing the file server to make changes to printer port configurations. This method of printing usually must be scheduled after normal working hours to minimize any downtime inconvenience to other users. Reserve core printing for smaller, low-traffic situations that do not require extended control.

Setting Up Core Printing in a 2.2 Server

Core printing in a 2.2 server requires that you choose this option when you install NetWare. If you choose Basic installation, core printing is initialized automatically for LPT1. Core printing enables you to attach up to five printers directly to the file server. To use these printers, the Administrator must be aware of the following commands:

699

◆ **P** *n* **CREATE** *port.* Assigns a printer number to a port on the file server. If you want LPT1 assigned as printer 0 and COM1 assigned as printer 2, type the following:

```
P 0 CREATE LPT1
P 1 CREATE COM1
```

If you need to set a COM port for anything other than the parameters listed here, use this command to reset parameters for the port:

```
P n CONFIG BAUD=a WORDSIZE=b STOPBIT=c PARITY=d XONXOFF=e
```

Options	Values
BAUD	300, 1200, 4800, 9600
WORDSIZE	7, 8
STOPBIT	1, 2
PARITY	Even, Odd, NONE
XONXOFF	Yes/No

◆ **Q** *name* **CREATE** *line.* Enables the Administrator to make a queue on the network. If you want to create a queue for a laser printer, for example, type **Q LASERQ CREATE.** A hexadecimally named subdirectory is created automatically on the network for storing print jobs.

◆ **P** *n* **ADD** *queuename* **AT PRIORITY** *x.* Hooks up the queue with the appropriate printer. Type the following command to attach printer 0 with the LASERQ queue:

```
P 0 ADD LASERQ
```

Normally, each printer has one queue. Other configurations are available, depending on the needs of the users on your network. Queues also can have priorities. Priority 1 is the highest. No other queues are serviced until the queue with priority 1 is empty. Then the queue with priority 2 is serviced. To add a queue called DRAFTMODE to PrinterQ at priority 2, for example, use the following command:

```
Q ADD DRAFTMODE AT PRIORITY 2
```

All the preceding commands can be entered into the file server at the DOS prompt. The best place for these commands, however, is the AUTOEXEC.SYS file, which you can edit in the SYSCON Supervisor Options. When entered at the prompt, these commands are valid only while the file server remains running. Downing the file server loses all the command's information except queue names. Placing these commands in the AUTOEXEC.SYS file ensures that they are executed whenever the file server is rebooted.

Section Review Questions

36. Which of the following commands adds a queue called ACCOUNTING to the network?

    a. CREATE Q ACCOUNTING

    b. ADD Q ACCOUNTING

    c. Q ACCOUNTING CREATE

    d. Q ADD ACCOUNTING

37. The printing service in NetWare 2.2 that lets you connect a printer to a server is called:

    a. Core

    b. Server

    c. Remote

    d. Local

38. Which file is NOT used for printing and print services?

    a. CAPTURE

    b. ENDCAP

    c. NPRINT

    d. RCONSOLE.VAP

39. What action (considered a drawback of using core printing) must you take with the file server if you attach a printer before bringing up a print server?

   a. Reset port parameters

   b. Down the server

   c. Choose dedicated server option

   d. Install a special printer port

40. How many queues are normally assigned to one printer?

   a. 1

   b. 3

   c. 5

   4. 6

41. Which statement is NOT necessary to fully enable a printer using core printing?

   a. P 0 CREATE LPT1

   b. Q 0 ADD DOTMAXQ

   c. S 0 TO DOTMAXQ

   d. CAPTURE Q=DOTMAXQ

Answers

36. d

37. a

38. d

39. b

40. a

41. d

Creating Custom Menus

Menus make access to applications easy for end users. By using menus, users never have to learn what drives a program. Instead, they can focus their efforts in more productive areas. Many third-party menu programs are available, but few have the simplicity and network compatibility that the menus in NetWare offer. One of the most appealing features of NetWare menus is the cost—they are free with the NetWare operating system.

If you can write DOS batch files, you have an excellent background for writing a menu in NetWare. Almost anything that you can accomplish using a batch file you also can do—with the same syntax—using a menu script.

Note Menu files are DOS text files with the extension MNU. All the files displayed in figure 10.7 are menus.

```
F:\MENUS>dir *.mnu

   Volume in drive F is SYS
   Directory of  F:\MENUS

12-2     MNU     557   7-31-91   2:40p
ADMINS   MNU     494  10-04-90   6:23p
SALES    MNU    1314   8-07-89   4:44p
BACKUP   MNU     425   8-13-90   1:21p
ACCOUNT  MNU    5171   4-15-91   1:05p
WORK     MNU    2072   7-25-90   1:36p
         6 File(s)   32436224 bytes free

F:\MENUS>
```

Figure 10.7

Examples of menu files.

By calling a batch file from within a menu, you might experience unreliable results. You should replicate all commands within a batch file in the menu script for smooth execution.

Menu Format

This section discusses the format that you can use to create a menu. In NetWare, you can create menus by using any text editor. The following list outlines the format of a menu file:

◆ Precede menu and submenu names with a percent sign (%) and line them up with the left margin.

◆ Left-align the options you want to use as items that users can choose from a menu.

◆ Make sure that all executable statements appear on their own lines and are indented at least one space.

◆ Indent and use a percent sign (%) when calling a submenu.

◆ Make sure that no spaces exist between the percent sign (%) and a menu name.

◆ When defining a submenu, make sure that the menu name is identical to the way it is called. If you call a submenu %UTILITIES, for example, you must match the name when you later define it.

You can place menus and submenus anywhere on-screen and use one of eight colors as defined in NetWare's COLORPAL utility. After you name the menu, you must define three fields, which are separated with commas.

 The syntax used for defining a menu's placement on the screen and which color palette it should use is as follows:

%MENUNAME , ROW# , COLUMN# , COLOR#

The order is row (from 1-24), column (from 1-80), and color. The row and column fields make up the size of the computer screen.

Do not use any spaces on this line.

In NetWare, the on-screen coordinates 12,40 are the default coordinates of menus. This point is the middle of a typical screen. You can place menus at any location on-screen; they will not wrap if you do not give the menu enough room. The coordinates 1,1 place the menu in the upper left corner, 1,80 in the upper right corner, 24,1 in the lower left corner, and 24,80 in the lower right corner.

To determine where you want to place your menu on-screen, you need to plan on a screen that has coordinates of 24 rows and 80 columns. You calculate menu positions by specifying the point at which the center of the menu should be placed.

You then need to determine the size of the menu. Figure the number of lines you want above the menu by making a rough sketch of the menu on lined paper. Your menu should be large enough to accommodate the desired text for the menu. The size of the menu is determined by the length of the menu text and the number of options in the menu. You need to determine where the middle of the menu needs to be placed.

You now need to decide the number of blank lines on the monitor you want above the menu. Next, count the number of lines you want in the menu and divide that number by two. This step locates the starting point of the menu at the middle of the screen. Add these two numbers together to determine the placement of the menu on the vertical axis, known as the *vertical placement*, as follows:

> # of lines above menu + (# of menu lines / 2) = row

If you want a menu that has six lines above the menu and six lines in the menu, for example, the vertical placement is 9.

Next, determine the number of columns you want before a menu. Count the number of characters in the longest menu item and divide by two. Add these two numbers together to determine the placement of the menu on the horizontal axis, known as the *horizontal placement*, as follows:

> # of columns before menu + (# of columns in longest menu option / 2) = column

The following is the syntax of a menu in NetWare:

```
%main menu name,row,column,color
option
  %submenu
option
    executable
%submenu,row,column,color
option
    executable
```

In the preceding syntax, the %main menu name,row,column,color line specifies the name of the menu. It also specifies the placement of the menu on-screen and the color of the menu. The option line specifies the names of the available options that you want to display on the menu. The %submenu line calls a submenu option, where an additional menu is defined. The executable line specifies the commands that can call the menu option.

Menu Requirements

 NetWare requires you to have Read and File Scan rights in the directory that holds the *menu* (MNU) files. In addition, you need Read, Write, Create, Erase, Modify, and File Scan rights in the directory in which you call a menu.

In the optimum condition, MNU files are flagged as Read Only, and Read, Write, Create, Erase, Modify, and File Scan are the user's trustee rights in that directory.

Two sets of files are created when you use the NetWare MENU utility: GO*.BAT and RESTART*.BAT. These pointer files are used to call programs from a menu. The system creates one of each of these files for each user running the menu. These files tell the system where you are when you call a program and the way to get back when you are finished.

 These files are *recyclable*—you never have more on your system than you have users using the menus. When a user exits the menu properly by pressing Esc and selecting Yes, or by selecting the logout option, these files are erased.

Limiting where a user can call a menu is a good idea; otherwise, you might find these files scattered throughout the network. To limit a user to one directory for calling menus, make sure that the user is aware of the acceptable location (directory) if the user calls a menu from a DOS prompt. Another way to make sure that a user is in the proper directory is to place him there in a login script and call the menu from the login script. This method is discussed in the section on menu-calling procedures.

NetWare enables you to exit from a menu by using the LOGOUT command. The network knows the way to close all open files, including the GO*.BAT and RESTART*.BAT files. When you exit in this manner, however, you are disconnecting yourself from the place where these files are kept. As a result, the menu program that was brought into the workstation's memory gives two error messages. The message Batch File Missing displays twice. The program is searching for the GO*.BAT and RESTART*.BAT files, but now you are logged out of the network.

 Because users often are frightened by error messages, NetWare enables you to use the !LOGOUT command from a menu. The exclamation point (!) simply blocks the error messages from the screen.

Menu-Calling Procedures

Now that the menu is created and the rights are established, you need to bring the menu up on-screen. This step enables you to use the menu on your workstation. To call a menu from the DOS prompt, use the MENU command and type the name of the menu file name, as follows:

```
MENU filename
```

The MNU extension is optional, because MENU knows to look for a file with an MNU extension. In figure 10.8, for example, the menu SALES is called from the menu subdirectory.

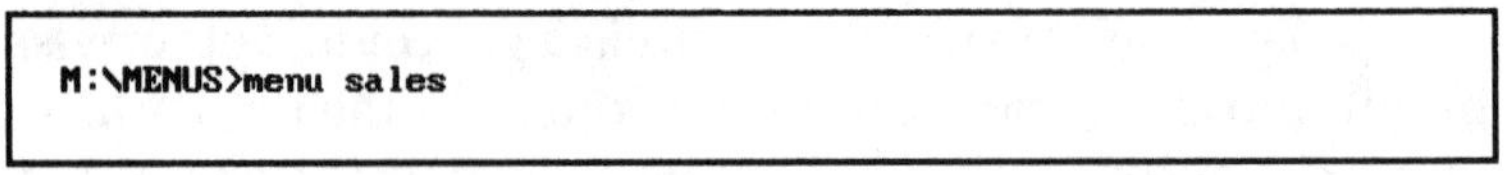

Figure 10.8

Calling a menu from the DOS prompt.

```
M:\MENUS>menu sales
```

NetWare offers several ways to call a menu from a login script. The best method is to create a batch file that calls the menu. You then should call the batch file from the EXIT statement, as follows:

```
EXIT NETMENU
```

In this example, the file NETMENU.BAT is in a directory mapped earlier in the menu. It contains the following command:

```
MENU NETMENU
```

Another method to call a menu is to use the # call. This method enables you to return to the login script when you exit from the menu. The following is an example of calling up a menu by using the # call:

```
#MENU NETMENU
```

This method does require more workstation memory, however. For more information, see the earlier section on login commands.

Techniques for Setting Up Menus

Many methods are available for setting up menu options. In this section, you examine a menu and learn a few hints for creating a clean, smooth-working menu environment. The following example is a menu created for the Sales department. The following file is called SALES.MNU:

```
%Sales Dept Main Menu
Applications
    %Application Menu
Utilities
    %Utilities Menu
Logout
    !LOGOUT
%Application Menu,1,1,3
Data Base
    map insert s3:=sys:apps\db
    map f:=sys:data\sales\db
```

```
          f:
          datab
          m:
          map del s3:
          map del f:
Spread Sheet
          map insert s3:=sys:apps\s2
          map f:=sys:data\sales\ss
          f:
          ssheet
          m:
       map del s3:
          map del f:
%Utilities Menu,24,80,5
Send a Message
          Send " @1"Type a message" " @2"Send it to?"
Capture Settings
          Capture q=@1"Type Queue Name" c=@2"# of Copies?" @3"FF or
                      NFF?"
Ncopy a File
          NCOPY @1"Source path/file" @2"Destination"
```

After you create this menu as a text file, type **MENU SALES** at the DOS prompt. The screen that appears is shown in figure 10.9. Notice that NetWare puts the options in alphabetical order. If you want options listed in a different order, you must place numbers in front of the options; MENU will display the items in numerical order.

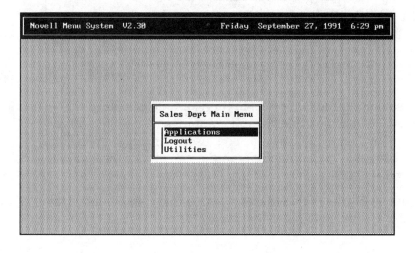

Figure 10.9

The Sales Dept Main Menu screen.

Note If you number the menu options, you need to remember the way a computer counts. Numbering the options 1, 2, 3, and so on works fine as long as you do not use the number 10. When a computer reads the number 10, 10 falls between 1 and 2. Use two-digit numbers, such as 01, 02, 03, and so on if you need more options. A more conventional method is to use letters instead of numbers.

When you press Enter while the Applications option is highlighted, NetWare calls up the Application menu (see fig. 10.10). In this menu, two options are available—Data Base and Spread Sheet. You now can choose one of these options by highlighting it and pressing Enter. This action executes the commands contained under the option you select.

Figure 10.10

The Application menu.

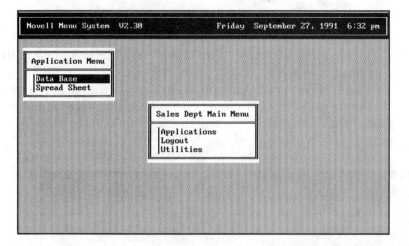

The idea behind the mappings in this example is to keep the system as lean as possible. Search mappings take up file server memory. By leaving drives mapped, users can get at them from DOS more easily. Keeping the mappings in menus instead of the login script works well.

In figure 10.11, the system maps a search drive and a data drive. Then the system changes to the data drive and calls the program.

710

At this point, the application, such as the Spread Sheet option, starts. You then exit the spreadsheet program after you finish working in it.

```
M:\MENUS>map insert s3:=sys:apps\ss

SEARCH3:  = X:. [CDI286\SYS:  \APPS\SS]

M:\MENUS>map f:=sys:data\sales\ss

Drive  F: = CDI286\SYS:  \DATA\SALES\SS

M:\MENUS>f:
```

Figure 10.11

Choosing the Spread Sheet option.

As figure 10.12 shows, when you exit from the application, the system returns to the default directory. This ensures that GO*.BAT and RESTART*.BAT are deleted properly. The network then deletes the search drive and the data drive. The last step takes the user back to the menu.

```
F:\DATA\SALES\SS>m:

M:\MENUS>map del s3:

The search mapping for drive X: was deleted

M:\MENUS>map del f:

The mapping for drive F: has been deleted.

M:\MENUS>
```

Figure 10.12

Exiting the application to display the remaining executables.

Press Esc to close the option menu and to return to the Sales Dept Main Menu. The next choice is the Utilities option (see fig. 10.13). Under this option, several commands have been added that need user input. To get the user to answer questions, the menu utility allows input variables designated as @1 through @9.

Input Variables

Input variables enable the user to type information into a window from the menu. This information is sent to the DOS prompt for execution. This feature is helpful if users have different needs for calling programs. A good example is printing by using the CAP-TURE command. Different users might need to print to different queue names. The following option enables the users to input the appropriate queue name:

```
CAPTURE Q=@1"ENTER QUEUENAME"
```

Figure 10.13

The Utilities menu.

You can use up to nine windows for each command, such as @1, @2, ..., @9. Enter the prompt that the user sees on-screen between the quotation marks in the preceding syntax.

The next item that you can choose is the Capture Settings option, which enables you to see the Type Queue Name prompt (see fig. 10.14). This prompt asks you for the name of the printer queue you want to use. When you created the menu, you placed the input question within quotation marks. No space exists between the input variable and the quotation marks. For the prompt to work, make sure that you do not insert spaces between the input question and the quotation marks. Spaces cause the window to fail to appear, and the command will be issued with an error.

As you answer each prompt that appears on-screen, NetWare stores the information until you answer all the questions. NetWare then sends the information to the DOS prompt.

712

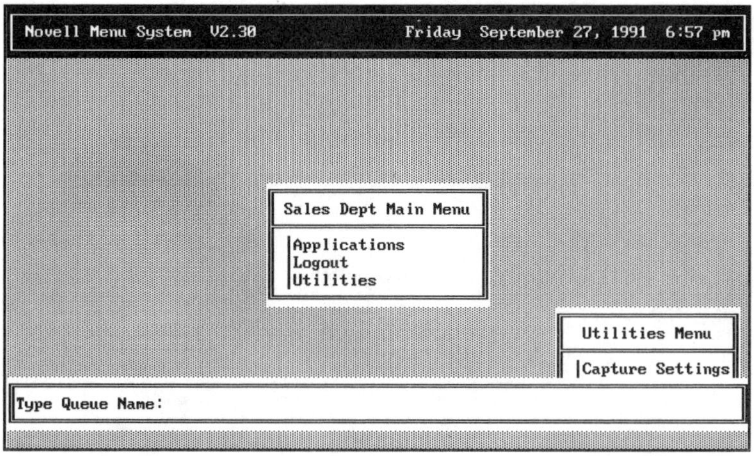

Figure 10.14

The Type Queue Name input box.

In figures 10.15 through 10.18, for example, NetWare prompts you for the printer queue name, number of copies, and whether you want form feed. After you answer the last question, NetWare returns you to the DOS prompt. You now can print by using the CAPTURE options.

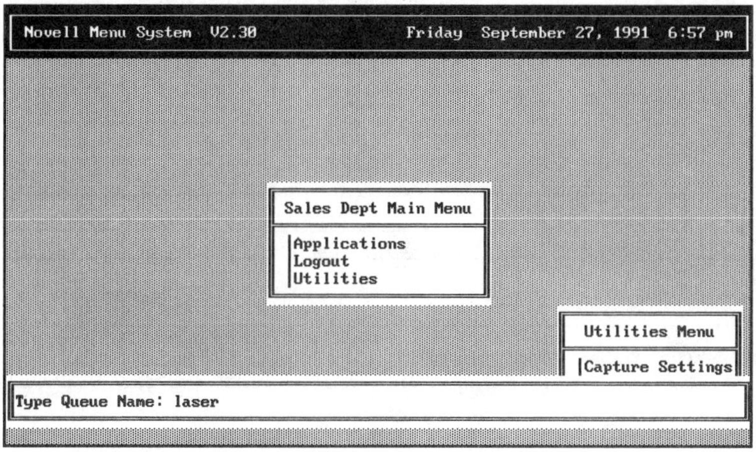

Figure 10.15

Inputting the name of the queue.

713

Figure 10.16

Inputting the number of copies for the printer.

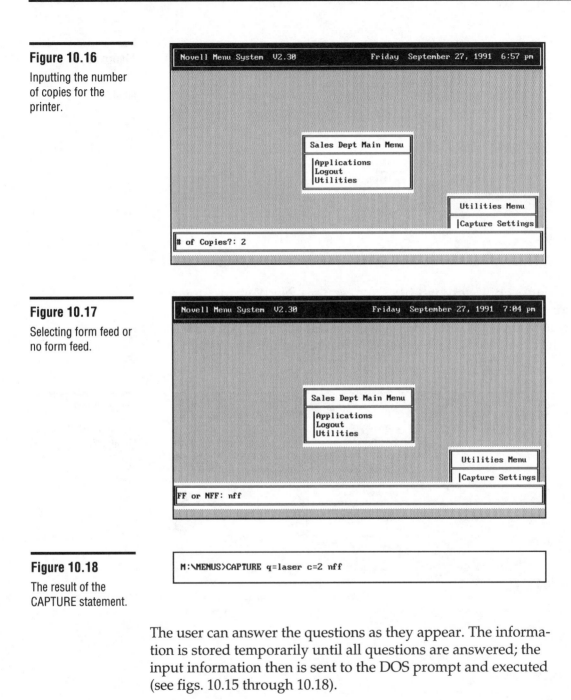

```
Novell Menu System  V2.30              Friday  September 27, 1991  6:57 pm


                                    Sales Dept Main Menu

                                    Applications
                                    Logout
                                    Utilities

                                                           Utilities Menu

                                                          Capture Settings

 # of Copies?: 2
```

Figure 10.17

Selecting form feed or no form feed.

```
Novell Menu System  V2.30              Friday  September 27, 1991  7:04 pm




                                    Sales Dept Main Menu

                                    Applications
                                    Logout
                                    Utilities

                                                           Utilities Menu

                                                          Capture Settings

 FF or NFF: nff
```

Figure 10.18

The result of the CAPTURE statement.

```
M:\MENUS>CAPTURE q=laser c=2 nff
```

The user can answer the questions as they appear. The information is stored temporarily until all questions are answered; the input information then is sent to the DOS prompt and executed (see figs. 10.15 through 10.18).

This example shows you the way to create a menu that enables you to set up a CAPTURE statement. This type of statement helps you automate NetWare for yourself as well as for all end users on the network. To take full advantage of NetWare's utilities, look for ways to automate every repetitious or time-consuming task. Be creative with menus. The interface truly helps users become comfortable with using network utilities.

Section Review Questions

42. Which statement about menus is false?

    a. All items to be chosen from one menu must be left-aligned.

    b. All executable statements must be on their own line.

    c. A space is necessary between the % and the menu name.

    d. Submenu names must match identically where they are defined and then called for use.

43. The program used to change the colors for menus is called:

    a. COLORPAL

    b. PALETTE

    c. COLORMNU

    d. COLORS

44. The default position for a menu is:

    a. 12,40

    b. 24,80

    c. 1,24

    d. 40,12

45. Which of the following is NOT a valid way to call the menu CDI.MNU from a login script?

    a. `#MENU CDI.MNU`

    b. `MENU CDI`

    c. `EXIT "MENU CDI"`

    d. `EXIT "CALLMENU"`, where `CALLMENU` is a batch file that contains the command MENU CDI

46. Which of the following is NOT one of the commands for specifying menu placement or color?

    a. ROW#

    b. COLUMN#

    c. CELL#

    d. COLOR#

47. How many color options for menus does NetWare 2.2 provide?

    a. 2

    b. 5

    c. 6

    d. 8

Answers

42. c

43. a

44. a

45. b

46. c

47. d

Running WSGEN to Create Workstation Files

In this section, you learn to use the *workstation generation program* (WSGEN) to generate IPX drivers, part of the workstation files required to log in to a NetWare 2.2 file server. Many NetWare 2.2 sites now use the NetWare DOS Requester, and no longer need to use WSGEN. However, if you should work at a company that uses WSGEN, then this information may be of some use to you.

Running WSGEN to Generate IPX

WSGEN is not available in NetWare 3.12.

The WSGEN utility configures a file that DOS workstations must use to gain access to the network. When you use WSGEN, you generate a file called IPX.COM. IPX stands for *Internetwork Packet Exchange*.

The WSGEN program and the NetWare 2.2 install program are actually menu-driven linkers. These programs enable you to select the program modules and link them to the customized executable files needed to log in to the network. In the case of WSGEN, you are linking the network board drivers with a file named IPX.OBJ to form IPX.COM.

You can run the WSGEN program from a floppy drive or hard disk. If you run the program from a floppy drive, you first must create a copy of the original disk. The original Novell disk is write-protected, and WSGEN must create a new IPX.COM file for you. Novell supplies a number of network card drivers with the

WSGEN program. If the driver you need is not included with the Novell disks, you also need a driver disk from the hardware manufacturer. Network card drivers generally are found on a disk shipped with the interface card and must be placed on a floppy disk with the electronic label LAN_DRV_*xxx*, in which *xxx* is a three-digit number designated by the manufacturer.

The syntax for the DOS LABEL command is LA-BEL A:LAN_DRV_*xxx*. Refer to your DOS reference manual for more information.

When WSGEN runs, it searches all floppy drives for disks with these labels and includes the appropriate drivers in the lists presented to you for selection.

System Administrators can set up a directory on their local hard drive or on the network to provide a fast method for creating network shells when needed. To set up the required directories, you need a main directory. The examples in this section assume you name this directory SHELLS.

After you use the DOS MD command to create a SHELLS directory, create a subdirectory named WSGEN. Then copy the contents of the Novell WSGEN disk into the \SHELLS\WSGEN directory. If any optional LAN drivers are required, you must copy them into directories that have the same name as the floppy disk that contains the drivers. To allow for a floppy name with more than eight characters, place a period (.) before the last three characters or numbers, as in the following example:

```
\SHELLS\WSGEN\
            |
            |-LAN_DRV_.001
            |
            |-LAN_DRV_.002
```

Novell's WSGEN program looks for this label to locate the driver files.

Next, copy the WSGEN.EXE file into the SHELLS directory. You then can execute the WSGEN program from this directory by typing **WSGEN** and pressing Enter. NetWare displays a screen like the one shown in figure 10.19.

When this screen appears, press Enter to continue.

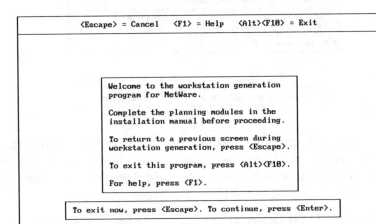

```
      <Escape> = Cancel    <F1> = Help    <Alt><F10> = Exit


              Welcome to the workstation generation
              program for NetWare.

              Complete the planning modules in the
              installation manual before proceeding.

              To return to a previous screen during
              workstation generation, press <Escape>.

              To exit this program, press <Alt><F10>.

              For help, press <F1>.

         To exit now, press <Escape>. To continue, press <Enter>.
```

Figure 10.19

The WSGEN opening screen.

> **Note**
>
> If WSGEN appears to lock up while searching the floppy drives, reboot the computer and check your directory structures. This problem is common when you try to run the WSGEN program from the wrong directory.

The next screen that appears is the driver-selection screen (see fig. 10.20). At this screen, select the appropriate network board driver required by your network interface card. Simply use the arrow keys to scroll up or down until you find the correct driver.

If the driver you need does not appear in the selection window, the driver might not be included with NetWare or the driver disk might not be installed correctly. If you install a LAN_DRV_.*xxx* directory, make sure that the underscores (_) and the period (.) are correct. If you create a LAN_DRV_.*xxx* directory, make sure that you do not confuse the underscore character (_) with the dash character (–).

Figure 10.20

The driver-selection screen.

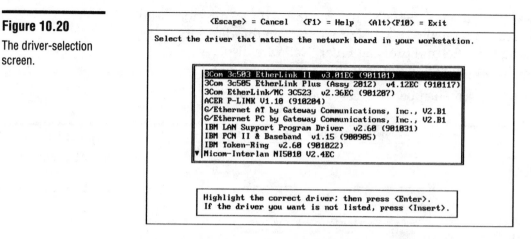

```
          <Escape> = Cancel    <F1> = Help    <Alt><F10> = Exit

Select the driver that matches the network board in your workstation.


      3Com 3c503 EtherLink II   v3.01EC (901101)
      3Com 3c505 EtherLink Plus (Assy 2012)  v4.12EC (910117)
      3Com EtherLink/MC 3C523   v2.36EC (901207)
      ACER P-LINK V1.10 (910204)
      G/Ethernet AT by Gateway Communications, Inc., V2.B1
      G/Ethernet PC by Gateway Communications, Inc., V2.B1
      IBM LAN Support Program Driver   v2.60 (901031)
      IBM PCN II & Baseband   v1.15 (900905)
      IBM Token-Ring   v2.60 (901022)
    ▼ Micom-Interlan NI5010 V2.4EC


      Highlight the correct driver; then press <Enter>.
      If the driver you want is not listed, press <Insert>.
```

Another way to handle the addition of new drivers is to press Ins while the driver-selection screen is visible. NetWare then prompts you to insert the disk that contains the additional drivers. The new drivers then are added to the list of available drivers.

When you locate the desired driver, press Enter. The screen shown in figure 10.21 appears.

Figure 10.21

The hardware configuration screen.

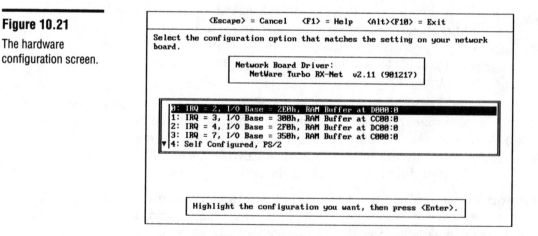

```
          <Escape> = Cancel    <F1> = Help    <Alt><F10> = Exit

Select the configuration option that matches the setting on your network
board.
            Network Board Driver:
               NetWare Turbo RX-Net  v2.11 (901217)


      0: IRQ = 2, I/O Base = 2E0h, RAM Buffer at D000:0
      1: IRQ = 3, I/O Base = 300h, RAM Buffer at CC00:0
      2: IRQ = 4, I/O Base = 2F0h, RAM Buffer at DC00:0
      3: IRQ = 7, I/O Base = 350h, RAM Buffer at C000:0
    ▼ 4: Self Configured, PS/2


      Highlight the configuration you want, then press <Enter>.
```

You need to know a few things about the particular workstation on which you are working. This screen provides you with the hardware options supplied by the interface manufacturer. These options include interrupts, base memory address, I/O address, and DMA channels. The default option, 0, is usually a good choice for a standard workstation configuration. If your workstation has a modem, terminal emulator, or other special hardware, you need to have all the equipment settings available. When selecting a configuration option, you need to be aware of all the additional interface card settings in the computer.

 You should make a list of all card settings. This list can help you locate unused hardware settings that your network interface can use.

If none of the available choices appears to provide all the settings, select option 0. From here, you should be able to install a customized configuration with the JUMPERS utility, which is discussed in *NetWare Training Guide: Networking Technologies* and in *Inside Novell NetWare*, both from New Riders Publishing.

Use table 10.3 to determine the standard PC hardware settings. The table includes I/O addresses, memory addresses, interrupts, and DMA channels used by common equipment.

Table 10.3
Common Hardware Configurations

Device	INT	I/O Decode (h)	MEM Decode	DMA
Com1	4	3F8-3FF	-	-
Com2	3	2F8-2FF	-	-
LPT1	7	378-37F	-	-
LPT2 (cannot be used with XT controller)	5	278-27F	-	-
If LPT3 exists, LPT1	7	3BC-3BE	-	-
LPT2	5	378-37A	-	-
LPT3	-	278-27A	-	-

continues

721

Table 10.3, Continued
Common Hardware Configurations

Device	INT	I/O Decode (h)	MEM Decode	DMA
XT controller	5	320-32F	C800:0000-3FFF	3
AT controller	14	1F0-1F8 170-177	- -	- -
Floppy controller	6	1F0-1F8 3F0-3F7	-	2
Tape controller	5	280-28F	-	3
Novell disk coprocessor	11.10, 12, or 13	#1 340-347 #2 348-34F	-	-
Novell SCSI adapter	2, 3, or 5	340-343 (enhanced only)	D000:0000-7FFF	1, 3, or none
EGA	2	3C0-3CF	A000:0000-1FFFE or B000:0000-7FFF or B800:0000-7FFF	0
Monochrome adapter	-	3B0-3BF	B000:0000--7FFF	0
Color graphics adapter	-	3D0-3DF	B800:0000-7FFF	0
Hercules	-	3B4-3BF	B000:0000-7FFF	-
monochrome (286A server)	-	-	B800:0000-7FFF	-

After you select a configuration option, press Enter to begin the linking process. After you select the hardware option, NetWare displays your choice and prompts you for confirmation. Select Yes to confirm your selection or No to abort (see fig. 10.22).

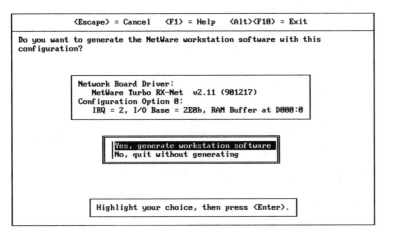

Figure 10.22

Confirming your selection.

If the link process runs without error, NetWare displays a screen that informs you when workstation software generation is complete. At this time, you can copy the IPX.COM file from the \SHELLS\WSGEN directory to your workstation boot disk along with the appropriate shell: NETX.COM, XMSNETX.EXE, or EMSNETX.EXE.

Logging In through DOS

After you successfully generate your workstation files and copy them to your boot disk, you are ready to attach to the NetWare file server.

You can issue the following commands manually or place them in a batch file in the order listed (you can replace NETX with the optional XMSNETX or EMSNETX):

```
IPX
NETX
F:
LOGIN fileserver name/username
```

723

The drive letter F might not be available on some workstations; the number of drive letters available depends on the number of locally attached hard drives or on the CONFIG.SYS file's LASTDRIVE setting. The login drive is the first available unused drive letter.

When you issue the IPX and NETX commands, NetWare displays the information shown in figure 10.23.

Figure 10.23

A sample screen that appears after you successfully attach to the file server.

```
[DR DOS] C:\SH386>ipx
Novell IPX/SPX v3.04 (910703)
(C) Copyright 1985, 1991 Novell Inc.  All Rights Reserved.

LAN Option: NetWare Turbo RX-Net  v2.11 (901217)
Hardware Configuration: IO: 350; MEM: D800; IRQ: 5 (Jumpers Config)

[DR DOS] C:\SH386>netx

NetWare V3.22 - Workstation Shell (910731)
(C) Copyright 1991 Novell, Inc.  All Rights Reserved.

Running on DOS V3.31

Using configuration file SHELL.CFG
SHOW DOTS ON

Attached to server CDI
09-30-91    5:06:13 pm

[DR DOS] C:\SH386>
```

First, examine the NetWare LOGIN command. The LOGIN command is located in the SYS:\LOGIN directory, and you can issue the command from that directory to access the file server's resources.

After your workstation loads the NetWare shell, it transparently attaches to the nearest file server. After moving to the LOGIN drive (which usually is drive F), issue the LOGIN command. At the F:\LOGIN\> prompt, for example, enter the following:

        LOGIN

NetWare prompts for your login name and password. After you successfully enter the requested information, you have access to the other services for which you have privileges. If your system utilizes more than one file server, you can prefix your login name with the file server's name. You can, for example, enter the following at the F:\LOGIN\> prompt:

`LOGIN SALES\TOM`

After the preceding information is entered, the program prompts Tom to enter his password. After Tom enters his password, NetWare processes the request for access to the SALES file server.

If your login script attaches you to more than one file server, LOGIN determines whether all passwords are valid. If a password has expired, you are prompted to change it. If you change your password, LOGIN asks if you want to synchronize all passwords on all servers. If you answer Yes, the password becomes the same on all attached servers.

The IPX, NETX, XMSNETX, and EMSNETX programs each have optional command-line switches that can simplify the network Administrator's job.

IPX

IPX.COM provides five options, as shown in figure 10.24:

- **-I or /I**—Displays an informational screen. This option is handy for determining the version and hardware setting of the IPX you are using (see fig. 10.25).

- **-D or /D**—Displays all available options.

- **-O or /O*x***—Use this option to set IPX to use a hardware setting displayed with the D option.

- **-C or /C**—Enables advanced users to use a special configuration file rather than the Novell default SHELL.CFG or NET.CFG.

- **-? or /?**—Displays all available options (see fig. 10.25).

725

The /D and /O*x* command-line switches are handy when you need to test a shell or when a shell is included in the batch file. These switches enable you to use any standard configuration without relinking the IPX program.

Figure 10.24

The IPX options.

```
C:\SH386>ipx ?
Novell IPX/SPX v3.04 (910703)
(C) Copyright 1985, 1991 Novell Inc.  All Rights Reserved.

LAN Option: NetWare Turbo RX-Net  v2.11 (901217)
Hardware Configuration: IO: 350; MEM: D800; IRQ: 5 (Jumpers Config)


Usage: IPX [options]
valid options:
          -I or /I                  Display version information
          -D or /D                  Display hardware options
          -O or /O<num>             Load using hardware option <num>
          -C or /C=[path]<filename> Use an alternate configuration file

          -? or /?                  Display this help screen

C:\SH386>
```

Figure 10.25

Displaying version information.

```
C:\SH386>ipx i
Novell IPX/SPX v3.04 (910703)
(C) Copyright 1985, 1991 Novell Inc.  All Rights Reserved.

LAN Option: NetWare Turbo RX-Net  v2.11 (901217)
Hardware Configuration: IO: 350; MEM: D800; IRQ: 5 (Jumpers Config)

C:\SH386>
```

Permanently configuring the IPX program for normal use is still a good idea. Doing so saves confusion if the user attempts to load IPX without the batch file.

NETX, XMSNETX, and EMSNETX

NETX, XMSNETX, and EMSNETX provide the following three options:

◆ **-I or /I**—Displays an informational screen (see fig. 10.26).

◆ **-U or /U**—Uninstalls or removes the shell from memory.

◆ **-PS or /PS (Preferred Server)**—Specifies the server from which you get the LOGIN command.

```
C:\SH386>netx i

NetWare V3.22 - Workstation Shell (910731)
(C) Copyright 1991 Novell, Inc.  All Rights Reserved.

C:\SH386>
```

Figure 10.26
Displaying version information.

NetBIOS

NetBIOS provides the following two options:

- **-I or /I**—Displays an informational screen.
- **-U or /U**—Uninstalls or removes NetBIOS from memory.

When using the /U command-line switch, make sure that the programs are removed in the opposite order from which they were installed. You might receive unpredictable results if you unload any memory-resident program that might have another program loaded in after it.

Section Review Questions

48. What is an identifier variable?

    a. A variable used in creating menus that enables the user to answer questions.

    b. A variable that returns known information about NLMs.

    c. A variable that returns known information about network objects, such as time of day and login name.

    d. A variable used in NET.CFG files.

49. Which statement about menus is false?

    a. All items to be chosen from one menu must be left-aligned.

    b. All executable statements must be on their own line.

c. A space is necessary between the % and the menu name.

d. Submenu names must match identically where they are defined and then called for use.

50. The program used to change the colors for menus is called:

a. COLORPAL

b. PALETTE

c. COLORMNU

d. COLORS

51. The default position for a menu is:

a. 12,40

b. 24,80

c. 1,24

d. 40,12

52. Which of the following are valid switches for IPX.COM?

a. /X, /D, /?, /C

b. -I, -D, -?, -U

c. /I, /D, /O, /C

d. -I, -D, -O, -U

53. Which of the following is the correct order to load the following files to log in to the network?

a. IPX, NETX, F:, LOGIN

b. NETX, IPX, F:, LOGIN

c. IPX, F:, NETX, LOGIN

d. NETX, F:, IPX, LOGIN

54. Which of the following is the correct order to load the following files to log in to the network?

    a. LSL, IPXODI, NE2000, NETX, F:, LOGIN

    b. NE2000, LSL, IPXODI, NETX, F:, LOGIN

    c. LSL, NE2000, IPXODI, NETX, F:, LOGIN

    d. NE2000, IPXODI, LSL, NETX, F:, LOGIN

Answers

48. c

49. a and c

50. a

51. a

52. c

53. a

54. c

Case Study

1. Why would you want to use a dedicated server rather than a nondedicated server?

2. List the steps necessary to add a VAP.

3. Describe the process of removing a VAP.

4. List and describe SFT Level II options.

5. Set up an AUTOEXEC.SYS that allows core printing to use two parallel printers and one serial printer. Use one queue per printer and make one of the parallel printers the default printer.

6. Create a menu with the following parameters:

   ◆ Provides access to three applications—one for spreadsheets, one for accounting, and one for word processing. Use applications with which you are familiar.

   ◆ Has a submenu with several NetWare menu utilities.

   ◆ Has a submenu with SEND, NCOPY, and NDIR. Use input variables.

   ◆ Places submenus in different positions on the screen and makes them in different colors.

Understanding NetWare 2.2 Advanced System Manager Functions

CHAPTER 11

This chapter focuses on NetWare 2.2 Advanced System Manager issues, which differ from the NetWare 3.1*x* Advanced Administration objectives. The topics covered in this chapter are as follows:

- ◆ NetWare 2.2 installation
- ◆ Network management using FCONSOLE
- ◆ NetWare 2.2 memory

Installing NetWare 2.2

Choose the correct installation mode for your network environment.

You can install NetWare 2.2 from floppy disks, hard disks, or a network drive.

Install NetWare 2.2 in the chosen mode.

When you install from floppies, first make disk copies of the following disks: SYSTEM-1, SYSTEM-2, OSOBJ, and OSEXE. Program files are written to these four disks as they are created by the installation program.

When installing from a local hard drive or a network drive, you must copy the appropriate floppies into the directories having the same name as the floppies. This procedure can be done manually, but NetWare 2.2 has a utility that does this for you automatically. This utility is called UPLOAD and is found on the SYSTEM-1 disk.

When you finish generating the operating system and want to put the changed files onto the appropriate disk, you must run the DOWNLOAD program on the SYSTEM-1 disk.

The installation program for NetWare 2.2 is broken into four modules, each having a specific function. These modules are as follows:

◆ Module 1: Operating System Generation

◆ Module 2: Linking and Configuring

◆ Module 3: Track Zero Test (ZTEST)

◆ Module 4: File Server Definition

Module 1: Operating System Generation

This module enables you to do the following:

◆ Select Dedicated or Nondedicated mode for the file server

◆ Select the number of communications buffers (discussed later in this chapter)

+ Select and configure the network boards

+ Select and configure the disk controllers

Module 2: Linking and Configuring

This module creates executable files from the configuration information set up in Module 1. The linked and configured files include the following:

+ **ZTEST.EXE.** This file performs the ZTEST in Module 3.

+ **INSTOVL.EXE.** This file is the INSTallation OVerLay used when you install NetWare 2.2.

+ **COMPSURF.EXE.** This file performs a COMPrehensive SURFace analysis. Many hard drives are *NetWare-ready*, which means that they have been tested thoroughly and do not require another exhaustive surface test. Older drives and drives not known to be NetWare-ready should be tested to ensure integrity. COMPSURF tests the entire disk for bad blocks.

+ **VREPAIR.EXE.** VREPAIR is used to repair problem volumes. In NetWare 2.2, VREPAIR is configured for the hardware options you choose when you generate the operating system.

+ **NET$OS.EXE.** This file is the NetWare 2.2 Operating System.

Module 3: Track Zero Test

This module performs the ZTEST, which is used to check the integrity of Track Zero on the hard drive. *Track Zero* is the boot track on a hard drive and must be clear of defects for NetWare to load.

Module 4: File Server Definition

This module is used to fine-tune file server parameters. With Module 4, you can perform the following tasks:

◆ Name the file server

◆ Limit hard drive space

◆ Assign volumes

◆ Set up the drives for mirroring

◆ Set a flag to prompt for loading the Macintosh VAP

Starting the INSTALL Program

The modules described in the preceding section are accessed through the INSTALL menu or command-line variables.

Understand the options available during operating system installation.

The following list explains each installation option and which modules they execute.

-E: Expert—Advanced Installation

Use this option to install a new system. This option completes modules 1 through 4 if you answer Yes to the question, "Will this machine be the server?"

This question appears in the first input screen of the install option. Figure 11.1 shows an example of this screen.

The -E option completes modules 1 and 2 if you answer No to the question, "Will this machine be the server?"

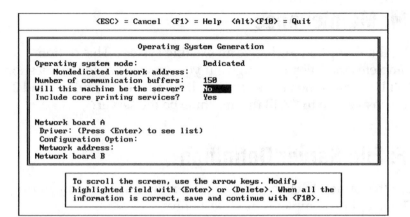

Figure 11.1

The first input screen of Advanced installation.

-L: Linked or Linking Complete

This option is used when you answer No to "Will this machine be the server?" with another option, and you are attempting to complete the installation. Variables that -L can follow include -M and -U. Make sure that -L follows another letter; do not use this option alone. If you put -L first, it automatically performs the ZTEST on the drive. This option completes modules 3 and 4.

-N: No Linking

Use this option if you are configuring an operating system for someone else and they will complete the installation. This option completes module 1. Follow this up with INSTALL -C.

-C: Configuration Complete

Use -C to finish an INSTALL -N. This completes modules 2 through 4.

-M: Maintenance

Use the -M option to change an existing system. This option completes modules 1 through 4 if you answer Yes to the question "Will this machine be the server?" It completes modules 1 and 2 if you answer No to "Will this machine be the server?"

-F: File Server Definition

Use this option to change volumes, server names, and mirroring. The -F option completes module 4 only.

-U: Upgrade

Use this option to upgrade from a 2.*x* system.

No version of NetWare earlier than 2.0a can be upgraded by using the UPGRADE option of INSTALL.

Changing from 3.*x* to 2.*x* is not considered an upgrade. No utility facilitates going backward from 3.*x*.

The -U option completes modules 1 through 4 if you answer Yes to "Will this machine be the server?"; it completes modules 1 and 2 if you answer No to this question.

Investigating the INSTALL Options

Choose the correct installation options for your network environment.

In the main menu of the INSTALL program, as shown in figure 11.2, you see four options: Basic installation, Advanced installation, Maintain existing system, and Upgrade from NetWare v2.*x*.

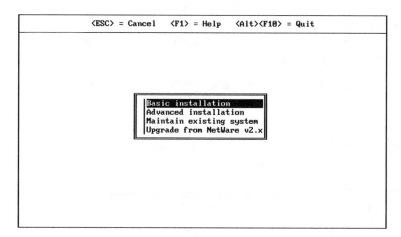

```
           <ESC> = Cancel    <F1> = Help    <Alt><F10> = Quit




                         ┌──────────────────────────┐
                         │Basic installation        │
                         │Advanced installation     │
                         │Maintain existing system  │
                         │Upgrade from NetWare v2.x │
                         └──────────────────────────┘
```

Figure 11.2
The INSTALL menu.

Basic Installation

You are asked only three questions when you install by using the Basic installation option. These questions ask for the following information:

- ◆ File server type: Dedicated or Nondedicated
- ◆ File server name
- ◆ Network board type

This method is the easiest and most restricted method of installation. When using Basic installation, the INSTALL program assumes that the following points are true:

- ◆ Only one file server is on the network. INSTALL sets the network number to 1.

- ◆ The file server has only one network board. (Each network board needs a unique number, and Basic installation does not give you the option to change the network number.)

- ◆ The file server has only one hard disk controller.

- ◆ The file server has one parallel printer attached.

Basic installation sets up everything needed for printing to one parallel printer attached to the file server.

◆ Basic installation expects all workstations on the network to run DOS. With the Basic installation option, you cannot load the Macintosh VAPs.

◆ The file server does not use internal routers (multiple network boards) or an external disk subsystem.

If any of the preceding statements are not true of your network, you will need to run Advanced installation.

 The Basic installation interrogates the CMOS in the file server to discover the disk controller type. Basic installation defaults to Option 0, or factory default settings.

Filling in the Blanks

This section guides you through both a basic and an advanced installation of a new file server. Complete your hardware installation and resolve any conflicts before proceeding.

 Install the NetWare 2.2 operating system in the chosen mode.

Basic Installation Demonstration

After you prepare your installation method, whether it is the floppy-drive, hard-drive, or network-disk method, you can start the install programs. The main INSTALL menu appears, as you saw in figure 11.2.

After you select the Basic installation option, you see the introduction screen, as shown in figure 11.3. This screen has a welcome and a warning message that confirms your choice.

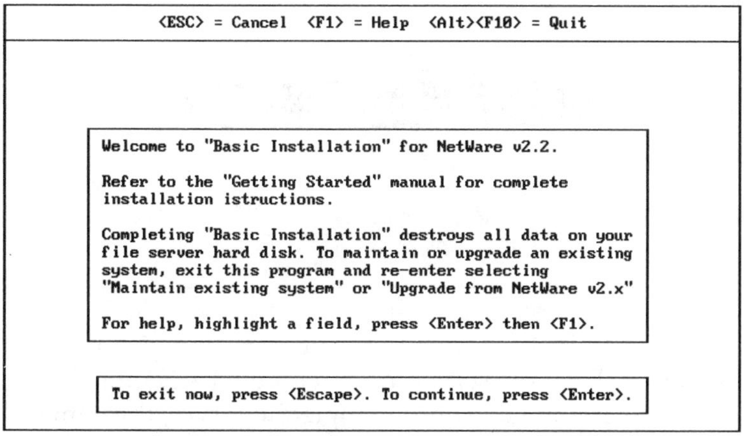

```
┌────────────────────────────────────────────────────────┐
│        <ESC> = Cancel  <F1> = Help  <Alt><F10> = Quit   │
├────────────────────────────────────────────────────────┤
│                                                         │
│                                                         │
│   ┌──────────────────────────────────────────────────┐ │
│   │ Welcome to "Basic Installation" for NetWare v2.2.│ │
│   │                                                  │ │
│   │ Refer to the "Getting Started" manual for complete│ │
│   │ installation istructions.                        │ │
│   │                                                  │ │
│   │ Completing "Basic Installation" destroys all data on your│ │
│   │ file server hard disk. To maintain or upgrade an existing│ │
│   │ system, exit this program and re-enter selecting │ │
│   │ "Maintain existing system" or "Upgrade from NetWare v2.x"│ │
│   │                                                  │ │
│   │ For help, highlight a field, press <Enter> then <F1>.│ │
│   └──────────────────────────────────────────────────┘ │
│                                                         │
│   ┌──────────────────────────────────────────────────┐ │
│   │ To exit now, press <Escape>. To continue, press <Enter>.│ │
│   └──────────────────────────────────────────────────┘ │
└────────────────────────────────────────────────────────┘
```

Figure 11.3

The introduction screen.

After confirming that you want to continue (by pressing Enter), you are asked to select the file server mode (see fig. 11.4), either dedicated or nondedicated. A *dedicated* file server is dedicated to the task of being a file server. Unless the system you are installing is small (up to five users) and has lightly used disk access, you should install in the dedicated mode. The option of using the file server as a workstation can sometimes be a problem rather than an advantage. To choose an option, simply highlight your choice and press Enter.

Many System Administrators do not realize the critical liability of operating a nondedicated file server. A nondedicated file server's processing power as a file server is greatly reduced by switching between the workstation and file server modes.

With a nondedicated file server, the system runs a much higher risk of system failure and data corruption. The single workstation user who operates programs on the file server has the ability to disrupt all other users if a program crashes or "hangs."

739

Figure 11.4

The file server mode menu.

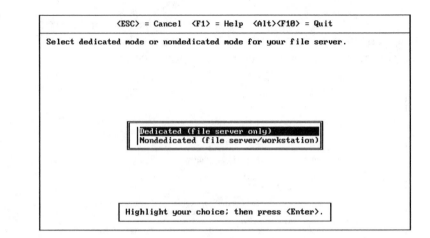

```
                    <ESC> = Cancel   <F1> = Help   <Alt><F10> = Quit

   Select dedicated mode or nondedicated mode for your file server.




                        ┌──────────────────────────────────────┐
                        │Dedicated (file server only)          │
                        │Nondedicated (file server/workstation)│
                        └──────────────────────────────────────┘




                   ┌──────────────────────────────────────────┐
                   │ Highlight your choice; then press <Enter>.│
                   └──────────────────────────────────────────┘
```

After you select the file server mode of operation, you must name the file server. Each file server located on the LAN must have a unique name. If you have only a single file server, the name is simply a label and is not used by the users (as in a multiserver environment).

The file server name screen, as shown in figure 11.5, is self-explanatory. The name given to your file server is not limited to any particular words. The name can be as simple as your company's name or the name of a department the file server is servicing. You can use any name containing two to 45 characters. No spaces or periods are permitted as part of the server name.

Next, you need to select the network interface card installed in your file server. The NetWare install program presents you with a list of drivers supplied with NetWare, as in figure 11.6. If the driver you need is not shown, press Ins and provide the required driver from the disk supplied by the manufacturer or Novell.

After you complete the network card selection, the linking and configuration information appears on the screen as each process is performed.

After module 2 or the Link and Configure processes finish, you are prompted with the ZTEST screen, as illustrated in figure 11.7. This screen warns you about data loss that occurs if you proceed.

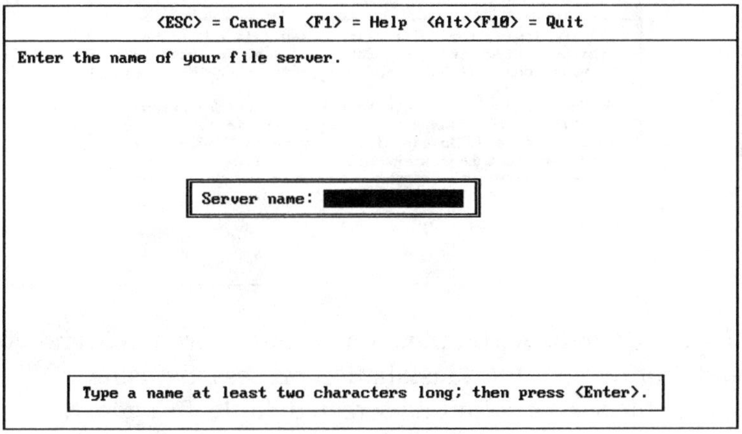

```
        <ESC> = Cancel   <F1> = Help   <Alt><F10> = Quit
 Enter the name of your file server.




              ┌──────────────────────────────────┐
              │ Server name: ████████████████     │
              └──────────────────────────────────┘




         ┌──────────────────────────────────────────────┐
         │ Type a name at least two characters long; then press <Enter>. │
         └──────────────────────────────────────────────┘
```

Figure 11.5

The file server name screen.

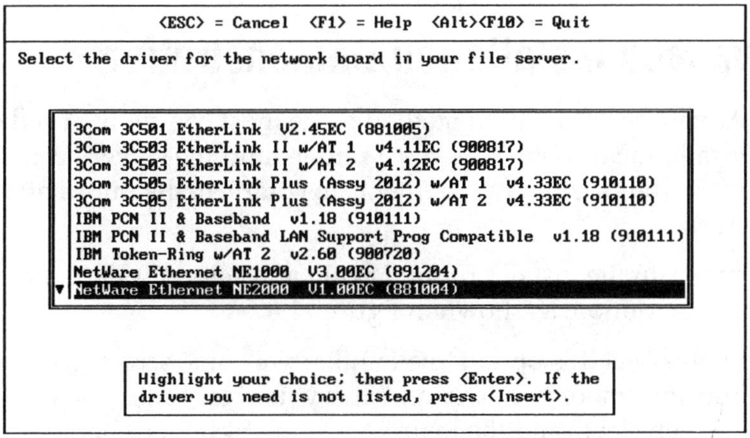

```
        <ESC> = Cancel   <F1> = Help   <Alt><F10> = Quit
 Select the driver for the network board in your file server.

    ┌──────────────────────────────────────────────────────┐
    │ 3Com 3C501 EtherLink  V2.45EC (881005)                │
    │ 3Com 3C503 EtherLink II w/AT 1  v4.11EC (900817)      │
    │ 3Com 3C503 EtherLink II w/AT 2  v4.12EC (900817)      │
    │ 3Com 3C505 EtherLink Plus (Assy 2012) w/AT 1  v4.33EC (910110) │
    │ 3Com 3C505 EtherLink Plus (Assy 2012) w/AT 2  v4.33EC (910110) │
    │ IBM PCN II & Baseband  v1.18 (910111)                 │
    │ IBM PCN II & Baseband LAN Support Prog Compatible  v1.18 (910111) │
    │ IBM Token-Ring w/AT 2  v2.60 (900720)                 │
    │ NetWare Ethernet NE1000  V3.00EC (891204)             │
  ▼ │ NetWare Ethernet NE2000  V1.00EC (881004)             │
    └──────────────────────────────────────────────────────┘


         ┌──────────────────────────────────────────────┐
         │ Highlight your choice; then press <Enter>. If the │
         │ driver you need is not listed, press <Insert>.    │
         └──────────────────────────────────────────────┘
```

Figure 11.6

Network card driver selection.

741

Figure 11.7

The ZTEST
warning screen.

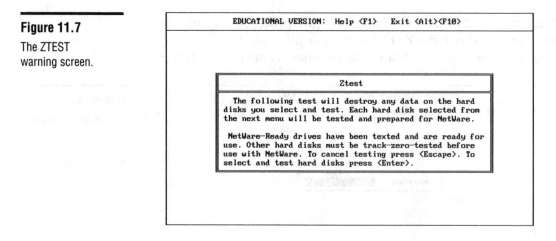

```
EDUCATIONAL VERSION:  Help <F1>    Exit <Alt><F10>


           ┌──────────────────────────────────────────┐
           │                  Ztest                   │
           ├──────────────────────────────────────────┤
           │   The following test will destroy any data on the hard │
           │ disks you select and test. Each hard disk selected from │
           │ the next menu will be tested and prepared for NetWare.  │
           │                                          │
           │   NetWare-Ready drives have been texted and are ready for │
           │ use. Other hard disks must be track-zero-tested before  │
           │ use with NetWare. To cancel testing press <Escape>. To  │
           │ select and test hard disks press <Enter>.               │
           └──────────────────────────────────────────┘
```

At this point, you have completed modules 1 through 3, and you are ready for the module 4 installation process. By using the Basic option, the file server definition screen defaults to a generic configuration, and the loading of all files begins automatically.

Advanced Installation Demonstration

The Advanced installation method is the most commonly used of the installation options. You must understand file server hardware and your system requirements to complete the information on-screen.

To begin, run the install program again and select the Advanced installation option, as shown in figure 11.8.

After you select this option, the familiar welcome screen appears and informs you of your choice. After you press Enter, the welcome screen clears and the main Operating System Generation screen appears. This screen, as shown in figure 11.9, offers hardware configuration options.

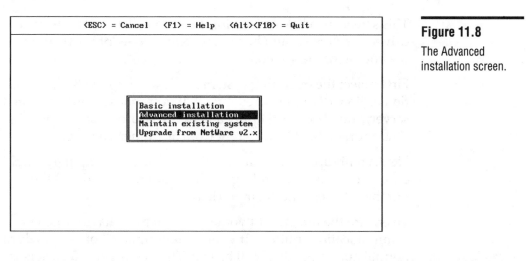

Figure 11.8

The Advanced installation screen.

Figure 11.9

The Operating System Generation window.

The Operating System Generation screen contains the following options:

◆ Operating system mode: Dedicated or Nondedicated

◆ Nondedicated network address

◆ Number of communication buffers

◆ Will this machine be the server?

◆ Include core printing services?

743

This screen also has options for disk controllers, network card drivers, addresses, and hardware. Note the set of instructions at the bottom of the screen.

First, select the operating system mode (as with the Basic installation option, discussed previously). If you choose a nondedicated server, you also must supply a network address for this process. This address must be different from any other you use.

Next, configure the communication buffers. The required number of buffers varies, depending on the equipment used and the number of users and their work load.

To ensure the integrity of your data, you must have sufficient communications buffers. If your system runs out of buffers during normal operation, data will be lost. The default of 150 buffers is sufficient for most installations.

You can estimate the number of required buffers by using two buffers for each user and ten buffers for each file server network card. If this number is fewer than 150, use the default.

NetWare 2.2 gives you the option of generating the operating system on a machine other than the file server, and then transferring the linked and configured files to the server. If you have chosen this method of OS generation, answer No when prompted as to whether this machine will be the server. If you are performing the installation on the server itself, respond Yes to this question.

Next, NetWare asks if you want to include core printing. If you only need a couple of printers connected to a file server, core printing might be the best solution. If your printing requirements are more involved, and you need printers distributed throughout the office, you can use the server VAP rather than core printing.

You should know the hardware configuration of your network and disk controllers, because you must insert a network-interface driver for each of the four LAN cards you might have installed. To select a network driver, highlight the Network board A field and press Enter. The driver option window appears (see fig. 11.10).

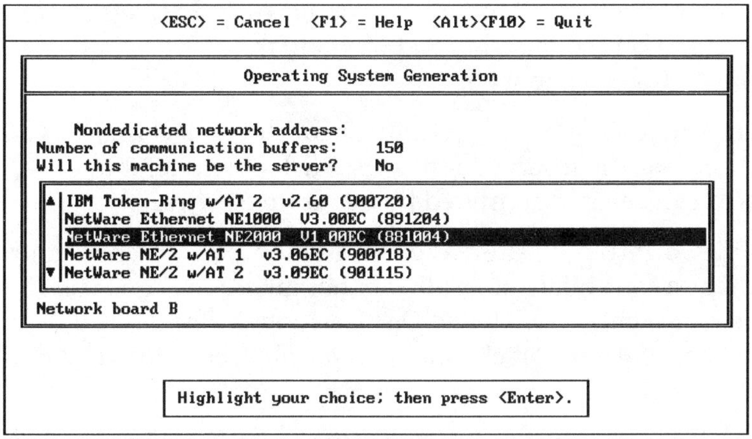

Figure 11.10

The network board driver selection window.

This window enables you to scan through the Novell-supplied drivers and choose the one required. If your driver is not listed in this window, you can press Ins and supply the INSTALL program with the appropriate disk.

In this example, the Novell NetWare Ethernet NE2000 driver (see fig. 11.10) and the first configuration option (0) are chosen (see fig. 11.11).

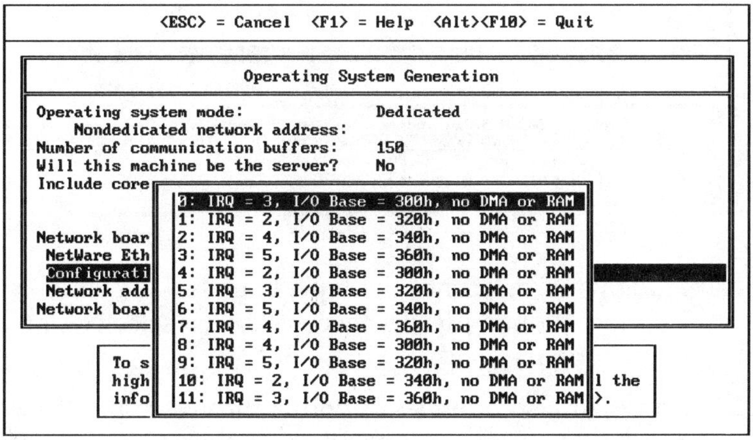

Figure 11.11

Hardware options.

In the Network address field, enter an address different from any other network segments to which your system might be connected. This process is repeated for network boards B, C, and D, if needed.

Next, enter configuration information for disk channels 0 through 4. Because you are selecting an ISA standard disk controller in this instance, choose channel 0.

Novell provides support for four concurrent disk channels. Channel 0 generally is reserved for an ISA disk controller, but other devices can use it if permitted by the driver software.

Channels 1 through 4 are designed for high-performance controllers. These controllers normally are not intended for use on DOS-based computers. The Novell *Disk Coprocessor Board* (DCB) was the first to make use of channels 1 through 4, and does not support channel 0.

Press Enter and the disk driver selection window appears. For this example, select the Industry Standard ISA controller choice, as shown in figure 11.12.

Figure 11.12

The disk driver selection window.

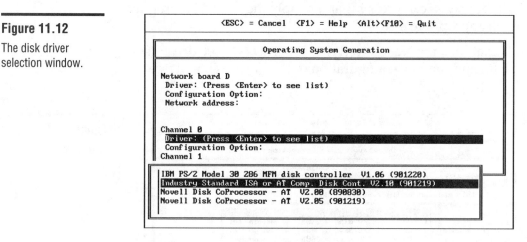

After selecting your disk controller type, you need to configure hardware options. For an ISA disk controller, the selected option is 0, as shown in figure 11.13.

The ISA controller also provides options 1 through 9, but these options might not be supported on all controllers. Currently, the only ISA disk controller certified to use all options is the standard Compaq controller.

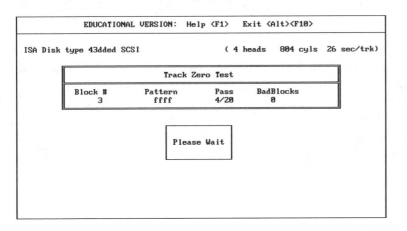

Figure 11.13
Disk driver options.

After you complete the disk controller information fields, press F10 to save the selections and continue with module 2. You see the link and configuration information scroll as the different steps take place. If you selected the option that identifies the machine you are working on as the file server, you see the same ZTEST screen that appeared in the Basic installation method.

Figure 11.14 shows the screen that appears as each drive is tested. If you selected the option that your machine is not the file server, Advanced installation is almost complete.

Figure 11.14
The ZTEST testing screen.

The next step is to set up the hardware on the machine that will be a server. Boot the server under DOS and put in the SYSTEM-1 disk. Type **INSTALL -M-L** to complete the steps in creating the server.

The last step is performed in module 4 and is the actual file server definition screen. It is used in both maintenance and installation.

Figure 11.15 shows the first part of the form in module 4. In this screen, you are asked for the file server name, the maximum number of open and indexed files, Transaction Tracking information, and information on limiting disk space and setting the flag to install NetWare for Macintosh.

Figure 11.15

Module 4 Part 1.

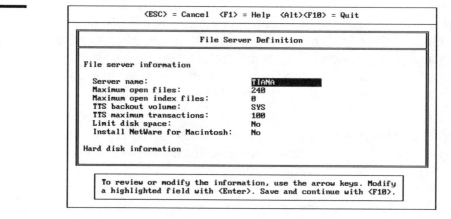

Figure 11.16 shows you the default information that the INSTALL program filled in for the demonstration. Much of this information can be modified. Other entries provide information about the drives. The important information you should notice in figure 11.16 is the size, type, and current status of the drives, which channel they are on, if they are mirrored, and the amount of space set aside for Hot Fix.

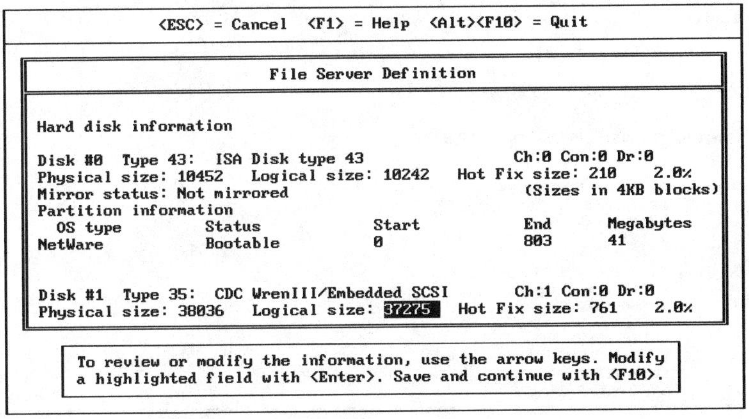

```
<ESC> = Cancel  <F1> = Help  <Alt><F10> = Quit

┌──────────────────────────────────────────────────────────┐
│                  File Server Definition                   │
│                                                           │
│  Hard disk information                                    │
│                                                           │
│  Disk #0  Type 43:  ISA Disk type 43        Ch:0 Con:0 Dr:0│
│  Physical size: 10452  Logical size: 10242  Hot Fix size: 210   2.0%│
│  Mirror status: Not mirrored                    (Sizes in 4KB blocks)│
│  Partition information                                    │
│    OS type        Status        Start      End      Megabytes│
│  NetWare         Bootable        0          803       41   │
│                                                           │
│                                                           │
│  Disk #1  Type 35:  CDC WrenIII/Embedded SCSI   Ch:1 Con:0 Dr:0│
│  Physical size: 38036  Logical size: 37275  Hot Fix size: 761   2.0%│
│                                                           │
│   ┌────────────────────────────────────────────────────┐ │
│   │ To review or modify the information, use the arrow keys. Modify│ │
│   │ a highlighted field with <Enter>. Save and continue with <F10>.│ │
│   └────────────────────────────────────────────────────┘ │
└──────────────────────────────────────────────────────────┘
```

Figure 11.16
Module 4 Part 2.

Figure 11.17 shows the final input portion of module 4. Here you can modify the volume information. You can view and modify the volume names and size, and determine if they should be cached and how many directory entries are allowed. Each volume also shows which drive it is on.

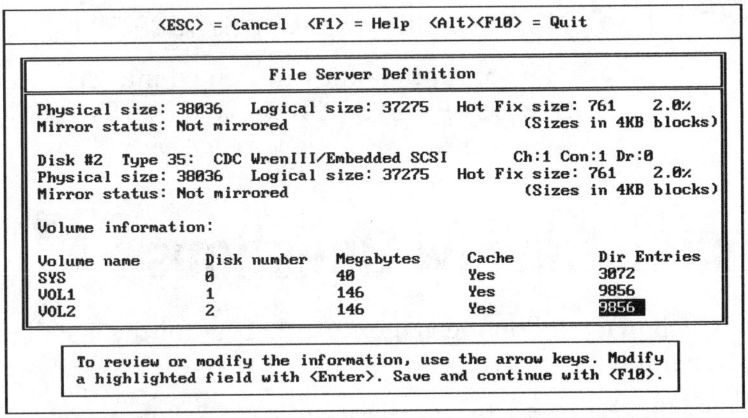

```
<ESC> = Cancel  <F1> = Help  <Alt><F10> = Quit

┌──────────────────────────────────────────────────────────┐
│                  File Server Definition                   │
│  Physical size: 38036  Logical size: 37275  Hot Fix size: 761   2.0%│
│  Mirror status: Not mirrored                    (Sizes in 4KB blocks)│
│                                                           │
│  Disk #2  Type 35:  CDC WrenIII/Embedded SCSI   Ch:1 Con:1 Dr:0│
│  Physical size: 38036  Logical size: 37275  Hot Fix size: 761   2.0%│
│  Mirror status: Not mirrored                    (Sizes in 4KB blocks)│
│                                                           │
│  Volume information:                                      │
│                                                           │
│  Volume name     Disk number    Megabytes   Cache   Dir Entries│
│  SYS             0              40          Yes     3072   │
│  VOL1            1              146         Yes     9856   │
│  VOL2            2              146         Yes     9856   │
│                                                           │
│   ┌────────────────────────────────────────────────────┐ │
│   │ To review or modify the information, use the arrow keys. Modify│ │
│   │ a highlighted field with <Enter>. Save and continue with <F10>.│ │
│   └────────────────────────────────────────────────────┘ │
└──────────────────────────────────────────────────────────┘
```

Figure 11.17
Module 4 Part 3.

After all the screens are completed, you see messages similar to those shown in figure 11.18. In this figure, you see that the cold boot loader was successfully installed on the hard drive. This procedure allows NetWare 2.2 to boot up without a bootable floppy disk.

Figure 11.18

Successful load
of files.

```
Installing NetWare v2.2 operating system files:

Installing the Cold Boot Loader.

Cold boot loader successfully installed.


Copying NET$OS.EXE to SYS:SYSTEM


Copying Files to SYS:LOGIN
        LOGIN.EXE
        WHOAMI.EXE


Copying Files to SYS:PUBLIC
        LOGIN.EXE
        WHOAMI.EXE
        MAP.EXE
        VOLINFO.EXE
        FCONSOLE.EXE
        LOGOUT.EXE
        SYSCON.EXE
```

Next, you see the files as they are copied to their appropriate
directories.

Note   The following events take place during a successful
installation:

♦   NET$OS.EXE is copied to SYS:SYSTEM

♦   The appropriate files are copied into the
SYS:LOGIN, SYS:PUBLIC, and SYS:SYSTEM
directories

Section Review Questions

1.   Which of the following is the correct order for the installation modules?

a.   Operating System Generation, ZTEST, Linking and
Configuring, File Server Definition

b.   Operating System Generation, Linking and Configuring, ZTEST, File Server Definition

c.   File Server Definition, Linking and Configuring,
ZTEST, Operating System Configuration

d.   File Server Definition, ZTEST, Linking and Configuring, Operating System Configuration

2. Which of the following is NOT a valid INSTALL command-line parameter?

    a. INSTALL -U

    b. INSTALL -N

    c. INSTALL -L-M

    d. INSTALL -F

3. Which INSTALL command-line parameter takes you straight to Module 4?

    a. INSTALL -M

    b. INSTALL -M4

    c. INSTALL -F

    d. INSTALL -L

4. Which of the following questions is NOT asked during a Basic installation?

    a. What is the name of the file server?

    b. What type of network adapter is in the file server?

    c. Will the file server be dedicated or nondedicated?

    d. Will this machine be the file server?

5. Which item on the Install Main Menu is incorrect?

    a. Basic installation

    b. Expert installation

    c. Maintain existing system

    d. Upgrade from NetWare 2.*x*

6. In which module are you asked to load the Macintosh VAP?

    a. Module 1

    b. Module 2

    c. Module 3

    d. Module 4

7. Which utility automatically copies the installation files from the disks to the network?

   a. UTILCOPY

   b. XCOPY/SUB

   c. UPDATE

   d. UPLOAD

8. Which module requires you to choose between Dedicated and Nondedicated mode for the file server?

   a. Operating System Generation

   b. Linking and Configuring

   c. Track Zero Test (ZTEST)

   d. File Server Definition

9. Which of the following install options should you use if you are updating an existing NetWare 2.2 server?

   a. -C

   b. -M

   c. -F

   d. -U

10. Which of the install options should you use if you are updating an existing NetWare 2.x server to a 2.2 server?

    a. -C

    b. -M

    c. -F

    d. -U

11. Which of the following is NOT assumed when running the Basic installation?

    a. Only one file server exists on this network.

    b. The file server has one parallel printer attached.

    c. The file server will be duplexed.

    d. Only one network board is installed in this file server.

12. When is installing a nondedicated file server considered an advantage rather than a problem? (Mark only the two best answers.)

    a. When the system has five or fewer users

    b. When the file server disk will be accessed very little

    c. When the file server does not need to also be run as a workstation

    d. When only one person will be using this particular workstation as a workstation, even though the network has 20 or more users

Answers

1. b
2. c
3. c
4. d
5. b
6. d
7. d
8. a
9. d
10. d
11. c
12. a and b

Managing NetWare 2.2 Using FCONSOLE

In this section, you learn to use some simple tools and methods that help you monitor your file server. Careful monitoring and knowledge of your file server enables you to prevent many problems before they happen. Except for hardware failures, most file server problems are visible through monitoring utilities long before the critical stage.

The network Administrator's main responsibility is to monitor and record any file server problems. In most cases, if the Administrator does not watch out for these problems, no one will. System monitoring and troubleshooting is enhanced by a wide range of Novell NetWare diagnostic and monitoring utilities. These utilities can give both users and System Administrators the data required to maintain a file server efficiently. By monitoring a few of the system's resource statistics, you can make adjustments to the file server that can prevent system failure and increase performance.

Use the FCONSOLE utility to master performance management techniques.

The Administrator easily can monitor and change NetWare's active parameters to maintain a properly operating file server. With a simple understanding of the following parameters, many system problems can be prevented:

♦ File service processes

♦ Disk cache performance

♦ File server utilization

♦ Communications buffers

♦ Dynamic memory pools

Using FCONSOLE for Management Operations

The File Server Console, or FCONSOLE menu utility, enables the System Administrator to maintain and fine-tune the file server. This command finds all file servers and places them in a list. FCONSOLE enables you to view user connections, memory management statistics, and LAN I/O statistics. FCONSOLE also can provide advanced diagnostic information that can assist debugging procedures.

User limitations depend on the user's security level. All functions and submenus are open for use by the System Supervisor or equivalent. Selected functions and submenus are locked and not functional if you are a normal system user. Users designated as FCONSOLE operators in the SYSCON Supervisor options have limited use of FCONSOLE, but more options than the normal end user.

Being aware of FCONSOLE's specific tools for management operations should help you filter out the screens of detailed technical information that are of reduced importance in day-to-day administrative concerns. After executing the FCONSOLE command, you are presented with the opening menu (see fig. 11.19).

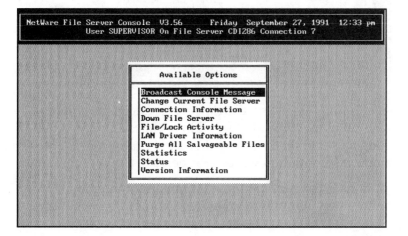

Figure 11.19

The FCONSOLE main menu.

The first menu option, Broadcast Console Message, enables you to send a message to every user currently logged in to the file server. This feature is useful when you need to inform users of scheduled downtime or other global announcements.

The second option is used in a multiserver environment. It enables the FCONSOLE user to attach to other file servers from within the FCONSOLE utility. This option enables you to use FCONSOLE to examine multiple file servers. The interface follows the NetWare utility standard by making use of Ins to add other file servers to the pick list. After choosing a file server from the list, you then are required to supply both a login name and password.

The Connection Information option provides a submenu that enables operations on that particular connection. The Connection Information menu, shown in figure 11.20, shows the Current Connections submenu, which lists the options provided.

Figure 11.20

The Connection Information menu.

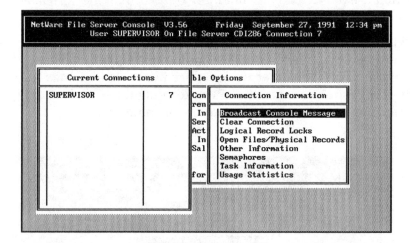

When entering this menu, the Current Connections window displays all users currently logged in to the file server. After selecting a user by highlighting that user's name, press Enter. The Connection Information window appears.

The options listed here are useful when attempting to inspect connections on the system. From here, you can broadcast messages, clear connections, and inspect a user's open files.

The most commonly used options of FCONSOLE are Broadcast Console Message, Clear Connection, and Open Files/Physical Records. These options are often used while requesting users to log off the system for maintenance. You can, for example, broadcast a message that asks users to please log off the system. After a reasonable period of time, you then can check the Open Files option to determine if they are still in an application. You can decide whether their connections should be cleared by using the Clear Connection option.

If a user does not log out properly, files might be left open on the system. If a user's workstation is turned off, that person's workstation continues to show on the FCONSOLE and an improper logout procedure has probably occurred. In this case, clearing the connection is the proper solution to the problem.

Not all applications show up as an open file on the system. Due to the nature of the program, a user can use Lotus 1-2-3, for example, and show no files open. This fact should be considered when deciding to clear a connection.

Some older technology application programs might be more sensitive to clearing a connection than others. You always should test or confirm this process with the software developers to prevent having to rebuild data files if damaged.

The other Connection Information options are used by advanced system developers when troubleshooting problems related to file sharing and the proper operation on a network. This specialized information is generally useful to programmers and applications development people. A brief description of these other options follows.

The Logical Record Locks option displays the logical record locks that the connection has logged to the file server. This information can be useful when debugging a network application sharing data files.

The Open Files/Physical Records option displays the connection's open files. This option also displays tasks and file status information. By highlighting a particular file and pressing Enter, various status messages appear, depending on the file's open state. More detailed information about this option can be found in the NetWare manuals.

The Other Information option shows additional information about the connection, including login name, full name, login time, and network address.

The Semaphores option enables you to get a list of semaphores that might be used. A *semaphore* is used by system tasks to limit the number of tasks that can use a resource at one time and to limit the number of workstations that can run a program at the same time.

The Task Information option shows which tasks are active at the selected workstation.

The Usage Statistics option shows the total disk usage and packet requests since the selected user logged in. This option can determine the activity of a workstation.

Use FCONSOLE to determine if there is enough memory in a file server to run efficiently.

The Statistics option in FCONSOLE's main menu calls up the File Server Statistics menu (see fig. 11.21). This menu has several useful choices for getting information about network performance and system integrity. In particular, the Cache Statistics, Disk Statistics, and Summary options are important monitoring and diagnostic tools.

Figure 11.21

The FCONSOLE Server Statistics menu.

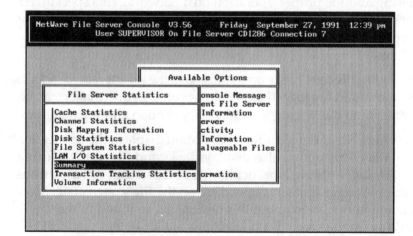

Cache Statistics

The Cache Statistics screen deals almost exclusively with memory usage. This screen tells you about NetWare file caching in the current server. Several of the screen parameters help you determine if enough memory is available in your file server. An example of the Cache Statistics screen is shown in figure 11.22.

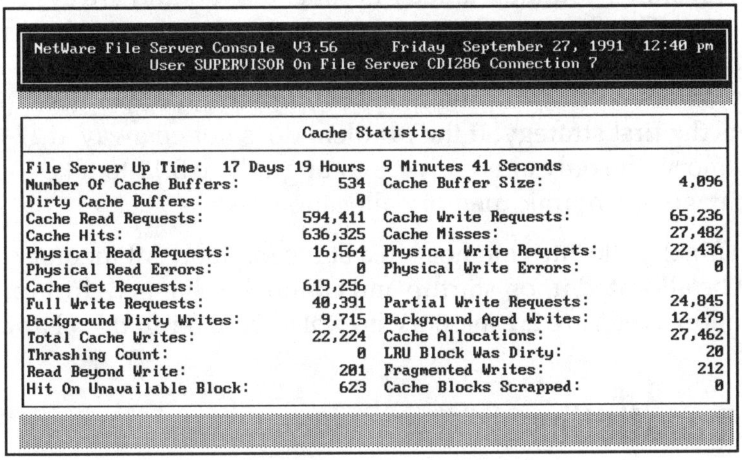

```
NetWare File Server Console  V3.56       Friday  September 27, 1991  12:40 pm
           User SUPERVISOR On File Server CDI286 Connection 7


                               Cache Statistics

File Server Up Time:  17 Days 19 Hours  9 Minutes 41 Seconds
Number Of Cache Buffers:            534  Cache Buffer Size:         4,096
Dirty Cache Buffers:                  0
Cache Read Requests:            594,411  Cache Write Requests:     65,236
Cache Hits:                     636,325  Cache Misses:             27,482
Physical Read Requests:          16,564  Physical Write Requests:  22,436
Physical Read Errors:                 0  Physical Write Errors:         0
Cache Get Requests:             619,256
Full Write Requests:             40,391  Partial Write Requests:   24,845
Background Dirty Writes:          9,715  Background Aged Writes:    12,479
Total Cache Writes:              22,224  Cache Allocations:        27,462
Thrashing Count:                      0  LRU Block Was Dirty:          20
Read Beyond Write:                  201  Fragmented Writes:           212
Hit On Unavailable Block:           623  Cache Blocks Scrapped:         0
```

Figure 11.22

A typical Cache Statistics screen.

The Cache Hits and Cache Misses parameters show you the number of times a memory cache handled a read-write request and the number of times the hard disk had to be accessed instead. In other words, a *cache hit* occurs when the requested information is found in memory, and a *cache miss* occurs when the information has to be taken from the hard disk. Because the minimum requirement for the network is 80 percent or more of requests serviced from cache, the amount of misses should never be more than 20 percent of the total. Make sure that you have allotted enough memory for cache buffers in the server.

The Physical Read Errors and Physical Write Errors parameter values always should be low, if not zero. An increase in these numbers indicates a communication problem with the hard disk when cache is requesting a read or write.

Physical Read and Write Errors, along with Hot Fix blocks (discussed in the next section), should be zero in a healthy system.

An occasional error or Hot Fix block might occur with normal equipment wear, but continual errors or Hot Fix blocks used weekly and daily indicate possible future failure. Errors can occur over a period of time and then stop. This problem generally indicates a media failure that NetWare handled properly. When errors continue and do not stop, however, you should be concerned.

The Thrashing Count parameter number also should always be near zero. *Thrashing* occurs when a cache block is needed but is not available. File server performance is seriously degraded when this problem occurs. Adding memory until this number goes to zero is the first strategy. If the problem does not go away at 12 MB of memory, the only alternative is to upgrade to 3.11 to take advantage of dynamic memory allocation.

NetWare 2.2 allocates memory in a static manner. All memory must be allocated upon startup and cannot be changed during operation. NetWare 2.2 memory is explained later in this chapter.

Disk Statistics

 Find other statistics in FCONSOLE to help manage memory and other functions of the network file server.

Two important parameters in the Disk Statistics screen are IO Error Count and Hot Fix Table Size/Hot Fix Remaining. Figure 11.23 shows the information available for a typical physical disk.

The IO Error Count parameter figure indicates the number of problems encountered when trying to read or write to the hard disk. A separate information screen appears for each drive.

The Hot Fix Table Size parameter tells you exactly how many Hot Fix blocks were allocated when the system was generated. The Hot Fix Remaining parameter tells you how many of those blocks are left. Every time a bad block is encountered on the hard disk, the Hot Fix Remaining parameter decreases.

```
NetWare File Server Console  V3.56     Friday  September 27, 1991  12:41 pm
              User SUPERVISOR On File Server CDI286 Connection 7

                         ┌─────────────────────┐
                         Physical Disk  0

       File Server Up Time:  17 Days 19 Hours 10 Minutes 39 Seconds
       Disk Type:  16. Vertex V185/A4070
       Non-Removable Drive
       Disk Channel:  1   Controller Number:  0   Drive Number: 0
       Controller Type: 6.
       Drive Size (less hot fix area): 106,475,520 bytes
       Drive Cylinders:  1,166  Drive Heads:  7   Sectors Per Track:  26
       IO Error Count:      0
       Hot Fix Table Start: 25,995       Hot Fix Enabled
       Hot Fix Table Size:  531 blocks   Hot Fix Remaining: 492 blocks
```

Figure 11.23

The FCONSOLE
Physical Disk 0.

As part of a normal maintenance schedule, System Administrators should check Hot Fix Remaining once a month. If the number goes down by more than five blocks, check the Hot Fix numbers once a week. The nature of hard disks is that they will accrue an occasional bad block, but if a problem exists, they usually accumulate bad blocks quickly. If you see a steady decrease in the number of blocks remaining, be prepared to repair or replace the drive.

File Server Statistics Summary

Choose the Summary option from the File Server Statistics menu to get to the File Server Statistics Summary screen. As figure 11.24 illustrates, this summary screen provides the technical summary data gathered since the file server has been up. This tool is helpful when monitoring the operation and reliability of your server.

The File Server Up Time parameter shows the amount of time the file server has been running. This time resets if the server is downed or shut off.

The Number of *File Service Processes* (FSP) parameter tells you the number of processes the file server has. A file server should have at least three processes, but four is recommended and is the average. NetWare 2.2 has a maximum of ten FSPs. Although three

761

processes enable your file server to operate, a slow CPU, a single heavily used disk controller, or a low amount of cache memory might require more.

Figure 11.24

The File Server Statistics Summary screen.

```
NetWare File Server Console   V3.56      Friday  September 27, 1991  12:39 pm
                 User SUPERVISOR On File Server CDI286 Connection 7

                           File Server Statistics Summary

File Server Up Time:  17 Days 19 Hours  8 Minutes 59 Seconds
Number Of File Service Processes:    6  Current Server Utilization:        6%
Disk Requests Serviced From Cache:  96%  Packets Routed:                    0
Total Packets Received:         527,763  File Service Packets:              6
Total Number Of Cache Buffers:      534  Dirty Cache Buffers:              0
Total Server Memory:          4,194,304  Unused Server Memory:          3,072

                           Maximum      Peak Used    Currently In Use
Communication Buffers        150           13              0
Open Files:                  240           41             21
Indexed Files:                 5            0              0
Bindery Objects:             500           69             41
Connections:                 116           10              1
Dynamic Memory 1:         12,232        2,374            994
Dynamic Memory 2:         26,576        6,124          5,264
Dynamic Memory 3:         59,500        1,130            694
Dynamic Memory 4:         63,646          944            144
```

 Change certain user-definable variables to possibly increase File Service Processes.

This number can be manipulated by adjusting devices that used memory from Dynamic Memory Pool 1, described later in this chapter.

If your file server appears to have a problem with File Service Processes, a system reconfiguration generally is required. Consult a Novell engineer who is familiar with this problem if reconfiguring the system does not correct the situation.

Note The following factors can decrease the number of FSPs available on a network:

◆ Network board packet size is too large

◆ Network boards using DMA

◆ An overabundance of directory entries

Be cautious about reducing directory entries. You can lose files, directories, and trustee rights if this number is reduced drastically.

The most complete reference about all the factors that affect FSPs is the September 1991 *NetWare Application Notes*. The *Notes* can be purchased from the Novell Research Order Desk. For more information, call (800) 453-1267, extension 5380.

The Disk Request Service from the Cache parameter is the disk cache performance indicator. This number shows the number of requests received at the file server that are taken from the cache memory. The remainder of the requests received go to the hard disk. Accessing information from cache is 100 times faster than going to the hard disk. The more the file server can get from memory, the faster the network functions. If disk cache performance drops below 93 percent, you should add more memory. According to Novell recommendations, this number should never fall below 80 percent. The actual number of cache buffers your system needs depends on your applications and the load created by the users. If users request more data than their cache buffers can handle, file server performance suffers.

A good rule of thumb is to have between 800 and 1000 cache buffers. You might need to adjust this number after monitoring system statistics.

Note In some cases, you can have too much memory. In a NetWare 2.2 file server, more than 10 MB of memory can be almost as slow as direct disk I/O, but normally is not a problem.

The Current Server Utilization parameter shows the percentage of use of the file server processor. A utilization that continually reaches a high percentage might require making hardware changes or splitting the network load.

The Communication Buffers parameter also is an important area to watch. These numbers tell how many buffer areas have been set aside to hold incoming packets while currently held packets are being processed. These buffers are necessary to handle both incoming and outgoing packets. If no buffer is available, that packet is lost and a retransmit is required, which can greatly decrease performance.

You should have at least 100 communication buffers, plus one for each workstation. If the Peak Used is equal to the maximum, increase the number of buffers. An overabundance of these buffers is a waste of cache memory.

The Open Files parameter tells you how many open files the server can track. As the Peak Used reaches the maximum, users are not able to run applications.

Four dynamic memory pools are at the bottom of the File Server Statistics Summary screen. The dynamic memory pools are important to monitor, but in most cases difficult to adjust. Make sure that the Peak Used number is always at least 2 KB below the Maximum number.

Dynamic memory pools are 64 KB memory segments defined by NetWare 2.2. These segments hold information such as drive pointers, file handles, print queue pointers, and other system housekeeping information.

 Explain what a File Service Process is.

Dynamic Memory Pool 1, the all-purpose memory pool, is used for global allocated data, process stacks, packet buffers, volume tables, and general purpose workspace. This number is not user-configurable.

Dynamic Memory Pool 2 is used for file and record locking. You can modify this number by reducing the maximum number of open files.

Dynamic Memory Pool 3 contains Router and Server tables. It is not user-configurable.

Dynamic Memory Pool 4 is used for drive handles. Each mapping you create uses 16 bytes of memory. This number is not user-configurable, but if you decrease the number of mappings you keep, you can reduce this number.

Section Review Questions

13. What can you NOT do from FCONSOLE?

    a. Load a VAP

    b. Down the file server

    c. Clear a connection

    d. View Hot Fix statistics

14. Which function of FCONSOLE can be performed only by a Supervisor equivalent?

    a. Clear a connection

    b. Down the file server

    c. Reset the file server time

    d. a and b

15. In which FCONSOLE screen can you find Hot Fix information?

    a. CACHE STATISTICS

    b. SUMMARY

    c. DISK STATISTICS

    d. LAN I/O STATISTICS

16. In which FCONSOLE screen can you best see memory performance?

    a. CACHE STATISTICS

    b. SUMMARY

    c. DISK STATISTICS

    d. LAN I/O STATISTICS

17. In which FCONSOLE screen can you see Dynamic Memory Pool Maximums and Peak Used?

    a. CACHE STATISTICS

    b. SUMMARY

    c. DISK STATISTICS

    d. LAN I/O STATISTICS

18. Which of the following tasks CANNOT be done using the FCONSOLE utility?

    a. Broadcast console messages

    b. Restart the install program to update the file server

    c. Purge all salvageable files

    d. Change from one file server to another

19. How can you determine if the hard disk on a network file server might be going bad and needs to be replaced?

    a. By checking the thrashing count parameter to see if it is near or above zero

    b. By looking at the number of Hot Fix blocks allocated when the system was generated

    c. If you see a steady decrease in the number of Hot Fix blocks remaining

    d. If users begin to complain about lack of disk storage space

Answers

13. a

14. d

15. c

16. a

17. b

18. b

19. c

Exploring File Server Memory

The personal computer has gone through many changes since its introduction. With each class of microprocessor released by Intel came a new way of handling memory. The 8086, 8088, and 80x86 series of Intel microprocessors each brought a higher level of functionality. Conventional memory, extended memory, and high memory areas all are available to the applications programmer depending on the Intel microprocessor being implemented.

The original IBM PC design, based on the Intel 8086 and 8088, allowed a total memory capability of 1 MB. This original design reserved the upper 384 KB of this 1 MB for items like system *Basic Input/Output System* (BIOS), video memory, and adapter cards such as network adapters. This configuration left the 640 KB with which you already are familiar. Although the Intel 80286 can access 16 MB of memory and the 80386 4 GB, the 640 KB limit still is present for many DOS applications that remain compatible to all previous versions of the Intel microprocessor.

The Intel 80486 microprocessor is a highly optimized version of the 80386 machine that owes most of its performance to a faster instruction execution and integrated math coprocessor. The 80486SX version provides the increased instruction speed without the math coprocessor benefit.

Before you can understand NetWare's memory usage, you need a basic understanding of memory itself.

Conventional memory is the memory you use every time you run your PC—the memory area up to 640 KB. This area is used by the real-mode operating system DOS and also is the area that presents the common problem of application memory shortage. This 640 KB must be shared by programs such as DOS itself, disk drivers, LAN card drivers, and many others you might require to run your applications. All applications load into this memory area by default. This configuration sometimes presents a problem, because it does not leave enough free memory to properly run the desired application.

The *upper memory*, or *upper memory blocks* (UMB), is the area between 640 KB and 1 MB. This area is accessible by DOS, but reserved for special functions. This memory area starts at hexadecimal A000 through FFFF and is used by many common PC hardware interfaces. Many common VGA adapters, for instance, use from A000h to CBFFh. The BIOS, which every PC has, normally is located at F000h to FFFFh, although IBM uses a larger area of E000h to FFFFh.

Note Anyone who uses computers runs into hexadecimal numbers sooner or later. They are easy to recognize, because they usually mix the letters A through F with digits 0 through 9.

Hexadecimal number notation represents numbers in base 16, in contrast to base 10, which we use in most everyday numeric activities. Base 16 requires digits with values ranging from 0 to 15, and the letters A through F are used to represent values from 10 through 15 (A equals 10, B equals 11, and so forth).

Hexadecimal or *hex* notation is popular, because it is easier for humans to read than binary. You probably will agree that CBFF is easier to scan than its binary equivalent, 1100101111111111.

The other areas can be used for other interface cards, such as LAN adapters, which might require a memory address; this varies depending on the manufacturer. This UMB area also can be used to load drivers and *terminate-and-stay resident* (TSR) programs. This feature is supported by DOS 5.0, DR-DOS 6.0, and many third-party memory managers. Figure 11.25 illustrates some of the resources that utilize the UMB.

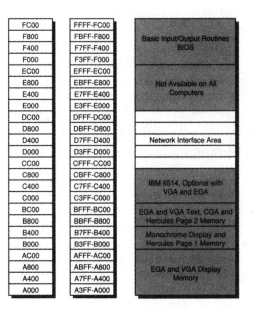

Figure 11.25

UMB memory utilization.

Extended memory is the area above 1 MB, and is not directly addressable to DOS while running in real mode. This memory area is available directly to applications written by using DOS extenders, and to memory manager programs that provide access through special driver software. Extended memory, however, is directly accessible when operating in protected mode. This extended memory is what Novell's NetWare products require to supply the performance and functionality for which they are known.

Write the minimum and maximum memory requirements for NetWare 2.2.

Note The term *real mode* came about when the 80286 processor was developed to operate like *real* 8088/ 8086 processors, which could utilize a maximum of 1 MB of memory. DOS is a real-mode operating system, and the old 640 KB memory limit is a holdover from the oldest IBM PCs and the oldest versions of DOS.

Protected mode was introduced when the 80286 processor was given the capability to manage 16 MB of memory as a continuous memory block. The 80386 and 80486 processors also offer protected mode and can manage even more memory—up to 4 GB in the case of the 80486. DOS programs cannot work with this mode, but more advanced operating systems such as NetWare require far more memory than DOS and utilize protected mode.

Expanded memory, used by many applications, is not actually part of the directly addressable memory, but is accessed through a "page frame" setup in the UMB area. This page frame allows applications to access the expanded memory area by mapping in 64 KB pages. This memory standard is used by many popular applications such as Lotus 1-2-3 and Ventura Publisher. Expanded memory is not used in any of the NetWare operating systems, but can be used on the workstation.

NetWare 2.2 Memory Model

Currently, NetWare 2.2 is the workgroup solution provided by Novell. This product offers many high-performance features and is intended for the smaller workgroup in which multiple communications protocols and large amounts of disk storage are not required.

Note The minimum amount of memory required for NetWare 2.2 is 2.5 MB.

Memory usage in NetWare 2.2 has been modified from earlier NetWare 2.*x* products to improve performance and prevent running out of *file server processes* (FSPs).

To properly calculate the amount of memory needed to operate, a NetWare 2.2 file server requires the information discussed in the following sections.

Directory Entries

Each directory entry is made up of a 32-byte entry stored in the *directory entry table* (DET) and located on the drive itself. This DET is loaded into cache memory. The number of total directory entries is determined during installation.

Note The number of directory entries refers to the total number of directories, subdirectories, and files that can be created on a particular volume.

Directory Hashing

The *hashing table* is a simple index stored in memory to the directory entry table. This table requires 8 bytes of memory for each directory entry.

Directory Caching

This feature requires 32 bytes for each directory entry and improves the disk file access time. This option is not implemented if the file server does not have enough memory.

Volume Bit Maps

The *volume bit map* is created for each volume on the file server. This table increases performance by informing the server if a particular disk block is free.

Hot Fix Tables

The *Hot Fix tables* store information pertaining to data redirected because of a bad disk block.

 By default, two percent of the hard drive is set aside for Hot Fix.

Hot Fix is also known as *dynamic bad block remapping*.

File Caching

File caching is the process that stores often-used file blocks in memory for quicker access. This process also attempts to bring the next most likely accessed data block into memory in case it is needed.

Disk Cache Buffers

After all memory is allocated, the remaining memory is used as disk cache buffers to service file caching. This number should be between 800 and 1000.

 Limited memory results in poor performance because of insufficient file cache; too much memory can result in poor performance because of increased system overhead. You can adjust this balance by increasing communication buffers or directory entries if needed.

Cache Memory Work Area

This area is a general work area used to manage disk cache buffers. The size of this area can be determined by multiplying the number of disk cache buffers by 32 and adding 4.7 KB.

File Allocation Table (FAT)

The *File Allocation Table* (FAT) is an index or link to the disk storage locations. Each FAT entry contains a sequence number and a pointer to the corresponding block for the file. This table requires 1 KB of memory for each megabyte of disk space.

File Handles (Dynamic Memory Pool 2)

File handles are used to track open files on the file server. Each file handle requires 56 bytes of memory. The maximum number of open files supported by NetWare 2.2 is 1000.

Workstation Tables

This area maintains information pertaining to users and connections to *value-added processes* (VAPs). This area is not configurable. Approximately 170 bytes are allocated per possible connection.

Index File Tables

This area is used to maintain Turbo Indexes or Turbo FATs. These indexes are built into RAM to speed disk access to large files. When a file larger than 262,144 KB (64 blocks) is marked with the I file attribute, NetWare maintains a Turbo FAT for the file.

 Note Specifying more indexed files than you need wastes memory.

Operating System

When calculating memory requirements, be sure to include the memory requirements for the operating system files.

The following worksheet can help you to calculate server memory requirements:

Server Resource Memory Requirements	Your Server Requirements
Directory Entries (KB) = directory entries x 32 / 1024	KB
Directory Hashing (KB) = directory entries x 8 / 1024	KB
Directory Caching (KB) = directory entries x32 / 1024	KB
Volume Bitmaps (KB) = 32 x volume size (MB) / 1024	KB
Hot Fix Tables (KB) = 14.5 KB x # of drives /1024 + 32 x volume size + 4096	KB
File Caching (KB) = Minimum of 40 cache blocks or 160KB	KB
Cache Memory Work Area (KB) = Minimum of (40 cache buffers x 32) / 1024 + 4.7 KB	KB
Caching FAT (KB) = 1 KB memory per MB disk space	KB
File Handles (File Control Blocks) (KB) = 7 KB file control workarea + # of open files x 56 /1024 *(default is 240, maximum is 1000)*	KB
File Locking (KB) = 2.5KB *(support for 100 WS)* + # open files x 100 /1024	KB
Workstation Tables (KB) = 174 bytes per possible service connection *5 user OS (32 x 174 = 5568) / 1024* *10 user OS (32 x 174 = 5568) / 1024* *50 User OS (60 x 174 = 10440) / 1024* *100 user OS (110 x 174 = 19140) / 1024*	KB
Index File Tables (KB) = (1040 x # indexed files) / 1024	KB
Operating System (KB) = size varies between 460 - 560 KB *(obtain size from SYS:SYSTEM\NET$OS.EXE file size)*	KB
Additional OS Memory (KB) = *To include the following:* Interrupt and Segment table: 35.25KB Dynamic Memory 1: 64KB Dynamic Memory 3 and 4 *(96KB for 5-10 user system* *128KB for 50-100 user system)*	KB
Non-Dedicated Workstation (KB) = If using Non-Dedicated WS 640KB	KB
VAP (KB) = *Depends on VAP requirements*	KB
Communications Buffers (KB) = Three buffers per WS and 50 per network interface *1 buffer = 64 + 42 + (maximum packet size)* *(# WS x 3 buffers) + (# NIC x 50 buffers) =* *Communications Buffers / 1024*	KB
Total Server Memory Required	KB

VAP Requirements

VAPs require memory and occasionally buffer space. When determining the total memory to be used, consult the software developer to determine the actual requirements.

Communication Buffers (Routing Buffers)

This memory area is used as a temporary storage area for data arriving from the network. It ensures that data is not lost during file server busy times. The actual number of buffers to be configured varies with each installation, but you should start with three for each user and 50 for each network interface.

 Note The optimum amount of communication buffers is to have 25 percent more than the peak used.

File Service Process

 Explain what a File Service Process is.

In NetWare, a *File Service Process* (FSP) is used to service a file service packet. This process normally is a *NetWare Core Protocol* (NCP) request from a workstation. An FSP is the only process that can service an NCP request. If an FSP is not available to service the request, then the request is stored in an FSP buffer until it can be serviced. If these buffers fill up, all NCP requests are ignored and requests are lost. This problem was common with previous versions of NetWare 2.*x* and resulted in the restructuring of NetWare 2.2's memory.

NetWare 2.2 memory is allocated into *dynamic memory pools*. Because of limitations imposed by the Intel 80286 microprocessor, these pools are limited to 64 KB in size. NetWare 2.2 contains four

775

separate dynamic memory pools; earlier versions of NetWare contained only three. The fourth pool was added to solve a problem that caused file servers to run out of FSPs when supporting many resources.

Dynamic Memory Pools

These dynamic memory areas are used for many functions. The following sections briefly describe each pool. These areas are not directly configurable, but when troubleshooting, you should understand what each group affects.

Dynamic Memory Pool 1

Dynamic Memory Pool 1 is considered a general purpose workspace. It is used for global static data, process stack information, volume information, and packet buffers. Because of the limitations of the Intel 80286 processor, this memory pool is limited to 64 KB. The memory in this pool is collectively referred to as the DGROUP.

Dynamic Memory Pool 2

This memory pool is used to maintain the file and record locking features of NetWare. Dynamic Memory Pool 2 also is used for the workstation tables. This memory pool can be as large as 64 KB.

Dynamic Memory Pool 3

Dynamic Memory Pool 3 contains the router and file server tables. This table lists the other file servers that might be on the network and the different routes available. This memory pool is fixed in size and can present a problem if connected to a large internetwork that contains many servers and routers.

Dynamic Memory Pool 4

Dynamic Memory Pool 4 was previously part of Dynamic Memory Pool 1. With the growth of networks, the size of disk drives available became a problem that resulted in file servers with too few FSPs. In NetWare 2.2, this memory pool handles user drive mappings. Thus, Dynamic Memory Pool 1 has more memory to allocate to packet buffers, resulting in more FSPs and higher performance. The size of this dynamic memory pool is fixed and determined by the number of users your version supports.

Section Review Questions

20. Which Dynamic Memory Pool is responsible for File Handles?

    a. Dynamic Memory Pool 1

    b. Dynamic Memory Pool 2

    c. Dynamic Memory Pool 3

    d. Dynamic Memory Pool 4

21. Communication buffers also are known as:

    a. Routing buffers

    b. Communication cache

    c. Cache buffers

    d. Routing cache

22. Which dynamic memory pool can be decreased by limiting the number of drive mappings a user has?

    a. Dynamic Memory Pool 1

    b. Dynamic Memory Pool 2

    c. Dynamic Memory Pool 3

    d. Dynamic Memory Pool 4

23. Which dynamic memory pool is most affected by a large number of servers and routers?

    a. Dynamic Memory Pool 1

    b. Dynamic Memory Pool 2

    c. Dynamic Memory Pool 3

    d. Dynamic Memory Pool 4

24. Which dynamic memory pool is responsible for file and record locks?

    a. Dynamic Memory Pool 1

    b. Dynamic Memory Pool 2

    c. Dynamic Memory Pool 3

    d. Dynamic Memory Pool 4

Answers

20. b

21. a

22. d

23. c

24. b

Case Study

1. Figure out the memory requirements for the following scenarios by using the memory worksheet in this chapter. Determine if the file servers have enough memory. If you determine a need for more memory, state how much more is adequate.

A. File Server #1
   OS: Nondedicated 50-user NetWare 2.2
   Hard Drive: One 300 MB hard disk
   Volumes: SYS: 255 MB and SYS1:45 MB
   SYS: 5,000 directory entries
   SYS1: 1,000 directory entries
   20 users
   20 open files per user
   NET$OS.EXE is 500 KB
   1 Ethernet Network Board

B. File Server #2
   OS: Dedicated 100-user NetWare 2.2
   Hard Drives: Two 300 MB hard disks
   Volumes: SYS: 255 MB, SYS1: 45 MB, SYS2:
   255M, SYS3: 45 MB
   SYS: and SYS2: 4,000 directory entries each
   SYS1: and SYS3: 1,000 directory entries each
   40 users
   35 open files per user
   NET$OS.EXE is 500 KB
   6 indexed files
   One VAP using 100 KB
   2 Ethernet Network Boards

Appendixes

Getting Your Certification

Networking knowledge is a commodity that is in ever-increasing demand in the computer industry. Every day, corporations with local-, municipal-, and wide-area networks discover the value of relying on current staff to maintain the network's integrity. Security issues, reliability concerns, and general maintenance problems all need to be resolved quickly and efficiently.

Companies always have been concerned with the ways in which they can best address the needs that arise from using a network. Rarely is the solution to skip over current staff and hire an outsider to fit the bill. Hidden somewhere in most computer departments is an individual with the aptitude and drive to manage the network. A program that trains this individual on the company's specific operating system is valuable. Of even greater value to the business is a way to assess the knowledge this person has obtained.

Occasionally, the need arises to look beyond the in-house staff for a network-support person. When shuffling through résumés, employers cannot always ascertain the exact amount of network knowledge applicants have. The applicants might have a broad knowledge of service, support, administration, and more, or they might only have expertise in administering specific versions of operating systems. An established method for employers to spot the type of individual for which they are searching definitely eases the difficult task of filling network support positions.

Novell, Inc., recognized these problems and instituted several certification programs to help place the necessary information in the hands of the people supporting the network. If you have a Novell network that needs a competent Administrator or technician, Novell's certification programs can help you get the most-qualified people into those positions. If you are responsible for managing a NetWare network, Novell's certification programs can help enhance the knowledge and skills you need. If you are considering a career as a network manager, Novell's CNA, CNE, and ECNE certifications can make it easier for you to get started in that career.

This appendix briefly provides an overview of Novell's certification programs and the benefits of earning a certification. Details about Novell's certification programs and processes, and in-depth information on studying for and taking Novell's certification tests are available in *New Riders Guide to Novell Certification*, by New Riders Publishing.

Choosing the Right Certification

Novell offers four certification programs, including its *Certified NetWare Instructor* (CNI) program. The CNI program is for individuals who want to teach Novell certified courses. This appendix only discusses Novell's three certifications intended for individuals who want to work in a Novell NetWare environment. These certifications include the following:

◆ *Certified NetWare Engineer* (CNE)

◆ *Enterprise Certified NetWare Engineer* (ECNE)

◆ *Certified NetWare Administrator* (CNA)

 Note   The Novell CNI program is extensively covered in *New Riders Guide to Novell Certification*.

The Certified NetWare Engineer

The Certified NetWare Engineer program was created by Novell so NetWare customers can easily distinguish people committed to learning about NetWare. Achieving CNE status means that you have passed Novell's rigorous testing requirements. Through the certification programs, you can establish a special relationship with *Novell Technical Support* (NTS) not available to the general public.

Anyone who works with PC hardware and Novell products is a candidate for the CNE program.

The Novell certification process generally requires the following skills and knowledge:

◆ CNE candidates must have a thorough understanding of DOS and microcomputer concepts.

◆ CNE candidates are responsible for planning their own curriculum within Novell guidelines. Tests are taken at *Drake Authorized Testing Centers* (DATC).

◆ Novell has individual classes that relate to all tests except DOS and micro hardware. These courses are offered through *Novell Authorized Education Centers* (NAEC) and *Novell Education Academic Partners* (NEAP) nationwide. Call (800)233-3382 for more information about NAECs and NEAPs in your area.

◆ As NetWare makes advancements in networking technology, CNEs are responsible for fulfilling continuing education requirements. You have one year to complete these requirements.

Novell mails you notification of continuing education requirements, so make sure that you send any address changes to the following address:

Novell CNE/ECNE/CNA Administration
Mail Stop E-31-1
122 East 1700 South
Provo, UT 84606

You also can fax address-change information to (801) 429-5565.

The biggest benefit to becoming a CNE is industry recognition. The network-computing industry recognizes individuals who have earned the Certified NetWare Engineer credential as LAN technicians capable of providing superior network support.

Some less obvious benefits also are available. After you become NetWare certified, for example, you own the certification even if your employer paid for it. A company cannot become certified—only an individual. You can, therefore, take your certification with you no matter which company you choose to work for. Novell NetWare certifications can enhance your résumé and your chance of being hired if you plan to search for a NetWare networking position.

Other more tangible benefits also come with the CNE certification, including the following:

◆ **The Network Support Encyclopedia.** This electronic information database contains valuable technical information.

◆ **Novell Technical Support.** CNEs receive two free support incidents and the ability to purchase additional support incidents for a 50-percent discount. The two free support calls are good for one year from the date you receive your certification.

◆ **Authorization to use the CNE logo.** After you have achieved CNE status, you can use the CNE logo on your business literature. This identifier lets your customers know that you are a Novell-certified service provider.

◆ **Eligibility as a CNEPA member.** Novell encourages all CNEs to join the *CNE Professional Association* (CNEPA). The CNEPA is a nonprofit organization created to help you keep your technical skills current. Only CNEs can join this organization. With your membership, you can access a special CNE forum on NetWire. *NetWire* is a special-interest group on CompuServe.

The Enterprise Certified NetWare Engineer

The *Enterprise Certified NetWare Engineer* (ECNE) program is a significant level above the CNE program. This certification enables the CNE to specialize in several different areas of networking, including TCP/IP, communication, and troubleshooting. The ECNE program generally requires the following:

◆ You must already be a CNE.

◆ You must earn 14 credits of elective tests.

The network computing industry recognizes individuals who have earned the Enterprise Certified NetWare Engineer credential as LAN specialists: the greatest benefit in spending the time to become an ECNE. NetWare clients recognize that the ECNE belongs to individuals who have surpassed the level of CNE and possess a wide range of networking expertise.

You also can use the ECNE logo. This logo helps you advertise the fact that you successfully completed the rigorous testing regimen that Novell requires of ECNEs.

The Certified NetWare Administrator

The CNA program is Novell's entry-level certification program. It is designed to show that an individual has obtained a minimum level of knowledge about networking by using one of Novell's NetWare products—NetWare 2.2 or NetWare 3.1*x*.

The CNA program also is Novell's newest certification program. Since its inception in late 1992, over 3,500 individuals have successfully met the program's requirements and been granted the status of Certified NetWare Administrator.

The Certified NetWare Administrator program is for individuals who manage a NetWare network and are responsible for its day-to-day operation. The CNA is responsible for system administration and fine-tuning. If you are skilled at administering a 2.2 or 3.1*x* NetWare LAN, then this program is the one you should pursue.

The CNA path is appropriate for the person who manages the LAN, but not for the hardware technician. Though the CNA program is not intended as a stepping stone to the CNE program, it helps you learn valuable information that can assist you later if you choose to get your CNE certification. In fact, many of the CNA candidate's NetWare 2.2 and 3.1x course objectives are identical to CNE program objectives. As a CNA, however, you are not required to meet many of the advanced networking course objectives that the CNE candidate is required to meet.

As a CNA candidate, you must know DOS and basic microcomputer concepts. Although you are not specifically tested on these concepts, you need a working knowledge in these areas in order to successfully administer a NetWare LAN.

Estimates indicate that approximately three million LANs exist today. Most LANs need someone to administer them, whether that individual is a dedicated or part-time LAN Administrator. Your CNA certification gives you industry recognition. The computer networking industry recognizes that Novell has set a standard of competence for network administration. Your CNA certificate proves that you have made a commitment to learning ways to manage NetWare.

You also gain improved job performance through increased knowledge. When you learn about the network's intricate workings, you automatically learn ways the network can best function in your own customized environment. This knowledge makes your network easier to manage and makes you more productive.

Your increased networking knowledge and the CNA designation tell your current or future employers that you are qualified to handle the tasks of administering a NetWare network. They also increase your potential for career advancement and make you more eligible for a position as a NetWare Administrator in another company. Your certification also might contribute to increases in your current or future salary.

Using this Book to Study for the Certification Exams

Two principles apply when you are studying for the certification exams. If you follow these maxims, the process of studying and actually learning the material is easier and less fatiguing:

♦ You must completely and thoroughly understand, in the context in which it is presented, any fact that you must remember.

♦ You must consciously decide that you want to remember the information and know why it is important.

The information presented in this book is here for two reasons. First, the information is important to anyone who needs to understand the way Novell NetWare works, specifically in the following areas:

♦ Networking, network workstations, and DOS

♦ Security

♦ Printing

♦ Memory configuration

♦ Hardware and software basics

♦ Utilities

♦ Backup

♦ Login scripts

♦ Applications installation

♦ Prevention and maintenance

This information comprises the fundamental knowledge on which everything else you learn about NetWare is based. This book is the first step to ensuring your success in administering a network.

Second, the information contained in this book is not trivial. It includes all the objectives stated by Novell on which the tests are based. Everything presented in this book is based on a hierarchy of knowledge. Each small piece of information contributes to the total concept that must be learned.

Studying for the certification tests is not to be taken lightly. On the adaptive tests, you are asked between 10 and 25 questions per test. If you take three tests, you encounter between 30 and 75 unique questions. You cannot predict which questions you will get or even which specific topics will be covered. The questions are designed so that you must understand the entire concept to answer the selective questions. Ultimately, you need to know and understand all the information in this book not only for the test, but for the sake of any network with which you come in contact.

This book is designed to teach you the whole concept from beginning to end, and then the specifics for each operating system. The method of this book helps you learn all the information, then take the tests all together.

This appendix also provides some recommended study techniques that you can use to help you prepare for the certification tests.

 For more information on studying for Novell certification tests, read *New Riders Guide to Novell Certification*.

Study Techniques

Many techniques for remembering things are available. This section introduces you to several techniques used throughout this book to aid you in remembering key topics.

Repetition

Repetition is an incredibly strong method for retaining information. In this book, you read about a concept and are asked questions about items relating to that topic. You might also notice that some key concepts are discussed several times throughout the book. This repetition helps you understand the topic's details.

To further enhance your learning by using repetition, consider making NetWare flashcards. On one side of a 3-by-5 card, write a question; write the answer on the other side. This method differs from the review question procedure because you do not give yourself multiple-choice answers. It also ensures that you are learning the concept, not simply making an educated guess. The more cards you create, the less likely you are to be surprised by a test question.

Another way to create questions for flashcards is to develop fill-in-the-blank questions. When creating these questions, replace key words with a blank. Write the key words on the backs of the cards. You also can reverse this study method by looking at the key words and placing them in a sentence that describes their function.

Linking

When you need to remember something elusive, try relating it to something with which you are familiar. This process is called *linking*. The more outrageous the comparison, the easier it becomes to remember. Take a look at the following examples for Hot Fix and bridge.

To remember what Hot Fix means, picture yourself moving a hot pan from an extinguished fire to a newly lit fire. Imagine slightly singeing your fingers on the pan handle. You have just "fixed a hot problem," or "hot fix." In NetWare terms, *Hot Fix* involves moving a piece of data written to a bad hard drive block over to a good hard drive block.

To remember what a bridge does, think of why concrete bridges are created. Normally, a bridge is built to connect two or more roads that otherwise cannot be connected. The Mackinac Bridge was built to connect Michigan's upper and lower peninsulas. In networking, a *bridge* connects two similar network topologies.

Mnemonics

Another type of linking is *mnemonics*—a method of remembering a list of items by assigning the first letter of each word to a common word and linking the words together to form an easily remembered sentence.

A common mnemonic in Novell's Networking Technologies class is used to remember the *Open System Interconnect* (OSI) model's seven layers. A list of these seven layers follows:

- Application
- Presentation
- Session
- Transport
- Network
- Data Link
- Physical

When you take the first letter of each word, you have APSTNDP. Next, each letter is assigned to a word that makes up a sentence that you can remember easily:

All

People

Seem

To

Need

Data

Processing

This simple, pertinent sentence helps you remember the seven layers in their correct order.

Keep a notebook handy as you go through this book. Keep any notes you take in one place; you can use them as a quick reference to points important to you. Be sure to note, in particular, the objectives shown throughout these chapters, and the information pertaining to those objectives.

Comparison Charts

B
APPENDIX

	Table B.1 *Rights*
2.2	*3.1x*
Read	Read
Write	Write
Create	Create
Modify	Modify
Erase	Erase
File Scan	File Scan
Access Control	Access Control
	Supervisory

Table B.2
Rights and Attributes

2.2	3.1x
Inherited Rights Mask	Inherited Rights Mask
Directory Rights	Directory Rights
	Directory Attributes
File Attributes	File Attributes
	File Rights

Table B.3
Minimum/Maximum File Server RAM Requirements

2.2	3.1x
2.5 MB/12 MB	4 MB/4 GB

Table B.4
Maximum Disk Storage

2.2	3.1x
2.2 GB	32 TB

Table B.5
File Attributes

2.2	3.1x
ALL	ALL
Normal (NsRw)	Normal (NsRw)
Shareable	Shareable
Read/Write	Read/Write
Read Only	Read Only
Archive Needed	Archive Needed
Indexed	
Hidden	Hidden
SYstem	SYstem
Transactional	Transactional
Read Audit	Read Audit
Write Audit	Write Audit
	Purge
	Copy Inhibit
	Delete Inhibit
	Rename Inhibit

Test Objectives

This appendix contains Novell's list of test objectives for the following tests:

- ◆ NetWare 2.2 System Manager
- ◆ NetWare 2.2 Advanced System Manager
- ◆ NetWare 3.1x Administration
- ◆ NetWare 3.1x Advanced Administration

Before you take any test, consult this list as a final study measure. Make sure that you understand each point.

These objectives are current as of the publication of this book. The objectives are subject to change at Novell's discretion, and the presence of the objectives in this book does not constitute an endorsement by Novell, Inc. Readers are cautioned to obtain the current objectives from Novell when they begin to study for a course.

NetWare 2.2 System Manager: Test #50-20

1. List the responsibilities of a system manager.
2. Relate course topics to those responsibilities.
3. Fill in a NetWare log.
4. Use general system management resources provided by Novell.

5. Define a network.

6. List the hardware components of a network.

7. Choose the best option for expanding your network.

8. List the software components needed to access the network from the DOS environment.

9. Choose and load IPX and the shell.

10. Create a distributed processing environment.

11. Use various tolerance features of NetWare 2.2.

12. Diagram the levels of the NetWare directory structure.

13. Name the required volume, the four required directories, and their contents and location in the directory structure.

14. Diagram possible directory structures given an organization and its needs.

15. Create an organized and efficient directory syntax.

16. Construct a directory path using the required syntax.

17. Work with DOS and NetWare commands related to directory structures and their contents.

18. Identify the default drive pointers in both the DOS and NetWare environments.

19. Use the MAP command to move through the directory structure.

20. Differentiate between drive mappings and search drive mappings.

21. Understand the effects of the DOS CD command on MAP.

22. List the levels of NetWare security.

23. Use command-line utilities to apply NetWare's security to a basic directory structure.

24. Understand security features implemented on the system through "user types."

25. Understand the correlation between NetWare command-line utilities and NetWare menu utilities.

26. Identify the workstation commands incorporated in these menus.

27. Recognize the specific tasks that can be accomplished within each menu utility.

28. Use the appropriate menu utility to create trustees, make trustee assignments, adjust all aspects of security, view directories and their contents, copy files, send messages, and manipulate drive pointers.

29. Describe the purpose of specific Supervisor commands.

30. Identify the directory where Supervisor commands are located and the limitations of other users to this directory.

31. Function within the special menu utilities reserved for Supervisor use.

32. Recognize the function of console commands and where they are issued.

33. Identify the two printing services available.

34. Identify parameters for choosing the right service.

35. Create print queues.

36. Assign queues to printers.

37. Create spooler assignments.

38. Create a system AUTOEXEC.SYS file.

39. Print files by using CAPTURE, ENDCAP, and NPRINT.

40. Create, control, and monitor queues through PCONSOLE.

41. Determine application compatibility with NetWare.

42. Recognize the features necessary to allow multiuser access.

43. Determine the placement within a directory structure for easiest access and maintenance.

44. Perform the steps required by security to ensure safe and reliable results.

45. Contrast the three login scripts used on the network.

46. Identify and use login script commands to create a system and user login script.

47. Debug problems in login script logic.

48. Identify vital mappings that must exist in the system login script.

49. Customize a user environment using menus.

50. Recognize the menu option file format and syntax.

51. Create custom menus.

52. Execute custom menus.

53. List the functions of the NBACKUP utility.

54. Identify the rules for running NBACKUP.

55. List the basic steps for backing up a file server.

56. Identify the basic steps for restoring backed-up data.

57. Use NBACKUP to protect your data.

58. Configure a network.

59. Control security.

60. Organize login scripts.

61. Create menus.

62. Understand and use the commands introduced in this course.

NetWare 2.2 Advanced System Manager: Test #50-44

1. Choose the correct installation mode for your network environment.

2. Install NetWare 2.2 in the chosen mode.

3. Install the workstation software that best fits each user's needs.

4. Update workstation files from an earlier version of NetWare to be used on a NetWare 2.2 workstation.

5. Use multiple methods for creating and defining trustees.

6. Use multiple methods to restrict or control user access and use of your Novell network.

7. Use the FCONSOLE utility to master performance management techniques.

8. Expand your printing options and capabilities by installing and configuring a NetWare print server.

9. List the hardware requirements for a file server.

10. List the software requirements to install the operating system.

11. Understand the options available during operating system installations.

12. Choose the correct installation options for your network environment.

13. Install the NetWare 2.2 operating system in the chosen mode.

14. Understand the environment of the workstation.

15. Select the appropriate shell files for each workstation.

16. Use WSGEN to create the workstation files required for different environments.

17. Use WSUPDATE to update your shell and other files.

18. Define and create a router.

19. Create specialized configuration files for individual users' needs.

20. Restrict the number of workstations that can use the same login name at one time.

21. Restrict users to specific workstations.

22. Control minimum password length.

23. Control the frequency with which the password must be changed.

24. Restrict the times when users can be logged in.

25. Restrict network disk storage by users.

26. Set parameters to help detect and deny intruder logins.

27. Use SYSCON to view the File Server Error Log.

28. Use NDIR to access network information on files and directories.

29. Use options of NDIR to find files with specific characteristics.

30. Establish resources for NetWare resource sharing.

31. Control and monitor the use of file server resources.

32. Create charges to be assessed against users for use of those resources.

33. Use the ATOTAL command to track summaries of file server resource use.

34. Use the PAUDIT command to view details of resource use.

35. Use advanced utilities to set up users.

36. Recognize which utility is best suited for a particular situation.

37. Establish defaults that fit your own users' needs.

38. Write the minimum and maximum memory requirements for NetWare 2.2.

39. Explain what a file service process is.

40. Explain the way in which DGroup memory affects the number of file service processes.

41. Change certain user-definable variables to possibly increase file service processes.

42. Use FCONSOLE to determine if there is enough memory in a file server to run efficiently.

43. Find other statistics in FCONSOLE to help manage memory and other functions of the network file server.

44. Determine if a network performance problem is indicated, given individual statistics from the Statistics Summary, Cache Statistics, and Disk Statistics screens.

45. Identify the possible course(s) of action to take when specific problems are indicated in the statistics screens.

46. Identify printing services and specifications.

47. Describe the purpose and functions of specific printing utilities.

48. Implement the appropriate steps in the NetWare 2.2 printing setup process.

49. Identify and use command-line utilities with the correct syntax for printing-related tasks.

50. Use PRINTDEF to create customized printer definitions, modes, and forms.

51. Use PRINTCON to create customized print jobs.

52. Print files using the jobs created in PRINTCON.

NetWare 3.1x System Administration: Test #50-130

1. Describe the basic function and services of a network.

2. Identify the client types supported in NetWare 3.12.

3. Describe workstation communications with the network and list the files required to connect a DOS workstation to the network.

4. Describe the function of the software necessary to connect a workstation to the network, including local operating systems, NetWare DOS Requester, communications protocols, and network.

5. Connect a workstation to the network by loading the appropriate DOS workstation files.

6. Explain and perform the login procedure.

7. Identify, navigate, and perform similar basic functions using a DOS text utility, a command-line utility, and a graphical utility.

8. Activate and navigate Help for each type of utility.

9. Activate and navigate Novell ElectroText.

10. Explain the basic concepts of network file storage, including volume and directory structures.

11. Describe a volume and its technical specifications.

12. Describe a directory, including its main functions, hierarchical structure, directory name, and directory path.

13. List the system-created directories on the SYS: volume and describe their contents.

14. Access file systems by mapping network drives to volumes and directories.

15. Navigate volumes and directories by using network drives.

16. Access network applications by mapping search drives to application directories.

17. Display and modify the display of file system information on volumes, directories, and files.

18. Perform directory management tasks such as creating, deleting, and renaming directories.

19. Perform file management tasks such as copying, moving, deleting, salvaging, and purging files.

20. Identify the levels and functions of network security.

21. Describe login security, including user account restrictions, time restrictions, station restrictions, and intruder detection.

22. Set up network user accounts and apply account restrictions.

23. Set up group accounts and user account management.

24. Describe packet signature.

25. Describe NetWare 3.12 file system security, including the concepts of trustees, directory and file rights, inheritance, Inherited Rights Mask, and effective rights.

26. Make a trustee assignment and apply rights in SYSCON and FILER.

27. Calculate effective rights.

28. Describe directory and file attributes and their use in a file system security plan.

29. Implement a file system security plan using command-line and menu utilities.

30. Describe the function of the CONFIG.SYS, AUTOEXEC.BAT, and NET.CFG configuration files.

31. Alter workstation configuration files so that they contain all pertinent information to automate the process of connecting to the network, loading the DOS requester, and logging in to the network.

32. Perform a DOS and MS Windows client installation using the NetWare client installation software.

33. Describe the types of login scripts and how they coordinate at login.

34. Explain each login script command, propose standard procedures that are executed through login scripts, and plan a system of login scripts for user login.

35. Build and execute the plan using system and user login scripts.

36. Describe the components of a user menu system.

37. Describe NetWare 3.12 menu command language, and plan a simple user menu.

38. Build and execute a NetWare 3.12 menu.

39. Convert menu files from earlier versions of NetWare into the new menu utility.

40. Describe the function of a server, its interface, and its communication with the network.

41. Describe console commands, and identify the function of commands commonly used by Administrators.

42. Describe NLMs, explain how they are loaded, and identify their types.

43. Identify the purpose and function of the major NLMs, such as INSTALL, MONITOR, and UPS.

44. Describe remote console management, and list the steps necessary to set up a server for both SPX and asynchronous remote connections.

45. Use RCONSOLE.EXE to connect remotely to the server, and describe the purpose and function of the available options in RCONSOLE.

46. Implement console security features on the server by assigning a console password and placing the server in a secure location.

47. Describe the basic components of network printing and the way they interrelate in processing a print job. Describe the general steps necessary for setting up the components.

48. Set up a network printing environment by creating and configuring a related and functional print queue, printer, and print server.

49. Set up network printing hardware by bringing up a print server on a dedicated workstation or NetWare server and connecting a printer to the network through a NetWare server or a DOS workstation.

50. Send print jobs to network printers by redirecting print jobs with CAPTURE or NPRINT.

51. Perform basic network printing maintenance tasks, such as viewing and modifying printing information in PCONSOLE.

52. Manage print jobs in the print queue by viewing their properties, pausing, rushing, delaying printing, and deleting jobs in the queue.

53. Describe the way you use PRINTDEF and PRINTCON to customize print jobs.

54. Explain *System Fault Tolerance* (SFT) and describe the way to implement it.

55. Describe SMS and strategies for implementing successful storage management.

56. Use SBACKUP, NetWare's utility for implementing SMS, to perform a simple backup and restore.

57. Describe NetWare *Basic Message Handling Service* (MHS).

58. Describe the steps required to install Basic MHS on a NetWare server.

59. Perform administrative tasks, such as adding a user and creating a distribution list, using the Basic MHS Administration software.

60. Send, read, and file mail in First Mail.

61. Identify basic guidelines for selecting application software.

62. List basic steps to be completed when loading applications.

NetWare 3.1*x* Advanced Administration: Test #50-131

1. Identify and describe the server components.

2. Perform a server startup procedure.

3. Identify and describe server configuration files.

4. Identify commands and options used to customize the appropriate server configuration file.

5. Select the appropriate utility and edit the server configuration files.

6. Create server batch files that perform specific tasks, such as remotely downing the server.

7. Describe the communication and name space protocols supported by a NetWare server.

8. Identify the default Ethernet frame type and match the appropriate frame type to the communication protocol supported.

9. Identify the ODI support architecture and related files that are used at a NetWare server.

10. Describe the services provided by the NetWare protocol suite, including IPX, SPX, RIP, SAP, NCP, and Packet Burst.

11. Display and explain routing information with the TRACK ON utility.

12. Install TCP/IP support on a server.

13. Identify the components and requirements involved in name space support.

14. Install OS/2 and Macintosh name space support.

15. Identify optional multiple protocol products used for file and print sharing.

16. Describe the tables, blocks, and buffers important to the workings of server memory.

17. Determine NetWare 3.12 server memory requirements for given cases.

18. Identify NetWare 3.12 memory pools, and describe the features, content, resource use, and effect of each.

19. Use MONITOR to view server memory statistics.

20. Describe server console commands related to memory.

21. Identify components that affect server and network performance.

22. Identify the relationships and balances needed between server memory components to maintain optimum server performance.

23. Use MONITOR to verify server and network performance, and to view resource and processor utilization.

24. List interactions between various SET parameters and the considerations for changing settings.

25. Select and implement the appropriate SET parameter needed to alter network performance based on a given case.

26. Describe the ways in which the *Large Internet Packet* (LIP) and Packet Burst protocol affect network performance.

27. Identify the performance implications associated with the NCP Packet Signature.

28. Identify the purpose and procedures of server maintenance utilities such as BINDFIX, BINDREST, VREPAIR, and SBACKUP.

29. Analyze the data presented on the disk information screen of MONITOR to determine the health of the server's hard disks.

30. Repair the server bindery using BINDFIX and BINDREST.

31. Describe the reasons you would use VREPAIR.

32. Use VREPAIR to remove name space support from a volume.

33. Back up and restore a server bindery and trustee assignments using SBACKUP.

34. Load the components needed to perform a client backup using SBACKUP.

35. Describe the utilities used to set time and time zone support.

36. Describe the utility used to support read-only devices.

37. Perform printing maintenance tasks with PCONSOLE and PSC.

38. Compare the steps required to set permanent and temporary settings for print queues and notification lists.

39. Use PRINTCON to create default print job settings to be used by CAPTURE and PCONSOLE.

40. Print a document using print job configurations that have been created in PRINTCON.

41. Identify advanced printing setup and management design considerations.

42. Summarize the capabilities of the NetWare DOS Requester modules.

43. Modify the NET.CFG file to configure the ODI environment.

44. Customize the NET.CFG file with parameters that affect the NetWare DOS Requester.

45. Identify the options available to load the NetWare DOS Requester.

46. Describe the changes made to a client station during the client installation for Microsoft Windows.

47. Update existing client files using WSUPDATE, and describe the procedures and login script commands used to automate the process.

48. Describe the procedures used to protect against virus intrusion.

49. Describe the method used to support diskless client stations, and identify the files used with the method.

INDEX

C

833

O

USERDEF, 365-367
WSUPDATE, 387-388
Utilities Reference book, 533
utility commands (DOS), 167-171

V

value-added processes (VAPs), 674,
679-680, 773
VAP command, 683
VAPs (value-added processes), 674,
679-680, 773, 775
VER command, 168
VERSION command, 560
vertical placement of menus, 705
VESA (Video Electronic Standard
Association) bus, 45-46
VGA (Video Graphics Array) display,
84-86
video displays, 81-86
View File Server Error Log option
(SYSCON Supervisor options),
327-328
viewing
directories (DOS), 145-146, 152-165
PDF (printer definition files), 440
text files (DOS), 153
Virtual Loadable Modules (VLMs),
199, 496
viruses (backup systems), 608-609
VLM.EXE DOS Requester,198, 497
VLMs (Virtual Loadable Modules),
199, 496, 501-507
BIND.VLM, 503
DOS redirection, 503
DOS Requester, 502
LITE.VLM, 503
NDS.VLM, 503
PNW.VLM, 503
service protocols, 503
transport protocols, 503
VOLINFO (Volume Information)
command, 237-238
volume bit maps, 772

Volume Information menu (FILER),
356
Volume/Disk Restrictions option
(SYSCON User Information), 344-345
volumes, 204-205, 207
labels, changing, 136-137
names (DOS), 139
naming and setting up, 206
NetWare, 204-205
NetWare 2.2 installation, 749
VOLUMES command, 560
VREPAIR utility (backup systems), 614
VREPAIR.EXE, 733

W

WA (Write Audit) attribute, 531
WANs (Wide Area Networks), 97-98
warm boots, 120-121
WATCHDOG command, 683
wildcards, 156-159
DIR command, 145
XCOPY command, 163
Windows support, 512-513, 666
workgroup managers (security), 259
Workgroup Managers option
(SYSCON Supervisor options), 328
Workstation Communication software,
94
workstation generation program
(WSGEN), 717-727
workstation tables, 773
workstations, 197
ACONSOLE utility, 538
ADMIN utility, 538-541
ALLOW utility, 537-538
attached status, 210
blank status, 210
CHKDIR utility, 541
default status, 210
diskless workstations, 212, 513
distributed processing, 675
DSPACE utility, 541-543
file updates with WSUPDATE,
387-388

X–Y–Z

NetWare Training Guide
Managing NetWare
Systems, Third Edition

REGISTRATION CARD NRP

Fill out this card to receive information about future NetWare books and other New Riders titles!

Name _____ Title _____

Company _____

Address _____

City/State/ZIP _____

I bought this book because: _____
_____

I purchased this book from:
☐ A bookstore (Name _____)
☐ A software or electronics store (Name _____)
☐ A mail order (Name of Catalog _____)

I purchase this many computer books each year:
☐ 1–5   ☐ 6 or more

I currently use these applications: _____
_____
_____
_____

I found these chapters to be the most informative: _____
_____

I found these chapters to be the least informative: _____
_____

Additional comments: _____
_____

☐ I would like to see my name in print! You may use my name and quote me in future New Riders products and promotions. My daytime phone number is:_____

New Riders Publishing 201 West 103rd Street • Indianapolis, Indiana 46290 USA

Fold Here

New Riders Publishing
201 West 103rd Street
Indianapolis, Indiana 46290
USA

WANT MORE INFORMATION?

CHECK OUT THESE RELATED TITLES:

	QTY	PRICE	TOTAL

Inside Novell NetWare, Special Edition. This #1 selling tutorial/reference is perfect for beginning system administrators. Each network management task is thoroughly explained and potential trouble spots are noted. The book also includes a disk with an extremely easy-to-use workstation menu program, an MHS capable e-mail program, and workgroup management tools. ISBN: 1-56205-096-6.

_____ $34.95 _____

NetWare 4: New Business Strategies. The ultimate guide to planning, installing, and managing a NetWare 4.0 network. This book explains how best to implement the new features of NetWare 4.0 and how to upgrade to NetWare 4.0 as easily and efficiently as possible. ISBN: 1-56205-159-8.

_____ $27.95 _____

Downsizing to NetWare. Get the real story on downsizing with *Downsizing to NetWare*. This book identifies applications that are suitable for use on LANs and shows how to implement downsizing projects. This book lists the strengths and weaknesses of NetWare—making it perfect for managers and system administrators. ISBN: 1-56205-071-0.

_____ $39.95 _____

LAN Operating Systems. Learn how to connect the most popular LAN operating systems. All major LAN operating systems are covered, including: NetWare 3.11, Appleshare 3.0, Banyan VINES 5.0, UNIX, LAN Manager 2.1, and popular peer-to-peer networks. The following client operating systems are covered as well: MS-DOS, Windows, OS/2, Macintosh System 7, and UNIX. This book clears up the confusion associated with managing large networks with diverse client workstations and multiple LAN operating systems. ISBN: 1-56205-054-0.

_____ $39.95 _____

Name _____

Company _____

Address _____

City _____ State ____ ZIP _____

Phone _____ Fax _____

☐ Check Enclosed ☐ VISA ☐ MasterCard

Card #_____Exp. Date _____

Signature _____

Prices are subject to change. Call for availability and pricing information on latest editions.

Subtotal _____

Shipping _____

$4.00 for the first book and $1.75 for each additional book.

Total _____
Indiana residents add 5% sales tax.

New Riders Publishing 201 West 103rd Street • Indianapolis, Indiana 46290 USA

Orders/Customer Service: 1-800-428-5331
Fax: 1-800-448-3804

- Fold Here -

New Riders Publishing
201 West 103rd Street
Indianapolis, Indiana 46290
USA

Become a CNE
with Help from a Pro!

The NetWare Training Guides are specifically designed and authored to help you prepare for the **Certified NetWare Engineer** exam.

**NetWare Training Guide:
Managing NetWare Systems**

This book clarifies the CNE testing process and provides hints on the best ways to prepare for the CNE examinations. *NetWare Training Guide: Managing NetWare Systems* covers the following sections of the CNE exams:

● NetWare 2.2 System Manager

● NetWare 2.2 Advanced System Manager

● NetWare 3.*x* System Manager

● NetWare 3.*x* Advanced System Manager

ISBN: 1-56205-069-9, **$69.95 USA**

**NetWare Training Guide:
Networking Technology**

This book covers more advanced topics and prepares you for the tough hardware and service/support exams. The following course materials are covered:

● MS-DOS

● Microcomputer Concepts

● Service and Support

● Networking Technologies

ISBN: 1-56205-145-8, **$69.95 USA**

NETWORKING TITLES

#1 Bestseller!

INSIDE NOVELL NETWARE, THIRD EDITION

DEBRA NIEDERMILLER-CHAFFINS & DREW HEYWOOD

This best-selling tutorial and reference has been updated and made even better!

NetWare 2.2, 3.11, & 3.12
ISBN: 1-56205-257-8
$34.95 USA

MAXIMIZING NOVELL NETWARE

JOHN JERNEY & ELNA TYMES

Complete coverage of Novell's flagship product...for NetWare system administrators!

NetWare 3.11
ISBN: 1-56205-095-8
$39.95 USA

NETWARE: THE PROFESSIONAL REFERENCE, SECOND EDITION

KARANJIT SIYAN

This updated version for professional NetWare administrators and technicians provides the most comprehensive reference available for this phenomenal network system.

NetWare 2.x & 3.x
ISBN: 1-56205-158-X
$42.95 USA

NETWARE 4: PLANNING AND IMPLEMENTATION

SUNIL PADIYAR

A guide to planning, installing, and managing a NetWare 4.0 network that best serves your company's objectives.

NetWare 4.0
ISBN: 1-56205-159-8
$27.95 USA

GO AHEAD. PLUG YOURSELF INTO
MACMILLAN COMPUTER PUBLISHING.

Introducing the Macmillan Computer Publishing Forum on CompuServe®

Yes, it's true. Now, you can have CompuServe access to the same professional, friendly folks who have made computers easier for years. On the Macmillan Computer Publishing Forum, you'll find additional information on the topics covered by every Macmillan Computer Publishing imprint—including Que, Sams Publishing, New Riders Publishing, Alpha Books, Brady Books, Hayden Books, and Adobe Press. In addition, you'll be able to receive technical support and disk updates for the software produced by Que Software and Paramount Interactive, a division of the Paramount Technology Group. It's a great way to supplement the best information in the business.

WHAT CAN YOU DO ON THE MACMILLAN COMPUTER PUBLISHING FORUM?

Play an important role in the publishing process—and make our books better while you make your work easier:

- Leave messages and ask questions about Macmillan Computer Publishing books and software—you're guaranteed a response within 24 hours

- Download helpful tips and software to help you get the most out of your computer

- Contact authors of your favorite Macmillan Computer Publishing books through electronic mail

- Present your own book ideas

- Keep up to date on all the latest books available from each of Macmillan Computer Publishing's exciting imprints

JOIN NOW AND GET A FREE COMPUSERVE STARTER KIT!

To receive your free CompuServe Introductory Membership, call toll-free, **1-800-848-8199** and ask for representative **#597**. The Starter Kit Includes:

- Personal ID number and password

- $15 credit on the system

- Subscription to CompuServe Magazine

HERE'S HOW TO PLUG INTO MACMILLAN COMPUTER PUBLISHING:

Once on the CompuServe System, type any of these phrases to access the Macmillan Computer Publishing Forum:

GO MACMILLAN	**GO BRADY**
GO QUEBOOKS	**GO HAYDEN**
GO SAMS	**GO QUESOFT**
GO NEWRIDERS	**GO ALPHA**

Once you're on the CompuServe Information Service, be sure to take advantage of all of CompuServe's resources. CompuServe is home to more than 1,700 products and services—plus it has over 1.5 million members worldwide. You'll find valuable online reference materials, travel and investor services, electronic mail, weather updates, leisure-time games and hassle-free shopping (no jam-packed parking lots or crowded stores).

Seek out the hundreds of other forums that populate CompuServe. Covering diverse topics such as pet care, rock music, cooking, and political issues, you're sure to find others with the same concerns as you—and expand your knowledge at the same time.

WINDOWS TITLES

GRAPHICS TITLES

INSIDE CORELDRAW! 4.0, SPECIAL EDITION

DANIEL GRAY

An updated version of the #1 best-selling tutorial on CorelDRAW!

CorelDRAW! 4.0

ISBN: 1-56205-164-4

$34.95 USA

CORELDRAW! SPECIAL EFFECTS

NEW RIDERS PUBLISHING

An inside look at award-winning techniques from professional CorelDRAW! designers!

CorelDRAW! 4.0

ISBN: 1-56205-123-7

$39.95 USA

CORELDRAW! NOW!

RICHARD FELDMAN

The hands-on tutorial for users who want practical information now!

CorelDRAW! 4.0

ISBN: 1-56205-131-8

$21.95 USA

INSIDE CORELDRAW! FOURTH EDITION

DANIEL GRAY

The popular tutorial approach to learning CorelDRAW!...with complete coverage of version 3.0!

CorelDRAW! 3.0

ISBN: 1-56205-106-7

$24.95 USA

Using the New Riders Electronic TestPrep Disk

The *New Riders Electronic TestPrep* testing program is designed to help you become a *Certified NetWare Engineer* (CNE) or a *Certified NetWare Administrator* (CNA) by simulating the types of questions you are likely to face on the CNE or CNA exams. If you are already a CNE or a CNA, *Electronic TestPrep* will help you keep your skills sharpened by presenting you with up-to-date topics and information presented in an easy-to-use graphical format.

Before you install *New Riders Electronic TestPrep* disk, remove the disk from the plastic sleeve and make a copy of it. Store it in a safe place. This is your backup copy.

Installing the New Riders Electronic TestPrep Disk

The *Electronic TestPrep* is a Windows-based application that has the following system requirements:

Any IBM PC-compatible computer running Microsoft Windows version 3.0 or above (standard or enhanced mode). DOS version 3.1 or above, 2 MB or more of RAM. A Microsoft Windows-compatible mouse. An EGA, VGA, or compatible monitor (color is recommended). A hard disk drive with at least 3 MB of free space. A 3 1/2 inch high-density floppy disk drive. A Microsoft Windows-compatible printer is recommended.

Steps to Follow

The following steps reference floppy drive A. If your floppy drive is B, just substitute B whenever A is mentioned.

1. Place the Electronic TestPrep disk into drive A.

2. From the Windows Program Manager, choose **F**ile, then **R**un.

3. In the Command Line box, type **A:\SETUP.EXE** and press Enter.

4. Follow the instructions on the screen. When the license agreement screen displays, read it and click on the "agree" button if you agree. Also, be sure to enter your name correctly in the Enter Your Name field.

5. Specify the start-up directory where you want the TestPrep to be stored. The default is NRP2. Click on Continue.

TestPrep will now install on your hard disk. After TestPrep installs, a program group named New Riders is created in your Program Manager. From here, you can start the TestPrep program by double-clicking on its icon. Or, if you want to review additional books published by New Riders Publishing, double-click on the NRP Books icon.